SUPPLEMENT V
Russell Banks to Charles Wright

AMERICAN WRITERS
A Collection of Literary Biographies

JAY PARINI
Editor in Chief

SUPPLEMENT V
Russell Banks to Charles Wright

Charles Scribner's Sons
An Imprint of The Gale Group
New York

Charles Scribner's Sons
An Imprint of The Gale Group
1633 Broadway
New York, New York 10019

1   3   5   7   9   11   13   15   17   19   20   18   16   14   12   10   8   6   4   2

Library of Congress Cataloging-in-Publication Data

American writers: a collection of literary biographies.

Suppl. 5 edited by Jay Parini.
The 4-vol. main set consists of 97 of the pamphlets originally published
as the University of Minnesota pamphlets on American writers; some have been
rev. and updated. Supplements I–V cover writers not included in the original
series. Retrospective Supplement I includes original articles by new
contributors on nineteen of the subjects in the 4-vol. main set.
Includes bibliographies.
Contents: v. 1. Henry Adams to T. S. Eliot — v. 2. Ralph Waldo Emerson to Carson McCullers — [etc.] — Supplement[s] — 5. Russell Banks to Charles Wright.
American Literature — History and Criticism. 2. American literature — Bio-bibliography. 3. Aluthors, American — Biography. I. Unger, Leonard, ed. II. Baechler, Lea. III. Parini, Jay. IV. Litz, A. Walton. V. Weigel, Molly. VI. University of Minnesota. Pamphlets on American writers.

PS129.A55 810'.9 73-1759
ISBN 0-684-80625-8

The paper in this publication meets the requirements of ANSI/NISO Z39.48-1992 (Permanence of Paper).

Acknowledgment is gratefully made to those publishers and individuals who have permitted the use of the following material in copyright.

"Philip Levine"

Excerpts from "Sierra Kid," "On the Edge," and "The Horse" in *On the Edge* by Philip Levine, copyright © 1964 by Philip Levine, reprinted by permission of Philip Levine.

Excerpts from "A New Day" and "Silent in America" in *Not This Pig* by Philip Levine, copyright © 1968 by Philip Levine, reprinted by permission of Philip Levine.

Excerpts from "Red Dust" in *Red Dust* by Philip Levine, copyright © 1971 by Philip Levine, reprinted by permission of Philip Levine.

Excerpts from "They Feed They Lion" and "To P. L., 1919–1937" in *They Feed They Lion* by Philip Levine, copyright © 1972 by Philip Levine, reprinted by permission of Philip Levine.

Excerpts from "1933" in *1933* by Philip Levine, copyright © 1974 by Philip Levine, reprinted by permission of Philip Levine.

Excerpts from "No One Remembers," "On the Murder of Lieutenant José del Castillo by the Falangist Bravo Martinez, July 12, 1936," and "New Season" in *The Names of the Lost* by Philip Levine, copyright © 1976 by Philip Levine, reprinted by permission of Philip Levine.

Excerpts from "Starlight" in *Ashes* by Philip Levine, copyright © 1979 by Philip Levine, reprinted by permission of Philip Levine.

Excerpts from "You Can Have It" in *7 Years From Somewhere* by Philip Levine, copyright © 1979 by Philip Levine, reprinted by permission of Philip Levine.

Excerpts from "On My Own" in *One for the Rose* by Philip Levine, copyright © 1981 by Philip Levine, reprinted by permission of Philip Levine.

Excerpts from "Sweet Will" in *Sweet Will* by Philip Levine, copyright © 1985 by Philip Levine, reprinted by permission of Philip Levine.

Excerpts from "A Walk with Tom Jefferson" in *A Walk with Tom Jefferson* by Philip Levine, copyright © 1988 by Philip Levine, reprinted by permission of Alfred A. Knopf, a Division of Random House, Inc., and Philip Levine.

Editorial and Production Staff

Senior Editor
STEPHEN WAGLEY

Copyediting
VISUAL EDUCATION CORPORATION
LOUISE B. KETZ
JESSICA HORNIK EVANS

Proofreader
SUSAN GILAD

Indexer
IMPRESSIONS BOOK AND JOURNAL SERVICES

Production Supervisor
JANE ANDRASSI

Publisher
KAREN DAY

List of Subjects

Introduction

In the original incarnation of *American Writers,* nincty-scven authors were treated in a series of sharply conceived, compact, and popular pamphlets published between 1959 and 1972. The Minnesota Pamphlets on American Writers attracted a devoted following, and the series proved invaluable to a generation of students and teachers, who could depend on reliable and interesting critiques of major figures. The idea of reprinting these essays occurred to Charles Scribner Jr. (1921–1995). The updated and revised series appeared in four volumes entitled *American Writers: A Collection of Literary Biographies* (1974).

Since then, four supplements have appeared, covering more than two hundred poets, novelists, playwrights, essayists, short-story writers, and autobiographers. The idea has been consistent: to provide lucid, informative essays aimed at the general reader. Each of the essays, which often rise to a high level of craft and critical vision, is meant to introduce a writer of some importance in the history of American literature, and to provide a sense of the scope and nature of the career under review. A certain amount of biographical context is also offered, so that readers can appreciate the historical ground that provides the texts under review with air and light, soil and water.

Most of the critics who have contributed to these supplements are professionals: teachers, scholars, and writers. As anyone glancing through this volume will see, they are held to the highest standards of good writing and sound scholarship. Each essay concludes with a select bibliography intended to direct the reading of those who want to pursue the subject further.

The present volume is mostly about contemporary writers, many of whom have received little sustained attention from critics. For example, Maxine Hong Kingston, Erica Jong, A. R. Gurney, Robert Stone, Tim O'Brien, Ann Beattie, and Russell Banks have been written about in the review pages of newspapers and magazines, but their work has yet to attract significant scholarship. The essays included here constitute a beginning.

The poets included here, such as Charles Wright, Philip Levine, and Louise Glück, are well known in the poetry world, and their work has in each case been honored with major literary prizes, but the real work of assimilation, of discovering the true place of each writer in the larger traditions of American poetry, has only begun. Each of these poets is here presented by an established poet-critic, and the depth and eloquence of their essays should be obvious even to casual readers.

The reader will also find essays on important older writers such as Upton Sinclair, who for various reasons were neglected in previous volumes and supplements. It is, in fact, a goal of this series to double back, as necessary, to include earlier writers. One recent supplement (1997), for example, was devoted to revisiting major authors from the earlier volumes. The reason for this, of course, is that scholarship continues to grow and change on these figures, and they often look very different in the light of decades of new criticism.

Supplement V is a rich and varied collection that treats authors from a wide range of ethnic, social, and cultural backgrounds. The critics who contributed to this collection in themselves represent a range of backgrounds and critical approaches, although the baseline for inclusion was that each essay should be accessible to the non-specialist reader or beginning student. The work of any culture involves the continuous assessment and reassessment of major texts produced by its writers, and our belief is that this supplement performs a useful service here, providing substantial introductions to American writers who matter to readers, and who will be read well into the twenty-first century.

—JAY PARINI

Contributors

Charles R. Baker. Poet, short story writer, and essayist. Author of *What Miss Johnson Taught*. LARRY McMURTRY

Cates Baldridge. Professor of English, Middlebury College. Author of *The Dialogics of Dissent in the English Novel* and *Graham Greene's Fictions: The Virtues of Extremity*. ROBERT STONE

Christopher Buckley. Professor and Chair of the Creative Writing Department, University of California at Riverside. Author of ten books of poetry, most recently *Fall from Grace*, and *Appreciations: Reviews, Views, & Interviews: 1975–2000* (forthcoming). Editor of *On the Poetry of Philip Levine: Stranger to Nothing*. PHILIP LEVINE

Shelley Fisher Fishkin. Professor of American Studies and English, University of Texas at Austin. Author of *From Fact to Fiction: Journalism and Imaginative Writing in America, Was Huck Black? Mark Twain and African-American Voices, Lighting Out for the Territory: Reflections on Mark Twain and American Culture*; coeditor of *Listening to Silences: New Essays in Feminist Criticism* and *People of the Book: Thirty Scholars Reflect on Their Jewish Identity*; editor of *The Oxford Mark Twain*. ERICA JONG

John Gatta. Professor of English, University of Connecticut. Author of *American Madonna: Images of the Divine Woman in Literary Culture, Gracious Laughter: The Meditative Wit of Edward Taylor*; and articles on American literary culture and religion. PETER MATTHIESSEN

Henry Hart. Mildred and J. B. Hickman Professor of Humanities, College of William and Mary.

Author of *The Poetry of Geoffrey Hill, Seamus Heaney: Poet of Contrary Progressions, Robert Lowell and the Sublime, James Dickey: The World as a Lie* (biography), *The Ghost Ship* (poems), and *The Rooster Mask* (poems). Editor of *The James Dickey Reader* and *Verse* magazine. CHARLES WRIGHT

Brian Henry. Assistant Professor of English, Plymouth State College. Author of critical essays in numerous publications, including *Contemporary Literary Criticism, The Times Literary Supplement, The Kenyon Review*, and *Boston Review*. RICHARD FORD

Jerome Klinkowitz. Professor of English and University Distinguished Scholar, University of Northern Iowa. Author of *Literary Disruptions, Structuring the Void*, and forty other books on contemporary literature, art, music, philosophy, sport, and military historiography. ROBERT COOVER

Erik Kongshaug. Author of *The Path* (1998), a novel; articles on Upton Sinclair and Liberty Hill, labor, community, politics, and literature. Editor of *Random Lengths: Harbor Independent News*. UPTON SINCLAIR

Tony Magistrale. Professor of English, University of Vermont. Author of *The Poe Encyclopedia, Poe's Children: Connections Between Tales of Terror and Detection; A Dark Night's Dreaming: Contemporary American Horror Fiction*, and several books and articles on Stephen King. STEPHEN KING

Brenda Murphy. Professor of English, University of Connecticut. Author of *Congressional Theatre: Dramatizing McCarthyism on Stage, Film and Television*; *American Realism and American Drama, 1880–1940*; *Tennessee Williams and Elia Kazan: A Collaboration in the Theatre*; *Miller: Death of a Salesman,* and other books and articles on American drama and fiction; editor of *The Cambridge Companion to American Women Playwrights* and other books. A. R. GURNEY

Robert J. Niemi. Associate Professor of English, St. Michael's College. Cocompiler (with Daniel Gillane) of *The Bibliography of Weldon Kees* and author of *Russell Banks.* RUSSELL BANKS

Bill Roorbach. Associate Professor of English, The Ohio State University. Flannery O'Connor Award in Short Fiction; author of *Loneliness, Summers with Juliet, Writing Life Stories*. Essays in *The New York Times Magazine, Granta, Missouri Review, Harper's*. Fiction editor for the Sandstone Prize, Ohio State University Press. MAXINE HONG KINGSTON

Victor Strandberg. Professor of English, Duke University. Author of *The Poetic Vision of Robert Penn Warren*; *A Faulkner Overview: Six Perspectives; Religious Psychology in American Literature: A Study in the Relevance of William James*; and *Greek Mind/Jewish Soul: The Conflicted Art of Cynthia Ozick*. Essays on numerous American writers. CYNTHIA OZICK

Lee Upton. Professor of English, Lafayette College. Author of *Jean Garrigue: A Poetics of Plenitude, Obsession and Release: Rereading the Poetry of Louise Bogan*, and *The Muse of Abandonment: Origin, Identity, Master in Five American Poets.* LOUISE GLÜCK

Dana Cairns Watson. Teacher of twentieth-century American literature at University of California, Los Angeles. TIM O'BRIEN

Robert S. Wilson. Since 1996 the editor of *Preservation* magazine, winner of a National Magazine Award for general excellence in 1998. Founding literary editor of *Civilization* magazine and longtime book critic for *USA Today*. Essays about Peter Taylor in *The Atlantic Monthly, Shenandoah*, and *The Craft of Peter Taylor* (1995). PETER TAYLOR

Natasha Wimmer. Freelance editor at *Publishers Weekly*. Translator of *Dirty Trilogy of Havana*, by Pedro Juan Gutiérrez. (forthcoming fall 2000). ANN BEATTIE

SUPPLEMENT V
Russell Banks to Charles Wright

Russell Banks

1940–

*A*s a writer of mostly proletarian fiction in a literary marketplace dominated by middle-class tastes, Russell Banks had the cards stacked against him from the outset. His ascendance to international stature would have to be considered miraculous if it were not for Banks' prodigious talent, tenacity, and a ferocious work ethic. Though middle-aged, well-off, a retired Princeton University professor, even a self-confessed "bourgeois snob," Banks is one of only a handful of writers to come out of the U.S. working class, become successful, and yet never really relinquish his working-class outlook. Such an outlook, which he has aptly described as that "of powerless people who look up from below," has informed virtually all of Banks' writing—American Dream ideology notwithstanding, which dictates that those who "make it" should repress their humble origins. Russell Banks has made a career of *not* repressing his roots. Looking into the past, Banks vividly describes what he sees there: the often harrowing reality of growing up poor, pitied, brutalized, and forsaken in a society that worships money and success.

BANKS' BACKGROUND

Russell Earl Banks was born on March 28, 1940, in Newton, Massachusetts, the first of four chil-

dren to Earl and Florence (Taylor) Banks. Banks' father, Earl, was a plumber all his working life, as was Banks' grandfather. Described by the author as "a very bright man, talented in many ways," Earl Banks had to go to work at sixteen to help support his family as it struggled to survive during the Depression years. Cheated out of the possibility of further schooling by dire poverty, Earl Banks soon found himself stuck in a tedious job he hated, his station in life fixed by marriage and the responsibilities that come with a growing family. Frustrated with his lot and feeling trapped, Earl sought escape through alcohol. When he got drunk, his barely suppressed rage surfaced, resulting in paroxysms of verbal and physical violence wreaked on his wife and children. Florence Banks coped with her surly husband as well as she could, but home life at the Banks residence was one of unremitting turmoil. Both parents fought constantly and drank too much, inflicting unspeakable pain on themselves and their hapless children. Russell Banks remembers his parents acting "like hysterical children, stuck in a permanent tantrum. Everyone cried and shouted a lot. There was never enough money, and they were always packing up and moving out of an old place, where things had gone wrong, into a new [place] where everything would improve."

Things did not improve, but they did change.

In 1952, when Russell was twelve, his father took up with a girlfriend in Florida, abandoning the family forever. Florence Banks sued for divorce and took custody of her four children. The drunkenness and violence ended with the divorce but so did Earl Banks' steady financial support. Florence Banks was forced to go to work as a bookkeeper, a job that did not pay well enough to sustain a single parent and her four young children. Nerve-racking money shortages became a fact of life, as did constant changes of address in and around Wakefield, Massachusetts, when Florence fell behind with the rent.

As the oldest child, Russell assumed his absent father's role as male head of household. Taking care of his mother and his younger siblings was a responsibility he took with utmost seriousness. His strong sense of duty carried over to school. Banks was a hard-working, attentive student who earned good grades. He also showed artistic talent, a trait that won him praise from teachers and other adults. By his middle teens, Banks was thinking seriously about becoming an artist, a career path that he now believes allowed him "to separate himself from the conventional expectations for a bright kid" from his social class.

Banks' excellent grades eventually earned him a full, four-year scholarship to Colgate University in Hamilton, New York. He started at Colgate in the fall of 1958, "an early affirmative action kid" at "a preppy, neo-Ivy school for upper-middle-class white boys," as Banks later described it. Though he had more than enough intelligence to make good grades, Banks lacked the social skills and self-confidence needed to hold his own in such a privileged environment. Some thirty years later, in a quasi-autobiographical narrative sardonically entitled "Success Story," Banks explained what happened to him: "In this Ivy League school . . . among the elegant, brutal sons of the captains of industry, I was only that year's token poor kid, imported from a small . . . mill town like an exotic herb, a dash of mace

for the vichyssoise. It was a status that perplexed and intimidated and finally defeated me, so that after nine weeks of it, I fled into the night."

After hitchhiking back to Wakefield in a snowstorm, Banks had to endure two months of shame and embarrassment in the forlorn company of his heartbroken mother, disappointed teachers, and pitying friends. It all got to be too much. Shortly after Christmas, Banks packed some things in a duffel bag and set out to hitchhike his way to Florida. His plan was to join Fidel Castro's revolution against the Cuban dictator, Fulgencio Batista Zaldívar, which was just then reaching its climax. When he left Colgate, Banks was merely running away from unbearable pressures and expectations. When he went off to join Castro, however, Banks was following the classic Huck Finn fantasy, "the run from civilization, in which a young fellow in tweeds at Colgate University lights out and becomes a Robin Hood figure in fatigues in the Caribbean jungle." Banks now sees the myth he was chasing as "a very basic American story, as well as a basic white-male fantasy."

Banks' daydream of escape and heroism finally fell apart in Miami. He suddenly realized he did not know how to get to Cuba or what he would do if and when he got there. He had no contacts, did not speak Spanish, and knew next to nothing about the country or its people. At a loss as to what to do with himself, Banks got on the road again and hitchhiked 250 miles north to St. Petersburg on the Gulf coast. There he found work as a furniture mover at a downtown hotel, the only able-bodied young man amongst a crew of middle-aged alcoholics. After a few weeks of heavy lifting, Banks quit the hotel and took a job as a window trimmer, dressing mannequins and constructing facades for the display department of a downtown department store.

Working at the same store was a pretty seventeen-year-old salesgirl and bathing suit model named Darlene Bennett, the daughter of a local carpet installer. Banks and Bennett began to date and soon fell in love. In the late summer of 1959, only a few months after they met, the young couple married and moved into an apartment in Lakeland. Within weeks Darlene Banks was pregnant. As the year wore on—and Darlene's condition became more obvious—Banks grew more restive and panicky. He hated the cultural wasteland that was central Florida, hated his menial job, and could see himself being trapped, like his father, in a soul-destroying situation by the heavy responsibilities of marriage and a looming family.

In February 1960 Banks gathered his courage, loaded Darlene, now six months pregnant, into his old Packard, and headed north to Boston. They took a small basement apartment in the Back Bay. Banks found work at a local bookstore and, as he later put it, "sort of eased into a community of young artists, painters, musicians, writers and hangers-on—most of them wannabes—between the ages of twenty and thirty." Immersed in an exciting urban scene at an auspicious cultural moment, Banks started to take himself seriously as an artist and began to write in earnest.

Things were less sanguine at home. Though they had been married for only a few months, Banks and his teenage wife were discovering that they were fundamentally incompatible; Darlene was suited to suburban life in Florida while Banks was becoming a fledgling intellectual with literary aspirations. The birth of their daughter, Leona (nicknamed Lea), on May 13, 1960, only added further stress to the Bankses' crumbling marriage. Six months later Banks told his wife that it was all over. She departed Boston in a fit of rage and hurt and returned to Florida with the baby to live with her parents. Darlene Bennett soon remarried, to a man Banks knew. After that, a resentful Bennett shut Banks out of her life. He would have no contact with her or his daughter Lea for many years. Banks later admitted to an interviewer that he "essentially replicated" his fa-

ther's behavior toward himself and his siblings. Escaping his father's orbit was proving to be an extremely difficult thing to do.

Shortly before the breakup of his family, Banks met an Emerson College theater major named Mary Gunst. The two plunged into an emotionally charged and tumultuous relationship that was beyond Banks' frail emotional resources. That summer he had something akin to a nervous breakdown, probably a delayed reaction to the accumulated emotional trauma of his life. Deeply depressed, Banks packed his duffel bag once again and returned to Florida. Intent on solitude and quiet so that he could write and put himself back together, Banks spent the latter half of 1961 at Islamorada Key, fifty miles north of Key West. He lived in a trailer, read and wrote during the day, and pumped gas at a filling station at night to earn his living. After a trip to Key West, Banks journeyed cross-country to visit his mother, who had relocated to San Diego to take a job with Raytheon. Once again at a loss as to what to do with himself, Banks called his father, then living in Concord, New Hampshire. Earl Banks advised his wayward son to return to New England, learn a useful trade, and "stop all this goofing around." Banks had to admit that, for once, his father was right.

Upon arriving in New Hampshire, Banks joined the union as a plumber's apprentice, bought a pickup truck, and settled into an apartment in Concord. A pipe fitter by day, Banks worked on his first novel in his off-hours. He had kept in contact with Mary Gunst in the course of his travels, but the relationship seemed to him to be "broken." At any rate, Gunst was no longer living in Boston; she had transferred to Virginia Commonwealth University for her senior year. Banks called her one night in October to bring closure to the romance. Much to his surprise, she showed up on his doorstep the next day, having dropped out of school to be with him. They were married on October 29, 1962.

EARLY WRITING

Over the next year Banks finished his first attempt at a novel that he has since described as "quite simply awful." In August 1963 Banks took off a week from work to attend the Breadloaf Writers' Conference near Middlebury, Vermont. His mentor at Breadloaf was the noted proletarian writer Nelson Algren, winner of the first National Book Award in 1950 for *The Man with the Golden Arm.* Algren went over Banks' manuscript, pointed out the better passages, and made it clear to Banks that he had to do the rest himself. Because Algren did not drive, he appealed to Banks for a ride into town, to escape the stuffy confines of Breadloaf. The two adjourned to a bar in Middlebury, became acquainted over beers, and ended up as friends. Banks credits Algren with validating him, publicly and privately, as a genuine writer at this crucial stage in his early development. In 1990 Banks paid homage to Algren (who died in 1981) by writing the Foreword to a new edition of Algren's *A Walk on the Wild Side.*

Banks continued to write and to toil at his plumber's job over the next year. He and Mary Gunst had their first daughter, Caerthan, on July 7, 1964. In September, six years after the Colgate debacle, Banks returned to college, thanks to the extraordinary generosity of his well-to-do mother-in-law, who offered to pay his way. There was only one stipulation: that Banks go to a college in the South so that Mary could be near her family. Banks considered Duke and the University of Virginia but finally chose the University of North Carolina at Chapel Hill because it was coed, less self-consciously elitist, and more cosmopolitan than the other schools.

Chapel Hill proved to be an auspicious choice. Banks remembers anticipating a "sleepy but interesting southern town and a large but nonetheless fairly elite state university." What he walked into was "a hotbed of radicalism." The Civil Rights movement was at its height and the anti-war movement was just getting underway. Besides a crash course in radical politics, Banks also got a vivid education in race relations. He had known no African Americans in New Hampshire (there hardly were any). Consequently, like many white Americans, he saw black people as "exotic, mysterious . . . more emblematic, symbolic . . . than real." Surrounded by blacks in North Carolina, he began to see them as human beings and began to understand "the political reality of their lives." He also began to see American society as a deeply racialized society—a fact generally suppressed and denied by the white majority, which takes whiteness as a universal given. It was an epiphany that affected Banks deeply and would have a profound effect on much of his subsequent writing.

In every way, Banks' stint at the University of North Carolina (1964–1967) marked a major turning point in his life. Now in his mid-twenties, remarried, a father again, with numerous adventures and three continuous years of blue-collar work behind him, Banks had come of age. Attacking his studies with a tremendous sense of purpose, Banks graduated in just three years, Phi Beta Kappa. He also flourished outside the classroom. He wrote a second novel and found a literary agent named Ellen Levine, who—much to Banks' surprise—was able to place the book with Random House. Just as Banks' novel was about to be typeset, his editor, Steven M. L. Aronson, left Random House to take another job. Without an in-house editor supporting and promoting the book, Banks decided to withdraw it and try to sell it elsewhere but found no takers. Upon rereading the manuscript, he came to the conclusion it was "quite a terrible novel" and decided to put it aside until a later time. The abortive novel was, however, only a minor setback. Banks was busy on other fronts. He and a close friend, the poet William Matthews, cofounded a small publishing house they called Lillabulero Press and began to publish poetry chapbooks and a small magazine also called *Lillabulero,* "a periodical of Literature and the Arts" that soon attained a 1,000-copy circulation nationally.

Banks published his own work as well. In 1967 he and his coeditors, Newton Smith and William Matthews, each contributed five poems to *15 Poems* (1967), a Lillabulero Press chapbook. In style and subject matter, Banks' poems were prosaic in the extreme. One dealt with the view from his bed, others were about a maudlin drunk singing in a bar, a girl failing to catch a Frisbee, a disappointing beach trip, and eight sad haiku (arranged as one poem) on what would emerge as a favorite Banks topic—the rigors of New England in winter. Banks was no poet but he did exhibit nascent talent as a writer of short fiction. Of much more interest than the banal verse in *15 Poems* is a story Banks published in the July 1967 issue of *Lillabulero* called "The Adjutant Bird." The story deals with the career of Yankee sea captain Frederick Tudor, who pioneered the shipping of ice from New England to the South, the West Indies, and India in the early 1800s. Banks' interest in Tudor is telling in several ways. One attraction was the sheer oddity of Tudor's story; marketing ice in the tropics before the advent of modern refrigeration was a strange, quixotic adventure. Another attraction for Banks, no doubt, was the fact that Tudor was ultimately successful in his endeavors, success that bespeaks a man of remarkable resilience and determination, a questing hero in a world of comfortable mediocrity. Concerned with the intersection of alien worlds, particularly the northern and southern hemispheres, "The Adjutant Bird" also manifested a theme that would mark much of Banks' later fiction.

After his graduation from the University of North Carolina, Banks and Mary Gunst lived in Chapel Hill for another year. A second daughter, Maia, was born on May 17, 1968. A few months later Banks and his family moved to Northwood Narrows, New Hampshire, a small town in the southeast corner of the state that was not far from Barnstead, where Banks had spent a significant part of his youth. The family settled into a large Victorian-style farmhouse, and Banks found work teaching writing at Emerson College, Boston, and the University of New Hampshire in Durham. Soon Banks was joined in New Hampshire by two Lillabulero cohorts—poets Doug Collins and Charles Simic—and the three formed their own intellectual community.

In 1969 Banks edited and contributed to a second poetry chapbook called *30/6* (Winter/Spring 1969), so named because it featured five poems each by Banks, Peter Wild, Charles Simic, Robert Morgan, William Matthews, and Doug Collins. The poems that Banks contributed were by no means great, but they did show a clear advance in imagination and daring over the uninteresting verse he had published two years earlier. One poem, called "Waiting to Freeze," was a murky exploration of male estrangement from the world of women. Another was a farce about a bear lured to a teenaged girls' campsite by the smell of menstruation. A third poem described a balmy fall day after a snowfall. A fourth poem, "On Acquiring Riches," constituted a sly satire of materialism. Banks' final and most intriguing contribution to *30/6* was his "Homage to Che Guevara." To Banks, the fallen revolutionary leader seemed to embody the heroism and political passion conspicuously lacking in bourgeois America. The poem he wrote was, tellingly, equal parts homage to Che and satire of himself as a gringo dilettante, dabbling in fantasies of heroic radicalism. "Homage" ends with a sobering vision of the late Che Guevara "drowning / quickly before my eyes in a sea of blood." By contrast, the speaker perches, safe and secure, in his figurative life raft of American affluence, "munching saltines," "nipping from a water tap," and sailing his "rubber craft with remarkable skill" as if he "were a Kennedy / a few miles off Cape Cod."

Soon after the publication of *30/6* Banks published *Waiting to Freeze: Poems* (1969), his first chapbook devoted entirely to his own work. Comprised of some new and some previously published work, the collection also recycled its title poem and three other poems from *30/6*. All ten poems were steeped in the bleak atmospherics of New England in winter, a real landscape but also the psychic terrain of Banks' tortured youth. In a poem entitled "Purchase," Banks speaks of his need to return to New England for chances "To bicker with memories, / To re-enter the lists / Armed with the cool gigantic force / Of dead anger, / Making messes of the past, / Remaking everything / In my own images." As Banks later told Wesley Brown, "I can see my life as a kind of obsessive return to the 'wound' . . . Going back again and again trying to get it right, trying to figure out how it happened and who is to blame and who is to forgive."

The Banks family was filled out with the birth of another daughter, Danis, on January 13, 1970. Though now a husband, the father of three young girls, and a commuting college professor, Banks still found the time and energy to write. His routine was to write from ten o'clock at night until two o'clock in the morning, sleep for a few hours, get up, deal with domestic matters, and then set out for his teaching job. Though this schedule put inordinate stress on his marriage, Banks' remorseless self-discipline soon paid off in terms of professional recognition. In 1971 one of his stories, "With Che in New Hampshire," was chosen for inclusion in Houghton Mifflin's *Best American Short Stories* annual. Somewhat typical of Banks' work at this time, "With Che" was in the postmodernist mode, a reflexive story about the imaginative process of writing a story. Two years later Banks won the Fels Award for fiction. In 1974 another Che-inspired story entitled "With Che at Kitty Hawk," was selected for an O. Henry Prize.

That same year Banks published a long poem in chapbook form called *Snow: Meditations of a Cautious Man in Winter* (1974), a poem that revisits the emotional desolation already broached in *Waiting to Freeze*. Written in short, spare, telegraphic lines, *Snow* begins as a discourse on the hardness of winter in northern New England. Halfway through, though, memory takes over and the frosty, snow-covered landscape becomes the primal scene of the poet's fearful childhood: "*Hands*! I'd looked for / *hands*! Fisted, / like knotted wet rope. / Hands pounding down on me, the / face fading above." Reliving the terror and pain of his past, the speaker—clearly Banks—engages in guilty self-interrogation: "Are you, have you ever been, a violent man? / Yes. Of course. My father / beat me. / . . . Yes, I was, have been, am still, a violent man. But I've only beaten/ women and men. / I've never been anything / but kind to my children." The speaker's declaration is not some perverse fiction that is meant to shock; it is a real confession. In a 1989 interview with Wesley Brown, Banks admitted that when he was much younger he had been "violent against the people I loved. But I was never violent against my children. That's as specific as I can be." Clearly, the abuse visited upon him by his father had made Banks abusive in turn. It was a theme that would haunt Banks' imagination and writing for many years to come.

Though Banks continued to write poetry and short stories in a relatively straightforward realist idiom, he had begun to embrace metafiction for some of his stories. The literary fashion du jour among serious American writers in the seventies, metafiction was a narrative style that eschewed the conventional devices of realism. Instead of building up a convincing illusion of life through conventional characterization, scene painting, and plotting, metafiction often admitted, even advertised, its own contrived and artificial nature as narrative. The idea was not only to call into question the conventions of realism but also to destabilize accepted notions concerning consciousness, cognition, language, identity, even reality itself. Accordingly, metafictional narratives often tended to be cerebral in tone and complex and cryptic in form and content. For Banks, the authorial detachment that metafiction afforded was a welcome refuge from his own uncertainties as a struggling writer. As he later told the interviewer Robert Faggen, "I became a writer without a clear sense of entitlement . . . . It wasn't a trade I could imagine myself into very easily. So in order to do it, I felt I had to reject a lot of my background . . . and willfully learn the techniques of fiction. In my early years as a writer, I was a lot more self-conscious and deliberate in my attempts to acquire craft." Because it tended to be abstract and ratiocinative, metafiction also allowed Banks to distance himself from subject matter that would have been too painful to explore and articulate in a more direct way, at least at this point in his career.

EXPERIMENTS IN METAFICTION

Banks' first extended experiment in metafiction was also his first published novel, *Family Life* (1975). Like *Snow, Family Life* explores the psychological and emotional anguish of a family ruled by an erratic, emotionally destructive patriarch. But because the material was so close to his own heart and experience, Banks had to cloak it all in the guise of an absurd, satiric fable set in contemporary America. Thus *Family Life* features fairy-tale characters with silly names: King Egress the Hearty (sometimes "The Bluff"), his wife, Naomi Ruth, their three sons, Princes Egress (the Wild), Dread, and Orgone (the Wrestler). Other characters include a mysterious Green Man, and King Egress' drinking buddy (and gay lover), Loon, a hashish-smoking hippie who lives in a tree house. Highly episodic and largely devoid of a recognizable plot, *Family Life* was, on the surface, a wisecracking, high-spirited romp. The core story it told, though, was of the gradual dissolution of a marriage and family, destroyed by violence, alcohol, and neglect. The most striking feature of *Family Life* is the weird disjunction between the book's excessively breezy tone and its dark subject matter, a disjunction that becomes tiresome rather than engaging.

As a novel, *Family Life* simply did not work; it garnered scathing reviews. Banks would later declare the book "apprentice work, more useful to the writer, perhaps, than the reader." He did better with *Searching for Survivors,* his first collection of short stories, also published in 1975. Six of the fourteen stories are quasi-autobiographical. The other eight stories consist of five moral or political parables and a trio of tales that invoke Che Guevara as a kind of talismanic presence. Most of the stories in the collection are cast in varying modes of metafiction. A few are rendered in something akin to traditional realism. The split in narrative approaches and styles reflected a larger split in Banks himself, between the battered proletarian who took pride in his blue-collar pedigree, and the iron-willed, upwardly mobile careerist desperate for success, status, and respectability. It was a schism that would take Banks years to resolve.

As often happens with apprentice fiction, *Searching for Survivors* is an uneven collection, sometimes pretentious, sometimes profound. Certain stories, such as "The Investiture," "The Nap," and "The Drive Home," are overly elaborate and unnecessarily abstruse; their complexity promises a payoff that never quite materializes. Other stories, like "The Masquerade" and "With Che at the Plaza," are supposed to be cleverly witty metafictions but come off as merely awkward and cloying. More consistently successful are the stories grounded in real life experiences. One of the best of these is "Searching for Survivors (II)," Banks' quasi-fictionalized account of the death of his younger brother, Christopher, in a train wreck outside of Santa Barbara, California, in 1968. Banks had already eulogized his brother in an obscure poem called "Trains" (from *Waiting to Freeze*) that dramatized the emotional devastation the surviving family members experienced. This story—written some six years after the event—attests to the fact that Banks was a still long way from resolving his grief over Christopher's horrific death. Like "Searching (I)," "Searching (II)" is realistic in tone and voice but metafictional in terms of structure. Banks divides his story into eleven distinct segments and then arranges them in seemingly random order so as to violate a traditional chronological presentation. For example, one section recounts Reed (Banks) flying home from California after a futile search for Allen's (Christopher's) body. A later section flashes back to Reed dropping Allen off at a bus station in New Hampshire for his return trip to California the previous summer. Still another section focuses on Reed leaving his father's house after Allen's memorial service. The effect of such a structure is to create a disjointed series of arrival and departure scenarios. These transitory meetings underscore the appalling fragmentation of the narrator's family, a clan separated by divorce, geography, and a chronic inability to communicate—even when the family members were in proximity.

In the end, "Searching for Survivors (II)" is not so much about Christopher's death as it is about the emotional repression that is so endemic in American culture. In the name of some absurd decorum that affirms stoicism as the greatest good, familial love is generally kept under wraps. Reed (Banks) finds it "pathetic that we surviving children, we survivors, loved Allen only in secret and never had the pleasure . . . of uttering it full-faced to him. Pathetic that his death didn't free us to do for each other now what we were unable to do for him then . . . I can't believe that we have been so incredibly stupid and weak, that we go on doing it!" In sum, "searching for survivors" is an ironic aspiration that takes on global proportions. Here the expression means searching for emotionally vibrant human beings in a spiritually blunted and dehumanized culture.

Though hardly an unqualified literary triumph, *Searching for Survivors* was Banks' first fully realized achievement as a writer. The book was well received by critics and won the St. Lawrence [University] Award for Fiction, where Banks was a writer-in-residence. When Banks applied for a prestigious Guggenheim Fellowship in 1976, he won it on the strength of his short fiction, not on the somewhat dubious merits of his first novel or his poetry. The Guggenheim turned out to be a watershed event beyond the obvious boost to Banks' reputation as a writer. Banks used the $25,000 cash award to install himself and his family on the island of Jamaica for a year and a half, from May 1976 until September 1977. During this period he completed two book-length manuscripts (*Hamilton Stark* and *The Relation of My Imprisonment*) and most of the stories that would form his second collection, *The New World: Tales* (1978). When he was not writing, Banks sought to immerse himself in the life of the island by learning to play dominoes with the local workmen. He also ventured into the mountainous interior, sometimes to live and work in deliberate isolation, sometimes to socialize with friends he made among the Maroons (an isolated group descended from Ashanti slaves who successfully rebelled against the British in the late 1700s). An admitted "library rat," Banks supplemented his travels with extensive reading on the history, culture, and religion of Jamaica, Haiti, and the Caribbean in general—knowledge that he would draw upon extensively in the years to come.

Undoubtedly a tremendous boon to his career, Banks' Jamaican sabbatical had the opposite effect on his already shaky marriage to Mary Gunst. By the early seventies their relationship had largely disintegrated. By the time they left for Jamaica, they were staying together mainly for the sake of the children. The numerous distractions the island offered only widened the fissure between them. In June 1977 Gunst took the children back to Northwood in a parting that was less than amicable. Banks stayed on alone for another four months. Barely a month after he returned to New Hampshire, Banks moved out of the house and bought a small farmhouse just down the road, to stay close to his young daughters. After almost fifteen years, his second marriage was over.

Banks' teaching job at the University of New Hampshire had been discontinued during his absence, but he immediately found work at New England College in Henniker, forty miles west of Northwood. Though his personal life had once again run aground, Banks' literary fortunes continued to flourish. In 1978 he published two of the books he had worked on in Jamaica: *Hamilton Stark,* his second novel, and *The New World: Tales,* his second collection of short stories.

With *Hamilton Stark,* Banks fashioned a novel that eschewed the conventional, unified narrative in favor of a parcel of narrative approaches. He merged the geological, economic, and political history of the region with anecdotes from the childhood of his protagonist, Hamilton Stark; parts of an "unpublished novel" by Stark's daughter, Rochelle; transcripts of taped interviews with two of Stark's five wives; and philosophical digressions, authorial asides, and other kinds of discourses. *Hamilton Stark* turned out to be not so much a novel as a fictive journal about the entire investigative and imaginative process of novel writing. Inevitably, with such a complex and variegated approach to storytelling, Banks ran into problems of structure. He remembers having to rewrite and revise *Hamilton Stark* a number of times over a period of years before he began to discern patterns that he was able to shape into a coherent form.

In addition to employing a labyrinthine structure, Banks further distanced himself (and his readers) from his protagonist by mediating Stark's story through the narrative voice of an unnamed friend who becomes obsessed with Stark after the man's mysterious disappearance. Thus, in true postmodernist fashion, Hamilton Stark is present only in his absence, a subject that inspires extensive commentary and speculation by virtue of his mysteriousness and inaccessibility. Indeed, Banks uses a quote from the existentialist philosopher Søren Kierkegaard as the novel's epigraph to suggest that the unfathomable enigma of Stark's identity applies to every person: "The individual is a host of shadows, all of which resemble him and for the moment have an equal claim to authenticity."

Highly imaginative experiments in metafiction, Banks' elaborate strategies of narrative indirection also served a more personal agenda. In many ways, the elusive Hamilton Stark was yet another, albeit exaggerated, version of Banks' father, Earl—with aspects of the author included in the admixture. Consequently, Banks needed to use all kinds of distancing devices to keep the emotional content manageable for himself. Even so, Stark comes across as larger than life. A five-times-married misanthropic Yankee, Hamilton Stark is a mass of contradictions, "self-centered, immature, violent, cruel, eccentric, and possibly insane," but also physically imposing, handsome, meticulously well groomed, funny, quick-witted, honest, even a good dancer. In short, Stark is that rare soul: a man who had managed to gain "control over his life without suppressing his life."

Stark's adult daughter, Rochelle, shares the narrator's fascination with her father. Their mutual obsession leads them into an intense and turbulent love affair, which affords Banks the opportunity to explore the desperately complicated psychology of male-female relationships. As his involvement with Rochelle deepens, the narrator is confronted with overwhelming evidence that Stark was an emotional sadist, especially in his treatment of the women around him. Suffering a crisis of faith in his idol, the narrator chooses to emulate Stark's misogyny by rejecting Rochelle in an abrupt and cruel way—a move that hurts him as much as it does Rochelle. The narrator's disintegrating myth of Hamilton Stark as masculine role model is further blasted by his friend C., who suggests that Stark's behavior was not some heroic display of will but actually the result of weakness and neurosis. The myth is at low ebb when Stark actually disappears, his tracks abruptly ending in the snows of Blue Job Mountain. Much like the prying journalist in Orson Welles' *Citizen Kane,* Banks' narrator tries to reconstruct Hamilton Stark in all his contrariness and complexity but never succeeds in defining the man's character. But that is precisely Banks' point: that no one can be known to satisfaction. What *does* matter is the paradoxical quest for self through passionate involvement in the life of another person. That involvement may be abstract or deeply personal, even abortive or futile (as it is for Banks' narrator), but it is always instructive because it leads away from the trap of self-absorption.

The experimental style of *Hamilton Stark* continues with *The New World: Tales,* a collection of ten short stories divided into two equal sections, one headed "Renunciation," the other headed "Transformation." Banks describes the book in rather lofty terms, as "a carefully structured gathering of ten tales that dramatize and explore the process and progress of self-transcendence, tales that . . . embrace the spiritual limits and possibilities of life in the New World." By "self-transcendence," Banks seems to mean self-mastery, the triumph of the conscious will over tumultuous emotions and unconscious impulses, an impossible ideal perhaps, but an ideal worth striving for. By "the New World," Banks refers, of course, to the Western Hemisphere but also to the Brave New World of American corporate society, where religion has faded as a moral and spiritual arbiter of life and unbridled self-interest reigns supreme.

The five stories in the "Renunciation" section are indeed about types of moral and emotional abnegation. The sardonically titled "A Sentimental Education," features Veronica Stetson, the "only and pampered" daughter of a Texas oil tycoon. "Blonde and blue-eyed, long and tanned of limb," Veronica has gone to the best schools, is fluent in five languages, and is "a concert-level pianist and an Olympic-quality freestyle swimmer." Yet two years out of college, Veronica is suffering from the "colossal boredom" that comes from being able to predict "practically every word and act" of everyone she meets. Insulated from life by her wealth, education, and good looks, Veronica is beginning to understand that a world without real contingency or peril is a world without excitement or hope. In a desperate attempt to stave off a crushing cynicism, Veronica temporarily renounces her true identity and transforms herself into "Martha," a low-budget divorcée. At a working-class bar she meets a "hawk-faced" auto mechanic named Vic. After bouts of furious, degrading sex at Vic's dirty house trailer and in the grease pit of his garage, Veronica almost loses her grasp on her real self. Deeply shaken by her brief immersion in the brutal and alien culture of the working class, she comes out of her ordeal with a newfound appreciation of her enormous privilege; comfortable boredom seems quite preferable to life in the raw.

In marked contrast to the purely fictional "Renunciation" tales, the stories that comprise the "Transformation" section of *The New World: Tales* are all based in real persons and events. The inexplicably titled "Rise of the Middle Class" deals with an unsuccessful assassination attempt on the life of Simón Bolívar in 1815 that dramatizes the unique risks of being a man in history. In a decidedly feminist vein, "Indisposed" imagines what marriage might have been like for an eighteenth-century Englishwoman, in this case, Jane Hogarth, wife of the London engraver William Hogarth. With "The Caul," Banks explores the guilt-ridden psychology of Edgar Allan Poe, a man haunted by the death of his mother when he was only two years old. The title story of the collection compares the lives of two seventeenth-century Jamaicans: a Catholic prelate named Bernardo de Balbuena and a Sephardic goldsmith named Mosseh Alvares. Both men were writers after a fashion. Balbuena penned *El Bernardo,* a "bizarrely mediocre epic poem" some 40,000 lines long. Alvares wrote "The Patriarch," "a rather shapeless and morose version of a medieval tale." What fascinates Banks in the story of these obscure literary amateurs confined to a "stagnating backwater" is their shared impulse to enlarge the self and transcend banal circumstances by exercise of the imagination.

RETURN TO REALISM

The full flowering of Banks' Jamaican sabbatical occurred in 1980, with the publication of his third novel, *The Book of Jamaica.* Banks later told the interviewer Curtis Wilkie that, while on the island, he found himself "absolutely fascinated" by ordinary Jamaicans, "the carpenters, pipe fitters, the storekeepers. Just the average Joes and their wives." Though he brought an extraordinary "quality of care and attention" to the lives of these people, he found that he could not penetrate their world: "I couldn't eliminate my white-ness, my American-ness, my middle-classness." One of the primary reasons Banks wrote *The Book of Jamaica* was to deal with and articulate the racial and cultural alienation he felt while he was there.

Like *Hamilton Stark, The Book of Jamaica* centers on a mystery—this time not of an individual, but of an entire society. Heretofore, Banks' work had focused on moral and perceptual evolution within the context of marriage and family. To do justice to Jamaica as subject, Banks was forced to widen his scope as a writer, to become overtly political, and to shift emphasis to content as opposed to form. Consequently, Banks

resorted to a relatively straightforward realism idiom for *The Book of Jamaica,* a narrative style largely bereft of the convoluted metafictional tropes that mark his earlier fiction. What remains consistent, though, is Banks' tendency toward a loose, elliptical structure and the hybridization of genre. His Jamaica novel shifts gears and meanders. It also defies easy categorization, being a combination travel book, fictionalized memoir, detective story, and sociopolitical allegory.

Banks models his protagonist on himself: a thirty-six-year-old white college professor, politically progressive and morally scrupulous, in Jamaica on a foundation grant (in this case, to study the Maroons). The first part of the book deals with a mystery involving Jamaica's most famous white resident in the 1950s: notorious movie star Errol Flynn. Banks' protagonist gets wind of a rumor that has been circulating on the island for twenty years, that Flynn and two accomplices murdered and dismembered a young Jamaican woman. Fascinated equally by Flynn's mythic stature and the lurid murder case, the professor conducts an exhaustive investigation but ends up much like his counterpart in *Hamilton Stark,* confused and empty-handed, so much so as to be in doubt about the merits of Western logic.

In the same way that Flynn embodies the impenetrability of individual identity and the evils of colonialism, the Maroons manifest anticolonial resistance in its purest form. But Banks does not fall back on an easy moral dichotomy that simply elevates good over evil. The remainder of the novel traces the protagonist's increasing identification with the exploited Maroons, an identification that compels him to try and mediate a treaty dispute between rival Maroon factions that almost gets him killed. In the end, he is forced to flee Jamaica for his life. Summarizing the novel himself in his *Paris Review* interview with Faggen, Banks noted that the book "leaves the protagonist at the end stunned into self-recognition by his confrontation with what people call the 'radical other.' " For Banks' protagonist, that self-recognition is the same one that Banks had at Chapel Hill, only to be reiterated with greater force in Jamaica a few years later, that "you can't escape your skin color in a racialized society, even if you're white."

After *The Book of Jamaica,* Banks switched back to short fiction with *Trailerpark* (1981), his third collection and his first book in a wholly realist style. The thirteen stories that comprise *Trailerpark* form a story cycle somewhat in the manner of Sherwood Anderson's famous collection, *Winesburg, Ohio* (1919). Each story deals with one or more of the dozen denizens of Granite State Trailerpark in central New Hampshire, all of whom are ostracized from bourgeois society because they are in impoverished retirement, unemployed (or unemployable), involved in petty crime, black, homosexual, or mentally ill. In the last category is Flora Pease, in trailer number 11, a bedraggled Air Force retiree who breeds guinea pigs until they take over her trailer. Rather than let her neighbors dispose of the animals, she burns her trailer to the ground, guinea pigs and all, and reverts to a squatter's shack in the woods nearby. Equally psychotic is Noni Hubner, a drug-addled young woman who lives with her mother, Nancy, in number 7. Noni hallucinates a telephone conversation with Jesus instructing her to dig up her late father's grave. Tom Smith, in number 9, is burdened with a shiftless, parasitic criminal for a son; Tom eventually commits suicide. Bruce Severance, in number 3, is a diehard hippie-romantic who sings the praises of organic gardening, solar energy, and transcendental meditation. Less wholesome is his self-employment dealing marijuana; after a misunderstanding, his business partners come to his trailer and murder him.

Carol Constant, in number 10, is a black nurse from West Roxbury who has migrated to New Hampshire to take the unsavory job of caring for a dying rich white man. Living with her is her good-for-nothing brother, Terry. Briefly the lover of Noni Hubner, Terry is a "friend" of Bruce Severance who leaves Severance to his own devices when the man is put in mortal danger by his homicidal business associates. Marcelle Chagnon, in number 1, the trailer park manager, is the survivor of marriage to an abusive alcoholic and the grief-haunted mother of a son who died in childhood from spinal meningitis. Leon LaRoche, in number 2, is a deeply closeted gay bank teller who is rebuffed by Tom Smith's volatile son and laughingly dismissed by Dewey Knox, the army retiree in number 6. Doreen Tiede, living in number 4 with her young daughter, is divorced from Buck Tiede, an otherwise macho working man made impotent by excessive sexual repression in his youth. Merle Ring, in number 8, is a retired carpenter whose one great obsession is ice fishing alone on the lake adjacent to the trailer park. When he wins $50,000 in the state lottery, Ring is besieged by his desperate neighbors and most of the money is accidentally lost.

As Merle Ring's saga demonstrates, the trailer park is American society writ small, a miscellaneous collection of people in search of a sense of community that eludes them. The residents live in proximity but mostly live for themselves, in their own worlds. When they do interact, nothing positive seems to come of it. But then all of Banks' trailer people are damaged human beings—intellectually malnourished, emotionally blighted, psychically scarred. For the most part, their problems are the result of bigotry, ignorance, poverty, and abuse, but some are self-inflicted, owing to elaborate delusional systems adopted to cope with intolerable circumstances. Yet Banks never condescends to his characters. The tone he adopts throughout is one of slightly amused irony, an implicit acknowledgment that these people—the human detritus of a brutal and decadent business civilization—are more sinned against than sinning. The self-defeating irrationality of their lives reflects the overall irrationality of their society.

In 1983 Banks finally found a publisher for *The*

Relation of My Imprisonment (1983), a novella he had written in Jamaica in 1976 and 1977, while still enthralled with the metafiction vogue. The long delay in getting the book published might have been because of its cryptic nature and extreme peculiarity. Reading extensively in the literary and cultural history of early New England during the 1970s, Banks discovered the "Relation," a genre of personal narrative written by seventeenth-century Puritans jailed for deviations from religious orthodoxy. Typically, in these Relations, the narrator would confess, often in lurid detail, his fall away from faith into sin, debauchery, or criminality and then would go on to describe his subsequent spiritual recovery through a regimen of self-mortification and penance. The Relation would be read aloud to the Sabbath congregation in order to impart religious inspiration and instruction.

Taken with the Relation's schizoid mixture of piety and titillation, Banks adapted the form to his own purposes. In his *Relation* Banks expertly imitates the dry formality of seventeenth-century English prose and even retains the overall narrative structure, but his unnamed first-person narrator is no Puritan. The man has been imprisoned not for some hedonistic transgression but because he belongs to a heretical religious cult that worships the dead. A coffin maker by trade, Banks' narrator builds coffins for himself and other members of his cult, who lie in them to pray, meditate on mortality, and (presumably) to prepare for their own deaths. Imprisoned for years in a dark, damp cell, the sensory-deprived coffin maker succumbs to an insatiable fantasy life that revolves around lust, greed, and gluttony. Eventually he suffers a fragmentation of mind and personality and becomes "that pathetic and sorrowful figure, the man of time." By the end of his narrative, the coffin maker is still in jail, alone and in mourning for his recently deceased wife, seriously ill with numerous, painful maladies, and threatened by other prisoners. Nonetheless, after a long and intensive period of self-analysis

and meditation, he has managed to recover his religious zeal for the worship of the dead. Having regained self-transcendence and release from earthy cares and concerns, the man is not pitiable but triumphant. Like Job or King Lear, the coffin maker has been reduced in the material world while being elevated spiritually. The nature of his faith is also instructive. Worshiping the dead is no morbid preoccupation but an existentialist recognition of death's finality that stands in marked contrast to the evasive wish fulfillment fantasies of an afterlife promulgated by conventional religion. Banks succinctly encapsulates the meaning of *The Relation of My Imprisonment* with an epigraph taken from an old headstone he found in a New Hampshire cemetery: "Remember death."

ACHIEVING MAINSTREAM STATUS

Until the mid-1980s Banks' fiction swung back and forth between New England and the tropics and generally oscillated between realism (for his short stories) and metafiction (for the novels): a tendency he has since characterized as "bipolarity." With his fourth novel, *Continental Drift* (1985), Banks resolved these dichotomies of setting and form by creating two protagonists and setting them on migratory journeys that ultimately intersect.

Banks' main protagonist is Bob Dubois, a thirty-year-old oil burner repairman from New Hampshire. Married with two children, a mortgage, a mistress on the side, and a low-status job he hates, Dubois is Banks' type for the blue-collar American male—and doubtless another version of Earl Banks. Coming to the realization that "his life has died," Bob decides to start all over again. He sells his house and moves his family to Florida, where he takes a job at his brother's liquor store. Formerly a white man in a white world, Bob is shocked to find himself in a racialized society where whites are not necessarily in the majority. In Florida Bob Dubois' American

Dream soon turns into a nightmare. The job at the liquor store involves long hours and poor pay. He quits after being forced to shoot and kill a man trying to rob the store. Soon thereafter, Bob's brother, Eddie—hopelessly indebted to mobsters—commits suicide. Bob has a doomed affair with a black woman, his marriage disintegrates, and one of his children is diagnosed as "emotionally disturbed." His prospects steadily diminishing, Bob's life unravels to the point that he finds himself supplementing his income by smuggling Haitians to Florida on his fishing boat.

Doleful as it is, Bob Dubois' downward spiral pales in comparison to the horrors faced by Banks' other protagonist, Vanise Dorsinville, a young black woman from Haiti trying to migrate to Florida with her infant son and nephew in tow. Dubois' narrative occupies the lion's share of the novel, but Vanise's story—told in brief interchapters—is vitally important to the book's overall meaning. While Bob Dubois embodies the plight of the American working-class male, Vanise Dorsinville globalizes the American Dream quest by personifying the Third World, which is mostly young, nonwhite, female, desperately poor, and politically disenfranchised. Bob Dubois may be relatively powerless but Vanise Dorsinville is at the utter mercy of everyone she encounters on her exodus. Relentlessly robbed, raped, exploited, and terrorized, she and her baby end up on Bob Dubois' fishing boat with thirteen other illegal aliens trying to get to Miami.

Thus the two narratives converge—with horrifying results, as it turns out. When a Coast Guard cutter appears on the scene, Dubois gives his first mate permission to drive the terrified Haitians from the boat at gunpoint. All immediately drown in the rough seas, except Vanise, who washes up on shore demented and half-dead. In the novel's climactic episode, Bob Dubois attempts to assuage his terrible guilt by seeking out Vanise in Miami's Little Haiti to give her the money the Haitians paid for their passage. Bob eventually locates Vanise and tries to hand her

the money to "remove the sign of his shame," but she refuses it and turns away. He is then set upon by a gang of thugs and stabbed to death. As tragic as it is, Bob Dubois' death does involve at least a kind of moral redemption; he dies trying to expiate his sins. In his *Paris Review* interview, Banks was asked if he foresaw Bob Dubois' demise when he started writing the book. He replied, "I saw the boat, the collision of two worlds and the people drowning . . . and [the fact that] Bob was going to have to deal with that. I didn't know the meaning of it, but I trusted that the meaning would be acquired through getting there. The journey itself would be the truth and meaning of the ending. As in life."

Though *Continental Drift* was easily one of the most depressing novels published in the 1980s, it was a major success for Banks. A strong seller (15,000 copies in hard cover, 100,000 in paperback), the book was generally praised by critics, won the John Dos Passos Award, the American Academy of Arts and Letters Award, a Pulitzer Prize nomination, and was named one of "the best books of 1985" by *Library Journal.* Formerly a little-known writer of academic fiction, Banks was suddenly elevated to mainstream status with the novel's resounding success. The Hollywood director Jonathan Demme promptly bought the film rights to the book and hired Banks to write the screenplay. Soon thereafter, Robert B. Wyatt, editor in chief at Ballantine Books, bought the rights to Banks' earlier books and reissued them in standardized paperback editions.

After completing *Continental Drift,* Banks returned to short fiction, publishing his fourth collection, *Success Stories,* in 1986. Another example of Banks' "bipolarity," the dozen tales contained in *Success Stories* divide equally between quasi-autobiographical stories and political parables that deal with global issues, especially the relationship between the First and Third Worlds. Banks calls himself "Earl Painter" in the stories of the former category, perhaps to invoke the dark influence of his father but also to suggest the counterbalancing impulse of the artist in him. In "My Mother's Memoirs, My Father's Lie, and Other True Stories," Banks links his mother's delusions about knowing famous people to a lie his father told him about the origin of his name and concludes that both parents lied, consciously or otherwise, to make themselves more lovable to their children. With "Success Story" Banks recounts his quixotic journey to Florida to join Fidel Castro's revolution. "Adultery" chronicles Banks' angst-ridden sexual coming-of-age involving an affair with his landlord's wife shortly before his marriage to Darlene Bennett ("Eleanor Hastings"). "Firewood" fictionalizes a turning point in Banks' relationship with his father that occurred in the winter of 1977. Offered a Christmas present of a cord of firewood by his father, Banks reluctantly went over to his father's house to pick up the wood, some of which was already frozen into the snowy ground. In his *Paris Review* interview, Banks recalls that the "old man was in the kitchen watching me. Finally, he put his coat on and came out and worked alongside me. I was working pretty furiously, ignoring him, but after awhile I looked over at him and saw that it was very difficult for him. I suddenly saw him as an old man, and very fragile. We reversed our polarity at that moment." In "Firewood" Banks removes himself from the story and imagines what would have happened if he had never come to collect his wood. His disappointed father, drunk and alone, struggles to get the neglected wood into his barn before the snow covers it—an image of heartbreaking loneliness and desolation.

Earl Banks died of liver disease in 1979 but he still continued to haunt his son's memory and imagination. Banks' next novel, *Affliction* (1989), contrasts two adult sons of an abusive, alcoholic patriarch. As Banks told Robert Faggen, "The two brothers, Wade and Rolfe [Whitehouse], can be seen as equal and opposite reactions to the same conditions. Rolfe manages not to inflict on others the same violence that was inflicted on him—but he does it by withdrawal

and an absence of connection. Whereas Wade doesn't keep other people safe from him; he has relationships, an ex-wife, a lover, a child—he puts himself into the fray of life." Rolfe becomes Banks' narrator but the novel centers on Wade, a depressive, rage-filled alcoholic in his early forties, living alone in a house trailer in the aftermath of a marriage destroyed by his own drunken violence. Despite his best efforts to right himself, Wade sinks deeper into paranoia and violence until he finally snaps, killing his hated father and a coworker. To a degree, the novel was an emotionally purgative experience for Banks. He told Laurel Graeber he wrote *Affliction* "to understand my own life, and also my father's and grandfather's. I wanted to know what brought them to be the human beings they were, and why they inflicted so much suffering."

Two years after the publication of *Affliction*, Banks brought out his seventh novel, *The Sweet Hereafter* (1991). A book that manages to exceed its predecessor in sheer grimness—no mean feat—*The Sweet Hereafter* focuses on the aftermath of a horrifying school bus accident that has claimed the lives of fourteen children in the mythical Adirondack town of Sam Dent. Banks told the interviewer Richard Nicholls that he wrote the novel "to explore how a community is both disrupted and unified by a tragedy." In keeping with a more dispersed focus, Banks uses four consecutive first-person narrators, each of whom embodies an essential perspective on the tragedy. Dolores Driscoll, the bus driver responsible for the accident, comes to serve as the town scapegoat. Billy Ansel, a father who lost his two children in the crash, represents all of the grieving parents. Mitchell Stephens, a high-powered lawyer who specializes in negligence cases, takes on the task of assigning legal blame. Nicole Burnell, a young cheerleader and beauty queen crippled in the accident, represents the victims and survivors. Stephens lines up townspeople for a massive lawsuit, but Nicole Burnell destroys his case by falsely claiming that she saw Dolores Driscoll speeding. The lie is meant to hurt and repudiate her sexually abusive father but ironically has the salutary effect of liberating Sam Dent from its legal entanglements so that it can get on with the business of healing and accepting the unacceptable.

For his eighth novel, a bildungsroman entitled *Rule of the Bone* (1995), Banks used a first-person narrator named Chapman "Chappie" (a.k.a. "Bone") Dorset, a fourteen-year-old "mall rat" from upstate New York who sports a mohawk, a nose ring, and a massive marijuana habit. A product of divorce, Chappie leaves home to escape an abusive stepfather and embarks on a journey of self-discovery that plunges him into the world of bikers, drugs, child pornography, and homelessness. Befriended by a middle-aged black Rastafarian named I-Man who comes to serve as his mentor, Chappie ventures to Jamaica with I-Man and there finds his long-lost father, "Doc," only to discover that the man is hopelessly self-interested and corrupt. Indeed, Doc has I-Man murdered in a pique of jealous rage after Chappie—in an act of misplaced allegiance—informs him that I-Man has slept with Doc's girl-friend. Though undeniably tragic, I-Man's death liberates Chappie from his romantic fantasy of father–son reconciliation; he comes to realize that chosen loyalties can be more valuable than blood ties.

Banks' ninth novel, *Cloudsplitter* (1998), signaled a new direction for him as a writer. Ever since his Chapel Hill days, Banks had been fascinated by John Brown, the fiery abolitionist who martyred himself and most of his followers at Harpers Ferry in 1859. After his marriage to the poet Chase Twichell in 1988, Banks took up residence in Keene, New York, a short distance from John Brown's Adirondack homestead and grave. Brown's proximity rekindled Banks' interest in him. As he told Robert Faggen, "The ghost of John Brown returned to haunt me." In about 1990 Banks undertook a fictionalized account of

Brown's life that would involve seven years of research and writing and result in Banks' longest (758 pages) and most ambitious book to date. Told from the point of view of Owen Brown, the only son to witness Osawatomie and Harpers Ferry and survive, *Cloudsplitter* is a richly detailed portrait of an enormously energetic, complex, morally ambiguous, and ultimately baffling man—for Banks, "the last Puritan and the first modern terrorist." Banks' book does not resolve the long-standing controversy over the question of Brown's sanity but it does make a powerful case for Brown's heroism and historical importance.

Russell Banks retired from his position as the Howard G. B. Clark '21 University Professor at Princeton University in 1998 and now devotes his full energies to writing. The author of thirteen books over a twenty-five-year period, Banks has been more productive than most of his contemporaries and shows no signs of slowing down. Two of his novels—*Affliction* and *The Sweet Hereafter*—were made into award-winning films in the late 1990s and three more—*The Book of Jamaica, Continental Drift,* and *Rule of the Bone*—were in the works. Banks' stature as a major American writer continues to grow and the passion that fuels his art continues unabated. In his *Paris Review* interview, Banks said that he was driven by two "ongoing perplexities . . . First, Is there such a thing as wisdom? And second, Is there such a thing as heroism?"

Selected Bibliography

WORKS OF RUSSELL BANKS

NOVELS AND SHORT STORIES
Family Life. New York: Equinox Books/Avon, 1975.

Searching for Survivors. New York: Fiction Collective, 1975.
Hamilton Stark. Boston: Houghton Mifflin, 1978.
The New World: Tales. Urbana, Ill.: University of Illinois Press, 1978. (Contains "The Custodian," "The Perfect Couple," "A Sentimental Education," "About the Late Zimma (Penny) Cate: Selections from Her Loving Husband's Memory Hoard," "The Conversion," "The Rise of the Middle Class," "Indisposed," "The Caul," "The Adjutant Bird," and "The New World.")
The Book of Jamaica. Boston: Houghton Mifflin, 1980.
Trailerpark. Boston: Houghton Mifflin, 1981. (Contains "The Guinea Pig Lady," "Cleaving, and Other Needs," "Black Man and White Woman in Dark Green Rowboat," "Dis Bwoy, Him Gwan," "What Noni Hubner Did Not Tell the Police about Jesus," "Comfort," "God's Country," "Principles," "The Burden," "Politics," "The Right Way," "The Child Screams and Looks Back at You," and "The Fisherman.")
The Relation of My Imprisonment. Washington, D.C.: Sun & Moon Press, 1983.
Continental Drift. New York: Harper & Row, 1985.
Success Stories. New York: Harper & Row, 1986. (Contains "Queen for a Day," "My Mother's Memoirs, My Father's Lie, and Other True Stories," "The Fish," "Success Story," "The Gully," "Adultery," "Hostage," "Mistake," "Children's Story," "Sarah Cole: A Type of Love Story," "Captions," and "Firewood.")
Affliction. New York: Harper & Row, 1989.
The Sweet Hereafter. New York: HarperCollins, 1991.
Rule of the Bone. New York: HarperCollins, 1995.
Cloudsplitter. New York: HarperFlamingo, 1998.

UNCOLLECTED SHORT STORIES
"Crossing the Line." *New York Times Magazine,* December 20, 1992, p. 21.
"Just Don't Touch Anything." *GQ,* May 1993, pp. 126–131.
"Plains of Abraham." *Esquire,* July 1999, pp. 78–85.
"That." In *Statements: New Fiction from the Fiction Collective.* Compiled by John Baumbach. New York: George Braziller, 1975. Pp. 28–33.
"The Visitor." In *Disorderly Conduct: The VLS Fiction Reader.* Edited by M. Mark. New York: Serpents Tail, 1991. Pp. 15–24.

"Xmas." *Antaeus* 64/65: 176–180 (Spring–Autumn 1990).

POETRY
15 Poems. With William Matthews and Newton Smith. Chapel Hill, N.C.: Lillabulero Press, 1967.
30/6. With Peter Wild, Charles Simic, Robert Morgan, William Matthews, and Doug Collins. Supplement to *The Quest* 3, 2 (Winter–Spring 1969).
Waiting to Freeze: Poems. Northwood Narrows, N.H.: Lillabulero Press, 1969.
Snow: Meditations of a Cautious Man in Winter. Hanover, N.H.: Granite Publications, 1974.

OTHER WORKS
[Coedited with Michael Ondaatje & David Young] *Brushes with Greatness: An Anthology of Close Encounters with Greatness.* Toronto: Coach House Press, 1989.
[Photographs by Arturo Patten; text by Russell Banks] *The Invisible Stranger: The Patten, Maine Photographs of Arturo Patten.* New York: HarperCollins, 1999.

BIOGRAPHICAL AND CRITICAL STUDIES

Aldridge, John W. "Blue Collar Enigmas." [Review of *Success Stories.*] *New York Times Book Review,* June 22, 1986, p. 22.
Atlas, James. "A Great American Novel." [Review of *Continental Drift.*] *Atlantic Monthly,* February 1985, pp. 94, 96–97.
Bair, Deirdre. "Parable from the Coffin." [Review of *The Relation of My Imprisonment.*] *New York Times Book Review,* April 1, 1984, p. 8.
Benvenuto, Christine. "Mapping the Imagination: A Profile of Russell Banks." *Poets & Writers* 26: 20–27 (March/April 1998).
Birkerts, Sven. "Bleak House." [Review of *Affliction.*] *New Republic,* September 11, 1989, pp. 38–41.
Birstein, Ann. "Metaphors, Metaphors." [Review of *Hamilton Stark.*] *New York Times Book Review,* July 2, 1978, p. 12.
Brown, Wesley. "Who to Blame, Who to Forgive." *New York Times Magazine,* September 10, 1989, pp. 53, 66, 68–70.

Domini, John. Review of *Success Stories. Boston Review* 11, 4: 27–28 (August 1986).

Douglas, Christopher R. "Reciting America: Repetition and the Cultural Self-Sufficiency of the United States in the Fiction of Russell Banks, Ralph Ellison, Maxine Hong Kingston, and T. Coraghessan Boyle." Ph.D. diss., University of Toronto, 1997.

Eder, Richard. "A Small Town Copes With Tragedy." *Los Angeles Times Book Review,* September 1, 1991, pp. 3, 8.

———. Review of *Success Stories. Los Angeles Times Book Review,* June 22, 1986, pp. 2, 10.

Graeber, Laurel. "The Perspective of the Perpetrator." *New York Times Book Review,* September 17, 1989, p. 7.

Graham, Julie, ed. "Russell Banks." *Current Biography Yearbook, 1992.* New York: H. W. Wilson, 1993.

Haley, Vanessa. "Russell Banks' Use of 'The Frog King' in 'Sarah Cole: A Type of Love Story.'" *Notes on Contemporary Literature* 27: 7–10 (May 1997).

Henson, Beth. "Ploughshares into Swords: John Brown and the Poet of Rage: an Appreciation of the Work of Russell Banks." *Lip* 9: 58–62 (August 1998).

Hitchens, Christopher. "The New Migrations." [Review of *Continental Drift*.] *Times Literary Supplement,* October 25, 1985, p. 1203.

Klinkowitz, Jerome. "From Banks, a Novel That's the Real Thing." *Book Week—Chicago Sun Times,* March 9, 1980, p. 12.

Leckie, Ross. "Plot-Resistant Narrative and Russell Banks' 'Black Man and White Woman in Dark Green Rowboat.' " *Studies in Short Fiction* 31, 3: 407–414 (Summer 1994).

LeClair, Thomas. Review of *Searching for Survivors. New York Times Book Review,* May 18, 1975, pp. 6–7.

Lee, Don. "About Russell Banks." *Ploughshares* 19, 4: 209–213 (Winter 1993).

May, Charles. "The Sweet Hereafter." *Magill's Literary Annual, 1996.* Pasadena, Calif.: Salem Press, 1992.

Nicholls, Richard. "The Voices of the Survivors." *New York Times Book Review,* September 15, 1991, p. 29.

Niemi, Robert. "Cloudsplitter." *Magill's Literary Annual, 1999.* Vol. 1. Pasadena, Calif.: Salem Press, 1999. Pp. 190–193.

———. "Rule of the Bone." *Magill's Literary Annual, 1996.* Vol. 2. Pasadena, Calif.: Salem Press, 1996. Pp. 668–671.

———. *Russell Banks.* New York: Twayne Publishers, 1997.

Pfeil, Fred. "Beating the Odds: The Brechtian Aesthetic of Russell Banks." In his *Another Tale to Tell: Politics and Narrative in Postmodern Culture.* New York: Verso, 1990.

Rosenblatt, Roger. "An Inescapable Need to Blame." [Review of *The Sweet Hereafter.*] *New York Times Book Review,* September 15, 1991, pp. 1, 29.

Strouse, Jean. "Indifferent Luck and Hungry Gods." [Review of *Continental Drift.*] *New York Times Book Review,* March 24, 1985, pp. 11–12.

Towers, Robert. "Uprooted." [Review of *Continental Drift.*] *New York Review of Books,* April 11, 1985, pp. 36–37.

———. "You Can't Go Home Again." [Review of *Affliction.*] *New York Review of Books,* December 7, 1989, pp. 46–47.

Vandersee, Charles. "Russell Banks and the Great American Reader." *The Cresset* 53: 13–17 (December 1989).

Wachtel, Chuck. "Character Witness." [Review of *The Sweet Hereafter.*] *Nation,* December 16, 1991, pp. 786–788.

Wilkie, Curtis. "Grit Lit." *Boston Globe,* August 25, 1991.

INTERVIEWS

Benedict, Pinckney. "Russell Banks." *Bomb* 52: 24–29 (Summer 1995).

Boyers, Robert. "Talking About American Fiction." *Salmagundi* 93: 61–77 (1992). (An edited transcript of a panel discussion among Marilyn Robinson, Russell Banks, Robert Stone, and David Rieff, August 1990, New York State Summer Writer's Institute, Skidmore College.)

Brinson, Linda. "Obsession—Author Russell Banks Tells Writers: Find Yours." *Salem [N.C.] Journal,* November 1, 1987.

Checkoway, Julie and English 497. "An Interview with Russell Banks." *AWP Chronicle* 28, 6: 1–8 (Summer 1996).

Faggen, Robert. "The Art of Fiction CLII: Russell Banks." *The Paris Review* 40: 50–88 (Summer 1998).

Reeves, Trish. "The Search for Clarity: An Interview with Russell Banks." *New Letters* 53, 3: 44–59 (Spring 1987).

Thiebaux, Marcelle. "PW Interviews Russell Banks." *Publishers Weekly,* March 15, 1985, pp. 120–121.

FILMS BASED ON THE WORKS OF RUSSELL BANKS

Affliction. Screenplay by Paul Schrader. Directed by Paul Schrader. Lion's Gate Films, 1997.

The Sweet Hereafter. Screenplay by Atom Egoyan. Directed by Atom Egoyan. Fine Line Features, 1997.

—ROBERT NIEMI

Ann Beattie

1947–

WITH THE simultaneous publication in 1976 of *Distortions,* a collection of stories, and *Chilly Scenes of Winter,* a novel, Ann Beattie embarked on a dual career. As a writer of short stories, she slipped immediately into a distinctive and assured style, which, though it has gone through a series of modulations, has retained a remarkable consistency; as a novelist, her path has been more uneven, but her novels expand her literary project, broadening her reach and pushing her to experiment in ways that often enrich her stories as well.

From the beginning it was clear that Beattie had an uncanny ability to express the longings and disappointments of a generation that came of age in the 1960s and moved all too quickly into the downtrodden 1970s; in her early work, she captures the half-resigned, half-aimless spirit of disenchanted upper-middle-class twenty- and thirty-year-olds between jobs, between marriages, and between emotions, with consummate skill. As time passed, Beattie moved on too, registering the attitudes and currents of the 1980s and the 1990s, and not always from the perspective of members of her generation—some of her most memorable characters are children and adolescents coming of age in the last decades of the twentieth century. The power of her stories to heighten their contexts, no matter the era, and to point up the idiosyncrasies of a particular climate is unquestionable. But when viewed over a quarter of a century, the cumulative impact of her fiction owes as much to small shifts and gestures— the clasping of a hand in one story, a quick glance in another—as it does to broader truths. Identity is not set by the usual defining characteristics of job, appearance, or family history. Instead, it is the quality of characters' movements, the timbre of their conversations, and the way they relate to lovers, children, and friends that fix them in the reader's mind.

Beattie's ability to suggest, to approach her subjects indirectly, and to allow revelation to creep in on an unexpected slant is central to her work. Her narrative style is most pared down and oblique in her early novels and stories, growing more textured and complex as her career progresses, but she has always been motivated by a desire to catch her subjects off guard, to illuminate them from a surprising angle; she has said that she hopes her characters are "the animated equivalents of outtakes during a portrait shoot." To succeed, she must surprise herself: her stories, and even her novels, are most often inspired by a visual detail or a mood, and she writes without knowing what the plot will be. The more inevitable and effortless the end product seems, the better she has succeeded.

BEATTIE'S BACKGROUND

Beattie's own story is simple, in outline at least. Born on September 8, 1947, to James A. and Charlotte (Crosby) Beattie in Washington, D.C., she had what she has called a very ordinary, middle-class childhood. Her father was an administrator at the Department of Health, Education, and Welfare, and her mother was a housewife. Beattie was an only child, and growing up in the D.C. suburbs, she spent much of her time alone or with her parents. "I probably saw a lot of things that other kids didn't see because I was alone. Being integrated into an adult world happened very early on in my life, and it made me a watcher. I saw things as being wrought with significance, in one situation after another." She was, she has said, "an extremely shy person back then," but she read, drew, and wrote stories and was a generally happy child, until she started public high school. Uninspired by her classes there, and generally depressed, she graduated in the bottom tenth of her class. Luckily, her father had a connection at American University, or she might not have been able to go to college at all. Once there, she majored in journalism, which she chose as a kind of default option, and switched to English a few years later. Though she claims to have had no literary aspirations in college, she was the editor of the university literary journal, and she was chosen by *Mademoiselle* magazine to be a guest editor in 1968.

Unsure of what to do when she graduated in 1969, she went on to graduate school at the University of Connecticut with the vague idea that she would get a doctorate in literature and teach; she would receive a master's degree in 1970, but abandon her doctoral studies in 1972. "I've never had a job in my life. I never wanted one then, and I don't want one now," she explained in an interview with Josh Getlin in 1990. "I stayed in school not because of a love of the academic life or even because I wanted to buy time as a writer. I stayed

in school because I didn't want to work." She was writing stories, but she had never considered the possibility that she might make a living as a writer. It was only when some other graduate students mentioned her stories to a professor, J. D. O'Hara, and he took an interest in her writing, that she began working seriously at it.

> He really became my official editor. He taught me more about writing than I could have imagined learning elsewhere. He did it all by writing comments in the margin of my manuscripts. We never once sat down and talked about things. I would put a story in his faculty mailbox, and he would return it, usually the next day, in my student teaching assistant mailbox.

Nevertheless, Beattie has always stressed that she knew practically nothing about writing at the beginning of her career. "I think I had very little sense of what other people were doing. I didn't read much contemporary literature and I had very little sense of what other writers sounded like." She was so oblivious to the mechanics of the craft, she claims, that when the interviewer Neila Seshachari asked her why she had decided to write *Chilly Scenes of Winter* in the present tense, she answered, "It's not written in the present tense." (It is, of course.) *Western Humanities Review* published her first story in 1972, but the official start of her career came in 1974, when *The New Yorker* published "A Platonic Relationship," picking it out of the slush pile after rejecting twenty-two previous submissions. For years, her relationship with the magazine was a charmed one, and under the editor Roger Angell, she became one of a select group, along with contemporaries such as Raymond Carver, Richard Ford, Mary Robison, and Tobias Wolff.

The New Yorker had cultivated such a distinctive brand of short story that readers in the know felt they could sanction or dismiss the fiction the magazine published as "*New Yorker* stories." The kind of story they had in mind was clean, spare, and understated, and soon the writers whose prose could be described in those terms came to be identified as part of a literary movement called minimalism. Beattie and her contemporaries did share many qualities, but they resisted being lumped together indiscriminately. Minimalism, which was originally the name given to a movement in the visual arts, postulated that absence and empty space were central to the work's impact, and minimalist fiction correspondingly centered on what was left unsaid, investing small gestures and details with the force of what was not directly expressed. This was an enticing formula—perhaps too enticing. "If I had to generalize, I'd say what I dislike about a lot of so-called minimalist writing is that it has no clear trajectory," Beattie said. "With a Carver story, I could at least tell you where I think something is being said that isn't verbalized, and how I think he's led into that." Because work by writers like Beattie and Carver seemed deceptively simple, it was tempting for lesser writers to churn out facile approximations of their stories.

The spareness of Beattie's own early prose was a response to the tenor of her times as much as it was to any literary imperative. The one writer she spent real time studying in graduate school was the stripped-bare Samuel Beckett, but asceticism was part of the climate of the 1970s, too. "The whole idea of antimaterialism was much in the air when I was going to college. So if we're talking about stories that I wrote in the early or mid-70s, I was often surrounded by a lot of people who professed not to want material possessions." Even so, they couldn't help but cling to some symbolic object, something they owned, however small: "What they tended to do, on however sad or humorous a level, was often to fixate on their pen, or something like that . . . . I never failed to see that." Like the small objects her characters focus on—a bunny-rabbit soap dish, potted violets, and a white scarf, for example, from her first collection of stories—Beattie's short sentences

are slender supports shoring up whole avalanches of sentiment. The spaces and silences echo, too, the disenchantment of Beattie's generation. "My friends and most of the people I know," she explained in a *Village Voice* interview with Bob Miner in 1976, "all feel sort of let down, either by not having involved themselves more in the 60s now that the 70s are so dreadful, or else by having involved themselves very much to no avail . . . and these are the people I'm writing about."

The people she was writing about certainly recognized themselves in her work. From 1974 until the simultaneous release of her first collection of stories, *Distortions,* and her first novel, *Chilly Scenes of Winter,* in 1976, her *New Yorker* stories were so popular that it was said circulation increased when one was scheduled to appear. Readers identified with her hapless protagonists, their makeshift lives, their shaky marriages, their nomadic habits. It was as if Beattie, like Francie in "Friends," a story from Beattie's second collection, *Secrets and Surprises* (1979), was the host of an open-ended house party, guests wandering in and out, drinking Gallo wine, sleeping, listening to Bob Dylan, eating breakfasts of eggs Benedict and leftover champagne mixed with ginger ale. Like F. Scott Fitzgerald and J. D. Salinger earlier in the century, she was hailed as the voice of a disaffected, postwar generation, and at the same time, as a kind of literary offspring of John Cheever and John Updike, chroniclers of suburbia. Interviewers loved to portray her as a character in one of her own stories, and in the process, she and her writing came close to being caricatured. In the *New York Times Book Review* in 1980, Joyce Maynard describes how a dog runs to Beattie's door when she knocks, and music is playing loudly. Maggie Lewis, in 1979, lingers over a description of Beattie in the stuffy lounge of the Algonquin hotel, decked out in Adidas running shoes and army surplus fatigue pants.

Beattie's real life in the 1970s involved quite

a bit of hard work, including several long years of teaching, which she did not particularly enjoy. She and her husband, David Gates, a musician she met in graduate school in 1973, bumped around from the University of Virginia in 1975 and 1976, to Harvard in 1977 (where Beattie was the Briggs-Copeland lecturer). Beattie found it hard to write while she was teaching creative writing: "When I see 20 bad student stories a week, I think, 'Oh there's too much bad writing in the world already.' And then I don't do my work either." In 1978 she was awarded a Guggenheim Fellowship, which allowed her to support herself for a few years without taking a teaching job. A second stint at the University of Virginia in 1980 was her final full-time position; since then, she has been able to lead a life focused on her writing.

After a difficult divorce in 1982 ("Getting divorced affected everything, my writing included. It affected the way I walked the dog. I did not recover from it quickly"), Beattie left New York, where she had settled, and moved to Charlottesville, Virginia. It was there that she met her second husband, the artist Lincoln Perry. Both were wary of marriage, but in 1988 they tied the knot in an impromptu ceremony. Known among her friends for her quirky sense of humor and love of practical jokes, Beattie lured a few guests to a rented summerhouse, had a justice of the peace drop by, and was married on the spot. One friend, Beattie later chuckled, was so shocked that "it took him five days to get composed enough to board a plane back to New York. Lincoln and I both like to shock people." Since neither Beattie nor Perry is tied down by their work, they now split their time between Maine and Key West, Florida.

Beattie objects to any direct equation of her life and fiction: her work "obviously does have to do with me, but it has more to do with what's captured my attention, what seems possible to transform into art." More vexing has been the notion that she is a spokesperson for her generation, a conclusion that not only suggests that her literary achievements are subverted by a kind of sociological urge, but also implies that her fiction is dated and of interest mainly in the context of her age. The mixed critical reception of *Distortions* and *Chilly Scenes of Winter* marked the beginning of Beattie's often frustrating history with the literary establishment, which has acknowledged her as one of the major writers of the late twentieth century but has also seemed to dismiss her on the grounds of her own popularity. As the critic Carolyn Porter explained in 1985: "It is fashionable these days . . . to express a superior disdain for Beattie." Toward the end of the 1990s, as her short stories became longer, she had trouble placing them in magazines before they appeared in book form, and she lamented, "Any notion that this gets easier, or that people treat me nicer—it's exactly the opposite of what really is the case." The reception of *Park City,* however, a collection of new and selected short stories published in 1998, was overwhelmingly positive and sparked a number of thoughtful overviews of her career.

BEATTIE'S EARLY WORK

While most reviewers of *Distortions* and *Chilly Scenes of Winter* praised the effortless glide of Beattie's prose, the more conservative took issue with her morally neutral perspective, simultaneously condemning the culture she depicted and her failure to judge it. The circumstances her fiction took for granted—divorce, adultery, lack of meaningful employment, and alienation—were deplored, and the stories were criticized for offering no redemption or escape. It was not Beattie's project, however, to provide solutions or to judge, but rather to record the world as she saw it. At the same time, her perspective is not entirely cool and reportorial, as it has often been described. In her early fiction, sentences are short and simple, associations are abrupt, and descriptive passages are few and far between, but the detachment thus achieved is empathic rather than clinical. Warmth is implicit, too, in her characters' attitudes toward each other: as alienated as they may be, they long for attachment but are unable for one reason or another to achieve it, or to allow themselves to feel it.

The malaise of the characters in the stories that make up *Distortions* may be related to 1970s discontent, romantic disappointment, or even tragedy, but there is an underlying, existential dissatisfaction that cannot be fully explained by external circumstances. Michael, in "Fancy Flights," has retreated almost entirely from adult life. He is unemployed, separated from his wife, uninterested in his daughter, and always smoking hash, and while any of these things might plausibly be the cause of his depression, it is equally likely that they are the result of it. There is a job he could have, but he doesn't want it; his wife tries to get him to reestablish a friendly relationship with his daughter, but he won't. He is so unhappy that he envies his daughter's plastic bunny soap dish, because it has something— soap—to hold on to, but he refuses to hold on to anything himself. Then there is the unnamed protagonist of "Vermont," whose husband, David, leaves her; some time later she ends up with another man, Noel. She realizes, finally, that "David makes me sad and Noel makes me happy," but she can't stop herself from thinking about David or feeling slight scorn for Noel. And in "The Lifeguard," a married couple at the beach with their children are vaguely dissatisfied with each other; after a terrible incident claims the lives of two of the children, their dissatisfactions are eerily transferred into the tragedy's aftermath, and they grow neither closer together nor farther apart.

Still, none of the stories in the collection are so bleak that they are not leavened by Beattie's wry humor. Even characters who are not happy

are amusing, and often they are amusing about being unhappy. In "Vermont," Noel describes how he once tried unsuccessfully to kill himself, first with a scarf he borrowed from the narrator's then-husband. "The truth was that he couldn't give David his scarf back because it was stretched from being knotted so many times. But he had been too chicken to hang himself and he had swallowed a bottle of drugstore sleeping pills instead. Then he got frightened and went outside and hailed a cab." Beattie is interested in the shock value of comedy, too, and indulges in it more fully in *Distortions* than anywhere else, in a series of uncharacteristically experimental stories covering exotic terrain: a college dropout lures his sister's friend's cat-loving maid to the Grand Canyon; a movie ticket taker leaves his wife for a Puerto Rican woman with orange lipstick; MacDonald visits his brother, who is a dwarf; and a team of aliens come down to Earth to take nude pictures of Estelle and Big Bear, a couple on their way home from a party. Beattie explains that at the time she was "writing about things that I was curious about, and I was writing about people who weren't exactly like me . . . . I was interested in an almost speculative thinking about those people."

Though her more experimental stories are not her most successful, the consistency and polish of the work collected in *Distortions* are impressive, with stories like "Vermont," "The Parking Lot," and "Imagined Scenes" introducing readers to the basic themes and settings of her fiction. Reviewers sometimes joked that anyone could write an Ann Beattie story if they followed certain rules and included certain props: a dog, a snowstorm, a song on the radio, a house in the woods, a phone call, a lover, an apartment in the city. Though this is a reductive way to look at the stories, Beattie's concerns do hold remarkably steady from one book to the next, and she has the uncanny ability to conjure up a seamless fictional reality. The echoes from one story to the next, and from one book to the next, foster a sense of continuity and a faith in the existence of a coherent imagined universe.

Chilly Scenes of Winter slips directly into an easy familiarity.

> "*Permettez-moi de vous présenter Sam McGuire,*" Charles says. Sam is standing in the doorway holding a carton of beer. Since Sam's dog died he has been drinking a lot of beer. It is raining, and Sam's hair streams down his face.
> "Hi," Susan says without looking up.
> "Hi," Sam says.

Beginning with dialogue, and built around dialogue, the novel moves loosely from one conversation to the next, the intervening passages most often recording inner deliberation or associative thought. Beattie has always found dialogue easier to write than exposition, and that ease is evident here. In comparison with her later novels, which are more elaborately constructed, the progress of *Chilly Scenes of Winter* is linear. Like much of her early work, and especially her short stories, which were often written in a few hours, the novel was composed very quickly, the rough draft reportedly finished in three weeks. Also like many of the short stories, but like none of the other novels, *Chilly Scenes of Winter* is written in the present tense. Effortless and immediate as the narration may seem, the selection of detail and the jumps from one idea to the next are subtly calibrated. Charles, Beattie's protagonist, can think of few things that do not remind him of his ex-lover, Laura, and sequences of obliquely related thoughts almost always lead to images or memories of her. In the car, on the way to a highway rest stop to rescue Pamela Smith, an old girlfriend who's been robbed, "he looks out the side window at a big blue truck rolling by. If he were Jack Nicholson in *Five Easy Pieces* he could hop a truck, start a new life. What new life would he like? The same life, but married to Laura. Or even living with Laura. Or even dating Laura."

Jack Nicholson in *Five Easy Pieces* is the link between the truck and Laura; there are references throughout the novel to Richard Nixon, Janis Joplin, John Lennon, and Bob Dylan. Much has been made of Beattie's allusions to pop culture, and in *Chilly Scenes of Winter* they are everywhere. It is the 1970s, and the chill of the decade can be felt deep in the bones of the novel. "The song is over. Janis Joplin is dead. Jim Morrison's *widow* is dead." The plot itself revolves around 1970s concerns: economic downturn, fraught relationships with parents, and the mutation of the nuclear family into looser associations of friends and relatives. Charles lives alone, but his best friend, Sam, is like family; when Sam loses his job as a jacket salesman (he was overqualified in the first place; he graduated Phi Beta Kappa), he moves in with Charles. Charles' mother lives across town with his stepfather, Pete; she is gradually losing her mind and must be coaxed out of bathtubs and convinced to wear clothes. Charles' younger sister, Susan, a straight-arrow college student, is the most grown-up member of the family, and Charles turns to her for advice. When Pamela Smith moves in briefly with Charles, too, after her adventures in California as a new-fledged lesbian turn sour, she brings with her the trappings of the sexual revolution, which seem oddly exotic. The truth is, as much as Charles is part of a new, more complicated world, the things he yearns for are simple and even traditional: he wants Laura back, and he wants her to make a dessert for him, a dessert she made when they were together and happy, an orange and chocolate soufflé. The pervasive melancholia of the 1970s merges with a timeless romantic longing. "It occurs to Charles that songs are always appropriate. No matter what record is played, it is always applicable. Once, on a date in high school, when he was going to tell his date he loved her, Elvis Presley came on the radio singing 'Loving You.' It always happens: politicians are always crooks, records are always applicable to the situation."

In his way, Charles is a great American dreamer, and as such he is created in the mold of Jay Gatsby, the most famous American dreamer of all. The parallels Beattie draws between Charles' quest for Laura and Gatsby's quest for Daisy are explicit and playful. Charles tries to convince Sam one night to drive with him past Laura's house:

"The light might be on."
    "Of course the light will be on. She wouldn't be in bed this early."
    "Then I want to see the light."
    "What's this, *The Great Gatsby* or something?"

But Charles wants to believe he is not really like Gatsby. "Gatsby waited all his life, and then Daisy slipped away. Charles has only been waiting for two years, and he'll get her back. He has to get her back. He will get her back and take her to Bermuda." At the end of *Chilly Scenes of Winter,* it seems Charles might be right. A miracle has occurred: he is with Laura, and Laura is making her soufflé. But Charles is not so different from the characters in *Distortions,* and though he is where he wants to be, he and Laura both are and are not the couple they used to be—and it is hard to say which prospect is most disturbing.

Romantic longing is a quintessential Beattie theme, and in *Secrets and Surprises* stories like "A Vintage Thunderbird," "Colorado," and "Friends" give it a bitter new twist. Nick, of "A Vintage Thunderbird," has loved Karen for years, but he does not know how to convince her that they should be more than friends. "It took him a long while to accept that she thought he was special, and later, when she began to date other men, it took him a long while to realize that she did not mean to shut him out of her life." Robert, of "Colorado," loves Penelope in the same hopeless, long-term way, but he finally wins her when he agrees to make a senseless move with her from New Haven to Colorado. The day before they

leave, Penelope's ex-boyfriend Dan calls to tell Robert, "She'll wear you down, she'll wear you out, she'll kill you." Perry, of "Friends," again, has loved Francie for years, but her final capitulation is as half-hearted as Penelope's. Beattie writes perceptively and convincingly from the male perspective, and her male characters are frequently men like Nick, Robert, and Perry: earnest, thoughtful, well-meaning dreamers. Her women can be more distant and harder to fathom. Karen, Penelope, and Francie, in any case, are not prepared to be objects of yearning, and there is a suggestion that they themselves do not know what they want. Even Francie, who does seem to know—she is determined to be a successful painter—equivocates with the personal. "I don't know what I want. . . . I want to be left alone, but I need to have people around." All three women are evasive, unwilling to communicate. As a result, even though Nick never wins Karen, and she sells the white Thunderbird that has become the symbol of their friendship, at the end of the story she finally looks him straight in the face and a note of hope, however tardy, is struck. "He looked at her sadly for a long time, until she looked up with tears in her eyes. / 'Do you think maybe we could get it back if I offered more than he paid me for it?' she said. 'You probably don't think that's a sensible suggestion, but at least that way we could get it back.' "

Hope has little place in "Weekend" and "Octascope," two of the bleakest stories in the collection, and in all of Beattie's fiction. In each one, a younger woman lives with an older man, for reasons that have more to do with need than love. Lenore, in "Weekend," has lived with George, a former English professor, for years, and they have two children. On the weekends, he invites old students to visit and drinks too much. Lenore knows he sleeps with some of the women, and once she heard him tell one of them that Lenore stayed with him because she was "simple." Several people ask her why she does stay, and she gives different answers. What she tells her brother is close to the truth—"She has a comfortable house. She cooks. She keeps busy and she loves her two children"—but even closer is what she says to George: "I'm the only one you can go too far with." The unnamed protagonist of "Octascope" knows exactly why she and her baby daughter stay with Carlos, a marionette maker: they have nowhere else to go, and Carlos is "a kind person who wanted a woman to live with him." All the protagonist wants to find out is whether they are to stay "always, or for a long time, or a short time." If dreams bring only grief, these two stories suggest that unblinking acceptance of reality is even harsher.

BREAKING NEW GROUND

With the publication of her second novel, *Falling in Place,* in 1980, Beattie's work won new approval from critics; the *New York Times* reviewer rhapsodized that it was "like going from gray television to full-color movies." Set between suburban Connecticut and New York City, *Falling in Place* is peopled by two interlocking sets of characters. John Knapp lives in Connecticut with his wife, Louise, and two of their children, teenage Mary and ten-year-old John Joel. The marriage is unhappy, and John's estrangement from his family is barely concealed. During the week, he lives with his mother (his youngest son, five-year-old Brandt, lives with her, too) on the pretext that her home in Rye is closer to his advertising job in the city, and most nights he stays late in New York with Nina, his young lover, who works as a salesgirl at Lord and Taylor. Mary is taking a summer school class, and her teacher, Cynthia, lives with Peter Spangle, a man who used to be Nina's lover. Beattie develops each character's story from his or her own perspective, including as still another counterpoint the story of a half-crazy magician who falls in love with Cynthia.

Despite all the shuttling back and forth of characters, the novel's mood, as the title suggests, is one of stasis. John is waiting for the right time to leave his wife and children, but that right time never seems to come. Cynthia is waiting for Spangle, who has been away for a suspiciously long time, to return from a trip. Nina is killing time working at Lord and Taylor, waiting for John. Even the magician is waiting, lurking outside Cynthia's apartment. John Joel and his friend Parker see a George Segal exhibit in the city, plaster figures frozen in the throes of domestic life. Meanwhile, up above, Skylab is falling, SLOWLY, and the same song, Blondie's "Heart of Glass," is always on the radio.

Finally, it is John Joel who shatters the uneasy calm. Overweight and lonely, with Parker, a maladjusted boy who plays disturbing pranks, as his only friend, John Joel is consumed by two passions. One is his love of food, and the other is his hatred of his sister, Mary, who taunts him mercilessly. When Parker puts a gun in John Joel's hand, and John Joel aims at Mary and pulls the trigger, the shot blasts the family out of its torpor. It is not a coincidence that it is John Joel who precipitates the novel's climax; like many of Beattie's child characters, he is preternaturally grown-up, while his parents cling to childish fantasies. After a long conversation of a kind mothers are not generally thought to have with their children, Louise looks at John Joel. "You must think I'm really silly," she says. "Do you think I make a good adult?" John, meanwhile, dreams of escaping to Nina, who he believes can save him from his adult life, and while talking to Mary in the hospital after she is shot, he abdicates decision-making power to her: "You want things to change—how? By my being in Connecticut?" "Be where you want to be," she says.

With its broader narrative sweep and more complex construction, *Falling in Place* did break new ground for Beattie. The hops from one character's perspective to the next in the third-person omniscient show up again later in *Love Always* (1985), and Beattie anticipates the split perspective of later novels like *Picturing Will* (1989), told from multiple points of view. Also like *Picturing Will* and *Another You* (1995), *Falling in Place* is punctuated with italicized sections. In *Falling in Place,* these sections fall at the end of each chapter, and though their function is questionable—ostensibly they express feelings the characters cannot openly voice, but in form and content they are not much different from the main text—they underscore Beattie's formal ambitions. Beattie has always struggled more with novels than with short stories, and when *Falling in Place* was published in 1980, she admitted: "I really do feel like a bumbler with the novel form. . . . I wonder if there are novelists who feel they know how to write novels. I wonder if this knowledge exists." Ten years later, she reiterated: "The novel form is not the one that comes to me most naturally. I normally rev myself up by having some complex idea, not in terms of plot, exactly, but in terms of how I'll approach writing the book."

While experimenting with the novel, she continued to produce short stories, and her third volume, *The Burning House,* was published in 1982. As Beattie's characters grow older, they generally become more affluent and established, and though they are not much happier than the characters of *Secrets and Surprises,* there is a new luminescence to their misery. The consolations of friendship, central to Beattie's work, are given particularly lyrical expression in stories like "Playback," which begins with an image of two friends. "One of the most romantic evenings I ever spent was last week, with Holly curled in my lap, her knees to the side, resting against the sloping arm of the wicker armchair." This picture is especially poignant because the narrator later betrays Holly in an attempt to hold on to her, though her attempt fails. "Jacklighting," too, evokes bittersweet memories of friendship, as a

group of friends gather to remember Nicholas, who died in a motorcycle accident. Without Nicholas, who saw things no one else noticed, there are fewer revelations. What the narrator understands now, sitting on the porch of a country house at night, is that "you can look at something, close your eyes and see it again and still know nothing—like staring at the sky to figure out the distances between stars."

The glow of the stories in *The Burning House* is heightened by their carefully crafted conclusions. Beattie has always been especially concerned with conclusions, which, she feels, should be revealed rather than planned: "Some stories or books fail simply at that point. They have to be thrown away if the ending doesn't reveal itself to me." Some of the narratives in this volume still end with a telling but ordinary detail, without explanation, but in several of them Beattie expresses herself more directly, refracting the characters' actions through a carefully slanted interpretation. More than one of the stories suggest entrapment, the feeling of being in the wrong skin, the mistaking of urges for emotions. In "Desire," the protagonist heads up the stairs to his lover: "Things began to go out of focus, then to pulsate. He reached for the railing just in time to steady himself. In a few seconds the first awful feeling passed, and he continued to climb, pretending, as he had all his life, that this rush was the same as desire." An eerily similar feeling is captured in "Afloat," when its protagonist, floating in a lake between her lover and her lover's daughter, remembers her lover spinning a child in the air, "knowing that desire that can be more overwhelming than love—the desire, for one brief minute, simply to get off the earth." The desire to escape, to literally get off the earth, repeats throughout the collection, and the book ends with a farewell speech delivered when the narrator of the title story asks her husband whether he's staying or going. "Men think they're Spider-Man and Buck Rogers and Superman. You know what we all feel inside that you don't feel? That we're going to the stars." / He takes my hand. "I'm looking down on all of this from space," he whispers. "I'm already gone."

Beattie's next novel, *Love Always,* came as a surprise. On one level it is a transposition of familiar characters and situations from her previous work into a new key: the plot revolves around the staff of a cultishly popular magazine called *Country Daze,* which is based in rural Vermont and staffed by a group of friends. The editor, Hildon, claims that he sees the magazine as "an extended family, a continuation of the life he and his friends had led in college," and the clublike atmosphere does recall the house parties of Beattie's earlier fiction, though the houses are more expensive, the gatherings more formal, and the drug of choice is now cocaine instead of hash. But the tone of the novel is quite different from anything that has come before. *Love Always* is a comic novel, a sharply imagined satire of East Coast post-hipster yuppies and West Coast Hollywood types in the 1980s, and a many-layered scrutiny of artifice.

There are few characters who do not wear some kind of mask or maintain an alternate persona: Lucy, the protagonist, writes a tongue-in-cheek lonely hearts advice column as "Cindi Coeur"; Hildon, her best friend and sometime lover, likes to dress up as white trash and roam summer street festivals; Lucy's fourteen-year-old niece, Nicole, visiting her aunt in Vermont for the summer, is a teen soap opera star. Under all the paint, romantic love becomes more farce than drama. Hildon and Les, Lucy's ex-lover, just want her to play along with them: Hildon, because he needs an "emotional chameleon"; and Les, because he is deeply insecure. When Nicole tells Lucy that she has no friends and doesn't want any, Lucy is appalled, shocked by Nicole's lack of "excess or passion or even the belief that something might be fun," but her horror rings a little false. The people Lucy loves best, after all,

have always been distant, the kinds who move on: Les, Hildon, Lucy's sister Jane, even Nicole. Lucy, herself, does not risk much. Perhaps the most cruelly accurate description of Lucy is the bitter picture painted by Maureen, Hildon's wife and Lucy's enemy: "Everything Lucy wore and did was perfect. Even Lucy's lover's departure had been perfect . . . . The column Lucy wrote was also perfect: it was exactly the right endeavor for the society girl who wanted to stay sour."

Lucy knows her life is about maintaining a weary equilibrium. "She would not pass judgment . . . . And since there were no particular ground rules, even those who were malicious couldn't zip the rug out from under and topple her, because she had made no firm assumptions about where she stood to begin with." In her ruthless self-awareness, Lucy is even more cut off from surprise than someone like Piggy Proctor, Nicole's Hollywood agent and surrogate father and the novel's reigning priest of superficiality. Notably, it is Piggy who is given one of the most heartfelt epiphanies in the novel, after Jane is killed in a motorcycle accident: "Through his tears he saw a neon burger with beads of light blinking around it. The lettuce that ruffled out from under the roll was blue. The bun was yellow. Piggy looked away, up at the sky. The sky was blue. He blew his nose. Thank God: the sky was blue."

If *Love Always* broadens the scope of Beattie's fiction, *Where You'll Find Me, and Other Stories* (1986), the writer's fourth short story collection, focuses its energies inward. Tight, short, and mostly swept clean of the interpretative conclusions of *The Burning House,* the stories rely on plain exposition and Beattie's trademark allusive shorthand. The knowledge that one thought leads to the next is what Carol and Vernon fear most, in "In the White Night," because all thoughts eventually lead to the memory of their young daughter, who died of leukemia. The result is a clever, subtle battle between the protagonists and the flow of the narrative. The story begins with a silly game played by one of Carol and Vernon's friends: "Don't think about a cow . . . don't think about a river, don't think about a car." They try not to think, but of course they must, and the only relief comes when they bed down in the living room for the night, altering the pattern of their lives "as a necessary small adjustment." In "Skeletons," a final allusive leap is so abrupt that Beattie seems to rely on sheer faith that there will be a resonance with what has come before, and the result is stunning. The image of a woman Kyle Brown has not seen for years metamorphoses before him as his car goes into a skid. "*Nancy Niles!* he thought, in that instant of fear and shock. . . . In a flash, she was again the embodiment of beauty to him."

A few stories take simplicity of exposition too far, failing to ever quite spring to life. "Cards," in which two women lunch together in the city, is ordinary, and "Times," about a young couple celebrating Christmas with the wife's parents, echoes similar stories from earlier collections but lacks their depth. Then, however, there is "Janus," which moves simplicity in an entirely new direction, telling the story of a perfect bowl. The bowl's owner, Andrea, is a real estate agent, and when she is showing a house, she always puts the bowl somewhere, on a table or a counter. She thinks it brings her luck.

"But the bowl was not at all ostentatious, or even so noticeable that anyone would suspect that it had been put in place deliberately. They might notice the height of the ceiling on first entering a room, and only when their eye moved down from that, or away from the refraction of sunlight on a pale wall, would they see the bowl." And when she is alone in the living room at night, "she often looked at the bowl sitting on the table, still and safe, unilluminated. In its way, it was perfect: the world cut in half, deep and smoothly empty. Near the rim, even in dim light, the eye moved toward one small flash of blue, a vanishing point on the

horizon." The bowl is so transparent a metaphor—for the way Beattie's fiction works, attracting attention only indirectly to its subject; for Andrea's paralyzingly perfect balance, which keeps her from choosing between her husband and her lover; and for the pure cool satisfaction of art itself, as a substitute for human attachment—that it might be expected to collapse under the weight of its significance, but instead radiant new life is bestowed on the most commonplace of analogies.

NOVEL WRITING: PHASE TWO

A process of renewal was underway in the composition of *Picturing Will:* Beattie's fourth novel went through three years of revisions and five major changes and lost fifteen chapters in the composition process; the third section alone was revised seventy-five to one hundred times. If work habits indicate anything, the writer who spent three weeks on a first draft of *Chilly Scenes of Winter,* and little more on *Falling in Place* and *Love Always* was attempting something different. And in fact, *Picturing Will, Another You,* and *My Life, Starring Dara Falcon* (1997) clearly belong to a second phase in Beattie's novel-writing career. On the one hand more conventional—written in complex sentences and allowing for a more extended passage of time, suggesting a historical past—and on the other hand structurally inventive, the texture of these three novels is both denser and looser. The impulse behind the change, as Beattie described it, was a new willingness to show her hand. "I'm more interested in formal issues now, and in how things are put together, and what I might do on that level to get a trajectory that is more clearly the author's." *Picturing Will,* she felt, marked "probably the first time in a novel I so clearly let myself be the manipulator." Critics received *Picturing Will* with almost universal acclaim, maintaining that Beattie had at last achieved a novelistic breadth and depth to rival the achievements of her short stories. If the three later novels lack some of the freshness of the first three, they demonstrate, nevertheless, a consistency and maturity of tone.

The progress of a career, dedication to a creative vision, and the price exacted for that dedication all come under investigation in *Picturing Will.* It is rare in Beattie's fiction for a character to show devotion to a career, even an artistic one—Francie, the painter in "Friends" is one of the few exceptions—and the picture that emerges of Jody, the photographer protagonist of *Picturing Will,* is a complicated one. As the novel begins, Jody is a single mother, divorced from her deadbeat first husband Wayne and living alone with her six-year-old son, Will, in Charlottesville, Virginia, photographing weddings for a living and doing her own work on the side. Her lover, Mel, flies down from New York as often as he can to see her and to try to persuade her to move to the city. As she is often told, Mel is the perfect lover, generous and considerate, and Jody loves him as much as she loves anyone, but even this early, before she can know she will be a success, she worries, "not that he would take her for granted, but that she would take him for granted." Already she knows that love for family will come second in her life. And as much as she loves Will, she is perturbed by the falseness she senses in her voice when she talks to him sometimes—she is not insincere, but it is as if she is somehow out of character. "She had a sense, too, of how ridiculous she sounded every time she tried to cajole Will. For some reason Mel never sounded ridiculous, but she did."

Jody observes herself; Will watches Jody; Mel looks out for Jody and Will. Though in the end Jody is at the center of the circle, in a sense *Picturing Will* has no protagonist—only multiple observers. The novel is divided into three sections, and in the first, "Mother," the observer is Jody, peering through her camera lens. The second,

"Father," follows Will on a trip to Florida to visit Wayne, over the course of which he witnesses two harrowing scenes: first, when he is left alone in a hotel room with another boy, the slightly older Spencer, and with Jody's dealer, Haverford ("Haveabud"), who is revealed to be a pedophile; and second, when Wayne is arrested while Will is staying at his house. The third section, a very short one, is "Child," but it is in a series of italicized passages appearing throughout the novel that the third observer is introduced. Musing in the second person singular about the experience of raising a child, the mysterious narrator is finally revealed at the end to be Mel.

The relationship between parent and child—or, just as often, between surrogate parent and child—is one that Beattie probes with great feeling and skill, and the many children in her stories and novels are so intimately drawn that readers are often surprised to learn that Beattie herself has no children. She has always affirmed that though she loves children she decided early on not to have any of her own, and that her ease in writing about them comes from memories of her own childhood and her closeness to the children of friends. Will, in fact, was modeled on a real boy named Will, born to good friends of Beattie's on the writer's birthday. Imagining Will from the inside out, Beattie speaks thus through Mel:

> *"What if your world was a comedy routine gone out of control? What if you experienced the world as a dwarf? . . . What if you lacked the ability to judge whether people were drunk or sober, and if your plans for the following day were changed when another person announced a change of plans?"*

It is Jody whose plans always change Will's, and Jody's plans inevitably involve photography, as she becomes a successful artist. Jody's ideas about photography, which are elucidated at some length, shed an interesting light on Beattie's ideas about writing—though they suggest most about her short stories, which are closer in concept to photographs, with their compression of action and mood. In her work, Jody is wary of trying too hard for effect, but at the same time she seeks out the unusual, the image fraught with unlikely significance: "The best of them were synergistic, or they didn't work at all." Like Beattie, who finds that "time and time again . . . what seemed a digression I decided to follow after . . . resolves itself by becoming an important element of the plot I could never have anticipated," Jody allows herself to "work her way into feeling something about a place by photographing in a perfunctory way."

Whether it is the effect of Beattie's new expansiveness in *Picturing Will,* or a renewed dedication to the digressionary tactics explained above, a new liberation is felt in *What Was Mine* (1991). The stories are longer on average ("A Windy Day at the Reservoir" is almost a novella), and looser, and there is more variation in the narrative voices. The characters, too, though they are mostly familiar types, are brought into contact with other, less familiar types outside their usual tight circles. In "You Know What," Stefan is drawn into the world of his daughter's elementary school teacher; in "Windy Day at the Reservoir," Chap has an understanding with Mrs. Brikel, a woman who lives with her grown-up retarded son; and in "Television," a young couple has lunch with an old man, a lawyer, on his birthday. The narrator of "Installation #6" is a blue-collar worker; the narrator of "Imagine a Day at the End of Your Life" is a retired delivery man.

The expansiveness is emotional, too. Though marriages still fail, and husbands and wives take lovers, there are a significant number of happy couples in *What Was Mine,* and an underlying sense that it is possible to be happy; characters who work things out are not just making do, they really love each other. In an interview in 1989, Beattie laughed that she was wary about writing about divorce since her marriage to Lincoln

Perry. "I get in trouble with my husband now if I do that. He reads the rough drafts of my stories and says, 'I hope these people don't get divorced.'" Whatever the reason for their creation, the happy marriages in the collection are as well observed as the unhappy ones in her earlier work, and it is pleasing to see that Beattie's world allows for their existence. In "You Know What," again, Stefan is overwhelmed by his love for his wife, Francine, as they are ice-skating, satisfied too that they have planned their lives carefully enough so they are both still happy: she is a successful executive, and he works at home and cares for their daughter, Julie. The retired delivery man in "Imagine a Day at the End of Your Life" has a wonderful time with his wife, Harriet, who is a mystery writer, and is always surrounded by the friends she makes doing research, people with interesting stories to tell.

As Mrs. Angawa, Julie's teacher, says "People talk quite a lot, but you often have to wait for their true stories. To be more specific, I think that it is all right to let Julie go on a bit. Eventually we will hear stories beneath those stories." And like Jody, in *Picturing Will,* Beattie takes her time, sidling in from the side or dropping down in front, creeping up on the perfect moment. Surrounded by her husband, daughter, granddaughter, and friends at a barbecue in her backyard, Elizabeth, the protagonist of "Honey," surveys the food she has prepared, hears the boys next door shouting to each other, watches her daughter and the baby. And then, suddenly, a swarm of bees attacks, and without realizing it, she and her lover rise in unison and clasp hands across the table.

Not all marriages are happy in *Another You,* but then again, there are no divorces, as Beattie takes her novelistic explorations a little farther. Chronicling the interlinked adulterous adventures of Marshall Lockard, a professor at a small New England college; his wife, Sonja, a real estate agent; and Jack McCallum, an unbalanced colleague of Marshall's, Beattie punctuates her tale with mysterious italicized letters from a certain M. to someone called Martine. As the novel progresses, small clues link the letters and the main text, and it gradually becomes clear that M. and Martine have something to do with Marshall's early life. Dealing for the first time with a historic past—the letters date from the 1940s—Beattie succeeds remarkably well in bringing characters of an era not her own to life. The rest of the novel lacks the intensity of the letters, but it paints a convincing picture of the relationship of a childless married couple heading into middle age.

When Marshall picks up one of his students hitchhiking, it is the thought of encroaching middle age that causes him to toy with the idea of an affair; he goes so far as to take her out for a drink and kiss her. But she confides that she is worried about her roommate, who claims she has been raped by McCallum, and soon Marshall is mixed up in something both more serious and less intimate—and as a result, somehow less interesting—than a simple affair. "Unemotive" Marshall is the kind of man whose wife is afraid to tell him she's been sleeping with another man because she's worried he will insult her by not caring enough, and it is somehow fitting that Marshall is suddenly forced by McCallum to live the ultimate vicarious existence. McCallum's problems eventually encroach so severely on Marshall and Sonja's life that he is stabbed nearly to death by his wife in the Lockards' living room, and in the final third of the novel, McCallum and Marshall head off together on a supposedly restorative vacation to Florida. The trip does not turn out quite as planned, and when McCallum departs abruptly, so that Marshall is no longer goaded into action, he sluggishly returns to his usual placid habits.

Unlike Mel, Marshall is not a nurturer; here, the roles are reversed, and Sonja is the compassionate one. It is she who visits Marshall's elderly stepmother, Evie, in the nursing home, keeping her company and seeing that she is well cared for. Evie herself is a strong, compelling character, given unexpected depth in the novel's brief final flashback section. The two women provide the novel with its few flashes of passion. Marshall's final visit to his brother Gordon, who is "doing a credible imitation of a lowlife" in Key West, and the small revelations of the trip—he and Gordon are "two mocking people: he used a vehicle, language, to mock; his brother lived his life by invoking a stereotype he knew was absurd"—are unexpectedly poignant, but lack force. Beattie has taken power out of her characters' hands from the beginning, and keeps the revelations of the letters from them, while revealing all to the reader.

Lack of momentum ails *My Life, Starring Dara Falcon,* too, which, in a semi-return to an earlier Beattie world, is set in the late 1970s, making a slightly musty nod to a familiar milieu. Protagonist Jean Warner marries young and moves to Dell, a small New Hampshire town where she becomes part of her husband, Bob's, large extended family. Jean is an orphan, and for a while, she is satisfied by the novelty of domestic duties, but just as she begins to wonder whether things are quite as rosy as she had imagined, she meets Dara Falcon, an aspiring actress with a talent for turning everyday life into thrilling drama. Dara, it is clear, is untrustworthy, but Jean is fascinated by her and by the wider world that she represents.

That wider world, and the narrower world of Dell too, become too capacious, as if hindsight has clouded rather than clarified Beattie's vision of the 1970s, leading her to paint the era in broader and less convincing brushstrokes. Detail is still meticulously observed, but there is so much of it that it becomes undifferentiated. A little crispness is lost in *Picturing Will* and *Another You,* too, for the same reason, but the forward motion of the former compensates. The basic tension of *My Life* resides in the relationship between Jean and Dara, but as the novel progresses, the balance of their friendship only shifts and the action never quite builds to a climax. Jean sums up her feelings about Dara at the beginning of the novel, from the vantage point of the 1990s, and over the course of the story, she is never either entirely taken in nor wholly disenchanted. Even at the end, when she finally states that Dara "was the most manipulative person I have ever met," she continues to be oddly ambiguous. Finally, their friendship peters out, and Jean explains that Dara had, if anything, a very indirect effect on her decision to leave Bob.

Though the novel is missing a central thrust, there is a fair bit of action, and at times it turns consciously soap-opera-ish, in a playful way. Each member of Bob's extended family is a well-developed character, and Dara and her boyfriend and his ex-girlfriend provide more fodder for gossip. As Jean muses at a stoplight: "Was Bernie right to insist upon having the baby? Should Dara have fought with Tom so much about his decision to remain loyal to Bernie? Would Dara and Tom eventually marry?" Even Jean's fate is faintly daytime-TV-like: she marries a hotel manager and lives in a series of immaculate hotel rooms. In its less serious moments, *My Life* relaxes into comfortable comedy.

PLUNGING INTO A NEW WORLD

By 1998, Beattie had been writing steadily for twenty-five years, and the fruit of her short story labors was handily gathered up in *Park City,* a collection of eight new stories and twenty-eight selected from her published work. The sharp, highly colored new stories included in the volume make it plain that *Park City* is not a valedictory effort. If *What Was Mine* was generally placid in tone, its characters ready to settle down into old age, happy matrimony, or pleasant melancholy, *Park City* is marked by fresh agitation and a plunge into a heterogeneous 1990s world. The

two longest and most notable stories, "Cosmos" and "Park City," take on surrogate parenthood, a familiar topic for Beattie, but elaborated here with the kind of offbeat humor (tinged, in "Park City," with menace) that has not been so fully indulged since *Love Always. Love Always,* however, seems brittle in comparison to the rich, fluid roll of the *Park City* stories, in which the new openness of Beattie's expression reaches full flower.

The surrogate parent in "Cosmos" is Alison Woodruff, a junior high school teacher who gets herself into trouble by telling her class of Japanese girl students exaggerated stories about her lover Carl's eight-year-old son, Jason. To better connect with the students, she turns Jason into such a character that one of the girls, Moriko, becomes obsessed with him, and sets a fire in a garbage can behind Alison and Carl's garage to get Jason's attention. References to cartoons, television, and movies underscore the goofy drama of the story and anchor it firmly in the 1990s (an episode of *Frasier* is on in the background during one of Alison's confusing telephone conversations with Moriko's father), but the humor is bound up with a serious examination of Alison's relationship to Carl, and especially, Jason, as she feels herself growing inevitably closer to the son of someone she may not be with forever.

Television and cartoon references point toward darker dilemmas in "Park City." On a weeklong vacation in Park City, Utah, with her sister Janet, her sister's lover, Damon, her sister's three-year-old daughter, Nell, and Damon's fourteen-year-old daughter, Lyric, the narrator watches a cartoon with Nell in which a bear is swallowed headfirst by an alligator. "I watch . . . to see the bear regurgitated. Nothing happens." When the narrator asks Nell to turn the television off ("it's awful"), Lyric says, "She might as well learn the way of the world." Lyric has learned—like Nicole, in *Love Always,* she is coolly adult, making plans to leave her violent father and move to Brooklyn with one of his old girlfriends. Janet has not yet learned—though she knows about Damon's tendencies, she is considering having his baby. The potential for disaster that haunts earlier stories is heightened here by the sinister trappings of an artificial wonderland like Park City, where even hotel bedrooms are decked out like theme parks. Things have changed since 1976, as the narrator wryly notes:

> *"May you build a ladder to the stars and climb on every rung,"* Dylan sings. I'm actually hearing the song, not just remembering it. It's floating on the breeze—from where? From somewhere distant.
>
> But oh, Bobecito, we are already no longer young. Which might not be so bad in itself, except that the world doesn't seem young any longer, either.

Except that it does, when Beattie turns it into fiction. So long as she continues to catch us in motion, the world as we know it will never quite age.

Selected Bibliography

WORKS OF ANN BEATTIE

NOVELS AND SHORT STORIES

Distortions. New York: Doubleday, 1976.

Chilly Scenes of Winter. New York: Doubleday, 1976.

Secrets and Surprises. New York: Random House, 1979.

Falling in Place. New York: Random House, 1980.

The Burning House. New York: Random House, 1982.

Love Always. New York: Random House, 1985.

Where You'll Find Me, and Other Stories. New York: Linden Press/Simon & Schuster, 1986.

Picturing Will. New York: Random House, 1989.

What Was Mine. New York: Random House, 1991.

Another You. New York: Knopf, 1995.

My Life, Starring Dara Falcon. New York: Knopf, 1997.

Park City. New York: Knopf, 1998.

All of Beattie's novels and short story collections, except for *Secrets and Surprises* and *Where You'll Find Me,* are available in Vintage Contemporary paperback editions.

OTHER WORKS

Spectacles. New York: Workman Publishing, 1985. (Children's book.)

Alex Katz. New York: Abrams, 1987. (Art criticism.)

"Introduction." In *At Twelve: Portraits of Young Women.* Written by Sally Mann. New York: Aperture, 1988.

"Where Characters Come From." *Mississippi Review* 1(1) (April 1995).

"Introduction." *Ploughshares* 21(2–3) (Fall 1995).

BIOGRAPHICAL AND CRITICAL STUDIES

Epstein, Joseph. "Ann Beattie and the Hippoisie." *Commentary* 75(3): 54–58 (1983).

Ford, Richard. "Beattie Eyes." *Esquire,* July 1985, pp. 107–108.

Gelfant, Blanche H. "Ann Beattie's Magic Slate or the End of the Sixties." *New England Review* 1: 374–384 (1979).

Iyer, Pico. "The World According to Beattie." *Partisan Review* 50: 548–553 (1983).

Lee, Don. "About Ann Beattie." *Ploughshares* 21(2–3): 231–235 (Fall 1995).

Locke, Richard. "Keeping Cool." *New York Times Book Review,* May 11, 1980, pp. 1, 38–39.

Montresor, Jaye Berman (ed.). *The Critical Response to Ann Beattie.* Westport, Conn.: Greenwood, 1993.

Moore, Lorrie. "A House Divided." *New York Times Book Review,* June 28, 1998, p. 15.

Murphy, Christina. *Ann Beattie.* Boston: G. K. Hall (Twayne), 1986.

Olster, Stacey. "Photographs and Fantasies in the Stories of Ann Beattie." *Since Flannery O'Connor: Essays on the Contemporary American Short Story.* Edited by Loren Logsdon and Charles W. Mayer. Macomb: Western Illinois University, 1987. Pp. 113–123.

Parini, Jay. "A Writer Comes of Age." *Horizon* 25: 22–24 (1982).

Porter, Carolyn. "Ann Beattie: The Art of the Missing." *Contemporary American Women Writers: Narrative Strategies.* Edited by Catherine Rainwater and William J. Scheick. Lexington: University Press of Kentucky, 1985. Pp. 9–28.

Schapiro, Barbara. "Ann Beattie and the Culture of Narcissism." *Webster Review* 10(2): 86–101 (Fall 1985).

Stein, Lorin. "Fiction in Review." *The Yale Review* 85: 156–166 (1997).

Updike, John. "Seeresses." *The New Yorker,* November 29, 1976, pp. 164–166.

Wyatt, David. "Ann Beattie." *Southern Review* 28(1): 145–159 (Winter 1992).

INTERVIEWS

Centola, Steven R. "An Interview with Ann Beattie." *Contemporary Literature* 31(4): 405–422 (Winter 1990).

Getlin, Josh. "Novelist Focuses on Childhood Isolation." *Los Angeles Times,* January 18, 1990, sec. E1, pp. 14–15.

Hill, Robert W., and Jane Hill. "Ann Beattie." *Five Points: A Journal of Literature and Art* 1(3): 26–60 (Spring–Summer 1997).

Hubbard, Kim. "For Writer Ann Beattie, Winters Are Anything but Chilly Since Her Marriage to Artist Lincoln Perry." *People Weekly* 33: 89–94, 1990.

Lewis, Maggie. "The Sixties: Where Are They Now? Novelist Ann Beattie Knows." *Christian Science Monitor,* October 23, 1979, pp. B6–B10.

McCaffery, Larry, and Gregory Sinda. "A Conversation with Ann Beattie." *The Literary Review, an International Journal of Contemporary Writing* 27(2): 165–177 (1984).

Maynard, Joyce. "Visiting Ann Beattie." *New York Times Book Review,* May 11, 1980, pp. 1, 39–41.

Miner, Bob. "Ann Beattie: I Write Best When I Am Sick." *Village Voice,* August 9, 1976, pp. 33–34.

Murray, G. E. "A Conversation with Ann Beattie." *Story Quarterly* 7/8: 62–68 (1978).

Plath, James. "Counternarrative: An Interview with Ann Beattie." *Michigan Quarterly Review* 32(3): 359–379 (Summer 1993).

Samway, P. H. "An Interview with Ann Beattie." *America* 162: 469–471 (1990).

Seshachari, Neila C. "Picturing Ann Beattie: A Dialogue." *Weber Studies* 7(1): 12–36 (Spring 1990).

FILMS BASED ON THE WORK OF ANN BEATTIE

Head Over Heels. United Artists, 1979. (Recut version released as *Chilly Scenes of Winter* in 1982.)

—NATASHA WIMMER

Robert Coover

1932—

"LANGUAGE HAS invaded reality, remaking it," Robert Coover noted in his September 25, 1983, *New York Times Book Review* coverage of Robert Pinget's novel *Between Fantoine and Agapa;* "a strange sign has invoked a plot." Throughout his career as a fiction writer, Coover has been attracted to literature such as Pinget's, self-conscious experiments that delight in the chicken-and-the-egg question of which comes first, an event in life or the phrase for it? Not surprisingly, Coover's own fiction explores such issues relentlessly, yet with one major difference. Unlike many of the European and South American writers he so admires, this son of the American Middle West roots his innovations in popularly accessible contexts and develops them in tune with his country's common culture. Baseball, Wild West lore, Dr. Seuss' Cat in the Hat: these are the materials of what might otherwise be abstract metafiction.

"Metafiction" is belletristic narrative that explores the process of its own making, and Robert Coover's birth in 1932 places him at the center of a generation of American writers who have dedicated their careers to such exploration, including John Barth, Donald Barthelme, and Ronald Sukenick. As with these other writers, Coover's fiction first came to prominence in the mid- to late 1960s, when social, political, and cultural disruptions created a welcoming context for such unconventional works as Barth's *Giles Goat-Boy* (1966), Barthelme's *Snow White* (1967), and Sukenick's *Up* (1968).

There is a definite sixties feel to the author's first novels, *The Origin of the Brunists* (1966) and *The Universal Baseball Association, Inc., J. Henry Waugh, Prop.* (1968), and even more so to the pieces collected as *Pricksongs & Descants; Fictions* (1969), which as a volume of "fictions" rather than "short stories" called attention to their overtly fabricated nature. Coover's 1960s, however, are always based in a widely shared experience. Unlike Barth's and Sukenick's postmodern university and Barthelme's and Sukenick's hiply arty Greenwich Village, the settings for Robert Coover's early work are almost mundanely familiar: a small town in downstate Illinois, a baseball field imagined from a shabby apartment, and—in the short fictions—anything from an elevator to a suburban home where the babysitter is watching television. What happens in these locales and later in Coover's somewhat more wide-ranging writing is also familiar because actions evolve within the structure of popular myths and mass media culture. Showing how these latter phenomena constitute a usable language is Robert Coover's contribution to the development of American fiction.

COOVER'S BACKGROUND

The son of Grant Marion Coover (a newspaper editor) and Maxine Sweet Coover, Robert Lowell Coover was born in Charles City, Iowa, on February 4, 1932. The family did not stay long in the Hawkeye State; neighbors recall the Coovers as itinerants who moved around in search of new opportunities while escaping unwanted accumulations of debt. Subsequent residences included towns in Indiana and Illinois, most significantly the southern Illinois coal mining region surrounding Herrin, where both a mine disaster and his father's work at the newspaper provided materials for Coover's first novel.

Having enjoyed an adolescence characterized by the cultural typicalities of small-town American life, such as comic books and Saturdays at the movies, Coover pursued an equally unexceptional higher education at nearby state universities. After two years at Southern Illinois University in Carbondale (1949–1951), Coover transferred to Indiana University, where by 1953 he had completed his Bachelor of Arts degree. Following graduation he enlisted in the U.S. Navy, acquiring a reserve commission and reaching the rank of lieutenant while serving on cruisers. After leaving military service in 1957, Coover continued to spend much time abroad, marrying a Spanish woman, Maria del Pilar San-Mallafre, in 1959, and the next year having his first published work appear as "One Summer in Spain" in the small-press journal *Fiddlehead*. The combination of his naval officer background, extended residencies abroad (with no obvious means of support), and close friendship with the even more elusive writer Thomas Pynchon prompted literary gossip about possible cloak-and-dagger work; to Richard Elman's query in *Namedropping: Mostly Literary Memoirs* (1998) as to whether he had ever worked for the Central Intelligence Agency, Coover is reported as responding, "Alas yes." In any event, a Master of Arts degree from the University of Chicago (earned during the years 1958–1961 and awarded in 1965) made less of an impression on the critical and academic worlds than the fact that he was publishing in both high-powered intellectual journals (such as *The Noble Savage*) and relatively tawdry men's magazines (*Cavalier* and *Nugget*), all the while maintaining an air of fascinating mystery.

Of his many teaching positions, which have included appointments at Bard College, Columbia University, and Princeton University, Coover's most important pedagogical associations have been with the University of Iowa Writers' Workshop (1967–1969) and Brown University (as writer in residence), both of which included colleagueship with narrative theorist Robert Scholes. As author of *The Fabulators* (1967), Scholes was the first scholar to focus attention on the innovators whose company Coover would soon join: Kurt Vonnegut, Terry Southern, John Hawkes, and John Barth.

Fabulation, like metafiction, blurs lines between the actual and the artificial by placing an emphasis on the storyteller's art. Such emphasis was just what Scholes' junior colleague was perfecting during the two years spent back in his native state, reorienting himself from a decade and a half of worldwide travels by teaching creative writing and working on his own fiction just a few hours' drive from where he was born. Following another international period, during which he lived most of the time in England, Coover rejoined Scholes just as the older man's interests turned to semiotics, the study of how signs function within the larger grammar of a culture. From Brown University, Coover perfected his fictive mastery of semiotic technique, using his novel *Pinocchio in Venice* (1991) as a playground for signs and symbols known from fairy tales and current experience. In tune with postmodern theory yet accessible to the same popular readers whose culture he would exploit, Robert

Coover has always been ideally positioned for his literary experiments to succeed.

THE EARLY WORK: FABULATION AND METAFICTION

"Write what you see in a book and send it to the Seven Churches"—this verse from the Bible's Book of Revelation serves as an epigraph to Robert Coover's first novel and, in some respects, to his entire literary career. Although his subsequent books were less conventionally realistic and more reliant upon both the author's and his readers' self-conscious play with objects of popular culture, *The Origin of the Brunists* announced an interest in the mystifying properties of narrative that Coover has maintained through more than three decades of writing.

Much like Kurt Vonnegut's novel *Cat's Cradle,* published just three years before, *The Origin of the Brunists* begins with the end of the world, metaphorically of course. Whereas Vonnegut's protagonist is introduced as writing a book about the atomic bombing of Hiroshima that he intends to call *The Day the World Ended,* Coover's first characters are seen gathering for a religious apocalypse. In *Cat's Cradle* all life is eventually destroyed, not with a bang but a whimper, not consumed in fire but frozen in ice, with its hero leaving his own writing as a testament to human folly. Coover's work, which shares this same mindset of the times, follows *Cat's Cradle* in another respect. Just as he assumed the older man's instructorship at the University of Iowa's Writers' Workshop (when in 1967 Vonnegut departed with a Guggenheim Fellowship for the writing of *Slaughterhouse-Five*), Coover adopted the technique of using the beliefs of a religious cult to articulate his own thoughts on humankind's propensities for mythmaking. Vonnegut's Bokononists thus became Coover's Brunists, the former's fictively isolated Caribbean turning into a simi-

larly out-of-the-way corner of the southern Illinois coalfields made exceptional by its confrontation with disaster and unique in its metaphysical response. A catastrophic explosion destroys a mine, killing nearly one hundred; one man, Giovanni Bruno, has inexplicably survived. How can this be accounted for? Bruno's answer is that he has been spared to announce the Second Coming, and an increasing number of people believe him. Their response fascinates a local newspaper editor, who parlays the event into a national story, which in turn enlarges the cult and its effect. On both fronts, these narratives take on a life of their own, until they become Coover's favored chicken-or-the-egg question of which is preeminent, the story or the event. As happens in Coover's subsequent novels that rely on overtly ready-made materials of popular culture, the Brunists themselves and the editor who writes about them are relying on cultural myths that are fabricated rather than being in any sense natural, even though both God and Nature are assumed to stand behind them.

A God-figure actually appears in Coover's second novel, *The Universal Baseball Association, Inc., J. Henry Waugh, Prop.,* but in manner and appearance he is hardly Godlike. J. Henry Waugh is a wimpish accountant, an archetypal Walter Mitty figure who lives a secret life not so much of fantasy as of metafiction, creating and playing a tabletop baseball game that takes on two lives of its own: one in the imagination of its creator, the other within the constructed world of its players. As a bookkeeper, Coover's protagonist has to be a stickler for detail—which is why the book's title, with its abbreviations for "incorporated" and "proprietor," is so fussily correct. As sole owner and operator of this made-up baseball league, Waugh rolls dice, turns cards, and follows a mathematical chart for the fictive baseball game he plays. But things become metafictive when he keeps records, compiles league histories, and personalizes each pitcher, catcher, and other figures down there on the make-believe field. Here is where the author's talent for epitomizing American popular culture comes into play, as Waugh is made to understand:

You roll, Player A gets a hit or he doesn't, gets his man out or doesn't. Sounds simple. But call Player A "Sycamore Flynn" or "Melbourne Trench" and something starts to happen. He shrinks or grows, stretches out or puts on muscle. Sprays singles to all fields or belts them over the wall. Throws mostly fastballs like Swanee Law or curves like Mickey Halifax. Choleric like Rag Rooney or slow and smooth like his old first-base rival Mose Stanford. Not easy to tell just how or why.

Such characterization makes the players seem real to readers, as conventional literature should do. But it also makes J. Henry Waugh fall in love with one of them and forces a rule-breaking intercession lest the young pitcher be hit by a fatal line drive.

Waugh's intercession makes what was fiction become metafictive. In terms of the tabletop game, which has been projected by rolls of the dice and sequences of card turning, something now exists outside of statistical probability; this need to explain the event refocuses attention from the game's inventor to the game itself, where the ballplayers struggle to make sense of what has happened. Not surprisingly, they construct a myth, one that on their own level serves well to keep the game (and the life it breeds) going. The narrative is metafictive because the reader knows what they don't, everything from who J. Henry Waugh is and why he intervened to an explanation of something else that puzzles the ballplayers: why the sun is emblazoned with a manufacturer's trademark and wattage.

Robert Coover's first two novels thus display the traits of fabulation and metafiction that were so in vogue at the University of Iowa during Robert Scholes' directorship of the School of Letters and Kurt Vonnegut's teaching in the Writers' Workshop. Coover's recruitment to this faculty and his experience with this style of literary experimentation reinforce its key tenet: a reader's willing suspension of disbelief is not required for a fiction writer to exploit the artistic resources of the novel or the short story. Indeed, with readers in the know about his fiction making, Coover can indulge in self-conscious virtuosity, as when he allows his otherwise meek protagonist a riotous sexual fling that is motivated as much by language as by physical pleasures.

Pricksongs & Descants; Fictions gives its author's bravado even greater scope, complete with a prologue in Coover's own voice (saved until well into the collection) where colleague Robert Scholes is credited with explaining how fiction "must provide us with an imaginative experience which is necessary to our imaginative wellbeing," because "We need all the imagination we have, and we need it exercised and in good condition." A good example of such exercise is "The Elevator," in which a protagonist transforms his everyday experience with a self-service elevator in his office building into an elaborate fantasy in which he falls to his death, the fabricated nature of which is foregrounded when at the last possible moment he steps away from his imaginative structure and lets it (with the elevator car itself) fall away from him. Another example introduces a technique Coover shares with Donald Barthelme and develops at greater length later—retelling a commonly known fairy tale in a way that clarifies its magic for the reader. "The Gingerbread House" as redrafted by Robert Coover shifts attention from the event itself to its telling as a story. A father narrates; his children listen, even as in their identities as Hansel and Gretel they approach an actual witch's cottage with an entirely different initiation in mind. Immensely more sexual than the Grimms' tale, Coover's overt narrative is fragmented into forty-two numbered paragraphs that segment perspective and let readers be more knowledgeable than the children.

This what an adult reading of the old, familiar tale would achieve anyway; Coover just builds this process into the structure of his story.

Robert Coover is never an antirealistic writer. When in his later work he adopts the cartoon style action and characterization of the American cinema, it is always with figures his readers know as well as any other references in their lives. If the writer John Updike's suburban couple the Maples behave like so many other middle- to upper-middle-class people who read the same *New Yorker* magazine stories in which the Maples appear, then Coover should be seen as an author whose stock in trade comes from an equally accessible store, that of the myths and fantasies expressed in the popular culture of movies, television shows, comic books, and other forms of mass entertainment. And just as Updike manipulates manners to tell readers something they may not have understood among their practitioners, Coover replays the signs of this same culture's mass diversions to make the same point. The difference is that the stories of *Pricksongs & Descants* and many of the novels that follow are developed in a way that foreground the constructed nature of their form. This explains why "The Gingerbread House" is divided into numbered paragraphs that fit together while maintaining a strong sense of their separate identities, from the father's sense of narrative planning to the children's fascination with the budding sexual elements of their own manipulation.

"The Babysitter" demonstrates how such foregrounding can take a natural course in narrative once our attention is directed to it. The scene for Coover's story is as simple and as unexceptional as can be, as a babysitter arrives to care for a couple's children for a few hours in the evening. She's ten minutes late, the first line tells us, but that's not much of a complication because the kids are still eating dinner and the parents themselves aren't ready to leave. "Harry!" the wife calls to her husband. "The babysitter's here al-

ready!" This last word is the giveaway that the otherwise familiar scene will be disruptive because the action has just begun and already everyone's schedule is out of sync. This information, framed as a separate scene, is marked off as a freestanding paragraph on page 206; after this clearly marked segmentation a second one begins, centered on Mr. Tucker crooning love songs to the mirror as he steps from his shower. This paragraph stands alone as well, followed by a third telling of the babysitter's boyfriend "wandering around town, not knowing what to do." Three paragraphs, three locations, three distinct points of view—the makings for great potential complexity are here, causing no trouble yet because they have yet to come together. But within the next segmented section a subtle form of disruption is getting under way:

"Hi," the babysitter says to the children, and puts her books on top of the refrigerator. "What's for supper?" The little girl, Bitsy, only stares at her obliquely. She joins them at the end of the kitchen table. "I don't have to go to bed until nine," the boy announces flatly, and stuffs his mouth full of potato chips. The babysitter catches a glimpse of Mr. Tucker hurrying out of the bathroom in his underwear.

In terms of social manners, the family scene is at the border of dysfunction. But Coover's narrative plan is semiotic rather than social, and so from these initial conflicts he will present not just schizophrenically disconnected dialogues ("What's for supper?" / "I don't have to go to bed until nine") but emblematic displays of cultural practice, from the randy teenage boyfriend to the drunken cocktail party and the balding husband's seven-year itch, all of which comes crashing down on the hapless babysitter at the center of it all.

The 104 separate paragraphs of "The Babysitter" alternate a minimum of exposition with a maximum of action. The action itself, like J.

Henry Waugh's tryst in *The Universal Baseball Association,* is a chance for Coover to display his exuberance of style, a series of occasions that call for the utmost talent with language. Though a literary product of the 1960s, Robert Coover is less of a countercultural rebel (such as were Richard Brautigan, Ronald Sukenick, and so many others) than a supracultural adventurer, a James Bond figure armed with pen and paper and given a license not to kill but to write. As in an Ian Fleming novel or James Bond film of the time, none of the action is totally impossible; the fact that the improbable does happen (with such spectacular results) is thanks to the fissure that opens in the otherwise solid surface of what passes for reality. Coover as writer, much like Agent 007 as intelligence agent, spots a telltale sign, takes control of it, and uses it to infiltrate a culture's carefully built structure, showing off his technical mastery in the process. The power to accomplish such feats comes from understanding how language can maintain control over events. It can't when mythology takes over and leaves an imaginatively calcified form—that's the lesson dramatized in Coover's play, *A Theological Position* (1972). Like most of the sixties innovators, Robert Coover shatters the bonds of this calcification; few others, however, would use the consequent freedom to construct such lavish displays of their own virtuosity at the task.

SEMIOSIS: POLITICS AS CARNIVAL

Politics as a ludicrous sideshow is a subject dear to the hearts of American writers. Flavored by the performative nature of the tall tale, nineteenth-century narratives by Augustus Baldwin Longstreet and Mark Twain combined caricature with fabulation in ways that made public service seem like a great disservice to the people's concerns. Yet in a democracy people tend to get what they deserve, and in his political fictions of the 1970s

Coover delivers these just desserts with relish. *The Public Burning* (1977) and *A Political Fable* (1980) describe the formal extremes of their author's canon, respectively his longest novel and shortest novella, but share the technique of overkill that would characterize much subsequent work. Its 534 closely set pages mark *The Public Burning* as what some critics have called the meganovel and others the novel of excess; within such interpretations it shares company with similarly encyclopedic works as *Gravity's Rainbow* (1973) by Thomas Pynchon and *The Tunnel* (1995) by William H. Gass. Yet its same effect is accomplished in the eighty-eight half-sized pages of *A Political Fable,* showing how Coover does not feel compelled to inundate his readers with tidal waves of knowledge, wisdom, and expertise. Instead, his excessiveness is measured as action, action that is soon too much but keeps on coming like the winsome mayhem in a Dr. Seuss story, the model for each of these works.

A Political Fable first appeared as "The Cat in the Hat for President" in a 1968 issue of *New American Review,* a paperback journal that was introducing many fresh and startling innovators, among them Walter Abish, Donald Barthelme, Steve Katz, and Ronald Sukenick. *The Public Burning* also made its initial in-progress appearance as a novella, "The Public Burning of Julius and Ethel Rosenberg: An Historical Romance," that was featured in the Winter 1973 issue of another magazine devoted at the time to experimental literature, *TriQuarterly.* The two were meant to be published with another pair of novellas as a book, but as the countercultural disruption of the 1960s turned into the political corruption of the early 1970s, Coover's "public burning" project grew, while his "cat in the hat" stepped aside for a while as no longer adequate to the age's shenanigans.

The Watergate scandal that occupied America's attention through 1973 and 1974 shocked many writers, but to someone like Robert Coover the events generated by Richard Nixon and the White House "plumbers" (who were convicted of breaking into and bugging Democratic Party headquarters in an attempt to locate the source of presidential news leaks) appealed to his fabulative sense of the ridiculous. Twenty years earlier, the House Un-American Activities Committee's and Senator Joseph McCarthy's investigations of communism in U.S. government agencies had led certain writers to despair that fiction could no longer equal reality in imaginative quality. Philip Roth, only a year younger than Coover and a graduate of the same University of Chicago Master of Arts program, had despaired quite early in his career over trying to equal the entertainment value of any single day's news. Speaking at Stanford University in 1960, Roth looked back at the previous decade for his remarks on "Writing American Fiction," which would be published in the March 1961 issue of *Commentary* and collected in *Reading Myself and Others,* and found something quite dismaying:

> that the American writer in the middle of the twentieth century has his hands full in trying to understand, describe, and then make *credible* much of American reality. It stupefies, it sickens, it infuriates, and finally it is even a kind of embarrassment to one's meager imagination. The actuality is continually outdoing our talents, and the culture tosses up figures almost daily that are the envy of any novelist.

Among the figures Roth mentioned were Richard Nixon, who had by that time served two terms as Dwight D. Eisenhower's vice president after saving his place on the 1952 ticket by means of a televised speech defending the acquisition of his family's pet dog, Checkers, and criticizing Julius and Ethel Rosenberg, convicted of passing secrets about the atomic bomb to the Soviet Union and executed in the electric chair for their crimes. With Nixon again in office, this time at the top, and with recriminations over the Rosen-

bergs still a traumatic issue, Robert Coover did not despair at trying to equal them as caricatures. Instead, he appreciated how Nixon and the Rosenbergs and so many others from recent times had become cultural signs, as susceptible to manipulation as any other icon within popular awareness (such as Uncle Sam and any number of stars from the entertainment world). In *The Public Burning* he would take what Roth considered their excesses and make those excesses worse, turning imaginative fascination back upon itself in a way that told readers much about the world they had created.

Richard Nixon himself narrates parts of *The Public Burning,* his manner of presentation saying as much about him as about the events described. He is ruthless and cunning, yet ever unsure of his own place in the drama, something to be argued for as ponderously as Richard III's soliloquies in Shakespeare's play. He comes off best as agent for the novel's principal icon, Uncle Sam, who is at once America's savior and its Yankee Peddler exploiter. Yet action takes precedence over character, reducing the latter to cartoonish stylization in the service of an unending series of pratfalls and other narrative indulgences.

The result has been called historiographic metafiction, whereas in E. L. Doctorow's popular and critically successful novel *Ragtime* (1975), chronicled events and fictive inventions are mixed together in a way that emphasizes the artificial nature of each. Indeed, Coover's blend of the real and the fantastic prompts a productive confusion in the reader's mind. Yes, Julius and Ethel Rosenberg were executed on June 19, 1953, the day after their fourteenth wedding anniversary; and yes, the whole country knew about this coincidence of dates and reflected, either somberly or with vindictive glee, on the fate of their marriage and the two children it had produced (and who would survive both in real life and as characters in another novel, E. L. Doctorow's 1971 masterpiece, *The Book of Daniel*). But did their visit to the electric chair take place in Times Square with Tex Ritter singing "Do not forsake me, oh my darling," the theme song from the early 1950s' most popular movie, *High Noon,* from which lead actor Gary Cooper would make a guest appearance? Of course not, but there is a familiarity of association that Coover develops, initially for shock value but later in a way that subverts memory and encourages a fascination with possible connections, in the same way that certain demagogic politicians of the time cultured a sense of paranoia about communist conspiracies that might undermine the land of the free and the home of the brave.

As in Coover's first two novels, a serious theme underlies both this book's lofty mystifications and its vaudevillian pranks. There is what critic Lois Gordon describes in *Robert Coover: The Universal Fictionmaking Process* (1983) as "a fanatical core of American life" that breeds unsettling fears and sometimes vile instincts; in response "one creates political, social, or religious mythologies which then structure and orchestrate his or her culture and mentality." The gamelike aspects of small town newspaper writing and the actual board game that Coover's baseball fan plays are now realized in more disturbing fashion in the very real (and quite dangerous) game of politics. In J. Henry Waugh's ludic exercise, there is a fictive, ritual atonement; in the anticommunist hysterias of the early 1950s, Coover reminds us, there were actual flesh-and-blood sacrifices that for all their news media carnivalization might as well have been conducted at high noon in the center of New York City, at the crossroads of its streets and avenues dedicated to information and entertainment. *The Public Burning* offers not so much a report on this phenomenon as a re-creation of it, with mythmaking functions radically exaggerated for effect. As the fiction writer and theorist Ronald Sukenick was warning, we have to be careful about safeguarding our rights of imagination—otherwise somebody else will do our imagining for us, as Coover's Richard Nixon has done here.

A Political Fable is milder stuff, more of an entertainment than an indictment—a reminder that the 1960s, when it was conceived and first published, were a less foreboding time than the early 1970s of the Vietnam War's wind-down and the White House's immersion in Watergate. Its performative joy comes in Coover's having fun with the qualities of voice. The novella's narrator is a hard-bitten political professional named Brown (no first name, just Brown) who speaks in the blunt rhythms of backroom fixing; his job is to let the coming election be won by the opposing party's locked-in incumbent while preparing the ground for a more logical presidential campaign four years hence (a strategy that some historical analysts believe the actual Republican Party followed in 1964). But Brown's gruffly pragmatic spokesmanship is countered by the voice of a surprise candidate, someone who sincerely believes he can win it all now. Who is this archetypal dark horse, coming out of nowhere but capturing everyone's fancy as the figure they've been looking for all along? It's the Cat in the Hat, fresh from his latest fable in one of Dr. Seuss' children's books. "I CAN LEAD IT ALL BY MYSELF," the Cat proclaims, and in singsong rhythms that accompany his slapstick pranks, he not only wins the party's nomination but (with Brown's reluctant help) also launches a campaign for the United States presidency that promises to be an unqualified success.

How the Cat gets to this point is as funny and as telling as his ridiculous stunts, but the process lets Coover sound out many of the same points developed in *The Public Burning.* Brown himself does his job as an inside organizer with the full knowledge that terms such as "liberal" and "conservative" are merely fictions that pros like himself manipulate according to need—not even the candidate's need, but by measuring the dynamics of force "to which politicians sooner or later and in varying ways adapt," based on things an oracle like him can perceive:

> Politics in a republic is a complex pattern of vectors, some fixed and explicable, some random, some bullish, some inchoate and permutable, some hidden and dynamic, others celebrated though flagging, usually collective, sometimes even cosmic—and a politician's job is to know them and ride them. So instinctive has my perception of the kinetics of politics been, so accurate my forecasts of election outcomes, I have come to be known jocularly as Soothsayer Brown among my colleagues, or, more spitefully, Gypsy.

With his infectious rhymes and deconstructing rhythms, the Cat in the Hat conveys this knowledge up front to the public, in effect letting the cat out of the bag. What previously gullible voters once accepted as truths are now paraded about as unapologetic shams, mere signs to be juggled like any number of wonders to be produced by the magician's sleight of hand. "Signs are signs," Donald Barthelme's narrator had learned earlier in the 1960s, and by the decade's end when "The Cat in the Hat for President" was first published and certainly by 1980 when it was revised and issued as *A Political Fable,* Coover could strongly agree that "some of them are lies." But they are necessary lies, if a culture is to retain its functionality. Because the Cat exposes the underlying fraud, he suffers; as funny as his revelations have been, they cannot be allowed to take a redirective role, because it would mean the end of political parties and perhaps of polis altogether. In such a case there's only one way to skin a cat, and in the novella's conclusion that quite literally happens; the winsome but unacceptably disruptive creature is dismembered in a ritual sacrifice to be commemorated every October 31, otherwise known as the Halloween that precedes regular fall elections.

THE FICTION OF SELF-REFLECTION

Is Robert Coover himself a Cat in the Hat? In the way he has managed both his life and his writing career there is a definite spunkiness to him. Never fearful of offending vested interests, he could take on the powers of the Nixon administration in one novel and move at once to offend proponents of feminism, women and men who presumably would have shared his disgust with the abuses that characterized both the anticommunist crusades of the 1950s and the Watergate abuses twenty years later. *Spanking the Maid* (1982) turns directly against the rising sentiment in the 1980s that brought new prominence to women's issues. Male mastery, female submission; sexual relations as the violation of women by men; endless repetitions of practices that after their first revelation should be condemned and forgotten—all these things that happen in Coover's novella seem intended to shock the newly emerging sensibility that for the first time in American cultural history was objecting to such apparently sexist orientations. Yet Coover is no sexist. Had he simply told the story once, critics might have made the charge stick. Instead he transforms reflection on a sexual theme into a reflexive act, one that by turning back on itself makes concern about supposed subject matter irrelevant.

The narrative voice for this self-reflection is as different as can be from the lively mix of *A Political Fable.* For his new novella, Coover adopts a tone already half a generation out of date: the flat, phenomenologically descriptive style of the French *nouveau roman,* the "new novel" pioneered by Alain Robbe-Grillet in the 1950s. Experiencing a story this way, by sticking with a painstaking literalness to an observable surface with no attempts to project attitudes or delve for inner meanings, can be a maddening affair for both writer and reader. But that is the effect

Coover wants. Even as sexual interest threatens to leap from the page, the author puts it back there where it must be studied as an object rather than felt as a sensation. Any sensational response, whether pleasurable or horrific, is out of bounds for such a work. "She enters, deliberately, gravely, without affection, circumspect in her motions (as she's been taught)," the narrative begins, segmented into Coover's now classically discrete paragraphs that in this case allow an alternation in focus between the maid and her master. To her "She enters" is counterposed "He awakes from a dream," a dream about being whipped as a student. Everything needed to generate the action is here, and a routine is at once off and running, as predictable as the "he thrusts, she heaves" of John Cleland's erotic classic *Fanny* that was back in fashion. Yet the only erotics for Coover's work are in the text itself; it is the paragraphs that interface, not the people, something that the seemingly endless repetitions (with only minor variations) mandate.

While feminist objections to content could thus be put aside, the tedium of this novella's self-reflection remains a problem. John O'Brien paired it with Alain Robbe-Grillet's *Djinn* in the *Chicago Sun-Times Book Week* for June 7, 1982, praising the authentic French "new novel" but disparaging the American effort at adapting these same techniques:

> The Coover novel is a failed attempt to employ the methods of the *nouveau roman;* the repetitions, the variations upon images, the structural loops, the shifts in perspective, all seem wearily imitative, forced, and pretentious. Each morning a maid enters her employer's bedroom, and each morning she is spanked for her failures. As in Robbe-Grillet, there is an implicit invitation to see how the book is constructed. Here, however, the machinery creaks, sputters, and grinds; the tricks are telegraphed, even to the ending in which the employer and maid exchange roles. Finally, I began to suspect that some grand metaphor was rearing its ugly head. Or a fable: the man and his maid are supposed to represent

the relationship between man and woman, between husband and wife, children and parents; or between artist and society, and artist and critic. No matter how well the artist does some things, so the fable might go, the critic will spank him for not doing others.

After taking his blows from the feminists, Coover may well have welcomed a gentle paddling from the customarily acerbic O'Brien. Yet the sting remains. "*Spanking the Maid* can be seen as new and inventive only if one forgets a dozen or so French novelists of the past thirty years," O'Brien concluded. "It is a simplification of the technique of the French writers, and should not be viewed as much more." The key distinction, as many other critics agreed, was not between the old and the new "but between that which is executed well and that which isn't. *Djinn* is well executed, *Spanking the Maid* is not."

Spanking the Maid and its poor critical reception in 1982 mark the low point in Robert Coover's professional life. Always highly regarded as an academically serious, innovative writer, he had hoped to break through to a wider public with *The Public Burning,* timed as it was to coincide with the country's bicentennial celebration. His publisher's worry about possible litigation and perhaps even covert government interference delayed the book's release and also prompted some expensive rewrites that the author, who had been living in England with no obvious means of support, could ill afford. Having returned to the United States to pursue his writing career, complications developed between several Ivy League universities over his employment, in which the assurance of some support was compromised by English Department faculty squabbling of the worst order.

With disappointing book sales and employment prospects temporarily suspended, Coover had to scratch out what income he could on the college reading circuit. For such occasions there were eminently performable excerpts from his novels, but even the stories of *Pricksongs & Descants* were too long for attention-holding live readings. For an audience warm-up the writer needed something shorter, something quick and to the point, with its techniques demonstrable in just a few minutes of presentation time. For this purpose Coover developed the instant fictions collected as *In Bed One Night & Other Brief Encounters* (1983). With many of them less than a thousand words long, his immediate access to the audience was ensured—but not as a prose poet or miniaturist. The materials here are coherent fictions, true narratives that initiate action and take it to a conclusive point, all the while demonstrating the nature of their composition. As self-reflection they are at the far distance from what John O'Brien described as the tedium in *Spanking the Maid;* as entertainment, they are as lively as *A Political Fable* and without its somber moralizing at the end. Prompted by adversity and written to order for a specific economic need, they put Robert Coover onstage as performer, where the pratfalls would be most appealingly his own.

More than one of these pieces begins with the most obvious sign of conversational intimacy: "So one night he comes in from using the bathroom"; "So the driver eases off the interstate up the exit ramp"; "Now Tom's in an elevator in a great hotel." The reader is made very much a listener by this device; something special is about to be shared. But as spoken by an utter stranger, it has to be a come-on; why should this person, who speaks with such authority but who I don't know from Adam, let me in on the big secret? Thus Coover not only chooses his narrative voice, but he puts his readers just where he wants them, listening to the Cat in the Hat or Sam Slick the Yankee Peddler or Richard Nixon himself, knowing they shouldn't believe in these murmured confidences but captivated nonetheless. It's the manner of apparently offhand but in fact carefully planned and paced storytelling—and

hours later, in the poker game with friends that customarily followed his campus readings, he'd be using it again, spinning a tale while raking in the chips.

The strategy worked: before long Coover had regained his richly colored narrative voice and bluffed his way past department conservatives into a more secure position at Brown University, teaching in Robert Scholes' refuge from English professor fustiness, the Program in Semiotics. As an adept reader of signs and how they function in both society and culture, Coover was in his natural element, and he returned wholeheartedly to the exuberant play with signs and symbols of popular mythology that characterized *The Public Burning,* yet without that novel's sinister implications of political control. But first there would be a transitional work, the author's last swirling dance with self-reflection, the astonishing farrago of a novel known as *Gerald's Party* (1986).

The party in question is at first a liberating affair, a freeing of both its characters and their author from restraining semblances of control. Events are soon almost totally out of control, but that seems to be the point, qualifying the narrative as reflexive: freedom is not license, but when everything *is* allowed, intelligence itself is eclipsed and eventually effaced, leaving nothing but a riot of sensations parading themselves as signs. For the cool, perceptively appraising former naval officer who writes the book, the occasion must have been a surrender to a long withheld temptation. Rather than plumb a culture's essence for its secret organization, the author blows his cover entirely by letting go with a riot of excess, a surrender to the fascination of the abomination that quite literally lets this party wreck the house that holds it.

Like any self-reflective novel, *Gerald's Party* announces its plan of composition. The opportunity comes relatively early, about a quarter of the way into the 316-page narrative that will be unrelenting in its permutational formula for disaster, having everything that could go wrong do so in a manner even worse than feared. Recalling a sexual escapade with the woman who has been discovered dead in the midst of the party's increasingly riotous doings, the narrator confesses to his favorite style of action—not the type that focuses on coherent characterization (however attractive the choice of character might be)—but instead the "kind of odd stuttering tale that refused to unfold" and became "ever more mysterious and self-enclosed, drawing us sweetly toward its inner profundities." What are these profundities? More than two hundred pages later, the reader still can't be sure, other than that readerly attention has been consumed by a vast machine—or, even more aptly, by a monstrous beast, as the party has taken on a life of its own. Yet there is writerly advice for this predicament too, an admission that in all artistic entertainment a certain amount of sacrifice is taking place, not of the author or the characters or of (in this case) Gerald's poor house but of the audience for all of this. "A proscenium arch," the narrator confides, "is like a huge mouth, but the sensation is that it is the audience that is being fed through it is just another of theater's illusions. Theater is never a stripping down . . . but always a putting on: theater fattened on boxed time." To watch a play or read a novel, then, "was a form of martyrdom," a situation *Gerald's Party* exploits to the fullest.

AMERICAN SIGNS

Although the major accomplishment of his maturity as a writer would feature the nightmares of an art historian metamorphosed into the Italian fairy-tale character Pinocchio visiting an ageless Venice at carnival time, Robert Coover's work of the later 1980s and through the next decade would take quiet confidence in the simple enjoyment of American cultural signs. To someone of Coover's generation, Pinocchio is as familiar a childhood character as the heroes of cowboy stories and sports mythology and just as reliable a source of entertainment as anything seen at the movies. Hence the puppet-turned-boy's story is European only in setting; Coover's execution of the tale is as thoroughly American as Walt Disney's film version, albeit in a way that uses postmodern understanding to highlight the grammar and syntax that make possible such an interesting language of signs.

The best preparation for understanding Coover's most fully realized work would be to spend a night at the movies, preferably in a theater showing a revival of popular American classics, ranging from a preview of coming attractions, a weekly installment from the ongoing adventure serial, a selected short subject or two, and a cartoon for the kids to a travelogue, a musical interlude, and finally the feature film, hopefully a romance. Such a program fills the table of contents for the author's third collection of short fiction, the aptly titled *A Night at the Movies, or, You Must Remember This: Fictions* (1987). Unlike the fabulations and metafictions of *Pricksongs & Descants* and well beyond the reflective exercises of *In Bed One Night,* the stories from Coover's movie house let the signs of popular culture speak (almost) for themselves. The writer's art is in doing all he can with their language to make the spectacle of signs at play both entertaining and mildly instructive, which is just what so many American films of the 1940s and 1950s did. At the time, these cinematic masterpieces also asked viewers to suspend their disbelief—not to be devoured like viewers of the mad theatrics in *Gerald's Party,* but to be carried away from troubles and responsibilities into a magic kingdom of visual play.

As a preview of coming attractions, "The Phantom of the Movie Palace" notes both action and camera angles. On the screen itself, a Tarzan-like creature finds himself being fed Bogart lines by an actress much like Lauren Bacall, interrupted by quick cuts to a mad scientist out to destroy the world. By viewing every cinematic cliché in a kaleidoscopic manner, Coover's protagonist experiences not so much the films themselves as their free-floating grammar, a machine standing ready at all times to generate whatever effect is desired. As the collection proceeds, familiar movies are rerun in unfamiliar ways, letting readers see what has been taking place (in their heads) all along. Yet unlike so much of Coover's previous work, nobody is seriously hurt. As the book's epigraph promises, *"Ladies and Gentleman May safely visit this Theatre as no Offensive Films are ever Shown Here."* As if a Decency Code is proscribing limits for harmless fun, Coover's narratives can proceed without fears for underlying conspiracies or the manipulations of a malign central intelligence. At the very most he shows these films to viewers who, like himself, have been freed from unsuspected manipulation by an aesthetic Freedom of Information Act; what the makers of culture have done for our entertainment is now the entertainment itself.

Whatever Happened to Gloomy Gus of the Chicago Bears? (1987) recasts the Richard Nixon–like nemesis of *The Public Burning* as a more manageably comic figure, a football player bred for success and programmed to perform by rote. What makes this version more like *A Political Fable* is its narrator, a leftist who tries to guide his friend Gus through the entire panoply of Chicago's Depression-era cultural signs, from sports to socialist politics. Sympathy soon turns to making use of Gus' talents, and when they are used in street politics rather than within the safe bounds of the football field disaster almost inevitably follows. The big difference in terms of Robert Coover's development is that Nixon need no longer be an evil genius, nor slave to another evil genius such as Uncle Sam. The problem with what so many other writers were calling Tricky Dick is not himself, but his lack of self: his total

blankness, ready to be filled amorally (and therefore immorally) with a formula for succeeding that has no substance to it beyond the formulaic factors alone.

A similarly tolerant understanding informs *Pinocchio in Venice*. The puppet-turned-boy is no longer a boy, nor are his adventures those of childhood and beckoning adolescence. In Coover's version he is an old man, rounding out a brilliant international career as a scholar of art by coming home to write his magnum opus, a work to be titled *Mama*. By struggling to produce a text, Pinocchio invites readings as a text himself. Indeed, Coover asks, how can we consider this particular character and what he is doing without thinking of a great number of narratives, from the original Collodi fairy tale to Walt Disney's cartoon feature and even Thomas Mann's novel *Death in Venice,* including its cinematic adaptation by Luchino Visconti? These images are both in our minds as readers and matters for Pinocchio's subconscious. That his masterwork will be a tribute to the Blue Fairy underscores this already obvious intertextuality, and it is no surprise that in his search for her he once again faces distractions and deceits—goodness is, as it always was, difficult and elusive. Because it is carnival time, everyone wears masks; hence it will be easy for the Cat and the Fox to rob him, but also for the old dog Lido to save him. Is true goodness forever out of reach, even as old age slowly turns Pinocchio back into wood? Because he does find the Blue Fairy in death, readers can be granted hope without having to sanitize or sentimentalize the debaucheries that attend even these last moments of an admirable, if all too human, life.

Despite its party atmosphere, *John's Wife* (1996) marks a similar consolidation in Coover's work, a step back from the riotous behavior of *Gerald's Party* in order to more properly appraise the system of relationships that have come to characterize life among the middle class successes of 1990s Americans. The setting is small town/Midwest, but with none of the cultural and economic meanness that flavored *The Origin of the Brunists,* published thirty years before and conceived from Coover's teenage experience even earlier. Times are now good, people are flush, and everything's right for building and development, especially for those with political connections. John himself sits at the top of this pyramid, acting like a combination medieval lord and Renaissance Machiavellian. The only thing he isn't is an egalitarian democrat, the charade of which veils a rapacious capitalism underlying all the professional action. Personally, John's wife (who is, significantly, never named) informs the novel as a vague presence, never sharply defined in herself but central to many people's fantasies, whether of sex, wealth, or cultural achievement. The narrative style is freewheeling, pouring on flowing descriptions of anyone and everyone in the town; each of these folks is given his or her fifteen minutes of fame in a paragraph, then it's off to the next character, part of a dizzying roundelay that only toward the end turns morbidly violent.

Who are these people? Knowing the Coover canon, one might guess they are Brunists without a Giovanni Bruno to inspire them and even more so without a local newspaper editor to organize their story. In the half century since Robert Coover first began measuring the mythologies of Midwestern small town life, much had intervened: in the culture, much disruption but also real improvement in the qualities of life, while the literary tools for expressing such life had been reoriented and redeveloped by any number of artistic and philosophical movements, from deconstruction and postmodernism to a more fluid understanding of how signs function in society. *John's Wife* joins *The Public Burning* and *Gerald's Party* as one of the author's huge, even excessive, deliberately overwritten works, with the heft of something that readers had come to expect

from him as well as from Thomas Pynchon, William Gaddis, and William H. Gass. Yet in his delivery of the product Coover shows that he still prefers the small set piece—in this case brilliant portraits that swing by as if animated on a merry-go-round, in his next two novels more self-contained (in the manner of *Spanking the Maid* and *Gloomy Gus*).

Briar Rose (1996) is a reminder that there's more than one way to tell the Sleeping Beauty story. Coover's way is to counterpoint the prince's action with the Beauty's reflection. The prince plots his course and wonders about his fate; she dreams in fragments and remembers even less. By cutting back and forth between these two focuses, the author lets his readers entertain various ways of proceeding: maybe the princess is better off dying in her sleep, or perhaps she'll awake not to love but to rape. As for the prince, he must judge whether his progress is in fact true; whether he is about to call at the correct address (what would happen if he has the wrong castle?); or, and only Robert Coover could be expected to introduce such thoughts, what if his Sleeping Beauty is having her menstrual period just now? There's a rhythm to these speculations that's much like sex itself, involving repetition and variation, all of it saved by a certain amount of virtuosity within what are tightly circumscribed bounds. The fact that a third point of view comes from the fairy who first entranced the Beauty makes it obvious that Coover still values the storyteller's role most of all, for it is her metafictive fabulation that motivates everything that can possibly happen.

America's native mythology is its Wild West, the scene for Coover's short novel *Ghost Town* (1998). At 147 pages (to *Briar Rose*'s 86), it allows a longer track for the protagonist's journey, a trip through sagebrush and scrub with distant buttes that only help to profile the lone rider against the "bleak horizon under a glazed sky." Like a Marlboro cigarette commercial or the opening credits for a John Wayne or Clint Eastwood movie, *Ghost Town* speaks at once in the language not so much of the West but of how the West has been portrayed (for how old-time and modern cowboys actually speak, one must go to the novels and film scripts of Thomas McGuane). The rider himself soon comes to inhabit a ghost town of cultural signs, all of which are easily readable but none of which coheres in the proper language of narrative. Instead, Coover's story has set them askew, confusing the protagonist (if not the reader, who knows it all so much better than he). Farcical pratfalls and occasionally hideous violence follow, thanks to this sense of deliberate linguistic indirection; what prevail are the signs themselves, a stage set for the drama that Coover steadfastly refuses to supply. Like the earliest precursors of postmodernism, Gertrude Stein and Samuel Beckett, our contemporary author puts it plainly: what you see is what there is. Signs are signs, and (several accidents later) his protagonist learns that some of them are lies. Is there a secret pattern to all of this? Only the shadowy, mysterious author knows.

"The central thing for me is story," Robert Coover told Larry McCaffery for the collection *Anything Can Happen: Interviews with Contemporary American Novelists* (1983), which McCaffery compiled with Tom LeClair. "I like poems, paintings, music, even buildings, that tell stories." To be good with stories, you have to master their materials; but only some of their materials are words. "I'm much more interested," the author confessed, "in the way that fiction, for all its weaknesses, reflects something else—gesture, connections, paradox, story. I work with language because paper is cheaper than film stock. And because it's easier to work with a committee of one." And there are ways to tell a story without words: "We all learned that as kids at our Saturday morning religious experience in the local ten-cent cinemas."

Although he has dabbled at times in both film

and theater, fiction remains Coover's most common medium. And while the cost of film stock remains high, words with their encodings of gesture and connections now come cheaper than ever, thanks to such innovations as fax machines, cellular phones, electronic mail, and of course word processing. To Coover's delight, these new technologies also allow something else: what he calls in his *New York Times Book Review* essay "The End of Books" (June 21, 1992) "true freedom from the tyranny of the line." For centuries novelists had been trying anything to win such freedom, from marginalia and footnotes to radical displacements of space and time. Now, Coover found that a simple computer offered any number of infinitely forking paths for narrative development. The style even had a name, *hypertext,* which with suitable equipment he had begun teaching in his fiction classes at Brown University. Here the text could loop around, gradually accrete, or completely deconstruct, "just as the passage of time in one's lifetime." Structure becomes the new focus, for writer and reader alike. Linkage, routing, and mapping replace style. Texts themselves survive as fragments, but only as stepping-stones for safety during the real business of taking part in all the narratives that flow around them.

Ghost Town is a conventionally published novel that implies the workings of hypertext. Here the stepping-stones are the familiar swinging saloon doors, assay offices, and other fixtures of the old Wild West. But their setting has become a ghost town that only the protagonist's passage can activate. That activation is multidirectional and almost infinitely expansive; only the printed form of the book's 147 pages contains things, and we know that if the narrative possibilities were set out on computer there would be no limits at all. Hypertext is Robert Coover's new ideal, a place where his love for signs of culture can play endlessly in the fields of imaginative chance.

Selected Bibliography

WORKS OF ROBERT COOVER

NOVELS AND SHORT STORIES

The Origin of the Brunists. New York: Putnam, 1966.

The Universal Baseball Association, Inc., J. Henry Waugh, Prop. New York: Random House, 1968.

Pricksongs & Descants; Fictions. New York: Dutton, 1969. (Contains "The Door," "The Magic Poker," "Morris in Chains," "The Gingerbread House," "Seven Exemplary Fictions," "The Elevator," "Romance of the Thin Man and the Fat Lady," "Quenby and Ola, Swede and Carl," "The Sentient Lens," "A Pedestrian Accident," "The Babysitter," and "The Hat Act.")

The Public Burning. New York: Viking Press, 1977.

A Political Fable. New York: Viking Press, 1980.

Spanking the Maid. New York: Grove Press, 1982.

In Bed One Night & Other Brief Encounters. Providence, R.I.: Burning Deck, 1983. (Contains "Debris," "The Old Man," "In Bed One Night," "Getting to Wichita," "The Tinkerer," "The Fallguy's Faith," "An Encounter," "The Convention," and "Beginnings.")

Gerald's Party. New York: Simon & Schuster, 1986.

A Night at the Movies. New York: Simon & Schuster, 1987. (Contains "The Phantom of the Movie Palace," "After Lazarus," "Shootout at Gentry's Junction," "Gilda's Dream," "Inside the Frame," "Lap Dissolves," "Charlie in the House of Rue," "Cartoon," "Milford Junction, 1939: A Brief Encounter," "Top Hat," and "You Must Remember This.")

Whatever Happened to Gloomy Gus of the Chicago Bears? New York: Simon & Schuster, 1987.

Pinocchio in Venice. New York: Simon & Schuster, 1991.

Briar Rose. New York: Grove Press, 1996.

John's Wife. New York: Simon & Schuster, 1996.

Ghost Town. New York: Henry Holt, 1998.

PLAY

A Theological Position. New York: Dutton, 1972. (Contains "The Kid," "Love Scene," "Rip Awake," and "A Theological Position.")

SELECTED CRITICAL WRITINGS

Review of *Bartlett's Familiar Quotations. New York Times Book Review,* December 8, 1968, pp. 8, 72.

Review of *Between Fantoine and Agapa* and *That Voice,* by Robert Pinget. *New York Times Book Review,* September 25, 1983, pp. 15, 21.

Review of *The Real Life of Alejandro Mayta,* by Mario Vargas Llosa. *New York Times Book Review,* February 2, 1986, pp. 1, 28.

Review of *Six Memos for the Next Millennium,* by Italo Calvino. *New York Times Book Review,* March 20, 1988, pp. 1, 29–31.

"The End of Books." *New York Times Book Review,* June 21, 1992, pp. 1, 23–25.

CRITICAL STUDIES

Anderson, Richard. *Robert Coover.* Boston: Twayne, 1981.

Cope, Jackson I. *Robert Coover's Fictions.* Baltimore: Johns Hopkins University Press, 1986.

Dewey, Joseph. *In a Dark Time: The Apocalyptic Temper in the American Novel of the Nuclear Age.* West Lafayette, Ind.: Purdue University Press, 1990.

Elman, Richard. *Namedropping: Mostly Literary Memoirs.* Albany, N.Y.: State University of New York Press, 1998.

Gordon, Lois. *Robert Coover: The Universal Fiction-making Process.* Carbondale, Ill.: Southern Illinois University Press, 1983.

Hutcheon, Linda. *A Poetics of Postmodernism.* New York and London: Routledge, 1988.

Kennedy, Thomas E. *Robert Coover: A Study of the Short Fiction.* New York: Twayne, 1992.

LeClair, Tom. *The Art of Excess: Mastery in Contemporary American Fiction.* Urbana, Ill.: University of Illinois Press, 1989.

McCaffery, Larry. *The Metafictional Muse.* Pittsburgh, Pa.: University of Pittsburgh Press, 1982.

Maltby, Paul. *Dissident Postmodernists.* Philadelphia: University of Pennsylvania Press, 1991.

Saltzman, Arthur M. *Designs of Darkness in Contemporary American Fiction.* Philadelphia: University of Pennsylvania Press, 1990.

———. *The Novel in the Balance.* Columbia: University of South Carolina Press, 1993.

Scholes, Robert. *Fabulation and Metafiction.* Urbana: University of Illinois Press, 1979. (Expanded, with additions on Coover's work, from *The Fabulators* [New York: Oxford University Press, 1967].)

Walsh, Richard. *Novel Arguments: Reading Innovative American Fiction.* Cambridge and New York: Cambridge University Press, 1995.

INTERVIEWS

Gado, Frank. *First Person: Conversations with Writers.* Schenectady, N.Y.: Union College Press, 1973.

LeClair, Tom, and Larry McCaffery. *Anything Can Happen: Interviews with Contemporary American Novelists.* Urbana: University of Illinois Press, 1983.

Ziegler, Heide, and Christopher Bigsby. *The Radical Imagination and the Liberal Tradition: Interview with English and American Novelists.* London: Junction Books, 1982.

—JEROME KLINKOWITZ

Richard Ford

1944–

RICHARD FORD'S FIVE novels (*A Piece of My Heart* [1976], *The Ultimate Good Luck* [1981], *The Sportswriter* [1986], *Wildlife* [1990], *Independence Day* [1995]) and two collections of short fiction (*Rock Springs* [1987], *Women with Men* [1997]) aptly demonstrate the qualities that make him a unique and unpredictable writer. The restlessness of Ford's work has divided and thwarted critics since the beginning of his career, causing Michael Mewshaw to remark, "Described in *Granta* as a devotee of 'dirty realism,' invariably characterised as a macho figure from Marlboro country, frequently linked with laconic stylists such as Ernest Hemingway or Raymond Carver, Ford has been hilariously misrepresented." Since the publication of his first novel, Ford has sent critics scrambling for categories and, in the process, has elicited conflicting critical responses while becoming increasingly popular.

The most frequent charge leveled against Ford's fiction is that it is overly masculine. In an interview in *The Writer,* Ford asserts, "There is no such thing as a guy's book. . . . Literature is an attempt to try to make communicable—by which I mean shareable—something that is true about us all." His defensiveness about the charge of being a "guy's" writer stems from his skepticism of gender differences: "My basic feeling is women and men are more alike than unalike, and the ways they're different are both obvious and

comprehensible and not as interesting as they're made out to be." He is more concerned with having "sympathy" for his characters than with "gender sensitivity."

Whether male or female, Ford's characters are always ordinary, nonheroic people, often confused and unmoored. His challenge is to write about these characters in a way that gives their unspectacular lives dignity and beauty. In his fiction Ford records worlds in which people's thoughts rarely mesh with their words; even his most educated characters cannot articulate their feelings. This failure to communicate precipitates much of the drama in Ford's fiction, especially the drama of male/female relationships. Infidelity courses through his work, establishing a thematic link from book to book and demonstrating that Ford is concerned, above all, with desire and its ramifications. Erotic desire in particular drives, haunts, and ruins his male protagonists, who tend to be troubled, unfaithful men in their thirties and forties.

FORD'S BACKGROUND

The only child of Parker and Edna Ford, Richard Ford was born in Jackson, Mississippi, on February 16, 1944. He started to move between Jackson and Little Rock, Arkansas, where his grandparents operated a hotel, after his father's first heart attack in 1952. When a second heart attack killed his father in 1960, Ford remained primarily in Arkansas until he moved to Michigan in 1962 because, in his own words, he was "not brave enough or committed enough or selfless enough to stay . . . during the civil-rights movement." Ford attended Michigan State University to study hotel management and there met his future wife, Kristina Hensley (now Ford). During his undergraduate years, he enlisted in the Marine ROTC but was given a medical discharge after contracting hepatitis. He then decided to study literature.

After graduation in 1966, Ford drifted unhappily from job to job; he taught middle school and worked as a science editor for *American Druggist* before attending law school at Washington University. Although he quit after one semester, the experience was not futile. "Going to law school was probably very important to me because, when I started to try to write stories, I realized how much writing stories was like writing briefs. It's writing to persuade someone." Ford then returned to Little Rock and worked as a substitute teacher, disliked the job, and decided to try writing, which he had enjoyed as an undergraduate but had not pursued seriously. He applied to graduate school for creative writing, and in 1970 he received his Master of Fine Arts in fiction writing from the University of California at Irvine, where he studied with the novelists E. L. Doctorow and Oakley Hall. After graduate school, however, Ford could not publish his stories in magazines (a dilemma humorously retold in his introduction to *The Pushcart Prize, XIII* [1988]), so he started to write a novel. Part of his first novel, *A Piece of My Heart,* was published in *The Paris Review,* which helped him find a publisher for the book. Ford wrote another novel before his first "decent" short stories were accepted by magazines.

Since *A Piece of My Heart,* Ford has published four more novels and two collections of short fic-

tion. He has taught briefly at Princeton University, the University of Michigan, Goddard College, Williams College, and Northwestern University, but he has not taught regularly since 1981, when he quit teaching and writing fiction to write for *Inside Sports* magazine. Ford started *The Sportswriter,* his third novel, on Easter in 1982, after *Inside Sports* became defunct and *Sports Illustrated* declined to offer him a job. The end of Ford's sportswriting career has seen his status as a fiction writer rise significantly.

THE EARLY NOVELS: *A PIECE OF MY HEART* AND *THE ULTIMATE GOOD LUCK*

Ford's first novel, *A Piece of My Heart,* demonstrates both the benefits and the dangers of a Southerner writing about the South. Although Ford has denied being a Southern writer, asserting "there is no such thing as Southern writing or Southern literature," his first novel owes an obvious debt to William Faulkner. Critics have described the novel as an example of "neo-Faulknerism" that "shows obvious promise, but also exhibits all the characteristic vices of Southern fiction" and "reads like the worst, rather than the best, of Faulkner" and as a work that "suffers from its own excesses, excesses seen far too often in Southern fiction of the last 30 years." Despite some positive responses and a nomination for the Ernest Hemingway Award for Best First Novel, the critical reception of *A Piece of My Heart* did not bode well for Ford.

While identifying the Faulknerian elements in *A Piece of My Heart* can help readers contextualize Ford's work, attempting to place Ford in Faulkner's shadow after his first novel will prove fruitless. As Bonnie Lyons noted in her introduction to an interview with Ford, "Since [*A Piece of My Heart*] his novels . . . and his much acclaimed collection of short stories, *Rock Springs,* have proved him a much less predictable writer and one harder to categorize." The diversity of his later work notwithstanding, *A Piece of My Heart* limits itself largely to the Mississippi/Arkansas border. The novel's themes—incest, identity, familial destruction, personal downfall, and violence—recall those of some of Faulkner's novels, especially *The Sound and the Fury, Absalom, Absalom!,* and *Sanctuary.*

Although unhappy with comparisons between himself and Faulkner, Ford has acknowedged his predecessor's importance to his development as a writer. In his essay "The Three Kings: Hemingway, Faulkner, and Fitzgerald" (in *Esquire,* December 1983), Ford writes, "Reading Faulkner was like coming upon a great iridescent glacier that I had dreamed about"; and in an interview in *The Paris Review* he admits that *A Piece of My Heart* was "probably directly influenced by Faulkner and Eudora Welty and Flannery O'Connor" and that it "was about the South and was captivated by certain traditional Southern themes—search for place, freedom of choice, s-e-x—all inherited literary concerns." But Ford also points out, "I pretty quickly realized that I wasn't going to be able to write very much about the South because it had already been written about so well by all the greats."

The novel's two protagonists—Robard Hewes, an incestuous adulterer, and Sam Newel, a gloomy law student living in Chicago—meet at an uncharted island on the Mississippi River, where much of the novel's action takes place. Having left his wife in California in order to pursue sexual relations with his married cousin, Beuna, Hewes responds to a help wanted ad looking for someone to guard the island, which is owned by the quarrelsome Mr. Lamb, from poachers. Hewes wants to maintain a low profile, and this job seems ideal because the island is miles from Beuna's town, Helena.

Hewes' decision to go to Arkansas becomes the novel's most consequential act. Early on, he asks himself the book's central question: "What

happens when she manages to infect you with something dangerous, keeping it alive for years on the strength of gardenia odor and a few flourishing letters? What happens when you recognize it's important—what you did and what she did and would do, and when and how and to whom?" Hewes' obsession with Beuna fills him "with a kind of ruinous anxiety that just one thing will satisfy." For Hewes, this "one thing" is sex, and its lure is strong enough to bring him from California to Arkansas. Attempting to justify his decision to leave his wife, he convinces himself "he was not finished with this part of his life yet, wife or no wife, this part left with Beuna." Beuna, though, is a destructive force, a person who has fallen from grace and propriety.

Not content with her own fall, Beuna wishes to pull Hewes down with her: "I want you to tear me up. . . . I want to do it in the back of the truck in the dirt and the rocks and the filthiness." At the beginning of their affair, Hewes worries about this aspect of Beuna: "He looked at her and thought maybe the best thing to do was to get back in the truck and out of there right then. . . . Except that whatever it was she had, badness or disappointment or meanness, was the thing that was indispensable now, and he wanted to draw in to her and glide off in infinitude and just let loose of everything." Ford portrays Hewes as having little capacity for decision making, casting Beuna in the role of the siren singing to him from the rocks; Hewes knows she will bring disaster upon him, but he cannot resist her song.

Ford structures the novel so chapters are alternately narrated through Hewes' and Newel's perspectives. Although different in many regards, each character is possessed by his past. In Hewes' chapters, the past frequently interrupts the present, and nostalgia propels him on his dangerous journey to Beuna. Newel, a native of Mississippi, has come to Lamb's island to "be part of something happening, not something [he] remembered," to try to learn how to make use of his past, which "is supposed to give you some way of judging things." Newel's obsession with his memories has crippled him, transforming him into a hermit in his room in Chicago. Hewes' attitude toward the past, however, becomes more enabling, at least in his encounters with Beuna.

Ford further stresses Newel's inability to avoid thinking about the past by including brief subchapters (in italics) narrated omnisciently. In these vignettes, Newel is always a boy, and his relationship with his parents, particularly his father, seems awkward and distant. The significance of these memories lies in the adult Newel's recollection of them, in his belated awareness of their importance and failure to gather them into something cohesive.

Because of Hewes' nocturnal jaunts to Helena, he and Newel rarely see each other on Lamb's island, from which Newel does not venture until Lamb electrocutes himself in his fishing boat. However, they talk enough for Newel to annoy Hewes, especially when he tries to warn Hewes about the likely result of his relationship with Beuna. Although the book is divided between Hewes and Newel, Hewes receives most of Ford's attention and interest. The novel's structure calls for a meaningful engagement between Hewes and Newel; however, because Newel eventually emerges as a minor character—one whose fate the reader is only mildly interested in—while Beuna's consequence to the novel increases, that engagement does not materialize. Part of Newel's relative insignificance is a result of his disconnectedness: he cannot react to the world around him, persisting in pessimism and cynicism and always believing "nothing good lasts very long."

One of Ford's signal achievements in *A Piece of My Heart* is his blend of seriousness and humor. The novel is infused with outrageous, sometimes offensive humor, courtesy of Beuna and Lamb. Indeed, Beuna and Lamb become the most complex and compelling characters in the novel. Despite his cantankerous demeanor and swag-

gering skepticism, Lamb is more optimistic than any other character in the book: "You know why the birdies wake up singing . . . ? . . . Because they're happy to be alive one more day. You can't count on that, Hewes. Them little birdies know it, too. That's why they're out there singing all the time. They're trying to tell us something. 'Tweet, tweet, you're alive, you ignorant asshole.' "

The novel's title, too, arises from a humorous moment. Early in the book, a truck passes Hewes with "large writing on the sides through dirt and coagulated grease, WHACK MY OLD DOODLE, and below that, TAKE ANOTHER LITTLE PIECE OF MY HEART." Although both phrases are colloquial (the second coming from a Janis Joplin song), the phrase that gives the novel its title becomes a symbol for Hewes' life: driven by lust and nostalgia, he cannot avoid leaving his wife to see his cousin. Thus, a piece of his heart has been taken, as if he had no will. Similarly, Beuna's letters to Hewes—always brief, always importunate and flirtatious—become a force he no longer can resist, leading him from his wife and toward a woman who will lead him, in turn, to his downfall.

Beuna emerges as the novel's main enigma, and Hewes wants to understand her behavior and her motivation. But Beuna remains inexplicable, and Hewes' presumptuousness ruins him: if he would acknowledge that he cannot understand her, he would not become so dangerously vulnerable to her seductiveness. When separated from Beuna, he thinks of her in psychological terms: "There was some mystery to Beuna still, some force that drew him, made him want to find her out, like a man plundering a place he knows he shouldn't be but can't help but be for the one important thing he might find." But when he is with Beuna, he thinks primarily, if not solely, of sex and of the mysterious bag she has been saving for him and promising him in her letters. When Hewes learns what the bag is for—to cover Beuna's mouth while he urinates or defecates on her face—he is disgusted. Her fantasy denied, an enraged Beuna guides Hewes unknowingly back to her mobile home, from which her husband, W. W., chases him with a rifle. Hewes speeds back to Lamb's island, hoping W. W. does not follow him there, or at least does not persist in trying to kill him once Hewes is on the island.

While fleeing from W. W., Hewes realizes why Beuna turned against him: "If he refused whatever included her little plastic bag, then he refused that he and she were in the same boat. And that was what had made her lead him right to W. W., a desire to end the dispute by cutting the knot." Hewes arrives at the dock across from Lamb's island, takes a boat, and sets out across the water. Expecting to see W. W. when he turns to look at the dock, he sees instead the teenage boy who once worked for Lamb but was fired for killing a poacher. The boy is holding a rifle, taking careful aim at Hewes in the boat. In an attempt to remind him of who he is (he met the boy the day he applied for the job guarding the island), Hewes "cut the throttle, and offered the boy a perfect broadside of the boat." When he stands up and spreads his arms "so the boy could see him clearly in the prism of his scope, see his face, and recognize him as the old man's employee," the boy, thinking him a poacher, shoots Hewes, who, feeling "a great upheaval, a tumult of molecules being rearranged and sloughed off in rapid succession," falls into the water, mutters "Oh, oh," and dies.

The epilogue of *A Piece of My Heart* does not follow the events of the novel, but precedes them. Italicized, the passage describes a scene with Newel as a boy and his father in a hotel in New Orleans. They see a crowd of people, one of them repeatedly taking photographs, around a dead man. When the photographer moves the body for a different angle, Newel's father says, "Listen, now listen, and you can hear him rattle in his throat." By ending the novel with a flashback about Newel's childhood that focuses on a death and on the idea of paying careful attention, Ford

skillfully guides his readers to listen closely, in case Hewes, who has died on the previous page, makes a noise. But, like the rattle in the corpse's throat, which Newel "wasn't ever sure if he had heard it or not," the sound of Hewes' dying is so faint ("Oh, oh") it immediately fades into the sound of water.

With its explosions and gunfights, Ford's cinematic second novel, *The Ultimate Good Luck,* makes much more noise than *A Piece of My Heart.* Concerned with being perceived as a Southern novelist, Ford purposefully moves his field of concern to Oaxaca, Mexico. *The Ultimate Good Luck* possesses the elements of a thriller; taut and suspenseful, couched in a spare, muscular prose, it carries more action than Ford's first novel and has been compared to the work of Robert Stone and Dashiell Hammett, two writers Ford never resembles again. Written in a mode and set in a place to which he has not returned, *The Ultimate Good Luck* seems an aberration in Ford's career. When he finished the novel, he stopped writing fiction and started to write for *Inside Sports* magazine, signaling a crisis in his life as a fiction writer.

The protagonist, Harry Quinn, a thirty-one-year-old Vietnam veteran, has gone to Oaxaca, Mexico, to help free the brother of his estranged girlfriend, Rae, from jail in the hope of reconciling with Rae in the process. The brother, Sonny, has been arrested for smuggling cocaine into Tijuana and now is in physical danger because Deats, the drug dealer Sonny was working for, arrives from Los Angeles claiming that Sonny took half the cocaine before he was arrested. The plot progresses through various twists, some unexpected, after Quinn hires Carlos Bernhardt, a Mexican lawyer, to bribe a judge to authorize Sonny's release. Everyone wants a part of the bribe, and Quinn, naturally wary, cannot decide whom to trust. His suspiciousness increases as he witnesses several acts of violence: a particularly brutal boxing match in which one of the boxer's eyeballs is knocked loose; a deadly explosion at a Baskin-Robbins; a murdered young man in a hut; and Bernhardt's murder. Violence characterizes Quinn's arena of awareness. A Marine in Vietnam, he has seen an unusual amount of killing; during the course of the novel, Quinn recalls his previous encounters with violent acts. Quinn moves in a world where he is perpetually at risk.

Quinn attributes his survival—in Vietnam, in Oaxaca—to "good conduct," a phrase tattooed on his arm. For him, this is "what kept you in the picture, kept ground underneath you instead of on top." To Quinn, good conduct entails restraint in the face of violence; but good luck serves as his savior as much as good conduct does, hence his frequent references to luck in the novel— "Luck was infatuated with efficiency," "everybody lives in some relation to the luckless," "Quinn knew he needed to get lucky." Good conduct and good luck together allow Quinn to survive all the deception and double-crossings of the novel, especially the climactic scene in which the wife of a crime boss takes Quinn to see a young terrorist, Muñoz. By now Bernhardt has been killed, Sonny has been attacked in prison and is likely to be murdered, and Quinn has begun to realize the futility of all his efforts.

This scene marks the one point in *The Ultimate Good Luck* where Quinn actually commits an act of violence: when Quinn aims his pistol at Muñoz and tells him not to touch his gun, Muñoz seems not to understand and raises his own gun. Quinn then shoots him, more out of exasperation ("Come on, for Christ's sake") than out of fear or anger. Muñoz's bodyguard, who shot Bernhardt the night before, opens fire into the room, killing the crime boss's wife before Quinn can shoot him. Now responsible for three deaths, Quinn "wondered, as he walked, if he'd perfected something in himself by killing three people he didn't know, when he had come at the beginning, simply to save one." The novel ends with Quinn and Rae preparing to leave the hotel, finally acknowledging that they cannot save Sonny.

The novel's impetus—Quinn's regret over allowing his relationship with Rae to end—becomes its true focus. This secondary plot consists of Quinn's attempts to overcome the aloofness that caused Rae to leave him. His emotional detachment resembles that of Newel in *A Piece of My Heart*—"Intimacy just made things hard to see, and he wanted things kept highly visible at all times"—but he recognizes his problem and wants to change his frame of mind after he decides he cannot be happy without Rae. The habit of solitude has become natural for Quinn, and his struggle with his own personality develops into the most compelling tension in the novel.

The Ultimate Good Luck has received the most negative critical reaction of any of Ford's books. According to one of the novel's more thoughtful critics, Walter Clemons, "Ford has jimmied himself into the confines of the existentialist thriller with a conspicuous sacrifice of his robust gift for comedy." Furthermore, Clemons does not consider the novel's protagonists successful as characters: "Quinn and Rae seem laboratory animals in a demonstration that Quinn's belief in living without attachments is an insufficient code." The anonymous reviewer for *Kirkus Reviews* criticizes the novel for its "flat, clichéd characters . . . surrounded by Ford's dreadful macho/psychological prose, a syrup boiled down from the worst tendencies of everyone from Hemingway to Robert Stone." The same reviewer also asserts that Ford's mixture of "pretentious/empty verbiage with the existential-thriller formula becomes a numbing one." Despite some strengths, *The Ultimate Good Luck* emerges as Ford's weakest book.

THE BASCOMBE NOVELS: *THE SPORTSWRITER* AND *INDEPENDENCE DAY*

Ford's third novel, *The Sportswriter*, and its sequel, *Independence Day*, changed Ford's status among critics and proved to be popular successes as well. The two novels have emerged as his most celebrated and most accomplished books to date: *The Sportswriter* was selected as one of the five best books of 1986 by *Time* and has sold nearly 200,000 copies, and *Independence Day* won both the 1996 Pulitzer Prize in fiction and the 1996 PEN/Faulkner Award for fiction, the first and only book to win both prizes. The success of these novels stems from Ford's protagonist/narrator, Frank Bascombe, who has been called "the perfect 1980s suburban hero"; "one of the most finely etched characters in recent fiction"; "a great mythic American character"; and "one of the most complex and memorable characters of our time."

Bascombe's complexity and memorableness arise from his acute and chronic self-consciousness, which results in a constant stream of interruptions in and interpretations of the events of the novel. Because Bascombe tries to be as inconspicuous as possible, he emerges as resolutely unremarkable. Even critics enthusiastic about the Bascombe novels have been ambivalent about Bascombe, viewing the solipsistic dimension of Ford's character as a drawback: "It's terribly difficult to sustain the reader's interest in a narrator/protagonist who is not himself interesting." Michiko Kakutani, otherwise enthusiastic about *The Sportswriter*, thinks Bascombe's "existential gloom and talent for self-pity can sometimes make him an irritating (not to mention long-winded) narrator," and Barbara Ehrenreich has called him "a typical mid-80s case of intimacy-phobia complicated by a full-blown fear of commitment." A few critics also have objected to Bascombe's attitude toward women, his relationship with his children, and his lack of participation in the lives of others.

Bascombe's sexism remains a hotly contested issue among critics, with Ford himself occasionally weighing in to argue against his character being sexist. Whether he is a "neo-sexist lug,"

Bascombe does reveal a problematic attitude toward women, whom he refers to as "girls" throughout *The Sportswriter*. He describes his current lover, Vicki Arcenault, as "a wonderful bunch," "a treasure trove for a man interested in romance," and "a nice bundle." He also makes preposterous statements about women, such as "the best girls oftentimes go unchosen, probably precisely because they are the best"; and, despite the overwhelming evidence to the contrary, he presumes to understand what women are thinking and feeling. Bascombe's problem with women, according to critic Vivian Gornick, is that he "feels compassion for women but not empathy." When his compassion gives way to pity, Bascombe becomes sentimental and insincere.

It is a measure of Bascombe's richness as a character that he can engender so many different responses from readers. At times, he can become his own harshest critic: "I don't think I have any ethics at all, really. I just do as little harm as I can"; "I have become more cynical than old Iago, since there is no cynicism like lifelong self-love and the tunnel vision in which you yourself are all that's visible at the tunnel's end." Bascombe's ethical universe seems empty; he is concerned about being, or seeming, ethical, more out of vanity than out of goodwill. He never willingly penetrates others' lives, fearing any personal attachment that might bring his life into meaningful contact with another's. Bascombe confides more to his fortune-teller, Mrs. Miller, than to anyone else, including Vicki. He has little capacity for friendship—"Friendship is a lie of life"—and because of his cynicism, he does not produce faith in those around him. He is absolutely compelling.

The Sportswriter is narrated by Bascombe in a present tense saturated with flashbacks. Ford's expansive style in *The Sportswriter* has garnered much praise, with one reviewer deeming the novel "a remarkably gentle and meditative book" composed in a "relaxed, colloquial style" that "moves easily from description to commentary."

Bascombe floats in his memories and speculations about the past as he guides the reader through an Easter weekend—from Good Friday to Easter Sunday—that is light on action and heavy with recollection and speculation. Despite the novel's religious backdrop, however, Bascombe's thoughts remain completely secular; he does not approach his problems spiritually or existentially, but domestically and psychologically.

Like Ford himself, Bascombe has turned to sportswriting following a brief career as a fiction writer. After publishing a book of twelve short stories, selling film rights to the book, and receiving an advance for a hazily planned novel (all while he is still in his early twenties), Bascombe moves to New York because he thinks that is what writers do. Feeling stifled by the city, he stops writing, then moves with his new wife to the suburban town of Haddam, New Jersey, where he still cannot write and begins to suspect he has written everything he would ever write. When the managing editor at a sports magazine offers him a full-time job writing about sports, he accepts, never returning to fiction writing. In retrospect, he believes "It is no loss to mankind when one writer decides to call it a day."

But the issue persists in Bascombe's mind: "Why did I quit writing? Forgetting for the moment that I quit writing to become a sportswriter . . . Was it just that things did not come easily enough? Or that I couldn't translate my personal recognitions into the ambiguous stuff of complex literature? Or that I had nothing to write about . . . ?" Bascombe acknowledges "there are those reasons and at least twenty better ones." His reasons for not writing fiction are central to the novel, because the change this decision invokes in his life also ripples through the lives of his family.

Bascombe believes the main reason he quit writing is because he "somehow lost [his] sense of anticipation at age twenty-five." This loss pushes him into silence; it renders his novel still-

born and prohibits him from writing any more stories. Because Bascombe loses interest in whatever he "might write next—the next sentence, the next day," he dies as a writer. For him, sportswriting "is more like being a businessman, or an old-fashioned traveling salesman . . . since in so many ways words are just our currency, our medium of exchange."

Sportswriting becomes the ideal occupation for Bascombe, who does not participate but observes, does not act but reports on action. He learns to respect athletes, who "by and large, are people who are happy to let their actions speak for them, happy to be what they do." Bascombe admires athletes for their penchant for detachment, "a rare selfishness that means he isn't looking around the sides of his emotions to wonder about alternatives for what he's saying or thinking about," which is what Bascombe does. He believes his life would improve if he could learn "the necessity of relinquishing doubt and ambiguity and self-inquiry in favor of a pleasant, self-championing one-dimensionality." This blankness appeals to Bascombe because during the last year of his marriage he "was always able to 'see around the sides' of whatever [he] was feeling." Whenever he became aware of an emotion, he realized he "could just as easily feel or act another way . . . even though [he] might've been convinced that the way [he] was acting probably represented the way [he] *really* felt."

This type of thinking becomes a symptom of one of Bascombe's main problems: an emotional relativism that is crippling yet rationalized as generosity of outlook. Bascombe's hypervigilance about his own emotions stems partly from his prior experience as a fiction writer: " 'Seeing around' is exactly what I did in my stories . . . and in the novel I abandoned, and one reason why I had to quit. I could always think of other ways I might be feeling about what I was writing, or other voices I might be speaking in." In a way, Bascombe has transformed himself into both character and author, authoring his own experience instead of living it.

The main drama of *The Sportswriter* is Bascombe's attempt to make his former wife (to whom he refers as "X," both an algebraic variable with infinite possibilities and the homophonic equivalent of the "ex" in "ex-wife") to feel anything positive toward him. After their son Ralph died of Reye's syndrome at the age of nine, Bascombe slept with eighteen women ("a number I don't consider high, or especially scandalous"). He attributes the demise of his marriage not to his infidelities but to his attempts "to simulate complete immersion." "What I was doing . . . was trying to be within myself by being as nearly as possible *within* somebody else." This, Bascombe claims, "leads to a terrible dreaminess and the worst kind of abstraction and unreachableness." Bascombe's dreaminess, which is "among other things, a state of suspended recognition," anesthetizes him while alienating his wife.

Bascombe's own feelings of isolation are magnified in several of the book's saddest and most colorful characters—Walter Luckett (a recent divorcé), Herb Wallagher (a former football player now in a wheelchair because of a waterskiing accident), and Wade Arcenault (Vicki's unstable father). Bascombe fails to connect with any of these characters, despite his attempts to learn about Wallagher (for a magazine profile) and Arcenault (to impress Vicki). While his encounters with Wallagher and Arcenault have minimal consequences, Bascombe's inability, or unwillingness, to connect with Luckett indirectly contributes to Luckett's suicide.

When Luckett, a new member of the Divorced Men's Club to which Bascombe belongs, confides to him that he slept with a man two nights earlier, Bascombe says, "It doesn't matter to me." This quality, or lack, in Bascombe is precisely what compels Walter to confide in him: "I think I wanted to tell you, Frank, because I knew you wouldn't care." Luckett tries to become close to Bascombe, but Bascombe rebuffs him. Even after Luckett's suicide, Bascombe admits, "I still cannot think a long thought about Walter." Instead of helping Luckett before his suicide, Bascombe visits his now-abandoned house in a belated attempt to understand something about him—as Ehrenreich points out, "physical structures are easier to deal with than their residents." This forthright callousness, like Bascombe's behavior throughout the novel, simultaneously alienates him from and endears him to the reader; he has severe inner flaws, but at least he acknowledges them. However, the critic D. G. Myers feels this detachment signals a flaw in the novel and argues that Bascombe's "crippling, complacent limitation is, finally, the trouble not only with him . . . but with the book of which he is the hero."

Because of his inability to communicate with her, Bascombe's already tenuous relationship with Vicki disintegrates (after Easter dinner at her father's house, she calls an end to their romance, and when he tries to persuade her otherwise, she hits him in the face). Ironically, Bascombe's behavior toward Vicki is a cultivated insincerity, since he closely analyzes what he says while and after he says it. Most of Bascombe and Vicki's conversations have followed a "jokey-quippy-irony style" that precludes revelation and truthfulness. Accustomed to his facility with language, Bascombe is shocked when he cannot sway Vicki through words: "Words, my best refuge and oldest allies, are suddenly acting to no avail." This failure parallels the end of his career as a fiction writer; but whereas Bascombe has come to terms with his inability to write fiction, he has not yet acknowledged the possibility of language failing him in his love life, although it has done so for years.

Bascombe's portrait of his small New Jersey town, Haddam, is as convincing as his self-portrait. Through Bascombe, Haddam emerges as a 1980s version of a 1950s small American town, run by Republicans and Italians, served by an adequate number of doctors and schools. If one loses a wallet in Haddam, it is returned with nothing missing the same night. Bascombe acknowledges the town's dullness but claims its dullness is what he likes about it: "Haddam in fact is as straightforward and plumb-literal as a fire hydrant, which more than anything else makes it the pleasant place it is."

However, later in the novel, after Luckett's suicide and Bascombe's failure with Vicki, he sees Haddam differently: "I am . . . struck by an unfriendliness of the town, the smallish way it offers no clue for how to go about things—no priority established, no monumental structures to determine a true middle, no Main Street to organize things." His acknowledgment of the town's faults highlights his feelings of despair. Previously, Haddam served as a harbor—from New York, from crime, from his past—but when Haddam has no "true middle," the town offers nothing for Bascombe to hold onto. He also realizes Haddam "is not a good place for death. Death's a preposterous intruder. A breach. A building that won't fit with the others."

Without improving or being redeemed by any of the novel's events, Bascombe's final possibility for redemption occurs late Easter night at the train station, when he watches people arrive from their various travels and a woman, whom he believes is Walter Luckett's sister, disembarks from a train. He believes he and she "are the same vintage," and he waits for her, "ready to be used" and hoping to be helpful. But when she approaches him, he leaps unexpectedly onto the train, saying, "I'm sorry . . . I've got to catch a train," thereby failing to connect to her or redeem himself. His nonchalance at this failure—the one point in the novel where he does not second-guess his actions—speaks volumes about how little he has changed.

In the novel's final chapter, Bascombe explains his reasoning for recording the events of that Easter weekend:

I realize I have told all this because unbeknownst to me, on that Thursday those months ago, I awoke with a feeling, a stirring, that any number of things were going to change and be settled and come to an end soon, and I might have something to tell that would be important and even interesting.

Despite all the benefits of telling his story, Bascombe realizes "I am at the point of not knowing the outcome of things once again." Although Bascombe claims "things occur to me differently now, just as they might to a character at the end of a good short story," he still sees around things rather than to their center, acknowledging all possible emotions rather than choosing one. In effect, he remains his own protagonist, a character in his own life. Bascombe's spiritual stasis is not a failure of the novel; rather, it is the novel's primary achievement that it can occupy almost 400 pages and refuse to bring its protagonist to a state of emotional or spiritual resolution.

Although the last chapter of the novel, entitled "The End," offers some narrative, if not emotional, closure by providing updates on the main characters and by offering more of Bascombe's observations about his life, the novel truly ends with chapter thirteen. Bascombe goes to the office of the magazine for which he works, meets a college-age intern, and asks her out for a drink and a sandwich. While she prepares to leave with him, Bascombe stares out the window of the office building, "hoping for even an illusion of a face, of someone there watching me here," but he sees nothing. The chapter's final sentence—"No one's noticed me standing here at all"—is an anti-epiphany, since the reader's expectation that Bascombe would become more virtuous, or at least more present—ethically if not spiritually—in the world, is defeated. By closing with "no one" and the failure of vision, the novel reinforces the spiritual void it attempts to fill. This starkness illuminates the moral blindness Bascombe acknowledges and bemoans but does nothing to change.

The Sportswriter is ultimately a tour de force of self-regard.

By taking place on a secular holiday, Ford's sequel to *The Sportswriter, Independence Day,* forgoes the promise of redemption but, ironically, provides it. In the five years since the events of *The Sportswriter* occurred, Frank Bascombe has realized sportswriting "is at best offering a harmless way to burn up a few unpromising brain cells" and has quit his job and moved to Florida and then to France with a lover. Upon his return to Haddam, his ex-wife (now identified as Ann Dykstra) remarries and relocates to Deep River, Connecticut, with the children, and Bascombe moves into her former house. "Aquiver with possibility and purpose," Bascombe now sells real estate, owns a hot dog stand, rents out two homes in the Black section of Haddam, and has a "lady friend," the "blond, tall and leggy" Sally Caldwell. In his words, his life "at least frontally, is simplicity's model."

In many respects, *Independence Day* answers to Bascombe's situation in *The Sportswriter.* The country is in worse condition, economically and morally, but Bascombe has entered what he calls his "Existence Period," "the high-wire act of normalcy" during which he has learned "to ignore much of what [he does not] like or that seems worrisome." According to Steve Brzezinski, "Through Frank's ruminations, Ford describes a country that seems to have lost its way in some fundamental sense: hope is put on hold, civility is in disrepair, and violence and ugliness are ubiquitous." Being a realtor allows Bascombe to observe and comment on American life, on the malaise and discontent of the late 1980s, a time when everyone seeks safety and security—for their children, for themselves—but finds only confusion and contradiction. Reflecting the state of the country, Haddam is not as safe as it was five years ago. Several months before the novel's plot begins, Bascombe himself has been assaulted by teenagers, two houses have been burglarized

(twice), and one of his business associates, who also was Bascombe's lover for a short time, has been raped and murdered. Yet Haddam pretends to prosperity, trying to "convince us our worries aren't worries, or at least not ours alone but everyone's." Bascombe's skepticism about this attitude, and about the condition of the country in general, reinforces D. G. Myers' comment that *Independence Day* "unashamedly offers a moral commentary upon the American present."

In this regard, Ford's Bascombe novels have more in common with John Updike's fiction than with any other writer's. The sense of bourgeois despair and ennui that have become Updike's signatures appears in *The Sportswriter* and *Independence Day,* but Ford's Bascombe emerges as a more complicated figure than Updike's Harry Angstrom. According to Douglas Kennedy, "No one writes better [than Ford] . . . about the bland wasteland of U.S. suburbia"; and Ehrenreich has commented that "Everything in this universe is just as it seems, as banal and soul-crushing as a Sunday afternoon spent shopping for garden tools." While he remains "almost a caricature of a self-absorbed leading-edge babyboomer," the Bascombe of *Independence Day* is less self-absorbed than his earlier incarnation in *The Sportswriter,* which signals that he has become, by virtue of his new professions and civic interests, less detached from the society he critiques. Bascombe is now brimming with good intentions, though he lacks the ability to follow through on them. His reintegration into society—his nonspiritual, nontranscendent version of redemption—occurs only at the novel's end, when he admits to enjoying "the push, pull, the weave and sway of others."

Bascombe's plans for the holiday weekend are to finish some personal and professional business and then pick up his troubled fifteen-year-old son, Paul, at his mother's house and drive to the basketball and baseball halls of fame in Springfield, Massachusetts, and Cooperstown, New York. The purpose of this secular pilgrimage is for Bascombe to offer Paul the wisdom of experience while referring to figures like Ralph Waldo Emerson and Thomas Jefferson in an effort to bring home to his son the true meaning of independence, "independence from whatever holds him captive." The holiday also gives Bascombe the opportunity to mull over the meaning of personal, rather than national, independence, and to analyze how his chronic detachment affects his own state of independence.

Before he goes to Connecticut to pick up Paul, Bascombe visits Sally for dinner, shows a house to an irresolute couple from Vermont, tries to collect rent on one of his rental properties, and checks on his hot dog stand. Each of these tasks proves disappointing or troubling: Sally sends him home unsatisfied and half-intoxicated, the Vermonters are impossible to please, the tenant responsible for payment pretends to be away, and the operator of the hot dog stand fears a robbery and now carries a gun. Bascombe's holiday begins most unpromisingly.

And it never improves. Because of Paul's nature and current behavior—he recently has been arrested for shoplifting condoms and for assaulting the security guard who confronted him; he hits his stepfather with an oar and drives the family Mercedes into a tree; he copes with the death of both his older brother and the family dog by barking; he has tattooed the word "insect" on the inside of his wrist; and he has become fat and unkempt—the father/son trip becomes little more than a vehicle for their sarcasm and cynicism. This means Bascombe can reach his son only through platitudes; when he attempts to be original or interesting with his advice, Paul mocks him. Although Bascombe fails to instill in Paul the lessons he had hoped to convey, the tension between them produces several consummately humorous scenes.

Bascombe's Independence Day weekend goes completely awry when Paul purposely steps into a 75-mile-per-hour fastball in a batting cage in Cooperstown. Bascombe spends the rest of the afternoon in the hospital in a nearby town, wondering if Paul will lose vision in the eye struck by the ball, talking to his stepbrother (whom Bascombe has not seen for several years but who happens to be near the batting cage when Paul is hurt), and waiting for Ann to arrive from Deep River to see Paul and decide if he should be flown to a hospital in Connecticut. After he learns that Paul's detached retina is reparable and that Ann forgives him for allowing Paul to harm himself, Bascombe realizes "there's nothing like tragedy or at least a grave injury or major inconvenience to cut through red tape and bullshit and reveal anyone's best nature." In a novel studded with such minor discoveries, Bascombe's redemption is achieved almost imperceptibly yet gracefully.

FORD'S MONTANA: *ROCK SPRINGS* AND *WILDLIFE*

Ford's short stories differ from his novels primarily in length. The protagonists and narrators in his stories, as in his novels, are male. They have problems with women and infidelity, with work and money, with alcohol and responsibility and violence. They tend to brood on their pasts, they have bad luck, and they lack a sense of purpose. They have seen opportunity diminish to the point of vanishment.

Yet they survive. The most striking aspect of Ford's short stories is how they illuminate the human capacity for survival. Despite the threads of desperation and alienation that run throughout *Rock Springs,* Ford's primary achievement in these stories is allowing his characters a small measure of hope in the face of hardship and ruin.

Given its brevity, the short story provides a formal challenge that novels, with their sprawl and depth, cannot offer. Ford, though, views the short story less as a formal alternative than as an economical complement to the novel. He claims not to assign much weight to the short story form; for him, writing short stories is "a minor contribution to the saga of mankind," and he admits to writing approximately one short story per year, primarily to have new work available at public readings. However, Ford's own achievements with his short stories in *Rock Springs* demonstrate a studied proficiency despite his apparent casualness.

Most of the stories in *Rock Springs* occur in Montana, in or near Great Falls. Ford's Montana is a state where people go to jail for writing bad checks, where catastrophe is as common as boredom, and where the vastness of the landscape reinforces the individual's feeling of insignificance. Also known as Big Sky Country, with its wide expanses and interminable horizon, Montana serves well as a locus of isolation: the large physical distances are mirrored by an equally large emotional distance between the characters.

Although Raymond Carver is frequently mentioned in relation to Ford because of the bleakness of the stories in *Rock Springs,* some critics have recognized the crucial differences between Carver and Ford: Ford "doesn't seem to need the 'existential' alienation and tight-jawed bitterness that preside over the knowing silences in so much 'minimalist' fiction"; "Ford is not the minimalist writer some critics have taken him to be. . . . He resists the tempting rhetoric of abrupt ends, and lets his characters mull over their losses." Indeed, Ford's style is more expansive and digressive than Carver's, his sentences longer and more sweeping. And where Carver has become associated with minimalism—with concision, compression, distillation, and understatement—Ford's stories are concerned with exploring his characters' motivations, thereby producing voices more ruminative than in Carver's work. While most of Ford's characters in *Rock Springs,* like those in much minimalist fiction, are marginals on the wrong side of luck, they feel a persistent need to understand their situations and to unravel their responses to those situations.

Eight of the ten stories in *Rock Springs* are narrated in the first-person voice, the other two ("Fireworks" and "Empire") in the third person. Every narrator is a white male, near Ford's age or younger. Characters like Eddie Starling ("Fireworks"), who has been unemployed for half a year, and Earl Middleton ("Rock Springs"), who steals a Mercedes for a Montana–Florida excursion with his lover and daughter and breaks down near Rock Springs, are typical. Many of Ford's male characters seem interchangeable, like parts in a machine. Yet these characters never become predictable, fulfilling Ford's wish "to write only characters which have the incalculability of life."

In these stories, Ford strives for intimacy between his characters as well as tension—narrative and psychological. The stories are consistently sad, because their characters, even if they begin as a member of a family or in a relationship, or if they meet someone significant during the story, usually end up alone—abandoned, divorced, transient. But a surprising amount of empathy appears in the stories, such that the narrator of "Sweethearts," after helping his lover escort her ex-husband to jail, remarks: "I knew, then, how you became a criminal in the world and lost it all. Somehow, and for no apparent reason, your decisions got tipped over and you lost your hold. And one day you woke up and found yourself in the very situation you said you would never ever be in." Ford deftly navigates these situations, garnering substantial praise in the process.

Ford's fourth novel, *Wildlife,* shares its unforgiving Montana setting and its mood with most of the stories from *Rock Springs.* Set in 1960, the year Ford was sixteen years old, the novel portrays a family's collapse and a teenager's attempt to understand what makes a life. The novel's narrator, Joe Brinson, is a sixteen-year-old boy who, along with his parents, is a recent transplant from Lewiston, Idaho. The end of Joe's childhood begins when his father, Jerry, a golf pro teaching at a local country club, loses his job. Jerry sulks for a while, grows distant from his wife, Jean, then suddenly and against Jean's wishes decides to leave to help fight the forest fire that has been raging for months north of Great Falls. Immediately after Jerry's departure, Jean starts sleeping with Warren Miller, a wealthy, older, and slightly crippled but threatening man.

The fire, caused by arson, becomes a heavy symbol of the lack of control humans have over the natural world and over their own lives. Jerry's rash decision stems from his desire to take control of something for once; but after three days he realizes the fire will not be subdued: "We just watch everything burn." This lack of control deepens when he returns home and learns about Jean and Miller.

Although Ford's work has explored varieties of love triangles, this one becomes complicated by Joe's mother flaunting her infidelity in front of her son; she brings Joe to dinner at Miller's and allows Miller to come to their house later that night. By involving Joe in her affair with Miller, she transforms him into both witness and accomplice. The least judgmental of narrators, Joe remains stoic in the face of both his mother's infidelity and his father's temporary inability to cope with circumstances. Joe is chronically agreeable, and he habitually answers "I know it," "All right," "I understand," and "Okay" when he really does not understand, when things are not "okay" or "all right." In a way, Joe is civilized to a fault, seeking the path of least resistance whether he believes, understands, or agrees with what he hears. This trait becomes significant when Joe sees Miller, naked, in the bathroom of his own house, and feels guilty and helpless, like "a spy—hollow and not forceful, not able to cause anything." His mother later catches him in the hallway watching her and says "Oh God damn it," slaps him twice, and then says "I'm mad at you." Instead of becoming angry or upset, Joe meekly responds, "I didn't mean it . . . I'm sorry."

Joe emerges as a lonely, emotionally detached teenager whose entire social life revolves around his parents. He respects and loves his father, and steadfastly wishes for his return, especially after his mother's infidelity threatens to destroy the family and, therefore, his social network. But Joe also loves his mother and withstands her misplaced rage and frustration, even as she becomes increasingly cynical and bitter toward him. Jean knows her actions with Miller are immoral, especially since her son has seen them together, and fears her son's judgment; but she becomes angry when he seems not to judge her. In fact, Joe's primary reaction to his mother's behavior is forbearance.

Because of the violence of so much of Ford's work, the gradually increasing tension in *Wildlife* seems destined to culminate in a final act of violence. But when Joe's father, confused and anguished, tries to set fire to Miller's house, he fails to ignite anything but the front porch, briefly, and is humiliated and almost arrested. Though formally taut, *Wildlife* sags with resignation, and its close is anticlimactic, with Jean's and Miller's affair ending, Miller eventually dying of an extended illness, and Jean drifting and finally returning to Jerry. The novel stops rather than ends, with none of Joe's emotional dilemmas resolved.

According to Ford, "*Wildlife* got the most effusive praise of any book I'd written before *Independence Day,* but it also got the widest variety of responses—some very negative, which I found perplexing." Ford attributes this critical divergence to the novel's "sensitive subject," which "some readers simply couldn't deal with." Yet some critics, like Sheila Ballantyne, who considers *Wildlife* "a thin book rather than a rich one," have found fault in the book's structure and the choice of Joe as its narrator. The novel's eye as well as its "I," Joe witnesses all of its pivotal events, a strategy that transforms him into a fictional construct and requires his presence at the novel's important moments. According to Mark Spilka, Joe's "narrative sensibility," which is "plainly earnest and only moderately intelligent," weakens the novel because it cannot present "richly and deeply drawn characters in a felt complex world"; Joe's shortcomings as a narrator, then, produce characters who "come through like thinned-out versions of their short story origins, attenuated rather than enriched."

THE LONG STORIES: *WOMEN WITH MEN*

In the three long stories in *Women with Men,* Ford keeps one foot in Montana (with "Jealous") while extending his vision to Paris in the book's two longer pieces, "The Womanizer" and "Occidentals," his first pieces set in Europe. Perhaps because Ford ventures into new territory here, the critical response to *Women with Men* has been mixed, with some critics hailing Ford's continual honing of his skills and others complaining about redundancy or "diminution of ambition." The book's title, which reverses that of Hemingway's *Men without Women,* has engendered substantial discussion about the roles of women in Ford's fiction, with Michael Gorra claiming "Ford has throughout his work acknowledged the central importance that women and marriage have in the lives of men" and Paul Quinn asserting "strong women characters in the stories ultimately exist only to mark the shifts in sensibility of one or other troubled male. Despite the promise of the volume's title, then, we do not get women with men, no communion of spirits, but a sense of self-absorbed men moving *around, against* or *through* women."

According to Quinn, "Jealous," the shortest of the stories, "could almost be read as a parody of the hegemonic, all-American short story: a first-person narration by a confused adolescent . . . in transition and in transit." In "Jealous," seventeen-year-old Lawrence and his aunt Doris are planning to take the train to visit Lawrence's mother, who has separated from Lawrence's father and moved to Seattle. While waiting for the train,

Lawrence and Doris see police officers shoot a man to death in a bar and Lawrence experiences Doris' incestuous passion for him, an attraction that acquires additional complexity because Doris has slept with Lawrence's father several times. Despite the story's potential for disaster, it ends with Lawrence and Doris on the train, her passion for her nephew unfulfilled. Doris falls asleep as Lawrence watches her and then nearly succumbs to "the scary feeling . . . that you're suffocating and your life is running out," a feeling he overcomes such that, "for the first time in my life, I felt calm."

Although older than Lawrence, the men in "The Womanizer" and "Occidentals" seem especially inept and callous. Where Ford's stories and novels set in Montana, New Jersey, and Mexico convincingly evoke those places, "The Womanizer" and "Occidentals" purposely fail to recreate Paris because their protagonists, Martin Austin ("The Womanizer") and Charley Matthews ("Occidentals"), cannot progress beyond their expectations and tourist guides. In effect, the stories' shortcomings are the protagonists' shortcomings, since their inability to speak French, or any language other than English, illuminates their inability to communicate effectively with anyone.

In "Occidentals" Charley Matthews, author of one unsuccessful novel and a former professor of African-American literature (he is neither African American nor especially interested in African-American literature), has come to Paris with his lover, Helen Carmichael. Intending to visit the office of his French publisher, Matthews learns his editor has suddenly decided to leave the country, stranding him in Paris with no plans but a possible lunch with his translator. Disappointed, he and Helen wander the city dazed by fatigue.

Although Helen has accompanied him to Paris, Matthews does not have strong feelings for her: "He hadn't really fallen for [her]; he simply liked her." When Helen, whose cancer has been in remission for a year, begins to feel sick in Paris, Matthews tries not to think of her illness; but the cemetery outside their hotel window serves as a morbid reminder of the inevitability of death. He begins to pity her, which makes him "feel fond toward her, fonder than he'd felt in the entire year he'd known her," and he tells her he loves her, a pronouncement she resists because she knows it is false. When Helen sleeps in very late the next day, Matthews leaves her in the hotel room. Her cancer has returned with such force that she decides to commit suicide by overdosing on her medicine. Her decision and her suicide occur while Matthews is wandering around Paris, considering arranging a tryst with a former lover and shopping for a Christmas gift for his daughter. When he returns to the hotel, he finds her corpse and a letter ("We were never in love. Don't misunderstand that"), realizing too late "what marriage meant."

In "The Womanizer," Martin Austin, a married American in Paris on business, tries to seduce Joséphine Belliard, an assistant editor for a French publisher. Joséphine is in the process of a divorce because her husband has published a "scandalous" novel "in which Joséphine figured prominently: her name used, her parts indelicately described, her infidelity put on display in salacious detail." Austin pursues Joséphine not out of passion but out of a compulsion arising from ennui. This halfhearted attempt at seduction, though unsuccessful, is sufficient to raise his wife's suspicions; she tells him he has become "unreachable" after he returns home. When Austin responds, "I'm sorry to hear that. . . . But I don't think there's anything I can do about it," her reaction is both decisive and unexpected: "Then you're just an asshole. . . . And you're also a womanizer and you're a creep. And I don't want to be married to any of those things anymore." She leaves and stays away from the house, unwittingly giving him the opportunity to take advantage of the situation: "free to do anything he wanted, no questions asked or answered," he packs his bags and flies back to Paris, hoping to initiate a relationship with Joséphine.

While in Paris, Austin desires Joséphine but thinks "normally, habitually, involuntarily" of his wife, who "occupied . . . the place of final consequence—the destination to practically everything he cared about or noticed or imagined." He still thinks "he could never really *love* Joséphine," who has become too preoccupied with her divorce to register any passion for Austin. When she leaves her four-year-old son with Austin to visit her lawyer, Austin's distractedness has nearly tragic consequences when he forgets about the boy, whom he has taken to a park, and the boy is almost molested. Joséphine's reaction is one of total rage and disgust: "You are a fool . . . You don't know anything. You don't know who you are. . . . Who do you think you are? You're nothing."

"The Womanizer" ends with Austin in Paris, alone, thinking of his life "almost entirely in terms of what was wrong with him, of his problem, his failure—in particular his failure as a husband, but also in terms of his unhappiness, his predicament, his ruin, which he wanted to repair." In this regard, Austin's situation recalls the human dilemmas faced by many of Ford's characters, thus illuminating the common elements of life that abound in and bind his works of fiction.

Selected Bibliography

WORKS OF RICHARD FORD

NOVELS

A Piece of My Heart. New York: Harper and Row, 1976.

The Ultimate Good Luck. New York: Houghton Mifflin, 1981.

The Sportswriter. New York: Vintage, 1986.

Wildlife. New York: Atlantic Monthly Press, 1990.

Independence Day. New York: Alfred A. Knopf, 1995.

SHORT STORIES
Rock Springs. New York: Atlantic Monthly Press, 1987.
Women with Men. New York: Alfred A. Knopf, 1997.

OTHER WRITINGS
American Tropical. Antaeus 66:75–80 (Spring 1991). Produced at Actors Theatre of Louisville, Louisville, Kentucky, 1983. (A play.)
Bright Angel. Directed by Michael Fields. Hemdale, 1991. (Screenplay.)
My Mother, in Memory. Elmwood, Conn.: Raven Editions, 1988. (A limited edition memoir.)

EDITED WORKS
The Best American Short Stories, 1990. With Shannon Ravenel. Boston: Houghton Mifflin, 1990.
The Granta Book of the American Short Story. London: Granta Books, 1992.
The Essential Tales of Chekhov, by Anton Chekhov. Hopewell, N.J.: Ecco, 1998.
Eudora Welty: Complete Novels, by Eudora Welty. With Michael Kreyling. New York: Library of America, 1998.
Eudora Welty: Stories, Essays, and Memoir, by Eudora Welty. With Michael Kreyling. New York: Library of America, 1998.
The Granta Book of the American Long Story. London: Granta Books, 1999.

BOOK INTRODUCTION
The Pushcart Prize, XIII: Best of the Small Presses. Edited by Bill Henderson. Wainscott, N.Y.: Pushcart Press, 1988.
Juke Joints, by Birney Imes. Jackson: University Press of Mississippi, 1990.
Aren't You Happy for Me? and Other Stories, by Richard Bausch. London: Macmillan, 1995.
The Fights, by Charles Hoff. New York: Chronicle, 1996.

UNCOLLECTED SHORT STORIES
"Privacy." *The New Yorker,* July 22, 1996, pp. 58–59.
"Crèche." *The New Yorker,* December 28, 1998, pp. 72–85.

UNCOLLECTED ESSAYS
"The Three Kings: Hemingway, Faulkner, and Fitzgerald." *Esquire,* December 1983, pp. 577–587.

"A Stubborn Sense of Place." *Harper's Magazine,* August 1986, pp. 42–43.
"So Little Time, So Many Rooms." *Money,* May 1989, pp. 102–108.
"Stop Blaming Baseball." *The New York Times Magazine,* April 4, 1993, pp. 36–42.
"In the Face: A Metaphysics of Fisticuffs." *The New Yorker,* September 16, 1996, pp. 52–53.
"Where Does Writing Come From?" *Granta* 62: 249–255 (Summer 1998).
"Good Raymond." *The New Yorker,* October 5, 1998, pp. 70–79.
"In the Same Boat." *The New York Times Magazine,* June 6, 1999, pp. 106–109, 111–113, 146, 148, 151–152, 170.

BIOGRAPHICAL AND CRITICAL STUDIES

ARTICLES ABOUT RICHARD FORD
Blades, John. "House Calls." *Chicago Tribune,* June 22, 1995, p. 9C.
Lee, Don. "About Richard Ford." *Ploughshares* 22, nos. 2 and 3: 226–235 (Fall 1996).
McQuade, Molly. "Richard Ford: Despite the Dark Strain in His Work, the Footloose Author Says He Is an Optimist." *Publisher's Weekly,* May 18, 1990, pp. 66–67.
Schneider, Wolf. "*Bright Angel:* Richard Ford Ups the Ante." *American Film,* May 1991, pp. 50–51.
Schumacher, Michael. "Richard Ford's Creative Spark." *Writer's Digest,* May 1991, pp. 32–35.
Shelton, Frank W. "Richard Ford (1944–)." In *Contemporary Fiction Writers of the South: A Bio-Bibliographical Sourcebook.* Edited by Joseph M. Flora and Robert Bain. Westport, Conn.: Greenwood, 1993. Pp. 147–155.
Smith, Dinitia. "A Nomad's Ode to Soffit and Siding." *New York Times,* August 22, 1995, pp. C13, C17.
Weber, Bruce. "Richard Ford's Uncommon Characters." *The New York Times Magazine,* April 10, 1988, pp. 50–51, 59, 63–65.

CRITICAL ARTICLES
Crouse, David. "Resisting Reduction: Closure in Richard Ford's *Rock Springs* and Alice Munro's *Friend of My Youth.*" *Canadian Literature* 146: 51–64 (Autumn 1995).
Dupuy, Edward. "The Confessions of an Ex-Suicide: Relenting and Recovering in Richard Ford's *The*

Sportswriter." *Southern Literary Journal* 23, no. 1: 93–103 (Fall 1990).

Gornick, Vivian. "Tenderhearted Men: Lonesome, Sad, and Blue." *The New York Times Book Review,* September 16, 1990, pp. 1, 32–35.

Schroth, Raymond A. "America's Moral Landscape in the Fiction of Richard Ford." *The Christian Century,* March 1, 1989, pp. 227–230.

Trussler, Michael. " 'Famous Times': Historicity in the Short Fiction of Richard Ford and Raymond Carver." *Wascana Review of Contemporary Poetry and Short Fiction* 28, no. 2: 35–53 (Fall 1994).

BOOK REVIEWS

Anonymous. Review of *The Ultimate Good Luck.* *Kirkus Reviews* 49, no. 4: 230–231 (February 15, 1981).

Ballantyne, Sheila. "A Family Too Close to the Fire." *The New York Times Book Review,* June 17, 1990, pp. 3, 12.

Bonner, Thomas, Jr.. Review of *Independence Day.* *America,* December 9, 1995, pp. 26–27.

Bowman, James. "One Man's Cavalcade of Really Deep Thoughts." *Wall Street Journal,* June 16, 1995, p. A12.

Bryan, C. D. B. "Mexican Coke Rap." *The New York Times Book Review,* May 31, 1981, p. 13.

Brzezinski, Steve. Review of *Independence Day. The Antioch Review* 54, no. 1: 114 (Winter 1996).

Clemons, Walter. "Uneasy Rider." *Newsweek,* May 11, 1981, pp. 89–90.

———. "The Divorced Men's Club." *Newsweek,* April 7, 1986, p. 82.

Ehrenreich, Barbara. "Reality Bites." *The New Republic,* September 18, 1995, pp. 48–51.

Flower, Dean. "In the House of Pain." *The Hudson Review* 41, no. 1: 209–210 (Spring 1988).

Giles, Jeff. "Seems Like Old Times." *Newsweek,* June 12, 1995, p. 64.

Gorra, Michael. "Evasive Maneuvers." *The New York Times Book Review,* July 13, 1997, pp. 5–6.

Gray, Paul. "Return of the Sportswriter." *Time,* June 19, 1995, p. 60.

Green, Michelle. "Transient Writer Richard Ford Lets His Muse Roam Free in *Wildlife.*" *People Weekly,* July 9, 1990, pp. 63–64.

Hardwick, Elizabeth. "Reckless People." *The New York Review of Books,* August 10, 1995, pp. 11–14.

Hoffman, Alice. "A Wife Named X, a Poodle Named

Elvis." *The New York Times Book Review,* March 23, 1986, p. 14.

Johnson, Charles. "Stuck in the Here and Now." *The New York Times Book Review,* June 18, 1995, pp. 1, 28.

Kakutani, Michiko. Review of *The Sportswriter. The New York Times,* February 26, 1986, p. C21.

———. "Afloat in the Turbulence of the American Dream." *The New York Times,* June 13, 1995, p. C17.

Kazin, Alfred. "Fallen Creatures." *The New York Review of Books,* November 5, 1987, p. 12.

Kennedy, Douglas. Review of *Independence Day. New Statesman and Society,* July 14, 1995, p. 39.

Lehmann-Haupt, Christopher. "A Triangle of Mother, Father, and Son." *The New York Times,* June 1, 1990, p. C27.

———. "Men Behaving Badly, or at Least Not Too Well." *The New York Times,* June 16, 1997, p. C16.

McMurtry, Larry. "With the Vices of the Genre." *The New York Times Book Review,* October 24, 1976, pp. 16, 18.

Mewshaw, Michael. "Bad Baby-sitting." *New Statesman,* October 17, 1997, p. 55.

Myers, D. G. "Midlife Crises." *Commentary,* November 1995, pp. 130–134.

Quinn, Paul. "The Troubled Males of Montana." *Times Literary Supplement,* August 29, 1997, p. 23.

Reed, John Shelton. "Frankly, My Dear . . . " *National Review,* September 25, 1995, pp. 93–94.

Ross, Cecily. "Flames of Desire." *Maclean's,* September 10, 1990, p. 82.

Rubin, Merle. "Frank Bascombe Awakes to Lessons of Independence." *The Christian Science Monitor,* July 3, 1995, p. 13.

Schechner, Mark. Review of *Independence Day. Tikkun,* March–April 1996, pp. 74–77.

Schroth, Raymond A. "The Poetry of Real Estate." *Commonweal,* October 6, 1995, pp. 27–28.

Sheppard, R. Z. "Dreamworld." *Time,* March 24, 1986, p. 86.

Smith, R. J. "You Can't Drive Home Again." *Los Angeles Times Book Review,* July 2, 1995, pp. 1, 7.

Spilka, Mark. "Bad Mothers Great and Small." *America,* November 17, 1990, pp. 380–382.

Towers, Robert. "Screams and Whispers." *The New York Review of Books,* April 24, 1986, pp. 38–39.

Toynton, Evelyn. "American Stories." *Commentary,* March 1993, pp. 49–53.

Wideman, John. "Love and Truth: Use with Caution."

The New York Times Book Review, September 20, 1987, pp. 1, 35.

Wood, Susan. Review of *A Piece of My Heart. Washington Post Book World,* February 20, 1977, p. N3.

Yardley, Jonathan. "The Agony of Defeat." *Washington Post Book World,* March 30, 1986, p. 3.

INTERVIEWS

Bonetti, Kay. "An Interview with Richard Ford." *The Missouri Review* 10, no. 2: 71–96 (1987).

Cuagliardo, Huey. "A Conversation with Richard Ford." *The Southern Review* 34, no. 3: 609–620 (Summer 1998).

Gilbert, Matthew. "Interview with Richard Ford." *The Writer,* December 1996, pp. 9–10, 22.

Lyons, Bonnie. "Richard Ford: The Art of Fiction CXLVII." *The Paris Review* 140: 42–77 (Fall 1996). Reprinted in *Passion and Craft: Conversations with Notable Writers.* Edited by Bonnie Lyons and Bill Oliver. Urbana: University of Illinois Press, 1998. Pp. 1–22.

—BRIAN HENRY

Louise Glück

1943–

SINCE THE PUBLICATION of her first book of poems in 1968, Louise Glück has focused most often on the trials of one sensibility and the contours of its psychic structure. She has worked with a sensibility of aggrievement—largely an autobiographical one—charting the spiritual and psychological development of a twentieth-century American woman. "Poems *are* autobiography," she wrote in *Proofs and Theories: Essays on Poetry* (1994), "but divested of the trappings of chronology and comment, the metronomic alternation of anecdote and response." Emerging from the "base matter" of autobiography, at times her poems voice desires to abandon the body's demands to perfect the voice's orphic potential. Although her cast of characters—biblical, mythical, and archetypal—has included such figures as Moses, Aphrodite, Achilles, Penelope, Eurydice, Gretel, and Joan of Arc, whoever speaks in her poems echoes the concerns of a central female figure who must brood upon deprivation, deceit, and abandonment.

Glück's poems, whether characterized by intense anger or distanced, almost ethereal witnessing, never seem casually constructed; each is a condensed psychological drama. Her bitter eloquence and complex intelligence enliven and deepen her work. The paradoxes of her poems, troubling and anguished or stately and dryly distant, resist consolation in favor of powerful insinuations that disturb and provoke.

In some ways a Freudian, Glück grants the family romance immense explanatory power for her speakers' experiences of emotional deprivation in adulthood. She pursues a psychoanalytic understanding, questioning received knowledge, and finding in the roots of early childhood the most potent elements of psychic violation to color later life. Glück relies on logical reversals, specifically reversals of common assumptions: in her poems, food starves selfhood, sight blinds, sexuality detaches. Often her poems seem to occur in timeless interior landscapes or against a horizon of mythic dimensions. Nevertheless, her work reflects on contemporary mores dealing with marital infidelity and the breakdown of common faith in religion and community. As Ann Townsend notes, "Her lyric mode combines song and harsh psychological realism, expressed in terms of dramatic performance, a mode which includes rather than excludes the social world."

Glück's assumption of mythic postures is prominent in much of her work, lending resonance to contemporary domestic scenes. Indeed, Glück has been attracted to mythic and archetypal elements since the beginning of her career. Elizabeth Dodd insightfully describes Glück's poetic as "postconfessional personal classicism—one in which the voice of the self is muted by an amplified sense of the mythic, the archetypal . . . , without losing the compelling presence of an individual, contemporary 'I,' a personal voice addressing the reader." Her treatment of myths strikes many readers as artfully static, as Helen Vendler suggests: "Glück's manner suits her matter; the manner is as stationary, as foreseen in its pastness, as her myths." Emulating the effect that we ascribe to myths, Glück gives her poems an aura of permanence and "inevitability." As she has written, "My own work begins . . . at the end, literally, at illumination, which has then to be traced back to some source in the world. This method, when it succeeds, makes a thing that seems irrefutable. Its failure is felt as portentous." Often her poems have the quality of gravestone rubbings; they are meant to remind us of our mortality and fragility.

Although she is a meticulous craftsperson, to Glück the poem is not a product of simple human agency, because ultimately poems are oblivious to the wishes of their authors. Their source is mysterious, resisting human intentionality. She argues in her prose that writing an authentic poem is not an exercise of will. "The only real exercise of will is negative: we have toward what we write the power of veto." As a consequence, poets are besieged by silences: "The fundamental experience of the writer is helplessness" in "a life dignified . . . by yearning." How could it be otherwise, she asks: "When the aim of the work is spiritual insight, it seems absurd to expect fluency." From the beginning, her work has dealt with the difficulties of assuming voice. The poem arrives as an uncontrollable visitation. The ideal poem is "given" to the poet by a force outside the human will; her insistence on a connection to such a force idealizes and sacralizes the poem.

GLÜCK'S BACKGROUND

Louise Glück was born in New York City on April 22, 1943, to Daniel, an executive, and Beatrice (Grosby) Glück. She was raised on Long Island. Her background suggests precocity and privilege. According to her essay "Education of the Poet," by the age of three she was well acquainted with classical mythology. Her childhood reading taste would reflect her later writing style: "From the beginning I preferred the simplest vocabulary." She and her younger sister were encouraged by their mother in artistic pursuits and given various lessons (for a time Glück wanted to be a painter). Despite her parents' willingness to encourage her interests, by Glück's account she experienced intense frustration in childhood; in a voluble household, she was unable to finish her sentences. "I was born into an environment in which the right of any family member to complete the sentence of another was assumed." As a consequence, her voice was continually "cut off, radically changed—transformed, not paraphrased." Her frustration is significant; even in childhood she recognized that a life dedicated to language, specifically writing, would serve as her route to claiming a self-sufficient identity. Her mature poems are so ingeniously compressed and so startlingly assertive that they seem to have been honed by a sensibility dedicated to training itself from childhood to exert maximum semantic pressure on the minimal number of words.

She read at an early age and with a sense of dedication. Her earliest literary influences were Shakespeare, John Keats, William Blake, William Butler Yeats, and T. S. Eliot. Since childhood, she writes in "Education of the Poet," she has displayed a preference for paradox and riddling ambiguities.

As an adolescent she suffered from anorexia nervosa at a time when little was known about the condition. In her poetry she has translated anorexia into a metaphor that echoes an aesthetic of perfectionism. As Lynn Keller notes, "Glück's poetics were founded on the anorexic's renunciative orientation, and though flexed and stretched somewhat, they remain largely unchanged." Glück's descriptions of her adolescent anorexia, as many readers have noted, duplicate the tenor of her mature poetry, particularly in frequent enactments of scenes of rejection. As she writes of her anorexia: "What I could say was *no*: the way I saw to separate myself, to establish a self with clear boundaries, was to oppose myself to the declared desire of others, utilizing their wills to give shape to my own." She dealt with anorexia through intensive therapy. As a senior in high school she began psychoanalysis, leaving high school to pursue it. "For the next seven years, analysis was what I did with my time and with my mind; it would be impossible for me to speak of education without speaking of this process." Her commitment to poetry apparently grew with her ability to analyze her own motives and preoccupations. For two years she attended Léonie Adams' poetry workshop at the School of General Studies at Columbia University, moving on to study with Stanley Kunitz, her most influential mentor, for five years. She has credited the latter poet as being instrumental to her development, particularly for his insistence on freshness and unpredictability in poetry. Her first book is dedicated to Kunitz.

The line of descent to Glück is a fascinating one. It is evident that some aspects of Emily Dickinson's highly compressed, hermetic structures are reproduced in Glück's poetry. Yet Dickinson's contrary explorations, her experiments in adopting a variety of philosophical positions, seem hardly comparable with Glück's more absolutist perspectives. Furthermore, Glück is not a poet of linguistic experiment in the same vein as Dickinson, nor would the tenor of her poems recall us to the sometimes playful expressivism that her nineteenth-century predecessor mastered.

With T. S. Eliot, Glück shares a commitment to poetry as spiritual quest. When noting elements of Eliot's aesthetic, she might be writing of her own: "Eliot's particular spirituality, his intense wish to be divested of temporal facts, may seem to contemporary readers not simply irresponsible but immoral: an indulgence of privilege and omen of our collective ruin." Her own rebellion from flesh is echoed in her assessment of Eliot's, as well as her recognition that her preoccupations may likewise disturb her readers.

Certainly Glück shares affinities with H. D. (Hilda Doolittle) in her interest in classical literature and in her attempt to dignify her female personae. In turn, she conveys aspects of Louise Bogan's intense examination of emotions and her commitment to presenting female personae that express extreme psychological states in a seemingly coded manner. She takes from Sylvia Plath some of her more explicitly and openly aversive tones—and yet it is the restrained Plath of *The Colossus* that we may hear in muted form in Glück's poems as much as we hear the more invasive Plath of *Ariel*. Curiously, Glück's poems bear some relation to Diane Wakoski's for their focus on the myth of selfhood and for their enactment of self-disgust and self-abjection. Yet while Wakoski's style is epistolary and explanatory, Glück's is distinguished by absolute condensation and an exploitation of nuance.

SUPPORTERS AND DETRACTORS

Glück's poetry has been rewarded with high honors. Critics have praised the significance and dignity of much of her work, as well as her introspective urgency and her originality of stance and tone. *The Triumph of Achilles* (1985) received the National Book Critics Circle Award, the Poetry Society of America's Melville Kane Award, and the Boston Globe Literary Press Award. *Ararat* (1990) received the Rebekah Johnson Bobbitt National Prize for Poetry. *The Wild Iris* (1992) was awarded the Pulitzer Prize and the Poetry Society of America's William Carlos Williams Award. Her essay collection, *Proofs and Theories: Essays on Poetry,* received the PEN/Martha Albrand Award for Nonfiction. In 1999 she was named a chancellor of the Academy of American

Poets. Among the institutions at which she has taught are Goddard College, the University of North Carolina at Greensboro, the University of Iowa, the University of Cincinnati, Columbia University, and Williams College.

Despite Glück's many awards, her poetry does not often inspire warmth in appraisals. The tone of repulsion that her speakers claim as their own seems to affect the ways in which her poetry is received. That is, her strongest supporters laud the nearly classical purity and austere paradoxes of her work, while her detractors tend to react with an almost visceral distaste to those same elements. Some readers resent the "chill" of her poems; they find her seeming repulsion from physicality and the female body not only threatening but also inexplicable.

Unfortunately, Glück has not been adopted wholeheartedly by most feminist critics, perhaps in part because she herself is leery of categorization and has resisted such appropriation. "I'm puzzled, not emotionally but logically, by the contemporary determination of women to write as women," she notes in "Education of the Poet." She argues that just as the historical epoch in which the writer composes will be imprinted upon the poem, so too will be the writer's gender. The sexes differentiate themselves in the writing of poetry through unconscious means. In her insistence on the inevitability of an artist's inscribing her gender and historical epoch on the poem, we may hear her primary assumption: the poet cannot entirely control the poem.

In the early stages of feminist criticism, at the time when her first work was appearing in the late 1960s, Glück's refusal to celebrate womanhood or to assert political change caused her to be ignored by some critics who preferred a more declarative and openly feminist poetic. Lynn Keller has been particularly insightful on this subject: "[Glück's] often extremely negative sense of womanhood—as both a biologically and socially determined experience—has been crucial in

shaping the language, tone, and style, as well as the thematic content of her poetry." Such a focus makes many readers uneasy. As Keller puts it, "Glück has not passed beyond self-loathing, and this makes reading her work still a profoundly uncomfortable experience." Nevertheless, this very struggle "electrifies her poetry," Keller argues, and it accounts for some measure of its uncanny power.

Glück has written of her frequent desire to recast her strategies as a poet. "Each book I've written has culminated in a conscious diagnostic act, a swearing off." Such a practice contradicts somewhat her perceptions of the poem as inspired rather than willed. As one reads through her work it becomes clear that she has created a severe self-accounting, adjusting her stylistic predilections with each new volume. She seems to be conducting a dialogue between herself and her critics as well, attempting with each new book to engage in another fresh rhetorical strategy that attests to her self-awareness. Her poems are less about exorcising parts of the self than about voicing emergent attitudes toward the self and its place among others, a process that calls for a readiness for re-envisioning the possibilities of identity and of poetry.

FIRSTBORN (1968)

Glück's first collection is remarkable for its repulsion of the family and the abjection of all signs of nourishment. Femaleness is a violation and control is essential—control of the body and of the poem. A barely withheld violence is suggested through frequent monosyllabic, clipped end rhymes and a jarring mix of colloquial and highly sophisticated diction. Verbs are invasive: *biting, prying, clamping*. The emphatic line breaks and consonantal effects create a staccato impression, further heightened by blunt questions ("Done?," "How long?").

Birth ultimately conflates with death in *First-born*, which makes the frequent image of children suggestive of a rejected self. Most often children in the collection are viewed as unwanted intrusions, figured as latching onto a mother's body somewhat in the manner of parasites. Strikingly, images of infants and men collide. Women are threatened by their own relationships to both. In "Returning a Lost Child," a man is figured as a gun. In other poems, children seem to be men's accomplices in containing or depleting women's energies, a conspiracy unmistakably figured in the description of wallpaper as patterned like "a *plot* / of embryos" (emphasis mine) in "The Wound."

Images of food and cooking appear often, contextualized to suggest physical revulsion and the speaker's psychic diminishment. Thanksgiving as a holiday dedicated to consumption is presented as horrific and sacrificial. A mother in "Thanksgiving" appears with "skewers in her hands / . . . . tucking skin / . . . over the pronged death." Glück makes the family holiday of consumption a ritual that elevates food (such a problematic substance in her poems) above family, or mistakes the family for the food it consumes. Cooked meats seem, curiously enough, like ghosts: "All day I smell the roasts / Like presences." The speaker's environment is quick to spoil and rot. An onion is Ophelia, a roast is a sacrifice, and "rice congeals" in the atmosphere, as if humans and food were within one conceptual category and waste inflected all aspects of corporeality. Although Glück creates a varied cast of speakers—a prioress of Ursuline nuns, a nurse, a bride, a widow—each revolts against the fleshly and stakes her claim in opposition to nature.

The forty-two poems in the collection are notable for their hint of malice and bravado. One hears a young poet tuning her voice to make a startling impact. The world inhabited by the woman who speaks in most of these poems threatens. It too readily restrains her energies. The references to abortion, particularly in the book's first section, seem emblematic of the central speaker's self-perception as a rejected being who has been thrust from any vital connection to others.

The concerns of this first book will arise with alternate solutions in later books. Among such concerns are abjection, including preemptive rejection of others; need disguised as self-sufficiency; memory as an isolating faculty; and the female body as object. The young speaker, at times appearing to be bored and contemptuous, can only partially disguise her yearning to be known and valued.

Firstborn made it clear that Glück had surely learned aesthetic lessons from her readings of both Robert Lowell and Sylvia Plath. Many reviewers noted Robert Lowell's influence on Glück in the muscular, confessionalist tone of *Firstborn* and in its emphatic rhythms. We can hear cries of complaint in the poems that are reminiscent of Plath as well. Yet for all their debts to other poets, Glück's debut poems proved greatly promising; the book presented a fierce and ambitious sensibility in the process of development.

In an author's note fronting *The First Four Books of Poems* (1995), Glück describes her later reaction to *Firstborn* as "embarrassed tenderness." In her second book she wished to work more fully with the sentence as a composition unit, rather than with the fragmentary declaratives that dominate her first book. She would choose, in turn, a radical departure in tone.

THE HOUSE ON MARSHLAND (1975)

With her second book, Glück emerged as a composed and original voice. What was and remains most striking about the collection is Glück's manipulation of tone, her assertion of an authoritative and yet often intimate voice, whether subtly pleading or clearly threatening. She crafted poems out of elemental materials: a spare vocabulary, a stately free verse, subtle aural echoes, and a haunting cache of images. Here are aspects of a contemporary reappropriation of medievalism: the fairy tale, the saint's story, the aubade transformed to utter thwarted desires.

The House on Marshland includes thirty-five poems organized in two parts. Silence hovers over the poems, as does a sense of bewitchment. "All Hallows," one of her most frequently anthologized and discussed poems, sets the tone with the notes of the strange birth of other and of self, an anguished coming-into-being, presented with minimal context. As Helen Vendler notes: "Glück's independent structures, populated by nameless and often ghostly forms engaged in archaic or timeless motions, satisfy without referent." The uncontextualized quality of the poems contributes to their aura of mystery. Glück's shifts in meaning through her enjambments impart insinuations more often than explorations of the dynamics of situations. Her poems call for an alert reader who will fill in the outlines that she traces. Her imagery, seldom detailed, is simple and yet resonant.

Extreme longings, matricidal as in "Gretel in Darkness," or for maternal merging, as in "For My Mother," undergird the collection. And here too are the signature poems with the family imprints that she chooses to depict in most of her work. The family had emerged in *Firstborn,* but in *The House on Marshland* it takes on a mythical status. Psychological profiles with their sources in autobiography are sketched in what seems like indelible ink: a mother as an absorbing force that the daughter needs and fears; a father as a withdrawn figure represented by a face in the act of turning away; and a daughter as a stern and implacable witness to her family's struggles. A dead infant sister is a source of original mystery, firstborn in the family, about whom Glück has written in prose in "Death and Absence." "The dead sis-

ter died before I was born. Her death was not my experience, but her absence was." These are the occupants of the "house on marshland." The marsh of inchoate and unmet desires jeopardizes the family, which dwells on unstable ground.

The volume presents Glück's unmistakably mixed feelings about womanhood. Reproductive energy is unopposable and violating, a fruit that stains, as in "Flowering Plum," in which a girl's developing sexuality draws out familial wrath and initiates her own self-objectification and self-division. Glück's mixed feelings also are invested in mythic retellings—the "re-envisioning" of stories in Adrienne Rich's famous phrase—through such characters as Persephone and Demeter, Hansel and Gretel, and Abishag. In "Abishag" a girl's body betrays her, and in "Pomegranate" a girl's body is contested space between a mother's and a lover's claims.

Despite surfaces that are formalized and clipped of excess, the poems' depths suggest violence through the imagery of blood: a mother's murder of her child; a girl's menstruation; a mother knitting red scarves for a son ("afraid of blood, your women / like one brick wall after another"). Nature is an antagonist—a further source of violence.

Frequently the speaker views herself as object rather than subject. Things simply and ineradicably occur to her, for she is less an agent of change than a figure at the mercy of large natural and historical forces. "Love / forms in the human body" a woman claims in "The Fortress," as if she has no responsibility or will in the matter whatsoever. In "The Swimmer" lovers are swept up, whether they wish to be or not: "The waves come forward, / we are traveling together." Volition appears as if entirely localized outside the self, as unopposable as the approach of seasons.

In its uncluttered exhumation of voice, *The House on Marshland* signaled a new arrival in American poetry. Glück housed her poems in sentences that are notably longer than those of her previous work and grafted with multiple connectives in which meaning hovers and logical closure is withheld. At times the voice expresses the calm that we might associate with a person who speaks after having fully vented her anger. The tone at points is remote and quietly determined, bespeaking a sense of fatedness. As Steve Burt has argued, "Depressive realism is the secret strength of Louise Glück's work: it is what connects Louise Glück's stark, straitened tones to the insights her poems contain. Her distance from those she describes (herself included) lets her see them with cold acuteness; coming to love a Glück poem means coming to empathize with the bitter self-consciousness her skeletal arrangements reflect."

Part of the authority of the poems rests in Glück's reversal of conventional expectations, particularly with regard to victors and victims. In their eloquence, her women seem ultimately victorious over their victimizers. In the poems' scale of values, it is the inner world that rules. She with the richest inner life triumphs. Her speakers, while recording the workings of seasonal change, most often appear to exist outside of nature and beyond the flow of time. The unforced and unapologetic beauty of Glück's language emerges as a form of impassioned restraint and suggestive testament.

DESCENDING FIGURE (1980)

In an author's note to *The First Four Books of Poems* Glück has acknowledged *Descending Figure* as her favorite of her first four books and an attempt to work with "questions and contradictions." A collection of twenty-six poems, *Descending Figure* is divided into three parts: "The Garden," "The Mirror," and "Lamentations." The concerns of each section overlap, but the collection divides broadly along the following lines. Part I deals with the seductive lure of both death

and oblivion and the ineffectuality of words to counter a Freudian death instinct. Calls of warning or benediction are issued to endangered beings, but such calls appear alien and ineffectual; no rescue is in sight. The body in the poems is paralyzed, and images of nature are cold and dry. Voices intimate a dreadful knowledge of death as inevitable and the human as irredeemable. As Glück observes in "Thanksgiving," all creatures "have their place in the dying order." The volume's title poem addresses the death of Glück's sister in infancy—and here the dead infant, birdlike, seems to haunt, and the speaker imagines her own helplessness. The garden, the title image of the section, is an infertile formalized sphere, human-made and corrupted.

The second part of the book, "The Mirror," is concerned with hunger as diffuse yearning, physical and spiritual. Most important, the second section concerns the means of denying hunger, of staking selfhood upon habits of refusal: refusal not only of food but also of comfort and common fellowship. "Dedication to Hunger" reflects on a child's distance from her father, who won't touch her; a psychological muting of a wife in conventional marriage; and a child's most assured power—that of renunciation, as it combines with her desire to control her body: "the same need to perfect, / of which death is the mere byproduct." In "Dedication to Hunger" Glück refers directly to her experience with anorexia as an adolescent, and we are led to acknowledge that the effort to control and restrain the body in her poems is not only symptomatic of anorexia but also constitutive of a worldview. The way the body is treated reflects the way Glück's speaker sees all being. The body appears deadened, an art object itself as in the image of a "Ceramic / hand in the grass" of "Porcelain Bowl." Like the body, language emerges as alien and estranging. Identity as manifested through language is contested: "My name / was like a stranger's, / read from an envelope." Just as the body itself appears to be an object separable from being, a static entity to be studied, so too is the speaker's environment. She places herself at a radical remove from others; perpetually, she is a vigilant outsider.

The third part of the book, "Lamentations," is autumnal in atmosphere, drawing together the book's earlier images and statements enacting psychic detachment from the body. The female body is seen as an object separated from the woman's perception of her own identity, as noted in Glück's commentaries on anorexia in prose and poems; tellingly, in part two of the poem "Lamentations," God divides "the man, the woman, and the woman's body." Unmistakably, the body proves a source of frustration as both a physical and a conceptual burden of sorts.

Glück asserts her imaginative distinction and independence from what she sees as nature's plan for women, a plan that makes both sexual intercourse and reproduction forms of violation. In this part of the book, Glück discovers a response to the injustices of implacable nature—the seduction of oblivion. The lure of oblivion, the state of being unknown and unbounded, the desire to enter "the stable dark of the earth" (with all the implications of the word *stable* kept intact, as stationary and unchanging, and as site of Jesus' birth) arises in "The Dream of Mourning." Death is repeatedly presented as a force pulling speakers toward oblivion, and oblivion is seen as mysteriously compelling. Glück is somewhat reminiscent of Stevie Smith in this manner; for both poets, writing about oblivion serves as a productive obsession.

In telling fashion, Glück ends her third collection by imagining God's vision of humans, a vision that emphasizes both human smallness and, paradoxically, the immense beauty of creation. Her God, pointedly, is an invention of humans. In section four of "Lamentations" she envisions a creation story in which lovers give birth to a child and then to God, who rises from their bodies and their awareness: "How beautiful it must have

been, / the earth, that first time / seen from the air." With this detached God's-eye view, Glück closes the collection with a remarkable vision of ascent, countering the book's downward trajectory as a whole with its multiple descending figurations: dead children, Glück's dead infant sister, Jesus descending, the self's descent toward oblivion.

The stance of *Descending Figure*—resignation at points rather than defiance as in *Firstborn*—and its broader, more ambitious philosophical view than that of *The House on Marshland*, established Glück as a poet mastering a severe and complex vision.

THE TRIUMPH OF ACHILLES (1985)

Comprised of three parts, *The Triumph of Achilles* signals an interesting departure for Glück in its focus on sexual love. The book is more invested in narrative and in the extended sequence than her earlier collections, and it is her most imagistically rich and erotically focused collection. Its dominant imagery is of summer, markets, water, fruit, and flowers. The poems seem to be written out of a psychic need to locate and erect an incorruptible self, but only after detailing the sensual temptations that threaten self-awareness. While the poems record attraction to and immersion in oblivion, they simultaneously chart the self's willingness to be extricated from the sensual commands of the body. The first poem, "Mock Orange," startlingly sets up the collection's essential arguments: sensual feeling is overwhelming and seductive and thus obliterates the clear boundaries of identity.

It is not the moon, I tell you.
It is these flowers
lighting the yard.

I hate them.
I hate them as I hate sex,

The man's mouth
sealing my mouth, the man's
paralyzing body

"Brooding Likeness," a poem of self-definition for Glück, reveals a duality of reference between stubborn animal flesh and heavenly unfleshed aspiration. She invests her astrological sign, Taurus, with the qualities that her poems seek to explore: a fiery recalcitrance, a drive to distinguish the self, and a hunger for the eternal. The sign of Taurus refers to the bull in the ring doomed to destruction despite its bold display. Taurus also signals the constellation set in the heavens. As such, the poem suggests the twin poles of flesh and spirit around which Glück's *Triumph of Achilles* revolves.

The collection's title poem reveals a dynamic that would balance the desire for absolute self-sovereignty that pervades her work. After the death of his friend Patroclus, Achilles grieves. It is his immersion in grief, in lost love, that accounts for what Glück identifies as his triumph even as he is "a victim / of the part that loved, / the part that was mortal." This emphasis on triumph as the outgrowth of the discovery of human weakness, emotional permeability, and psychic imperfection is essential in Glück's work at this point. She labors to reveal vulnerability and longing. To become human, as such, would mean to triumph over the neurotic quest for perfection in oneself and others.

The plotline of the collection reveals a persona's gradual assertion of her freedom from sensuality. The story that she tells within the poems—of the great pull of sexual desire—is the story of sexuality as it menaces, most specifically, the poet's assumption of voice. The artist must not simply live in the sensation of oblivion that sexual congress creates; the artist must cultivate an ability to detach and analyze experience rather than be absorbed by it. Tellingly, after "Marathon," a poem of sexual oblivion in nine parts,

the collection's succeeding poems are charged with biblical stories; Jesus and Mary emerge, as do Moses and Joseph of Egypt. These biblical stories of sacrifice and the struggle to assert heroism weigh against the erotic; they become parables linked to artistic creation. Even nature itself, as in "Elms," performs a narrative of struggle and ascension:

> . . . the process that creates
> the writhing, stationary tree
> is torment, and have understood
> it will make no forms but twisted forms.

Near the book's conclusion, the story of fleshly ecstasy through sexual union takes on an unquestionably sinister cast. In "Hawk's Shadow," the shadow of a hawk flying with its prey reminds the speaker of the shadow that she and her lover make when he holds her. The paeans to sexual love in *The Triumph of Achilles* are mediated by the accumulative view of sexual love as a threat to being and creation and to the establishment of an effective and powerful self. The image of the hawk's shadow casts in condensed form the ambivalence toward sexual union that distinguishes the book.

In the summer of these poems, as in the story of Achilles, the human is divided by "the part that was mortal." So too, Glück enacts a tendency for her speakers to break into parts, to dissolve, or to merge with another. She finds a disturbing power of metamorphosis within her speakers and a contrary desire to stall change through self-analysis, as in "Marathon," in which a woman regards herself in Narcissus-like fashion at a pond: "Nakedness in women is always a pose. / I was not transfigured. I would never be free."

The Triumph of Achilles differs significantly from her three earlier books: its often longer lines, greater number of figures, and more developed sequential and narrative patterns suggest her willingness to once again cast off an earlier style in favor of expanding her stylistic strategies. Yet her preoccupation with the singular, separate, withheld self reemerges at the book's end, as if the summer markets were only a hiatus in a long journey.

ARARAT (1990)

Ararat, a collection of thirty-two poems, is anomalous in Glück's work for its proselike rhythms and for its unrelieved focus on one family, without presenting a counterbalancing myth. In her fifth collection, Glück centers on pairings: mother and daughter; father and daughter; father and mother; aunt and mother; and grandmother and aunt. The intimate voice of her speaker examines these dyads repeatedly. Bald perceptions recur. The father, recalled as stonily inert, withholding and silent, given to rehearsing death, has himself now died. The mother, emotional and vulnerable, tends her grief but seems unavailable to her children. The family's two daughters envy one another. The older of these daughters, Glück's persona, explores how early psychological imprinting in the family has conditioned her to expect emotional deprivation. Her preference, like her father's, is for silence, secrecy, and disguise in relationships. It is an unabashedly unattractive portrait that Glück presents of her speaker in childhood: a sullen, withdrawn child with polished manners in public who knows full well in private how to harm her sister but chooses more often to harm herself.

In one of the most successful poems in the collection, "A Fable," Glück recasts the story of Solomon. (The poem is anomalous in *Ararat* for its use of an animating biblical story.) Solomon's decision to adjudicate two women's claims on an infant, deciding in favor of the mother who refuses to destroy her child, is transformed brilliantly. Glück's speaker asserts that her self-abnegation is a means by which she "rescues" her mother:

Suppose
you saw your mother
torn between two daughters:
what would you do
to save her but be
willing to destroy
yourself—she would know
who was the rightful child,
the one who couldn't bear
to divide the mother.

An uncanny logic of self-destruction informs the volume and refracts through poems on her speaker's son and her niece—both of whom take after their respective mothers. In "A Fable" the speaker's son and his mother are "living / experts in silence," employing silence to isolate others and to maintain a stable position of superiority over the more spontaneous and voluble.

What is remarkable about *Ararat* is its unremitting focus on the family and its detailing of inertia. The volume presents evidence of early psychic trauma. The speaker's weapons are simple ones that require stoic self-discipline: the ability to withhold love and to use herself as a witness of others' perfidies by being "a device that listened." We are left with the impression of a family home as a "grave" enclosing pain that seems to be only reluctantly understood. This portrait of repression, of contained emotional violence within a family, self-consciously announces itself as partial and distorted. We are to question the teller of the tale. In "The Untrustworthy Speaker" Glück reminds us to be suspicious readers: "That's why I'm not to be trusted. / Because a wound to the heart / is also a wound to the mind."

In total, *Ararat* seems to be the least accomplished of Glück's books. The emotions of the volume are stunted, processed too readily through conventional therapeutic channels of understanding. In her attempt at greater clarity, Glück has not created technical innovation. The work cedes too readily to a prose style; the fine aural echoes, the control of pacing through sentence length and line break, and the arrangement of arresting images that distinguished her earlier work are not in evidence. What is valuable, however, is the book's focus on sisterly envy (a topic rarely treated with candor and seriousness) and Glück's willingness to present for inspection two qualities that are generally deemed negative in relationships: silence and self-disguise.

The volume appears to have been a transitional endeavor for Glück, a necessary "outing" of the claustrophobic domestic, an archaeology of the childhood mind and an autopsy of familial relations. She has conducted a freeze-frame of an earlier self—accomplished before the spiritualized outpouring of one of her most triumphant collections, *The Wild Iris*.

THE WILD IRIS (1992)

The Wild Iris was written in ten weeks during the summer of 1991. Its speed of composition appears to be unprecedented in Glück's career. Glück has written frequently about her struggles with writing. In both prose and poetry she presents writer's block as an inevitable part of the genuine poet's experience. The writer who composes through inspiration and the dictates of the unconscious, through psychic need with spiritual understanding as primary goal, necessarily faces periods in which she cannot write. Access to the unconscious is not accomplished through will, she has argued. Her measure of the authentic poem is its link to unwilled creation. Given Glück's assumptions, the circumstances in which she wrote the fifty-four poems of *The Wild Iris* must have appeared to be miraculous. Arriving with such unprecedented fluency for Glück, the poems mark a turning point: her succeeding collections will seem to be less hampered by a perfectionism that would cramp her ability to execute her ambitions.

The Wild Iris marks this point of greater fluency, it may be suggested, by Glück's choice of vehicle. She discovers in the voices of the collection—many of them attributed to flowers and light—a freedom from flesh and an image of cyclic renewal that mirrors her view of the cyclicity of psychic life. Such seemingly "slender" vehicles paradoxically allow her a new depth of statement. She has succeeded in "unfleshing" her voice, a psychic effect that she had sought both as an adolescent anorexic and as a mature poet. As a writer who has used the topic of attaining voice—and the difficulty of doing so—as a major source of inspiration, she has imagined voice as a refined body of sorts in *The Wild Iris*. The garden's flowers are powered by voice freed from the human body's urgencies and impurities. In their physical form flowers are irredeemably alien to us, and by assuming to speak through their absolute otherness, she assumes a beguiling stance, representing nature as both secretive and irreducible to human formulae. As Judith Kitchen has asserted, "*The Wild Iris* returns to the distanced voice of Glück's early poetry—and to its restrained, meticulous observation of the natural world—but this volume is not recapitulation. It is a foray into new territory, from which emerges a personal mythology giving rise, in turn, to theology."

Glück opens the collection with the possibility of escape and change, and the direct address of the poems presents the illusion of intimacy. We might even think of the collection as presenting intimacy as a source of authority itself, even as the poems address the fear of speechlessness and abandonment. Her elemental voices carry vulnerability, a vulnerability that takes on dignity and, paradoxically, power because it harbors ancient cries against deprivation and death. The poems reflect on the act of responsiveness—a regeneration after a depressive interlude:

. . . whatever
returns from oblivion returns
to find a voice:

from the center of my life came
a great fountain, deep blue
shadows on azure seaward.

The garden in the poems seems folded into the body of the gardener through her acts of imaginative identification. The collection as a whole, bounded by a growing season and movement from dawn to nightfall, is posed toward spiritual quest.

Although *The Wild Iris* garnered Glück the Pulitzer Prize and admiring reception, it is imprinted with her fear of criticism. That she was concerned about the book's reception is evident in the poems themselves, most especially "Daisies," in which she alludes to likely objections to her practice. Perhaps her focus on the garden is out of date, escapist, and sentimentalist, a reduction of the poem to preciousness? By raising such objections she anticipates and inoculates her critics. In "Clear Morning" she answers critics who prefer parable, fable, and concrete images to a poetry of unadorned statement: "I am prepared now to force / clarity upon you." She replies to her critics by the declarative force of her lines. Her questions are pointedly forthright and unanswerable other than by faith.

Poems titled "Matins" (seven in all) and "Vespers" (ten in all) emphasize the prayer-like quality of the work. In part, the collection unnerves because of its unabashed tone of supplication to a godlike figure who shades into images of nature, a gardener, and a lover. She ends *The Wild Iris* with a note of belief in the ecstatic potential of love in "The White Lilies":

> Hush, beloved. It doesn't matter to me
> how many summers I live to return:
> this one summer we have entered eternity.
> I felt your two hands
> bury me to release its splendor.

In *The Wild Iris* Glück had found a way to speak of profound need. The frequent use of apostrophe and the relative brevity of the poems serve further to highlight the urgency of the voices that she created.

MEADOWLANDS (1996)

Meadowlands records a marriage and a divorce through the lens of the myth of Odysseus and Penelope, with particular attention to exploring Penelope as the spouse who grieves. Glück's Penelope is, for the most part, immovable in her grief. She is paralyzed at points by her will. She is also masterful at moments of detachment, displaying an acute emotional separation from those around her. Watchful, "stubborn," she sees in her own nature a strange corruption.

Glück's Odysseus is much less fully explored than her Penelope; at best he is a superficial man. While Penelope is an avatar of the inner life, he is without the gift of self-reflection. A self in perpetual movement, he seeks reflection through young lovers. The bickering that he and his wife engage in has taken on a ceremonial quality through the years. He assaults her temperament (her quiet reclusiveness, at least seemingly inert) as a means of effecting his own self-protection. His irritation with her appears to be perpetual, as is her quiet resentment. This futile pairing is commented on primarily by two outside sources: Telemachus, who looks on his parents' marriage and separation with self-protective bemusement; and Circe, Odysseus' most stubborn lover, who would seek to agitate and inhabit Penelope's mind. Despite the inherent interest that these sidebar characters pose, the main focus of the book is Penelope, and here we see Glück characteristically shifting traditional angles of attention in a myth from a male to a female character.

The few references to opera in the collection suggest that Glück wants the marriage's problems to be writ large and given high dramatic power. She conditions such a risk with her emphasis on comic carping between husband and wife. It is perhaps part of Glück's boldness to cast the daily trivialities and pettiness of a dissolving marriage against the outsized proportions of myth. Certainly it is a calculated risk. But it is indeed the more dramatic experience of ritualized containment, the theme of lost love and disabling grief, that one remembers most in contrast to the accounts of symptomatic prickliness between married partners. Despite the collection's somewhat lighter moments, Glück would make a "grasping, / unnatural song—passionate, / like Maria Callas" in "Penelope's Song."

Notably, the body in the poems is an encumbrance and an annoyance. It is a "troublesome body," hardly animate. In "Departure" a husband strokes his wife's body and the chair she sits on with equal attention. Like the chair, the wife's body would seem wooden and functional only. According to her husband, the wife has a secret fascination for meat, and in turn her body is meat-like and deadened to feeling. Her faithfulness appears to be a species of illusion, her patience a cryptic watchfulness before the impatient, erring husband who complains about her austerity, solitude, and routinized life.

Accompanying the collection's mythic contours are parables, nine in all. These serve as further commentary on the book's key polarities: revelation and secrecy, faithlessness and faith, departure and stasis, self-destruction and survival. Conventionally, the parable serves as a teaching device. Glück's "Parable of the King" attends to desire and the destruction of the past. "Parable of the Hostages" deals with the dream of the future as an entrapment and any delay as a bewitchment. "Parable of the Trellis" reflects on dependence and movement. In the ninth parable a gift is destroyed and the speaker seems unforgiven, for she has mistaken the conditions in which natural growth of any sort occurs; "Parable of the Gift" suggests resignation and, if not self-condemnation, the speaker's collusion in destroying her marriage.

The book details a climate of depressive stasis. The daily cruelties that are recorded here—a husband's greater feeling for the comfortable position of a cat on a bed than for his wife's very being (quarrels are mediated through pets)— are small and bitter strikes against a backdrop in which Glück surreptitiously defends Penelope's nature: her patience, her stoicism, and her solitude.

Penelope's revenge, finally, is poetry. She survives through poetry; it is the "loom" that Penelope works upon and unmakes while she waits for Odysseus' return in "Ithaca." Upon the "loom" of the poem, Glück is not only detailing the squalid infractions and petty insults of a contemporary marriage that is bound toward divorce; she is questioning the boundaries of identity and the resilience of desire. Penelope does not desire Odysseus; he seems quite unworthy, too boyish and fickle. It seems more accurate to say that she desires a vision of her own security in the past. For the future she desires the poem—which doesn't make her inchoate grief any less alarming but perhaps all the more poignant.

The innovations of *Meadowlands* are tonal. The humor that emerges and had been nearly absent from earlier collections is almost startling in context. It is important to note, however, that humor in the collection takes the form of verbal sparring in dialogues between husband and wife. These are complaints within a marriage, deflations meant to harm the other and to guard the self. Her insertions of contemporary details (previously her landscapes seemed mysteriously out of time) provide another layer of innovation in her body of work. Despite the mythic framing of the collection, the poems occur more clearly within a contemporary stream of time than do scenarios from her other collections. After all, in *Meadowlands* the mythic must cohabit with cuts of steak and neighborhood buglights. Perhaps most important, *Meadowlands* is her first book in which dialogue figures prominently. Although her contemporary Penelope gains our most fervent attention, we hear Odysseus' voice. The book presents these paired voices in what seem at moments like comic opera duets, albeit rather bitter duets, more like duels.

Glück ends the collection with "Heart's De-sire," an invitation to imagine affection and for-giveness through neighborly love. Although it's a dream of a backyard party—not a reality—it anticipates the curatives that she will pose in her eighth collection, *Vita Nova.*

VITA NOVA (1999)

Glück's eighth single collection is one of her most accomplished. It reflects on earlier images and themes (the beech tree and anorexia, for in-stance). While such repetitions might create an aura of redundancy in the collection, they more fully suggest culminating power. Glück has not abandoned poetry as a form of self-help, that is, as a practice of psychoanalytic self-study. But here her repeated images are focused toward a remaking of her poetic and a further experimen-tation with the possibilities of layering diverse tones within poems. The surprising insertion of humor, of daily detrius that marked *Meadow-lands,* survives into *Vita Nova.* The later poems, rather than being accounts of the breakdown of a long marriage, now register the speaker's self-reconstitution after she has separated from her husband. Sorrowful notes are even more pro-nounced in this collection, and yet here too are notes of hope for the new life that the collection's title announces.

Vita Nova is not only the title of the collection but also the title of its first and last poems and its eighth poem, translated as "New Life." What does new life mean in this context? What are the resonances that Glück chooses to explore in the phrase? Surely new life represents the season of spring, a season repeatedly depicted in the col-lection and a season that Glück has been drawn to representing even in her earliest work. More specifically, however, the new life is her speaker's life post–marriage, the poet's new life as it must take the imprint of change. Despite the desolation to which some poems in the collection allude, the prospect of a new life is more pow-erfully rendered as opportunity than devastation.

The thirty-two poems in *Vita Nova* reflect upon one another and ultimately present a persona's progression both inward and outward. The book opens with an immediate cry for intimacy and an immediate claim. "You saved me, you should re-member me." The line reappears in "Seizure," the twenty-ninth poem of *Vita Nova,* the repetition suggesting the power that Glück wishes to afford the claim. As such, we begin the book in *medias res,* after a rescue of some sort. To save and to remember are not necessarily linked, but in Glück's cosmology, human beings find them-selves inevitably responsible for one another, no matter how often they fail to uphold such an ideal.

The opening poem is especially important. Al-though it bears signature images that we have come to associate with her work, it is quite unlike any other poem Glück has written. It exemplifies the new life toward which the poems are aimed; it is a poem in which memory saves rather than decimates. The poem deals with the selectivity of memory and the way that an incident from the deep past may float up to consciousness with new and restorative power. The poem's nearly im-pressionistically arrayed details (ferryboats, blos-soms, tables), seen from a distance, are followed by a small discrete image that seemingly literal-izes sweetness to create a new appetite for life:

> Islands in the distance. My mother
> holding out a plate of little cakes—
>
> as far as I remember, changed
> in no detail, the moment
> vivid, intact, having never been
> exposed to light, so that I woke elated, at my age
> hungry for life, utterly confident—

In *Vita Nova,* the new life is the old life, re-seen, rediscovered, and reinterpreted. The act of revision is an act of reclamation. Her self-revision is an attempt to see multiples where previously she had focused on scarcity; literally, she now sees more than one cake on the plate. She detects sweetness offered up from the earliest moments of her life, rather than deprivation. In "Unwritten Law" the speaker takes pity on time, questioning what she calls her earlier "inflexible Platonism, / my fierce seeing of only one thing at a time." The book's first poem is an attempt to interrogate her speaker's earlier "readings" of her life. She is now, in a sense, her own redeemed Odysseus, for she must travel through a mental landscape, questioning her former preoccupations and methods of understanding, as in "The Mystery": "The passionate threats and questions, / the old search for justice, / must have been entirely deluded."

Although she chooses to allow feeling that had gone underground to reemerge, Glück continues in this collection to work with the grand opposites that have sustained her work: gods and men, absolutes and mutability, expectation and reality. Significantly, the word "shattered" appears twice in the book as if to suggest that the breaking of logic is now impelled. She has mastered statement and emblem, but she would now "break" into another, less expectant way of being. Stylistically, she employs filmic techniques through imagistic dissolves and "quick cuts" between scenes. She plays with scale—size and distance—and with isolated images as if to pictorially readjust her earlier impressions of the meaning of her life.

Auguries of the new life in the collection occur in part through dreams. A number of the poems depict dreams and argue covertly for their authority. The speaker's dreams assist her, presenting alternate scenarios and lovers and new embodiments of chaotic needs. Such dreams reassign meaning and possibility, and she reads them as parables that point toward psychological remedies.

Additionally, Glück suggests that one way in which the self is reborn is through a renewal of sight. As such, one should not overlook the many references to sight in this collection. The act of seeing proves to be aggressive and interrogative. Indeed, the shadowing myth of *Vita Nova* is that of Orpheus and Eurydice. The allusion to or partial retelling of the myth occurs in nine poems, and other poems bear at least some measure of the imprint of the myth's template.

When we read Glück's poems that circle about the story of Orpheus and Eurydice we are reminded that the myth is, on one level, a story about the power of sight. Seeking to return his wife to the living, Orpheus is allowed to enter the underworld to retrieve her, under the condition that he not turn to look at her before leaving the underworld. But because he turns to look at Eurydice, and by turning condemns her to her second death, the test he fails might be called a test of vision. Orpheus' failure, then, seems representative of failed perception, of a gaze turned backward to the past and to the material world too readily and too possessively. Orpheus' plight as one who loses and is responsible for his loss resonates through these poems. Yet Orpheus' loss in the context of Glück's poems is more than the loss of the beloved. Glück's Eurydice is an idea, a theme, a way of perceiving. Thus, the mourning that the poems enact is localized not only within the lost beloved but within a perspective, a way of seeing and a way of being within the world.

Together, Orpheus and Eurydice serve as adjuncts around the central figure of the book: a woman reliving the impact of her devastating divorce. Alternately, Glück assumes the voice or perspective of either member of the pair. For Glück, Orpheus is the type of the poet; he sings and he fails and his mourning conditions his music. Eurydice performs as a betrayed woman and a symbol of loss.

Glück's concluding poem in *Vita Nova* seems to be a concerted effort toward tonal departure, for here irony is raised to a level of comedic self-deprecation. In most endings of her books she leans toward the portentous. The contrary effect in *Vita Nova* is to literalize a new life, to shed tragic overtones, to outwit her critics by deflating, and even toying with, her own self-image—and to suggest survival as a commitment to advancing, both physically and spiritually, through space and time:

> Life is very weird, no matter how it ends,
> Very filled with dreams. Never
> Will I forget your face, your frantic human eyes
> Swollen with tears.
> *I thought my life was over and my heart was broken.*
> *Then I moved to Cambridge.*

While Glück has written most often of a state of being that resists consolation, after *The Triumph of Achilles* her poems have become less pressurized, less often about the pursuit of a debilitating perfection than about the process of becoming human by accepting imperfection and mortality. It is telling that *The Triumph of Achilles,* her fourth collection, depicts the process of becoming mortal by interrogating the godlike perfections and idealisms that trouble her speaker's psyche. Her fifth book, *Ararat,* exploits novelistic effects to create a linked narrative out of a blighted family romance. With *The Wild Iris* she launches her work toward a spiritualized voicing of anxiety, loss, and painful resignation. She tells the story of abandonment within a dignified and elevating poetic. The early work carries a daring explosive charge; the later, sometimes quietly aggrieved poems have had a devastating effect of another sort altogether.

Among the generation of poets of which she is a member, including James Tate, Mark Strand, Charles Wright, and Jean Valentine, Glück seems the darker alternative, displaying in her early work an almost primitive single-mindedness. She manages, paradoxically, to seem archaic without

being archaic. She has crafted a sensibility in a linked series of autobiographical poems that dwell on the great themes of mortality and abandonment. She has also given tragic dimension to elements often seen as comprising the lesser emotions: envy, disdain, and resentment.

In addition to being a poet of considerable influence, she is an accomplished essayist. Her prose style is remarkably similar to her poetic style: aphoristic, intimate, alert to irony. As she commented in her introduction to *Proofs & The ories,* her essays grow from strategies that she developed through poetry: "I wrote from what I know, trying to undermine the known with intelligent questions. Like poems, [these essays] have been my education." Similarly, the essays, like her poems, are born from "prolonged brooding" and an attempt to overturn conventional assumptions.

In the late 1990s Glück was widely regarded as a major contemporary poet. Her readers eagerly awaited each new book that she wrote, assuming it would be a reflection of her radical independence and her growing insights on her own inchoate but pressing need for spiritual understanding. She refers to books of poetry as "holy object(s)" and each of her own books as "a speaking whole." However seemingly splintered in different personae, Glück's voices struggle to attain insights about meaning: how to speak with the difficult truth of feeling as the most demanding guide.

Selected Bibliography

WORKS OF LOUISE GLÜCK
POETRY
Firstborn. New York: New American Library, 1968.

The House on Marshland. New York: Ecco, 1975.
Descending Figure. New York: Ecco, 1980.
The Triumph of Achilles. New York: Ecco, 1985.
Ararat. New York: Ecco, 1990.
The Wild Iris. Hopewell, N.J.: Ecco, 1992.
The First Four Books of Poems. Hopewell, N.J.: Ecco, 1995.
Meadowlands. Hopewell, N.J.: Ecco, 1996.
Vita Nova. Hopewell, N.J.: Ecco, 1999.

PROSE

Proofs & Theories: Essays on Poetry. Hopewell, N.J.: Ecco, 1994.
Glück's collected essays: "Education of the Poet," "On T. S. Eliot," "The Idea of Courage," "On George Oppen," "Against Sincerity," "On Hugh Seidman," "The Forbidden," "Obstinate Humanity," "Disruption, Hesitation, Silence," "Disinterestedness," "The Best American Poetry 1993: Introduction," "The Dreamer and the Watcher," "On Stanley Kunitz," "Invitation and Exclusion," "Death and Absence," and "On Impoverishment."

BIBLIOGRAPHY

Friedman, Paul. "Louise Glück: Primary Source Bibliography (1966–1986)." *Bulletin of Bibliography* 44.4: 281–285 (December 1987).

CRITICAL STUDIES

BOOKS

Dodd, Elizabeth. *The Veiled Mirror and the Woman Poet: H.D., Louise Bogan, Elizabeth Bishop, and Louise Glück.* Columbia: University of Missouri Press, 1992.
Upton, Lee. *The Muse of Abandonment: Origin, Identity, Mastery in Five American Poets.* Lewisburg, Pa.: Bucknell University Press, 1998.
Vendler, Helen. *The Music of What Happens: Poems, Poets, Critics.* Cambridge, Mass.: Harvard University Press, 1988.
———. *Part of Nature, Part of Us: Modern American Poets.* Cambridge, Mass.: Harvard University Press, 1980.

ARTICLES

Bedient, Calvin. "Four American Poets." *Sewanee Review* 84: 351–354 (Spring 1976).
Boland, Eavan. "Making the Difference: Eroticism and Aging in the Work of the Woman Poet." *American Poetry Review* 23.2: 27–32 (1994).
Bond, Bruce. "The Unfinished Child: Contradictory Desire in Glück's *Ararat.*" *New England Review* 14.1: 216–223 (1991).
Bond, Diane S. "Entering Language in Louise Glück's *The House on Marshland*: A Feminist Reading." *Contemporary Literature* 31.1: 58 (1990).
Burt, Steve. "The Dark Garage with the Garbage." *PN Review* 25.3: 31–35 (1999).
Doreski, William. "The Mind Afoot." *Ploughshares* 7.1: 157–163 (1981).
Gordon, Gerald. " 'Summoned Prey' in Louise Glück's 'Thanksgiving.' " *CEA Critic* 48.3: 68–72 (1986).
Hart, Henry. "Story-Tellers, Myth-Makers, Truth-Sayers." *New England Review* 15.4: 192–206 (1993).
Hix, H. L. "The Triumph of Louise Glück's 'Achilles.' " *Notes on Contemporary Literature* 22.2: 3–6 (March 1992).
Keller, Lynn. " 'Free / of Blossom and Subterfuge': Louise Glück and the Language of Renunciation." In *World, Self, Poem: Essays on Contemporary Poetry from the "Jubilation of Poets."* Edited by Leonard W. Trawick. Kent, Ohio: Kent State University Press, 1990. Pp. 120–129.
Kitchen, Judith. "The Woods Around It." *The Georgia Review* 47.1: 145–159 (Spring 1993).
Kuzma, Greg. "Rock Bottom: Louise Glück and the Poetry of Dispassion." *The Midwest Quarterly* 24.4: 468–481 (1983).
Landis, Joan Hutton. "The Poems of Louise Glück." *Salmagundi* 36: 140–148 (Winter 1977).
Mattson, Suzanne. "Without Relation: Family and Freedom in the Poetry of Louise Glück." *Mid-American Review* 14.2: 88–109 (1994).
McClatchy, J. D. "Recent Poetry: New Designs on Life." *Yale Review* 65: 95–100 (Autumn 1975).
Miklitsch, Robert. "Assembling a Landscape: The Poetry of Louise Glück." *Hollins Critic* 19.4: 1–13 (1982).
Muske, Carol. "The Wild Iris." *The American Poetry Review* 22.1: 52–54 (January–February 1993).
Raffel, Burton. "The Poetry of Louise Glück." *The Literary Review* 31.3: 261–273 (Spring 1988).

Reynolds, Oliver. "You Will Suffer." *Times Literary Supplement* 30: 23 (July 1999).

Stitt, Peter. "Contemporary American Poets: Exclusive and Inclusive." *The Georgia Review* 34.4: 849–863 (Winter 1985).

Townsend, Ann. "The Problem of Sincerity: The Lyric Plain Style of George Herbert and Louise Glück." *Shenandoah* 46.4: 43–61 (Winter 1996).

—*LEE UPTON*

A. R. Gurney

1930–

ONE UBIQUITOUS CLICHÉ dominates the discussion of A. R. Gurney's work. This is that he is the chronicler of American WASP culture, a way of life that was beginning to lose its centrality in the American consciousness when he began writing in the mid-1960s and that has continued to decline throughout his career as a playwright. Gurney was called the "John Cheever of the American stage" by several critics when his first play to achieve success in New York, *Scenes from American Life* (1970), premiered at Lincoln Center in 1971, and he acknowledges Cheever's influence warmly, having based two of his plays, *Children* (1974) and *A Cheever Evening* (1994), directly on Cheever's work. Gurney is also compared often to Philip Barry, John Updike, F. Scott Fitzgerald, J. P. Marquand, S. N. Behrman, and John O'Hara, comparisons to which he does not object, although he once made the important distinction that while writers such as Barry, Fitzgerald, Behrman, and O'Hara all wrote "from the outside looking in . . . trying to decode the world they wanted to get into," he is someone who "was there" and is "kind of glad to be a little bit out of it."

GURNEY'S BACKGROUND

When Albert Ramsdell Gurney Jr. was born on November 1, 1930, in Buffalo, New York, it was into the heart of WASP America and what he describes as a "comfortable, middle-class family" that included an older sister and would eventually include a younger brother. Both sides of the family had been among the prominent citizens of Buffalo since the mid-nineteenth century. Gurney's father owned a real estate and insurance firm, while his mother, Marion Spaulding Gurney, was what he once described as a "homemaker," meaning that "she organized the house. We had a few maids. She was . . . an excellent sports woman. She played tennis, rode horses and ran the symphony." The Gurneys were prominent in their social club and various cultural organizations and had the same pew in the Episcopal church for four generations. The same dancing school teacher who taught A. R. Gurney and his wife, Mary (Molly) Goodyear Gurney, also taught his mother and grandmother. It is typical of the family's circumspect way of life that Gurney did not discover the one irregular thing in the family history, his great-grandfather's suicide (to which he alludes in *The Cocktail Hour* [1988]), until he was in his forties, when it was revealed at his father's funeral in 1977.

Gurney admits that he brought some of the WASP stereotyping on himself in deciding early in his career to write about the people he knew best. In the 1970s, the increasing emphasis on ethnicity in the United States made him think beyond the insularity of the world in which he had grown up. He has said that the increasing pride of various ethnic groups made him realize that he came from an ethnic group too: "I realized that I was one of the variations and that I could explore the very specific local and parochial ethnic customs of upper-middle-class white Americans." In the thirty years since the premiere of *Scenes from American Life,* a satiric treatment of upper-middle-class Buffalo, there has hardly been a review, an interview, or a critical article on Gurney that does not mention WASPs. At times he bristles against what he has called this "compartmentalizing," but for the most part he accepts the role of "WASP laureate" with characteristic politeness, and he occasionally launches a civilized defense of his people. He points out that WASPs are a "neglected and in some ways prejudiced-against minority. Talk about slurs. People can say things about WASPs they wouldn't dare say about any other group in this country—and they do!" In the 1990s he noted the attempts of his group to come out of its self-imposed insularity and integrate themselves more with the larger American society, a trend that he has not only chronicled but has also helped to precipitate.

Gurney's position in relation to the WASP subculture is similar to his relationship with his parents, that of a rebellious but loving son. His plays often feature a parent and two sons in a Cain and Abel configuration, in which Gurney's autobiographical character is invariably the Cain figure. He has said that he played the "prodigal son role" in his family, and his character is a son who is starving for attention and approval, while chafing against his parents' demands and values to the extent that he ends up acting out his rebellion in ways that alienate his parents even further. This conflict is central to the plots of *The Cocktail Hour, The Middle Ages* (1977), *Children,* and *What I Did Last Summer* (1983), and also informs *Scenes from American Life* and *The Wayside Motor Inn* (1977). One of the prime impetuses in these plays is the question that John asks his sister Nina in *The Cocktail Hour:* "What went wrong

between my father and me? Where, when, why did he turn his countenance from me?" In one sense, as he suggests in *The Cocktail Hour,* Gurney's plays about WASPs have been a reflection of the kind of acting out that John has always done with his family. As Nina tells him, "You came here to stir things *up,* John. You came here to cause trouble. That's what you've done since the day you were born, and that's what you'll do till you die." Gurney admits to having gone, like John, from room to room in the family's large house, teasing people, stirring things up, and thereby getting attention, although not necessarily the kind he desired.

Early on, Gurney learned to get attention in a more approved way by writing plays. His first, written in kindergarten, was about a raccoon. As a boy, he would write plays and perform them in the family's basement, most often using marionettes, but sometimes persuading his sister and brother to act in them with him. At Williams College, he succeeded Stephen Sondheim as the writer of the annual musicals, and he wrote his first satiric treatment of WASP subculture as a musical, *Love in Buffalo* (1958), while completing his Master of Fine Arts at the Yale School of Drama in 1958. He worked briefly at the profession of musical comedy, writing *Tom Sawyer* (1959) for the Starlight Theatre in Kansas City in 1959, but the births of his four children in quick succession led him to abandon the precarious life of the musical theater in favor of a more prosaic life, first as a prep school teacher, and then as a professor at the Massachusetts Institute of Technology, where he remained on the faculty from 1960 until 1996, although he stopped teaching there in 1982.

A CONTEMPORARY TAKE ON THE CLASSICS

Gurney's position at the Massachusetts Institute of Technology required him to teach the classics as well as modern literature, both of which have a deep presence in his plays. He likes to use literary precursors for what he refers to as "a bass clef," an underpinning that can be used as a basis for irony and contrast. Several of his early one-acts were contemporary versions of classical and biblical stories, satirizing various aspects of American life in the 1960s. *The Comeback* (1964), set at the return of Odysseus, provides a protofeminist treatment of Penelope, who is deciding whether to "call [her] own shots" in the marriage game because she is "suddenly very tired of just . . . playing touch . . . tired of being just a thing—just a mechanical rabbit which you dogs are not supposed to catch up to." There is some Oedipal tension between her and Telemachus in the play, but the primary conflict is between him and the shadow of his absent father. Telemachus feels worthless and awkward, as if he were "trying to play some game by some terribly difficult rulebook, held all the time in [his] hand." "Forgive me, father. Forgive me, and tell me how to make it up," he prays to the absent Odysseus. There is a certain wish fulfillment for the wayward son Gurney in this play as Odysseus tells Penelope, "He's like a child put into our custody when we're too young for the responsibility. So you ignored him; and I asked too much of him. And now that we're older, he's making us pay for it." In the end, Telemachus embraces a patriarchal Judaism, going "off to Judea to find his father," while the Hellenistic family of Odysseus disintegrates.

Other early uses of the classics include *The Golden Fleece* (1967), an updating of the Medea story as a domestic suburban tale, and *The David Show* (1966), which, in 1968, was Gurney's first New York production and was savaged by the *New York Times* critic. Set in a television studio during the rehearsal for the crowning of David by the prophet Samuel, it is a satire of the moral vacuity of contemporary politicians, of what was referred to in the sixties as "selling out," and of the subordination of everything else to the media event.

Gurney's most significant use of the classics was to come twenty years later, in *Another Antigone* (1987), which bears the stamp of thirty years of studying and teaching the subject. The humorous self-reflexiveness in this modern Antigone play about a young woman who is writing a modern Antigone play cannot be missed. But it is also, as the Antigone character Judy's play is, meant to speak meaningfully to what the Creon character Henry calls "a world which seems too often concerned only with the meaning of meaning." Henry is quite an eloquent spokesman for the classicist point of view that "there are things beyond the world of management which are profoundly unmanageable," although he comes to realize that, like Creon, "in his commitment to abstract and dehumanizing laws, he has neglected the very heart of his life" by ignoring the human needs of the people around him. Judy, on the other hand, develops from a simple and rather juvenile defiance of authority for its own sake to an awakening sense of the failures of the American social system, but she can express this only through the rather useless gesture of refusing an award for her play with the words:

> Maybe my play hasn't influenced anyone else, but it sure has influenced me. I don't feel good about my life anymore. I don't feel good about my country. I can't accept all this *stuff* that's going on these days. I can't accept it. No, I'm sorry, but I just can't accept it.

At the end of the play, one of the characters says, "I have a feeling we may have lost them both forever."

This play may be self-reflexive, but it is not postmodern. Its form is that of classical tragedy, and its action is impelled by a clear conflict between two characters, which compels debate of fundamental moral questions. In fact, A. R. Gurney is a deeply moral playwright. Like the writers to whom he pays homage—Sophocles, Henry James, T. S. Eliot—he believes in a social contract and in human responsibility and in right conduct, and he is concerned with the basic ethical question of how one should act in this world. He is also a great respecter of what he refers to as "dancing in chains," creating art under the formal constraints of classical playwriting. "I am aware of the three unities," he told the interviewer John DiGaetani, "and most of my plays attempt to follow the traditional rules of playwriting: the unities, if possible, a clear line of action, and a 'hook'—that is, something at the end of the first act which will persuade the audience to come back for the second. These are old techniques, but they work."

Another Antigone is also about academic life, its power struggles and the moral dilemmas that arise from them, a subject that has interested Gurney since the sixties. In three lightly satirical one-act comedies, he portrayed academic life in the late 1960s and early 1970s. *The Open Meeting* (1965) is an absurdist play about three faculty members, Roy, Verna, and Eddie, who are attending a meeting that is really controlled by a fourth, offstage, character, Dick. As the power relationships unfold, the younger character Eddie comes to see "the democratic experience" as "simply the sum of a series of petty patricides, commencing at the local level." Another comic piece, *The Love Course* (1969), uses a team-taught course on "The Literature of Love" as a vehicle for discussing power relations both in the university and between men and women. While the male Professor Burgess exercises his control over the female Professor Carroway in the Curriculum Committee and a tenure vote, she conquers him by the power of art and love. "Oh woman, what have you done to me?" wails Burgess. "You have seduced me. With books! We have bathed in them, we have rolled in them, we have wallowed in them like lascivious Turks . . . . you are holding me in thrall! You're dragging me down! I'm drowning!" She frees him only after she has exercised her power, drawing him into a passionate moment by reading a scene from *Wuthering Heights* with him. *The Old One-Two* (1971), which Gurney has described as a precursor to *Another Antigone,* is modeled on the comedy of Menander. While it has the same rebellion of female student against male professor that *Antigone* has, it treats it much differently. The professor seduces the student by having her read book six of the *Odyssey.* On the brink of his resignation, the dean discovers a birthmark that reveals him to be the professor's long lost child; the student decides to move in with her boyfriend; and all the students are given the freedom to take any course they want.

GURNEY AS NOVELIST

Gurney's most serious treatment of academic life is his fine academic novel, *Entertaining Strangers* (1977). The novel, whose narrator is a teacher in the humanities department of a major institute of technology in the Boston area, has strong autobiographical underpinnings. Like Gurney in the late 1970s, Professor Porter Platt is a middle-aged WASP with four growing children and an intelligent wife who is just emerging from her years of full-time mothering into a career as a nutritionist. The novel is a deftly satiric inside account of academic life, with its hopelessly garrulous faculty meetings, its sycophantic faculty members posing as brave revolutionaries, its incompetent, cynical administrators, and its general air of petty, Byzantine intrigue. More fundamentally, however, it is about Porter's subject, the humanities, which was also Gurney's subject for twenty-five years, and about the general failure of universities to live by the values they teach. Porter extends himself to help what he takes to be a young Englishman who appears at his office door one day hoping for a job interview. Having gotten him a job, he takes Christopher Simpson under his wing, even inviting him into his home for an extended stay with his family.

Christopher quickly shows his Machiavellian

colors. He plays university politics with great skill, getting to know people, Porter among them, so that he can ascertain their weaknesses and play them against each other. Once he has stirred up discontent among students and junior faculty members, he can remove key opponents from power and then step into the positions himself, choosing the perfect moment at a faculty meeting to deliver a speech that will bring him to general prominence. In the end, Porter comes to see Christopher, who turns out to be a Rhodesian who has never had the position at Oxford that he claimed, for what he is, "bright, adept, and passionate as a Puritan to stake his claim in this strange profession, in this strange country, in these strange times." When asked by the university president for his opinion of Christopher's actions, the only accusation that Porter can make against Christopher is Caesar's sin of ambition. "What's wrong with that?" retorts the university president. "I'm ambitious, and I hope you are"— which, in a way, is exactly what's wrong. Porter feels betrayed by a man to whom he has reached out in friendship, to whom he has exposed himself, and who has not reciprocated, but who has simply made use of the situation and the information to advance his own interests. In Porter's view, Christopher has failed to honor the social contract, failed to live up to the humane values that he thought they shared. At the end of the novel, as Christopher, having obtained an offer from Harvard, walks out of the professor's office and his life, Porter says, "I really think I would have hit him again, but he was gone, on up the corridor, and I would have swung at nothing but thin air."

Gurney has written two other novels, *The Gospel According to Joe* (1974) and *The Snow Ball* (1984), which he also adapted as a play, but he has made it clear that he much prefers the theatrical medium to fiction:

> I think I'm more at home in plays, possibly because I've done more of them. The emotional payoff from

drama is obviously more immediate. With a play, you know where you are with an audience, for better or worse, very quickly. With a book, you don't. Maybe I'm just more at home with that kind of immediate gratification.

He has also pointed out that *Entertaining Strangers* "has certain theatrical things about it. It's the old *Tartuffe* plot, after all, transposed to academia."

MODERN LITERATURE AS THE BASS CLEF

The most significant effect of Gurney's academic career has been his tendency to use modern literature as his "bass clef," situating many of his plays in immediate dialogue with a literary as well as a theatrical tradition. The most straightforward use of modern literature occurs in the 1976 play *Richard Cory* (in the volume *Collected Plays, 1974–1983* [1997]), which is, according to the Author's Note, "an attempt to deconstruct and explore the poem by Edwin Arlington Robinson, using it as a tragic framework of inevitability within which the hero is doomed to die." Gurney has said that he was fascinated by the relationship between Cory and the townspeople in Robinson's poem—"he fluttered pulses when he said, / 'Good morning,' and he glittered when he walked"— and their puzzlement when Richard Cory "one calm summer night, / Went home, and put a bullet through his head." He begins the play with a sort of choral recitation of the poem by the townspeople, who treat Cory as an object of envy and awe, and consequently isolate him from the life of the town. Young men try to dress like him, and young women organize their days around his morning greetings, but when he tries to connect with the townspeople by sitting down to a cup of coffee in a diner, the jokes stop, the place goes silent, and soon everyone has left but him. He is emotionally isolated from his, predictably, WASP family, which goes off to the family summer home without a second thought, leaving him alone in the town. He suffers from "a perpetual ache" that his doctor cannot diagnose, and after a day of failed attempts at human interaction, he goes home and shoots himself.

Richard Cory is far from realistic. Much of its dialogue is in verse, and it has an expressionistic quality about it, with its self-conscious, sticho-mythic dialogue, flat characters, and clearly stated theme of modern isolation and alienation. Gurney's framing of the play's "literarity," or existence as art, was to be further developed as a technique in the 1980s. Gurney has made it abundantly clear in the presentation of six of his plays from the 1980s that he wants them to be seen as self-consciously metatheatrical, self-referential, or as he prefers to put it, self-reflexive. His introduction to the volume *Love Letters and Two Other Plays: The Golden Age* and *What I Did Last Summer* (1990) begins: "These are three plays about writing." To be even more precise, he later explains that "all three plays have to do with men who use writing as a mode of self-liberation, and their relationships with women who seem to be able to embrace a freer, more spirited life on their own." Asked about the then-yet to be produced *Cocktail Hour* in a 1988 interview, he commented:

> The conflict is about a man in his early middle years who comes home to his city to ask his parents' permission to stage a play he has written. He is sensitive enough to want to ask his parents. But they won't even read it. The idea of being made public is not to their liking. The name of the writer's play is "The Cocktail Hour." It's very self-reflexive.

In the introduction to the 1990 volume *The Cocktail Hour and Two Other Plays: Another Antigone and The Perfect Party* (1989), he carefully laid out the lines along which he wanted the self-reflexivity of the plays to be read:

> *Another Antigone* is about, and should constantly remind us that it is about, both its similarity to and difference from its Greek counterpart. *The Perfect Party,* written as a kind of satyr play to follow it, tries to underscore the connections between a social gathering and the very theatrical event the audience is actually attending. Finally, *The Cocktail Hour,* which ostensibly would seem to be the most realistic of the three, is, in another sense, the most theatrically self-conscious, since it is most of all about itself, and continually calls attention to its own stagecraft.

There are a number of subtexts in Gurney's conscious direction of the reader to see these plays in this way. One, of course, is the implied repudiation of the label "realist" for the works, a term that in the 1980s carried a heavy weight of implication itself—the realistic mode being assumed by many critics to be identical with a putatively smug, self-satisfied, bourgeois, misogynist, elitist, imperialist frame of mind that characterized many of the plays that were written by Europeans and Americans during the late nineteenth century, when realism was the most common dramatic idiom of the literary playwright. Gurney, trying to put some distance between himself and the ubiquitous epithet "WASP," naturally chose to put as much distance as possible between his work and realism. Indeed he sounds more like Gurney the professor than Gurney the playwright in his careful description of the plays' subversion of dramatic realism:

> These characters struggling to break the bonds of the world they were born into and these plays pressing against the limitations of their own form, give my work, I hope, a theatricality which undercuts the conventions of realistic drama and the complacencies of the upper-middle-class milieu which I tend to write about.

In the postmodern spirit of the eighties, Gurney also speaks of the "built-in 'playfulness' " of his self-reflexive forms. Another subtext emerges, however, from his concern that this playfulness, "along with the fact that I write about WASPS, seems to open me up to the charge of being shallow and superficial." Considering his postmodern emphasis of play, of formal subversion, of self-reflexivity, this concern seems misplaced, and its juxtaposition with these literary aims suggests a conflicted author and more complex aesthetics than he owns up to.

What remains unspoken in Gurney's introduction to *The Cocktail Hour* is the play's obvious reference to T. S. Eliot, a reference that is made explicitly in the play more than once. Perhaps it remains unspoken because Gurney's allusion, or *hommage,* to Eliot points the spectator or reader away from the playful, self-reflexive, constantly shifting world of the postmodern and back toward the more realistic aesthetics and the high-modernist quest for the sacred and the moral of Eliot's *Cocktail Party.* Gurney has made it clear that his vision is comic, in the formal sense, that he seeks closure for his plays in a "reconciliation . . . between the individual and the world." Noting that in the European tradition, in the plays of Jean-Baptiste Molière, William Congreve, and Noël Coward, for example, "the world is always put back together by the end," while in "American comedies, there's anarchism at the end— Huck Finn says goodbye and shoves off for the territories, Holden Caulfield ends up in the madhouse"—Gurney concludes that his seeking a reconciliation between the individual and the larger society goes "against the grain of the American embracing of private freedom." This is hardly the aesthetics of a postmodernist. It is in fact closer to that of a neoclassicist, and Gurney reveals his affinity with this point of view in a work such as *Another Antigone.*

The disjunction between the two versions of Gurney's aesthetics does not necessarily suggest a hopeless contradiction. It might point instead to an aesthetic dialectic, in which the playwright makes use of some of the literary methods of the postmodern milieu in which he lives to dramatize a fundamentally realistic vision. *The Golden Age* (1981), perhaps because it is the earliest of the self-reflexive plays about writing, provides the most clear-cut example of Gurney's allusive aesthetics. Gurney notes that the play was "suggested by a story of Henry James." The "story" is *The Aspern Papers,* a novella based on an anecdote that James had heard about Lord Byron's lover Jane Claremont and a Boston critic.

The narrator, who is a critic and the editor of the poet Jeffrey Aspern's papers, goes to Venice in pursuit of a cache of love letters that he believes is in the possession of Juliana Bordereau, who had been romantically involved with Aspern in the 1820s. He becomes acquainted with Juliana and her grandniece Tina by assuming a false identity and persuading them to rent him some rooms in their large palazzo, where he tries to insinuate himself into their confidence so they will show him the letters. A climactic scene occurs when Juliana catches the narrator trying to steal the letters; she hisses passionately, "Ah you publishing scoundrel!"

Following Juliana's death, the helpless Tina first leads the narrator to believe that if he will marry her, she will give him the Aspern papers, but she thinks better of it and destroys them. Throughout the story, James depicts the literary critic as a hypocritical liar and thief who will do almost anything to exploit the writer's life for his own profit. James' narrative technique allows the narrator to incriminate himself, inviting the reader to indict him, and by extension the whole critical profession. The narrator argues that the end justifies the means—in this case, bringing Jeffrey Aspern's intimate relationship with Juliana to light justifies lying and hypocrisy, the manipulation and exploitation of human weakness, and finally the commodification of himself as a unit of exchange in a marriage bargain. In constructing his narrative, however, James makes it clear that the justification is far from adequate, and the narrator is revealed as morally bankrupt at the end of the story.

In *The Golden Age,* Gurney examines many of the same moral issues, but with some crucial differences. Since the play is kept within the confines of realism, there is no privileged communication between any of the characters and the audience. Gurney capitalizes on this generic limitation, giving the female characters, in this case Isabel Hastings Hoyt and her granddaughter Virginia, as full development as he gives the critic Tom. Gurney changes the locale of the play to New York, and the focus of the critic's interest from a romantic poet to F. Scott Fitzgerald. Tom, who teaches American literature at Hunter College, has discovered that Isabel, a central figure in the jazz-age social set that Fitzgerald wrote about, is living in a New York brownstone. He approaches her with the idea of writing a book about her, which he thinks will reveal something new about the intimate lives of Fitzgerald and other artists. Isabel tantalizes Tom with the hint that a black folder she has contains a chapter from an early *Great Gatsby* manuscript describing an explicit sexual scene between Daisy and Gatsby. Meanwhile she maneuvers Tom and Virginia into a romantic relationship that she hopes will lead to marriage. In the course of the play she manages to reveal nothing about herself or Fitzgerald.

In developing the conflict between Isabel and Tom over the manuscript, Gurney focuses on issues that are similar to the ones James raises in *The Aspern Papers.* Isabel tells Tom, "I don't like academics. They're all so hungry . . . hungry for *life.* They suck your blood." By contrast, "a real writer brings *in* life. He creates it." Tom's defense of his pursuit of the manuscript—"I mean, is it a crime to love literature around here? Is it a major crime to want to preserve the past?"—is belied by the mercenary terms in which he conceptualizes his relationship with Isabel: "I am *speculating* on you. I'm not getting a nickel for doing this. Nothing. No publisher has been willing to cough up one red cent until we produce something tangible and concrete. . . . Now I'm *betting* on you,

Mrs. Hoyt. I'm putting my life on the line here." It is of course Isabel whose life is on the line, not Tom, but having converted that life into a potentially saleable commodity, he has lost sight of the human being to whom it rightfully belongs.

As in *Another Antigone,* Gurney voices in *The Golden Age* what he sees as a moral danger that is peculiar to the academic. Responding to Virginia's accusation that he is "lost in the lost generation," Tom says, "Maybe she's right. Maybe I'm so much in love with the past that I can't love anything else. . . . I think we're a greedy, vulgar society and we're spinning out of control." The danger that Gurney sees is the use of an idealized past—Tom's notion of the 1920s as a Golden Age—to escape the moral and social imperatives of the present, and in essence, withdraw from the responsibilities of the human social contract. In a world that is considered greedy, vulgar, and out of control, Tom has no ethical standards to meet either in his professional treatment of Fitzgerald and Isabel or in his personal treatment of Isabel and Virginia.

Unlike James, but in the spirit of his fundamentally comic aesthetics, Gurney allows Tom a moral redemption, although he does not go so far as to suggest that he and Virginia can have a future together. In his play, it is Tom who makes the Jamesian act of renunciation, when Virginia offers him the manuscript a month after her grandmother's death, unencumbered by any suggestion of marriage. Tom is able to say no because he is writing his own book now. The implication is that Tom's move from vampire critic to life-creating writer has begun the redemptive process that will allow him finally to "connect" with his own living world.

Gurney is also much more hopeful about Virginia's future than James is about Tina's. After Tom renounces the manuscript, she burns it, ending her dependency on her grandmother, and bids Tom goodbye. In a little self-reflexive gesture, Gurney has her tell Tom the manuscript was only a play called *The Golden Age,* by Walter Babcock McCoy. Gurney's subversion of the generic expectations of comedy in withholding the "boy gets girl" ending actually serves to emphasize the moral redemption of Tom and the empowerment of Virginia that suggest more hope for the future than their sexual union could. They have renounced each other as well as the fame and financial security represented by the manuscript, a genuine loss for both, but Gurney suggests that their development as human beings is well worth it.

In *The Cocktail Hour,* while maintaining the mimetic illusion, Gurney extends the "play" about the play from a single suggestion to the whole play. John has come to ask his parents' permission to produce a play about them called *The Cocktail Hour.* In the course of the action, he constantly reveals what will happen in Gurney's play by telling the characters what happens in his play. Although Gurney's allusion to Eliot's *Cocktail Party* is not made explicit, it is revealed in the characters' discussion of John's play. As his father says of the title: "It will confuse everyone. They'll come expecting T. S. Eliot, and they'll get John. Either way, they'll want their money back."

Although its aesthetics are playful, this work embodies a moral debate that is similar to that of *The Golden Age.* In this case it is the playwright rather than the critic who is on trial, but he also faces a moral dilemma. To what extent is the writer justified in exposing the private lives of people who would prefer to keep them private in order to create a work of art? Once again the form is comic, proceeding to the celebratory dinner at the end and John's reconciliation with his father, although once again a renunciation is required, in this case of John's real vision of the truth about his family. Visually, the comic celebration is also undercut by John's being left alone on the stage with his play while the rest of the family troops off to dinner.

Gurney's moral statement in these self-reflexive plays is clear. The reconciliation "between the individual and the world" is primary, and the individual who chooses to remain outside the social contract cannot be fully happy. But this reconciliation demands the renunciation of some individual desires and even the compromising of some personal principles. In his hope for the future, there is also a sense of loss. His comic vision, like James', is dark, subverted, and ironic, but it is a comic vision nonetheless, and one that is grounded on humanistic values and a belief in social responsibility. Gurney may use some of the techniques of the postmodern idiom, but the vision they help to realize complicates their aesthetic implications immensely. Beyond his playful structures, A. R. Gurney is a deeply serious playwright, negotiating a classical set of values through a murky postmodern moral landscape.

LITERARY ALLUSIONS

As a kind of gloss on his allusive plays of the 1980s, Gurney returned to Henry James in the 1993 play *Later Life.* Although both the program for the production and the published play bear the line "the author is indebted to Henry James," Gurney is a bit more enigmatic about the source for this play than for the earlier ones, perhaps because identifying it as James' "The Beast in the Jungle" would give away the ending. Interestingly, while only two of the New York critics recognized the source, almost all considered *Later Life* one of Gurney's best plays from a theatrical point of view, nearly perfect in its architectonics, with brilliantly witty and entertaining dialogue of the kind that, among contemporary American playwrights, only A. R. Gurney is capable of writing, and above all, a moving experience in the theater.

"Beast in the Jungle" is a novella about John Marcher, who conceives early in life of the idea that he has been singled out for a dark and special fate, a metaphorical "beast" that may spring at any time, and that his life's work is to watch and wait for the event. He renounces his chance for human fulfillment by preferring to have his friend May Bartram wait with him rather than forge a deeper relationship with her. The two spend their lives watching and waiting for the beast. It is only after May's death, when Marcher witnesses the deeply felt grieving of a man at his wife's grave, that he realizes that the beast has already sprung, and that his fate was to have been the man of his time "to whom nothing on earth was to have happened." He has given up, through his own invincible egotism, the one chance that he had to escape his fate, which was to love May.

Gurney presents the situation in the context of a Boston party where Austin, a lonely WASP divorcé, meets Ruth, whom he had known briefly many years earlier on the Isle of Capri. Ruth has just separated from her passionate but parasitic, and possibly abusive, husband, making the evening the single chance for them to break out of the destructive, well-worn grooves of their lives and form a meaningful connection with each other. Ruth tells Austin that when they first met, he had spent the whole evening talking about his belief that "something awful was going to descend on [him] and ruin [his] life forever." Austin reveals that his life has been conventionally successful; he became a banker, married the boss's daughter, raised two children, and then got divorced, "the best thing to happen in a long, long time." As Austin and Ruth talk, they come to realize that "a second chance" is being given to them, a chance for a deeply fulfilling relationship. When the time comes, however, Austin fails to rise to the occasion. Ruth's husband, who has flown in from Las Vegas, calls and asks her to meet him. It is a moment of challenge to the repressed Austin, who, in response to her husband's passionate pursuit, can only offer Ruth his guest room and suggest "if, when we're there, you'd

like to . . . to join me in my room, if you'd care to slip into my bed, naturally I'd like that very much." Ruth responds, "Oh, Austin. Austin from Boston. You're such a good man" and goes off to meet her husband. First, however, she tells Austin that the terrible thing has already happened to him, and she hopes that he will never find out what it was because he will go through "absolute hell . . . you'll clear your throat, and square your shoulders, and straighten your tie— and stand there quietly and take it. That's the hellish part." This is exactly what Austin does as the curtain closes on his realization that he has lost Ruth again, and he does not have it in him to pursue her as her husband has.

Like James, Gurney points out the dangers of renunciation in cutting oneself off from human contact. Like the WASPs, who, Gurney says, are trying now to come "out of their shells, out of their clubs" and join the rest of the democratic society, Austin can only save himself by getting off the terrace and joining the heterogeneous characters who keep emerging from the party and intruding on his isolation.

Gurney makes a similar point with the play *Overtime* (1995), a lighthearted "sequel" to Shakespeare's *Merchant of Venice,* which explores ethnic interaction in a multicultural society. The play begins at the end of Shakespeare's, with the pairing off of the young people that marks its comic ending. Gurney uses the situation in Venice to write about the splintering of modern democracy into wrangling groups based on ethnicity and gender. Jessica, a self-identified Jewish-American princess, breaks up with Lorenzo, a self-hating WASP who desperately wants to be Jewish, and goes off temporarily with a Chinese waiter. She ends up with Nerissa, who discovers her Hispanic heritage while Gratiano finds his African roots, and both become conscious of their exploitation by Bassanio and Portia. Antonio discovers that he is gay and Bassanio, who is ambivalent about his sexuality, decides to join the marines. Portia goes bankrupt and ends up with Shylock. They celebrate by giving a party for everyone, in celebration, as Shylock says, of "the social contract." This is hardly a serious study of the splintering of American society based on the overemphasis of difference, but it suggests that, and its ending implies that a new, more open, more tolerant, richer, and more varied society can be built if the various groups are willing to recognize the value of community as well as their own self-interest.

THE PROLIFIC PERIOD

In 1982, his children for the most part educated and out of the house, Gurney decided to take an extended leave of absence from the Massachusetts Institute of Technology and become a full-time playwright. He and his wife sold their house in Boston and moved into an apartment on the Upper West Side of New York, ending what he called his "hyphenated life" and beginning an extraordinarily prolific period as a playwright. In the years between 1982 and 1999, Gurney had no fewer than sixteen new plays produced, including those that critics consider his most significant—*The Dining Room* (1982), *The Perfect Party* (1986), *Another Antigone, The Cocktail Hour, Love Letters* (1988), and *Later Life*—as well as the commercially successful *Sweet Sue* (1986) and *Sylvia* (1995).

Fortunately for Gurney, the success of his "break-though play," *The Dining Room,* coincided with his move to New York. First treated as an experiment in the tiny upstairs space at Playwrights Horizon, it was quickly moved to the main stage there after it received very favorable reviews in the New York press, and it has since had a long production life in regional and college theaters. *The Dining Room* combines a number of Gurney's interests and strengths as a playwright. He has often said that plots don't particu-

larly interest him, and he has often experimented with ways of shifting the audience's interest and expectations from time to space, from the sequence of events to the locale in which they take place. This play focuses on the dining room as the physical representation for a vanishing culture, that of the northeastern American WASP that Gurney knows so well. In his Author's Note, he says that "it brings together in a single resonant space the fragmented, mosaic structure" he had explored in *Scenes from American Life, Richard Cory,* and *The Wayside Motor Inn.* "Like *Children,* it takes place over the course of one day, yet like *The Middle Ages,* it leaps through a number of years." Although he acknowledges the influence of Thornton Wilder's *The Long Christmas Dinner,* Gurney has said that the idea for the play originated in his own life, when, during the oil crisis of the 1970s, he and his wife decided to close off their living room and turn the dining room into a family room in order to conserve energy. He came to realize that in doing away with the dining room, they were saying goodbye to a whole way of life, the ritualized upper-middle-class world of their youth.

A number of critics have called *The Dining Room* an "anthropological study," and although it satirizes the anthropological point of view in one of its scenes, it does have this quality. The play, meant to be performed by six actors in multiple roles, consists of a series of scenes that reflect the changing manners, mores, and values in middle-class family life from the 1930s to the 1980s. Gurney notes that "the blending and overlapping of scenes have been carefully worked out to give a sense of both contrast and flow . . . . The play should never degenerate into a series of blackouts." Scenes in the present: a real estate agent trying to sell a house to a client who can't imagine what he will do with a dining room; two latchkey teenagers preparing to get drunk on gin and vodka; a grown daughter trying unsuccessfully to persuade her father to let her come back "home"; and an Amherst student filming his great-aunt for his anthropology class as she shows him her china and silver and explains what it was used for, blend with scenes in the past: a father makes his son late for school while he holds forth at breakfast; a boy eats lunch with his grandfather in an effort to convince him to pay for his boarding school tuition (per his parents' instructions); an elderly woman with Alzheimer's disease keeps trying to leave the family Thanksgiving dinner to go "home"; and a maid announces her retirement, among others.

While there is a sense of loss here, of a stability and structure that no longer exists, there is no sentimentality or nostalgia. The overall import of this comedy is to suggest that it is a good thing to have left the old culture of the dining room, with its oppressive manners and its exploited servants, behind, but that the dining room itself should not be abandoned. The celebratory image at the end is of a party where the hostess wants to invite "everyone we've ever known and liked. We'd have the man who fixes our Toyota, and that intelligent young couple who bought the Payton house, and the receptionist at the doctor's office, and the new teller at the bank. And our children would be invited too. And they'd all come back from wherever they are." Like most of Gurney's work, it suggests a better, more democratic society with a less rigid, more human family structure rather than a wholesale rejection of the past. Gurney sees value in the dining room and the civil human interaction it represents.

The Perfect Party is a kind of companion piece to *The Dining Room* as well as a sardonically autobiographical play. Tony, a middle-aged college professor, has quit his teaching job in order to devote himself to creating "the perfect party." He has invited a critic from "the major New York newspaper" to review his party in the hope that it will be a big hit and enable him to make a living as a professional party consultant. The parallel with Gurney's decision to become a full-time

playwright is obviously intentional. Although it has a realistic structure, the play is too self-reflexive to be contained in that mode. The dialogue is a self-conscious version of the witty drawing-room comedy of the 1930s, with many allusions to Oscar Wilde, and the action is a fable about the dangers of compromising one's artistic integrity for commercial success. To secure a favorable review from the critic, Lois, Tony disguises himself as a "bad" twin brother, Tod ("death"), who seduces her. When she gives the party a bad review anyway, he complains that "it's almost as if Lois had attended an entirely different party. Didn't she hear the singing? Jesus, what kind of a country do we live in where one person calls the critical shots? It's cultural fascism, that's what it is! It's Nazi Germany!" For Gurney, whose New York career began with a devastating review from the *New York Times*, which was not to be his last, this serves as a little warning against pandering to critics in order to secure commercial success by winning their approval. Interestingly, the New York critics loved the play, including Frank Rich of the *New York Times,* who praised it as a daring leap forward, which signaled the emergence of a new and inventive style for Gurney.

The play reaches somewhat beyond the fairly parochial concerns of the New York theater, indicating that the perfect party is also a metaphor for the ideal democratic society. Tony, a professor of American Studies, has tried to assemble a "microcosm for America itself, in the waning years of the twentieth century" in his guest list, so that, as Lois comments, "if the party succeeds, it will mean that America itself, as a social and political experiment, will have succeeded." The party at first breaks down and splinters into various hostile groups—the young people, the elderly, various ethnic groups, "the gays and the born-agains"—and the workers become resentful and sullen. One of the guests comments that it is like an image of America itself. Enlightenment comes when Tony's wife, Sally, explains to him that what he had been trying to do was an instance of cultural imperialism and that "this impulse to control, to shape, to achieve perfection permeates the fabric of this country." When Sally explains to him that it doesn't work, either at home or abroad, Tony realizes that all his party has done is "take American idealism, and reveal it for the dark, destructive dream it really is." However, as Tony begins to despair about the future, the doorbell rings and the guests arrive, assembled voluntarily this time, without Tony's imposition of the form of the "perfect party" upon them. Sally tells him "there will be no shaping or judging or interrupting unless someone gets physically violent or is obviously misinformed." There will be no caterer, and all of the guests have promised to bring ethnic dishes and help clean up afterward. When Tony worries that it will turn into chaos, Sally replies that it's the chance he'll have to take, and she forgives him because, in all his foolishness, she senses "a fundamental yearning to create a vital human community in this impossible land of ours."

If *The Perfect Party* was an unlikely hit with the critics, Gurney's next play, *Sweet Sue,* was an unexpected and devastating failure, although with two fine actresses and "big name" stars in Mary Tyler Moore and Lynn Redgrave, it ran for six months on Broadway, a commercial success. *Sweet Sue* is a further development of the subject of *What I Did Last Summer,* Gurney's treatment of the relationship between a middle-aged woman and a teenage boy, as well as an exploration of the mother–son relationship that he had touched on in *Children. Last Summer,* which is set in the summer of 1945, is a coming-of-age play in which the fourteen-year-old protagonist, Charlie, is caught between the values and demands of his upper-middle-class WASP family, embodied in his mother, Grace, and the influence of Anna, a free-spirited and iconoclastic art teacher who brings Charlie to some awareness of

the limitations and restrictiveness of his parents' world. A climax comes when Charlie is being pressured by Grace to go with her to a party where he can make connections that will "smooth the way" for him at the boarding school where his parents are sending him to curb his rebellious tendencies. After much tension between the two of them, Grace finally explodes and slaps Charlie, and he rips off his father's tie, and then the rest of his clothes, and runs down to the lake to dive in naked and get "really clean." Charlie temporarily refuses to go away to school and escapes to Anna's farm, where he says he can "live in her barn, and eat her tomatoes, and realize my potential any time I want!" Charlie comes to realize the folly of such unbridled freedom when he borrows Anna's car and crashes, putting himself and his fourteen-year-old girlfriend in the hospital.

Having suggested the danger of unbridled Dionysian freedom, Gurney's ending affirms traditional structures, with Grace refusing to accept Anna's description of her giving up painting to become a full-time wife and mother as "the shadow of a life," Anna being forced to sell her property and live in the city, and Charlie reluctantly bidding Anna goodbye and heading off to boarding school. Significantly, World War II is ending, and Charlie's father is coming back to reassert his control of the family. The value of Anna's influence is suggested, however, in Charlie's final line: "So I tried photography in boarding school. And took up writing in college. And finally, last summer, I wrote this play." The implication is that Charlie finally does realize his potential and that what he has absorbed of Anna's creative spirit has managed to evade his parents' and their culture's zealous efforts to repress it.

Sweet Sue presents a similar relationship, but from the woman's point of view. Susan is an illustrator of Hallmark cards who has never been able to draw a convincing nude. She has decided to take the summer off and work seriously on her art, trying to recapture the creative impulse that had originally inspired her and to push through the inhibitions that have kept her from developing. Unbeknownst to Sue, her son Ted, an off-stage character who spends all of his time with his girlfriend, has invited his college roommate Jake to spend the summer at Sue's house while the two boys paint houses. Sue and Jake become friends, eating meals and spending a good deal of time together, and gradually fall in love, although their emotions never find physical expression. Sue is physically repressed; Jake is emotionally repressed. He tells her that he is working on becoming "normal," that is learning to interact with a girl at other levels than sexually. This schematic interaction is heightened by Gurney's addition of the characters Susan Too and Jake Too. Unlike most plays with split or alternate characters, *Sweet Sue*'s second characters do not represent deeper, psychological doubles. Gurney makes a point of this in the stage directions, saying "it would be a mistake to break the parts down into different psychological aspects or alter-egos of the characters. Rather we should see two different but complete approaches to each role, as if we were attempting to sketch the human figure from two different perspectives." He has referred to his technique as a "double voice," allowing him to tell the same story from multiple perspectives at the same time.

Gurney has said the play started out as a retelling of the the myth of Phaedra and Hippolytus, but it became more of a study of the emergence of Sue's artistic and emotional freedom in which the cultural struggle that is enacted by Grace and Anna in *What I Did Last Summer* goes on within Susan herself. The most important relationship in the play is not between Susan and Jake but between Susan and Susan Too. In the end, Susan and Jake go their separate ways. Jake believes that their falling in love and her treating him "like a man" has freed them both to "start the ball rolling" in other relationships, he with a girl he has met in a bar and she with a longtime

suitor. It is possible to read the ending in several different ways, as Susan's account of her final meetings with Jake is intentionally unreliable, but their relationship seems to have freed something in her as an artist. Drawing Jake from memory, she is able to draw a male nude "with a sex organ" for the first time.

Sweet Sue was Gurney's first play to originate on Broadway, and he has indicated that he was unhappy with the changes he was forced to make during out-of-town tryouts in order to make the show viable commercially. The New York critics condemned it as pretentious and confusing, or simply an arty version of Robert Anderson's *Tea and Sympathy.* Nor did they care very much for *Another Antigone,* which followed it. Because of some advance publicity that backfired, *Antigone* was mistakenly viewed as primarily a play about anti-Semitism. Gurney's next two plays, however, were to prove his most successful, both with critics and with audiences. *The Cocktail Hour* and *Love Letters* were a return to his roots, in a sense, as analyses of the culture he knew best. He has said that there was no specific incident in his life that corresponded to the situation in *The Cocktail Hour,* but that his plays did produce tension in his relationship with his family. Gurney's father refused to speak to him for a time after seeing *Scenes from American Life,* a few scenes of which depicted incidents that had occurred in the Gurney family. Gurney has said that his father's death in 1977 made him feel freer to explore this territory as an artist, which he immediately did with *The Middle Ages,* a play that is set in the trophy room of a social club. It opens with a son's threat to make a speech denouncing the whole WASP way of life at his father's funeral and ends with his revelation that he had bought the club with the proceeds of his pornography business and had been planning to give it to his father.

In *Love Letters,* Gurney went back to an eighteenth-century literary form, the epistolary novel, and adapted it to the stage through the most minimal of conventions. The play consists of a series of letters between Andrew Makepeace Ladd III and Melissa Gardner, which record a rather Jamesian relationship lasting fifty years, from the age of seven until Melissa's death. Typical of Gurney, the play is a love story that dramatizes a series of missed opportunities and a brief sexual affair between two people who are fated by their own natures and the world in which they are brought up to constantly make choices that will not fulfill them or make them happy, although they might be the "right" choices for fulfilling the expectations of their families or their duties of one kind or another. The unhappy, emotionally neglected child of an alcoholic mother, Melissa becomes an alcoholic herself and, after several failed marriages, loses custody of her children. Andy marries a woman he doesn't love, becomes a lawyer and a U.S. senator, and when he and Melissa finally get together, gives her up because of his duty to his family and his desire to stay in office. The intriguing thing about the play is its technique. From its opening production with Stockard Channing and John Rubenstein, the play has been staged in an absolutely minimal way, with the two characters sitting side-by-side at a desk and reading their letters directly to the audience. This makes the audience into a third character in the play, creating a triangulated dynamic in the performance that makes the spectator's experience particularly immediate. Because there is no movement and it is not necessary to memorize the lines, the play can be staged with very little rehearsal, and in the original production, new actors were brought in every week to play the parts, which soon became choice roles for many of them.

Most critics mistakenly present Gurney as a fairly conventional, realistic playwright, partly because of his middle-class subject matter. In fact, very few of Gurney's plays fall within the mode of realistic drama, and he has experimented throughout his career with both dramatic form and theatrical technique. One of his earliest plays, *The Bridal Dinner* (1962), employs self-reflexive, Pirandellian techniques to achieve a Brechtian estrangement that will allow his audience to give the desired critical consideration to his treatment of contemporary marriage. In *The Rape of Bunny Stuntz* (1962), he broke through the realistic "fourth-wall illusion" by employing the device of having the protagonist address the audience as if it were at a meeting, as Clifford Odets did in *Waiting for Lefty,* although for humorous effect. His experiments with absurdism and with the disruption of time have been mentioned. In *The Wayside Motor Inn,* he also fragmented the concept of space, by using one set to represent five different motel rooms, with five sets of actors acting five different "actions" while present simultaneously on the same set.

In *The Fourth Wall* (1992), Gurney brought experimentation to the forefront, making it the subject of the play. This play is metatheater with a vengeance. It features what would be a typical living room set in a play that was in the mode of middle-class realism, except that all of the furniture is arranged to face the room's "fourth wall," the "invisible" wall that is the audience. The wall is the central thematic focus of the play, which has four characters, a married couple named Roger and Peggy, their friend Julia, and Professor Loesser, who is brought in as an expert in drama to help the other three understand the wall and find plot lines that they can enact in front of it. Loesser explains that Peggy is "subtly challenging western democratic capitalism" by setting up the wall, saying that "there is something more than material success and the quaint pleasure of hearth and home . . . there is a world elsewhere, a world beyond this wall, which is far more worth reaching for." There turn out to be two competing plots. Peggy is the subject of a Joan of Arc plot in which she yearns to save the democratic ideal by breaking out of the fourth wall and making connections with the audience and the larger society beyond. Julia hopes to involve Roger in what Loesser describes as "a cheap throw-back to the continental sex comedy." In the course of the evening, a number of walls are broken through, as Julia forms her first nonsexual relationship with a member of the opposite sex by bonding with the gay Loesser, Peggy breaks out of the living room, heading out into the audience and up the aisle to go to Washington and save democracy, and Roger follows her, deciding that he's "played the lead too long" and is ready to accept a supporting role in his marriage. The play is an entertaining comedy with classic Gurneyan dialogue—sophisticated, slightly satirical, witty, and funny—but it also raises serious questions about the theater's role at the end of the twentieth century.

In a way, Gurney came full circle in the thirty years between *The Bridal Dinner* and *The Fourth Wall*, using nonrealistic self-reflexive forms in both works to discuss the theater and its role in American society. But the questions he raised in the nineties were quite different from those that occupied him in the sixties. While the earlier questions were personal—Should I marry?—the later ones were public—What is the theater's responsibility to a democratic society? They are in some sense the measure of the broadening of Gurney's vision during his forty years as a playwright. Although he has done it with a light comic touch, like his Greek hero Sophocles, Gurney has tried to use the theater to investigate fundamental human values and responsibilities. His subject is the individual in relation to others, in the family, in the workplace, among friends, and in the larger society. He has dramatized his subject with a recognizable voice and from a particular vantage point, which might be defined as "upper-middle-class, northeastern, white Anglo-Saxon Protestant, classically educated, liberal humanist," and he has made it well worth attending to.

Selected Bibliography

WORKS OF A. R. GURNEY

COLLECTED PLAYS

A. R. Gurney: Collected Works.
Vol. I. *Nine Early Plays 1961–1973.* Lyme, N.H.: Smith and Kraus, 1995. (Includes *The Comeback, The Rape of Bunny Stuntz, The Golden Fleece, The David Show, The Problem, The Love Course, The Open Meeting, The Old One-Two,* and *Scenes from American Life.*)
Vol. II. *Collected Plays 1974–1983.* Lyme, N.H.: Smith and Kraus, 1997. (Includes *Children, Richard Cory, The Middle Ages, The Wayside Motor Inn, The Dining Room,* and *What I Did Last Summer.*)
Four Plays. New York: Avon, 1985. (Includes *Scenes from American Life, Children, The Middle Ages,* and *The Dining Room.*)
The Cocktail Hour and Two Other Plays: Another Antigone and The Perfect Party. New York: Plume, 1989.
Love Letters and Two Other Plays: The Golden Age and What I Did Last Summer. New York: Plume, 1990.
Later Life and Two Other Plays: The Snow Ball and The Old Boy. New York: Plume Press, 1994.

SINGLE PLAYS

Three People. In *Best Short Plays, 1955–56.* Edited by Margaret Mayorga. New York: Beacon Press, 1956.
Turn of the Century. In *Best Short Plays, 1957–58.* Edited by Margaret Mayorga. New York: Beacon Press, 1958.
Love in Buffalo. Produced, 1958.
Tom Sawyer (musical). Produced, 1959.
The Bridal Dinner. Produced, 1962; in *First Stage: A Quarterly of New Drama* 4.1: 33–56 (Spring 1965).
As "Peter Gurney," *Around the World in Eighty Days.* New York: Dramatic Publishing, 1962.
The Rape of Bunny Stuntz. Produced, 1962; New York: Samuel French, 1964.
The Comeback. Produced, 1964; New York: Dramatists Play Service, 1966.
The Golden Fleece. Produced, 1968; New York: Samuel French, 1967.

The Open Meeting. Produced, 1965; New York: Samuel French, 1968.

The David Show. Produced, 1966; New York: Samuel French, 1968.

The Problem. Produced, 1973; New York: Samuel French, 1968; published as *Public Affairs.* New York: Samuel French, 1992.

Tonight in Living Color (combines *The David Show* and *The Golden Fleece*). Produced, 1969.

The Love Course. Produced, 1970; New York: Samuel French, 1969.

Scenes from American Life. Produced, 1970; New York: Samuel French, 1970.

The Old One-Two. Produced, 1973; New York: Samuel French, 1971.

Children. Produced, 1974; New York: Samuel French, 1975.

Who Killed Richard Cory? Produced, 1976; New York: Samuel French, 1976; Produced as *Richard Cory,* 1986.

The Middle Ages. Produced, 1977; New York: Dramatists Play Service, 1978.

The Wayside Motor Inn. Produced, 1977; New York: Dramatists Play Service, 1979.

The Golden Age. Produced, 1981; New York: Dramatists Play Service, 1984.

The Dining Room. Produced, 1982; New York: Dramatists Play Service, 1982.

What I Did Last Summer. Produced, 1983; New York: Dramatists Play Service, 1983.

The Perfect Party. Produced, 1986; New York: Doubleday, 1986 and New York: Dramatists Play Service, 1986.

Sweet Sue. Produced, 1986; New York: Dramatists Play Service, 1987.

Another Antigone. Produced, 1987; New York: Dramatists Play Service, 1988.

The Cocktail Hour. Produced, 1988; New York: Doubleday, 1989.

Love Letters. Produced, 1988; New York: Dramatists Play Service, 1989.

The Snow Ball. Produced, 1990; New York: Dramatists Play Service, 1992. (adaptation of the novel)

The Old Boy. Produced, 1991; New York: Dramatists Play Service, 1992.

The Fourth Wall. Produced, 1992; New York: Dramatists Play Service, 1994.

Later Life. Produced, 1993; New York: Dramatists Play Service, 1994.

A Cheever Evening. Produced, 1994; New York: Dramatists Play Service, 1995.

Sylvia. Produced, 1995; New York: Dramatists Play Service, 1996.

Overtime. Produced, 1995; New York: Dramatists Play Service, 1996.

Let's Do It (musical). Produced, 1996.

Labor Day. Produced, 1998.

Darlene and *The Guest Lecturer.* Produced, 1998.

Far East. Produced, 1999.

FICTION

"Buffalo Meat." *Horae Scholasticae* 79.4: 89–90 (1945).

The Gospel According to Joe. New York: Harper & Row, 1974.

Entertaining Strangers. New York: Doubleday, 1977.

The Snow Ball. New York: Arbor House, 1984.

SCREENPLAYS

The House of Mirth, 1972.

Love Letters, Columbia, 1992.

Sylvia, Paramount, 1995.

TELEPLAYS

The Golden Fleece, N.E.T. Playhouse, National Educational Television, November 8, 1969.

O Youth and Beauty (adapted from the John Cheever story), Great Performances, PBS, 1979.

The Dining Room (based on his play), Great Performances, PBS, 1984.

The Hit List, Trying Times, PBS-TV, 1989.

ARTICLES

"Pushing the Walls of Dramatic Form." *New York Times,* July 27, 1986, pp. II, 1.

"The Dinner Party." *American Heritage,* September/October 1988, pp. 69–71.

"Conversation Piece." *Newsweek,* June 26, 1989, pp. 10–11.

"When the Final Act Is Only a Beginning." *New York Times,* October 27, 1991, pp. H5–6.

"Critical Condition." *American Theatre,* June 1991, pp. 24–27.

ADAPTATIONS

A musical version of *Richard Cory* by Ed Dixon was produced at O'Neill Theatre, 1997.

The Middle Ages was adapted by Percy Granger for the ABC television special *His Brother's Wife.*

SECONDARY WORKS

INTERVIEWS

Damsker, Matt. "A. R. Gurney, Jr. The Voice of WASPs." *Hartford Courant,* December 28, 1986.

DiGaetani, John L. "A. R. Gurney." In *A Search for a Postmodern Theater: Interviews with Contemporary Playwrights.* Westport, Conn.: Greenwood Press, 1991. Pp. 113–119.

Erstein, Hap. "In the WASPs' Nest with A. R. Gurney." *Washington Times,* August 29, 1989, pp. E2–4.

Forman, Debbie. "Breaking Through 'The Fourth Wall.'" *Cape Cod Times,* August 29, 1992, pp. C1–2.

Gale, William K. "He Takes a Swat at His WASP-ish Past." Providence *Journal-Bulletin,* February 15, 1991, pp. D14+.

Holley, Tim. "Gurney Puts WASPs Under the Microscope." *The Bridgeport* (Connecticut) *Post,* November 6, 1988, pp. F4–5.

Levett, Karl. "A. R. Gurney, Jr., American Original." *Drama* 149: 6–7 (Autumn 1983).

McCulloh, T. H. "The WASP Chronicler." *Los Angeles Times,* April 15, 1990, pp. G12–14.

Skinner, M. Scott. "Playwright Keeps It All So Civilized." *Arizona Daily Star,* November 26, 1989, pp. C12–13.

Sponberg, Arvid F. "A. R. Gurney." In *The Playwright's Art: Conversations with Contemporary American Dramatists.* Edited by Jackson A. Bryer. New Brunswick, N.J.: Rutgers University Press, 1995. Pp. 86–101.

———. "A. R. Gurney, Jr., Playwright." In *Broadway Talks: What Professionals Think About Commercial Theater in America.* Westport, Conn.: Greenwood Press, 1991.

Weiss, Hedy. "Stung WASPs." Chicago *Sun Times,* November 23, 1989, pp. D9, 11.

Welsh, Anne Marie. "Another Gurney for the Globe." *San Diego Union,* May 29, 1988, pp. A11, 13.

Witchel, Alex. "Laughter, Tears and the Perfect Martini." *New York Times Magazine,* November 12, 1989, pp. 42–43, 102–105.

CRITICAL STUDIES

Colakis, Marianthe. "Tragedy into Comedy-Drama: A. R. Gurney's Another Antigone." *Text and Presentation: The Journal of the Comparative Drama Conference* 12: 1–5 (1992).

Contemporary Literary Criticism. Detroit: Gale, 1985–89. Vol. 32, pp. 216–221; Vol. 50, pp. 174–185; Vol. 54, pp. 215–223.

Hornby, Richard. "Role Playing, Self Reference, and Openness." *Hudson Review* 39.3: 472–476 (Autumn 1986).

Laing, Jeffrey M. "Missed Connections in A. R. Gurney's *Love Letters.*" *Notes on Contemporary Literature* 25.2: 3–4 (1995).

McConachie, Bruce A. "*The Dining Room:* A Tocquevillian Take on the Decline of WASP Culture." *Journal of American Drama and Theatre* 10: 39–50 (Winter 1998).

Miller, Laura Hendrix-Branch. "Dancing in Chains: A. R. Gurney's 1980s Plays and How They Reflect Contemporary Culture." Ph.D. Diss, University of Nebraska, 1993.

—BRENDA MURPHY

Erica Jong

1942–

*W*HEN ERICA JONG published her first book in 1971, she did what many authors do: she held a publication party. But the publication party was held in a fruit and vegetable market, and the author read selections from the book—a collection of poems entitled *Fruits & Vegetables*—perched on a crate of grapefruits and oranges. It was a portent of things to come. Throughout her career Jong would continue to playfully explode conventional expectations about where poetry—and women poets—belonged, and whether embracing the flesh of fruits or the fruits of the flesh, in poetry or in prose, Jong would continue to create art that celebrated nature's earthy bounty.

Jong's poetry and fiction—particularly her 1973 bestseller *Fear of Flying*—ignited impassioned debate. Was it art? Was it pornography? And what was a woman doing writing this stuff, anyway? More than any other writer of this era, Jong came to embody the impulse to break out of the stultifying conventions that had so severely limited the roles women could play in American letters. Despite the freshness of her work, however, she is actually heir to a long line of women writers in America—one that begins with the seventeenth-century poet Anne Bradstreet and in the twentieth century embraces figures including Edna St. Vincent Millay, Meridel LeSueur, Sylvia Plath, and Anne Sexton. Despite the controversy it sparked, Jong's writing extends a literary tradition established by such quintessentially canonical figures as Walt Whitman, Theodore Dreiser, and Mark Twain.

With her iconoclastic challenges to a literary establishment that had never fully assimilated the achievement of these renegade precursors, Jong pushed American letters to be more open to the idea of a woman writer's aspirations to come out of the kitchen and dine at the table of literature in her own right. Her poetry, fiction, and essays, as well as her much-profiled personal life, depict a particularly robust version of "having it all": bread and roses; work and love; poetry and prose; children and career; laughter and lust; fortune and fame—and fun.

JONG'S BACKGROUND

Erica Jong grew up on Manhattan's Upper West Side in a home in which the arts were central. Her father, Seymour Mann (né Samuel Weisman), the child of Polish Jews, was a musician. Her mother, Eda Mirsky, the child of Russian Jews who had settled in England before moving to New York, followed the example of her own father (a successful portrait painter and commercial artist) and became a painter. The pair met in the Catskill Mountains when they were teenagers. During the early years of their marriage, Jong's mother worked as a painter and as a designer of clothing and fabrics, while her father got his first job on Broadway, performing "Begin the Beguine" on stage in Cole Porter's show *Jubilee.* But when Eda became pregnant with their first child in 1937, she persuaded her husband to give up show business for work that was more dependable and wouldn't keep him out at night. He became, as Jong put it, "a traveling salesman of tchotchkes" (household knickknacks, dolls, and gifts). Erica was born in 1942.

She spent much of her childhood in a rambling neo-Gothic apartment that took up the top three floors of a building across the street from the Museum of Natural History in Manhattan, in which her grandparents, as well as her parents, lived until shortly after her younger sister was born. Her grandfather's studio occupied the top floor, and Erica often painted alongside him as a child, with "an extra palette filled with such mellifluous colors as alizarin crimson, rose madder, viridian, cobalt blue, chrome yellow, raw umber, Chinese white," on a little canvas he would stretch for her next to his own. He would rage and roar, Jong recalled, "if I 'muddied colors' or failed to take my painting seriously." While Erica's grandfather had a studio, and her father had an office, her mother had to "set up a folding easel when and where she could and resented this bitterly."

Eda Mirsky had been the best draftswoman and painter in her art school class at the National Academy of Design and "had every reason to win the top prizes—including the big traveling fellowship—the Prix de Rome." But she was not sent to Rome.

> When she won the bronze medal and was told—quite frankly (no one was ashamed to be sexist then)—that she hadn't won the Prix de Rome because, as a woman, she was expected to marry, bear children, and waste her gifts, she was enraged.

Her mother sacrificed her art to domesticity and paid a constant daily price. "What I remember most about my mother was that she was always angry," Jong recalled.

> My mother's frustrations powered both my feminism and my writing. But much of the power came out of my anger and my competition: my desire to outdo her, my hatred of her capitulation to her femaleness, my desire to be different because I feared I was too much like her. Womanhood was a trap. If I was too much like her, I'd be trapped as she was. But if I rejected her example, I'd be a traitor to her love. I felt a fraud no matter which way I turned. I had to find a way to be like her and unlike her at the same time. I had to find a way to be both a girl and a boy.

Tillie Olsen once observed how "fortunate are those of us who are daughters born into knowledgeable, ambitious families where no sons are born." Jong was such a daughter. Her mother's stifled creativity and feminist rage, and her father's need for Erica "to be his son," combined to make a "potent brew" that fueled Erica's drive and ambition. "The ingredients were just right to make a girl who thought she was allowed to be a boy. But who also had to punish herself for this presumption."

(Jong would recognize the tensions that she felt as typical of her generation. "We held ourselves back in misplaced loyalty to our mothers," she wrote in *Fear of Fifty: A Midlife Memoir* [1994]. "Since they were not fully free to be assertive, we stayed chained to their limitations as if this bondage were a proof of love . . . . In midlife, with time beating its wings at our backs, we finally snatched the courage to break free. We finally let go of that ambivalence that was our mothers' collective lot—and we crashed through the glass ceiling inside ourselves, to real freedom.")

From her earliest years, Jong wrote as well as painted—notebooks, stories, journals, and poems. After graduating from the High School of Music and Art, she attended Barnard College, where she was the editor of the literary magazine and produced poetry programs for the campus radio station. She received her Bachelor of Arts in 1963 (Phi Beta Kappa and magna cum laude). Few women writers graced the syllabi in any of her literature courses. "Poetry meant William Butler Yeats, James Dickey, Robert Lowell. Without even realizing it, I assumed that the voice of the poet had to be male."

One of "the most notable and faintly horrifying memories" from Jong's college years was

> of the time a distinguished critic came to my creative writing class and delivered himself of this thundering judgment: "Women can't be writers. They don't know blood and guts, and puking in the streets, and fucking whores, and swaggering through Pigalle at five A.M. . . . ." But the most amazing thing was the response—or lack of it. It was 1961 or '62, and we all sat there, aspiring women writers that we were, and listened to this claptrap without a word of protest.

In 1965, two years after she graduated from Barnard, Erica earned a Master of Arts in English from Columbia University and planned to go on for a doctorate in eighteenth-century English literature when she found herself more drawn to the creative writing that was taking increasing amounts of her time and attention. In 1966, after marriage to a fellow graduate student, Michael Werthman, ended in divorce, Erica married Allan Jong, a Chinese-American psychiatrist. The military sent him to Germany shortly after the marriage, and Erica accompanied him there, where she taught at the University of Maryland Overseas Division and pursued her writing. (She had also taught English at the City University of New York from 1964 to 1965 and at Manhattan Community College from 1969 to 1970.)

Her first book of poetry, *Fruits & Vegetables,* was published in 1971 to critical acclaim. Before her second book of poems—*Half-Lives*—was published in 1973, Jong had won an award from

the American Academy of Poets, the Bess Hokin prize from *Poetry Magazine,* a Borestone Mountain Award in poetry, the Madeline Sadin Award from the *New York Quarterly,* and the Alice Faye di Castagnolia Award from the Poetry Society of America. But the event that would catapult Jong from a promising young poet to a world-famous writer was the 1973 publication of her boldly iconoclastic first novel, *Fear of Flying,* a book that would become one of the top ten bestsellers of the decade and that would earn Jong a permanent niche in American literary history.

"I started with poetry," Jong wrote in *What Do Women Want? Bread Roses Sex Power* (1998), "because it was direct, immediate, and short. It was the ecstasy of striking matches in the dark. I went on to fiction because fiction can contain satire and social comment and still tell stories." Other novels continued to appear every three or four years during the next two decades: *How to Save Your Own Life* (1977), *Fanny: Being the True History of the Adventures of Fanny Hackabout-Jones* (1980), *Parachutes & Kisses* (1984), *Shylock's Daughter: A Novel of Love in Venice* (formerly titled *Serenissima: A Novel of Venice*) (1987), *Any Woman's Blues* (1990), and *Inventing Memory: A Novel of Mothers and Daughters* (1997). Other volumes of poetry appeared as well—*Loveroot* (1975), *At the Edge of the Body* (1979), *Ordinary Miracles* (1983), *Becoming Light: New and Selected Poems* (1991)—as did memoirs (*The Devil At Large: Erica Jong on Henry Miller* [1993] and *Fear of Fifty: A Midlife Memoir* [1994]), a collection of essays entitled *What Do Women Want? Bread Roses Sex Power,* a multigenre book about witches, and a children's book about divorce.

During this enormously productive period, Jong also divorced her second husband, Allan Jong, married and divorced her third husband, writer Jonathan Fast, with whom she had a daughter, Molly Miranda Jong-Fast, and married her fourth husband, Ken Burrows, a lawyer. She was elected president of the Author's Guild, serving in that capacity from 1991 to 1993, and has been active in a number of other professional organizations including PEN, the Authors League of America, the Dramatists Guild of America, the Writers Guild of America, the Poetry Society of America, the National Writers Union, and Poets and Writers.

She was awarded the Premio Internationale Sigmund Freud (Italy) and the United Nations Award of Excellence for literature. She also became an increasingly visible presence on television talk shows and in the feature pages of newspapers and magazines, her life often receiving the kind of media scrutiny usually reserved for elected officials, movie stars, and royals.

Jong's famously autobiographical fiction, jarringly honest poems, and compellingly candid memoirs have been taken to heart by women readers around the world struggling with the age-old challenges that Jong's mother faced and that Jong herself negotiated with such aplomb. There is the challenge of how to have life and love, a satisfying role in the world, and a satisfying someone to share it with. And there is the challenge of how to combine meaningful work and maternity—in Jong's mother's case, art and children; in Jong's, art and a child. (Jong notes that she "waited until I was fledged as a writer before I succumbed to the seductions of motherhood. *Fear of Flying* was my emancipation proclamation—which also, by chance, gave me the material success to support the child I bore.") And there is the challenge, ultimately, of forging a sense of identity as a woman in the modern world. It is Jong's sensitive exploration of all of these challenges that allows her to connect so deeply with her readers.

Jong's strategy for overcoming the obstacles (ambivalence, mixed signals, timidity, fear) that threaten to thwart the aspiring woman writer involves a combination of artistic innovation, humor, courage, brutal honesty, and an unsparing willingness to mine her personal past for the stuff of poetry and fiction. This approach has been both highly effective and costly. As she observed, in *Fear of Fifty,* she has

> written openly about sex, appropriated male picaresque adventures for women, poked fun at the sacred cows of our society. I have lived as I chose, married, divorced, remarried, divorced, remarried and divorced again—and, still worse, dared to write about my ex-husbands! That is the most heinous of my sins—not having done these things, but having confessed to them in print. It is for this that I am considered beyond the pale. No PR can fix this! It's nothing more or less than the fate of rebellious women. They used to stone us in the marketplace. In a way, they still do.

Jong has received more than her share of harsh treatment from critics and still smarts from the pain. She has probably been the object of more acerbic ad hominem (or ad feminem) attacks than any woman writer of the late twentieth century from reviewers whose objectivity is compromised by the often barely masked misogynist, and sometimes anti-Semitic tone that underlies their attacks, as Charlotte Templin shows in her illuminating study, *Feminism and the Politics of Literary Reputation: The Example of Erica Jong.* And while some critics—usually but not always male—seem to have been incensed by the transgressive nature of Jong's work, other critics—usually but not always female—have taken issue with it for not being transgressive *enough.* Novels—like *Fear of Flying*—that were seen as revolutionary when first published sometimes appear to later feminist critics as retrograde or ultimately reactionary. Indeed female-initiated sex itself, a symbol of freedom during the heady heyday of women's liberation, would be construed by feminists in the 1980s and 1990s as a snare and a delusion that trapped women in their bodies with as much damage as the domesticity of the fifties trapped women in the home.

Targeted by traditionalist critics for being too subversive, and targeted by radical critics for being too reactionary, Jong has been wounded but not vanquished. She has dealt with change—change in her life, in American society, in gender relations, in women's roles in our culture—by writing about it. In 1998 in *What Do Women Want?* Jong writes,

[W]hen I look back on the years since I left college and try to sum up what I have learned, it is precisely that: not to fear change, nor to expect my life to be immutable. All the good things that have happened to me in the last several years have come, without exception, from a willingness to change, to risk the unknown, to do the very things I feared most. Every poem, every page of fiction I have written has been written with anxiety, occasionally panic, and always uncertainty about its reception. Every life decision I have made—from changing jobs to changing partners to changing homes—has been taken with trepidation. I have not ceased to be fearful, but I have ceased to let fear control me. I have accepted fear as a part of life, specifically the fear of change, the fear of the unknown. I have gone ahead despite the pounding in the heart that says: Turn back, turn back; you'll die if you venture too far.

Although in her fame, her visibility, and her achievement as a writer surely Erica Jong is exceptional, in her "fears and feelings," Jong claims to be "just like my readers." In *What Do Women Want?* she explains,

As a writer, I feel that the very source of my inspiration lies in my never forgetting how much I have in common with other women, how many ways in which we are all similarly shackled. I do not write about superwomen who have transcended all conflict. I write about women who are torn, as most of us are torn, between the past and the future, between our mothers' frustrations and the extravagant hopes we have for our daughters.

It is possible that some day there may come a time when the conflicts and challenges that animate Jong's work will strike readers as preposterously dated. When that time comes, her poems and novels and essays will provide the historian with invaluable information about that time in the distant past when (for example) women felt bold if they recognized and acted on their sexual impulses, but men felt normal; when achieving a sense of self independent of a partner of the opposite sex was harder for women than for men; when the challenge of having both meaningful careers and children was something men took for granted but women had to struggle with; and when critics tended to praise certain habits of prose when they encountered them in male authors but damn them when they encountered them in female authors. Until that time, however, Jong's willingness to grapple with these and other issues in person and in print will continue to pull readers into her orbit.

THE WOMAN POET

In her 1997 essay "*Fruits & Vegetables* Recollected in Tranquility," Jong describes the raison d'être of the title of her first book.

If I was going to spend time in the kitchen, I wanted to learn how to look into an onion and see my soul, to reclaim for poetry the humble objects of a woman's daily life . . . .

"Poetry," Jong believed, "had been an elitist upper-class men's club long enough. It was high time to welcome in the people who prepared the food!"

Before Jong—and before Plath—there was Anne Bradstreet, a seventeenth-century American poet who had also tried, as Jong put it, "to reclaim for poetry the humble objects of a woman's daily life." Bradstreet's most famous poem, "The Author to Her Book," is, like so many of Jong's poems, about poetry itself—and about the challenge of writing poetry as a woman. Here Bradstreet writes of her book as if it were her child, using images drawn from the quotidian tasks of the housewife and mother:

> I wash'd thy face, but more defects I saw,
> And rubbing off a spot, still made a flaw.
> I stretcht thy joynts to make thee even feet,
> Yet still thou run'st more hobling then is meet;
> In better dress to trim thee was my mind,
> But nought save home-spun Cloth, i'th' house I
>   find . . .

In nineteenth-century America, Walt Whitman and Ralph Waldo Emerson urged American poets to probe the meaning of the ordinary, the commonplace. ("A morning glory at my window, satisfies me more than the metaphysics of books," Whitman wrote in "Song of Myself.") Whitman also raised eyebrows and hackles—as Jong did—by writing the body in all its concrete specificity into his poems. All of this demonstrates not that Jong is a derivative poet, but rather that she is a very American one, expanding traditions whose roots stretch back to a Puritan on the one hand and a Transcendentalist on the other.

Fruits & Vegetables is a crazy salad of poems and prose and aperçus. Sometimes Jong's meditations skate the immediate surface at hand—letters on a page—while also delving into the metaphysics of the commonplace. Her reflections on the onion, for example, begin with the two letter o's in the vegetable's name, then explore the vegetable as metaphor for the psyche and the body, and finally merge the two perspectives unexpectedly, bringing it all together:

> I am thinking of the onion again, with its two O mouths, like the gaping holes in nobody . . . . a modest, self-effacing vegetable, questioning, introspective, peeling itself away . . . unloved for itself alone—no wonder it draws our tears! Then I think again how the outer peel resembles paper, how soul & skin merge into one, how each peeling strips bare a heart which in turn turns skin . . .

At various points in the book, the poet links cooking, copulating, and creating. In "Arse Poetica," for example, passages alternate between the gastronomic and the pornographic but are essentially about writing a poem:

> II
> Salt the metaphors. Set them breast up over the vegetables & baste them with the juice in the casserole. Lay a piece of aluminum foil over the poem, cover the casserole & heat it on top of the stove until you hear the images sizzling. Then place the poem in the middle rack in the preheated oven . . .

> III
> Once the penis has been introduced into the poem, the poet lets herself down until she is sitting on the muse with her legs outside him. He need not make any motions at all. The poet sits upright & raises & lowers her body rhythmically until the last line is attained . . . .This method yields exceptionally acute images & is, indeed, often recommended as yielding the summit of aesthetic enjoyment . . . .

One of the most arresting poems in this volume is "Bitter Pills for the Dark Ladies," which begins with an epigraph about Sylvia Plath. Jong identifies with Plath to some extent and appreciates her enormous talents (Plath's ghost hovers both on and beneath the surface of several poems). But Jong is also terrified of that identification—in part because of the struggle Plath endured to be taken seriously and to take herself seriously—but most of all because Plath ultimately took her own life. For Jong is, above all, determined to be a survivor—and a survivor *as a poet,* as well. Like Plath, and like Anne Sexton, Jong would pioneer in writing about a woman's body, in making visible aspects of human experience—such as menstruation—that had previously been largely absent from books.

In the concluding section, Jong bemoans the fact that the "ultimate praise" for the woman poet "is always a question of nots":

viz. Not like a woman
viz. "certainly not another 'poetess' "

What they really mean, Jong writes, is, "she got a cunt but she don't talk funny."

But how *should* a woman poet talk? In "The Objective Woman," the poem that immediately follows "Bitter Pills," Jong erupts in a wild Whitmanesque celebration of woman as consumer of the language and products with which advertisers target her.

For I praise the women of America . . . .
For I praise the firmessence of their ultralucence
& the ultralucence of their firmessence

How does a woman artist surrounded by critics who assume she has nothing important to say go about finding her own voice? This question will preoccupy Jong throughout her career as a writer.

Sylvia Plath is still a visible presence in the poems in Jong's second collection of poetry, *Half-Lives,* which appeared in 1973. "The Critics," for example, subtitled "For Everyone Who Writes About Sylvia Plath Including Me," parodies the unsatisfying theories critics have generated to explain Plath and concludes with the lines: "She is patient. / When you're silent / she'll crawl out." And food is still a central element as well. In place of the onions of her first book, this collection features some very memorable eggplant ("The Eggplant Epithalamion" makes real and imagined eggplants more vivid than any previous eggplant in literature). There are poems about women who cook, about searching for poems, about divorce, about the challenge of maintaining wholeness, about paper cuts, birth, mothers, orphans, widows, love, and death.

Jong's two debut books of poetry received positive reviews. Margaret Atwood, in *Parnassus: Poetry in Review,* wrote that she read the poems in *Fruits & Vegetables*

the way you watch a trapeze act, with held breath, marvelling at the agility, the lightness of touch, the

brilliant demonstration of the difficult made to look easy.

In *Half-Lives* Atwood found more of an edge, and more pain—but also much of the same whimsy, verbal dexterity, and engaging self-mockery that she had enjoyed in the earlier volume.

FEAR OF FLYING

Both books of poetry, however, would be quickly overshadowed by Jong's explosive first novel, *Fear of Flying.* Shocked typesetters refused to set the book in type. Meanwhile, employees of her publisher stole copies of the galleys and excitedly shared them with their friends. Early reviews were lukewarm. But then the encomiums began to appear—from fellow writers such as John Updike and Henry Miller.

Updike said the book "feels like a winner. It has class and sass, brightness and bite." Updike compared the book to Philip Roth's *Portnoy's Complaint* and J. D. Salinger's *Catcher in the Rye,* and he characterized Jong as a modern-day incarnation of Chaucer's Wife of Bath. Updike applauded the book's "cheerful, sexual frankness," writing that the author "sprinkles on four-letter words as if women had invented them." The poet who ransacked her kitchen cupboards for metaphors must have been particularly gratified by one that Updike invented: "Containing all the cracked eggs of the feminist litany, her soufflé rises with the poet's afflatus."

Henry Miller declared that Jong was "more forthright, more daring than most male writers." He found the novel "full of meaning and . . . a paean to life." He compared it to his own novel *Tropic of Cancer,* finding it "not as bitter and much funnier." "It is rare these days," Miller said, "to come upon a book written by a woman which is so refreshing, so gay and sad at the same time, and so full of wisdom about the eternal man-woman problem." He predicted that the book "will make literary history, that because of it women are going to find their own voice and give us great sagas of sex, life, joy, and adventure." *Time* called *Fear of Flying* "a raunchy, anarchic account of a woman's sexual escapades conducted with a Tom Jones lusty disregard for convention, taste or conscience . . . . It is also an ICBM in the war between the sexes." By 1999, there were fifteen million copies in print.

Fear of Flying is the story of Isadora Wing, an aspiring writer in her twenties who accompanies her noncommunicative psychiatrist husband to a professional conference in Vienna. At the conference she finds herself madly attracted to a British Laingian analyst, Adrian Goodlove. After much soul-searching and indecision, Isadora takes off on a two-and-a-half-week camping trip through Europe with Adrian, during which period disillusionment begins to set in. Her disenchantment crests when Adrian (who has been largely impotent) abandons her in Paris to go to a prearranged meeting with his wife and children in Cherbourg. Isadora then tracks her husband down in London and takes a bath in his hotel room, awaiting his return. In her capacity to stray from conventional morality and land on her feet, Isadora is a late twentieth-century sister to Sister Carrie, the eponymous heroine of Theodore Dreiser's 1900 novel who, rather than suffer for the choices she made, became the toast of Broadway. But while Carrie seemed to drift passively into both perdition and triumph, Isadora was clearly the author of her destiny—whatever that destiny held.

Isadora (like Jong) is a Barnard-educated, middle-class, nice Jewish girl who is unafraid to break the rules: she is open about her body, candid about her sexual fantasies, honest about male sexual performance, and unafraid to express herself in four-letter words. In *Fear of Flying* food and sex still mingled in Jong's store of metaphors, much as they did in her poetry; but poetry reaches an infinitely smaller audience, and her earlier work hardly prepared the mass public for the frankness it encountered here. When the culinary-copulating images resurfaced in the novel, the results were explosive:

> What was it about marriage anyway? Even if you loved your husband, there came that inevitable year when fucking him turned as bland as Velveeta cheese: filling, fattening even, but no thrill to the taste buds, no bittersweet edge, no danger. And you longed for an overripe Camembert, a rare goat cheese: luscious, creamy, cloven-hoofed.
>
> I was not against marriage. I believed in it in fact. It was necessary to have one best friend in a hostile world, one person you'd be loyal to no matter what, one person who'd always be loyal to you. But what about all those other longings which after a while marriage did nothing much to appease? The restlessness, the hunger, the thump in the gut, the thump in the cunt, the longing to be filled up, to be fucked through every hole, the yearning for dry champagne and wet kisses . . . .

One of Isadora's most engaging qualities (to her fans—perhaps one of her most exasperating qualities to her critics) is her self-consciousness, her insight into how gender roles are constructed in contemporary society:

> Growing up female in America. What a liability! . . . What litanies the advertisers of the good life chanted at you! What curious catechisms!
>
> . . . "Love your hair." . . . "That shine on your face should come from him, not from your skin." . . . "How to score with every male in the zodiac." . . . "To a man they say Cutty Sark." . . . "If you're concerned about douching . . . ." "How I solved my intimate odor problem . . . ."
>
> What all the ads and all the whoreoscopes seemed to imply was that if only you were narcissistic *enough,* if only you took proper care of your smells, your hair, your boobs, your eyelashes, your armpits, your crotch, your stars, your scars, and your choice of Scotch in bars—you would meet a beautiful, powerful, potent, and rich man who would satisfy every longing, fill every hole, make your heart skip a beat (or stand still), and make you

misty, and fly you to the moon (preferably on gossamer wings), where you would live totally satisfied forever.

The backdrop, then, for Isadora's life and worldview, if you will, is none other than what Charlotte Perkins Gilman referred to as the ubiquitous "love plot" that tyrannized over every heroine in literature: the dream of total fulfillment through a man. That is what women in literature are supposed to do, Gilman told us in the early 1900s: fall in love. Convention dictates that it's their most promising role. Jong's Isadora, rather than breaking free of conventions, is, in this sense, completely conventional. Society tells her she is to seek fulfillment through a man. Very well, then, that's exactly what she does. But Isadora comes up with a distinctive fantasy to deal with the contradictory "itches" she feels (she is "itchy for sex and itchy for the life of a recluse," "itchy for men, and itchy for solitude"):

> My response to all this was not (not yet) to have an affair and not (not yet) to hit the open road, but to evolve my fantasy of the Zipless Fuck. The zipless fuck was more than a fuck. It was a platonic ideal. Zipless because when you came together zippers fell away like rose petals, underwear blew off in one breath like dandelion fluff. Tongues intertwined and turned liquid. Your whole soul flowed out through your tongue and into the mouth of your lover.
>
> For the true, ultimate zipless A-1 fuck, it was necessary that you never get to know the man very well . . . . So another condition for the zipless fuck was brevity. And anonymity made it even better.

Isadora enjoys sex and is open about that fact; but her obsession with the fantasy of the Zipless Fuck so directly mirrors the male fantasies that have objectified women throughout literary history that it is impossible to miss Jong's satirical thrust: What if we turn the tables for a spell, she seems to be saying—just to see what it looks like when women treat men as men have always treated women? To say that Jong is at root a sat-

irist is not to say that she fails to take her heroine seriously. Isadora is a fully realized character whose motivations are as clear or confusing to the reader as they are to herself. But through Isadora and her frantic efforts to find herself, Jong mounts an acerbic critique of the hand women are dealt (and have learned to deal themselves) in contemporary society. (Along the way Jong deftly satirizes many other things as well, from advertising to psychobabble.)

Jong makes the time period covered in the novel—a little less than a month—resonate with the biological rhythms of the 28-day menstrual cycle that the book's narrator lives. The body Jong writes into her text with such concreteness and immediacy is thus much more than a body who seeks and receives sexual gratification; it is a body that experiences ovulation, menstrual bleeding, tension, release. Isadora's attraction to Adrian Goodlove coincides with the onset of ovulation. She tells the reader,

> I seem to be involved with all the changes of my body. They never pass unnoticed. I seem to know exactly when I ovulate. In the second week of the cycle, I feel a tiny ping and then a sort of tingling ache in my lower belly. A few days later I'll often find a tiny spot of blood in the rubber yarmulke of the diaphragm. A bright red smear, the only visible trace of the egg that might have become a baby. I feel a wave of sadness then which is almost indescribable. Sadness and relief.

The cycle was, of course, familiar to every woman the narrator's age, but absent from American literature until that time.

Isadora's journey cannot be reduced to a quest for sexual fulfillment—although sexual fulfillment is certainly an important part of it. Rather, her journey is one of self-definition. She needs to understand what makes her who she is and what kind of person she wants to be. That understanding takes her back into a past that she shares with the reader in fresh and poignant ways.

Really, I thought sometimes I *would* like to have a child. A very wise and witty little girl who'd grow up to be the woman I could never be. A very independent little girl with no scars on the brain or the psyche. With no toadying servility and no ingratiating seductiveness. A little girl who said what she meant and meant what she said. A little girl who was neither bitchy nor mealy-mouthed because she didn't hate her mother or herself . . . .What I really wanted was to give birth to *myself*—the little girl I might have been in a different family, a different world . . . .

Feeling very alone, in a pup tent with a sleeping man who she knows is no solution to her problems, Isadora tries to "remember who I was: Isadora Zelda White Stollerman Wing . . . . B.A. M.A., Phi Beta Kappa. Isadora Wing, promising younger poet. Isadora Wing, promising younger sufferer. Isadora Wing, feminist and would-be liberated woman. Isadora Wing, clown, crybaby, fool . . . . slightly overweight sexpot, with a bad case of astigmatism of the mind's eye . . . ." Women readers in the 1970s could identify richly with Isadora's lack of confidence, her self-doubt, her ambivalence, and her confusion. The "zipless fuck" may have gotten all the press, but readers probably found the larger drama of the search for identity at least as compelling, if not more so.

Isadora Wing embarked on her quest for identity at a time when almost every aspect of a woman's identity was contested and up for grabs. During the 1970s the women's movement would transform American society profoundly. Jong's novel, appearing as that movement was beginning to come into its own, became an instant icon, a cultural document. It wasn't so much that it contained four-letter words or was candid about sexual gratification and the lack thereof. It was that all this sex talk happened inside a woman's head and was told from a woman's point of view. The sex object—the role into which women had traditionally been cast in literature in the United States—was talking back. What's more, she was talking back assertively and aggressively. She was taking the initiative and suiting herself, no matter that her results were decidedly mixed. What mattered was the audacity of the venture. Conflicted, confused—much as her readers probably were—Isadora nonetheless broke out of the role in which society had cast her and gave birth to a new self. It was brazen and adventurous to be sure. And it was as American as apple pie—if you were a male. Self-invention (the self-made man) had been a staple enterprise on the part of American writers from Benjamin Franklin to Walt Whitman to F. Scott Fitzgerald. But it was largely a novelty for women. (There were exceptions, to be sure: one thinks of Fanny Fern's wonderful novel—*Ruth Hall*—about how she invented herself as a newspaper columnist. Fern published it in 1855, the same year Whitman published "Song of Myself." But Fern was one of those exceptions that prove the rule.)

And if self-invention was a largely male prerogative, talking dirty in print was even more so. Four years before *Fear of Flying* appeared, Philip Roth published *Portnoy's Complaint,* a book that foregrounded a man's candidly described sexual obsessions while aspiring to be more than mere pornography. Can a writer do this? Pack a book with sex and four-letter words and still get taken seriously as literature? Roth proved it could be done—if you were male. As Erica Jong found out when she wrote a novel that tried to do just that—but from a woman's point of view—the same rules don't apply. Roth evoked titillation while Jong provoked outrage. (Critics Alfred Kazin and Paul Theroux, for example, both called Jong's book hopelessly "vulgar.") While Roth was celebrated for breaking the rules, Jong was castigated. Jong, the sly poet who mined her vegetable bin for the stuff of seventeenth-century conceits, now found herself at the barricades of the sexual revolution, poster-girl for an Equal Rights Amendment for writers.

Critics who admired the book have looked at

elements it shares with journeys penned by Homer and Dante and have compared its author to Rabelais. They have valued the book as a feminist bildungsroman, a novel of female growth and development. Meanwhile, conservative critics who approved of the status quo in gender relations welcomed the chance to attack feminism by attacking this book. Jean Larkin Crain, for example, writing in *Commentary,* saw the novel as an attack on marriage as an institution and accused Jong of having falsified reality when she suggested that women were victims of forces beyond their control. (Benjamin Demott, writing in the *Atlantic,* also saw the book as a "diatribe against marriage.") Patricia Coyne, writing in *The National Review,* charged Jong with having been brainwashed by the "Women's Lib" movement, writing that "the author sees in life precisely what the women's movement has told her to see." Meanwhile, liberal critics such as Ellen Hope Meyer writing in the *Nation,* complained about the solipsistic "Dear Diary" quality of the novel, maintaining that the heroine's self-indulgent subjectivity provided no blueprint for social change.

MOVING THROUGH A PARALLEL UNIVERSE

As Jong's character Isadora Wing observes in *How to Save Your Own Life,* published in 1977, "Books go out into the world, travel mysteriously from hand to hand, and somehow find their way to people who need them at the *times* when they need them." Clearly millions of women needed *Fear of Flying* in the early 1970s. By early 1975 it had hit number one on the *New York Times* Bestseller List. Jong became a high-voltage celebrity, and celebrity would be the target of her deft satire in her second novel, *How To Save Your Own Life.*

Like *Fear of Flying, How to Save Your Own Life* is narrated by Isadora, who will also be central to *Parachutes & Kisses* (1984) and will "au-

thor" *Any Woman's Blues* (1990), a manuscript brought to print by a fictitious feminist critic after a plane Isadora is piloting disappears mysteriously over the South Pacific. But in none of these sequels will Isadora be as much of an "amanuensis to the Zeitgeist" (as she puts it) as she turned out to be in *Fear of Flying.*

Jong, who in her first book of poems celebrated the multilayered nature of the onion, creates onionlike layers of authorship and authenticity in her "Isadora" tetralogy. By the time *How to Save Your Own Life* comes out, Isadora Wing, the fictional heroine of *Fear of Flying,* is herself the author of the novel *Candida Confesses,* a book that (like *Fear of Flying*) contained many autobiographical elements and brought its author celebrity, notoriety, ill-fated movie deals, and kinky mash notes from flakes in all corners of the country. Isadora, who is herself Jong's creation, spends much time discussing the ways in which Candida Wong (Isadora's creation) is and is not modeled on Isadora Wing. Meanwhile, back in real life, Erica Jong moves through a distinctly parallel universe during these years, spending much time discussing the ways in which Isadora Wing is and is not Erica Jong.

Critical responses to these volumes almost always veered into "did she or didn't she" speculations about the extent to which Isadora's experiences reflected Jong's. As Jong told *Playboy* interviewer Gretchen McNeese in 1975, "Sure, there's a lot of me in Isadora, but a lot of characters and events in the book are totally invented. I didn't set out to write autobiography; I set out to write a satirical novel about a woman in search of her own identity, and I did not stick to facts very closely—frequently not at all." Correspondences between Jong's life and that of her heroine were striking: both had grown up in a family of painters in a middle-class Jewish home in Manhattan; both had gone to Barnard; both had published poetry before turning to fiction; both had been married to Chinese-American psychoanalysts; and both had published an exuberantly bawdy first novel that triggered endless probing into what, exactly, was taken from life and what was made up. In the family of "portraitists and still-life painters" in which she grew up, Isadora observes in *How to Save Your Own Life,* "It was family wisdom that you painted what you had at home . . . .You could learn chiaroscuro, color, composition as well from an apple or an onion or your own familiar face as from the fountains of Rome or the storm clouds of Venice." Isadora tells us that

> I had modeled Candida after myself, yet she was both more and less than the real Isadora. Superficially, the likeness was easy enough to spot: a nice Jewish girl from the Upper West Side, a writer of poems and stories, a compulsive daydreamer. Yet Candida was frozen in a book, while I was, I hoped, growing. I had outgrown many of the desires that motivated her, many of the fears that trapped her. Yet my public insisted on an exact equivalency between her and me—because my heroine, astoundingly enough, had turned out to be amanuensis to the Zeitgeist.
>
> This amazing development surprised no one more than me. When I invented Candida Wong (with her wise-ass manner, her outspokenness about sex, and her determined bookishness), I was convinced that she was either unfit for print or else so precious that no one but a few other wise-ass Jewish girls from the Upper West Side could relate to her. But I was wrong. As Candida felt, so felt the nation. And no one could have been more surprised than her creator.
>
> Millions of copies later, I began to wonder whether I had created Candida or whether she had, in fact, created me.

Clearly Isadora had done much to catapult Jong to the celebrity that she chronicled in the sequels—but that celebrity turned out to be a decidedly mixed blessing.

Jong herself was trapped, in some ways, by the success *Fear of Flying* had enjoyed. First, she was trapped by the impossible demand of coming up with a second act to the revolution: *Fear of Flying* helped usher in such fresh possibilities for honesty in women's writing, helped open the culture to so much that had been repressed before, that by the time *How to Save Your Own Life* came out four years later, it couldn't help but seem at least somewhat derivative as it continued doing more of the same. Second, the sheer enormity of the sales of *Fear of Flying* led some critics to think of her work as "popular culture" rather than "literature," as if mass appeal somehow disqualified a novel from being taken seriously as art; this classification gave critics an excuse to focus on the heroine's sexual exploits, or the roman à clef aspects of the book, rather than focusing on Jong's talents as a satirist of contemporary manners and mores. This is unfortunate, since those talents are considerable.

How to Save Your Own Life finds Isadora still married to a psychiatrist "who regarded life as a long disease, alleviated by little fifty-minute bloodlettings of words from the couch." There was something in her husband's "very manner, carriage, and monotonous way of speaking" that Isadora finds "life-denying." But she doesn't have the courage to leave him and set out on her own until he confesses to having had a long-term affair back in Heidelberg with a mutual friend, a housewife to whom he made love in Isadora's study, amidst her unpublished manuscripts. Outraged by this betrayal, Isadora sets out for Hollywood lured by a possible motion picture deal.

En route Jong paints a gallery of unforgettable figures with walk-on parts, one of whom—Jeannie Morton—is a thinly veiled version of the poet Anne Sexton, whose "images (even of God) were kitchen images, plain aluminum utensils to serve the Lord, Pyrex casseroles to simmer the Holy Spirit." Morton, Isadora tells readers,

> was easy to mock. Where a male poet would have been taken seriously—even if he saw God in a hunting knife or the wound of a war buddy—she was

mocked because it is harder for many people to understand that the womb (with its red blood) is as apt a vessel for the muse or for God as the penis (with its white sperm).

Another memorable character is Gretchen, a tall, blonde Marxist-feminist lawyer who "has so much life-force that she makes everyone else in the room feel drained." Gretchen is the owner of a loft reserved for romantic assignations and inventor of the "F" questionnaire, "a simple quiz designed for feminists to determine which men are safe to fuck." Then there is Holly, a painter who lives surrounded by African violets, potted avocados, lemon trees, and gardenias, and who has often explained to Isadora, "with considerable passion, that the fern, that ancient botanical specimen, has the ideal life situation. It is self-nourishing, self-fertilizing, contains sexual and asexual life-styles within its own lifetime, and it is actually immortal. Or at least some part of it is always alive." Isadora has "never met anyone who clearly wanted to be a plant, but Holly makes it seem extremely attractive." And then there is Hope, an old family friend "who gave everything away. She was a human potlatch." It is Isadora's relationships with these intensely caring, vividly drawn women friends that prompted Craig Fisher to describe the book (in the *Los Angeles Times*) as "a paean to friendship."

How to Save Your Own Life is also a lively satire on Hollywood. Isadora tells readers, for example, that "there is a certain kind of grayish, stoop-shouldered beaten screenwriter one meets in Hollywood," who once (he says) could have written a novel, but who believes it is now too late.

He was rich, but he was not happy. He had seen his lifework rewritten by illiterate producers, his best aphorisms mangled by arrogant actors, his philosophical nuggets crushed by directors, mushed by assistant directors, and trampled to dust by the Italian-leather soles of executive producers' shoes. He

was a beaten man, an intellectual derelict, a Bowery bum of letters. They had taken away his words and given him money instead. And it was a lousy bargain. He spent an hour wishing he were me.

Then there is the self-made "millionaire with a weakness for trendy self-improvement and a tendency to sound like a California Khalil Gibran" who spouts platitudes while joined by Isadora and others "all naked and simmering in a great redwood tub of bubbling water—like kreplach bobbing in a vat of chicken soup." Isadora writes,

We live in a society where everyone habitually lies about their feelings—so there is an immense gratitude toward anyone who even *tries* to tell the truth. I suppose this is why certain authors are worshipped as cult figures. We may disdain truth in our daily lives but we are that much more relieved and exhilarated when we find someone at least *trying* to express it in a book.

Telling the truth about her feelings is something Isadora does well. "There was all sorts of sex in my life and not very much intimacy," she writes, before Josh Ace, the new love of her life, enters the scene. (As Jong told the *Playboy* interviewer, "Men consider intimacy as a weakness. That's part of the sexist brainwashing our society subjects men to.") The movie doesn't materialize but the new man does. *How to Save Your Own Life* ends with Isadora enthralled by her new love, an aspiring writer several years her junior who is good at both intimacy and sex.

Seven years later, however, Isadora's fortunes have changed. When *Parachutes & Kisses* begins, Josh has left, blaming Isadora for the gap between his modest reputation and her exploding one. Thirty-nine-year-old Isadora is a single mother struggling to work, find love and companionship, and raise a bright three-year-old with the help of a motley series of nannies (including one obsessed with hellfire and brimstone and another obsessed with a loutish carpenter). As Jong observed to Gill Pyrah of the (London) *Times,* the book "is about having it all in the 1980s. Isadora exemplified the 1970s woman and now, in the 1980s, we are trying to be single parents, bread-winners, and feminine at the same time."

There is still a lot of sex in the book despite the fact that, as Isadora tells us, "it isn't fashionable to write too much about sex anymore."

> In the seventies, post-Portnoy, you couldn't pick up a novel, it seemed without getting sperm on your hands. Not only the hacksters and fucksters, but *literary* writers, good writers, had to chart the interiors of vaginas as if they were the caves of Lascaux (and all primordial truth were writ therein). Women were discovering the poetry of penises; men were unmasking before the Great Goddess Cunt.

> But then the hacksters got hold of sex and ruined it for everyone—like condominium developers ruining Florida. They took the license to explore Lascaux as a license to kill little girls; they turned the poetry of the penis into stag films so loathsome they made you want to become a nun. Before long the puritans were howling—"See! We told you how awful sex is! You should have listened to us! We were right about censorship! Put the mask back on!"

> And all the poetry of the penis, the sweet sexuality that peeked out of the fly of the Brooks Brothers pants for a brief decade was in danger of being covered up again . . . . And Isadora's old buddies, the feminists, are passing out leaflets on street corners protesting pornography, trying to make the world believe that people molest little girls *because* of pornography (rather than pornography flourishes because people want to molest little girls), and in general doing their best to blur the distinction between sex and rage.

Times had changed since 1973—and not only when it came to writing about sex in literature. By 1984, feminism itself was increasingly subject to new attacks, and this hostility inevitably rubbed off on the most famous feminist heroine of the previous decade, Isadora Wing.

In *Parachutes & Kisses* Isadora does much more than jump in and out of bed (she survives single parenthood, develops a sustaining relationship with a new love, travels to Russia in search of her roots, and so on. One critic, Lillian Robinson, even credits her with embarking on her own version of the *Odyssey*). She still seeks the same combinations of work and love that eluded her in her earlier incarnation. But if Isadora's needs remain basically the same, the feminism that helped validate and fuel them had, by 1984, to some extent gone out of fashion. Whether due to changes in the Zeitgeist or changes in Jong's own style or both (this book, unlike the others, has a third-person, rather than a first-person narrator), the book received decidedly mixed reviews. Citing the "postfeminist" political climate of the eighties, Charlotte Templin noted that "A number of reviewers fault Isadora for her failures in family life" and criticize her lack of sympathy for the midlife crises of men.

Isadora herself is presented as the author of *Any Woman's Blues,* published in 1990 and introduced by an imaginary feminist scholar who found the manuscript after Isadora's plane disappeared. Jong told the *Chicago Tribune* writer Lynn Van Matre that

> I knew I wanted to write a fable of a woman living in the Reagan era of excess and greed and avarice, an artist at the height of her powers who is hopelessly addicted to a younger man and goes through all the different states of change to get free.

The book's protagonist, Leila Sand, is a successful artist and a self-described addict, addicted to alcohol, drugs, and a manipulative, parasitic younger lover. She embarks on a self-help regime to pull her life together, and to a limited degree, she succeeds. Some critics found the main character self-indulgent and shallow and the writing pedestrian; others, however, found the character important and compelling and the narrative structure innovative and fresh.

IMAGINING THE PAST

If the sequels to *Fear of Flying* won their author the gratitude of readers around the world who appreciated Jong's willingness to tell truths (about women's fantasies, realities, aspirations, and frustrations), the two highly imaginative works of historical fiction she published during the 1980s, *Fanny* in 1980 and *Serenissima* in 1987, won her the gratitude of readers who appreciated her ability to spin such wildly entertaining, lush, and vibrant lies.

Fanny: Being the True History of the Adventures of Fanny Hackabout-Jones is a tour de force pastiche made possible by Jong's impressive command of the conventions of canonical eighteenth-century literature. A heady, zany blend of Samuel Richardson's *Pamela* and *Clarissa,* Henry Fielding's *Shamela* and *Tom Jones,* Daniel Defoe's *Moll Flanders,* Laurence Sterne's *Tristram Shandy,* and John Cleland's *Fanny Hill* (with more than a few dollops of the Marx Brothers thrown in as well), *Fanny* takes the reader on an exhilaratingly exhausting romp through country houses, city brothels, masked balls, witches' covens, and pirate ships. In something of the spirit of Virginia Woolf, who imagined "Shakespeare's sister" in *A Room of One's Own,* Jong imagines a female counterpart to these male authors and lets her rewrite the eighteenth-century novel in her own words from the inside out. Jong's feel for the archaic language is superb, her characters glow with vitality, and her plot perks along with just the right number of twists and turns and spirals to take her exactly where she wants to go.

Fanny, "the Beauteous Heroine" of the novel, is smart as well as stunning. She reads enough to be titillated that Alexander Pope is showing up for dinner—and she's sufficiently tempting that Pope, along with virtually every heterosexual male who marches across the page, continues marching into her bedroom with high hopes pinned to his flag-at-full-mast. Fanny has her share of major-league trauma: she is raped by her stepfather, she watches her women friends murdered by misogynist cutthroats, and her beloved infant daughter is kidnapped. But she is also a major-league survivor, and her ability to bounce back from these setbacks with resilience and humor makes her memoirs "mock-heroical" and "tragicomical" rather than tragic.

Like Vladimir Nabokov's *Lolita, Fanny* is as much about the joys of language as the pleasures of lust. It is a Nabokovian pacan to the pleasure of words. For example, Jong tells us that her picaresque heroine "has been called a woman of the town, a tart, a bawd, a wanton, a bawdy-basket, a bird-of-the-game, a bit of stuff, a buttered bum, a cockatrice, a cock-chafer, a cow. . . . " Fanny herself launches into a Nabokovian riff to demonstrate that "a Man's Estimation of his own Privy Member" may not be "necessarily infallible":

> The Politician who boasts of his Member-for-Cockshire, the Butcher who praises his Skewer, the Poet who prates of his Picklock, the Actor who loves his Lollipop, the Footman who boasts of his Ramrod, the Parson who praises his Pillicock, the Orator who apotheosizes his Adam's-Arsenal, the Archer who aims his Love-Dart, the Sea Captain who adores his own Rudder—none of these Men, howsoe'er lively these Mental Pars, is to be trusted upon his own Estimation of his Prowess in the Arts (and Wars) of Love!

There is a verbal energy here that surpasses anything Jong has written previously—although there are clear resonances with her earlier novels, particularly when it comes to the way Fanny wears her sense of feminist entitlement with grace and confidence. Fanny says, for example,

> In a Day when Girls were commonly thought to need no Education but the Needle, Dancing, and the

French Tongue (with perhaps the Addition of a little Musick upon the Harpsichord or Spinet), I was plund'ring My Lord's Library for Tonson's *Poetical Miscellanies,* new Books by Mr. Pope and Mr. Swift, as well as older ones by Shakespeare, Milton, Boccaccio, Boileau, and Molière . . . . I could never understand why Daniel, a rather dull-witted, lazy Boy, but a Year my senior, should be sent to Day School to learn Latin, Greek, Algebra, Geometry, Geography, and the Use of Globes, whilst I, who was so much quicker, was encouraged only in Pastry-making, Needlepoint, and French Dancing and laugh'd at for being vain of my fine Penmanship . . . .

Published after *Fear of Flying* and *How to Save Your Own Life, Fanny* demonstrated Jong's daunting command of both the style and substance of eighteenth-century literature as well as her marvelously inventive gifts as a satirist.

Jong drew on texts such as Captain Charles Johnson's 1724 volume, *A General History of the Robberies and Murders of the Most Notorious Pyrates from Their First Rise and Settlement in the Island of New Providence to the Present Year,* for example, as well as the anthropological research of Dr. Margaret A. Murray on the practices of eighteenth-century English witches, and Norman Himes' *A Medical History of Contraception* to lend accuracy to her reconstruction of the period and Fanny's adventures in the "skin trade"—although she admits to having "often stretched (though I hope not shattered) historical 'truth' in order to make a more amusing tale." Far from being weighed down by Jong's efforts at historical verisimilitude, however, the epistolary novel Fanny Hackabout-Jones writes for the benefit of her daughter, Belinda, soars with marvelous élan and energy. Fanny, as Jong admits in the afterword, "is not a typical eighteenth-century woman. . . . In many ways her consciousness is modern." But that is part of her charm. Jong expresses the hope that "this book will convey something of the fascination I have had with eighteenth-

century England, its manners and mores," but notes that "above all, it is intended as a novel about a woman's life and development in a time when women suffered far greater oppression than they do today." Along the way, the book wittily engages eighteenth-century aesthetics and moral philosophy, and even assigns walk-on roles to such towering figures of the age as the writer Jonathan Swift and the artist William Hogarth.

The book's feminism provoked familiar hostility: some male reviewers were evidently threatened by Jong's efforts to reclaim the eighteenth-century novel's sexual candor for women. But the book also won the admiration of critics as distinguished as the British novelist Anthony Burgess, who found Jong's reconstruction of the eighteenth century "imaginative and always convincing." Writers who were themselves known for a finely honed sense of humor, linguistic dexterity, and a fascination with the past tended to appreciate Jong's achievement. Judith Martin (a.k.a."Miss Manners"), for example, recognized that Fanny was larger than her "lusty Appetite." She was also a person of "Learning, Courage, Curiosity, Kindness, Wit, and good Chear," a "true heroine" with broad appeal.

Jong wrote in her introduction to an excerpt from *Fanny* published in *Vogue* (August 1980), "Having explored our right to anger and sexuality in literature, having asserted our right to tell the truth about our lives, we must now also assert our right to explore imaginary and invented worlds." The imaginary and invented world of sixteenth-century Venice is the setting of the historical novel Jong published in 1987, *Serenissima: A Novel of Venice,* which was later reissued under the title, *Shylock's Daughter: A Novel of Love in Venice.* Familiar themes surface in the novel—including the challenge of forging a sense of identity as a woman as well as the nature of love, death, aging, and imagination. Divorced actress Jessica Pruitt, who has traveled to Venice to judge a film festival, finds herself (through magic or the delirium of fever) transported to the sixteenth century. She meets William Shakespeare (who has fled to Venice to avoid the plague) and his patron/lover the Earl of Southhampton, and she helps inspire the Dark Lady of Shakespeare's sonnets and Shylock's daughter, Jessica, in *The Merchant of Venice* (a role that she has been anticipating playing). Jong revels in the opportunity to blend multiple levels of language (actual quotations from Shakespeare, modern English, pseudo-Elizabethan pastiches, snippets of Italian) with the typically fast-moving picaresque adventure plot that by then had become something of her signature. Although the novel did not receive as uniformly positive reviews as *Fanny,* many appreciated its inventive reach and entertaining energy. (Jong would return to her love affair with Venice in several essays in her 1998 collection, *What Do Women Want?*)

Jong's novel *Inventing Memory: A Novel of Mothers and Daughters* (1997) tracks four generations of Jewish women from the end of the nineteenth century to the early years of the twenty-first century, reprising a number of the themes that have animated Jong's earlier novels—particularly the challenge of forging a viable identity as an artist, a woman, a daughter, and a mother.

Although this novel foregrounds Jewish issues more prominently than any of Jong's prior books, Jewish concerns and themes have, in fact, been central to Jong's fiction from the start. In *Fear of Flying,* for example, Isadora often thinks about the residues of the Holocaust in modern Germany and holds forth on modern German amnesia about the Nazi past. Isadora's sense of herself as a Jew surfaces again in *Parachutes & Kisses,* when she makes a pilgrimage from Russia to Baba Yar. But even when she's not visiting the sites of anti-Semitic atrocities, Isadora is uncomfortably aware of anti-Semitic stereotypes in all

of the novels in which she is a central figure—and she is also prone to pepper her observations in all of these volumes with apt Yiddish phrases. A self-conscious awareness of Jewish history, humor, and language surfaces throughout Jong's novels. One might even argue that her decision as an artist to reject any reticence about the pleasures of the flesh may owe something to the traditionally Jewish acceptance of the earthy vitality of the body in all its robust physicality. After all, the daily morning prayer prescribed by Jewish tradition makes a point of thanking God quite specifically for having created pores, orifices, hollows, holes, openings, cavities, channels, and ducts that open and close according to a brilliant divine plan.

But if Jewish issues have been germane to Jong's writing from the start, in *Inventing Memory* they often take center stage. A pogrom—described in all its brutal rawness—propels the matriarch Sarah Solomon, born in Russia in the 1880s, to flee to America in about 1905, where she will move in and out of the downtown world of Jewish anarchists and bohemians. Four generations later, her great-granddaughter, Sara, born in 1978, researches family histories at New York's Council on Jewish History, searching for a "usable past" that she can both discover and invent. The narrative is punctuated with quotes from the Talmud, wry Yiddish proverbs, and comments on Jews and Jewishness from figures including Leo Tolstoy, Emma Lazarus, and Gershem Sholem.

The four women whose lives Jong chronicles have much in common with previous Jong heroines: they are honest, lusty, and all-too-human in their imperfections, and they aspire to forge new ways of being a woman in the modern world. The journeys on which they embark involve coming to terms with being a mother and a daughter and plotting those often vexed relationships on a rich canvas that stretches across the entire twentieth century. The novel lovingly savors, in all its sensuous concreteness, the texture of a past whose legacies reach into the present.

VOLUMES OF VERSE

Although she has become best known for her fiction, Jong has never abandoned her roots as a poet, publishing volumes of poetry at regular intervals after her two initial books of poems appeared. Indeed, as she notes in her preface to *Ordinary Miracles,* "I find that the volumes of verse tend to predict themes in the novels to come—almost as if I were distilling my life one way in poetic form, and another way in prosaic." Jong insists that "my poems and my novels have always been very much of a piece . . . . I am always hoping that someone will recognize the poet and novelist as two aspects of the same soul—but alas, the genres are reviewed by two different groups of people, so no one ever seems to notice this in print."

Loveroot takes its name from an evocative catalogue penned by Walt Whitman, whose joyful corporeality continues to inspire and empower Jong. The opening poem of the collection, "Testament (Or, Homage to Walt Whitman)," is Jong's celebration of her decision, very much in the spirit of Whitman, to "declare myself now for joy."

> I myself have been a scorner
> & have chosen scornful men,
> men to echo all that was narrow in myself,
> men to hurt me as I hurt myself.
> ....
> I resolve now for joy.
>
> If that resolve means I must live alone,
>   I accept aloneness.
> If the joy house I inhabit must be
>   a house of my own making,
>   I accept that making.

> No doom-saying, death-dealing, fucker of cunts
>   Can undo me now.
>
> No joy-denyer can deny me now.
>   For what I have is undeniable.
>   I inhabit my own house,
>   The house of my joy.
>
> "Unscrew the locks from the doors!
> Unscrew the doors themselves from their jambs!"

* * *

> Dear Walt Whitman,
>   Horny old nurse to pain,
> Speaker of "passwords primeval,"
> Merit-refuser, poet of body & soul—
> I scorned you at twenty
> But turn to you now
> In the fourth decade of my life,
> Having grown straight enough
> To praise your straightness
> & plain enough
> to speak to you plain
> & simple enough
> to praise your simplicity.

The volume's celebration of simple joy, self-sufficiency, and human resilence anticipate some of Jong's concerns in *How to Save Your Own Life.*

The poems in *At the Edge of the Body* (1979) are more concerned with death than any of Jong's previous poetry collections—a turn that should not surprise readers familiar with the centrality of the theme of death to the poetry of Whitman, whose rhythms and images still reverberate through Jong's poems. Like Whitman, Jong embraces death as a part of life, and this move propels her poetry to new levels of maturity and emotional depth.

In its clear, sharply observed attentiveness to the "ordinary miracle" of pregnancy, *Ordinary Miracles* (1983) may have more in common with the lucid prose of a figure like Meridel LeSueur than it does with obscurantist (male) poets more in favor in academe. Like the LeSueur who, in the 1935 story "The Annuciation," vividly brought to life a pregnant narrator who felt closer to the pear tree outside her window than to any of the beaten-down, sour human beings in her rooming house, the author of *Ordinary Miracles* etches the mystery and wonder of carrying another human being inside oneself. See, for example, her whimsical lyric to her unborn child in "The Birth of the Water Baby":

Oh avocado pit
Almost ready to sprout,
Tiny fruit tree
Within sight
of the sea,
little swimming fish,
little land lover,
hold on!
Hold on! . . .

Characteristically, here, as in all her other books, Jong tells truths that the rest of society is content to ignore, particularly about women's bodies and the world's response to them. In "Another Language," she writes,

The whole world is flat
& I am round.
Even women avert their eyes,
& men, embarrassed
by the messy way that life turns into life,
look away,
forgetting they themselves
were once this roundness
underneath the heart,
this helpless fish
swimming in eternity . . . .
What is this large unseemly thing—
A pregnant poet?
An enormous walking O?

In addition to collections of poetry and novels, Jong has published several volumes of nonfiction—*Fear of Fifty, The Devil At Large: Erica Jong on Henry Miller,* and *What Do Women Want? Bread Roses Sex Power.* Jong's nonfiction—both the autobiographical memoirs and the critical essays—shed light on her project as an imaginative writer and highlight her intelligence as a critic. In her essay "Deliberate Lewdness and the Creative Imagination," for example (in *What Do Women Want?*), Jong probes the links between pornography and creativity by exploring the importance of Mark Twain's 1876 pornographic sketch, "1601 . . . Conversation as It Was by the Social Fireside, in the Time of the Tudors." Twain wrote this bawdy Elizabethan fantasy during the same summer he wrote the first sixteen chapters of what would become *Huckleberry Finn.* Arguing that the "pornographic spirit is always related to unhampered creativity," Jong suggests that the "deliberate lewdness" of "1601" allowed Twain to sneak "up on the muse so that she would not be forewarned and escape," and helped awaken his "freedom to experiment, play, and dream outrageous dreams" that led directly that summer to the beginnings of his most lasting triumph as an artist. Here, as in her writing on Henry Miller, Jong champions the freedom necessary for creativity and stakes out a firm position against censorship of every stripe.

Through pathbreaking novels, radiant poems, lucid essays, and an indefatigable willingness to explain herself, in person and in print, to audiences continually startled by her honesty, her erudition, and her ambitious inventiveness, Jong has helped transform the role of the woman writer in our time.

Selected Bibliography

WORKS OF ERICA JONG

POETRY
Fruits & Vegetables. New York: Holt, Rinehart & Winston, 1971.
Half-Lives. New York: Holt, Rinehart & Winston, 1973.

Loveroot. New York: Holt, Rinehart & Winston, 1975.

At the Edge of the Body. New York: Holt, Rinehart & Winston, 1979.

Ordinary Miracles. New York: New American Library, 1983.

Becoming Light: New and Selected Poems. New York: Harper & Row, 1991.

FICTION

Fear of Flying. New York: Holt, Rinehart & Winston, 1973.

How to Save Your Own Life. New York: Holt, Rinehart & Winston, 1977.

Fanny: Being the True History of the Adventures of Fanny Hackabout-Jones. New York: New American Library, 1980.

Parachutes & Kisses. New York: New American Library, 1984.

Shylock's Daughter: A Novel of Love in Venice (formerly *Serenissima: A Novel of Venice*). New York: Houghton Mifflin, 1987.

Any Woman's Blues. New York: Harper and Row, 1990.

Inventing Memory: A Novel of Mothers and Daughters. New York: HarperCollins, 1997.

NONFICTION

The Devil at Large: Erica Jong on Henry Miller. New York: Turtle Bay Books (Random House), 1993.

Fear of Fifty: A Midlife Memoir. New York: HarperCollins, 1994.

What Do Women Want? Bread Roses Sex Power. New York: HarperCollins, 1998.

ARTICLES AND INTRODUCTIONS

"Ally McBeal and Time Magazine Can't Keep the Good Women Down." *New York Observer,* July 18, 1998, p. 19.

"The Awful Truth about Women's Lib." *Vanity Fair,* April 1986, pp. 92–93, 118–119.

"Changing My Mind about Andrea Dworkin." *Ms.,* June 1988, pp. 60–64.

"Colette—Connoisseur of Clutter, Chatter." *Los Angeles Times Book Review,* December 14, 1975, pp. 4–5.

"Daughters." *Ladies' Home Journal,* May 1975, pp. 60–65.

"Fame Fatale." *Mirabella,* August 1999, pp. 58, 60–61.

"*Fruits & Vegetables* Recollected in Tranquility." Introduction to new edition of *Fruits & Vegetables.* Hopewell, N.J.: Ecco Press, 1997.

"Introduction: *Fear of Flying* Fifteen Years Later." New York: Signet-NAL Penguin, 1988: xi–xv.

Introduction to *1601, and Is Shakespeare Dead? by Mark Twain.* In *The Oxford Mark Twain.* 29 vols. Edited by Shelley Fisher Fishkin. New York: Oxford University Press, 1996.

"Is There Life after Being a Good Girl?" *Glamour,* August 1987, pp. 268–269, 320.

"Is There Sexy after Forty? Erica Jong Unzips the Last Taboo." *Vogue,* May 1987, pp. 304–305.

"Jong Triumphant: In which the renoun'd Author of *Fear of Flying*—who has stunned All & Sundry by writing a huge, bawdy, historical Novel—here confeses to her ulterior Motives and the Pleasure of the Endeavor." *Vogue,* August 1980, pp. 229–230, 279–280 (Introduction to excerpt from *Fanny*).

"The Life We Live and the Life We Write." *New York Times Book Review,* February 10, 1985, p. 26.

"Marriage: Rational and Irrational." *Vogue,* June 1975, pp. 94–95.

"A New Feminist Manifesto." Review of *The Second Stage* by Betty Friedan. *Saturday Review,* October 1981, pp. 66–68.

"Notes on Five Men." *Esquire,* May 1975, pp. 69–73.

"Speaking of Love." *Newsweek,* February 21, 1977, p. 11.

"Succeed at Your Own Risk." *Vogue,* October 1975, pp. 216–217.

"Time Has Been Kind to the Nymphet: 'Lolita' 30 Years Later." *New York Times Book Review,* June 5, 1988, pp. 3, 46.

"Writer Who 'Flew' to Sexy Fame Talks about Being a Woman." *Vogue,* March 1977, pp. 158, 160.

"Writing a First Novel." *Twentieth-Century Literature* 20(4): 263–269, 1974.

"Ziplash: A Sexual Libertine Recants." *Ms.,* May 1989, p. 49.

OTHER WRITINGS

Megan's Two Houses. New York: New American Library, 1977. (Children's book, *formerly Megan's Book of Divorce: A Kid's Book for Adults*)

Witches. New York: Abrams, 1981. (poems, fantasy, fable)

BIOGRAPHICAL AND CRITICAL STUDIES

Aiken, Joan. "Erica Jong's Carnival of Venice." Review of *Serenissima. Washington Post Book World,* April 19, 1987, pp. 4–5.

Amis, Martin, "Isadora's Complaint." Review of *Fear of Flying. Observer Review,* April 21, 1974, p. 37.

Atwood, Margaret. *Parnassus: Poetry in Review,* Spring–Summer 1974. (Article in Contemporary Literary Criticism on-line database)

Avery, Evelyn Gross. "Tradition and Independence in Jewish Feminist Novels." *MELUS* 7(4): 49–55, 1980.

Burgess, Anthony. "Jong in Triumph." Review of *Fanny. Saturday Review,* August 1980, pp. 54–55.

Butler, Robert J. "The Woman Writer as American Picaro: Open Journeying in Erica Jong's *Fear of Flying.*" *The Centennial Review* 31, no. 3: 308–329 (Summer 1987).

Chapple, Steve, and David Talbot. *Burning Desires: Sex in America, A Report from the Field.* New York: Signet, 1990. Pp. 218–222.

Charney, Maurice. *Sexual Fiction.* London: Methuen, 1981.

Courtivron, Isabelle de. Review of *Fear of Fifty: A Midlife Memoir. Women's Review of Books* 12, no. 2: 15–16 (November 1994).

Coyne, Patricia S. "Women's Lit." Review of *Fear of Flying. National Review,* May 24, 1974, p. 604.

Crain, Jane Larkin. "Feminist Fiction." Review of *Fear of Flying* (and other works). *Commentary,* December 1974, pp. 58–62.

Cunningham, Valentine. "Back to Shiftwork." Review of *Serenissima. Times Literary Supplement,* September 18, 1987, p. 1025.

DeMott, Benjamin. "Couple Trouble: Mod and Trad." *Atlantic,* December 1973, pp. 122–127.

———."The Fruits of Sin." Review of *Any Woman's Blues. New York Times Book Review,* January 28, 1990, p. 13.

Evans, Stuart. "Fiction." Review of *Fanny* (and other works). (London) *Times,* November 27, 1980, p. 14.

Ferguson, Mary Anne. "The Female Novel of Development and the Myth of Psyche." In *The Voyage in Fictions of Female Development.* Edited by Elizabeth Abel, Marianne Hirsch, and Elizabeth Langland. Hanover and London: University Press of New England, 1983. Pp. 228–243.

Fisher, Craig. " 'Fear of Flying' Heroine Flies a New Flight Plan." Review of *How to Save Your Own Life. Los Angeles Times Book Review,* March 20, 1977, p. I12.

Friedman, Edward H. "The Precocious Narrator: Fanny and Discursive Counterpoint. In his *The Antiheroine's Voice: Narrative Discourse and Transformations of the Picaresque.* Columbia: University of Missouri Press, 1987. Pp. 203–219.

Gilder, Joshua. "*Fanny.*" Review of *Fanny. American Spectator,* March 1981, pp. 36–37.

Greene, Gayle. *Changing the Story: Feminist Fiction and the Tradition.* Bloomington: Indiana University Press, 1991.

Grossman, Anita Susan. "Sorry, Jong Number Three." Review of *Parachutes & Kisses. Wall Street Journal,* November 21, 1984, p. 28.

Haskell, Molly. Review of *Fear of Flying. Village Voice Literary Supplement,* November 22, 1973, p. 27.

Henderson, Bruce. "Erica Jong." In *Jewish American Women Writers: A Bio-Bibliographical and Critical Sourcebook.* Edited by Ann R. Shapiro, Sara R. Horowitz, Ellen Schiff, and Miriyam Glazer. Westport, Conn.: Greenwood Press, 1994. Pp. 133–141.

Hite, Molly. "Writing and Reading—The Body: Female Sexuality and Recent Feminist Fiction." *Feminist Studies* 14:1: 121–142 (Spring 1988).

James, Clive. "Fannikin's Cunnikin." Review of *Fanny. New York Review of Books,* November 6, 1980, p. 25.

Johnston, Carol. "Erica Jong." *Dictionary of Literary Biography.* Vol. 2, *American Novelists Since World War II,* First Series. Edited by Jeffrey Helterman and Richard Layman. Detroit: Gale Research, 1978. Pp. 252–255.

Kazin, Alfred. "The Writer as Sexual Show-off; or, Making Press Agents Unnecessary." *New York Magazine,* June 9, 1975, pp. 36–40.

Lehmann-Haupt, Christopher. "Books of the Times." Review of *How to Save Your Own Life. New York Times,* March 11, 1977, p. C25.

———"The Loves of Isadora." *Time,* February 5, 1975, pp. 69–70.

Malone, Michael. "The True Adventures of Shylock's Daughter." Review of *Serenissima. The New York Times Book Review,* April 19, 1987, p. 12.

Mandrell, James. "Questions of Genre and Gender:

Contemporary American Versions of the Feminine Picaresque." *Novel* 20(2): 149–170 (Winter 1987).

Mano, D. Keith. "The Authoress as Aphid." Review of *How to Save Your Own Life. National Review,* April 29, 1977, p. 498.

Martin, Judith. "The Pleasure of Her Company." Review of *Fanny. Washington Post Book World,* August 17, 1980, p. 4.

Miller, Henry, and Erica Jong. "Two Writers in Praise of Rabelais and Each Other." *New York Times,* September 7, 1974, p. 27.

Nitzsche, Jane Chance. " 'Isadora Icarus': The Mythic Unity of Erica Jong's *Fear of Flying." Rice University Studies* 64(1): 89–100 (Winter 1978).

Ostriker, Alicia Susan. *Stealing the Language: The Emergence of Women's Poetry in America.* Boston: Beacon Press, 1986.

Pétillon, Pierre-Yves. *Histoire de la littérature américaine: notre demi-siécle, 1939–1989.* Paris: Fayard, 1992.

Pritchard, William M. "Novel Reports." Review of *Any Woman's Blues* (and other works). *Hudson Review* 43: 489–498 (Autumn 1990).

Reardon, Joan. "*Fear of Flying:* Developing the Feminist Novel." *International Journal of Women's Studies* 1, no. 3: 306–320 (May–June 1978).

Robbins, Wayne. " 'Flying' High Again." *New York Now,* September 10, 1998, pp. 17, 48.

Robinson, Lillian. "Canon Fathers and Myth Universe." *New Literary History* 19, no. 1: 23–35 (1987).

Rubin, Merle. "Diving into the Shallows of Narcissism." Review of *Parachutes & Kisses. Christian Science Monitor,* October 24, 1984, pp. 21–22.

Schultz, Susy. "Jong's Zipping Along." *Chicago Sun-Times,* July 31, 1997, p. 33.

Steiner, Wendy. Review of *Fear of Fifty: A Midlife Memoir. Times Literary Supplement,* October 7, 1994, n4775: 44.

Stoffman, Judy. "Portnoy, Stop your Complaining. Writer Erica Jong Fights Stereotypes of Jewish Women." *Toronto Star,* November 2, 1997, p. C4.

Suleiman, Susan Rubin. "(Re)Writing the Body: The Politics and Poetics of Female Eroticism." In *The Female Body in Western Culture: Contemporary Perspectives.* Edited by Susan Rubin Suleiman. Cambridge, Mass.: Harvard University Press, 1985. Pp. 7–29.

Templin, Charlotte. "Erica Jong: Becoming a Jewish Writer." In *Daughters of Valor: Contemporary Jewish American Women Writers.* Edited by Jay Halio and Ben Siegel. Newark: University of Delaware Press, 1997. Pp. 126–140.

———. *Feminism and the Politics of Literary Reputation: The Example of Erica Jong.* Lawrence: University Press of Kansas, 1995.

Theroux, Paul. "Hapless Organ." *New Statesman* 87: 554 (April 19, 1974).

Thompson, Margaret Cezair. Review of *Any Woman's Blues. Elle,* January 1990, p. 69.

Updike, John. "Jong Love." *New Yorker* 49: 149–153 (December 17, 1973).

Walker, Nancy A. *Feminist Alternatives: Irony and Fantasy in the Contemporary Novel by Women.* Jackson: University Press of Mississippi, 1990.

INTERVIEWS

Burke, Karen. *Interview,* June 1987, pp. 95–96.

Cooper-Clark, Diana. *Interviews with Contemporary Novelists.* London: Macmillan, 1986. Pp. 114–143.

Fleishman, Philip. *Maclean's,* August 21, 1978, pp. 4–6.

Gardner, Ralph. In *Writers Talk to Ralph Gardner.* New York: Metuchen, 1989. Pp. 190–203.

Kern, John. "Erica: Being the True History of Isadora Wing, Fanny Hackabout-Jones, and Erica Jong." *Writer's Digest,* June 1981, pp. 20–25.

Kourlas, Gia. "From Fear to Eternity: Twenty-five Years after *Fear of Flying,* Erica Jong Wonders What Do Women Want?" *Time Out* no. 155: 208 (September 10–17, 1998).

Martin, Wendy. In *Women Writers Talking.* Edited by Janet Todd. New York: Holmes and Meier, 1983. Pp. 21–32.

McNeese, Gretchen. *Playboy,* September 1975, pp. 61–79, 202.

Packard, William. *The Craft of Poetry: Interviews from the New York Quarterly.* New York: Doubleday, 1974. Pp. 295–320.

Parker, Rozsika, and Eleanor Stephens. *Spare Rib,* July 1977, pp. 15–17.

Pyrah, Gill. "Erica Tries a Parachute." (London) *Times,* November 2, 1984, p. II.

Ross, Jean W. "Contemporary Authors Interview." In *Contemporary Authors,* New Revision Series. Vol. 26. Detroit: Gale Research, 1989. Pp. 189–192.

Showalter, Elaine, and Carol Smith. "An Interview with Erica Jong." *Columbia Forum,* Winter 1975, pp. 12–17.

Templin, Charlotte. "The Mispronounced Poet: An Interview with Erica Jong." *Boston Review,* March/April 1992, pp. 5–8, 23, 29.

Van Matre, Lynn. "Every Woman's Blues: Erica Jong Shows Why Every Book 'Should Be a Healing Experience.' " *Chicago Tribune,* April 25, 1990, Style, p. 8.

Virshup, Amy. "For Mature Audiences Only." *New York* 27, no. 28: 38 46 (July 18, 1994).

—SHELLEY FISHER FISHKIN

Stephen King

1947–

*I*N A CONVERSATION with Stephen King that took place several years ago, I made the mistake of asking him why he continues to live in Bangor, Maine. I reminded him that the year before he had made fifty million dollars; since he could afford to reside anywhere in the world, why Bangor? King took me in with a look that suggested he had just swallowed some particularly offensive species of bug—indeed, that perhaps I myself were a member of that insect species. His response was a sardonic, "Now, just where would you have me live—Monaco?"

This little anecode actually reveals a great deal about Stephen King, the man as well as the writer. Since 1974, the publication year of his first novel, *Carrie,* King has assembled a prodigious canon. By the late 1990s he had averaged more than a book a year for nearly three decades: 35 novels, 7 collections of short stories and novellas, and 10 screenplays. One consistent element that unifies this broad and eclectic landscape is that the majority of this fiction shares a Maine setting.

Born in Portland, Maine, on September 21, 1947, Stephen King has spent almost his entire existence in Maine. After his father, Donald, abandoned the family when Stephen was two years old and was never heard from again, his mother, Nellie Ruth Pillsbury King, was put in the sole position of raising Steve and his adopted brother, David. Stephen grew up in a succession of small towns, finally settling in Durham, Maine, when he was eleven. He was educated at the University of Maine, Orono, where he graduated with a Bachelor of Arts in English in 1970. His wife, Tabitha, is also a Maine native, a novelist, and University of Maine, Orono, alumna.

Over the years, the Kings have centered their lives—and the lives of their three children—in and around the Bangor community. Their sprawling Victorian mansion on West Broadway, a street that was once home to many of the region's nineteenth-century timber barons, is located almost in the center of town. Each year the Kings donate at least ten percent of their pre-taxable income to various charitable organizations, and a large number of these causes are local. In 1992, for example, Stephen King, an avid baseball fan, built a $1.2 million Little League ballpark for the city, and each year he spends another large sum of money to maintain its pristine upkeep. The Kings recently provided over two million dollars to renovate the Bangor Public Library. A pediatrics unit at Eastern Maine Medical Center, equipment for the Bangor Fire Department, music teachers for rural Maine schools, gym facilities for the Bangor YMCA, undergraduate scholarships for financially challenged students to study at universities in Maine and several other states—the list of community-bascd projects aided by the Stephen and Tabitha King Foundation is a long one. And several years ago, Stephen King began insisting that before he would sell the rights to one of his novels to a Hollywood producer, the contract had to stipulate that the film would be shot somewhere in Maine.

STEPHEN KING'S MAINE: STATE OF PLACE, STATE OF MIND

These illustrations are but a few examples of the obvious affiliation that Stephen King maintains with his native state. To a certain extent, however, the generous gifts to his community can be seen as a kind of payback for what the community has provided him in supplying material for a lifetime of writing. His most memorable characters are Maine natives. A novel such as *Dolores Claiborne* (1993) embodies the rugged spirit of Maine not only in its protagonist's powers of resiliency but in her very speech patterns, idioms, and diction. Even the supernatural creatures that have become signature features of King's horrorscape within the popular imagination are often Maine inspired: the Wendigo in *Pet Sematary* (1983) is a monster that owes its origins to regional Native American lore and a northeastern winter climate foreign to human habitation and survival. In an interview King conducted with me for the opening chapter of *Stephen King, The Second Decade: "Danse Macabre" to "The Dark Half"* (1992), he spoke at length about the importance of Maine as an influence on his writing: "If I decide I don't want to be in Maine for a story, my mind always seems to take me back there. If I am in Iowa or Nebraska, it is a place that is flat and empty. A place where I can still recognize a similarity to Maine. So place comes through, and place casts its own weight over whatever you are writing."

King's books and stories have been so strongly shaped by Maine's environment that it is impossible to imagine separating landscape from personality, climate from theme. Rather than evoking a chamber-of-commerce, pastoral relationship with the Maine landscape, however, King draws upon a nature that is hostile and savage, an environment where malefic energies reside in secret. In the novel *The Girl Who Loved Tom Gordon* (1999), nine-year-old Trisha McFarland is lost in the Maine woods. For days she wanders deeper into the wilderness in search of human beings or signs of civilized life. Her torment is heightened by her constant struggle against nature's elements: from swamp bogs, to incessant insect attacks, to her feeble efforts to forage food. Early in the novel, King reminds both Trish and her audience that "the woods were filled with everything you didn't like, everything you were afraid of and instinctively loathed, everything that tried to overwhelm you with nasty, no-brain panic." Trisha's greatest adversary stalks her until the end of the novel where she must confront and vanquish an adult bear. In her semi-hallucinogenic state brought on by fatigue, fever, and starvation, the bear metamorphoses into a supernatural embodiment of the woods itself, a shifting composite of nature's faceless and aggressively misanthropic spirit.

In an essay entitled "Beyond the Kittery Bridge," Burton Hatlen maintained that William Faulkner has remained one of King's favorite novelists from his days as an undergraduate. Modeling much of his canon after Faulkner's convoluted Yoknapatawpha cycle, King's "Maine books also suggest that he is more or less deliberately creating a 'myth of the South.'" Like Faulkner, the fictional cycle unifying King's Castle Rock microcosm often features families, characters, and events from one book that are referenced again in later books; certain plots are likewise dependent on events that have transpired in earlier narratives. For example, the haunting presence of Frank Dodd, the Castle Rock serial rapist in *Cujo* (1981) who merely haunts the perimeters of this novel, reappears in a much more central and substantial role in *The Dead Zone* (1979). The chef in *The Shining* (1977), Dick Hallorann, makes a brief appearance as a young man in *IT* (1987), and his role as sage survivor and rescuer of others is consistent in both texts. The 1958 Plymouth Fury featured in *Christine* (1983) is resurrected from the auto graveyard to ferry Henry Bowers to his early-morning assignation attempt at the Derry public library in *IT*. Even King's fictional towns—Castle Rock, Haven, Salem's Lot—share characteristics particular to small Maine communities. To a real extent, these Maine locales are all connecting points on the road to Derry, a city modeled on Bangor and the epicenter of evil on King's geo-literary map.

Understanding the importance of Maine as a shaping influence on King's fiction is an important starting point to appreciating his art. But his attitude toward Maine, at least in his fiction, is a decidedly bifurcated one. In characters such as Dolores Claiborne, John Smith (*The Dead Zone*), Frannie Goldsmith (*The Stand* [1978]), Alan Pangborn (*Needful Things* [1991]), and Trisha McFarland, King provides us with examples of heroism. Common men and women with few pretensions, these Maine natives embody an independent resolve sweetly tempered by a genuine commitment to others. Surrounded by situations that both torment and threaten their psychological stability, these characters—due in no small part to their obstinate streak of Yankee self-reliance—are in possession of unwavering moral centers. They maintain healthy psyches that stand in contrast to the forces of oppression, perversity, and corruption that often characterize their immediate familial and social relationships.

While King clearly admires their independent opposition, he also provides less flattering portraits of small-town Maine life to counterbalance their moral resolve. King seems to understand in-

tuitively that while the small-town Maine environment is capable of producing courageous individuals, it can destroy others because of its pride of isolation, pressures to conform, and lack of compassion. As the writer revealed in a 1980 interview, "Maine is different. Really different. People keep themselves to themselves, and they take the outsiders' money, and on the surface, at least, they're polite about it. But they keep themselves to themselves. That's the only way I can put it."

The towns of Derry, Haven, Salem's Lot, and Castle Rock are places where evil is challenged only by small groups of individuals. Throughout King's canon, evil manifests itself as a conforming presence, particularly appropriate to the social microcosm of Maine's small-town life. Whether it takes the form of a religious fanatic, the fascistic authority of Randall Flagg (*The Stand, The Eyes of the Dragon* [1987], *The Dark Tower IV: Wizard and Glass* [1997]), or the social homogeneity dictated by the Tommyknockers and It, evil thrives in closed, self-contained worlds. Malefic forces in King's work are remarkably consistent: they manipulate, restrict, and silence opposition. And usually the narrative itself, while projecting such a consciousness, is appropriately reduced to a single authoritarian voice. In novels such as *IT, The Tommyknockers* (1988), *Bag of Bones* (1998) and *Salem's Lot* (1975), the majority exerts a defining will that demands rigid conformity from all the inhabitants of the town—a monological merging in speech, thought, and action. The vampires that eventually take over Salem's Lot, for example, merely reflect the homogeneity of the town itself; the progressive degradation of individuals into a spiritless mass of hungry undead completes the moral disintegration of the community. Hatlen views these regional portraits as a kind of "chronic soul-sickness prevalent, King implies, throughout post-Vietnam America, but working away with a special insidiousness in the heart of Maine, beguiled by its myth of itself as the Pastoral Paradise."

THE BODY UNDER THE STREET: GIVING SHAPE TO KING'S CANON

Like Emily Dickinson, another New Englander who drew art from her close scrutiny of place, if Stephen King has found himself geographically isolated in rural Maine for most of his life, he has more than compensated by creating a multi-layered fictional landscape imaginatively rendered. Trying to generalize about King's extensive oeuvre is a daunting task. Nevertheless, for the sake of this present analysis, King's canon can be divided roughly in half, since the books prior to *Misery* (1987) constitute the first part of his career, while those narratives that follow tend to reflect a markedly different set of priorities for the writer.

The early novels are large, ambitious books that encompass enormous narrative scope and revolve around recognizable genre themes (sometimes conflating two or more in a single text): horror, dystopian technology, epic fantasy, and journey quest. King's first fifteen years of work produced novels such as *The Shining* (1977), *The Stand* (1978), *Firestarter* (1980), *The Talisman* (1984), and *IT* (1987). These are fictions that present a macrocosmic view of postmodern America, providing the reader with a journey to the center of a post–Watergate heart of darkness. These books are further linked because they are rendered from a tremendous narratological range and vision; King's epic propensities are never stronger evinced than in *The Stand, The Talisman,* and *IT,* texts that weave a vast historical, mythological, and social matrix into a journey quest.

Many of the books from this period are also unified by virtue of being road narratives; indeed, the reader would be well served in keeping a roadmap of the United States close at hand. In each of these tales, King takes us across contemporary America on a system of interstates fraught with danger. The concrete highways that criss-cross these books frequently come to symbolize the hard-hearted uniformity of American towns and the personalities populating them that King's young men and women—who often are no more than adolescent boys and girls—must somehow confront and overcome. The influence of the epic tradition, particularly J. R. R. Tolkien's *Lord of the Rings,* on these early King novels cannot be underestimated. Like Tolkien's Frodo, King's young American travelers encounter magical realms and dark challenges that they survive only at the expense of their innocence and in the sharpening of their wits.

It is in the context of this sobering portrait of a postmodern America that King's road epics sometimes point the way back to Maine. At the conclusion of *The Stand,* for example, Frannie Goldsmith and Stu Redman choose to return to the isolation of a depopulated Maine rather than remain a part of the new social order currently under construction in the Boulder Free Zone. Maine no doubt represents Frannie's image of a nostalgic past, and this is a partial explanation for her wish to raise her children there. But Maine also offers this post-plague first family a sanctuary from the complicated societal issues that are beginning to reemerge at the end of the novel and that were responsible for creating the superflu disaster in the first place: the rise of technology, the imposition of a paranoid technobureaucracy, and the anonymity of mass culture.

In contrast to this macrocosmic examination of America frequently considered from the off-ramps of its interstate highway system, the books that follow *Misery* (as well as *Misery* itself) show evidence of King's ability to produce highly circumscribed, tightly wrought fictions bearing few of his early epic tendencies toward narrative and thematic expansiveness. If *The Shining* and *The*

Stand can be likened to an epic saga played out on a big screen to accommodate their involvement with history and dramatic social dynamics, then books such as *Misery* or *Gerald's Game* (1992) are more like classic Greek drama presented on a circumscribed stage, employing a consistent scenic backdrop and a small cast of characters, and performed in front of an intimate theatre audience.

Moreover, King's work of the 1990s, in addition to being generally shorter and more compact, also tended to include a more realistic treatment of women. The novels *Gerald's Game, Dolores Claiborne,* and *Rose Madder* (1995)—a trio that should be considered together, because the narratives share similar themes as well as being written and published consecutively—differ markedly from King's previous fiction. Feminist in orientation, the novels present most of the action from a woman's point of view. If the first half of King's literary canon can be read as an accurate and potent rendition of Everyman wandering amidst the wastelands of postmodern America, the second half of this body of work can be read as a focus on representations of the American Everywoman and her disgruntled home life.

In their introduction to *Imagining the Worst: Stephen King and the Representations of Women* (1998), Kathleen Margaret Lant and Theresa Thompson wrote that King's female characters "often provoke hostility as well as admiration. When analyzing King's depiction of women, it is tempting to relegate him to the category of unregenerate misogynist or conversely to elevate him to the status of newly sensitive male." This lukewarm evaluation notwithstanding, Lant and Thompson were correct in noting that King's more women-centered novels are a clear departure from his precedent portraits of women. These books likewise represented a substantial risk in potentially alienating King's popular readership. After two decades, his loyal audience had come to expect tales of supernatural horror and

fantasy rather than reality-based stories depicting the horror of sexual fantasies.

In light of these differing orientations that can be said to distinguish the two halves of Stephen King's prolific career, it is worthwhile to speculate about their respective influences on the writer's popularity, especially as translated into book sales. How has King's considerable and diverse audience greeted the dual tendencies that separate his early work from his later efforts? The length of time each of his novels has spent on the *New York Times* Bestseller List serves as an interesting barometer for distinguishing King's first decade of work from that published after *Misery.* Each of King's narratives from *The Shining* to the publication of *Misery* maintained a miminum of 23 weeks on the *New York Times* list; most were on the list longer: for example, *Firestarter,* 35 weeks; *IT,* 35 weeks; *Misery,* 30 weeks. In contrast, none of his books published after *Misery* has remained on the *New York Times* list longer than 23 weeks, and most have been on the list for a much shorter period: for example, *The Dark Half* (1989), 19 weeks; *Dolores Claiborne,* 14 weeks; *The Regulators* (1996), 14 weeks. (These statistics were partly responsible for King's contentious decision in 1997 to abandon an eighteen-year publishing relationship with Viking and to sign a three-book contract with Scribner; King believed that Viking failed to market, promote, and package his books sufficiently to boost sales figures that have, for at least the past decade, clearly reached a plateau.)

There are, however, probably several other explanations for this sharp fluctuation, one being that King published a book a year for three decades, and the *New York Times* statistics underscore the market's saturation point. But it is also possible that this dramatic shift in volume sales, far more than being a consequence of inadequate packaging and promotion, reflects King's laudable efforts to challenge himself as a writer by composing narratives that are not neatly categorized into the horror–fantasy genre. Nor are the books of the 1990s similar in subject matter to the narratives that originally established King's massive audience and forged his reputation in the 1970s and 1980s as the master of the macabre. Because work after *Misery* so seldom resembles the novels that preceded it, King has apparently disappointed a large segment of the audience that expected from him a consistency in genre and style of fiction. And ironically, while the books published in the 1990s have tended to be more "mainstream" in subject matter—focusing on domestic and gender issues—because of King's established reputation as a popular male horror novelist, his audience base has not enlarged to the point where his work is now included (as it legitimately should be) on the syllabi of women's studies curricula.

EARLY NOVELS: THE REIGN OF TERROR BEGINS

The early novels of Stephen King underscore the prodigious energies that distinguish this writer's canon in the literal size of the books as well as in their ambitious narrative design. If King is frequently criticized for composing narratives that are undisciplined and perhaps overly digressive, they are that way because their author has attempted to accomplish so much within them. Early in his career King produced a body of work that would undoubtedly have benefited tremendously from some judicious editing and revising; this point notwithstanding, these novels are also informed by a depth of energy and range of imagination seldom found in a young writer.

King's initial publishing efforts are demarcated by a distinct fascination with children, perhaps reflective of the writer's immediate personal experience during the time of their composition as a father raising three young children. As King's children have entered adulthood, his own interest in writing about childhood has diminished accordingly.

In his first decade of publishing, however, King's most important books usually center on a child (or group of children) often imperiled by violence or oppressive codes of behavior imposed by families, social institutions, and jaded adults. Many of these early narratives are rites of passage featuring the innocence of adolescence confronting adult realities, a journey that is always fraught with violence and danger. King's children cling to their youthful idealism and romantic innocence, both of which come under fierce attack in his novels from the oppressive forces of societal institutions and the supernatural creatures that frequently emerge as a direct consequence of adult moral lapses. If these young people are to survive—morally as well as physically—they must somehow find a way to resist the prevailing values of a society that transforms its adults into monsters.

King's kids are not responsible for their parents' divorces or for governmental errors in judgment, but they are nonetheless forced into coping with the consequences of such events. King's children, like the female protagonist in an eighteenth-century gothic novel, appear as perfect victims—their confrontations with evil are initially overwhelming—and their plights elicit intense sympathetic responses from the reader. To offset the oppressive nature of their relationships with adults and social authority, King endows his young protagonists with tremendous energies; indeed, they often possess imaginative capacities or supernatural abilities so potent that the children who wield them must learn to "grow into" their powers. As Clive Barker has opined, "In King's work, it is so often the child who carries the wisdom; the child who synthesesizes 'real' and 'imagined' experience without question, who knows instinctively that imagination can tell the truth the way the senses never can." As King's children come to discipline their attributes, they evolve as human beings, slowly maturing into child-adults who exhibit traits of adaptability, survival skills, and most important, a level of sensitivity seldom present in King's adults. (When King does supply an adult with these qualities, as in the case of Johnny Smith in *The Dead Zone,* usually the adult has not progressed far beyond the realm of adolescence and maintains childlike loyalties and a romantic faith in life.)

In King's fiction, children embody the full spectrum of human experience. Many of his youthful protagonists occupy the epicenters of his books, and from them all other actions seem to radiate. Some represent the nucleus for familial love. They are often healing agents, as in the first halves of *The Shining, Pet Sematary,* and *Cujo,* enabling parents in unstable marriages to hold their union together. Moreover, King seems inordinately fond of testing the moral capacities of his adolescent protagonists; most of his child-heroes represent a Wordsworthian ideal of goodness struggling against the forces of a corrupt world.

In one of the most important books from King's early period, *The Shining,* we are introduced to a child who embodies both the spirit of endurance and the propensity for goodness that characterizes most of King's other youthful protagonists. As Samantha Figliola argued in "The Thousand Faces of Danny Torrance," "Danny epitomizes King's own mythos of childhood. He is the 'marvelous third eye' of childhood perception magnified ten thousand times, a seer who is nonetheless simple and innocent. A psychological sieve for his parents' most deeply buried emotions, a hero forced to enter and escape hell." Danny captivates us with his sweet innocence; his peril at the hands of a psychologically unstable father and agents of an evil design located at the Overlook Hotel only serves to endear him even more to the reader. Danny overcomes these obstacles, in part, because of his supernatural attribute—a precognitive ability to view the past and future called "shining"—and a tremendous ca-

pacity for love. Although he undergoes traumatic experiences throughout the better part of the novel, we never doubt his resiliency and place in the future once he is freed from his father and the spirits at the Overlook. Unlike his father, Jack, Danny has a solid support system in his mother and surrogate-father figure, Dick Hallorann, to help him move outside the shadow of his father's dysfunctional behavior.

In contrast, Jack Torrance is never freed from his own childhood traumas. *The Shining* is, in fact, a book that centers on the persistent importance of childhood experience. The novel issues a strong statement about environmental determinism in its portrayal of a severely disturbed adult male whose memory of his own father is dominated by violence and alcoholism. Jack's identification is certainly exacerbated through his involvement with the history of patriarchal abuse in place at the Overlook, but it is likewise clear that such behavior originated in Jack's childhood and that this past continues to haunt his present. The novel steadily details Jack's inexorable transformation into his father, adhering to his alcoholism and propensity for violence, as being at the hotel helps to reawaken and reanimate recollected patterns of domestic abuse that Jack has struggled to repress as an adult.

The Shining is a book that owes a great debt to the Gothic literary tradition. Not only does it revisit the haunted house as a conceit that centers all of the narrative action, it also advances the tradition by making the house-hotel into a malefic locus of energy capable of manifesting itself directly into the lives of its inhabitants. By the end of the novel, Jack's initial interest in the hotel's nefarious history and his own writer's dream to be rich and famous merge together into a single obsession: the hotel usurps the place Jack's family once held in his life. Unable to separate himself from the influences of the past—his own identification with his father as well as the hotel's infamous history—Jack surrenders his future. In order to survive, his family must move out from beneath the long shadow Jack casts and move forward in his absence.

The conclusion of *The Shining* ultimately embodies Stephen King's profound faith in the resiliency of human nature and the enduring power of love. This novel's ending is often repeated in other King texts; evil is either vanquished, or at least recognized and confronted by the force of human morality, whatever form it happens to assume. As King generally affirms throughout his novels as well as in *Danse Macabre* (1981), his nonfictional treatise on horror art, "If the horror story is our rehearsal for death, then its strict moralities make it also a reaffirmation of life and good will and simple imagination—just one more pipeline to the infinite."

This moral vision or "pipeline to the infinite" is a recurring resource available throughout King's fictional landscape. In *The Shining,* it is the energy of the shining itself that bonds Danny to Dick Hallorann and the latter with his mother. In *Salem's Lot,* this force is found in the "inevitable rightness, of whiteness" that Mark Petrie discovers when he assumes the role of the "white knight" by pouring holy water over the blade of an axe in preparation for battle against the vampires. In *The Stand,* this magical property radiates from Mother Abigail, the source of human faith and conduit for divine goodness who counterbalances the evil of Randall Flagg. While in the novel *IT,* it is the circle created by the sexual and emotional union of the Losers' Club and their unwavering faith in the turtle and one another that ultimately defeats the monster It. King may have achieved his reputation by writing about threatening and disconcerting subject matter, but this does not necessarily impose a corollary that his vision is hopeless. As he expressed in a 1981 interview, "I really do believe in the White force. Children are part of that force, which is why I write about them the way I do. There are a lot of horror writers who deal with this struggle, but

they tend to concentrate on the Black. But the other force is there, too."

In nearly every one of King's major novels, there exists the presence of goodness—the white force, blind faith, small group human solidarity, the power of a writer's or child's imagination, simple love—that essentially breaks the stranglehold of evil, regardless of how its corruption is manifested in human or supernatural form. This unselfish force is always expressed as a highly romantic, antirational impulse. In *The Shining,* for example, Hallorann's decision to rescue the Torrances is not a rational decision, as he knows it will jeopardize his very life: "Was he willing to chance the end of that—the end of him—for three white people he didn't even know?" Yet Hallorann chooses to make the journey to Colorado against his own best interests because "the boy was stuck in that place, and he would go. For the boy."

The life-affirming, emotionally charged choices that compel the heroes and heroines of King's early fiction into action stand in direct contrast to the highly rational powers of evil that seek to isolate individuals into states of moral indifference. *The Stand* is King's most persuasive statement on the struggle between these two opposing ideologies, but it is likewise a paramount concern in other early narratives such as *Firestarter, The Talisman, The Dead Zone, The Tommyknockers,* and "The Mist" (in *Skeleton Crew* [1985]). Randall Flagg and his followers are aligned with the same technobureaucracy that created *The Stand*'s superflu and its subsequent social devastation. According to Douglas Winter in *Stephen King: The Art of Darkness,* Flagg "wanders the corridors of the haunted castle of the American landscape, symbolizing the inexplicable fear of the return of bygone powers—both technological and, as his last name intimates, sociopolitical." Although Flagg is affiliated with ubiquitous forces of evil throughout the novel, he is best represented in technological terms. Glen Bateman, the novel's resident observer of social dynamics, describes Flagg as a natural consequence of the technological god that was worshiped prior to the plague and that ends up destroying most of the earth's population in the creation of the superflu itself: " 'Maybe he's just the last magician of rational thought, gathering the tools of technology against us.' "

The Las Vegas empire that Flagg re-creates revolves around reestablishing conduits of energy and communication. And while we learn of his success at reconnecting air conditioning systems and telephones, his ultimate goal is to reactivate the technologies of war. Highly capable of manipulating the deadly machinery that litters the landscape of postmodern America, Flagg's empire of "tech people [who] like to work in an atmosphere of tight discipline and linear goals" ironically can create nothing; it can only destroy. At the core of Flagg's nature are the same impulses toward self-destruction and betrayal that characterize King's elaborate portrait of technology throughout his canon. Thus, it is appropriate that the Dark Man himself is betrayed by Trashcan Man, Flagg's ideological "id," and by the very machinery of mass destruction that the two men would use to secure their conquest of the world. In the end, Flagg and Trashcan Man are emblematic of "blind science"; their personal madness is symptomatic of the greater insanity that has led to the construction and deployment of America's lethal gadgetry.

If Flagg and his Vegas denizens are linked to technology and the urge to re-create another version of the pre-plague world, the Free Zone unconsciously revels in the distinctions that separate it from modern Western societies: "Whole groups of people were living together in small sub communities like communes. Boulder itself was a closed society, a *tabula* so *rasa* that it could not sense its own novel beauty." Moreover, perhaps reflective of King's own progressive politics, the central protagonists based in the Free Zone rep-

resent a more democratic social and gender mix than the exclusively patriarchal world of Flagg's Las Vegas. While Flagg's followers in Vegas are attracted to their white male leader because of his technological affinity and expertise, the men and women who compose the Free Zone are drawn to an old black woman and her simple faith in a primitive Christianity. Mother Abigail's "white magic" is decidedly antitechnological. Her farm in Nebraska operates without electricity and she must pump her own well water; when she seeks aid in guiding the community in Boulder, she adheres to the examples of biblical prophets by wandering into the woods to request correspondence with the inhuman powers of the natural world. The four men from the Free Zone who make their "stand" against Flagg and who initiate the collapse of his dominion follow Abigail's lead: eschewing automobiles, weapons, and the machinery of modern America, they journey across the desert relying on their instincts and intuition.

In most of Stephen King's epic fantasies, the forces of "white magic" exist in Manichaean opposition to the powers of supernatural evil. The potential for King's characters to produce acts of good or evil is always dependent on the individual's ability to control his or her selfish impulses. In *The Stand*, perhaps more than any other King novel, free will and moral choice are solidly within the individual's purview; all of the major characters in this book participate directly in determining their own fates. And while this determination is never an easy one to make—*The Stand*'s most complicated and engaging characters are pulled in opposing directions simultaneously—personal choices become, nonetheless, a barometer for measuring an individual's capacity for ethical development. Two of the more interesting characters in this book, Harold Lauder and Larry Underwood, illustate this principle insofar as these young men travel in opposite moral directions through the novel's unfolding. Lauder rejects the potential available to him in the future, symbolized in his newly acquired nickname, "Hawk," by clinging to a need to avenge the accumulated insults from his past; in contrast, Underwood learns that his current condition is better than his sordid past, and he matures into manhood when he accepts responsibility for the future of the Free Zone. Late in the novel, Harold unconsciously acknowledges the full burden of free will in one of his ledger entries: "To follow one's star is to concede the power of some greater Force, some Providence; yet is it not possible that the act of following itself is the taproot of even greater Power? Your GOD, your DEVIL, owns the keys to the lighthouse; . . . but to each of us he has given the responsibility of NAVIGATION."

All through the novel readers witness illustrations highlight

ing this "responsibility of navigation" in personalized contexts. Nadine Cross chooses to sacrifice her sexuality and her soul to Flagg's destiny; the men who operate "the zoo," a motorized bordello where women are systematically drugged, raped, and executed, do so because in a world devoid of formal law they themselves lack the will to impose self-control; Mother Abigail supplies a plan of action that suggests Glen, Stu, Ralph, and Larry engage in direct confrontation against Flagg's empire, but it is up to each individual man to choose whether to trust that plan and head west. When Larry asks, "Do we have a choice?," Abigail's response is that "There is always a choice. That's God's way, always will be. Your will is still free. Do as you will."

Clearly, a paramount concern in King's early fiction is dramatizing the will of men and women making proactive choices to oppose the dictatorial design of evil. In one of King's largest and most ambitious novels to date, *IT,* the epic scope of *The Stand* is channeled into a single city. The history of Derry, Maine, is carefully documented and its legacy of corruption must be confronted by the child-adults who are also its principal victims. In preceding works, such as *The Shining* and *Salem's Lot,* King's portrayal of evil is defined in terms of the "accumulated sum" of its parts: a chronicle of human depravity occurs in one place over an extended period. This locale and patterned behavior enables maleficence to emerge as a living organism capable of sustaining itself on renewable instances of violence and corruption. This paradigm is repeated in novels such as *Needful Things* and *IT,* where a town or village assumes core aspects of the Gothic haunted house, including the need for heroes and heroines to do battle against its resident evil force.

The individual members of the Losers' Club choose to return to Derry (all except for Stan Uris, who commits suicide) because they recognize their commitment to one another and to the cause of destroying the shape-changing monster that feeds on children. They confront It not merely for purposes of self-preservation; Bill Denbrough wishes to avenge his brother's death, but he and the others also seem genuinely disposed to saving the lives of Derry's children. Like Dick Hallorann in *The Shining* and the Free Zone citizens who journey west at various points to confront Flagg in *The Stand,* the Losers in *IT* are united in a quest to vanquish evil for reasons that are nobler than themselves. As Thomas R. Edwards remarked in his review of the novel, "Only brave and imaginative children, or adults who learn to remember and honor their childish selves, can hope to foil It." The novel is arguably King's most persuasive argument for keeping open the passageway that connects adolescence to adulthood. As King remarked in his interview in *The Second Decade,* "I'm interested in the mythic power that childhood holds over our imagination and, in particular, the point at which the adult is able to link up with his or her own childhood past and the powers therein." This is why the seven friends must return to Derry: to defeat It once and for all, the Losers' Club members must reopen their personal and collective conduits to childhood.

LATER FICTION: CHALLENGES TO EMPHASIS AND FORM

Over the past several years, feminist scholars have observed that the roles King has traditionally allotted women in his fiction and specifically female sexuality itself are patronizingly restrictive and frequently negative. Critic Chelsea Quinn Yarbro was first to lament that "it is disheartening when a writer with so much talent and strength of vision is not able to develop a believable woman character between the ages of seventeen and sixty." Mary Pharr, in a seminal essay that broadens and deepens Yarbro's position, noted that "Despite his best efforts, King's women are reflective of American sterotypes. . . . His most convincing female characters are precisely those who are least threatening to men." In a critique devoted to language ideologies in King's novels, Karen Hohne likewise opined that his women characters

> are never allowed to speak themselves, to make themselves with words. They get little dialogue, their speech is generally flat and undistinguished or stereotyped, or, worse, their language is distinctive but it is not their own; it is instead that of officiality, a set of languages from whose power they are excluded by their very being.

Burns and Kanner were even more specific when they examined King's treatment of female sexuality: "Menstruation, mothering, and female sexual desire function as bad omens, prescient clues that something will soon be badly awry." And in her discussion of *IT,* Karen Thoens reduced the monster in the text to an essentially feminine archetype:

It could be sexual intercourse. It could be repulsive female sexuality. But mostly, it is actually She. . . . It is your mother. It, nameless terror. It is bloody, filthy, horrible. The boy-men heroes have returned to Derry to face IT again, HER, the bitch, the force that is really responsible for their lost youth.

Sharply aware of such criticism and generally concurring with it, Stephen King has labored to create more human and less stereotypical female personalities, at least since the publication of *Misery.* In *Dolores Claiborne,* for example, the writer completely eschewed his traditional third-person narrative form in order to provide Dolores with an autobiographical voice and consciousness. This departure from omniscient point of view to a first-person monologue signals the importance King is willing to invest in legitimizing Dolores' perspective and the domestic issues her narrative explores. Perhaps the truism that middle-aged males begin to explore their "feminine" side is another explanation for King's interest in developing better women characters. In focusing much of his energy on women's issues, King's later fiction became more circumscribed, centering on one or two individuals almost exclusively.

Misery holds a pivotal position in King's canon; the novel signals a transition that begins to emphasize a new significance for women characters, an intense scrutiny provided to the roles of writer and reader, and a willingness to experiment with a more restricted narratological structure and style. The book takes place almost entirely in the bedroom of a remote Colorado farmhouse. The principal characters—a famous writer named Paul Sheldon, who is held captive by his "number one fan," Annie Wilkes—could easily be figures in a one-act play, where the deliberately oppressive stage backdrop helps to highlight their verbal and physical conflicts. In *Misery,* the reader encounters one of King's first attempts to create a fiercely independent woman who is neither a madonna nor a whore. Her psychopathology notwithstanding, Annie Wilkes is one of the few women in King's canon who possesses real power, even if she ultimately fails to exercise it responsibly. In her systematic torturing of Paul Sheldon, Annie appears as a figure who demands to be taken seriously; she is a kind of revenging agent for all past Gothic heroines who have suffered physical and psychological abuse from men. Although *Misery* is not a feminist text, as it remains mired in the destructive, potentially castrating nature of women, its female character is a prototype—at least in terms of her strength, intelligence, and angry resolve—for King's female protagonists who follow her in a series of heroine-centered books published during the 1990s.

Until the publications of *Gerald's Game, Dolores Claiborne,* and *Rose Madder,* the hero in Stephen King's fictional microcosm was usually from the young, white, male middle class, an American Everyman, exemplified in characters such as Andy Dufresne in "The Shawshank Redemption" (in *Different Seasons* [1982]), Stu Redman in *The Stand,* John Smith in *The Dead Zone,* or Dennis Guilder in *Christine.* These individuals find themselves in situations where their ordinary lives have become suddenly extraordinary. What King appears most interested in testing in works such as "The Shawshank Redemption" and *The Dead Zone* is the mettle of these ordinary men faced with extraordinary circumstances, watching them struggle and become greater than they ever thought they were capable of becoming. Until the 1990s, King's landscape was populated almost exclusively with heroes rather than heroines. In *Gerald's Game, Dolores Claiborne, Rose Madder,* and *Bag of Bones,* however, the writer expands the center of his fictional universe to include women. The females in all these narratives—even the ghost women, Sara Tidwell and Jo Noonan in *Bag of Bones,* who do battle against one another in the afterlife—differ markedly from women characters who appear

elsewhere in King's fiction. All of these wives and mothers possess highly impressive levels of inner strength and independence. And like King's male hero counterparts in the earlier works, the heroines of these books are situated at crisis points in their lives where they must either rise above their oppression or capitulate to it entirely.

Gerald's Game and *Misery* should be viewed as bedroom bookends: both texts are intense psychological explorations of gendered relationships that feature very little physical action, as the protagonists of these narratives are literally tied to their beds. As Linda Badley accurately assessed: "*Misery* blamed a sadistic and all-devouring matriarchy for the protagonist's victimization. *Gerald's Game,* as its title announces, condemns the patriarchy. The latter 'corrects' the misogyny implicit in *Misery,* transporting its situation and setting into Female Gothic and taking the woman's point of view." *Gerald's Game* and *Misery* are two of the most complex and ambitious efforts King has yet undertaken. The tales concern nothing less than a wrestling with the destruction and re-creation of selfhood.

The first chapter of *Gerald's Game* is a beautifully orchestrated introduction to all of the major elements that will unfold in the remainder of the text. The major character, Jessie Burlingame, has her hands handcuffed to a bed by her husband, Gerald, during kinky sexplay that has gone terribly awry. Far from arousing her sexually, this particular instance of "Gerald's game" revivifies a deeply repressed episode in her childhood that underscores the self-induced psychological bondage she has imposed over her memory of this event. As a young girl, Jessie experienced a sexual molestation while sitting on her father's lap during a full solar eclipse. But even worse than acting on his incestual urge was her father's successful effort to cover his involvement by making his daughter into a coconspirator: "I guess we have a bargain," he said. "I say nothing, you say nothing. Right? Not to anyone else, not even to each other. Forever and ever, amen. When we walk out of this room, Jess, it never happened."

For many years, as the girl matures into a woman, the truth is repressed, even as Jessie's relationship with her father deteriorates. Her later involvement with Gerald's bondage fantasy, however, reawakens Jessie's feelings of being powerless and demeaned: "Her response was not so much directed at Gerald as at that hateful feeling that came flooding up from the bottom of her mind." While Gerald interprets her verbal objections as part of a scripted sexual scenario, "She was *supposed* to protest; after all, that was the game," Jessie is actually beginning to confront the secret she has maintained since adolescence. Her husband's unwillingness to consider her feelings, the undeterred urgency of his arousal, his line of spittle and its nexus to sperm, even the darkening windows of the late fall afternoon in a secluded cottage by a lake transport Jessie back to her father and the day of the eclipse. As a result, her lethal kick to Gerald's crotch, viewed in this context, is less of an accident than an unconscious urge to castrate her father. Gerald's death occurs in the novel's dramatic first chapter; the remainder of the book centers on Jessie's self-induced psychotherapy as she struggles to resolve the opposing voices in her head and to extricate herself from the bondage that literally and symbolically binds her to Gerald's bed.

Throughout the first half of *Gerald's Game*, an abandoned dog named Prince shadows Jessie's situation and even makes a meal out of her dead husband. The dog and woman parallel one another's situations: Jessie is the former Princess, as the dog is the former Prince. Both have been cast off by careless and cruel men-owners, the prerogative of those who exercise power and control in a disposable culture. Both pet and wife had at one time been insulated from hunger, harm, and self-responsibility. Now, however, Prince's emaciated body foreshadows Jessie's potential fate; without a man to protect them, Jessie and

Prince are alone, masterless, and in grave jeopardy. Like Donna Trenton in *Cujo* and Wendy Torrance in *The Shining,* two other women in King's canon who eventually realize that they cannot wait for a soap opera rescue from a white knight, Jessie decides that if she is to be rescued she must do it herself. Donna Trenton waits too long and sacrifices her son. Wendy Torrance's survival effort is aided by the timely arrival of Dick Hallorann. But Jessie remains entirely on her own and acts in time. The most feminist of King's heroines concentrate on saving themselves and saving others instead of waiting to be saved.

Gerald's Game and *Dolores Claiborne* are arguably the most effective illustrations of King's fascination with creating interrelated plots and subject themes in his work. These narratives share not only the issue of father-daughter incest and moments where Dolores and Jessie either view or sense each other's presence in each respective text, but they also employ the same 1963 eclipse as a defining moment. In *Gerald's Game,* the eclipse signals the start of Jessie's descent into the silent darkness of shame and loss, whereas in *Dolores Claiborne* it is the event that liberates both Dolores and her daughter from the oppressive shadow of their husband-father. It is important to note that a detailed map of the path of the eclipse through Maine is provided as a frontispiece to both novels. The point at which the "path of totality" begins is Dark Score Lake, where Jessie is molested by her father. In contrast, its solar path ends at Little Tall Island, where Dolores kills her husband because he has sexually abused their daughter, Selena. The movement of the eclipse parallels the movement of evolving female empowerment in these two texts: from the shadow that begins Jessie's passive victimization on the lap of her father to its passing in Dolores Claiborne's bid for freedom against an oppressive male.

For Jessie to follow Dolores' path of liberation,

she must return to the eclipse and recognize it not only as the moment of her father's betrayal, but also as a symbol of the "eclipsed" relationships she has since constructed between herself and her parents, her friendship with Ruth Neary (a lesbian feminist who suspects that Jessie harbors a dark secret), her gender positioning as a wife, and her own identity as a woman. While the actual physical eclipse in both narratives is important, its metaphorical significance is even more so. In each book, the father interposes himself between daughter and mother (essentially "eclipsing" the latter). In addition, the eclipse becomes a metaphor for the condition of being female in a patriarchal culture: cut off, blocked, obscured. Furthermore, as a solar eclipse creates an unnatural ambiance for those who observe it, the incestual acts that both fathers perpetrate upon their daughters wreck havoc on the natural order of the respective families and the psychosexual development of the victims.

If male abuse, by objectification and oppression, is what continues to eclipse women, then King argues in these feminist texts that women must face the truth, like facing the sun, even at the risk of "burning yourself without knowing you were doing it." It may seem easier for Jessie and Dolores to ignore gender oppression to get along in the world, but as Jessie remarks of Dolores, "She is in the path of the eclipse, too," as are all women. The eclipse in a woman's life, King suggests, occurs in that period when a man is sexually prominent in it: from Jessie's and Selena's adolescence to the end of Dolores' wifehood. Both novels argue that a woman is only free when she escapes from beneath the sexual shadow cast by a man—be that man her father or her husband. Silence is equivalent to darkness in these novels, and King insists that true survival depends not on silence, but in confronting the past by revealing its secrets. Remembering the past not only gives Jessie the solution to her current physical entrapment—the smoked glass

fashioned by her father to obscure the eclipse forms a nexus to the glass she uses to cut herself free—but also liberates her psychologically by challenging the privileged and passive bondage into which she has willingly submitted herself as a Republican housewife. Jessie gains her freedom through a literal shedding of her skin/former self. Extricating her hand by pulling it through Gerald's single handcuff is a bloody and painful birthing process, an especially interesting metaphor in light of the fact that Jessie has never been a mother.

Dolores and Jessie similarly emerge from their shadowed lives through the guidance offered by women around them. Vera (Latin for "truth") shapes Dolores' action as much as Ruth and Punkin influence Jessie. And although Jessie's "voices" are primarily extensions of herself, they serve in a role that is similar to Vera's relationship with Dolores: forming an often harsh, but always honest and sympathetic, support group. (A women's support group is also critical to the psychological recovery of Rose Daniels, the oppressed wife in *Rose Madder,* who finally summons the courage to leave her abusive husband.) In contrast to the singular actions that characterize male behavior in *Gerald's Game, Dolores Claiborne,* and *Rose Madder,* women are defined in each of these narratives by virtue of their relationships with other women. The bond that women form through their common experience is so important that King acknowledges it in the dedication to *Gerald's Game* by recognizing various female relatives who have borne his wife's maiden name—Spruce. Presumably, these are the women who have influenced her most profoundly, and at the same time, all the women whom Stephen King understands Tabitha to be. Moreover King's dedication may reflect upon himself as well as his wife; all these Spruce women have also exerted a shaping influence on King himself, as a writer and as a male. It's a simple acknowledgment of domestic evolution:

STEPHEN KING / 151

after enough years a husband comes to understand that his own life owes a debt to the wife—and to female relatives—with whom he has chosen to live.

MEDIUMS OF OUR SOCIETY: THE RECURRING WRITER-PROTAGONIST

Gerald's Game begins in King's typical third-person narration but concludes in a first-person letter that Jessie is writing to Ruth Neary. This is a significant signal to readers, since Jessie's new role as writer—telling her own story in her own voice and through her own words—is indicative of her continuing rehabilitation and promise of future recovery. As a writer, Jessie is linked to the many other authors who populate King's fictional landscape, all of whom are invariably invested with impressive powers of self-understanding, imagination, even magic. In the interview published in *The Second Decade,* King reminded me that "Wherever you go in my little part of the landscape, the writer is always there, looking back at the reader. [Writers] do have powers. [They] are the only recognized mediums of our society."

The plethora of writers—both private and professional—scattered across King's landscape share at least one thing with their creator: they view writing as a means for establishing control in a universe where madness always threatens to reign. In his essay on the role of writing in King's novella "The Body," Leonard Heldreth argued that "writing succeeds for Gordon [the protagonist] because it offers control over experience. . . . Writing permits a systematic formulation of the plan or world view and provides the means for keeping it before not only the author but all his readers." Heldreth's assertions about the stabilizing influence of writing in *The Body* apply to every fictional work in King's canon in which an author makes an appearance. The one excep-

tion to this thesis is really no exception at all: Jack Torrance in *The Shining* is a writer whose abrogation of his mind and spirit to the powers at the Overlook Hotel is paralleled in the loss of his desire to write. When he abandons all further efforts at writing by the novel's midpoint, Torrance loses the release that "let something out of him that might otherwise have swelled and swelled until he burst." Jack is initially seduced by the idea that the hotel is a subject worthy of inspiring his greatest written composition, when in reality his creative energies are being siphoned away. In Jack's case, writer's block signals the onset of psychosis.

Like the child-savants found in King's early novels, the writer-protagonists are similarly endowed with tremendous imaginative capacities. Indeed, King's writers often share much in common with his children; certainly both are distinguished from conventional adulthood by virtue of their relative independence and romantic optimism. As early as *Salem's Lot* King proposes that to combat evil an individual must first possess enough imaginative freedom to believe in its material existence—only then does evil become recognizable and therefore vulnerable. In this novel, it is a literary man, the novelist Ben Mears, who is one of the few inhabitants of the town with the childlike conduit to his imagination still open enough to believe in the reality of vampires. Other writer-protagonists occupy similar heroic status throughout King's canon. From Bill Denbrough in *IT,* to Paul Sheldon in *Misery,* to Mike Noonan in *Bag of Bones,* the writer's job is to reassert order in the midst of chaos and destruction. While these individuals may not possess the supernatural abilities of a divinity, their powers are considerable. Without his craft, Paul Sheldon could not have survived his sentence as a prisoner in Annie Wilkes' house of horrors; similarly, Jessie Burlingame's truest moment of survival occurs not in her release from Gerald's handcuffs, but in the act of writing to Ruth, in communicating her experience rather than continuing to hide it. For it is only after she finishes the letter (and here is King's constant emphasis on the importance of writing as a vehicle for self-control) that "for the first time in months her dreams were not unpleasant."

Long ago Stephen King ceased writing out of financial necessity. His consistent rate of production over the past three decades, however, indicates that writing is necessary to preserving some sort of equilibrium in his life and temperament. That he works at his art so diligently—at least half a day, seven days a week, except for his birthday, Christmas, and the Fourth of July—indicates that the composing process for Stephen King is much more than an occupation or mere pleasurable experience; it is a methodology for survival.

HE SPEAKS AMERICAN: SOME CONCLUSIONS

Over the past three decades Stephen King has produced a body of literature that is as diverse as it is popular. His work should not be labeled exclusively—and, for some, diminutively—as horror fiction, for it draws on many literary genres and traditions: epic fantasy (*The Stand, The Talisman,* and *IT*), classical tragedy (*The Shining* and *Pet Sematary*), feminism (*Gerald's Game, Dolores Claiborne, Rose Madder*), the romance novel (*Misery*), the American western (*The Dark Tower: The Gunslinger* [1984]), the fairy tale (*The Girl Who Loved Tom Gordon* and *Eyes of the Dragon*), naturalism (*Cujo* and the Bachman books) and political-history metafiction (*The Dead Zone* and "Apt Pupil" [in *Different Seasons*]). King is one of those rare artists who has managed to capture the defining spirit of his ear at the same time that he has influenced it. Of his contemporaries, perhaps only The Beatles, Steven Spielberg, and maybe Madonna can be said to have accomplished a similar feat. The admonishments of English teachers notwithstand-

ing, Stephen King has already influenced an entire generation of fiction writers, readers, and film students.

Vampiric monsters and supernatural phenomena may be the great popular attractions of King's canon, but at the heart of his fictional universe is a profound sensitivity to the most emotional and deep-seated American anxieties. King himself maintains that his novels, when "taken together, form an allegory for a nation that feels it's in a crunch and things are out of control." No less than Nathaniel Hawthorne a century earlier, King is a moralist rendering a vivid portrait of white, middle-class American life in the latter half of the twentieth century. He has tended to celebrate traditional bourgeois values—family, children, and heterosexual love are central to his work. On the other hand, his critique of American bureaucratic institutions and government itself suggests his continued commitment to the radical politics he first encountered as an undergraduate during the 1960s. The conclusions of his novels are often sentimental and overly optimistic; at the same time, his understanding of patriarchal abuses, particularly as they oppress women, children, and minorities, is uncompromisingly realistic. In the end, it is not just his phenomenal popularity that has made Stephen King America's storyteller, but also his vision of the possibilities and contradictions that are inherent in being American.

Selected Bibliography

WORKS OF STEPHEN KING

NOVELS
Carrie. Garden City, N.Y.: Doubleday, 1974.
Salem's Lot. Garden City, N.Y.: Doubleday, 1975.
The Shining. Garden City, N.Y.: Doubleday, 1977.
The Stand. Garden City, N.Y.: Doubleday, 1978; rev. and unexpurg. New York: Doubleday, 1990.

The Dead Zone. New York: Viking, 1979.

Firestarter. New York: Viking, 1980.

Cujo. New York: Viking, 1981.

Christine. New York: Viking, 1983.

Cycle of the Werewolf. Westland, Mich.: Land of Enchantment, 1983.

Pet Sematary. Garden City, N.Y.: Doubleday, 1983.

The Dark Tower: The Gunslinger. West Kingston, R.I.: Donald M. Grant, 1984.

[With Peter Straub] *The Talisman.* New York: Viking and G.P. Putnam's Sons, 1984.

The Dark Tower II: The Drawing of the Three. New York: New American Library, 1987.

The Eyes of the Dragon. New York: Viking, 1987.

IT. New York: Viking, 1987.

Misery. New York: Viking, 1987.

The Tommyknockers. New York: G.P. Putnam's Sons, 1988.

The Dark Half. New York: Viking, 1989.

Needful Things. New York: Viking, 1991.

The Dark Tower III: The Waste Lands. New York: New American Library, 1991.

Gerald's Game. New York: Viking, 1992.

Dolores Claiborne. New York: Viking, 1993.

Insomnia. New York: Viking, 1994.

Rose Madder. New York: Viking, 1995.

Desperation. New York: Viking, 1996.

The Green Mile. New York: New American Library, 1996.

The Dark Tower IV: Wizard and Glass. New York: New American Library, 1997.

Bag of Bones. New York: Scribner's, 1998.

The Girl Who Loved Tom Gordon. New York: Scribner's, 1999.

COLLECTIONS

Night Shift. Garden City, N.Y.: Doubleday, 1978.

Creepshow. New York: New American Library, 1982.

Different Seasons. New York: Viking, 1982.

The Bachman Books: Four Early Novels. New York: New American Library, 1985.

Skeleton Crew. New York: Putnam, 1985.

Four Past Midnight. New York: Viking, 1990.

Nightmares and Dreamscapes. New York: Viking, 1993.

NONFICTION

Danse Macabre. New York: Everest House, 1981.

"Introduction." *Nightmares in the Sky: Gargoyles and Grotesques.* New York: Viking, 1988. Pp. 7–35.

AUTHORED SCREENPLAYS

Creepshow. Directed by George Romero. Warner Brothers/Laurel Entertainment, 1982.

Cat's Eye. Directed by Lewis Teague. MGM/United Artists, 1984.

Silver Bullet. Directed by Daniel Attias. Paramount Pictures, 1985.

Maximum Overdrive. Directed by Stephen King. De Laurentis Entertainment, 1986.

Pet Sematary. Directed by Mary Lambert. Paramount Pictures, 1989.

The Golden Years. Directed by Josef Anderson. Laurel/King Productions, CBS seven-episode series, 1991.

Sleepwalkers. Directed by Mick Garris. Columbia Pictures, 1992.

The Stand. Directed by Mick Garris. Laurel/Greengrass Productions, ABC miniseries, 1993.

The Shining. Directed by Mick Garris. Warner Brothers, ABC miniseries, 1997.

Storm of the Century. Directed by Craig R. Baxley. Trimark Pictures, ABC miniseries, 1999.

STEPHEN KING WRITING AS RICHARD BACHMAN

Rage. New York: New American Library, 1977.

The Long Walk. New York: New American Library, 1979.

Roadwork. New York: New American Library, 1981.

The Running Man. New York: New American Library, 1982.

Thinner. New York: New American Library, 1984.

The Regulators. New York: Dutton, 1996.

CRITICAL AND BIOGRAPHICAL STUDIES ABOUT STEPHEN KING

INTERVIEWS

Magistrale, Tony. *Stephen King, The Second Decade: "Danse Macabre" to "The Dark Half."* New York: Twayne, 1992. Pp. 1–19. (First chapter consists of a two-hour interview conducted on November 2, 1989.)

Underwood, Tim, and Chuck Miller, editors. *Bare Bones: Conversations on Terror with Stephen King.* New York: McGraw-Hill, 1988. (Contains major interviews conducted with King from March 1979 to May 1985 reprinted from publications ranging from daily U.S. newspapers to popular national periodicals.)

———, editors. *Feast of Fear: Conversations with Stephen King*. New York: Carroll and Graf, 1989. (Contains major interviews conducted with King from May 1973 to July 1986 reprinted from publications ranging from daily U.S. newspapers to popular national periodicals.)

Winter, Douglas, editor. "Stephen King." *Faces of Fear: Encounters with the Creators of Modern Horror*. London, England: Pan Books, 1990. Pp. 287–313.

BOOKS

Badley, Linda. *Writing Horror and The Body: The Fiction of Stephen King, Clive Barker, and Anne Rice*. Westport, Conn.: Greenwood Press, 1996.

Beahm, George. *The Stephen King Companion*. Kansas City, Mo.: Andrews and McMeel, 1989.

Bloom, Harold, editor. *Stephen King: Modern Critical Views*. Philadelphia, Pa.: Chelsea House, 1998.

Browne, Ray, and Gary Hoppenstand, editors. *The Gothic World of Stephen King: Landscape of Nightmares*. Bowling Green, Ohio: Bowling Green State University Popular Press, 1987.

Collings, Michael R. *The Films of Stephen King*. Mercer Island, Wash.: Starmont House, 1986.

Davis, Jonathan P. *Stephen King's America*. Bowling Green, Ohio: Bowling Green State University Popular Press, 1994.

Lant, Kathleen Margaret, and Teresa Thompson, editors. *Imagining the Worst: Stephen King and the Representations of Women*. Westport, Conn.: Greenwood Press, 1998.

Magistrale, Tony, editor. *The Dark Descent: Essays Defining Stephen King's Horrorscape*. Westport, Conn.: Greenwood Press, 1992.

———, editor. *Discovering Stephen King's "The Shining."* San Bernardino, Calif.: The Borgo Press, 1998.

———. *Landscape of Fear: Stephen King's "American Gothic."* Bowling Green, Ohio: Bowling Green State University Popular Press, 1988.

———. *Stephen King, The Second Decade: "Danse Macabre" to "The Dark Half."* New York: Twayne, 1992.

Reino, Joseph. *Stephen King, The First Decade: "Carrie" to "Pet Sematary."* Boston: Twayne, 1988.

Russell, Sharon A. *Stephen King: A Critical Companion*. Westport, Conn.: Greenwood Press, 1996.

Underwood, Tim, and Chuck Miller, editors. *Fear It-self: The Horror Fiction of Stephen King*. San Francisco, Calif.: Underwood-Miller, 1982.

———, editors. *Kingdom of Fear: The World of Stephen King*. New York: New American Library, 1986.

Winter, Douglas E. *Stephen King: The Art of Darkness*. New York: New American Library, 1986.

ARTICLES

Barker, Clive. "Surviving the Ride." In *Kingdom of Fear: The World of Stephen King*. Edited by Tom Underwood and Chuck Miller. New York: New American Library, 1986. Pp. 55–63.

Burns, Gail E., and Melinda Kanner. "Women, Danger, and Death: The Perversion of the Female Principle in Stephen King's Fiction." In *Sexual Politics and Popular Culture*. Edited by Diane Raymond. Bowling Green, Ohio: Bowling Green State University Popular Press, 1990. Pp. 158–172.

Carvajal, Doreen. "Who Can Afford Him? Stephen King Goes in Search of a New Publisher." *New York Times,* October 27, 1997, Natl. ed.: sec D, pp. 1, 8.

Casebeer, Edwin F. "The Art of Balance: Stephen King's Canon." In *A Dark Night's Dreaming: Contemporary American Horror Fiction*. Edited by Tony Magistrale and Michael A. Morrison. Columbia: University Press of South Carolina, 1996. Pp. 42–54.

Edwards, Thomas R. Review of *IT,* by Stephen King. *New York Review of Books,* December 18, 1986, pp. 58–59.

Figliola, Samantha. "The Thousand Faces of Danny Torrance." In *Discovering Stephen King's "The Shining."* Edited by Tony Magistrale. San Bernardino, Calif.: The Borgo Press, 1998. Pp. 54–1.

———. "Reading Stephen King Darkly: Issues of Race in Stephen King's Novels." In *Into Darkness Peering: Race and Color in the Fantastic*. Edited by Elisabeth Anne Leonard. Westport, Conn.: Greenwood Press, 1997. Pp. 143–158.

Hatlen, Burton. "Beyond the Kittery Bridge: Stephen King's Maine." In *Fear Itself: The Horror Fiction of Stephen King*. Edited by Tim Underwood and Chuck Miller. New York: New American Library, 1982. Pp. 45–60.

Heldreth, Leonard. "Viewing 'The Body': King's Portrait of the Artist as Survivor." In *The Gothic World of Stephen King: Landscapes of Nightmares*. Edited by Gary Hoppenstand and Ray B. Browne. Bowling

Green, Ohio: Bowling Green State University Popular Press, 1987. Pp. 64–74.

Hohne, Karen A. "In Words Not Their Own: Dangerous Women in Stephen King." In *Misogyny in Literature.* Edited by Katherine Anne Ackley. New York: Garland, 1992. Pp. 327–345.

Kent, Brian. "Stephen King and His Readers: A Dirty, Compelling Romance." In *A Casebook on "The Stand."* Edited by Anthony Magistrale. Mercer Island, Wash.: Starmont House, 1992. Pp. 37–68.

Lant, Kathleen Margaret. "The Rape of Constant Reader: Stephen King's Construction of the Female Reader and Violation of the Female Body in *Misery.*" *Journal of Popular Culture* 30: 89–114 (Spring 1987).

Magistrale, Tony. "Teaching the Intellectual Merits of Stephen King's Fiction." *The Chronicle of Higher Education* June 19, 1998, p. B7.

Pharr, Mary. "Partners in the *Danse:* Women in Stephen King's Fiction." In *The Dark Descent: Essays Defining Stephen King's Horrorscape.* Edited by Tony Magistrale. Westport, Conn.: Greenwood Press, 1992. Pp. 19–32.

Senf, Carol A. "Donna Trenton, Stephen King's Modern American Heroine." In *Heroines of Popular Culture.* Edited by Pat Browne. Bowling Green, Ohio: Bowling Green State University Popular Press, 1987. Pp. 91–100.

Thoens, Karen. "*IT,* A Sexual Fantasy." In *Imagining the Worst: Stephen King and the Representations of Women.* Edited by Kathleen Margaret Lant and Theresa Thompson. Westport, Conn.: Greenwood Press, 1998. Pp. 127–142.

Yarbro, Chelsea Quinn. "Cinderella's Revenge—Twists on Fairy Tales and Mythic Themes in the Work of Stephen King." In *Fear Itself: The Horror Fiction of Stephen King.* Edited by Tim Underwood and Chuck Miller. New York: New American Library, 1982. Pp. 45–56.

—TONY MAGISTRALE

Maxine Hong Kingston

1940—

I N HER FIRST (and thus far only) novel, *Tripmaster Monkey: His Fake Book* (1989), Maxine Hong Kingston has her protagonist—an effusive performer-playwright who calls himself a "stand-up tragic"—tell a rapt San Francisco audience:

> When I hear you call yourselves "Chinese," I take you to mean American-understood, but too lazy to say it. You do mean "Chinese" as short for "Chinese-American," don't you? We mustn't call ourselves "Chinese" among those who are ready to send us back to where they think we came from. But "Chinese-American" takes too long. Nobody says or hears past the first part. And "Chinese-American" is inaccurate—as if we could have two countries. We need to take the hyphen out—"Chinese Americans." However. Not okay yet. "Chinese hyphen American" sounds exactly the same as "Chinese no hyphen American." No revolution takes place in the mouth or in the ear.

Born in Stockton, California, on October 27, 1940, Maxine Hong Kingston is an American writer through and through. Her Chinese heritage, though, is at the front of nearly all of what she writes, and it is the source of most of the controversy surrounding her work, work that is widely admired, much written about, and used extensively in college literature, sociology, anthropology, history, women's studies, Asian studies, and many other courses (according to the Modern Language Association, *The Woman War-rior: Memoirs of a Girlhood Among Ghosts* [1976] is the most widely taught book in American college courses). Her books, and in a way, her life, have been the focus of numerous scholarly articles, hundreds of Ph.D. dissertations, and neat stacks of monographs; they have been treated and respected as the most eminent literature. But her work also makes the best-seller lists—her first book, *The Woman Warrior,* a work of biography and autobiography, has sold well in excess of 500,000 copies since its publication in 1976—proving her to be that rare writer whose work appeals to both academic and popular audiences, a writer strongly situated both high and low in the contested hierarchies of literature.

Kingston's four books—*The Woman Warrior, China Men* (1980), *Hawai'i One Summer* (1987), and *Tripmaster Monkey: His Fake Book*—explore what it is to be Chinese American in a general culture that tends to think of race (when it is thinking of race) in terms of black and white. In these books, Kingston examines race, certainly, but also issues of gender, exclusion, class, and identity (to name but a few) by examining her own experience, and by examining the experience of her family members, past and present, and—in her novel—by transmuting experience into fiction.

At times angry, at times sad, at times joyous (and even ecstatic), always emotionally layered,

Kingston's work forcefully teaches its readers—her books are self-consciously didactic—what it means to grow up and live in two cultures at once, and how those two cultures become, perforce, one culture in the family and in the person. Always, Kingston puts the individual (that very American and not particularly Chinese notion) at the front of her work. And always, Kingston examines how one individual—herself (or her protagonist when it comes to *Tripmaster Monkey*)—has found identity by embracing both ethnic-Chinese and geographical-American selves, even when these selves must conflict. That both her ancestral and natal cultures are historically and continuingly imperial, and that both are historically and continuingly patriarchal, adds yet further complications and layers to Kingston's work and to the heated discussion it engenders.

On the textual level, Kingston's books explore the curious relationship between fact and invention, between truth and fiction, between self and self-image, between history and myth. Critics often refer to Kingston's work as postmodern, presumably for its self-consciousness (Kingston is not only writing autobiography—she is writing autobiography about writing autobiography; her novel is not only about a Chinese American's search for identity, but about a Chinese American commenting on his search for identity), and its strong consciousness of the invented and arbitrary quality of both self and culture. Kingston makes no claim on the truth, but openly sets out to examine multiple truths in order to create a single truth useful in her search for identity, a truth useful as well to her characters (who are versions of herself), and a truth useful to readers who would seek to understand Kingston and her characters, certainly, but who would seek to understand further the existential plight of all Chinese Americans, and in the end, perhaps, that of Americans of any description.

In both *The Woman Warrior* and *China Men* the reader learns much about Kingston's child-hood and upbringing, but also about the lives of her parents, and her parents' parents, and their ancestors, and about some of the myths and beliefs and folkways and stories and facts of life and laws and prevarications that contribute to the person who now finds herself writing. But the facts of Kingston's life and family history are, perhaps, not the most important thing here: Kingston conceives and delivers not works of history, and not works of genealogy, not works of sociology per se, and not works of anthropology, but works of art.

KINGSTON'S CHILDHOOD AND YOUTH

Maxine Hong Kingston is the oldest child of her parents' American family. (There were, she believes, two children born to her parents in China before their emigration, both lost in unclear circumstances—thus, Kingston is either the oldest of six children, or the third of eight children.)

Her father, who took the name Tom Lan Hong for his American life, died at an unknown age (as Kingston writes in *China Men:* "My father was born in a year of the Rabbit, 1891 or 1903 or 1915"), but he was probably near ninety when he passed away in September 1991. Her mother, who died in May 1997, at the age of ninety-one, kept her Chinese name, Ying Lan Hong (the first part of which Kingston translates as "Brave Orchid"). The parents didn't emigrate together; in fact, they emigrated fifteen years apart, her father in 1924—off with his three brothers to make their fortunes—and her mother in 1939.

In the intervening years, Kingston's mother left her village to be trained as a midwife at To Keung School of Midwifery in Canton. Back home after her studies were complete, she lived the comfortable life of a village doctor in those years before the Maoist revolution.

Tom Lan Hong was a scholar in China, the one son out of four that his family saw fit to educate, an expensive proposition. He taught in his village, Sun Woi, not far from Canton. But during a time of upheaval and privation, Gold Mountain (the traditional Chinese name for a land just like America or California) beckoned. In the United States, his education was of no use—Chinese immigrants weren't allowed to work in the professions, and certainly not to teach—and he was forced to take what work he could, finally ending up in a laundry operation with two new friends, who eventually (or so the family story has it) bilked him out of his equity in the business. He was also involved in gambling, it seems, and sometime after Ying Lan joined him in New York, they moved to the south side of Stockton, California, where he took a job as a dealer in an illegal but flourishing Chinese-American gambling establishment. Kingston has told several interviewers that she was named after a regular gambler in that sordid place—a lucky blond named Maxine.

At home, the Hong family spoke a dialect of Cantonese called Say Yup. Kingston's part of America was an immigrant neighborhood full of people from her father's village. Daily, she heard the stories of old China mixed with the stories of the immigrant generation's Gold Mountain, and she grew to love and appreciate the Chinese (and now Chinese American) tradition of "talk-story," within which fiction and fact, myth and experience, dream and hearsay, hope and fear mix in the mouth of the teller, most often in the service of a moral lesson, but also in the service of history, and also, importantly, in the service of plain old entertainment. One of the best talk-story practitioners Kingston knew was her mother. Her father, by contrast, was quiet about his life, about China, about his emigration, and about history both personal and public.

Interestingly, after *The Woman Warrior* and *China Men* had been published, Kingston's mother took exception to some of the stories her daughter had written, perhaps feeling some sense of competition with this new (if much Americanized) practitioner of talk-story. Kingston told the interviewer Paul Mendelbaum about one conversation she and her mother had after the books had long been public:

> Mother told me she came through Angel Island [in San Francisco Bay] and that she was locked up for three weeks and then took the train across the country to meet my father in New York. I always thought she came through Ellis Island because all her stories about America start with New York. My geography is all off in *The Woman Warrior* and I don't have it right in *China Men!*
>
> I finished writing *China Men,* and years later she says: "Oh, your father stowed away three times on that ship from Cuba to New York. They threw him in jail and deported him, and he got on another ship. He did it three times before he could land."
>
> Why didn't she tell me earlier? That's much more dramatic and interesting than the way I wrote it, which is that he did it once.

Kingston went to public grade school, where, like many other Chinese-American students of her generation, she struggled with language and customs dissimilar to her close familiar upbringing. She found certain stereotypical roles were imposed on her: math whiz, quiet person, practitioner of mysterious customs. So in the afternoons and evenings, and along with other Chinese-American children (and a couple of African Americans, to whom the teachers gave Chinese names), Kingston attended what in her writing she tells readers was called "Chinese School," an after-hours neighborhood school where she and the others were more able to be themselves, boisterous and combative and loud, and to speak their various dialects of Chinese. By third grade she began to write poems in English.

By her own estimation, Kingston's neighborhood in Stockton was rough-and-tumble, a little dangerous. Ethnic allegiances put strains on certain of Kingston's youthful friendships, and she could count on being hailed with slurs as she walked the streets to and from school and to her parents' business, a laundry in which she worked folding shirts and listening to talk-story from her mother, her aunt, and numerous visitors. It was here, she says, that she learned of the classical Chinese poets, heard the myths of old China transmogrified by the American experience, and heard various versions of the history of her family.

She attended Edison High School in Stockton (she was later inducted into that school's alumni Hall of Fame) and did so well academically that she won no fewer than eleven scholarships to attend the University of California, Berkeley. Her first weeks of college were nightmarish, as she recounts—she missed her boisterous and supportive and "exhilarating" extended family and fell ill, but she gradually found her way.

She had entered Berkeley as an engineering major but quickly changed her major to English literature, amazed that the activity she loved most—reading—could be turned into a scholastic career. Berkeley during the early 1960s was an exciting place, full of activists and proto-hippies and people working against what Kingston saw (and sees) as the immoral American military exercise in Vietnam. Kingston became active in the antiwar movement.

During these years too, the student named Maxine Hong (Cantonese nickname: Ting Ting) acted in a student production at Berkeley of Bertolt Brecht's *Galileo*. Also featured in that production was an actor named Earll Kingston, who had just finished a hitch as a photographer in the U.S. Navy and was becoming active against the war.

Maxine Hong was awarded a Bachelor of Arts in English in 1962. Soon thereafter, she married Kingston and went to work as an assistant claims adjuster for an insurance firm. Earll continued to work as an actor. In 1963, their son, Joseph, was born. Both parents turned to teaching. Kingston earned her California teaching certificate—the near equivalent of a master's degree—in 1965. She and Earll both taught in what she has referred to as a "ghetto school" in Hayward, California, with Maxine teaching high school English and math.

But in their belief, to work in any sector of the American economy, to own bank accounts, to shop in the stores, was to feed the war machine. So in 1967, they "dropped out" and moved to Hawaii. There, they made no effort to find jobs, because as Kingston tells readers in *Hawai'i One Summer,* "It was the duty of the pacifist in a war economy not to work." She and her husband and son lived in an inexpensive apartment, finding spilled rice at warehouses and collecting wasted food from supermarket dumpsters. The Kingstons continued their antiwar work by volunteering in a sanctuary project for soldiers who had gone AWOL.

But that life gradually must have lost its appeal, because the Kingstons returned to teaching. Maxine Hong Kingston held a series of positions: Kahuku High School, Kahaluu Drop-In School, Honolulu Business College, and the Mid-Pacific Institute (a private high school), always teaching English, and all the while working on the material that would become *The Woman Warrior,* her first book. It was while she was teaching at the Mid-Pacific Institute that she sent her hard-won manuscript to agents she picked blindly out of a book. One of these agents agreed to represent her and sold *The Woman Warrior* immediately to Knopf. The book was launched in a small printing of 5,000 copies, without fanfare.

THE WOMAN WARRIOR

Kingston originally conceived *The Woman Warrior* and *China Men* as one book, filled with the stories of old China she'd heard as a child, as well as the stories of her family and those of her own childhood and growing up. But as she worked and her material burgeoned, she came to realize that she really needed two books—one for the women's stories and one for the men's. She told the interviewer Paula Rabinowitz, "The women had their own time and place and their lives were coherent; there was a woman's way of thinking. My men's stories seemed to interfere. They were weakening the feminist point of view. So I took all the men's stories out, and then I had *The Woman Warrior.*" Of course, Kingston saved the excised men's stories, which, added to further material, would become *China Men.*

The structure common to both of Kingston's memoirs in their eventual incarnations reveals another aspect of Kingston's original plans. At one point the title for the greater work—male and female together—was "Gold Mountain Stories," which was to be a collection of stories, essays, autobiography, and re-imagined Chinese myths, loosely connected.

The Woman Warrior, when it emerged from the greater work, was still a mixed-genre collection, but Kingston's editor at Knopf, Charles Elliot, thought a single, more cohesive narrative would sell better, and he suggested publishing the book simply as nonfiction. The full title of the work as published is *The Woman Warrior: Memoirs of a Childhood Among Ghosts.* This move to publish the book as nonfiction was the source of much controversy. Critics of all stripes struggled to place the book in a genre but found it did not fit in the usual boxes. Many Asian-American critics felt and argued vociferously that by calling her memoirs "nonfiction" Kingston was playing into the stereotypes held by white America: her vision of the old China is too dark, they argued, and her vision of Chinese America is skewed and not representative or authentic—indeed, it is fiction. And in any case, these critics alleged, autobiography is not a traditional Chinese form. Worse, non-Chinese American readers might mistake Kingston's inventions for history. Some sinologists took the book and Kingston to task for al-

tering original Chinese myths, for bending them to her purposes, which were often taken to be feminist or self-indulgent.

But Kingston replied (in numerous interviews and an essay) that she was only trying to re-create and dramatize her own experience and that of her family, that she should not be called to speak for all Chinese Americans. Her use of altered myths, she said, reflects the "low" art of talk-story, the living and ever-changing art of immigrant discourse, rather than the "high" art of historically accurate literatures. Autobiography, she said, was in fact practiced by Chinese people—particularly monks writing of their faith. As for feminism, that is surely one of her interests in *The Woman Warrior,* but that interest, she felt, was used unfairly by critics to dismiss the art of her book, which was meant to give voice to the people of her life, and not merely to represent history or to take a political stance.

Kingston has had many supporters among scholars and readers for her point of view. Finding her structure elegant and deeply expressive of the way human beings remember and know, her supporters have praised her courage in breaking the silence that they say kept Chinese women captive to their patriarchal culture for so many generations, and that kept (and keeps) Chinese-American women captive, and that keeps all women captive. In *The Woman Warrior: Memoirs of a Childhood Among Ghosts,* the argument goes, Kingston gives voice to women formerly silenced.

The first section of *The Woman Warrior* is titled "No Name Woman." The first voice of the many in *The Woman Warrior* is Maxine Hong Kingston's mother's voice, carefully set off in quotation marks, telling an adolescent Maxine the tragedy of No Name Woman, Kingston's own aunt, her father's sister. Readers hear a living mother speaking, "talking story." Kingston's mother begins by telling the harrowing story of the awful and unfair death of Kingston's lost aunt. "You must not tell anyone," her mother starts. Of course, readers are aware that by making her mother's words part of this book, Kingston is disobeying her mother: she's telling everyone.

Kingston thus opens with a story that will pull readers in—a "low" strategy, but effective, and reflective of the talk-story style of her mother. Her aunt apparently disgraced her family by getting pregnant adulterously and consequently killed herself and her new infant by jumping into the family well. The aunt's story is yet another "story to grow up on": take heed, Maxine, her mother says implicitly, and be careful with boys, or you too might end up in a well!

Kingston proceeds, first giving the story through her mother's words, then offering alternative versions and conjecture about her aunt's life and motives. The basic story is: the young men have all left the village to go work in foreign lands (such as California, Hawaii, and elsewhere in the Pacific and the Americas), and hurry-up marriages have been arranged for all the available young women, who will stay behind. And when the men have been long gone, longer than nine months, the aunt turns up obviously pregnant. The village cannot allow this breech of its rules, this dishonor to a husband, and to men in general, because it knows such behavior will bring bad luck to everyone. The villagers don masks and costumes and destroy the farm of her family on the night the aunt gives birth—former friends and familiar neighbors destroy or steal everything. The disgraced aunt jumps in the well, her new baby girl in her arms.

This talk-story told, Kingston shifts to her own voice and tries to get inside the mind of her lost aunt. Why did she do what she did? Was she forced into love by a man of the household or of the village? Did she fall in love? Kingston imagines various scenarios from romance to rape, all well informed by her knowledge of Chinese cus-

tom and of what would have been possible and then probable in the young woman's impossible circumstances. Finally, readers learn that to jump into the well was a defiant gesture, and a powerful one: "The Chinese are always very frightened of the drowned one, whose weeping ghost, wet hair hanging and skin bloated, waits silently by the water to pull down a substitute." Even Maxine Hong Kingston is a little afraid of her aunt's ghost: "My aunt haunts me—her ghost drawn to me because now, after fifty years of neglect, I alone devote pages of paper to her, though not origamied into houses and clothes. I do not think she always means me well. I am telling on her."

In the second section of *The Woman Warrior*, "White Tigers," Kingston transports the reader to the world of her childhood. She was a California girl, certainly, but poor, and the daughter of immigrants. And she brings us into the mind of the child she was—the child who could not accept, not even at seven, the kind of slavery to men that her aunt's awful story represented to her. "When we Chinese girls listened to the adults talk-story, we learned that we failed if we grew up to be but wives or slaves. We could be heroines, swordswomen." And so the reader begins to understand the title *The Woman Warrior*.

Kingston proceeds page by page to bring alive her childhood imagination—a girl refusing to see the squalor of the ghetto life around her, but always imagining herself a warrior much like Fu Mu Lan, the warrior princess of Chinese myth (and now—for better or worse—a Disney cartoon movie)—specially trained, magically gifted, a superwoman. And the girl goes through warrior training on a mystic mountain with immortal teachers who feed her magical potions and put her through test battles and see her through her first period:

Menstrual days did not interrupt my training; I was as strong as on any other day. "You're now an adult," explained the old woman on the first one, which happened halfway through my stay on the mountain. "You can have children." I had thought I had cut myself when jumping over my swords, one made of steel and the other carved out of a single block of jade. "However," she added, "we are asking you to put off children for a few more years."

"Then can I use the control you taught me and stop this bleeding?"

"No. You don't stop shitting and pissing," she said. "It's the same with the blood. Let it run." ("Let it walk" in Chinese.)

The training continues until the girl-hero is twenty-two, at which time she is free to lead armies to destroy the evil powers-that-be.

This, of course, is not only the child Maxine's fantasy—nonfiction in that sense—but also an allegory about a girl who is going to throw over all the conventions in a new land and become educated and powerful. This lyrical fantasy comprises the greater part of "White Tigers"; from it readers learn not only about Kingston's young mind, but also about traditional Chinese culture, and especially about the expectations and limits on women. (Girls are called "maggots in the rice," and expressions such as "feeding girls is like feeding cowbirds" abound.) Kingston's woman warrior takes on all the mythological force of male heroes.

In the third section of *The Woman Warrior,* "Shaman," Kingston shifts modes once again, both remembering her mother and speaking through her mother's memories and stories, giving readers a picture of the turmoil in China during and after the Communist revolution. Concomitantly, Kingston shows readers the turmoil inside the girl she once was, young Maxine, as she struggles to find a fully American identity.

In China before Kingston was born, her mother goes off to medical school. There, Brave Orchid exorcises the living quarters of its resident ghost by spending a night in a closed room with the ghost and doing battle with it. And she tells Maxine and her sister many other such ghost stories— China is alive with ghosts. China itself is a ghost to the young Maxine; it is a place encountered in stories only. For Brave Orchid, as for other Chinese immigrants to America, the Chinese word that Kingston translates as "ghosts" (her critic Jeffery [*sic*] Chan has said it should be translated as "demons," or "assholes") applies to all non-Chinese. And so the ghosts of Kingston's subtitle multiply.

In the fourth section of *The Woman Warrior,* titled "At the Western Palace," Kingston's aunt— her mother's sister, named Moon Orchid—comes to America. The problem is that Moon Orchid has a husband who moved to America thirty years earlier but never sent for her, though he has always sent her money. Brave Orchid insists that Moon Orchid stand up for her rights as First Wife—and hatches a scheme to introduce her to her deadbeat husband.

Kingston (who says she was trying for an *I Love Lucy* kind of screwball comedy, if poignant) tells this story entirely in the third person from her mother's point of view—in fact, she goes so far as to relate Brave Orchid's thoughts. At the beginning of the next section, readers discover that Maxine was not even there to observe the events she reports, that she got the story from her brother and surmised her mother's feelings. Critics ask: Is this truly nonfiction?

In the book's fifth and last section, "A Song for a Barbarian Reed Pipe," Kingston turns her attention from her ancestors to herself as the girl growing up—our Maxine—and the book shifts subtly from biography to autobiography. Maxine is no perfect child; she torments a classmate— also Chinese American—who will not speak. Upon this girl the young Maxine vents her rage at all it means to be ethnic Chinese in America.

And though the narrative voice in this last section shifts from mother to daughter, the mode continues to be talk-story. Kingston gives herself the last word, saying: "Here is a story my mother told me, not when I was young, but recently, when I told her I also talk story. The beginning is hers, the ending, mine."

And so the traditions of China continue in a new land, thoroughly altered, ghostly, changed, and changing still, and thus ever alive, growing American.

LIFE AFTER *THE WOMAN WARRIOR*

The Woman Warrior, published so modestly, received enormous attention. John Leonard, then editor of the *New York Times Book Review,* gave it an explosive push in the daily *Times* on Friday, September 17, 1976, starting: "Those rumbles you hear on the horizon are the big guns of autumn lining up, the howitzers of Vonnegut and Updike and Cheever and Mailer, the books that will be making loud noises for the next several months. But listen: this week a remarkable book has been quietly published; it is one of the best I've read in years."

The Woman Warrior sold 40,000 copies even before it was given the prestigious Book Critics Circle Award for the best nonfiction book of 1976. In 1979, *Time* named it one of the top ten nonfiction books of the decade.

Kingston has told numerous interviewers that the "establishment" press insulted her with stereotyped remarks: her work, they said, was mysterious and inscrutable. They opined that east and west were never going to meet (à la Rudyard Kipling). They called her Chinese repeatedly, forgetting that she was American, and only ethnically Chinese. They placed her childhood in San Francisco's Chinatown, rather than in Stockton, where there were not even whole blocks entirely inhabited by Chinese Americans, much less a Chinatown. They made much of her size (she's four foot, nine inches tall) and her "foreignness,"

her "sweet and sour" disposition, and of course, her "inscrutability." They made of her and her book something exotic and foreign, anything but American. Still, they reviewed and admired it.

All of the attention and admiration from the mainstream (read: primarily Caucasian) press brought scholarly attention, particularly attention from the Asian-American scholarly community, some of it in the form of nasty denouncements of her method, her style, her accuracy, her allegiance to Chinese-American values and history, and more. Of these Chinese-American critics, perhaps Frank Chin, an actor and novelist who was at Berkeley in the same years as Kingston, was the most visible. His ideas about Kingston's work—that it plays into white stereotypes of Chinese Americans and Chinese, that it is overly feminist, that it disturbs the old Chinese myths, that it is not representative and should be—continue to have much currency among his allies, though he's seen as mainly jealous and misogynistic by others: in this view Kingston has stolen his considerable thunder, so he throws lightning bolts.

Through all of the stormy attention and attendant mudslinging, Kingston kept working on her new endeavor, which would continue the old "Gold Mountain Stories" project, a book about the men of her family, who were generally more silent and hidden than the women. She and her husband, Earll, newly comfortable as a result of the success of *The Woman Warrior,* continued to live in Hawaii, and even bought a house.

From 1977 to 1981, during which time *China Men* was published, Kingston was visiting professor of English at the University of Hawaii, Honolulu.

CHINA MEN

Maxine Hong Kingston wrote *China Men* to hear the stories her father never told. Working in their laundry business, at home in the evenings, during family outings, Tom Hong was silent. While Brave Orchid spun endless talk-story, endlessly recalling and reinventing China, defiantly keeping her Chinese name, Tom Hong only muttered—horribly cursing his customers, women in general, his daughters, his wife, using the basest terms ("those curses") for women and their anatomies. Or he was silent for months on end, except for terrifying, tormented screams in the night.

Remember that Tom Hong was still alive as Kingston wrote *China Men*. If he wasn't going to talk, she would talk for him. And, she would use *China Men* to talk to him:

> You say with the few words and the silences: No stories. No past. No China.
>
> You only look and talk Chinese. There are no photographs of you in Chinese clothes nor against Chinese landscapes. Did you cut your pigtail to show your support for the Republic? Or have you always been American? Do you mean to give us a chance at being real Americans by forgetting the Chinese past?
>
> You are a man who enjoys plants and the weather. "It's raining," you said in English and in Chinese when the California drought broke. "It's raining." You make us inordinately happy saying a simple thing like that. "It rains."
>
> What I want from you is for you to tell me that those curses are only common Chinese sayings. That you did not mean to make me sicken at being female. "Those were only sayings," I want you to say to me. "I didn't mean you or your mother. I didn't mean your sisters or grandmothers or women in general."
>
> I want to be able to rely on you, who inked each piece of our own laundry with the word *Center*, to find out how we landed in a country where we are eccentric people.
>
> On New Year's eve, you phone the Time Lady and listen to her tell the minutes and seconds, then adjust all the clocks in the house so their hands reach midnight together. You must like listening to the Time Lady because she is a recording you don't have to talk to. Also she distinctly names the present moment, never slipping into the past or sliding into the future. You fix yourself in the present, but I want to hear the stories about the rest of your life, the Chinese stories. I want to know what makes you scream and curse, and what you're thinking when you say nothing, and why when you do talk, you talk differently from Mother.
>
> I take after MaMa. We have peasant minds. We see a stranger's tic and ascribe motives. I'll tell you what I suppose from your silences and few words, and you can tell me that I'm mistaken. You'll just have to speak up with the real stories if I've got you wrong.

And Kingston proceeds to mingle prodigious research, talk-story, fiction, essays, and reinvented myths to go find the disappeared story of her father and her grandfathers, and even the stories of her wandering great-grandfathers. The book moves forward in time to its last long section, which is about a thoroughly American brother, who did a hitch in the U.S. Navy as a way of avoiding what he, like Kingston, regarded as immoral duty in Vietnam.

China Men was published in 1980, again by Knopf, and received gentler, more understanding, more race-and-culture sensitive, and more extensive reviews than had *The Woman Warrior*. Like *The Woman Warrior*, *China Men* is broken into sections, each with its own style, direction, and force, but each working with the next to create a complete and coherent work of art.

Kingston opens with pair of very short sections, less than five hundred words each, juxtaposed to create surprising narrative tension without setting a plot in motion, a strategy that will set the tone for the work as a whole. The first of these miniature chapters is a bravura allegorical tale, "On Discovery." This is a retold Chinese myth about Tang Ao, a man who left China for the land of women, which Kingston explicitly links with America, and implicitly with the idea that Chinese men were feminized—that is, made powerless—by Gold Mountain racism. Tang Ao's lips are sewn together so that he might not speak, and his feet are bound so that he might hobble daintily. Is Kingston's father, with all his hidden fury, a kind of Tang Ao?

The second and shorter of the opening movements is a surprisingly stirring autobiographical vignette, "On Fathers." In it, Kingston simply recalls a time when she and her siblings mistook a perfect stranger for their father coming home. Simple, but by placing it after the mythopoetic "On Discovery," Kingston announces her method and creates a resonance between the stories of old China and the stories of her America that will ring throughout the book.

The first long section of *China Men* (indeed, it comprises about one quarter of the total book) is titled "The Father from China," and its main character—for that's what she has made him, her character—is Kingston's father. At the time of the publication of *China Men,* she told the interviewer Timothy Pfaff, "I have a father character who comes up in various guises throughout the book. He is really only one character, but I call him different things, like 'the legal father,' 'the illegal father,' 'the father from China,' and 'the American father.' In the course of the book, I have him coming into this country in five different ways. I'm very proud of that."

Like *The Woman Warrior, China Men* was published as nonfiction, and while *China Men* does use many of the techniques of nonfiction (research, reportage, a central voice) and certainly echoes the structures and strategies of the more clearly and traditionally nonfictional *The Woman Warrior,* it also uses the techniques of the novelist—drama, dialogue, invention—and is perhaps more fiction, closer to a novel, than is *The Woman Warrior.*

Kingston's method, of course, admits to her ignorance of the specific histories of her male forebears. Still, she knows and can relate at least the probable stories of these men from both talk-story heard when she was young and from prodigious research she conducted as an adult into the emigration of Chinese men to the United States.

So "The Father from China" is a kind of investigation, which might or might not be properly seen as fiction, depending on which critic is talking. Did Kingston's father hide in a barrel stowed away on a freighter to New York (as did so many Chinese men of his generation)? Or did he make his way to American immigration officers in California, passing all their political and intelligence tests to be one of the one hundred men allowed into the country (as did fewer Chinese men)? Kingston is creating a new genre of nonfiction that can enclose fiction. Kingston vividly imagines her father's childhood and youth in China, and then his emigration, continuing into his difficult life in the United States.

After "The Father from China," Kingston places a very short section, "The Ghostmate," in which she tells a story—with, once again, the elevated sound of mythology—about a young male scholar who walks to an unnamed big city in China to take the "Imperial Examinations." Kingston's father would have had to take such harrowing exams. Is the tale history? Is it fantasy? Myth? *China Men* assiduously avoids answering such questions, but the implication is that in the absence of hard evidence about her father's life, in the presence of his silence, Kingston's myth-influenced imagination will have to do.

The next long section is called "The Great Grandfather of the Sandalwood Mountains." Kingston, pleased to mingle what might have happened with what did happen, starts this section with a story from her own life in Hawaii, familiar from *Hawai'i One Summer,* of her visit with her husband, Earll, to the little island called Chinaman's Hat. The island's name (she considers the term "Chinaman" to be a racial slur) provokes both her anger and her interest, and leads her to the stories of her great-grandfathers, living, breathing men, who, while working in the fields of Hawaii, most probably wore the sort of hat the island was thought to resemble. In the ensuing stories of their lives, Kingston lifts laborers in "Chinamen's" hats out of the concealing mists of stereotype and gives them warm human faces, sweet human pleasures, and black human suffering.

Next, Kingston weaves in two more short allegorical sections, "On Mortality" and "On Mortality Again." The first appropriates an old Chinese tale, the second, a Polynesian tale, and having read the stories of the great-grandfathers, the reader must unavoidably connect the tales with the sufferings of those men.

Then, in "The Grandfather of the Sierra Nevada Mountains," Kingston spins her own tale, that of her grandfather, Ah Goong. She starts, once again, in her own life, and this is perhaps where the reader begins to realize how unusual this history is in yet another way: the men of *China Men* are viewed entirely through the eyes of a woman, who might be seen either as Kingston or as her narrator. Kingston, or her narrator, depending from which theory one proceeds, tells readers of her childhood, "Once in a while an adult said, 'Your grandfather built the railroad.' "

And so he did. With numberless other Chinese men, Ah Goong leaves China during a time of upheaval. Kingston tells us how he signed up to work on the railroads for a dollar a day, and how the Chinese men stuck together, worked together, and were persecuted or rewarded together. They missed their families, they prided themselves on working harder and better than any other cultural or ethnic group, and they kept their Chinese culture alive around them, even as what was around them changed that culture forever.

The next section, "The Laws," is structurally daring. It is an essay with no characters or narrative, but a chronological list of the laws made in the United States to control and discriminate against Chinese people. "The Laws" shows the fierce racism faced not only by immigrants, but also by fully American people of Chinese ancestry over the last two centuries. Kingston merely traces the changing immigration laws, but as she does so, specific people come to mind—characters from the earlier sections of the book—whom the reader now clearly sees suffering from the laws the author lays out.

"Alaska China Men," a short section, tells how Chinese and Chinese American men went to Alaska for the famous Klondike gold rush, and how they tried to stay on but were forced out in various waves of racism and lawmaking.

"The Making of More Americans," which appeared as an essay in *The New Yorker* in February 1980, is the longest chapter of *China Men* and tells much of the story of Kingston's childhood—already visited in *The Woman Warrior* but here extended into the greater community of Chinese in California during and just after the Second World War. Making use of her own memory and of the memories of those who spoke talk-story, Kingston re-creates the Chinese-American society of the 1940s. The effect is a claiming of a territory as convincing and as American as William Faulkner's Yoknapatawpha County, or closer to Kingston's home, John Steinbeck's California. The section ends with the story of her mother calling a brother on New Year's Day and having a very shallow conversation, just small talk. "You could call again next year!" Kingston tells her mother, who is saddened by the call. "You could call anytime!" But China, it seems, is more lost than a simple phone call can change. Brave Orchid has become an American.

The next short section is "The Wild Man of the Green Swamp," wherein Kingston recounts the story of the eponymous wild man, whom residents in Green Swamp, Florida, started glimpsing in 1975. The Wild Man turns out to be an escapee from the Tampa mental hospital, a stowaway caught and detained. By now, the sections of *China Men* are resembling facets of a great jewel, which Kingston turns and turns, showing the reader more, and then more again, in hopes that he or she comes to understand the human enormity that is the Chinese-American psyche.

In "The Adventures of Lo Bun Sun," Kingston—or rather Kingston's mother, with Kingston (or her narrator character) only reporting (or "reporting")—appropriates the Robinson Crusoe story. Lo Bun Sun even ends up with a castaway helper named Friday. "The Adventures of Lo Bun Sun" not only advances and deepens the discussion of the lives of Chinese-American men, but also presents a grand opportunity in its familiarity (for non–Chinese-American readers) to think about the complicated reaction Chinese-American readers and critics have had to Kingston's appropriations of and changes to Chinese myths and tales.

The next long section of *China Men* is "The American Father." Here, Kingston fills in the details of her father's life around a set of facts that is becoming familiar. Yet, she also introduces alterations to those facts. Now readers learn that her father was born in the United States in 1903. Or was he only said to have been born in the United States, so as not to risk deportation as an illegal alien? Kingston remembers, once again, talk-story from her childhood as well as her own experience. She tells her father's Californian story: that he was a gambler; that he worked as a dealer in a gambling house until the cops busted it; that he had a period of depression and hard drinking (while MaMa worked in the canneries and fields); that he screams in his sleep; that finally he recovered himself enough to buy a laundry and become an American businessman.

In a short section called "The Li Sao, an Elegy," Kingston takes on the voice of an essayist describing a Chinese tale, then tells the tale as if authoritatively. This tale is carefully selected to link the Chinese with other Asian cultures, including the Vietnamese.

"The Brother in Vietnam" takes the book to the present of its writer. She speaks here of a singular brother, but in life she has two brothers, both of whom served what she would call the war machine in Vietnam. Kingston conflates her actual brothers, then imagines this character brother's

Navy hitch (this with seeming help from the man himself—she takes a reportorial tone, making the reader believe she has interviewed "The Brother" extensively), and presents the reader with an ethnic Chinese so American in such ingrained ways (and yet a pacifist) that the concept of China as birthright and heritage begins to fall complicatedly away.

China Men ends as it begins, with two very short sections, one allegorical, one autobiographical. "The Hundred-Year-Old Man" recounts the story of a man who at his 106th birthday party told assembled guests that he had come to Hawaii in 1885. Kingston elevates this old soul to the level of sage. A reporter asked him what had given him the most joy in his long years: "What I like best is to work in a cane field when the young green plants are just growing up." At last, the China men are talking.

The closing section is called "On Listening." And the last word of the book is "listen." To hear the silent men of Kingston's heritage, especially over the ebullient talk-story of the women in Kingston's life, she must listen; we all must listen.

LIFE AFTER *CHINA MEN*

China Men won the National Book Award for nonfiction in 1981, having changed forever the notion of the shape a nonfiction book could legitimately take. Shortly thereafter, Hoopa Hongwanji Temple, a Honolulu sect of Buddhists, named Kingston a Living Treasure of Hawaii for the body of her work. In 1980, *China Men* was runner-up for a Pulitzer Prize and a nominee for the National Book Critics Circle Award; in 1981, it won the American Book Award.

In 1982, Kingston traveled to Hong Kong—her first trip to Chinese soil. In October 1984, she took her first extended trip to China, this with a group of writers including Allen Ginsberg, Gary

Snyder, Francine Du Plessix Gray, Leslie Marmon Silko, William Least Heat Moon, and Toni Morrison. During her stay she visited her mother's village, bringing photos back to show Brave Orchid how things had changed (though some buildings were familiar to the old woman). Kingston was able to compare her imagined China to its actual counterpart, and found she'd done surprisingly well. That year, she and Earll left Hawaii and returned to California.

During breaks from working on the manuscript that would become *China Men,* Kingston wrote a series of essays. One was "Through the Black Curtain" (1987), an essay about her writing process, published in an expensive keepsake chapbook edition by the Friends of the Bancroft Library.

Most of the others were first published in *The New York Times Magazine* "Hers" column. These essays are light, topical, and diaristic, yet they allow Kingston to speak in her own voice about concerns both great and small. She emerges as a person in front of the reader, rather than as the powerful and perhaps intimidating artist behind *The Woman Warrior. Hawai'i One Summer* falls here in the chronology of her work—it was published as a deluxe, handmade chapbook in 1987 at $500.00 per slipcased copy—even though it was not truly available to the public until a trade paperback was published by the University of Hawaii Press in 1999.

HAWAI'I ONE SUMMER

Hawai'i One Summer is a small book, only seventy-two pages in the 1999 paperback edition, which was lightly but favorably reviewed. And while it casts light on the other books and gives us an intimate look at Kingston's daily adult life and mind, it cannot be treated as one of her major works. *Hawai'i One Summer* consists of eleven essays arranged in three groups under the headings of June, July, and August. The summer of the title is that of 1978. The paperback version includes a new preface, in which Kingston laments that she needs twenty years to get perspective on events—twenty years she didn't have when writing these essays, some of which reported on events not two weeks old. "Memory is artistic in the ways it arranges and sorts out." But memory wasn't fully in control here. Assessing the book from the vantage point of twenty years, she's not perfectly happy with it. But, she says, "Let it stand."

"Our First House" is about the house that she and Earll have bought in Hawaii, despite their earlier idealistic refusal to do so. "If we cannot bear the weight of ownership we can always sell." Kingston takes readers to her twentieth reunion in "My High School Reunion." The old faces make her remember slights and some problems with race, and force her to consider her own aging. In "War," Kingston discusses how traumatic it was for her when the United States was involved in Vietnam, fighting against an Asian people, themes that will turn up again in her novel, *Tripmaster Monkey: His Fake Book.*

There is a light piece about washing dishes, then "Chinaman's Hat," interestingly an early draft of the "Chinaman's Hat" section in *China Men.* In the essay, Kingston describes her surprise (which may be different from her *China Men* narrator's surprise) at discovering a word she'd always considered a slur—"Chinaman"—to be the name of a small island off Oahu, to no one's apparent consternation but her own. She and Earll swim out to Chinaman's Hat—which is used by the navy for target practice—and she uses the occasion to discuss racial attitudes in Hawaii (not as horrible, she finds, as in California), and what she sees as military excess. Once again, the reader sees Kingston's themes in force, but one is also struck by how different this material feels—how much lighter, how much more personal and less universal (and less about being Chinese American) than when it appears in *China Men,* where it takes on and pulses with the accreted force and themes of the rest of the book.

In "A City Person Encountering Nature," Kingston reminds readers of her California-urban roots: nature always surprises her. In further essays Kingston writes about her teaching and about a bellicose conference of Asian-American and Hawaiian writers (at which, she believes, the true battle was between men and women, and not a gender unified Chinese-American battle against the dominant race and culture). She writes about the mysteries of her adopted Hawaii, about her son's risky surfing there, and about a mentor, the poet Lew Welch, who had recently disappeared.

These essays are occasional pieces, meant as columns, not tightly structured, discursive, meandering pleasantly, and have the charm of giving a sense of the woman while informing readerly interpretation of her other books.

TRIPMASTER MONKEY

From the title forward, Maxine Hong Kingston's first novel, *Tripmaster Monkey: His Fake Book,* is a long series of tricks and puns and riddles and games, all overlayered not with the consciousness of its main character, Wittman Ah Sing, but by the consciousness of its omniscient narrator. In later interviews, Maxine Hong Kingston equates this narrator with Kuan Yin, the Chinese goddess of mercy. In any case, as in *China Men,* the narrator is distinctly female, and seems not only to report the protagonist's story but to actively put Wittman through difficulties running the range from race to romance to substance abuse to the rigors of public art.

Tripmaster Monkey: His Fake Book was published by Knopf in 1989. The story is set in the San Francisco of the early 1960s (the exact year is unspecified) and partakes frenetically of the hippie oeuvre and vocabulary. Wittman Ah Sing

speaks in long, post-beatnik monologues, and bumps and thrashes through his days—always searching, always unsure, histrionically suicidal, questing after love and acceptance, and (as always in Kingston's work) searching for identity. His angst arises from a huge desire to give not only himself but also his people an American identity in an America hostile to Chinese ethnics, even those who are fifth-generation Americans like Wittman himself.

Wittman Ah Sing—who sings the Chinese American body electric, who sings the Chinese American body from top to toe (who, that is, is an ethnic-Chinese incarnation of Walt Whitman—lines of Whitman's poetry and allusions to his life and work fill this book, and several of the chapter titles are straight from *Leaves of Grass*)—is in battle with nearly everything, including his moralizing narrator, who approves of him more and more as he matures through the book. Wittman is a playwright and an actor, son of show-business parents (they dressed him in a monkey suit for vaudeville skits). Like Kingston, he's a graduate of Berkeley. He's furious, at loose ends, unmoored, until he conceives his great work: a play to restore the self-image and self-worth of all Chinese Americans.

The creation of a male protagonist, of course, was a marked departure for Kingston, who previously had written almost exclusively in the first person. This move away from autobiography (and biography) to fiction frees her to take on the problems and celebration of Chinese Americans in a more general and perhaps more representative way than had heretofore been possible for her. Even Kingston's language is freed—she can take on a grand poet's voice. In *The Woman Warrior* and *China Men,* Kingston is remembering Chinese voices, sometimes directly quoting, often translating, and always approximating—in English—Chinese rhythms and patterns. In *Tripmaster Monkey,* she finally allows herself to write the demotic American English she speaks every day. And the language in this book is jazz, or more specifically, it is bebop—fluid, elastic, noisy, soulful, manic. Listen to the opening of chapter three, "Twisters and Shouters" (that title yet another Whitman reference):

> In the Tenderloin, depressed and unemployed, the jobless Wittman Ah Sing felt a kind of bad freedom. Agoraphobic on Market Street, ha ha. There was nowhere he had to be, and nobody waiting to hear what happened to him today. Fired. Aware of emptiness now. Ha ha. A storm will blow from the ocean or down from the mountains, and knock the set of the City down. If you dart quick enough behind the stores, you'll see that they are stage flats propped up. On the other side of them is ocean forever, and the great Valley between the Coast Range and the Sierras. Is that snow on Mt. Shasta?
>
> And what for had they set up Market Street? To light up the dark jut of land into the dark sea. To bisect the City diagonally with a swath of lights. We are visible. See us? We're here. Here we are.

A "fake book" is a jazz musician's collection or notebook of songs, with melodies and chord progressions written out, often with lyrics. The old jazz players would copy each other's books and trade songs around, trying to amass comprehensive collections. When sold, these books were illegal, violating copyright laws (though commercial versions with properly secured copyright permissions are now widely available). The term connotes something outside of mainstream culture, a book to share in an underground way, a book that will teach the reader what she needs to know to sing the body electric. Kingston and her wily narrator don't tell the reader any of this, which led some critics to put themselves out on a limb writing about how the book is meant as a kind of fake novel or fake memoir—just look at the title.

The term "tripmaster" is the hippie Californian term for the person who guided the LSD trips of others, keeping tripsters out of harm's way; therefore, by extension, Wittman is the guide for the trip readers take, and the trip on which he hopes to bring Chinese Americans along.

As for the monkey of the title, Kingston told the interviewer William Satake Blauvelt where the choice of that animal came from:

> As I wrote about the '60s, I began to understand that the spirit of the monkey has come to America. You see in the Buddhist story he goes to India, but I have him continuing on and he arrives in America in the '60s. You can see his spirit in the Chicago Seven, who were like seven monkeys bringing chaos to the establishment. All those love-ins and Woodstock—all that is the monkey. The monkey loves to go to parties, and if you have a wonderful enough party, you can change life.
>
> I think of the monkey as an underdog—he doesn't have a lot of power, so he uses trickery. He has to think of new ways to change things. I even think of Martin Luther King, when he thought of those demonstrations, nonviolent acts, new acts in order to change the world. To me, that is evidence that the monkey was here. I now think he continued around and did the Cultural Revolution. Sometimes he's not so nonviolent; he causes a lot of trouble.

Tripmaster Monkey: His Fake Book was not universally loved by critics upon its publication in 1989. Newspaper reviewers tended to find it too antic, too manic, too allusive, too strange. Wittman is often called obnoxious, especially for his views of women. Even those who liked the book found it too rich in places, too full of allusion, talk-story, mythos, wild monologue, bebop language, freaky characters. One otherwise admiring writer even called the book "*bloated,*" using italics to emphasize her point. Several wondered if the book were indeed a novel, and not some new form. Once again, Kingston was pushing the boundaries, perhaps acting the role of the monkey herself.

But even with reservations, most critics admired the book, finding in it a passionate and hopeful expression of Chinese-American angst wedded cleverly to the general mood of upheaval in 1960s America. Interestingly, some have wondered in print if the book is some kind of revenge parody of Frank Chin, Kingston's critical nemesis. Chin, like Wittman, is a Chinese-American actor and activist. Kingston says no—but notes that it's no wonder Chin and Wittman resemble each other—Kingston has a similar Northern Californian background to Chin, and both were Berkeley English majors in the same years and had the same teachers.

The story: Wittman Ah Sing struggles in 1960s America as a Chinese American. Nothing is right. The Chinese-American community is missing even the benefits of being a minority: "Where's our jazz? Where's our blues?" sings Wittman. He is good-looking, well spoken, and apparently desirable to the opposite sex. He gets a date with Nanci Lee, a fellow Chinese American (whom he finds exquisitely gorgeous), but the date goes comically awry when Wittman freaks out (as he might say)—he can't handle her equipoise in the face of racial and political realities.

And the freak-out ripples outward, alternately comic and tragic. At his miserable job as a floor clerk in a toy store, he lectures the customers, insults their children, and finally manages to get himself fired. Triumphant in his failure, he marches to the bus stop and heads across the Golden Gate Bridge to go to his friend Lance's party: Lance is an A.J.A.—an American of Japanese Ancestry, a designation Wittman admires for its accuracy.

On the bus Wittman meets a rather plain Chinese-American woman. She's a bit of the peasant, down-to-earth, plain-speaking. Thus quickly, readers see that every character in the book stands for something, some aspect of American and Chinese-American culture (some of them perhaps a little woodenly). At his friend's party, for example, Wittman meets Taña De Weese, a beautiful, golden, all-American girl, who is an assistant claims adjuster, as was Maxine Hong Kingston at that age and at that time.

Wittman tests Taña: Does she believe in movie stereotypes of what it is to be of Chinese ancestry? Is she truly sympathetic? Leaving her for the moment, Wittman goes off to try to pick a didactic political fight with his best friend, Lance, over minority issues. Wittman's sea of enthusiasms, lost causes, hurts, angers, frustrations, and loves washes over the reader as it washes over Lance. The party gets nearly forgotten in the wordplay. Some critics find Kingston gloriously in control, others find her prolix.

Wittman's date with Taña De Weese goes better than that with Nanci Lee; so well, in fact, that the two of them get themselves married by a draft-dodger fake minister. In a wild weekend (comprising a wild long chapter of the book), Taña meets Wittman's eccentric aunts, the Flora Dora Girls (these seem almost parodies), and his show-biz mom (Ruby Long Legs, who dances with the Wongettes), then later his father (whose name is Zeppelin), and in this way readers are drawn into the world of Chinese-American culture and history that is yet recognizably American.

In other scenes, variously antic, tragic, parodic—often in the form of a haranguing monologue by the protagonist—Wittman learns that his PoPo, that is, his grandmother, has been abandoned by his mother in Reno (but not to fear, she will find a man to marry there). There's a chapter in the unemployment office, where Wittman spends a whole day (and meets an old Chinese-American woman who needs his help—another symbolic placement) while he and his narrator comment on American social policy.

And so on, in a great rush to the big finish—Wittman is going to put on a huge play, guerrilla theater. His plan is to create community through theater. He has a cast of thousands who appear magically (and the novel is definitely coming within range of magical realism here). He has pyrotechnics (carefully controlled—no violence for Kingston). His actors—including Nanci Lee and Taña De Weese—put on skits and tableaux expressing the Chinese-American experience in all its many faces: alienation, confusion, racial victimization, racism toward other groups, delusions of grandeur, deep paranoia, horrid media representations, capacity for joy, for boisterous good times, for rich family life, for intellectual and commercial achievement, on and on. Wittman's play is a grand if unlikely success. The early reviews come in, even as the play continues. And in their racist tones ("Sweet and Sour," "Inscrutable," "East Meets West," all lines from reviews of Kingston's earlier work), they excite Wittman to heightened performance.

He sits commandingly on the stage when the play is done and delivers ad lib a (33-page!) monologue of brilliant (or is it merely wordy?) manic intensity, a manifesto for Chinese Americans. In the midst of this passion, he roughly cuts his hair in an act perhaps reminiscent of the Chinese "queue cutting" of 1911 (which symbolized allegiance to the republic and the renunciation of coolie slavery), but also, perhaps, representing a purposeful defeminization. The pace is frantic. Wittman is Molly Bloom (from James Joyce's *Ulysses*): he rises above and unites the jumble of the book that lies behind him.

AFTER *TRIPMASTER MONKEY*

Tripmaster Monkey won the PEN USA West Award in fiction and heightened Kingston's already considerable reputation as an American writer. Her alma mater, Berkeley, invited her to serve as a chancellor's Distinguished Professor in the English Department from which she was graduated so many years before. In 1991, the year her father died, her home in the Oakland Hills was destroyed in a wildfire. All of her manuscripts, including all of her primary work-in-progress, a monumental pastiche called *The Fourth Book of Peace*, were destroyed.

She began immediately to reconstruct a new manuscript, calling it *The Fifth Book of Peace.* The title refers to lost books of Chinese legend—books without which humans cannot remember how to stay out of war. In interviews, Kingston mentions no projected completion date for the postinferno work.

Meanwhile, Kingston continues to collect honorary doctorates and to lend her time to political and environmental causes. In 1997, President Clinton awarded her the National Humanities Medal for the body of her work.

"I was first published when I was fifteen," Kingston told William Satake Blauvelt. "It was an essay in *American Girl Magazine,* and as I look back, I see my concerns are very similar. My essay was titled, 'I Am an American.' "

Selected Bibliography

WORKS OF MAXINE HONG KINGSTON

BOOKS
The Woman Warrior: Memoirs of a Girlhood Among Ghosts. New York: Alfred A. Knopf, 1976.
China Men. New York: Alfred A. Knopf, 1980.
Hawai'i One Summer. San Francisco: Meadow Press, 1987. Reprint, Honolulu: University of Hawaii Press, 1999.
Through the Black Curtains. Berkeley, Calif.: Friends of the Bancroft Library, 1987.
Tripmaster Monkey: His Fake Book. New York: Alfred A. Knopf, 1989.

ESSAYS AND ARTICLES
"Duck Boy." *New York Times Magazine,* June 12, 1977, pp. 55 + .
"Reservations about China." *Ms.,* October 1978, pp. 67–68.
"San Francisco's Chinatown: A View from the Other Side of Arnold Genthe's Camera." *American Heritage,* December 1978, pp. 36 + .

"The Making of More Americans." *The New Yorker,* February 11, 1980, pp. 34+.

"The Coming Book." *The Writer on Her Work.* Edited by Janet Sternburg. New York: Norton, 1980. Pp. 181–185.

"Cultural Misreadings by American Reviewers." In *Asian and Western Writers in Dialogue: New Cultural Identities.* Edited by Guy Amirthanayagam. London: MacMillan Ltd., 1982. (Essay.)

"A Writer's Notebook from the Far East." *Ms.,* January 1983, pp. 85–86.

"Postscript on Process." *The Bedford Reader.* 2d ed. Edited by X. J. Kennedy and Dorothy M. Kennedy. New York: St. Martin's, 1985. Pp. 69–70.

"Personal Statement." In *Approaches to Teaching Kingston's "The Woman Warrior."* Edited by Shirley Geok-lin Lim. New York: Modern Language Association of America, 1991. (Essay.)

BIOGRAPHICAL AND CRITICAL STUDIES

BOOKS

Cheung, King-Kok. *Articulate Silences: Hisaye Yamamoto, Maxine Hong Kingston, Joy Kogawa.* Ithaca, N.Y.: Cornell University Press, 1993.

Gao, Yan. *The Art of Parody: Maxine Hong Kingston's Use of Chinese Sources.* New York: Peter Lang Publishing, 1996.

Simmons, Diane. *Maxine Hong Kingston.* Boston: Twayne, 1999.

Skandera-Trombley, Laura E., ed. *Critical Essays on Maxine Hong Kingston.* New York: G.K. Hall & Co. (Simon & Schuster Macmillan), 1998.

Skenazy, Paul, and Tera Martin. *Conversations with Maxine Hong Kingston.* Jackson: University of Mississippi Press, 1998.

Wong, Sau-ling Cynthia. *Maxine Hong Kingston's "The Woman Warrior": A Case Book.* New York: Oxford University Press, 1999.

ARTICLES OR BOOK SECTIONS

Chan, Jeffery [*sic*]. "Jeff Chan, Chair of San Francisco State Asian American Studies, Attacks Review [of *The Woman Warrior*]." *San Francisco Journal,* May 4, 1977.

Cheung, King-Kok. "The Woman Warrior versus the Chinaman Pacific: Must a Chinese American Critic Choose between Feminism and Heroism?" In *Conflicts of Feminism.* Edited by Marianne Hirsch and Evelyn Fox Keller. New York: Routledge, 1990. Pp. 234–251.

———. " 'Don't Tell': Imposed Silences in *The Color Purple* and *The Woman Warrior.*" *PMLA* 103: 162–174 (1988).

"Chin, Frank. "The Most Popular Book in China." In *Maxine Hong Kingston's "The Woman Warrior": A Case Book.* New York: Oxford University Press, 1999.

———. "This is not an Autobiography." *Genre* 18.2: 109–130 (1985).

Leonard, John. "In Defiance of Two Worlds." *New York Times Book Review,* September 17, 1976, p. C21.

Lowe, John. "Monkey Kings and Mojo: Postmodern Ethnic Humor in Kingston, Reed, and Vizenor." *Melus* 21.4: 103–127 (Winter 1996).

Smith, Jeanne Rosier. "Monkey Business: Maxine Hong Kingston's Transformational Trickster Texts," "Monkey Mothers and Other Paradoxes: *The Woman Warrior,*" "Trickster History: *China Men,*" "The Monkey and his Community: *Tripmaster Monkey,*" "Monkey Business: Revisionist Mythmaking," "Tripmaster Kingston: The Author as Trickster." In her *Writing Tricksters: Mythic Gambols in American Ethnic Literature.* Berkeley: University of California Press, 1997.

Smith, Sidonie. "Maxine Hong Kingston's *Woman Warrior:* Filiality and Woman's Autobiographical Storytelling." In *A Poetics of Women's Autobiography.* Bloomington: University of Indiana Press, 1987.

Tyler, Anne. "Manic Monologue." *The New Republic,* April 17, 1989, pp. 44–46.

Yu, Ning. "A Strategy Against Marginalization: The 'High' and 'Low' Cultures in Kingston's China Men." *College Literature* 23.3: 73–88 (October 1996).

Yuan, Yuan. "The Semiotics of China Narratives in the Con/Texts of Kingston and Tan." *Critique: Studies in Contemporary Fiction* 40.3: 29+ (Spring 1999).

Zhang, Ya-Jie. "A Chinese Woman's Response to Maxine Hong Kingston's *The Woman Warrior.*" In *Maxine Hong Kingston's "The Woman Warrior": A Case Book.* New York: Oxford University Press, 1999.

INTERVIEWS

Blauvelt, William Satake. "Talking with the Woman Warrior." In *Conversations with Maxine Hong*

Kingston. Edited by Paul Skenazy and Tera Martin. Jackson: University of Mississippi Press, 1998.

Brownmiller, Susan. "Susan Brownmiller Talks with Maxine Hong Kingston, Author of *The Woman Warrior.*" *Mademoiselle,* March 1977, pp. 148 +.

Mendelbaum, Paul. "Rising from the Ashes: A Profile of Maxine Hong Kingston." *Poets and Writers Magazine,* May–June 1998, pp. 48–53.

Pfaff, Timothy. "Talk with Mrs. Kingston." *New York Times Book Review,* June 15, 1980, pp. 1, 24–26.

Rabinowitz, Paula. "Eccentric Memories." In *Conversations with Maxine Hong Kingston.* Edited by Paul Skenazy and Tera Martin. Jackson: University of Mississippi Press, 1998.

—*BILL ROORBACH*

Philip Levine

1928—

SINCE THE 1960S readers of contemporary American poetry have known the poems of Philip Levine for their original style and voice, elegiac narrative, grit, and telling detail. A Levine poem is recognizable by its tight line, turns of imagery, and powerful rhetorical closure, as well as for its acerbic diction and forceful rhythms issuing from an anaphoric use of contemporary idiom. The poetry of Levine has been celebrated not only for its singular technical virtues but also for its willingness to engage the smug and ungenerous powers of society, to make anger and moral indignation stand up for the disenfranchised. Levine's ability to absorb himself in lives in addition to his has the "I" of the poem speaking for the working and under classes that rarely have a representative in politics or art. Powerfully and memorably, his poetry consistently offers "vivas" for the human spirit, which defies the conditions of the world and survives with essential dignity.

Levine has been a witness to much of the inhumanity in American life in the twentieth century through hands-on examples, culled firsthand in factories and in the cities. The stories of his life are the stories of many lives and have raised the fortitude of the worker, the common man and woman, to lyric, mythical, and spiritual levels.

By the age of seventy-two Levine had produced an unparalleled body of poetry. Beginning as a poet of anger and suffering, he progressed to become a poet of determination and spare celebration. From his original working-class subjects, he has expanded his style and vision to include an almost metaphysical vision, certainly one that cherishes and celebrates all elements of existence, and his poetry champions a secular and inclusive transcendence whether or not it finally understands life's shortcomings and ambiguities. The poet and critic Edward Hirsch (1993) wrote that Levine "has increasingly asserted a Keatsian faith in the boundlessness of human possibility. One might say that his work begins in rage, ripens toward elegy, and culminates in celebration. . . . What starts as anger deepens into grief and finally rises into joy."

By the end of the twentieth century, Levine was arguably the preeminent American poet living and writing in the United States. While there will always be a critic or reader who prefers the style or vision of another major poet of the time, Levine's preeminence rests on the facts that no poet is more acclaimed than Levine and that his publication of so many first-rate, influential, and original books of poetry is unmatched.

Book critics and readers alike have found Levine to be inventive, challenging, dynamic, and important to American letters and life. Of his many collections, those published since *The Name of the Lost* (1976) all met with critical acclaim, his style and range increasing from book to book. The critic Harold Bloom commented in a blurb on the book jacket of *The Simple Truth* (1994), "I am a long time admirer of Philip Levine's poetry, but until now thought he would never surpass *The Names of the Lost,* a book I love deeply. But *The Simple Truth* deserves its title—I wonder if *any* American poet since Walt Whitman himself has written elegies this consistently magnificent. The controlled pathos of every poem in the volume is immense, and gives me a new sense of Levine."

Levine's first collection was *On the Edge* (1963) and was published in a letterpress edition of 220 copies that soon became unavailable. The following year it was brought out as an offset trade edition of one thousand paperback copies. His second collection, *Not This Pig,* was published in 1968 by one of the most important publishers of poetry at the time, Wesleyan University Press, and that year Levine received the Chapelbrook Foundation Award in the Arts. Three books published by small presses followed: *5 Detroits* (1970), *Pili's Wall* (1971), and *Red Dust* (1971). Levine then moved to a major publishing house, Atheneum, which published his fifth book, *They Feed They Lion;* the collection drew significant critical response from the poets X. J. Kennedy, Thom Gunn, and Robert Dana.

In 1973 Levine received the first of three National Endowment for the Arts (NEA) grants in poetry. Atheneum brought out his sixth book, *1933,* in 1974, and that same year he received the first of two Guggenheim fellowships, as well as the Award of Merit from the National Society of Arts and Letters and the Frank O'Hara Memorial Prize. His next work, *The Names of the Lost,* was published in 1976, first in a letterpress edition and then in a trade edition from Atheneum; this book received the Lenore Marshall Poetry Prize from the Academy of American Poets as the best book of poetry published by an American in that year. *On the Edge and Over,* a book that reprinted Levine's first book with poems "old, lost, and new,"

was also published in 1976, and in 1978 the University of Chicago awarded Levine the Harriet Monroe Memorial Prize.

Capitalizing on Levine's popularity and success, in 1979 Atheneum brought out two new books by him, *7 Years from Somewhere* and *Ashes.* That same year Levine received a grant from the Columbia Translation Center to translate with Ernesto Trejo a book by the eminent Mexican poet Jaime Sabines—*Tarumba, Selected Poems of Jaime Sabines. Ashes* and *7 Years from Somewhere* together received the National Book Critics Circle Award for Poetry for 1979, and the following year Levine received the American Book Award for Poetry for *Ashes* as well as his second Guggenheim fellowship. In 1981 the University of Michigan Press published *Don't Ask,* a collection of interviews with Levine, in its Poets on Poetry series; Atheneum brought out *One for the Rose;*and Levine received the Levenson Memorial Award from *Poetry* magazine.

In 1984 Levine's *Selected Poems* was published, and one of contemporary poetry's most notable critics, Peter Stitt, concluded:

> Philip Levine certainly must be ranked with the finest poets America has produced. He also belongs with those who are most thoroughly American, writing in the great tradition of William Carlos Williams—eschewing opera in favor of jazz, the drawing room in favor of the kitchen, the silk-covered cushion in favor of the bus-station bench. His *Selected Poems* is a monument for our age.

Also in 1984 Levine published *Off the Map,* a selection of translations with Ada Long of the contemporary Spanish poet Gloria Fuertes.

From 1984 to 1985 Levine was chairman of the Literature Board for the National Endowment for the Arts. *Sweet Will,* his twelfth book, was published by Atheneum in 1985. In 1987 he was awarded the Ruth Lilly Poetry Prize for distinguished poetic achievements. That same year he received his third NEA grant and edited *The Essential Keats.*

When Atheneum folded in 1987, Levine moved, along with his editor of many years, Harry Ford, to the publishing house of Alfred A. Knopf, where he published *A Walk with Tom Jefferson* in 1988. In 1991 Knopf brought out *New Selected Poems,* a volume substantially enlarged beyond the long-out-of-print *Selected Poems* of 1984. At the same time, Knopf published *What Work Is,* which won the National Book Award for Poetry for 1991 and the Los Angeles Times Book Award for Poetry. Levine's next book, *The Simple Truth* (1994), received the Pulitzer Prize for poetry in 1995.

In 1997 Greenhouse Review Press brought out an edition of Levine's poetry titled *Unselected Poems,* which contains more than one hundred pages of poems not included in either of his selected poems collections but that Levine felt were worthy of keeping in print. Similarly, *One for the Rose* was republished in 1999 by Carnegie Mellon University Press in the Classic Contemporary book series, as was the double collection *They Feed They Lion; and The Names of the Lost* by Knopf.

It would be difficult to find a more substantial list of publications and awards or higher accolades for any poet. In 1997 Levine was elected a member of the American Academy of Arts and Letters. John Martone, reviewing *Selected Poems* (1984) in *World Literature Today* (no. 59:296–297, 1985), wrote:

> Whitman shouted, "Vivas for those who have failed." Levine, who uses Whitman's line as an epigraph, has gone on to show us a universe of failure and dignity in the face of failure. Of all contemporary poets, he has probably remained most faithful to the world of the American underclass and working class, who know as he does what it is to endure "a succession of stupid jobs." As I read through these poems, I found myself feeling again and again that a reader one hundred years from now

will learn more about the secrets of our time from this book than any other I know.

LIFE AND CAREER

Philip Levine was born on January 10, 1928, in Detroit, Michigan, the second of three children, and the first of identical twins, of Harry Levine and Esther Gertrude Priscoll, both parents born in Russia. His father fought with the British army in World War I, after which he settled in Detroit, where he met and married Levine's mother. His twin brother, Edward, a painter with a considerable reputation in Detroit, inherited the family business, and his older brother, Eli, retired in Santa Barbara after a career in the Chicago automotive parts trade. After his father's death in 1933, Levine and his brothers were raised by their mother and attended Detroit's public schools. Levine became a factory worker at age fourteen during World War II, and through his teens and twenties he worked at a succession of blue collar jobs—on a road repair crew; at a plumbing fixtures plating company, Chevrolet Gear and Axle, and Detroit Transmission; and as a boxcar loader. These jobs and the people who worked alongside him became a substantial portion of the subjects for his poems.

From 1946 to 1950, while still working, Levine attended Wayne University (later Wayne State University), where he discovered modern poetry and the beginnings of his own poems and earned a B.A. degree. He was married to Patty Kanterman from 1951 to 1953, and in 1952, because of financial difficulties, he was forced to reject a grant in fiction from the Writers Workshop at the University of Iowa. From 1950 to 1954 Levine worked on his M.A. at Wayne University, writing his thesis on Keats' "Ode on Indolence." He then went to the University of Iowa to study with Robert Lowell and also took a class there with John Berryman, about whom he wrote "Mine Own

John Berryman," which was published in the autobiographical prose collection *The Bread of Time* (1994).

On his twenty-sixth birthday in 1954, Levine met Frances J. Artley, an actress and costumer who was working on a teaching credential in Iowa City. On July 4 they were married in Boone, North Carolina, and Levine adopted her son, Mark. From 1954 to1955 Frances taught speech and drama at Florida State University while Levine concentrated on his writing; his first poems were published in *Antioch Review, Beloit Poetry Journal, New Orleans Poetry Review, Poetry,* and *Western Review.* In 1955 he got a job at the University of Iowa teaching technical writing, Greek, and the Bible, enabling Levine to attend the Writers Workshop, where he met Peter Everwine, Robert Mezey, and Ted Holmes and renewed friendships with Henri Coulette, Robert Dana, Donald Petersen, Donald Justice, and others. He received his M.F.A. degree from the University of Iowa in 1957 and traveled to California to attend Stanford University and study with Yvor Winters on a Jones Fellowship (now the Stegner Fellowship). Levine and his family—Frances, Mark, and John, who was born in Iowa in December 1955—moved to Fresno, California, in 1958, and he began a career as a professor at California State University, Fresno. He later taught at many other important universities across the country—Princeton, Columbia, Tufts, Vanderbilt, and the University of Houston—building a major reputation as a teacher of writing and numbering among his students such now-accomplished poets as Larry Levis, Gary Soto, David St. John, Herbert Scott, Roberta Spear, Sherley Anne Williams, Glover Davis, Ernesto Trejo, Greg Pape, Kathy Fagan, Jon Veinberg, Dixie Salazar, Luis Omar Salinas, Lawson Fusao Inada, Jean Janzen, and Robert Vasquez. He retired from Fresno in 1992 but continued to teach at a number of universities in a visiting capacity, most notably at New York University.

ON THE EDGE

Levine received the fellowship to Stanford because, in his own words, he had "mastered the poetry of princes," or traditional metered verse. Levine wrote about his poetic beginnings in an essay for the landmark contemporary poetry anthology *Naked Poetry* (1969). In this candid essay Levine reveals how difficult it was for him in the late 1950s to bring the language of his own experience and life into his poetry instead of writing the "poetry of princes." While at Stanford he worked at syllabic poetry, having been directed to the poetry of Elizabeth Daryush by Winters. Levine largely discounts his syllabic efforts, pointing out that even Winters did not know that no one could hear syllables and that almost no one could hear the rhymes in syllabic poems; nevertheless at this time he did write the tour de force syllabic "Sierra Kid," which was included in *On the Edge.* Although syllabic poetry does not require rhyme schemes, Levine's early training in traditional forms and the strong suggestion by Winters moved him to include end rhymes in the poem. In a 1999 interview with Ernest Suarez for the journal *Five Points,* Levine related how in 1956 while at Iowa and studying with Lowell, Lowell insisted that students master traditional forms; answering a question about Winters and syllabic poetry, he responded, "He [Winters] insisted that I use rhyme because the poetry was too loose without it. I had been writing only metrical poetry for three or four years. Syllabic poetry provided an avenue for me even though it has strict formal requirements."

The voice of the Sierra Kid is specific, colloquial, and American, everything that William Carlos Williams called for and everything that Levine himself realized he would have to allow his poems to become, if what he was writing would truly become "his" poetry. "Sierra Kid" is a narrative monologue that marshals the strictures of the form but never loses the natural and credible speech patterns of the speaker. At the end of the essay for *Naked Poetry,* Levine recounts a reading he gave with Gary Snyder in San Francisco in 1957 and how Snyder was much better received by the audience than he was: "I knew he gave them more, that his poems were more readable, more eloquent and looser at the same time, and more consistently in our common American language. He was writing for and about the people who were listening; I had technique."

In "Sierra Kid" we hear a mountain man of the Sierras early in the twentieth century lashing out against the encroachment of "progress" and commercialism. Even in this early poem—in its tightly mastered measures—we hear the anger, the greater moral and social conscience, and the concern for the individual and mythical consciousness that constitute the unique alloy of much of Levine's voice. The following excerpts are the last stanzas of section four, "Civilization comes to Sierra Kid," and the last stanza of section five, "Mad, Dying, Sierra Kid enters the capital"—the end of the poem.

Six weeks. I went back down
  Through my own woods
Afraid of what I knew they'd done.
  There, there, and A&P,
    And not a tree
For miles, and mammoth hills of goods.

Fat men in uniforms
  Young men in aprons
With one face shouting, "He is mad!"
  I answered: "I am Lincoln,
    Aaron Burr,
The aging son of Appleseed.

"I am American
  And I am cold."
But not a one would hear me out.
  Oh God, what have I seen
    That was not sold!
They shot an old man in the gut.

      *   *   *

I came to touch
The great heart of a dying state.
  Here is the wound!
  It makes no sound.
All that we learn we learn too late.
  And it's not much.

In "On the Edge" the anger and indignation that characterize Levine's early work are amazingly fluent inside three stanzas of iambic pentameter with an ABCABC rhyme scheme. Levine combines the "edgy" psyche of Edgar Allan Poe with his own and develops a poetry that bypasses the autobiographical baldness of the confessional school of the late 1960s and 1970s. Levine set a course toward the mythology of the self, the emblem and image enlarging the emotional center and communal implications of the poem. This is the beginning of an original "move" that has Levine following his imagination and combining autobiographical material with fictive underpinnings in order to amplify the narrative or complaint and enrich the emotion, humor, and themes. This strategy gave rise to such memorable and highly imaginative poems as "Animals Are Passing from Our Lives" (in *Not This Pig*); "Angel Butcher" (in *They Feed They Lion*); "Let Me Be" and "Let Me Begin Again" (in *7 Years from Somewhere*); "I Was Born in Lucerne," "One for the Rose," "On My Own," and "The Fox" (in *One for the Rose*); and "M. Degas Teaches Art & Science at Durfee Intermediate School, Detroit, 1942" (in *What Work Is*).

In the opening stanza of "On the Edge" the colloquial diction is an exact fit to the alienated conceit of the speaker, and it drives forward in short, hard-hitting bursts, despite the iambs and the rhymes.

My name is Edgar Poe and I was born
In 1928 in Michigan.
Nobody gave a damn. The gruel I ate
Kept me alive, nothing kept me warm,
But I grew up, almost to five foot ten
And nothing in the world can change my weight.

Poe is a perfect alter ego for *On the Edge,* because, as Levine said in an interview with Glover Davis and Dennis Saleh for *American Poetry Review* (November/December 1972), "If you look at *On The Edge* you find poetry of someone on the edge, on the edge of despair, the edge of breakdown, on the edge of his culture, of his own life."

The most memorable poem from *On the Edge* is "The Horse." A free verse poem using what would for some years become Levine's customary three-beat line, this poem recounts a myth from the dropping of the atomic bomb on Hiroshima as related to Levine by a survivor. The painful inventive imagery sets a scene in compelling detail, and although this is a poem of political outrage—and Levine has many such poems—the politics never supersedes the language or the story of the poem. In the 1999 interview for *Five Points,* Levine was asked about political poetry and how he kept his from becoming mannered. He replied, "by inventing stories which involve people. The first level of the poem that comes at you is the language and the second level is the narrative with its characters and behind all of this may come a slow recognition that all this has to do with the politics of living. . . . Whatever political implications might grow out of them I welcome, but I never begin with the political." In "The Horse" the speaker is looking at the people, seeing what they see, the mass hallucination of the apocalyptic white horse careening through the city following the bomb blast, and radioactive firestorms. Unsentimental and realistic, the conclusion of the poem conveys the theme and politics:

The horse would never return.

There had been no horse. I could
tell from the way they walked
testing the ground for some cold
that the rage had gone out of
their bones in one mad dance.

In his review in *Poetry* (February 1964), the poet and critic X. J. Kennedy wrote, "*On the Edge,* the long awaited first book by Philip Levine, is another with virtues hard to make too much of. I can't imagine that the ultimate anthology, *Cold War American Poetry* (or whatever the glum title), will be able to do without two or three poems from it."

NOT THIS PIG

In 1965 Levine and his family—he now had a third son, Theodore—went to live in Spain for a year, which changed his poetry and produced many of the poems that would make up *Not This Pig.* Whereas *On the Edge* was a book of fury controlled largely by formal patterns, *Not This Pig* finds a voice and strategies that accommodate greater experience and imagination. The long poem "The Cemetery at Academy, California," and "Heaven," "Winter Rains, Cataluña," and "Baby Villon" are such poems. The poem "Animals Are Passing from Our Lives" sets a tone of defiance for the book with its expansive imagination that allows a pig to speak, a pig who refuses to give in to the market and to commercialism, and who says at the end, "No. Not this pig."

But Levine's early formalism is still to be found, and "A New Day" is a successful poem that hits high lyric notes in praise of the old heavyweight boxing champion Jersey Joe Walcott. Out early one morning in Chicago, the speaker comes across the champ doing roadwork around the lake.

He takes off at a slow trot
And the fat slides under his shirt.
I recall the Friday night
In a beer garden in Detroit
I saw him flatten Ezzard Charles.

It is dawn and the day is therefore new; the champ, past his prime, is out there working anyway, defying the years. The speaker does not burden him with the details of his own life but realizes with the champ that this is the world and though nothing much is going to change, it is what we together make it.

> Here at the shore, the two of us,
> To make a pact, a people come
> For a new world and a new home
>
> And what we get is what we bring:
> A grey light coming on at dawn,
> No fresh start and no bird song
> And no sea and no shore
> that someone hasn't seen before.

The best-known poem from *Not This Pig* is another tour de force in syllabics. "Silent in America" chooses a famous line from Whitman as its epigraph—"Vivas for those who have failed." This poem had its genesis in the fact that Levine actually had a broken jaw that was wired shut, but from that prosaic beginning we are given original and lean music firmly in the American idiom. The first section of the poem is an example of the fluent and forceful Levine rhetoric:

> Since I no longer speak I
> Go unnoticed among men;
> in the far corners of rooms,
> greeted occasionally
> with a stiff wave, I am seen
> aslant as one sees a pane
>
> of clear glass, reflecting both
> what lies before and behind
> in a dazzle of splendid
> approximations. . . .
>
> . . . One woman,
> hearing me grunt for breath, sits
> by my side in a green dress,
>
> her hands cupped in the valley
> of her life. She would receive
> my sympathy and in my
> eyes sees—God knows what she sees

> in my eyes. Let them have
> all they find under the sky.

Later, in section four, we hear the irony, humor, and self-deprecation that, in concert, uniquely mark Levine's work:

> I am Fresno's
> dumb bard, America's last
> hope, sheep in sheep's
> clothing. Who names the past
> names me. Who sleeps
> by my side shall find despair
> and happiness, a twi-night double header.

The poem proclaims in its communal conclusion that, despite the conditions of the world, let us go into the world with dignity and know it for what it is:

> Come with us tonight
> drifters in the drifting crowd,
>   we shall arrive, late
> and tired, beyond the false lights
>   of Pasadena
> where the living are silent
>   in America.

PILI'S WALL AND RED DUST

In 1971 *Pili's Wall* and *Red Dust* were published by small presses. *Pili's Wall* is a volume that first appeared in a letterpress edition of 750 copies; it is a long poem in ten sections accompanied by photographs of images drawn on a wall in Spain by the child Pili. The poet's consciousness melds with the images that the child presents of her environment and herself. While this poem does not contain the scope or vision of other long poems by Levine, it is interesting to see the more open movement in the poem, the concentration of imagery that moves Levine's poetry away from his formal early work.

Red Dust also presents a transitional stage in Levine's writing. Reviewers have commented on the more associative, even surrealist touches in these poems, but Levine brings a more necessary music and compelling rhetoric to the semisurrealist poem of the 1970s; there is little that is arbitrary or indulgently abstract in these poems. "Clouds," "How Much Earth," and "The Sadness of Lemons" are three poems in this mode that are still engaging. "Holding On" and the title poem, both written in his clear, muscular style, are the strongest in the book. In "Red Dust," Levine characteristically takes an everyday event—a woman complaining in a bar—and by the poem's end transforms the situation and emotion into almost mythical results:

> If eagles formed now in the
> shocked vegetation of my sight
> would they be friendly? I can hear
> their wings lifting them down, the feathers
> tipped with red dust, that dust which
> even here I taste, having eaten it
> all these years.

This ending is anything but elliptical, and while it offers an atmosphere spawned from intense imagination, it is direct, declarative, and resonant.

THEY FEED THEY LION

Candor charged with a stinging, almost biblical rhetoric, modulated by lyric passages or a visionary closure, are the qualities for which *They Feed They Lion* was widely acclaimed. Many of the subjects are autobiographical, about his sons or wife, about himself alone with the world ("Alone"), but just as often the poems are about others, ourselves in terms of the external objects of the world. In "Renaming the Kings," the speaker has had an accident and struck his head on a stone along the river and passed out. He wakes and confronts the rock, and names "the stone John / after my mysterious second born."

The rocks, the element of nature, then relate to the speaker in pain, in myth, and in blood, like sons. Levine uses the power of all the industrial parts of the United States—the gas stations, junked cars, slag heaps, and burning factory stacks of Detroit—to have us see what we have done to the earth and to each other.

The title poem is one of the better known poems of contemporary poetry, and it is with this poem that Levine most forcefully begins to speak for the voiceless. "They Feed They Lion" testifies by example, in an almost prophetic cadence, but there are no platitudes; instead, there is a fresh slate of specifics that in their imagistic resonance indict what was then the social order. The poem was written in response to the riots and civil unrest in Detroit and other cities of the United States in 1967. Levine uses a shorthand rhetoric and is wise enough to find the music and fiery imagery of the black idiom. He is able to take on a truly difficult subject—the political subject of racism—in the poem by presenting the choruses of evidence and finding in the dialect the facts of the matter. The Lion becomes the symbol for the fury of the black community in Detroit or in any U.S. city during that time. The Lion is a symbol of power and strength, as it was in ancient texts. Levine knows the places from which the anger and despair come from, having worked the same jobs or having been out of work alongside many of these people, and thus the catalog that opens the poem with the specific motivations for rage:

> Out of burlap sacks, out of bearing butter,
> Out of black bean and wet slate bread,
> Out of the acids of rage, the candor of tar,
> Out of creosote, gasoline, drive shafts, wooden dollies,
> They Lion Grow.

The anaphora propels the poem forward; the stanzaic coda of "They Lion Grow" builds up a rhetorical tension that surges through the poem, that buoys the lists of grievances that may give rise to empowerment:

> From "Bow down" come "Rise Up,"
> Come they Lion from the reeds of shovels,
> The grained arm that pulls the hands.
> They Lion Grow.

Levine concludes this important poem by including himself by not standing apart from or above the situation—a realistic and honest move that allows the poem to have intellectual and thematic credibility and to be the coefficient of the incantatory fervor of the music:

> From my five arms and all my hands,
> From all my white sins forgiven, they feed,
> From my car passing under the stars,
> They Lion, from my children inherit,
> From the oak turned to a wall, they Lion,
> From they sack and they belly opened
> And all that was hidden burning on the oil-stained
>   earth
> They feed they Lion and he comes.

There are many Detroit poems in this collection that hit hard and witness the effects of industrial life. The especially memorable poem "Salami" is set in Spain and opens with one of the most concrete, grisly, and unflinching catalogs in contemporary poetry:

> Stomach of goat, crushed
> sheep balls, soft full
> pearls of pig eyes,
> snout gristle, fresh earth, worn iron of trotter, slate
> of Zaragoza, dried cat heart,
> cock claws.

"To P.L., 1916–1937" is an elegy to a distant cousin who was a soldier of the Republic in the Spanish Civil War; this is such a detailed and intensely imagined narrative of the death and aftermath of his cousin, so particular in its vision, that it places readers right there and compels

them to value each quotidian specific of life. In this poem Levine demonstrates his talent to mix the frank details of place and narrative with a lyrical resolution that lifts the poem, finally, far beyond its bleak particulars to a prayerlike closure.

> and on the road to Huesca in spring
> there is no one to look for you
> among the wild jonquils, the curling
> grasses at the road side,
> and the blood red poppies, no one
> to look on the farthest tip
> of wind breathing down from the mountains
> and shaking the stunted pines you hid among.

Although *They Feed They Lion* is known for its realism and for the authority of its rhetoric and forceful music, there are other quite remarkable poems in the book that demonstrate Levine's range. "Alone" is a poem of quiet pastoral lyricism. "To a Fish Head Found on the Beach near Malaga" is one of the strongest poems in the collection and is exceptional for its inventive imagery, which is a necessary component of the lyric, almost mystic, voice and theme of the cyclic nature of life. The last poem in the book, "Breath," is, for its lyric intelligence and visionary resolution, every bit as strong as the title poem; it offers a resolute wisdom, an understated determinism in the face of mortality:

> . . . I give
> the world my worn-out breath
> on an old tune, I give
> it all I have
> and take it back again.

1933

In *1933* Levine shifts his subject matter and his imagistic manner. The poems are autobiographical and there is by far more compassion than anger. A pronounced change in attitude is evident when a comparison is made between images of the father in *On the Edge* and *1933*. Levine was five years old in 1933 when his father died, and in the title poem we have a tender, poignant view of the father. In "Night Thoughts over a Sick Child" from *On the Edge* the image of fatherhood is centered in anger and defiance. In the 1972 interview with Davis and Saleh for *American Poetry Review,* Levine speaks to this shift in attitude in his work. "I want to be a poet of joy as well as suffering. . . . The image of fatherhood in that book [*On the Edge*] is the image of the father scared, hovering over the sick child and furious at creation for afflicting the child. I think later I'm more likely to cherish the child no matter what he is." This turn in emotion is best seen in the last part of "1933":

> my father stands on the porch in his last summer
> he holds back his tears
> he holds back my tears
>
> Once in childhood the stars held still all night
>   the moon swelled like a plum but white and
>   silken
>   the last train from Chicago howled through the
>   ghetto
>   I came downstairs
>   my father sat writing in a great black book
>   a pile of letters
>   a pile of checks
>   (he would pay his debts)
>   the moon would die
>   the stars jelly
>   the sea freeze
> I would be a boy in worn shoes splashing through
>   rain

The poem ends on solitude, abandonment, and personal anguish, but Levine is not angry with his father for his absence but instead offers us a vision of a father we can cherish with him. We have the image, almost archetypal, of an emotional communion we all desire and we all lose.

The rhythms are not as driving and tight as before, and the forms are not as strict. The reader is not overwhelmed and overpowered as in the magnificent title poem of *They Feed They Lion,* but the poems in *1933* have power, a subtle power of genuine empathy, one arising out of a larger vision of the human condition.

Levine's heightened use of image and symbol enables him to go from the personal to the metaphysical, to give us the emotive content and then spiral it outward through the image to a larger context. This final imaginative movement outward helps to objectify essentially subjective experiences and to raise autobiography to contemporary myth and to a larger consciousness emblematic of our history. In the title poem Levine moves us to the overwhelming implication of death and loss: "the moon would die / the stars jelly / the sea freeze." These are not the usual concrete images of a Levine poem up to this point; they are fresh and effective ones.

Another image indicative of Levine's shift in tone is that of the river. In "Alone," from *They Feed They Lion,* the poet is "following a broken trail of stones / toward the deep and starless river." And while this is a lovely and emotive image it remains grounded in the landscape. In the last poem in *1933,* "Hold Me," the image of the river blends with other images to become visionary: "we are / all the moon, the one planet, the hand / of five stars flung on the night river." In the earlier poem we stay on the earth; in the poem from *1933* we move out to the stars with the planets and approach the cosmos.

The new tone and approach in *1933* accommodate the country of memory, and many of the most memorable poems are about relatives, including "Zaydee," "Grandmother in Heaven," "Uncle," and "Late Moon." Less specific but more inclusive is the stunning long poem "Letters for the Dead," a series of vignettes connected by voice, theme, and texture rather than narrative, a structure of theme and variation that is echoed in later long poems, such as "Belief" from *One for the Rose*, "A Poem with No Ending" from *Sweet Will*, "28" and the title poem of *A Walk with Tom Jefferson,* and the Dantesque masterpiece "Burned" from *What Work Is*. Because of the immediacy, the pith, and raw energy of much of his work, Levine is not especially known for his long poems, which are some of his best. Richard Jackson explicates the workings and compositions of three of these long poems and Levine's overall achievement in his essay "The Long Embrace," first published in the *Kenyon Review* (n.s. II, no. 4, Fall 1989).

THE NAMES OF THE LOST

The reclaiming of the past continues with strength and expanded vision in *The Names of the Lost*. Levine's ability to detail a complete scene and dramatic event in a few short lines in resonant detail is illuminated in such poems as different as "No One Remembers," about his Uncle Joe from his Detroit childhood, and "On the Murder of Lieutenant José del Castillo by the Falangist Bravo Martinez, July 12, 1936," about an incident in Barcelona during the Spanish Civil War. There is still anger in these poems, but there is also forgiveness, especially in "No One Remembers," which begins with a visit to a graveyard and the brutish details of his Uncle Joe's life recalled, no punches pulled:

> . . . Uncle Joe, big cigar, fist
> on the ear, nodding *sure*
> *bitch* and coming at me.
> You can't touch her now,
> and she's a thousand miles
> from here.

But at the end of the poem Levine finds something of the dead to cherish, some connection to life that provides forgiveness for Joe as he, in

fact, remembers, as the anaphora of "no one remembers" provides the channel by which all the memory enters:

> No one remembers
> your hand, opened, warm
> and sweating on the back
> of my neck when you first
> picked me up and said
> my name, *Philip,* and held
> the winter sun up
> for me to see outside
> the French windows of
> the old house on Pingree,
> No one remembers.

But Levine knows it is his place—poetry's place—to witness and find communion or to raise the banner of a humane and moral order, to hold the dead's name in a prayer on his lips.

Levine's facility for telling detail cuts through the past and places a reader on the immediate dramatic spot, as is evident in "On the Murder of Lieutenant José del Castillo by the Falangist Bravo Martinez, July 12, 1936." The title gives you the politics; it is no secret in the poems in *The Names of the Lost* or in later books that Levine championed the anarchists and opposed Franco and fascism; this is, after all, a murder, one among thousands, and while he does not forgive the fascists, he cherishes the individual and the value of a life that stood up to them.

> When the Lieutenant of the Guardia de Asalto
> heard the automatic go off, he turned
> and took the second shot just above
> the sternum, the third tore away
> the right shoulder of his uniform,
> the fourth perforated his cheek. . . .
> The pigeons that spotted the cold floor
> of Barcelona rose as he sank below
> the waves of silence crashing
> on the far shores of his legs, growing
> faint and watery. . . .
>
> The Lieutenant can hear it, the prayer
> that comes on the voice of water, today

or yesterday, from Chicago or Valladolid,
and hangs like smoke above this street
he won't walk as a man ever again.

In this political vein there are the poems "For the Fallen" and "For the Poets of Chile," with Levine bearing witness to their deaths and to their lives. However, most of the poems are for family—for his wife, sons, and his aunt—and for men he worked with in Detroit and for a Polish high school girl in 1949. The centerpiece of the book is "New Season," a poem of three pages that moves back and forth in time celebrating the life of Della Daubien, a black woman saved from the racism of the 1940s by three white girls, and the life of his mother turning seventy, her life connecting to his, with the park he recalls from his childhood and every living thing looking for a new season, to be reclaimed by the light, to live again by the light of memory:

> . . . —to the dark pond
> where the one swan drifted, the woman
> is 70 now—the willow is burning,
> the rhododendrons shrivel
> like paper under water, all
> the small secret mouths are feeding
> on the green heart of the plum.

ASHES AND 7 YEARS FROM SOMEWHERE

For Levine the personal combines with the political, and the political is present to support the individual, with the memory to hold and make sense of our lives. This vision and strategy continued and was expanded into his next two books, *Ashes: Poems Old and New* and *7 Years from Somewhere*, both published in 1979.

Ashes rescues thirteen poems from the out-of-print *Red Dust* and balances them between new lyrical, mystical, and rhetorical poems of striking personal power. "The Rains" is a poem that concludes in a transcendent vision of the poet and his wife beyond this life. For pure lyric power and purity it is hard to surpass the poem "Starlight," and while this poem does not have the ambition of "1933," it captures a lyric moment—one of the last it would seem between the poet and his father—as poignantly as it can be done:

> My father stands in the warm evening
> on the porch of my first house.
> I am four years old and growing tired.
> I see his head among the stars,
> the glow of his cigarette, redder
> that the summer moon riding
> low over the old neighborhood. . . .
> Then he lifts me to his shoulder,
> and now I too am there among the stars,
> as tall as he. Are you happy? I say.
> He nods in answer, Yes! oh yes! oh yes!
> And in that voice he says nothing . . .
> holding his child against the promises
> of autumn, until the boy slept
> never to waken in that world again.

The title poem "Ashes" has somewhat the same rhetorical power and focus as "They Feed They Lion" at its end. "Lost and Found" celebrates the communion of father and son, Levine and his son, and is a fitting closure to the book that begins with the poem "Father," which is followed closely by "Starlight." Levine is rescuing lives from the ashes of the past, cherishing them for what they were and are in memory.

At this point in his career, Levine was not content with simply the well-made poem of witnessing; he is pushed through to a realization that the past is gone, that imagination and art might be all we have to preserve what we value or love. Just as he realizes in "Starlight" that the safe and ordinary world of the child is gone, in *7 Years from Somewhere* he comes to a number of realizations about his life and ideals.

One of the most memorable poems in the collection comes at the end of the book. "You Can Have It" calls up the old rage and indignation at a society and industrial world that breaks down its best people. Here, however, Levine lets his rage combine with imagination and takes his complaint to a higher level, challenging the fates or what might be the order of a world. He is recalling 1948, when he and his twin brother were working at lousy jobs, one on day shift, one on night shift, with the work stealing their youth and their lives—the incredulous waste of it all.

> . . . We were twenty
> for such a short time and always in
> the wrong clothes, crusted with dirt
> and sweat. I think now we were never twenty. . . .

> for there was no such year, and now
> that year has fallen off all the old newspapers,
> calendars, doctors' appointments, bonds,
> wedding certificates, drivers licenses.

> . . . I give you back 1948
> I give you all the years from then
> to the coming one. . . .

> Give me back my young brother, hard
> and furious, with wide shoulders and a curse
> for God and burning eyes that look upon
> all creation and say, You can have it.

This is almost a curse, and the imagination is rooted in hard fact—working that hard for nothing does in fact take away that year, that period of youth; working like men, they were never twenty.

A number of other poems are pitched in the rhetoric of prayer, that is, intense, incantatory, and addressed at the cosmos. "Let Me Be," "I Could Believe," and "Let Me Begin Again" abandon autobiography in favor of the imagination and almost mystical sweeps of imagery and yet conclude with an understanding of existence. "Let me begin again as a speck / of dust caught in the night winds / sweeping out to sea," Levine begins, intoning a view of continuance, even reincarnation.

> 1/10/28. Tonight I shall enter my life
> after being at sea for ages. . . .
> A tiny wise child who this time will love
> his life because it is like no other.

This expanded vision and imagination became more evident in Levine's later books, in which a spare and secular metaphysical mode was worked into Levine's poems much of the time and focused and shaped the actual events from his life that sparked the poems.

ONE FOR THE ROSE AND *SWEET WILL*

In this more fictive and imaginative vein, *One for the Rose* and *Sweet Will* expand the grit and detail of Levine's actual life to a larger and more mythical level; irony, humor, and even some spiritual dimensions enter and give us a poetry more expansive in image and line as well as vision and supposition.

More so than any previous book, *One for the Rose* contains poems without literal biographical detail and that employ fantastic narrative and imagery. While the critic Helen Vendler panned the book, finding it "All Too Real" (*New York Review of Books,* December 17, 1981), David Walker, writing for *Field* (no. 26, 1982)—and the vast majority of reviewers—found it to be exceptional because of its infusion of imagination. "I Was Born in Lucerne" takes up a completely different life for the speaker as a contrast to Levine's actual industrial life. "The Poem of Flight" and "The Conductor of Nothing" both are persona poems. "The Fox" is a poem in which the speaker is a fox in Central Park in New York City. "On My Own" radiates with mythic and imagined detail that leaves the particulars behind while amplifying the emotions, strains, and small glories of childhood:

> . . . I found my room
> and spread my things on the sagging bed:

the bright ties and candy-striped shirts,
the knife to cut bread, the stuffed weasel
to guard the window, the silver spoon
to turn my tea, the pack of cigarettes
for the life ahead, and at last
the little collection of worn-out books
from which I would choose my only name—
Morgan the Pirate, Jack Dempsey, the Prince
of Wales. I chose Abraham Plain.

But this is an exceptional child, and Levine has language and imagery to match the imagination of a scene at school:

. . . but they all hushed
in wonder when I named the 400 angels
of death, the planets sighted and unsighted,
the moment at which creation would turn
to burned feathers and blow every which way
in the winds of shock.

And those watching, seeing the child, those without imagination would only see his shabby clothes: " . . . to you I'd have been / just an ordinary kid." What an individual's imagination and self-reliance might lead him to despite the prosaic world is the point of the poem's conclusion:

. . . Sure, now you
know, now it's obvious, what with the light
of the Lord streaming through the nine
windows of my soul and the music of rain
following in my wake and the ordinary air
on fire every blessed day I waken in the world.

In "One for the Rose," Levine rises to the height of the mythic:

I could have been drifting among
the reeds of a clear stream
like the little Moses, to be found
by a princess and named after a conglomerate
or a Jewish hero.

And in the longest and most visionary poem in the book, "Belief," the speaker is all spirit, a voice that is part of nature, that is recycled with the elements and with the light, a voice that in a pantheistic mode, encourages the reader to follow in the larger and continuing vision of life:

Do you hear the wind
rising all around you? That comes
only after this certain joy. Do you hear
the waves breaking, even in the darkness,
radiant and full? Close your eyes, close
them and follow us toward the first light.

While Levine will never abandon the Detroit working poem, it is important to note that midway through his career each book offers poems with spiritual and transcendent subjects and focus.

Sweet Will continues this fictive amplification even in the autobiographical poems. Bits of history, stories, and facts are used for effect, that is, they serve no linear end in and of themselves but are mitigated by comment and speculation and even by the blatant altering of facts, disruption of chronological time, and conscious intrusion of the writer into the poem. "Voyages" offers a speaker who took a degree in library science and worked into old age for the county. "Salts and Oils" and "Those Were the Days" are personal but inflated and exaggerated far beyond what we know of Levine; they create personas who are imbued with determination, that individual spirit taking hold of the world despite hardship or privilege, respectively.

The most noteworthy extension of Levine's method occurs in the title poem, "Sweet Will." The setting is familiar from earlier poems—Detroit Transmission, one of the factories of Levine's working youth. Levine moves from detail and incident to metaphysical speculation; instead of allowing the story of his coworker Stach to be the only story of one beaten and dehumanized by work, instead of allowing witnessing to be the only force in the poem, Levine takes the long look over thirty-four years and speculates on the worth of it all. He looks hard into the face of an inscrutable force and sings a little praise to the indomitable spirit that survives it.

> And in truth I'm not worth a thing
> what with my feet and my two bad eyes
> and my one long nose and my breath
> of old lies and my sad tales of men
> who let the earth break them back,
> each one, onto dirty blood or bloody dirt.

> Not worth a thing! Just like it was said
> at my magic birth when the stars
> collided and fire fell from great space
> into great space, and people rose one
> by one from cold beds to tend a world
> that runs on and on at its own sweet will.

Characters and stories serve a controlling vision as opposed to having the emotion and understanding of the poem serve the people and events. What if we are not as instrumental to the workings of the planet as we once thought? What if we will to see outside the usual structures of our life? These questions and concerns are carried on in the fine long poem "A Poem with No Ending." In that poem and other longer poems such as "Last Words" and "Jewish Graveyards, Italy," we find poems that accommodate a larger and more reflective and inquisitive vision—a vision that admits contradictions of time and physical circumstance, one that relies on the spirit and the will to pull the past and present into focus.

A WALK WITH TOM JEFFERSON

The past is recovered again in *A Walk with Tom Jefferson,* recovered in terms of the soul and in terms of faith, as often as not unjustified by the experiences of the past. Although it is placed last in the book, the six-hundred-line title poem is the centerpiece. Levine is walking once-familiar neighborhoods in Detroit, looted in 1967 and now destroyed. His guide is a retired factory worker, "same name as the other one," he tells Levine. Together, they try to find the justifications for faith in the earth and, by extension, their lives in what is left of the old, largely abandoned neighborhood. The turns in fate, the seasons, the relations of father to son are "Biblical," Tom tells the poet. Indeed they are, for the figure of Job comes to mind here—keeping his faith in God despite the unjust afflictions he suffers—as Tom keeps faith with the earth in a little garden in the years spent surviving. There is little evidence that what they were told about why they worked and what they made is worthwhile or that it finally survives. Tom is the example, the one who keeps on going, who finds values in life, and thus by the poem's end Levine can manage to keep a portion of faith in his own life—what he made back there in the past in the factories is gone, but strong and good people survive, and Levine has found meaning in them and in the poems he makes.

> The place was called Chevy
>   Gear & Axle—
> it's gone now, gone to earth
>   like so much here—
> so perhaps we actually made
>   gears and axles
> for the millions of Chevies
>   long dead or still to die.
> It said that, "Chevrolet
>   Gear & Axle"
> right on the checks they paid
>   us with, so I can
> half-believe that's what we
>   were making way back then.

The long poem "28" opens the book with the story of Levine's move to California as a young man and his relationship with Yvor Winters, who gives him good advice: "Philip, we must never lie or we shall lose our souls." The young poet was "faithless," and the poem, the life of poetry, is a search to find that faith. In "The Rat of Faith" the poet discovers faith in simple life, even that of a rat; he remembers,

> . . . the bright city
> of beauty I thought I'd lost
> when I lost my faith that one day
> we would come into our lives.

Early in the collection there is also the inventive, speculative poem "The Whole Soul," a meditation questioning the shape and constitution of the soul, a poem that discovers the spiritual in the elemental:

> I give a shape to the air going
> out and the air coming in,
> and the sea winds scatter it
> like so many burning crystals
> settling on the evening ocean.

"Winter Words" is anchored to the earth, the physical landscape reflecting the emotional and spiritual landscape in the poet, and so is fittingly dedicated to Tu Fu, the great eighth-century Chinese poet, working in that modest and reflective mode, finding in memory and the natural imagery the best arguments in favor of a heaven. *A Walk with Tom Jefferson,* written in Levine's mature voice, is a book of faith, a book that offers an affirmation to life despite all the pain of the past.

WHAT WORK IS

What Work Is was one of the most popular and acclaimed books of poetry of the 1990s, going through eight printings in hardcover before the paperback was issued. It received the National Book Award and the Los Angeles Times Book Award in 1991. It contains brilliant trademark Levine poems about work—the desperate and shining humanity of the title poem; the poem

"Fear & Fame," with its vivid infernolike details of the chemical pickling vat; and "Coming Close," a poem that looks so squarely into the brute facts of industrial labor that the reader comes away marked, guilty by association, guilty by never questioning the necessity of such conditions:

> . . . she would turn
> to you and say, "Why?" Not the old *why
> of why must I spend five nights a week?*
> Just, "Why?" Even if by some magic
> you knew, you wouldn't dare speak
> for fear of her laughter, which now
> you have anyway as she places the five
> tapering fingers of her filthy hand
> on the arm of your white shirt to mark
> you for your own, now and forever.

One of Levine's most luminous poems is the long Dantesque poem "Burned." In twenty sections Levine examines his life and the burning industrial lives of others; it is actual, experiential as well as archetypal. This is a classic poem, for Levine knows that you must descend into hell and confront and recover the shades before you ascend into the light:

> I have to go back into the forge room
> at Chevy where Lonnie still calls
> out his commands to Sweet Pea and Packy
> and stare into the fire.

It is a brilliant physical poem of detail and vignette that leads to a final metaphysical acceptance. The punishing nature of work also comes through in "Among Children," as Levine shows us the children of Flint, Michigan, who already have taken on the weight and effects of work, even in their dreams.

Yet for all the virtuosity of these poems, the achievement of the book does not rest solely with them. It is the range and variation of Levine's vision that has made *What Work Is* a contemporary classic. There are poems of great irony and humor. "Gin" recounts some teenagers' first encounter with booze and its awful effects, and concludes:

> . . . Ahead
> lay our fifteenth birthdays,
> acne, deodorants, crabs, salves,
> butch haircuts, draft registration,
> the military and political victories
> of Dwight Eisenhower, who brought us
> Richard Nixon with wife and dog.
> Any wonder we tried gin.

And the poem "Facts" proceeds with a series of declarations, a theme and development with great good humor, and a wry social slant. "On The River" is one of Levine's most poignant elegies to his father, his brother, and the Detroit of his youth. "M. Degas Teaches Art & Science at Durfee Intermediate School," in its imagination and specificity, captures almost everyone's childhood in grammar school. We are given the child's sense of slowed time and hopelessness as well as a parting shot that adumbrates so much academic discussion:

> "You've begun
> to separate the dark from the dark."
> I looked back for help but now
> the trees bucked and quaked, and I
> knew this could go on forever.

While reviewers often first point to Levine's important dignified working-class poems, it is important to note that from mid-career onward Levine expanded both his vision and his style to include poems of humor, politics, and deep spiritual questioning.

THE SIMPLE TRUTH

The Simple Truth won the Pulitzer Prize for poetry in 1995. It offers the great truths that are more often than not the great ironies of our lives. The spiritual level to which these poems aspire is secular, tough, unsentimental, and unpredictable; the human spirit is glorious in inglorious situations, and the mysteries of life and death are revealed in knowledge only through experience and at length. Primarily, this is a book of elegies, a book to cherish and celebrate what little light these lives attained and at what price. The title poem is a stunning ars poetica and is everything but theoretical; rather, it takes the plain examples of the earth, those that sustain, and in looking at loss realizes that together they make a vocation and a life.

> Some things
> you know all your life. They are so simple and true
> they must be said without elegance, meter and
>   rhyme,
> they must be laid on the table beside the salt shaker,
> the glass of water, the absence of light gathering
> in the shadows of picture frames, they must be
> naked and alone, they must stand for themselves.
> . . .
> it stays there for the rest of your life, unspoken
> made of that dirt we call earth, the metal we call
>   salt,
> in a form we have no words for, and you live on it.

This poem, like many in this book, shows Levine working in a longer, graceful, more pensive line that befits a book of elegies. In "The Trade" we see how the true elements of the earth transform us and amplify our lives. On a boat from Genoa, still a young man, he trades his copy of Eliot's *Selected Poems* for a knife and two lemons, which it seemed he needed more—a trade that would make sense years later in a poem and that made for earthly transformation then:

> . . . Two lemons, one
> for my pocket, one for my rucksack, perfuming
> my clothes, my fingers, my money, my hair,
> so that all the way to Rapallo on the train
> I would stand among my second-class peers, tall,
> angelic, an ordinary man become a gift.

Like *What Work Is, The Simple Truth* is rich for its range of subjects and poetic strategies. Among many longer, more narrative elegies, there is the bright, short imagistic elegy for Miguel Hernandez, "The Return: Orihuela, 1965," and the lyric "February 14th," a moving love and anniversary poem in taut lines and phrasing. Levine's portraits and the attention he pays to the lives of others—his brother, his cousin, Garcia Lorca, his "sister," Senor Ruiz—lift, in clear and accessible detail, those lives into mythic significance. "In the Dark" is a truly memorable poem on the subject of first love and sex, for its fresh and symbolic phrasing, for its humor, for its irony directed at Saint Augustine and God, and for its honest and tender detail. "Photography" is a poem that rises from the specific to bring the full weight of mortality to bear. Levine is looking at old photos and the sense of loss, that past that held light and meaning now gone, is absolutely overwhelming. But the poem does more. The renowned photographer Richard Avedon has said that photography is fiction, and in this mode Levine enters and invites the reader into the poem—"Let's say we're writing this together. Let's say I turn / to you now with a question about the wife"—asking if the reader would have an answer for her loss, for her husband's, for "morning after morning a perfect sky until I think / I see heaven waiting at the end of the block." Heaven may have been there, at that time, in that photograph, in this memory.

> . . . The clock is moving
> its hands across the face of heaven. Aunt Yetta stops
> between one breath and another. I gather her clothes
> into a bundle smelling of talcum and cigarette
>   smoke,
> and place it at the foot of her bed. I did that then,
> I would do it now, I would do it again tomorrow
> if heaven would only look. I would lower the shades
> to let the room blossom in darkness, to let Yetta
> sleep on long past noon and even into the darkness
> of the next day and the next and the next
> while a name hangs in the brilliant morning air.

The penetrating sorrow of this scene expands in exact detail and gesture to include us all and to render the essence of loss palpable through imagery.

The truth of loss, of mortality, ends the book in large, inclusive elegies to his mother and to his father—"My Mother with Purse the Summer They Murdered the Spanish Poet" and "My Father with Cigarette Twelve Years Before the Nazis Could Break His Heart." In the poem for his father, Levine speaks to the reader in the direct and honest style of this book. He remembers the life in his childhood home, its quotidian detail juxtaposed to the history: "the Second World War, / the news that leaked back from Poland / that the villages were gone."

> . . . The truth is—
> if there is a truth—I remember the room,
> I remember the flame, the blue smoke,
> how bright and slippery were the secret coins,
> how David Copperfield doubted his own name,
> how sweet the stars seemed, peeping and blinking,
> how close the moon, how utterly silent the piano.

THE MERCY

There is no mercy, no grand abstract quality that will descend and make our lives clear and meaningful. Mercy in *The Mercy,* as the mainstay of all of Levine's work, is found in small and everyday events that give us a small portion of mercy, a bit of redemption, some part of joy, but without—Levine seems to say here—complete understanding. This is, as the book jacket notes tell us, a book of journeys—for Levine at different points in his life and for the people he preserves for us.

The telling moment representative of life's small transformations is found in the title poem about the journey of Levine's mother at age nine to the United States; a Scottish seaman gives her a piece of an orange, the first one she has ever seen. The *Mercy* is the name of the boat that brings her to America:

> She learns that mercy is something you can eat
> again and again while the juice spills over
> your chin, you can wipe it away with the back
> of your hands and you can never get enough.

Nonetheless, this is a book that scrutinizes the past and finds as much meaning and as much mercy as the world allows and so accepts and celebrates life, even in its shattered parts. The secret is, of course, our individual lives, so Levine concludes this book with a coda, a separate elegiac poem for his mother titled "The Secret":

> When you lived the secret
> was yourself. You gave away
> hours, days, years, 94 in all,
> but never that. Your secret
> is safe tonight. The earth turns
> toward darkness, and the earth
> asks nothing."

Probably the best evidence of Levine's expanded vision in his work—the willingness to accept life, to praise even its perplexing outcomes—is found in "The Return." Levine returns to Detroit, rents a car, and drives off into the country to find what his father never found traveling many unknown roads between Detroit and Lansing. Retracing his father's routes, he stops by an apple orchard where his father may have stopped and simply "marveled at what was here, / nothing at all except the stubbornness of things." For Levine it has always been the things, the concrete particulars of the world that set fire to the senses and shine with the secrets of another realm, if there is one beyond the earth.

The Mercy is a book with a wide range; there are poems of humor ("Philosophy Lesson"); poems in praise of jazz greats Clifford Brown ("And That Night Clifford Died") and Sonny Rollins; and poems of Detroit, Spain, and Fresno that again reclaim and examine the past, but now with a more open-ended joy. As he writes in "Northern Motive,"

> . . . How ordinary
> it all was, the dawn breaking each morning, dusk
> arriving on time just as the lights of houses
> came softly on. Why can't I ever let it go?

CONCLUSION

Levine has spent half his writing career uncovering an elementary metaphysics; it is a hopeful movement, one based on the brilliance of nature, the light shining from the best people he has known. He has no grand or orthodox ideals, but he will not let go of the light that cherishes and preserves our lives against time.

At the age of seventy-two Levine was still writing some of his best poetry— a poetry foremost among American letters and a poetry still founded in a pure, direct, and accessible language, but a language that knows music and invention every time. His later poems are not so quick to proclaim a resolution to the temporal or the spiritual, and he is always pushing ahead for as much joy and celebration and as much meaning as he can wrestle from experience, although he consistently takes on the thorniest and most soul-making subjects. He sees continuance in the earth, with or without us, and he has done his part to make sure that a humane and intelligent music accompanies the world. His tribute to Sonny Rollins, "The Unknowable" (in *The Mercy*), could well be his own:

> The years pass, and like the rest of us
> he ages, his hair and beard whiten, the great
> shoulders narrow. He is merely a man—
>
> after all—a man who stared for years
> into the breathy, unknowable voice
> of silence and captured the music.

Selected Bibliography

WORKS OF PHILIP LEVINE

POETRY

On the Edge. Iowa City: Stone Wall Press, 1963; Iowa City: Second Press, 1964.

Not This Pig. Middletown, Conn.: Wesleyan University Press, 1968.

5 Detroits. Santa Barbara, Calif.: Unicorn Press, 1970.

Pili's Wall. Santa Barbara, Calif: Unicorn Press, 1971.

Red Dust. Santa Cruz, Calif.: Kayak Books, 1971.

They Feed They Lion. New York: Atheneum, 1972.

1933. New York: Atheneum, 1974.

The Names of the Lost. Iowa City: Windhover Press, 1976; New York: Atheneum, 1976.

On the Edge and Over: Poems Old, Lost, and New. Oakland, Calif.: Cloud Marauder Press, 1976.

Ashes: Poems New and Old. Port Townsend, Wash.: Graywolf Press, 1979; New York: Atheneum, 1979.

7 Years from Somewhere. New York: Atheneum, 1979.

One for the Rose. New York: Atheneum, 1981.

Selected Poems. London: Secker and Warburg, 1984; New York: Atheneum, 1984.

Sweet Will. New York: Atheneum, 1985.

A Walk with Tom Jefferson. New York: Knopf, 1988.

New Selected Poems. New York: Knopf, 1991.

What Work Is. New York: Knopf, 1991.

The Simple Truth. New York: Knopf, 1994.

Unselected Poems. Santa Cruz, Calif.: Greenhouse Review Press, 1997.

One for the Rose. Pittsburgh, Pa.: Carnegie Mellon University Press, 1999.

They Feed They Lion; and The Names of the Lost. New York: Knopf, 1999.

The Mercy. New York: Knopf, 1999.

OTHER WORKS

Tarumba: The Selected Poems of Jaime Sabines. Translation with Ernesto Trejo. San Francisco: Twin Peaks Press, 1979.

Off the Map: Selected Poems of Gloria Fuertes. Translation with Ada Long. Middletown, Conn.: Wesleyan University Press, 1984.

The Essential Keats. New York: Ecco Press, 1987.

The Bread of Time: Toward an Autobiography. New York: Knopf, 1994.

BIOGRAPHICAL AND CRITICAL STUDIES

Atlas, Janet. "New Voices in American Poetry." *New York Times Magazine,* February 3, 1980, pp. 16, 19–20, 24, 51–52.

Bedient, Calvin. "Four American Poets." *Sewanee Review* 84: 351–359 (1976).

Berg, Stephen, and Robert Mezey, eds. *Naked Poetry: Recent American Poetry in Open Form.* Indianapolis, Ind.: Bobbs-Merrill, 1969.

Bloom, Harold. "The Year's Books: Part I." *New Republic,* November 20, 1976, pp. 20–26.

Borroff, Marie. "Recent Poetry." *Yale Review* 62, no. 1: 87–89 (1972).

Boruch, Marianne. "Comment: Blessed Knock." *American Poetry Review,* July/August 1988, pp. 39–41.

Buckley, Christopher. "The Extension of Method and Vision in Philip Levine's *Sweet Will.*" *Crazyhorse* 34: 64–79 (1988).

———. " 'Belief': The Expanded Vision of Philip Levine." *South Florida Poetry Review* 9, no. 1: 47–54 (fall 1991).

———, ed. *On The Poetry of Philip Levine: Stranger to Nothing.* Ann Arbor: University of Michigan Press, 1991. (A generous selection of critical essays and reviews of Levine's work from 1963 to 1991, including a bibliography of secondary works and biographical chronology.)

Caruth, Hayden. "Making It New." *Hudson Review* 21: 399–412 (1968).

Corn, Alfred. "Songs of Innocence and Experience." *Washington Post Book World,* July 14, 1991.

Costello, B. "Orders of Magnitude." *Poetry,* May 1983, pp. 108–110.

Dana, Robert. "Recent Poetry and the Small Press." *North American Review* n.s. I, no. 3: 76–78 (1964).

Davison, Peter. "Poet of the Factory Floor." *Atlantic Monthly,* April 1999, pp. 108–112.

Donovan, Laurence. "Accessible *What Work Is* Takes Its Toll." *Miami Herald,* June 30, 1991.

Gibson, Margaret. Review of *Ashes* and *7 Years from Somewhere. Library Journal,* August 1979, pp. 69, 72.

Gregerson, Linda. "Short Reviews." *Poetry,* December 1989.

Hall, Donald, ed. *Don't Ask.* Ann Arbor: University of Michigan Press, 1981. (A collection of eight interviews with Levine by various poets and editors.)

Hedin, Robert. "In Search of a New World: The Anarchist Dream in the Poetry of Philip Levine." *American Poetry* 4: 64–71 (1986).

Hirsch, Edward. "Standing Up for the Fallen." *New York Times Book Review,* August 5, 1984, p. 13.

———. "Naming The Lost: The Poetry of Philip Levine." *Michigan Quarterly Review* 28, no. 2: 258–268 (1989).

———. "The Visionary Poetics of Philip Levine and Charles Wright." In *Columbia History of American Poetry.* Edited by Jay Parini. New York: Columbia University Press, 1993.

Hitchcock, George. "A Gathering of Poets." *Western Humanities Review* 28: 403–409 (1974).

Hugo, Richard. "Philip Levine: Naming the Lost." *American Poetry Review,* May/June 1977, pp. 27–28.

Jackson, Richard. "The Signposts of Words." *American Book Review,* September 1982, p. 20.

Jarman, Mark. "The Trace of a Story Line." *Ohio Review* 37: 129–147 (1986).

———. "The Pragmatic Imagination and the Secrecy of Poetry." *Gettysburg Review* 1: 647–669 (1988).

Kalstone, David. "The Entranced Procession of the Dead." *Parnassus: Poetry In Review* 3, no. 1: 41–50 (1974).

Kennedy, X. J. "Underestimations." *Poetry,* February 1964.

Manguso, Sarah. "The Simple Truth." *Boston Book Review,* April 1999.

Marchant, Fred. "A Walk with Tom Jefferson." *Boston Book Review,* June 1988, pp. 28–29.

Martz, Louis L. "Ammons, Warren, and the Tribe of Walt." *Yale Review* 72: 63–84 (1982).

Matthews, William. "Wagoner, Hugo, and Levine." *Ohio Review* 26: 126–137 (1981).

Mills, Ralph J. "Back to This Life: Philip Levine's New Poems." *New England Review* 2: 327–332 (1979).

———. "The True and Earthy Prayer: Philip Levine's Poetry." *American Poetry Review,* March/April 1974, pp. 44–47.

Oates, Joyce Carol. "A Cluster of Feelings: Wakoski and Levine." *American Poetry Review,* May/June 1973, p. 55.

Parini, Jay. "The Small Valleys of Our Living." *Poetry,* August 1977, pp. 198–210.

———. "The Roses of Detroit." *Times Literary Supplement,* July 2, 1982, p. 720.

———. "The Simple and the Finite." *Times Literary Supplement,* January 24, 1986, p. 95.

Parisi, Joseph. Review of *One for the Rose. Booklist,* January 1, 1982, p. 582.

Pettingell, Phoebe. "Voices for the Voiceless." *New Leader,* September 17, 1984, pp. 16–17.

Pinsky, Robert. "The Names of the Lost." *New York Times Book Review,* February 20, 1977, pp. 6, 14.

Plumley, Stanley. Review of *The Names of the Lost. Ohio Review* 18, no. 3: 133–136 (1977).

Pritchard, William H. "They Feed They Lion." *New York Times Book Review,* July 16, 1972.

Root, William Pitt. "Songs of the Working Class." *St. Petersburg Times,* November 3, 1985.

Sadoff, Ira. "A Chronicle of Recent Poetry." *Antioch Review* 35: 241–244 (1977).

St. John, David. "Where the Angels Come Toward Us: The Poetry of Philip Levine." *Antioch Review* 44: 176–191 (1986).

Scheck, Lauri. "American Dream's Dark Side." *Trenton Times,* November 3, 1991.

Schramm, Richard. "A Gathering of Poets." *Western Humanities Review* 26: 389–393 (1972).

Skenazy, Paul. "Philip Levine's Poems Plumb Memory and Metaphor." *San Francisco Chronicle Book Review,* January 1, 1995.

Stafford, William. "A Poet with Something to Tell You." *Inquiry,* June 26, 1978, pp. 25–26.

Stitt, Peter. "Poems in Open Forms." *Georgia Review* 36: 675–685 (1982).

———. "My Fingers Clawing the Air: Versions of Paradise in Contemporary American Poetry." *Georgia Review* 39: 188–198 (1985).

———. "The Typical Poem." *Kenyon Review* 8, no. 4: 131–132 (1986).

Tillinghast, Richard. "Working the Night Shift." *New York Times Book Review,* September 12, 1982, p. 42.

———. "Poems That Get Their Hands Dirty." *New York Times Book Review,* December 8, 1991, p. 7.

Walker, Cheryl. "Looking Back, Looking Forward." *The Nation,* September 13, 1975, pp. 215–216.

Walker, David. "One for the Rose/The Southern Cross." *Field* 26: 87–97 (1982).

Yenser, Stephen. "Bringing It Home." *Parnassus: Poetry in Review* 6, no. 1: 101–117 (1977).

Zweig, Paul. "1 + 1 + 1 + 1." *Parnassus: Poetry in Review* 1, no. 1: 171–174 (1972).

—CHRISTOPHER BUCKLEY

Peter Matthiessen

1927–

A NOTED EXPLORER, naturalist, and writer, Peter Matthiessen has gained a wide readership in circles reaching beyond the usual domain of those interested in imaginative literature. By virtue not only of books such as *Wildlife in America* (1959) but also of his frequent contributions to magazines such as *Audubon* and *The New Yorker,* he has become recognized as an authority on wildlife and environmental issues. Still other readers are engaged by works that embody his personal responses to the character and practice of Zen Buddhism, or by his travel writings with their geographic, ethnographic, and ecological reflections on far-flung lands selected from every continent. His prolific output, now represented by more than two dozen book titles, also includes works of social criticism focused on topics such as the unionizing initiatives of César Chavez, the economic struggle of Long Island fishermen, and the failure of U.S. government interactions with Native Americans.

Matthiessen enjoys the rare distinction of having an established literary reputation in two major genres: fiction and nonfictional prose. He can claim the exceptional honor of having been nominated for the National Book Award in fiction (for *At Play in the Fields of the Lord* [1965]) as well as nonfiction (for *The Tree Where Man Was Born* [1972]). In 1979 Matthiessen won the award for *The Snow Leopard.* As William Dowie observes,

Matthiessen's primary desire to be recognized as a fiction writer has been ironically thwarted to some degree by his own earlier successes in publishing celebrated works of nonfiction. Yet the appearance of *Bone by Bone* (1999), the capstone novel in his highly esteemed Watson trilogy, promises to enhance his reputation as a leading novelist of the late twentieth century.

At first one may perceive some contradiction between Matthiessen's stress on immediacy and on a Buddhist resolve to savor life in the present moment, in books such as *The Snow Leopard* (1978) or *Nine Headed Dragon River: Zen Journals 1969–1982* (1986), and his preoccupation with the historical past throughout the Watson trilogy. In a 1989 interview, for example, Matthiessen confirmed that "we waste our lives regretting the past, anticipating the future," whereas "all Zen teaches is to pay attention to the present moment" so as to perceive "this humble subject" as "full of power and resonance." But the Buddhist principle of "mindfulness" actually connects these two sides of Matthiessen's imaginative sensibility. In 1948 a disciple of Gurdjieff first impressed upon Matthiessen the importance of cultivating disciplined mindfulness, of "paying attention to the present moment"; and books such as Thich Nhat Hanh's *The Miracle of Mindfulness: A Manual on Meditation* (1975) have given this element of the Eight-Fold Path even broader exposure in the West. In any case, the spiritual discipline of mindfulness involves qualities of concentration and attentiveness to detail that are applicable to Matthiessen's discipline as a writer in fictional as well as nonfictional modes. Moreover, the historicity of the Watson trilogy is not a matter of archival facticity so much as it is what Matthiessen calls "reimagined life," requiring attentiveness to the details of what indeed *might* have happened. The novelist's craft involves a concentration—or in this case, what Matthiessen calls "a twenty-year obsession"—that brings the potential past vividly to mind as a present experience of the reader.

In addition to mindfulness, a preoccupation with wildness could be identified as another keynote of Matthiessen's writing across a broad span of decades and subgenres. Plainly, much of the writing is concerned with representations of wildlife and with often exotic wilderness landscapes in Asia, Africa, or North and South America. Yet Matthiessen's imaginative sense of the wild extends beyond the physical wilderness of roadless areas. In both fiction and nonfiction, he shows himself drawn repeatedly toward the uncharted place that he calls, in the spirit of Thoreau, "the wildness of the world." Having presumably lost this sense of primal vitality in early childhood, Matthiessen writes of endeavoring to recover it through much of the rest of his life. In an early interview, he described his fiction as "realistic only in the most superficial sense; someone has called it surreal, in the sense of intensely or *wildly* real, and I think this is correct."

Accordingly, his writing shows a perennial fascination not only with wild places and animals, but with untamed or archaic human beings as well—and with deviations from the normative values, beliefs, and practices of middle-class Americans. Thus, the E. J. Watson of Matthiessen's trilogy is himself a violent, passionate figure whose story is mostly played out in the lawless territory of the Florida Everglades in the late

1800s. The urge to defend or to recover association with archaic peoples likewise remains prominent throughout the corpus of Matthiessen's work.

MATTHIESSEN'S BACKGROUND

In his family origins and early personal history, though, Peter Matthiessen appears to have been more nearly a child of privilege than a wild child. Born in New York City on May 22, 1927, to Erard A. Matthiessen and Elizabeth Carey Matthiessen, he was the second of three children in a family of some means and social standing. His father was a successful architect who became a trustee of the National Audubon Society. In addition to a house on the Hudson River, his family had a Fifth Avenue apartment facing Central Park as well as a summer retreat on nearby Fishers Island. His parents and brother encouraged his lifelong interest in animals and outdoor activities. As a child, he attended St. Bernard's School in Manhattan. Yet by the time he went to board at the fashionable Hotchkiss School in Lakeville, Connecticut, he was showing his wilder side in the unruly, rebellious way he reacted to adult authority. He would later confess that "despite kind parents, superior schooling, and all the orderly advantages, I remained disorderly." Much of his later work sustains his reaction against the controlling influence of establishment wealth and privilege. By the age of sixteen, he had nonetheless resolved to write and had already begun exploring this vocation by composing short pieces for school publications.

After leaving Hotchkiss, he enlisted in the navy toward the end of World War II and was stationed at Pearl Harbor during 1945 and 1946. Although he spent little time at sea, he later testified that his experience one night of facing the wild force of a Pacific storm left a lasting impression. After his discharge, he wandered briefly through a period of aimless desolation in New York before enrolling at Yale. There he advanced toward becoming a writer by pursuing major course work in English and contributing pieces on hunting and fishing to the *Yale Daily News.* He also fed his interest in the natural world by taking courses in zoology and ornithology, though most of what he came to know about wildlife and environmental science he learned on his own. As he told an interviewer in 1986, "I'm not really trained in any of the disciplines; I'm what the 19th century would call a generalist—I have a lot of slack information, and for my work it's been extremely helpful."

In 1950 Matthiessen earned a Bachelor of Arts degree from Yale. While teaching as a creative writing instructor at his alma mater, Matthiessen had his first taste of real literary success when the *Atlantic Monthly* published two of his short stories, one of which ("Sadie") won the *Atlantic* Prize for 1951. In that same year he married Patricia Southgate, a woman from Smith College whom he had met while spending his junior year of college at the Sorbonne. He then returned to Paris with the idea of living a writer's life in the company of other aspiring artists. A dazzling literary circle soon formed around Matthiessen's third-floor apartment. Among those in this talented group of young Americans who would win future renown were William Styron, James Baldwin, Terry Southern, Harold Humes, Ben Bradlee, and George Plimpton. From literary conversation mixed with alcohol (but through prompting from Matthiessen in particular) came the idea of *The Paris Review,* which Matthiessen cofounded with Humes in 1953. Plimpton served as the first editor in chief and Matthiessen as the first fiction editor for this noteworthy magazine.

By the mid-1950s Matthiessen had fathered two children and published his first two novels, *Race Rock* (1954) and *Partisans* (1955). Both novels, as well as a third work—*Raditzer*—that followed in 1961, reflect the autobiographical

preoccupations that are often prominent in a writer's early work. All three concern the trials and problems of identity confronting a privileged young man. For George McConville in *Race Rock,* respectable civilization is challenged in the wilder, less conventional person of a former childhood companion named Cady Shipman. In *Partisans,* journalist Barney Sand is searching for a viable idealism amid the intrigue of Cold War politics in Paris, a setting obviously familiar to Matthiessen. The circumstance of Charlie Stark in *Raditzer* as a young man who enlists in the navy during World War II plainly draws on the author's personal history even as the novel's nautical character, which reminded some reviewers of Joseph Conrad, anticipates the sea fiction represented more experimentally in *Far Tortuga* (1975).

By the time *Raditzer* appeared, Matthiessen had worked for three years on the South Fork of Long Island as a commercial fisherman and charter boat captain following his return from Paris. The disciplined, physical quality of the work appealed to him, as did the chance to share the experience of laboring people. He could also claim time for writing during winter months and intervals of bad weather. No wonder he described this period, 1954 to 1956, as "the happiest time of my life." But when he set off alone in a car in 1956 to explore U.S. wildlife refuges in the West, he initiated another satisfying enterprise that would inspire and sustain his creativity throughout the remainder of his career. This first trip to observe life in the wild led most directly toward publication of *Wildlife in America.* But it also began a pattern of travel, observation, and research that in subsequent decades would take Matthiessen to countless remote places around the globe.

The first five-year period of what he once called his "world wandering" had been provoked initially by the demise of his fishing business and the breakdown of his marriage. Soon, though, he learned to shape what he discovered while traveling beyond the bounds of industrial civilization into the very substance of his writing. His self-sponsored sojourn through the American West was followed by a *New Yorker*-sponsored trip to less settled regions of South America in 1959. These travels in South America gave rise to an important novel, *At Play in the Fields of the Lord*, as well as a nonfictional book, *The Cloud Forest: A Chronicle of the South American Wilderness* (1961). A Harvard–Peabody Expedition of 1961 enabled him to visit western New Guinea, where he observed an aboriginal people, the Kurelu, as described in *Under the Mountain Wall: A Chronicle of Two Seasons in the Stone Age* (1962). Among the many other journeys to exotic places captured through subsequent decades in Matthiessen's writing are trips to Mosquito Bank in the western Caribbean, a barren island in the Bering Sea, the Serengeti Plain of East Africa, and the high Himalayan reaches of Asia.

During a lifetime of peregrination, Matthiessen has endeavored to bring genuine mindfulness to his study of each locale that figures in his writing. Even if some of his writing qualifies as travel literature, he never intends to produce a literature of tourism. Typically focusing full attention on the relevant spot of earth, he develops a historically and scientifically grounded sense of place through research conducted both in the field and in books. Since 1960, when he settled permanently on a six-acre tract in Sagaponack, Long Island, he has also found a kind of geographic anchor for his wandering disposition by maintaining his home in this community once dominated by potato farming. Certain patterns of geographical and generic symmetry are discernible in Matthiessen's career thus far. He began writing fiction, then moved toward producing a large proportion of nonfiction, and then turned his major effort back toward fiction once again. In his traveling life after Paris he looked first toward untamed territory in the American West, extended his journeying to many distant territories abroad, and then returned to native ground with his intensive study of southwest Florida in the Watson trilogy.

ENVIRONMENTAL NONFICTION

Wildlife in America warrants recognition not only as Matthiessen's first major work of nonfiction, but also as a landmark of twentieth-century American environmental literature. First published just three years before Rachel Carson's *Silent Spring,* it sounds a similar note of prophetic warning about the deleterious effects on the non-human world of thoughtless human intervention. Matthiessen's compendious chronicle of natural history in America surveys the condition of wildlife and wildlife conservation across a vast range of species, geographic habitats, and time frames beginning with the era of European contact. Many have deemed it authoritative, including ornithologist Roger Tory Peterson, who judged that it "should be the number one source volume for everyone who embraces the philosophy of conservation." As Daniel Payne has noted, the achievement represented by this trailblazing study is all the more remarkable given Matthiessen's paucity of formal scientific training in contrast to the careers of other noted ecological writers in the twentieth century such as Aldo Leopold and Rachel Carson.

Ironically, Matthiessen's prevailing literary style in this book is even more objectively scientific and impersonal than that exposed in the best-known works of Leopold and Carson. For the most part, Matthiessen simply allows the sad tale of species extinction to speak for itself. He verifies the thesis that "however well-intentioned . . . man's efforts to improve upon the natural scene have usually succeeded in upsetting the balance of nature" with copious illustrations, ranging from famous instances such as that of the passenger pigeon, buffalo, and whooping crane to less favored cases of endangerment such as the prairie dog and Gila monster. Only rarely is language of the chronicler swept aside by expressions of feeling and moral judgment. Thus, Matthiessen describes the mass killing of American elk for their teeth alone as "shameful," and he bemoans the "greed and waste" accompanying the destruction of bison herds that "were almost certainly the greatest animal congregations that ever existed on earth." In the revised version's epilogue, prepared with help from Michael Bean of the Environmental Defense Fund, the author declares human beings responsible for the "unprecedented impoverishment of the diversity of life" and the "escalating loss of species" now facing the world.

Yet unlike some comparable works of environmental nonfiction, the book's controlling rhetoric is modulated to a pitch below that of apocalyptic cataclysm. It concedes that certain species, including large fish of the Great Lakes, are declining for reasons other than human interference. It recognizes that species may be endangered not only by wanton slaughter but also by human deformations of their habitat or by misguided attempts to redistribute herds. It even describes cases—the northern fur seal, for example—in which a species has successfully recovered from near-extinction. The 1987 edition also charts advances in the understanding and practice of conservation during recent decades, as illustrated through legislation such as the 1973 Endangered Species Act.

If the book's dominant impression is nonetheless somber, its literary character is finally more elegiac than apocalyptic—even in the last chapter, which bears the seemingly apocalyptic title of "Another Heaven and Another Earth." Lamentably, this world of astonishingly diverse animal forms may end not with a bang, or even a whimper, but with empty silence in places where beasts once stirred. Matthiessen conjoins his elegy for creatures like the black-footed ferret with another mode of literary rhetoric reminiscent of the Puritan jeremiad. In the twofold manner of the jeremiad, the revised book's concluding aim is to encourage readers that it is not too late to become effectively mindful of wild animals but simultaneously to warn that "If we fail to recognize them, marvel at them, and conserve for our descendants the opportunity to be part of the great wonder and diversity of life, we are fatally diminished as a species."

A corresponding attentiveness to the natural history of endangered wildlife and habitats in Africa informs Matthiessen's three nonfictional studies of that continent: *The Tree Where Man Was Born, Sand Rivers* (1981), and *African Silences* (1991). (A fourth volume, *Shadows of Africa* [1992], is a compilation of previously published work.) In these books, however, the author must write more as an outside observer than as a national chronicler and citizen. In *African Silences,* for example, he searches out what wildlife remains in Senegal's Niokolo Koba Park yet knows his readers can do little about the sad decline of large animals and fauna in West Africa. He is also troubled by the rapid destruction of forests in the Congo basin, observing that "almost half of the earth's living things, many as yet undiscovered, live in this green world" of rain forest communities. By joining a survey of forest elephants in central Africa, he is able to take a somewhat more active role. His scientific colleagues, working with international conservation groups, have even influenced the creation of new wildlife reserves in the Central African Republic to protect forest elephants and other endangered species. While economically powerful nations outside Africa affect the continent's ecological health through measures such as banning or restricting the ivory trade, much of what happens to Africa's wildlife will depend on Africans. Yet beyond his involvement in the empirical inquiry of scientific surveys, Matthiessen performs a crucial role as a conservationist writer by stirring humanity's sense of wonder over a world still animated by gorillas, rhinos, and elephants. What could ever replace that ancient mystery of life sustained behind the elephant's "masked gray visage," as presented in *The Tree Where Man Was Born*? Or who could fail to marvel at the prodigious journeys completed by migratory curlew, as described in *The Shorebirds of North America* (1967)?

WHEN THE CIVILIZED AND THE PRIMITIVE MEET

Published to general acclaim in 1965, *At Play in the Fields of the Lord* marked the author's breakthrough to accomplished maturity as a novelist. Reviewers praised this "fascinating story" for its "convincing and absorbing" physical descriptions and a seriousness that marked its author as "one who is not afraid to grapple with the more fundamental problems of human existence." Inevitably, the novel directs more attention to the human element than a book like *Wildlife in America*. Yet *Fields of the Lord* sustains a similar concern with the frequently tragic consequences of interaction between civilized and primitive worlds. Still more obviously, this fiction is linked to the nonfictional treatment in *The Cloud Forest* insofar as both works draw upon the author's experience of traveling for five months through untamed regions of South America in 1959 and 1960. *Fields of the Lord* evokes the overwhelming presence of the Amazonian jungle while vividly portraying the endangered life of its native inhabitants.

The action focuses initially on the efforts of two conservative Protestant missionary couples to evangelize the Niaruna, an Indian tribe clinging to archaic ways in a remote stretch of Amazonian jungle. Predictably, the missionary project is shown to be misguided. Leslie Huben, whose mission is already established when Martin Quarrier arrives from North Dakota, appears in an especially unfavorable light. The missionaries are generally portrayed as ignorant, controlling, and condescending toward traditional peoples. They seem motivated less by Christian love than by imperialist arrogance. In the deadly ambition of their enterprise, they lack all sense of the wilderness as a divine gift, an opportunity for joyous play in the field of God's creation. In fact, the book's opening mood seems to be largely satiric.

Nor is the satire terribly subtle. Leslie Huben's open letter "from the fields of the Lord" mixes hackneyed lament for Satan's influence on the "poor lost souls" of the Niaruna, "savages" who are "headed straight for Hell," with thanks to the Lord for "his new outboard motor" with which to penetrate the "dark rivers" of wilderness paganism. A typecast monster of rigidity, Huben ends up hardening so far as to manifest outright cruelty and deceit. If this "false witness" of God cannot succeed in subduing the Niaruna to his will, he would rather see them dead than permit them to live as free savages. When the Niaruna become infected with influenza transmitted by the Americans, Huben refuses to send medicinal aid. For him, the tribal territories are simply a field ripe for personal conquest and for the exercise of what amounts to cultural imperialism. Critic Richard Patteson aptly calls his mission "cultural aggression of the rankest sort."

Hazel, Martin Quarrier's narrow-minded wife, becomes so pathetically fearful of opening herself toward encounter with archaic wildness that she reaches a state of catatonic derangement. Rufino Guzmán, the military commandant who agrees to sponsor attacks on the Niaruna, presents a familiar satiric image of Latin American political corruption and intrigue. Matthiessen also satirizes the competitive compulsion of the Protestant missionaries to regard even their fellow Christians, the Roman Catholics in fictional Oriente, as satanic agents of "the Opposition." So entrenched are these zealous Protestants in their masculinist anti-Catholicism that for someone like Hazel the very name of Oriente's capital city, Madre de Dios (Mother of God), is offensive. Worse still, the missionaries become instrumental in destroying the Niaruna people and culture while presuming to "save" them. For the missionaries, engagement with the Niaruna turns out to be not only fatally damaging to the indigenous people but self-destructive as well. Like insects typically driven toward what they perceive as light, only to "flail themselves to death," the missionaries run toward their own demise. Martin Quarrier dies unglamorously at the hands of an Indian convert wielding a machete originally given by the missionaries. Martin's son, Billie, succumbs to death by fever, while Hazel retreats into psychosis. Leslie Huben ends up suffering an ignominious defeat and hopeless estrangement from his wife.

Although this free-spirited woman, Andy Huben, shatters the image of zealous missioner, her character is never fully developed. Of the missionary figures, Martin Quarrier looms largest in our attention and deviates most significantly from the interventionist ideology of his colleagues. As this Moody Bible graduate and former missioner to the Sioux begins to question the project of converting the Niaruna and ends up questioning almost everything, his character gains complexity. His sexual attraction to Andy Huben further confirms his humanity. Following the example of his son, he starts to develop a mindful appreciation of traditional peoples and their culture before he dies. And though he is too awkward, hesitant, and physically unattractive to qualify as heroic, he does meet his death while trying to protect Indians from whites. Gradually abandoning his plan to change the Niaruna, he gains sympathy when he lets himself be changed instead by an alien environment that opens up previously unsuspected depths of his own psyche. Quarrier finally admits to uncertainty about why he is in the jungle at all, though he thinks he was searching there "for something more important than my own life."

The book's most compelling character, Lewis Meriwether Moon, is similarly possessed by what the Catholic padre Xantes calls a "troublesome search for knowledge." As a mercenary soldier, Moon at first accepts the idea of conducting air-bombing raids on the Niaruna with his companion Wolfie. Soon, though, this character of passionate desperation, who is part Cheyenne and once lived on a reservation, recognizes his kinship with the South American Indians. During a reconnaissance flight over the Niaruna village, he is struck by a tribal member's audacity in shooting an arrow toward his plane. Under the hallucinogenic influence of locally obtained ayahuasca, he then flies east toward the sun and deep jungle, ecstatically declaring himself on the radio as "at play in the fields of the Lord."

In the novel's second half, after Moon parachutes into the Niaruna settlement, the prevailing mood shifts from satire toward a visionary yet graphically detailed evocation of traditional life and culture that issues finally in elegy for these "doomed people of the jungle." Though Moon's adaptation to traditional ways is complicated by the Niaruna's taking him for a god, he quickly learns to toughen his body to recover his elemental connection to nature. He ends up alone, painfully isolated from human society yet fully mindful of the physical world and capable now of direct sensation: "Laid naked to the sun and sky, he felt himself open like a flower."

Nevertheless, Matthiessen takes pains not to romanticize the Indians or the land they inhabit. The Niaruna are shown to be vengeful, quarrelsome, and superstitious as well as harmoniously adapted to their environment. Their jungle world is scarcely a paradise but must be respected as a challenging field of survival crowded with stinging insects, snakes, jaguars, chigger fleas, and piranhas. Still, the Niaruna are more passionately engaged with their surroundings than the whites. They also show greater mindfulness of how fragile and artificial human culture really is in the context of all life. Thus Aeore, the tribesman who shot his arrow at the plane and is later killed by Moon, gives this passionate answer to the question of why the Niaruna wear paint: "We are naked and have nothing! Therefore we must decorate ourselves, for if we did not, how are we to be told from animals?"

Beyond its satire of meddlesome missionaries, *Fields of the Lord* probes the inevitably complex relation between nature and civilization, between the biosphere and universal human culture. Much of Matthiessen's writing underscores the point that *any* initiative, including scientific exploration, by which industrialized peoples encounter primitive peoples must be intrusive if not destructive. Aeore's gesture in sending his arrow up against an airplane is a futile yet memorably poetic sign of resistance to the machine age. That protest is one the book itself in some sense supports. However, Matthiessen is not so atavistic as to suggest that his own Western culture ever could or should return to a premodern "state of nature."

LIFE AT SEA

That wild nature remains a powerful presence even amid the mechanization and environmental depredation of "modern time" is amply demonstrated in the later nautical novel *Far Tortuga.* This book chronicles the final, ill-fated voyage of the *Lillias Eden,* one of the few remaining ships with sail capacity still plying the Caribbean turtle trade in the late 1960s. Its skipper, Raib Avers, likewise belongs to a dying breed of wind captains who treat men "de back-time way." Though the schooner has been hastily outfitted with twin diesel engines, it is otherwise ill equipped to compete for a share of the ever-diminishing turtle catch in April, late in the turtling season. The *Lillias Eden* lacks a chronometer, cook, radio transmitter, running lights, adequate life jackets, and other apparent necessities. Worse still, most of its crewmembers are emotionally unstable, contentious, and readily disposed toward vio-

lence. Raib complains that "in dis goddom lot" of men, with their disparate racial-ethnic allegiances and checkered personal histories, "I got two drunkards, one thief, and five idiots."

Yet Captain Raib is desperate to seize his last turtling opportunity before the Nicaraguan government closes its turtle banks to all Cayman vessels, including the *Lillias Eden,* the following year. In his search for the nesting grounds of the green turtle, he plans to brave perilous waters near the Misteriosa Reefs to reach that uncharted island of dreams known as Far Tortuga. By the time he arrives, though, the idyllic spot has already been invaded by Raib's dissolute half-brother, Desmond Eden, and a party of Jamaican ruffians. This starving and unruly band of egg plunderers is now "foulin dis one, too!" as Raib says with disgust. They overrun the ship, terrorize its crew, and incite one defiant seaman to desert before they scramble ashore. With his ship now threatened by hostile seizure, Captain Raib tries to escape by running through the reefs under sail at night. His daring effort to break free almost succeeds when the ship strikes a "wild rock." In the consequent struggle to reach safety in two catboats, only one crew member, a black Honduran nicknamed "Speedy," survives.

As the central character of this grim tale, Raib shows stoic dignity in confronting both his own death and the death of old ways of living on the sea. The oversevere captain soars above his failings when he "flings his free arm wide, exalted" on the crosstrees just before the ship strikes. Earlier, his intuitive affinity with the nonhuman environment had enabled him to suspect that "Dis mornin sea tryin to tell me something." A creature of the sea, he does not shrink from venturing out to "de edge of de world," from facing that oceanic silence where "the world is empty."

In *Far Tortuga,* the sea's blank indifference to human welfare thus belies the traditionally romantic view of nature as a benign, organically unified presence wedded to the human soul.

Critic Bert Bender aptly describes nature's presence in this great sea novel as "sharkishly voracious" or Darwinian in ways that recall Melville and, still more, Stephen Crane in "The Open Boat." One crewman's statement of the Darwinian social ethos—"Every mon for hisself"—perfectly foretells the men's brutal competition for life in the catboats while Speedy, the sole survivor, sees diminishing space for human civility in "modern time" when a harsh world closes in and "dey ain't no place to hide."

Indeed, the wilder side of human nature is not always portrayed favorably in this book. The rapacious, predatory behavior of Desmond Eden, Brown (a crewman otherwise known as Miguel Moreno Smith), and other lawless men is abhorrent. Speedy laments that when "dey ain't enough of anything to go around" in the Caribbean economy, "den people start actin like wild animals." Yet the novel's unfettered humans typically do more harm than animals—and considerable harm *to* animals as well. Raib is disgusted by the recklessness of those who have destroyed the region's seals, crocodiles, snipes, and iguana, "just like dey killing off green turtle"—and who are fast stripping mahogany, logwood, and fustic from Caribbean forests. As a Caymanian, he also deplores "dat atomic trash and shit de Yankees puttin in de sky."

Despite these corrupting influences, nature retains its elemental beauty in *Far Tortuga.* Matthiessen's ocean inspires amazement not because it is always lovely but because it is always there. It is bleak yet endlessly variable, an ever-enduring source of life and death. The stark realism of the book's narration effectively lays bare this material reality. Matthiessen's fragmented syntax, reliance on dialogue rather than narrative description, mastery of colloquial speech, and unusual layout of spacing and typography contribute to an arrestingly vivid evocation of life at sea. The author also draws on his own large store of maritime knowledge and particularly on his 1967 Caribbean schooner voyage, financed by *The New Yorker,* in search of green turtles. By including a ship's register, rigging diagram, and maps in the novel, he anchors the more mystically elusive qualities of his tale in hard fact. These human constructs blend imperceptibly with natural images of birds, fish, reptiles, and other features of the seascape. Just as it is sometimes hard to distinguish individual speakers in the book's unconventional presentation of dialogue, so also the line between human and nonhuman frames of reference begins to blur.

The catastrophic failure of a few rugged men to complete their turtle voyage seems to matter in its own episodic moment, but that moment flows at last into nature's endless reservoir of life. What endures most memorably in Matthiessen's poetic account of nature are primal impressions of water, wind, stars, and the "wild" sun. Raib counsels his son at sea that the north star is "one thing you can count on" because "everything else in dis goddom world changin so fast dat a mon cannot keep up no more, but de north star is always dere, boy." And soon after reminding crew members of the fragility of human life at sea, he is moved to ponder the contrasting immortality of "dat ocean" that "look so *old* in de mornin time." Already too old for "de modern time" at age 54, Captain Raib will soon cede his body permanently to this water.

JOURNEY TOWARD DISCOVERY

Matthiessen's most celebrated book of nonfiction, *The Snow Leopard,* seems at first a straightforward journal of an arduous 1973 expedition across remote Himalayan regions of Nepal to the Tibetan Plateau. Enfolded within this factual chronicle of adventure, though, is a richly evocative version of the archetypal quest narrative. The journey–quest proceeds on at least three planes. On the first and most obvious level, the trip's purpose is to seek further knowledge of the Himalayan bharal, or blue sheep. This scientific aim had initially motivated Matthiessen's zoologist friend George Schaller to propose the trip. Schaller invited the author to join him because of their shared zoological interest, but Matthiessen would find other reasons, too, for joining the expedition. Thus, the author observes that "where bharal were numerous, there was bound to appear that rarest and most beautiful of the great cats, the snow leopard" and that "the hope of glimpsing this near-mythic beast in the snow mountains was reason enough for the entire journey."

The tantalizing mention of a "near-mythic beast" suggests at the outset motives for journeying that are less rationally determined than those encompassed by naturalistic science. On a second plane, this best-selling work unfolds the story of a spiritual and religious quest. Already committed to Buddhist meditative practice, Matthiessen welcomed the chance to journey "step by step across the greatest range on earth to somewhere called the Crystal Mountain" as "a true pilgrimage, a journey of the heart." Here, after all, in the Land of Dolpo, lay the Crystal Monastery, where one might find the Lama of Shey, "the most revered of all the *rinpoches,* the 'precious ones,' in Dolpo." Dolpo was "said to be the last enclave of pure Tibetan culture left on earth." Tibetan culture, in turn, represents for many Westerners a depth of spiritual possibility and interiority that seems elusive in today's commercial world. As the book proceeds, Matthiessen often interposes explanatory accounts of Buddhist belief and practice with physical descriptions of the journey. Such explanations offer a cultural–historical context for understanding particular versions of Zen, Mahayana, and Tibetan Buddhism. Yet Matthiessen also invokes a variety of Western writers—including Thomas Traherne, William Blake, Rainer Maria Rilke, Hermann Hesse, and Henry David Thoreau—to suggest the universality of the spirit-quest.

A third dimension of the book's journeying toward discovery is intensely interpersonal and emotional insofar as it focuses on the author's absent family. In the Prologue, Matthiessen mentions that his second wife, Deborah Love, had died of cancer in the winter before his departure. This apparently casual reference takes on considerable meaning as the author returns repeatedly in memory to Deborah and the time of Deborah's death even as he progresses physically on his trek to Shey. In other ways, too, the book shows recursive stylistic traits that play against its linear progress through time and space, a progress signified outwardly by the inclusion of maps and dates.

The author's search to comprehend his relation to Deborah reaches an emotional climax in the entry for October 11, where a poignant account of her final days marks a turning point in the author's own sense of life and mortality. Particularly insofar as Deborah had shared Matthiessen's engagement with Zen Buddhism, this interpersonal strand of the book's narrative is closely interwoven with its portrayal of the spiritual quest. Matthiessen constantly juxtaposes reminders of the existential solitude demanded in spiritual journeying with vignettes about the self-discoveries he has made, paradoxically, through encounters with other human beings—with Deborah, above all, but also with figures like Tukten, his Sherpa porter, and with his redoubtable, enigmatic, and sometimes exasperating companion George Schaller.

Further comment on the spiritual and interpersonal planes of quest narrative in *The Snow Leopard* may indicate the exceptional richness of Matthiessen's achievement in this book, which has been substantially rewritten from the initial journal entries. The book's spiritual note is sounded from the first, with an epigraph from Rilke extolling the courage to confront strangeness, visionary experience, and the divine "spirit world." In subsequent expositions on the historical character of Zen, and of Buddhism more generally, the work offers an admirable summary of belief systems unfamiliar to most Western readers. What lends this bookish account of spirituality genuine force, however, are Matthiessen's frequent insertions of personal testimony.

This personal narrative of spiritual journeying begins with a vague restlessness. It is as though "one were being watched" but cannot say who or what is watching. Matthiessen confides that he had still felt inwardly confused in his first books, having then pursued a kind of religious understanding by experimenting with hallucinogenic drugs during the late 1950s and early 1960s. He even admits he doesn't quite know why he has taken this long trip on the Tibetan Plateau: "To say I was making a pilgrimage seemed fatuous and vague, though in some sense that was true as well." He had earlier described his "wandering from one path to another with no real recognition that I was embarked upon a search, and scarcely a clue as to what I might be after." He knew only "that at the bottom of each breath there was a hollow place that needed to be filled." All the same, he comes increasingly to feel "that there is a source for this deep restlessness; and the path that leads there is not a path to a strange place, but the path home."

Beyond the book's exotic landscapes, the undiscovered country that matters most at the level of spiritual quest is a space or path in the psyche that Matthiessen associates with the classic Chinese way of Tao. Such mysteries are likewise evoked by Buddhist traditions of "a hidden kingdom—Shambala, the Center—in an unknown part of Inner Asia." In comparable terms of Western Christianity, one might recall that for John of the Cross mystical truth is that which is hidden from oneself. Augustine, too, captured the unsettling character of religious quest in his famous pronouncement that our hearts are restless until they rest in God.

As *The Snow Leopard* proceeds, then, Mat-

thiessen reflects deepening awareness that his goal is not simply to reach the physical destination of Shey in Inner Dolpo. In fact, his trip could be considered something of an outward failure. He never manages to see the snow leopard—and when, after endless delays and difficulties, he reaches the fabled Crystal Monastery, he cannot view its interior. It is actually vacant. Before the snows, its lama and monks had already retreated across the mountains to Saldang. His journey therefore involves not only movement toward a geographic target, but also a painful education in mindfulness and understanding along the way.

To be sure, the remote physical locale plays a critical role in this path of discovery pursued by what Michael Heim calls "the new mystical naturalist." Though the environment is often forbidding in a way that reduces life to lowest terms, there is indeed "a blessedness to this landscape" with its occasional rest walls and teahouses. And as the author testifies, the silence and sublime grandeur of the high places readily encourage his practice of meditation. He also cultivates an attentiveness to more ordinary features of the Asian setting: "In the glory of sunrise, spiderwebs glitter and greenfinches in October gold bound from pine to shining pine. Pony bells and joyous whistling; young children and animals jump as if come to life." Who could fail to be distracted from petty egotism by the thrill of encountering animals like the red panda, Asiatic black bear, wolf, and bharal ram? Still, the book shows wariness toward the lure of exoticism, toward the cultural mythology of escape to James Hilton's distant utopia of Shangri-La.

Accordingly, *The Snow Leopard* seeks in many ways to dispel images of the heroic adventurer who confronts spectacular perils while traversing exotic territory. As critic Lawrence Buell has observed in *The Environmental Imagination*, the typical hero of the wilderness quest-romance in classic American literature is a solitary male protagonist in the mold of James Fenimore Cooper's

Natty Bumppo and William Faulkner's Ike McCaslin. By contrast, the narrator of *The Snow Leopard* portrays himself largely as an antihero. Prone to error and fits of petty anger, he rarely behaves nobly. There is little glamorous adventure in what he tells us of his leaking tent, bad shoes, and soggy sleeping bag. He even tells tales on himself, as when he confesses that envy may have stirred him to quarrel with George Schaller. He accuses himself of having behaved badly toward his now-deceased wife, of neglecting his motherless children, and of foolishly refusing the better judgment of Tukten. Native peoples, too, are portrayed as decidedly fallible, in contrast to the Western stereotype of saintly Tibetans. Matthiessen often complains about the stubborn, unruly, slothful, and deceitful conduct of the porters. By the end, though, he conveys a profoundly unsentimental appreciation of the humanity embodied in figures like Tukten.

In this regard, the book's periodic comments about interpersonal relations enrich its narrative of spiritual quest and refute the American wilderness myth of solitary heroism. Matthiessen's sporadic musings on a dead wife and absent children may seem at first only to distract him from involvement in the current expedition, but they play a crucial role in helping him cultivate the sort of mindful discipline that embraces the whole of life. Thus, the apparently intrusive remembrances of Deborah Love offer vital sustenance for his inward journey toward universal acceptance and love.

The central recollection of Deborah Love surfaces abruptly in the entry for October 11. Here Matthiessen relates a moving episode in which Deborah responded appreciatively to his gift of an elegant ceramic bowl even while she lay drugged and in pain during the final stages of her illness. The Himalayan peaks stirred memories of another mountain trip, when he had visited the French Alps with Deborah the year before her death. In the midst of his stormy relationship to this woman "lovely in person and in spirit," he secretly purchased the antique bowl she had admired with him in Geneva. He had intended to surprise her with it on her birthday. When they quarreled, he set it aside indefinitely. He did not present his gift until she lay on her deathbed, when he feared she could no longer know or care what was happening. Yet her surprising recognition of the bowl, and by implication, of his love, now looms large in memory as a moment of grace. It becomes a critical landmark in the author's journey toward acceptance of his own pain, remorse, and mortality.

For Matthiessen, reflection on the death of Deborah Love also figures conspicuously in his growth toward that paradoxical spirituality in which the self can be at once sympathetically engaged with others and inwardly detached. At the summit of his trip, on Crystal Mountain, the contentment he enjoys in solitude is not an escape from the world but rather a transcendent acceptance of death, affliction, and the satisfaction available in life's "common miracles." That paradoxical capacity, as T. S. Eliot describes it, "to care and not to care" likewise describes an ideal to which the author aspires in his complex relationships to other figures, including George Schaller, Tukten, and his absent eight-year-old son.

Thus, in the painful process of seeking oneness with the whole creation, the author finds Deborah Love becoming at once a presence and a palpable absence in his consciousness. The snow leopard, too, takes on growing significance in this book as both presence and absence. Its living presence is confirmed by November 9, when the author finds its print and scat along the Black River Canyon beyond Tsakang. Persuaded that the unseen animal is watching them, Matthiessen and Schaller develop a strong sense of its proximity. "It is wonderful," writes Matthiessen, "how the presence of this creature draws the whole landscape to a point." Schaller finally manages to sight a snow leopard while traveling apart from Matthiessen.

Yet Matthiessen never does. Because this creature is "wary and elusive to a magical degree," its absence from his gaze assumes an ever-deepening spiritual meaning. He would like to see a snow leopard but ultimately accepts his deprivation with serenity: "In the not-seeing, I am content." Perhaps he is not yet inwardly prepared for such vision. Perhaps, too, the leopard's presence-in-absence corresponds to that pregnant emptiness of the universe recognized by the spiritual sages—the emptiness into which Lao-tzu and Bodhidharma both passed.

Or perhaps the snow leopard should remain unseen because it serves as presiding spirit of an elusive, mysterious wilderness threatened by imminent destruction. Along his way through Nepal and across the Tibetan Plateau, Matthiessen sees many signs of environmental degradation, including land erosion, deforestation, and diminishing wildlife. As long as the snow leopard remains unseen, one can celebrate its survival as an unconquered remnant of primitive nature in a world dominated by the meddlesome technocracy of "new barbarians" from the West. Anticipating a gesture likewise recorded by Barry Lopez in *Arctic Dreams* (1986), the author of *The Snow Leopard* finds himself bowing involuntarily before the still beauty of nature revealed in the Dhaulagiri snowfields.

Beyond his obvious failure to see the leopard, Matthiessen must confront other forms of diminishment toward the close of his narrative. Inevitably, the thrill of discovery wanes during the return phase of his two-month trip, as he descends from the high point of his contentment with the beauty of Shey and Crystal Mountain. He feels a strange sense of regret following his safe return. Finally, on the day appointed for his last rendezvous with Tukten at a nearby shrine, Tukten fails to appear.

Even this last note of absence is consistent, though, with the book's broader themes and with the spiritual challenge of accepting the world as it is. Though physically absent at the close of the narrative, Tukten had already affected the author's soul through his example of unencumbered simplicity and inner freedom. In fact, "this leopard-eyed saint" ends up becoming Matthiessen's teacher and spiritual guide in a way that partly supersedes George Schaller's guidance, while recalling the elusive freedom of the snow leopard. In an interview, the author later confirmed that he regarded Tukten as his teacher and, indeed, as a kind of snow leopard. What is more, Tukten's openhearted acceptance of life matches the affirmative outlook Matthiessen had encountered when he eventually met the disabled Lama of Shey.

A fundamental supposition of *The Snow Leopard* is that an unseen presence and unity subsists at the heart of the phenomenal universe. The goal of spiritual search is to discover one's identity with this "Jewel in the Heart of the Lotus," to participate in the cosmic rhythm evoked by the great "Om" mantra. In this regard the book, written before the full bloom of postmodernism, runs against more contemporary suppositions of discontinuity, de-centered reality, and indeterminacy. Yet the way in which the book's travel narrative effectively re-presents ancient spiritual teachings from Asia and elsewhere could raise doubts today about the extent to which postmodern theorizing is actually a transient, parochial construct of Western culture.

THE WATSON TRILOGY

After *The Snow Leopard* appeared in 1978, Matthiessen continued to publish books of nonfiction, including *In the Spirit of Crazy Horse* (1983) and *Indian Country* (1984), while extending his study and practice of Zen Buddhism. For him, Zen involves "a way of seeing the world that is closely tied in with the way American Indian people see the world." His published advocacy of American Indian interests and defense of AIM (American Indian Movement) activist Leonard Peltier against murder charges for which Peltier had been imprisoned drew him into a protracted legal struggle, which was finally resolved in his favor. In 1980 Matthiessen married Maria Eckhart. In addition to winning the National Book Award in 1979, he was awarded both the John Burroughs Medal and the African Wildlife Leadership Award in 1982 and the Academy of Natural Sciences Gold Medal for Distinction in Natural History in 1985. He also saw a reasonably faithful movie version of *At Play in the Fields of the Lord*, featuring Tom Berenger as Lewis Moon and Daryl Hannah as Andy Huben, released in 1991. *On the River Styx and Other Stories* (1989) marked the author's renewed commitment to fiction, though only two of the stories in this volume had been recently composed. One of these, "Lumumba Lives" is a compelling, richly elaborate tale that manages to connect its main character's drama of personal identity and memory with broader sociopolitical themes involving race relations, national idealism and corruption, and environmental degradation.

Yet Matthiessen's central achievement of the past decade is his monumental Watson trilogy. Read most profitably as a single unified work, the three novels deal exhaustively with the historical figure of Edgar J. (aka "Jack") Watson, a commanding personality who becomes a prosperous sugarcane planter and entrepreneur after he makes his home at Chatham Bend in the swamp country of the Florida Everglades in the 1890s.

Born in South Carolina in 1855, Watson soon becomes a fugitive when he must flee to northern Florida, together with his mother and sister, to escape his brutal father. He later spends time in Oklahoma and Arkansas before showing up in Arcadia, in southwest Florida. Though capable of adopting a gentlemanly and neighborly bearing,

"Jack" Watson also has a violent temper and the reputation of a cold-blooded killer. Word of his misdeeds follows him from his previous lives in the Oklahoma Territory and north Florida to south Florida, where tales of murder and illegitimate children grow so plentifully around "Bloody Watson" that he assumes almost mythological stature in the frontier settlements of the Ten Thousand Islands region.

Matthiessen's trilogy, which examines Watson from every conceivable angle, draws us especially toward the last dramatic episodes of his life. An apocalyptic mood develops as Watson's end follows the ravaging effects of the Great Hurricane of 1910, the return of Halley's Comet, and a triple murder attributed to Watson though committed by his foreman, Leslie Cox. Ironically, it is this crime that leads to Watson's showdown with a self-appointed "posse" of neighbors who shoot him with thirty-three bullets when he returns to Chokoloskee on October 24, 1910. *Killing Mister Watson* (1990) tells the story through a polyphonic array of ten voices that, along with documentary statements from a fictive historian, reveal disparate judgments of the central character. In *Lost Man's River* (1997), the narration also draws on multiple witnesses but operates from a single, albeit unstable, center of consciousness in the person of Watson's son Lucius, while *Bone by Bone* revisits the story one last time from Watson's own point of view.

Most reviewers have applauded the trilogy's compelling sense of authority and its power to revivify forgotten facts of regional history while capturing that sense of place peculiar to the wilds of southwest Florida at the turn of the century. Trip Gabriel has called *Killing Mister Watson* "a tour de force." Sven Birkerts observes that "together these novels make a dense digest of a community over a period of decades," while Christopher Camuto, in his review of *Bone by Bone*, concludes that "few novelists embed their characters as deeply in the American landscape as Peter Matthiessen can, plumbing the depths of the relationship between nature and human nature." Sam Gilpin describes *Bone by Bone* as "the final installment of a complex and significant trilogy" that is "ambitious not only in its scale, but also in the breadth of its thematic concerns." Matthiessen's re-creation of Edgar Watson as "a strongly realized presence, a convincing, multi-faceted character" is essential to the work's success.

Nevertheless, at least one reviewer, John Skow, has asked if Watson—whether a real or imagined character—truly warrants the enormous attention accorded him in this meganovel. To be sure, his life poses a fascinating enigma. One wonders just why he went wrong and which of the many murders attributed to him he actually committed. But what is really so noteworthy about Watson beyond his divided disposition as gentleman outlaw, as an apparently likeable neighbor and serial murderer? Why should the problem of Mr. Watson matter enough to occupy more than 1300 pages of novelistic scrutiny?

Matthiessen's preoccupation with Watson is fully warranted if one sees this larger-than-life desperado as the focal point for an even larger, and distinctively American, cultural drama. In himself, Watson is indeed a peculiar sort of folk hero. Though he embodies the wild energy of America's frontier, he lacks the natural innocence of a Natty Bumppo or Huck Finn. Nor does he fit the usual profile of notorious outlaw in his attentiveness to paperwork land claims or his zeal for Florida's economic and industrial development. More than one of Watson's murders is impelled by a desire to silence those he fears will harm his reputation as aspiring business leader or thwart his schemes to expand the production of high-grade sugar syrup.

Particularly in the last two novels, Matthiessen shows how Watson's lawless ambition is symbolically linked to the unfettered voraciousness of leading capitalists and to the nation's expansionist designs as epitomized by the Spanish-American War. Despite his killing and carousing, Watson is a hard worker with "big plans" who stands for "progress." As one of his old neighbors testifies, Ed Watson " 'never let nobody stand in the way of progress.' " Watson believes in paying his bills, in exploiting hired labor to grow and process his sugarcane efficiently, and in realizing optimal profit through whatever means he deems necessary. For the sake of promoting his own economic empire, he would like to see southwest Florida developed by draining the Everglades for new acreage and building new railways. No wonder he is eventually honored by agribusinessmen as a progenitor of Big Sugar—and as one who helped pave the way for Florida's great plenty of highways, causeways, speculators, malls, golf courses, and retirement dwellings. No wonder, too, he is said to have "looked like God" and "like Satan" and "like Uncle Sam, all three at once."

It is germane to the dream of white mastery implicit in this cultural fable that Watson should have planted his sugar farm on top of an Indian mound left by displaced Calusas, and that two field hands he later kills for the sake of "eliminating agitators who caused serious trouble" should have been black. Watson concedes there may be some truth in the claim of Mr. Clemens, an author revered by his second wife, that "our nation's bold new spirit of industrialism and imperialism was based on nothing more nor less than racism and greed." Such are the complications of race relations in America that even Lucius, despite all his scholarly training and progressive politics, betrays an obsession in *Lost Man's River* to know whether Henry Short, the only neighbor considered black in the group confronting his father, had fired the first shot.

Still, Watson "always spoke as a stern supporter of the capitalist system" since he "meant to become a capitalist" himself and knew that "rough methods were sometimes necessary in the way of progress." Watson invokes the precedent of those "great capitalists building America" who "let nobody and nothing stand in the way of progress, especially their own." "I have taken life," he confesses, and "for that I will always be sorry." Yet he claims that "Generally, I have not done it for financial reasons," and asks "How many of these 'robber barons' who are making America's great fortunes can say the same?" When Henry Flagler developed his Model Land Company at Palm Beach and completed his railway project in east Florida, he ignored the hundreds who labored and often died "in that humid heat to make his fortune." So to Watson it seemed "unjust—in fact, it enraged me—that a small cane planter on a remote frontier should be slandered for a few deaths among his workers when the powerful men building great empires were permitted to write off human life as simple overhead." As a champion of progress, Watson wants to think he has more in common with two distinguished Florida visitors, Henry Ford and Thomas Edison, than he does with any celebrity killer.

That Watson is self-deceived in this conceit cannot be denied. But he is scarcely the first or only American to believe that ethical scruples must be set aside to realize some grand ambition. In the first two novels, Matthiessen deftly leads readers to sympathize with Watson despite his evil reputation. His detractors often seem motivated by envy or vindictiveness, and one who has read only *Killing Mr. Watson* cannot say for certain that Mr. Watson has killed anyone. Toward the close of *Lost Man's River,* though, credible testimony from Watson's son Rob deepens our abhorrence of Watson and his misdeeds. Although Lucius had long refused to acknowledge his father's guilt, he must finally admit that Ed Watson bears blame not only for slaughtering his field hands Ted and Zechariah, but also for the heinous killing of his previous foreman, Wally Tucker, and Tucker's pregnant wife. As Watson confesses in *Bone by Bone,* he bears still more

blame for destroying Rob's soul when he forces Rob to kill Bet Tucker than for himself killing or helping to kill several others.

The sins of the fathers are indeed visited upon their sons and daughters, a pattern confirmed by Matthiessen's portrayal of E. J. Watson's own frightfully drunken, violent father in *Bone by Bone.* Lucius, too, bears the unspeakable weight of his father's sins insofar as he shares the existential melancholy of one "doomed to apprehend his ultimate solitude on earth as his ordained existence." One can better understand if not excuse Ed Watson's behavior after learning from *Bone by Bone* of a youth and family heritage steeped in violence, of Watson's grief at losing a beloved first wife within ten months of marrying her, and of other adversities that hardened Watson in self-hatred, fear, and nihilistic pride. One needn't wholly accept Watson's alibi that he "grew hard, having no choice about it" to perceive that this man with hair the color of dried blood has both suffered and caused extraordinary pain. Just after the bullets hit, the trilogy's final page of fragmented impressions hints at Watson's ample exposure to "how the world hurts."

Watson exemplifies both the self-confident individualism and the violence endemic to American culture. His relation to the natural environment is similarly paradoxical. On the one hand, he readily adapts to living in what critic John Cooley calls that "singular bioregion" of the Everglades. Protected by wild mangroves, he thrives in the lawless isolation of the subtropical frontier. As Lucius observes, he has more instinctive talent for working with "crops and farm animals" than anybody else in the islands. On the other hand, Ed Watson's zeal for "progress" and disregard for life incite him to destroy the very wilderness he loves. When he first reaches the islands, he confides that "Seeing so much wild, virgin coast awaiting man's domination, I felt better and better." He cannot perceive the beauty of wild creatures so clearly as Lucius or as Rob, who bemoans "the desecration of Creation" displayed in the wanton slaughter of alligators. Hungry to shoot up "the best rookeries in spring," he fails to match Bill Smallwood's recognition of how the loss of plume birds and eventual disappearance of large cats and bears will hasten the time when there "Ain't goin to be one bright-eyed bit of life left in south Florida."

One must therefore reckon with more than one sort of wildness, and Watson's version of untamed energy more often destroys than preserves the endangered remnants of aboriginal life. Matthiessen has elsewhere defined wild people and places as those "that still have their own integrity." In *Lost Man's River,* even the creation of Everglades National Park raises troubling questions about what is truly wild when park management tries to erase every sign of previous human settlement from this wilderness enclave. Matthiessen's searching analysis of the interplay between nature and culture in America is only one dimension of his formidable achievement in the Watson epic. This brilliant work, reflecting the dense empiricism of real-life investigation, also bridges the usual gulf between fact and fiction. Clear boundaries no longer exist by which the historical facts of Watson's case can be set apart from the Watson myths and from Matthiessen's own fictions.

Finally, this latest and perhaps greatest of Matthiessen's works stimulates readers to reassess what "nature writing" is all about. The term is still commonly equated with nonfictional prose, and above all, with writing from which human beings have mostly been evacuated. While challenging such assumptions in his colossal Watson novel, Matthiessen has continued to reap artistic benefit from his multidisciplinary training. And he will doubtless continue to live up to his Zen name, Muryo, which as Pico Iyer points out, is amazingly apt in its sense of one "without boundaries."

Selected Bibliography

WORKS OF PETER MATTHIESSEN

NOVELS AND SHORT STORIES
Race Rock. New York: Harper & Bros., 1954.
Partisans. New York: Viking, 1955.
Raditzer. New York: Viking, 1961.
At Play in the Fields of the Lord. New York: Random House, 1965.
Far Tortuga. New York: Random House, 1975.
Midnight Turning Gray. Bristol, R.I.: Ampersand Press, 1984.
On the River Styx and Other Stories. New York: Random House, 1989.
Killing Mister Watson. New York: Random House, 1990.
Lost Man's River. New York: Random House, 1997.
Bone by Bone. New York: Random House, 1999.

OTHER WORKS
Wildlife in America. New York: Viking, 1959. Revised, 1989.
The Cloud Forest: A Chronicle of the South American Wilderness. New York: Viking, 1961.
Under the Mountain Wall: A Chronicle of Two Seasons in the Stone Age. New York: Viking, 1962.
Oomingmak: The Expedition to the Musk Ox Island in the Bering Sea. New York: Hastings House, 1967.
The Shorebirds of North America. Edited by Gardner D. Stout. New York: Viking, 1967. Republished as *The Wind Birds.* Viking, 1973.
Sal Si Puedes: César Chavez and the New American Revolution. New York: Random House, 1969.
Blue Meridian: The Search for the Great White Shark. New York: Random House, 1971.
The Tree Where Man Was Born. New York: E. P. Dutton, 1972.
Seal Pool [children's book]. Garden City, N.Y.: Doubleday, 1972.
The Snow Leopard. New York: Viking, 1978.
Sand Rivers. New York: Viking, 1981.
In the Spirit of Crazy Horse. New York: Viking, 1983.
Indian Country. New York: Viking, 1984.
Nine-Headed Dragon River: Zen Journals 1969–1982. Boston: Shambhala, 1986.

Men's Lives: The Surfmen and Baymen of the South Fork. New York: Random House, 1986.

African Silences. New York: Random House, 1991.

Baikal: Sacred Sea of Siberia. San Francisco: Sierra Club, 1992.

East of Lo Monthang: In the Land of Mustang. Boston: Shambhala, 1995.

NOTABLE COLLECTIONS

Everglades. By Patricia Caulfield, editing and introduction by Paul Brooks, and selections from the writings of Peter Matthiessen. San Francisco: Sierra Club, 1970.

Shadows of Africa. With Mary Frank. New York: Harry N. Abrams, Inc., 1992.

SELECTED ESSAYS IN PERIODICALS

"Lignumvitae—The Last Key." *Audubon,* March 1967, 64–71.

"How to Kill a Valley." *New York Review of Books,* February 7, 1980, pp. 31–36.

"Our National Parks: The Case for Burning." *New York Times Magazine,* December 11, 1988, pp. 38.

"The Trials of Leonard Peltier." *Esquire,* January, 1992, pp. 55–57.

"At the End of Tibet." *Audubon,* March/April, 1994, pp. 40–49.

"Survival of the Hunter." *New Yorker,* April 24, 1995, pp. 67–77.

"The Cranes of Hokkaido." *Audubon,* July/August, 1995, pp. 36–47.

"The Island at the End of the Earth." *Audubon,* September/October 1999, pp. 98–107.

BIBLIOGRAPHIES

Nicholas, D. *Peter Matthiessen: A Bibliography: 1951–1979.* Canoga Park, Cal.: Oriana Press, 1979.

Young, James Dean. "A Peter Matthiessen Checklist." *Critique* 21: 30–38 (1979).

CRITICAL AND BIOGRAPHICAL STUDIES

Bender, Bert. "Far Tortuga and American Sea Fiction Since Moby-Dick." *American Literature* 56: 227–248 (May, 1984).

Birkerts, Sven. "Heart of the Swamp." *New York Times Book Review,* April 11, 1999, pp. 9–10.

Burroway, Jane. "Still Looking for Mr. Watson." *New York Times Book Review,* November 23, 1997, pp. 16+.

Camuto, Christopher. "Fiction, Forests, and Mountain Lions." *Audubon,* July–August 1999, p. 124.

Capouya, Emile. "The Bible and Bombs." *New York Times Book Review,* November 7, 1965, pp. 4, 66.

Cobb, John L. "Peter Matthiessen." *American Novelists Since World War II: Second Series.* Vol. 6, *Dictionary of Literary Biography.* Edited by James E. Kibler Jr. Detroit: Gale Research Co., 1980. Pp. 218–224.

Cooley, John. "Matthiessen's Voyages on the River Styx: Deathly Waters, Endangered Peoples." In his *Earthly Words: Essays on Contemporary American Nature and Environmental Writers.* Ann Arbor: University of Michigan Press, 1994. Pp. 167–192.

Dowie, William. *Peter Matthiessen.* Boston: Twayne-G.K. Hall & Co., 1991.

———. "Peter Matthiessen." *American Novelists Since World War II: Fifth Series.* Vol. 173, *Dictionary of Literary Biography.* Edited by James R. Giles and Wanda H. Giles. Detroit: Gale Research Co., 1996. Pp. 132–147.

Gabriel, Trip. "The Nature of Peter Matthiessen." *New York Times Magazine,* June 10, 1990, pp. 30+.

Gilpin, Sam. "Swamp Memories." *Times Literary Supplement,* July 23, 1999, p. 22.

Grove, James P. "Pastoralism and Anti-Pastoralism in Peter Matthiessen's Far Tortuga." *Critique,* 21: 15–29 (1979).

Heim, Michael. "The Mystic and the Myth: Thoughts on The Snow Leopard." *Studia Mystica,* 4: 3–9 (Summer 1981).

Hicks, Granville. "No Eden on the Amazon." *Saturday Review,* November 6, 1965, pp. 29–30.

Iyer, Pico. "Laureate of the Wild." *Time,* January 11, 1993, pp. 42–44.

Lynch, William J. "Review—At Play in the Fields of the Lord." *America,* December 25, 1965, pp. 728–729.

Patteson, Richard F. "At Play in the Fields of the Lord: The Imperialist Idea and the Discovery of the Self." *Critique* 21: 5–14 (1979).

———. "Holistic Vision and Fictional Form in Peter Matthiessen's Far Tortuga." *Bulletin of the Rocky Mountain Modern Language Association* 37: 70–81 (1983).

Payne, Daniel G. "Peter Matthiessen." In *American Nature Writers,* Vol. 2. Edited by John Elder. New York: Charles Scribner's Sons, 1996. Pp. 599–613.

Raglon, Rebecca. "Fact and Fiction: The Development of Ecological Form in Peter Matthiessen's Far Tortuga." *Critique* 35: 245–259 (Summer 1994).

Skow, John. "Lost Man's Tale: Peter Matthiessen Caps a Dense, Fascinating Trilogy about a Brawling Florida Planter." *Time,* May 17, 1999, p. 89.

Styron, William. "Peter Matthiessen." In his *This Quiet Dust and Other Writings.* New York: Random House, 1982. Pp. 249–252.

Winterowd, W. Ross. "Peter Matthiessen's Lyric Trek." In his *The Rhetoric of the 'Other' Literature.* Carbondale: Southern Illinois University Press, 1990. Pp. 133–139.

INTERVIEWS AND AUTOBIOGRAPHICAL ESSAYS

Allen, Henry. "Quest for the Snow Leopard's Secret: And Other Journeys into Meaning with Best-Selling Author Peter Matthiessen." *The Washington Post,* December 13, 1978, pp. D1, 15.

Anonymous. "Peter Matthiessen." *World Authors: 1950–1970.* Edited by John Wakeman. New York: H.W. Wilson Co., 1975. Pp. 956–958.

Bonetti, Kay. "An Interview with Peter Matthiessen." *The Missouri Review* 12: 109–124 (1989).

Houy, Deborah. "A Moment with Peter Matthiessen." *Buzzworm: The Environmental Journal* 5: 28 (March 1993).

Matthiessen, Peter. "New York: Old Hometown." *Architectural Digest* 46: 52ff. (November 1989).

Plimpton, George. "The Craft of Fiction in Far Tortuga." *Paris Review* 15: 79–82 (Winter 1974).

Rea, Paul. "Causes and Creativity: An Interview with Peter Matthiessen." *Re Arts & Letters: A Liberal Arts Forum* 15: 27–40 (Fall 1989).

Smith, Wendy. "PW Interviews Peter Matthiessen." *Publishers Weekly* 9: 240–241 (May 9, 1986).

White, Jonathan. "Talking on the Water" (excerpts from interviews with Matthiessen and five other environmentally concerned writers). *Sierra,* May–June, 1994, pp. 72–75.

FILMS, PLAYS, AND TELEVISION PRODUCTIONS BASED ON THE WORKS OF PETER MATTHIESSEN

"Adventure: Lost Man's River—An Everglades Journey with Peter Matthiessen." PBS television production, 1991.

At Play in the Fields of the Lord. Screenplay by Saul Zaentz. Directed by Hector Babenco. Metro-Goldwyn-Mayer Film, 1992.

Men's Lives. Play adaptation by Joe Pintauro. First production: Bay Street Theater Festival, Long Island, 1992.

—JOHN GATTA

Larry McMurtry

1936–

*I*N AN EARLY essay, "Take My Saddle from the Wall: A Valediction," published in the collection *In a Narrow Grave: Essays on Texas* (1968), Larry McMurtry dismisses genealogical backtracking as nonproductive. "I have never considered genealogy much of an aid to recognition, and thus have never pursued my lineage any distance at all." Some knowledge of his ancestors and the land they settled, however, is desirable for a better understanding and enjoyment of his work. In an interview with Mark Horowitz for the *New York Times Magazine,* McMurtry said, "It's still such a strong landscape for me. I can't escape it in my fiction. I can work away from it, but I always start here. And whatever place I'm writing about, I'm still describing this same hill." The people and landscape of his youth "bred" Larry McMurtry just as surely as, to this day, they breed cattle, cactus, roughnecks, rodeo riders, isolation, and loneliness.

Larry McMurtry's grandparents, William Jefferson McMurtry and his wife, Louisa Francis McMurtry, left Missouri in 1877 and settled about forty miles north of Dallas, in Denton County, Texas. In those days, that was as far west as one wished to venture into Texas, especially if one was planning to raise a family. The very real danger posed by the Comanches had only recently been laid to rest, and hostilities regularly erupted. In the late 1880s, however, the devel-

oping cattle industry made the area around Archer County, one hundred miles northwest of Denton, relatively secure and very desirable.

William, with his wife and their six children, moved there and purchased a half-section (half a square mile, or 180 acres) of land close to a good spring and an old military road used by cattle drivers, for three dollars an acre. Six more children were born, making a total of nine boys and three girls. The youngest boy, Jeff, married Hazel Ruth McIver, and their son, Larry, was born in Wichita Falls, Texas on June 3, 1936. McMurtry grew up helping his father and uncles as a cowhand on the family ranch just outside of Archer City. He realized early on that this was not the life for him. In a *Newsweek* interview by Malcolm Jones, McMurtry admitted, "I never aspired to be a rancher. I never really liked it. I knew, and my father knew, that it wasn't going to last another generation. He just barely survived doing the work he wanted." At some time during his attempts to master the finer points of ranch work, McMurtry discovered books and the rich oral traditions of his eight uncles and became, as he often describes himself, a "herder of words." He graduated with honors from Archer City High School in 1954, earned his Bachelor of Arts in English from North Texas State College (now the University of North Texas) in 1958, and his Master of Arts from Rice University in Houston in 1960.

At Rice, McMurtry took creative writing classes taught by George Williams. Writers John Graves and William Goyen were also students of Williams at one time or another. These academic achievements are quite remarkable for anyone, but especially for a bookish young man who grew up surrounded by $20-a-month cowboys who thought Ph.D. stood for "post hole digger."

A Wallace Stegner Fellowship in 1960 allowed McMurtry to travel to San Francisco and enroll in Stegner's writing program at Stanford University. Stegner, the novelist who had redefined the notion of the West as a desirable landscape for rugged individualists, established Stanford's writing program in 1946, believing, as he later wrote, that "minds grow by contact with other minds, the bigger the better, as clouds grow toward thunder by rubbing together." The Stegner Fellowship, which has existed since the program's inception, offers stipends as well as deferral of tuition to promising writers and poets. McMurtry supplemented his income by working as a book scout for some of San Francisco's rare book dealers, developing a knowledge and love of the business that serves him well to this day. Stegner's program, and Stegner himself, had an immediate and lifelong influence on McMurtry. Other authors who have reaped benefits from the program include Raymond Carver, Thomas McGuane, Scott Turow, Tillie Olsen, and McMurtry's classmate Ken Kesey, one of the people to whom *In a Narrow Grave: Essays on Texas* is dedicated. McMurtry left the ranch behind and set out into a territory as unknown and frightening as any frontier pioneered by his forefathers—a career in letters.

In 1959 McMurtry married Josephine Ballard, and the couple's only child, James Lawrence McMurtry, was born on March 18, 1962, in Fort Worth, Texas. The McMurtrys divorced in 1966. James went on to become a popular singer, songwriter, and musician in the style of Bob Dylan and Ian Tyson. James' success is such that today,

especially in Texas, when one hears news of McMurtry's "latest," it is just as likely to be James' compact disc as his father's book that is being discussed. Josephine McMurtry is a University of Richmond, Virginia, professor of English literature and author of several books on the subject.

By the time of the 1966 divorce, McMurtry, in addition to his work as a lecturer and associate professor of English at Rice University in Houston and Texas Christian University in Fort Worth, had published three novels that would change the way the West was thought of forever. These three, *Horseman, Pass By* (1961), *Leaving Cheyenne* (1963), and *The Last Picture Show* (1966), are sometimes referred to as the Thalia Trilogy (Thalia being the not-too-fictionalized version of McMurtry's hometown of Archer City). It should be remembered that Thalia is also the name of the Greek goddess of comedy and pastoral poetry, both strong elements in all of McMurtry's work.

THE THALIA TRILOGY

William Butler Yeats' poem "Under Ben Bulben" is an important starting point for any study of McMurtry. The poem, especially the fifth section, is Yeats' rallying cry for Irish artists, writers, and poets to remain true to their "Irishry." Yeats' exhortation is McMurtry's guiding principle: destroy the myth and preserve the truth. The poem concludes with these words: "Cast a cold eye / On life, on death / Horseman, pass by." McMurtry's *Horseman, Pass By* was as difficult for McMurtry as any first novel can be. Manuscripts housed in the University of Houston attest that the novel was rewritten at least five times. McMurtry eventually agreed to most of the editorial changes simply to get the book published, but he has never felt good about the finished product and he attempts to disown it and other early novels at every opportunity.

The story *Horseman, Pass By* tells is simple and straightforward. Three men, Homer Bannon, a lifelong cattle rancher now in his eighties, Lonnie Bannon, Homer's seventeen-year-old grandson and the narrator of the novel, and Homer's stepson, thirty-five-year-old Hud, are faced with the end of a way of life each believed, for better or worse, would last forever. This end comes quickly. The narrative spans only a few weeks in the summer of 1954. A heifer is found dead on the ranch, and after much discussion and disagreement, Homer reluctantly agrees to call in a government veterinarian. " 'I never figured on havin' to call in the government,' Granddad said. 'I ain't sure I want to, just for one heifer.' Granddad had got so he would walk a mile rather than involve himself with the government offices. . . .' " Homer is one the last of the cowboy-gods, who equate aid with interference and acceptance of it with loss of character and stature. Jimmy Burris, the state veterinarian, examines the dead heifer, takes several samples, and after the test results indicate hoof-in-mouth disease, informs Homer that his entire herd must be destroyed. The resulting conflict between Homer and Hud over what to do about this calamity bewilders Lonnie. Determined to hold onto what he has spent his life building up, Homer tries to convince Mr. Burris that he can keep his herd tightly quarantined and thereby control the spread of the disease. Hud, however, wants the old man to sell the herd to some unsuspecting rancher before word gets out. Neither of these solutions makes sense to Lonnie, who is being seduced away from the ranch by an imagined different and better life he believes is somewhere down the road and is being enjoyed by everybody but him. Lonnie had realized early in the novel: "Granddad and I were in such separate times and separate places. I had got to where I would rather go to Thalia and goof around on the square than listen to his old-timy stories."

By the novel's end, Lonnie, who has witnessed a rape, a murder, and the extermination of Homer's cattle, packs up and leaves the ranch to visit an injured friend in Wichita Falls and perhaps find that life for which he longs. "I took a few of my clothes and a few of my paperbacks and drove to town in the pickup." He leaves the pickup where Hud can find it, draws his savings out of the bank, and hitches a ride with a trucker. These lines, near the close of *Horseman, Pass By*, leave the reader wondering just how far he traveled and if he did not turn around and come back home: " . . . and I sat thinking about Thalia, making the rounds in my mind. At home it was time for the train to go by, and nobody was sitting on the porch." All we know for certain is that he eventually becomes the writer of his own life.

In *Leaving Cheyenne,* McMurtry returns to the same north central Texas ranchland outside Thalia (Archer City). The ranch is the central location of the action, and the principal male characters are a cowboy and a rancher. Instead of a conflict of generations, as in *Horseman, Pass By,* the characters in *Leaving Cheyenne* are all approximately the same age and are united in their common fate—the passing of time. In this novel, McMurtry attempts to expand his narrative abilities by extending the plot over a much longer period, in this case the decades from the early 1900s to the late 1950s. Borrowing his title from an old cowboy song, "My foot's in the stirrup, / My pony won't stand, / Goodbye, old partner, / I'm leaving Cheyenne," McMurtry follows quickly with his explanation that he is not writing about a town in Wyoming: "The Cheyenne of the book is that part of the cowboy's day's circle which is earliest and best: his blood's country and his heart's pastureland."

The story is one of friendship between Johnny McCloud and Gideon Fry. Both are in love with Molly Taylor. This situation would lead to jealousy, anger, and violence in most fiction but in McMurtry's novel, since neither man marries her and thereby stakes his claim, and since Molly

222 / AMERICAN WRITERS

shares her love for each man equally, the friendships last for some forty years with no signs of strain.

McMurtry divides his novel into three sections, allowing Gid, Molly, and Johnny equal time as narrator. Each section is introduced by epigraphs meant to describe the narrator's point of view. The epigraph to the first section, Gid's story, refers to "the high lean country, full of old stories that still go walking in my sleep." Molly's narrative is preceded by these lines from Shakespeare's Sonnet 64, "Ruin hath taught me thus to ruminate, / That time will come and take my love away." The two epigraphs preceding Johnny's story bring the novel to its end. Chaucer's Wife of Bath laments, "The flour is gone, there is namore to tell," and Teddy Blue requests "and while the boys are lowering me to rest, go turn my horses free." Taken together these epigraphs sum up McMurtry's literary themes of love, loss, and eventual recognition and resignation. *Leaving Cheyenne* received some good critical reviews, but it is essentially a young man's fantasy book—the sort, perhaps, that Lonnie Bannon would have enjoyed.

McMurtry leaves the ranch behind and moves into the city (Thalia) in the third novel of the Thalia Trilogy, *The Last Picture Show.* This novel is one of his strongest attempts to correct the myths of the West fostered by previous Texas writers, specifically the myth of the pastoral and romantic life to be found in a small Texas town. Thalia is shown to be desiccated and shabby and its population mean and brutally stupid. The one exception is Sam the Lion, the owner of the café, the pool hall, and the movie theater. No one in Thalia knows how he got his nickname (an old love, however, claims to have bestowed it on him during a moment of passion), but he is respectfully regarded as "the man who took care of things." Like life in the town itself, nothing much happens in this rambling, episodic novel. The basic story is quite simple. Sonny Crawford, the

focal character, is adrift in a society that has reached a point of complete degeneration. His father, a widower and drug addict, will not provide Sonny with even the bare essentials of life. Thus, Sonny, in addition to finishing his senior year and playing guard on the Thalia High football team, works on weekends, and some weeknights, driving a butane truck. Sonny's friend and roommate, Duane Moore, has been abandoned by his mother, is a senior, and plays fullback. Sam the Lion, "the man who took care of things," looks after these two in addition to Billy, a mentally deficient child who was left on the curb in front of Sam's picture show. Sonny and Duane seek to escape the stultifying monotony of their lives by engaging in various sexual escapades in town and on trips to Fort Worth and Mexico. After Sam the Lion dies of a stroke, Sonny and Billy inherit the pool hall, or rather, Sonny inherits the pool hall and Billy. Sonny's fate is sealed. He will never be able to leave Thalia. Even when Billy is accidentally hit by a truck and killed, Sonny's reluctance to leave the familiar controls him. Duane Moore, however, takes the escape route available to most boys in similar situations in the early 1950s—he joins the army to see the world.

The novel caused scandal in Archer City (Thalia) because most of the real-life inspirations for McMurtry's characters were easily recognized. McMurtry certainly succeeded in creating vivid portraits of the citizens, especially the women. Jacy Farrow and Ruth Popper are a far cry from the wooden Molly of the previous novel. One Archer City resident, Ceil Cleveland, in her 1977 book *Whatever Happened to Jacy Farrow?,* claims to be the outrageously amoral, bitchy, fantasy-obsessed object of Sonny and Duane's affections. This claim is validated in McMurtry's accompanying commentary. An interesting account of coming-of-age in a small Texas town in the 1950s, the book is of some value to students of McMurtry's early work.

In 1966, McMurtry, barely thirty years old, had

three published novels to his credit. Though none of them sold particularly well, each drew favorable reviews from the *New York Times,* and each was eventually re-created by Hollywood: *Hud* (*Horseman, Pass By*), in 1962, *The Last Picture Show,* 1971, and *Lovin' Molly (Leaving Cheyenne),* 1974. These movies, more than anything else, attracted the popular reading public of the time to McMurtry's work. *Hud,* filmed in and around the Texas Panhandle town of Claude (population 895 in 1962), was nominated for seven Academy Awards and won three—Best Actress, Patricia Neal (Alma, a white version of the novel's African-American character, Halmea); Best Supporting Actor, Melvyn Douglas (Homer Bannon); and Cinematography, James Wong Howe. In addition, McMurtry was awarded the Jesse H. Jones Award of the Texas Institute of Letters in 1962 for *Horseman, Pass By,* and in 1964 he became a Guggenheim Fellow. To all appearances, Larry McMurtry seemed to be a young man at the top of his form with a splendid future ahead of him. He was the darling of Texas letters and Hollywood. But in 1966, McMurtry's marriage collapsed.

The 1968 publication of McMurtry's collection of essays, *In a Narrow Grave: Essays on Texas,* established what he has called a line of demarcation in his life and literature: "*In a Narrow Grave* was my formal farewell to writing about the country." The book is a collection, a scattering he has called it, of previously published essays. They present a clear, poignant, humorous account of where McMurtry stands in relation to his novels, his family, his hometown, Hollywood, and all things Texan. The Dallas writer and book critic A. C. Greene had this to say, "Native son Larry McMurtry takes apart Texas with all the skill and sadness of a master surgeon performing a post mortem on his mother." With the publication of this collection, McMurtry hangs his saddle on the wall, brushes off the Texas dust on his cowboy boots, and rides off, not into the sunset, but to the urban area of Washington, D.C.

THE HOUSTON TRILOGY

What is regarded as the second stage in McMurtry's career began in about 1970. During this time he taught briefly at George Mason College (now George Mason University) and at American University. He also established the first of his rare, out-of-print bookstores, Booked Up, with his friend and fellow collector, Marcia Carter. The store, which now houses close to one million volumes, still does business in the Georgetown area. The first in what came to be known as McMurtry's Houston Trilogy, *Moving On,* was also published in 1970. This novel is a radical break with the traditional McMurtry genre. First of all, it is massive, containing more pages (794) than his first three novels combined. Second, the setting, for the most part, is urban. Finally, the focal characters, Jim and Patsy Carpenter, are fairly affluent and somewhat intelligent.

Moving On opens with Patsy Carpenter reading *Catch-22* in her car outside a rodeo arena in Markle, Texas. Her husband, Jim, is inside indulging in his latest career/hobby, photography. Jim has given up his halfhearted attempts to become first a novelist and later a linguist. Patsy is clearly uninterested in Jim and his search for self-fulfillment. The dissolution of their marriage is the focus of the next several hundred pages. The novel was a disappointment to McMurtry followers. It was felt that he had tried to put everything he knew about anything into one unwieldy book: rodeo life, the Houston academic scene, Hollywood, San Francisco, a brief treatment of the Thalia ranch country—on and on until the sheer variety becomes overwhelming and numbing. Critics have said that the material in *Moving On* would make a dozen good short stories, but as a novel it fails. John Leonard, in a

June 10, 1970, review of *Moving On* for the *New York Times* wrote, "The promiscuity of incident is fatiguing. . . . [i]t's a little like turning on the radio, and leaving it on for years."

Toward the end of *Moving On,* Patsy's friend Emma is reading John Updike and is suddenly reminded of someone she cares about deeply, the novelist Danny Deck. Emma tells Patsy that Deck "had written one book, had one child, broken up with his wife, and disappeared. His car had been found in Del Río, Texas, near a bridge that crossed the Rio Grande." *All My Friends Are Going to Be Strangers* (1972) takes the reader back to 1961 and tells Danny's story. The original dust jacket of this novel features a drawing in the upper left-hand corner of a young man who, except for the lack of eyeglasses and a tie, could be the Larry McMurtry in the photograph that graces the back of the original dust jacket of *Moving On.* This would naturally lead the observant reader to conclude that McMurtry is intending in this novel to provide a portrait of the artist. Indeed, the novel has some biographical parallels, but the best way to approach an understanding of the novel, and McMurtry at this stage in his artistic development, is by reading Wallace Stegner's 1964 essay, "Born a Square: The Westerner's Dilemma." In this essay, Stegner gives a detailed account of what is unique about writers whose roots are in the West and what can happen to them when they receive an "invitation from the great world." This invitation usually arrives in the form of a letter from a literary agent. The lure proves to be irresistible, and the writer grows away from the roots (values) that both sustained and restricted him or her. Once away, the writer will try to assimilate values that are foreign and people who appear "to specialize in despair, hostility, hyper-sexuality and disgust." At this point, the Western writer is in an intolerable situation—too proud to return home as a "quitter" and unable to remain and live a lie. Stegner's solution is to come home to the source, realize and accept that the Western writer is "an orphan with an inadequate tradition," and capitalize on that fact. Stegner writes, "The point is to do the best one can in the circumstances, not the worst." Danny Deck's story has all the elements of Stegner's assumptions. Even though McMurtry continues to rely heavily on his large cast of eccentrics and grotesques, some of whom appeared in *Moving On, All My Friends Are Going to Be Strangers* provides a glimpse of the maturity and tight narrative not seen since *Horseman, Pass By* and *Leaving Cheyenne.* With Deck, McMurtry also has the opportunity to examine the relationship between a novelist and his text.

The final installment in the Houston Trilogy is *Terms of Endearment* (1975). This comedy of manners centers on Aurora Greenway, a displaced New Englander, who delights in correcting others' manners and grammar and behaving in an imperious and neglectful way toward her many suitors. Aurora is outraged to learn of her daughter's (Emma, from *All My Friends Are Going to Be Strangers*) pregnancy, which will make a grandmother out of the ever-vain forty-nine-year-old woman. "Now I'll lose all my suitors!" is her reaction to the news. She does not, of course, and for most of this almost Shakespearean romp, McMurtry reveals her amorous adventures.

Just short of the end of this novel, McMurtry abandons Aurora in Houston and advances the reader nine years ahead to the Midwest (Iowa and finally Nebraska) where Emma and her husband, Flap, and their three children now live. Emma is stricken with cancer and Aurora comes to her side. Abruptly, McMurtry drops most of the comic elements and leads the reader through a somber story of academic failure, vengeful adultery, and death. In the end, Aurora, one assumes, returns to her interrupted life in Houston. McMurtry, however, leaves the state of Texas behind for his next three novels. In a 1975 essay in the *Atlantic,* "The Texas Moon, and Elsewhere," McMurtry says goodbye to the source of his inspiration: "I was halfway through my sixth Texas novel [*Terms of Endearment*], when I suddenly began to notice that where place was concerned, I was sucking air. The book is set in Houston, but none of the characters are Texans." He goes on to disparage Texas as a good place for literary mining by bemoaning "the kind of mental and emotive inarticulateness" found there. He concludes, "The move off the land is now virtually complete, and that was the great subject that Texas offered writers of my generation. The one basic subject it offers now is loneliness, and one can only ring the changes on that so many times."

THE TRASH TRILOGY

The next three novels, *Somebody's Darling* (1978), *Cadillac Jack* (1982), and *The Desert Rose* (1983), are sometimes referred to (perhaps correctly) as the Trash Trilogy. They certainly rest at the bottom of the list of McMurtry's significant work. In addition to the subject matter, the lack of a "Texas connection" left readers and reviewers disappointed. It was generally agreed that McMurtry's abilities had dried up and blown away.

Somebody's Darling, though set in Hollywood, is not in any sense a "Hollywood" novel. In a 1980 interview with Patrick Bennett, McMurtry said that writing *Somebody's Darling* was "an unpleasant experience," that it was "forced"—an "enjoyable read but an interesting failure." *Cadillac Jack,* the Washington, D.C., novel about an antiques scout/junk dealer, seems equally forced. The Las Vegas novel, *The Desert Rose,* revolves around the life and loves of a mother–daughter team of showgirls. The novel entertained few and irritated many. McMurtry admits he spent only

three weeks writing this novel, which was originally conceived as a film script.

The period from roughly 1970 through 1983 is a time of withdrawal from all things Texan for McMurtry. He firmly established himself as the "bad boy" of Texas letters in a startling essay, "Ever a Bridegroom: Reflections on the Failure of Texas Literature," published in the *Texas Observer* on October 23, 1981. In this essay, McMurtry distances himself from even his most ardent admirers. He attacks everyone and everything associated with Texas literature, including such giants as Katherine Anne Porter, J. Frank Dobie, Roy Bedichek, W. P. Webb, and the prestigious Texas Institute of Letters. McMurtry had dealt harshly with these Texas icons in previous essays, but "Ever a Bridegroom" was particularly caustic. The Texas press mounted a swift counterattack. The *Dallas Times Herald* ran a column by staff writer Bryan Wooley, entitled "Nuts To You Too, Mr. McMurtry." One of Kent Biffle's articles on the matter, published in the *Dallas Morning News,* was headlined "Bulldozing Texas' Literary Landscape." A. C. Greene, who drew a particularly sharp attack in the essay, wrote, "His [McMurtry's] weakness as a critic comes at those points where he seems to deny anyone the right to have a differing opinion." Despite the well-deserved retaliations, a close reading of the notorious essay reveals that McMurtry sees himself as the biggest failure at achieving the goal of Texas literary greatness. McMurtry admits in the essay, "It took me until 1972 to write a book that an intelligent reader might want to read twice, and by 1976 I had once again lost the knack." This mea culpa, coupled with the fact that the brilliant promise of the first novel steadily dimmed with each succeeding book, left the book world wondering what to expect from McMurtry next, if indeed, anything. McMurtry seemed to wonder as well.

By 1983, McMurtry had published nine novels. Although four of them had been adapted into award-winning motion pictures (*Hud, The Last Picture Show, Lovin' Molly, and Terms of Endearment*), the novels themselves were not bestsellers. It was Hollywood that was keeping McMurtry's name in front of the public, and in a 1971 interview by Alan Crooks, McMurtry acknowledges that he is aware of this. In that interview, McMurtry makes these statements: "I do want to go into screenwriting. I've found that I enjoy it, that it is less lonely and much less isolating than writing novels, and that it may turn out to be just as satisfying creatively." McMurtry and his cowriter, director Peter Bogdanovich, wrote the screenplay for *The Last Picture Show,* a script that was nominated for an Academy Award in 1971 (it lost to *The French Connection* screenplay by Ernest Tidyman).

McMurtry is certainly not the first novelist to be drawn to Hollywood and scriptwriting. Nathaniel West, F. Scott Fitzgerald, and William Faulkner are a few of many who made that journey and career adjustment with varying degrees of success. In the 1971 interview McMurtry admits, "I don't have any firm convictions about it yet, except that I am very fatigued with writing novels, and I would like to investigate screenwriting as a possible new line of work completely or, at the very least, as a balance to writing novels." Indeed, from this point on, all of McMurtry's novels appear very "cinematic." The reader "sees" more than he or she "feels." It seems as if McMurtry has one eye on the box office and one on the *New York Times* Bestseller List. The first two novels had surrendered to a literary style that provides entertainment by telling some interesting tales peopled with eccentric characters. Then in 1985 McMurtry, who was admittedly tired of writing novels, especially about Texas, and through his essays, was determined to turn all his friends into strangers, surprised everyone with an enormous novel about the very subjects he seemed to have gladly abandoned.

THE BIG COWBOY BOOK

Lonesome Dove (1985) has its origins in a 1971 screenplay entitled "The Streets of Laredo," which McMurtry wrote in the hopes of enticing Peter Bogdanovich to direct and John Wayne, Jimmy Stewart, and Henry Fonda to star as Woodrow Call, Gus McCrae, and Jake Spoon. McMurtry said, "It was an end-of-the-West western. Three old men stumble into a last adventure, and they're old, and the West is over. Everybody loved it except the three actors, so we didn't make it. I've sometimes thought I might see what would happen if I did it as a novel."

The novel relies strongly on the historic experiences of two of Texas' most famous trail drivers, Oliver Loving and Charles Goodnight. Goodnight, a former Texas Ranger, returned to his cattle business after fighting for the Confederacy in the Civil War. He was faced with the dilemma of rounding up his scattered herd and then bringing them to a market somewhere outside the war-ravaged South. He formed a partnership with an older rancher, Loving, who had driven herds to Louisiana, Illinois, and Colorado. Together, in 1866, they left Belknap, Texas, with two thousand head of cattle and arrived in Fort Sumner, New Mexico. This journey established the famous Goodnight-Loving Trail. The biggest debt *Lonesome Dove* owes to the Goodnight/Loving story is in the details of Loving's mortal wounding in a Comanche Indian ambush in New Mexico and Goodnight's fulfillment of his dying wish to be returned to Texas for burial. McMurtry was obviously quite familiar with the best-written account of this episode, *Charles Goodnight: Cowman and Plainsman* (1936) by J. Evetts Haley.

Although McMurtry does not specify a year for the action in *Lonesome Dove,* the reader can safely assume from a character's mention of Custer's fall at the Battle of the Little Bighorn that the events presented occur after 1876. Two former captains in the Texas Rangers, Woodrow Call and Augustus McCrae, have for nearly fifteen years operated the Hat Creek Cattle Company on the banks of the Rio Grande near the town of Lonesome Dove, Texas. McMurtry appropriated the name for the town from a church van he saw in Fort Worth, advertising the "Lonesome Dove Baptist Church." As middle age approaches, Woodrow is restless and yearns for at least one more great adventure. Gus, on the other hand, is content to live out his days on the porch with his jug and memories of their glory days. Into this setting rides Jake Spoon, who had rangered with them but chose not to settle down. Jake, on the run for shooting a dentist in Ft. Smith, Arkansas, regales his old friends with tales of the beauty and availability of the unspoiled country in the Montana Territory. The plan to pull up stakes and establish a cattle empire 2,500 miles to the north is agreed on, and they begin to gather a herd of 3,000 head of cattle and a remuda (most stolen from an old adversary on the Mexican side of the border).

The characteristics, motives, and desires of the participants in this cattle drive are familiar to those who have read McMurtry's previous novels. Woodrow and Gus are strong, reliable men (Homer Bannon and Sam the Lion) who love the same woman (Johnny and Gid). The town whore, Lorena, lives in a Jake Spoon–induced fantasy of life in San Francisco (Jacy Farrow). Newt is a boy in search of a father or at least a father figure (Lonnie, Sonny, and Duane). Jake Spoon is a charming but essentially violent man (Hud). Clara, Gus' love of long ago, is well established in Nebraska, motherly, loving, and able to take on all situations (Aurora Greenway). McMurtry's stock-in-trade eccentrics are in good supply as well: buffalo hunters, riverboat men, and whiskey peddlers. What is less familiar is McMurtry's ability to portray acts of extreme violence and cruelty and the men who carry out those acts. The fearsome Comanche, Blue Duck, and the outlaw Suggs brothers are new types to the McMurtry

cast of characters and are some of the worst villains in literature. McMurtry's strong anti-mythic stand, his refusal to glorify the West and the people who inhabited it, makes this story far more credible than the old familiar adventures of Gene Autry and Roy Rogers.

After a lukewarm reception of his previous nine novels and his book of essays, McMurtry— just shy of fifty years old—received an immediate and positive response. *Lonesome Dove* spent twenty weeks on the *New York Times* Bestseller List, and reviews were, for the most part, adulatory. McMurtry's lecture fee jumped from his usual $1,500 to $4,000, he was featured in *People* magazine, and he was invited to (and attended) the White House reception of the Prince and Princess of Wales. He won the Spur Award of the Western Writers of America, the Texas Institute of Letters Prize for Fiction, and the 1986 Pulitzer Prize in fiction. The other nominated finalists for the Pulitzer were *The Accidental Tourist,* by Anne Tyler and *Continental Drift,* by Russell Banks. McMurtry's Booked Up bookstores (in 1986 there were three others, in Dallas, Houston, and Tucson in addition to the flagship store in Georgetown) were visited by avid fans hoping that the proprietor was in and that he would inscribe their copies of the "big, cowboy book." McMurtry had the habit of rarely staying in one place very long, so finding him in his bookshop was nearly impossible. Determined autograph seekers did, however, leave their books, and McMurtry would inscribe them when he passed through.

Lonesome Dove captured the imagination of people worldwide. Lonesome Dove restaurants sprang up. There were fashions, furniture, and theme parties based on the novel. Sales figures for the novel remained high through the 1990s. The book's popularity was strengthened by the production of a television miniseries written by William Wittliff and starring Tommy Lee Jones as Woodrow Call, Robert Duvall as Gus McCrae, and Robert Urich as Jake Spoon. The series aired on CBS in four parts beginning on February 5, 1989, and was the recipient of seven Emmy Awards, a Peabody Award, and two Golden Globes.

In spite of this critical acclaim, McMurtry was disappointed. Thinking he had written the ultimate anti-western, he discovered that critics and readers took it to be the greatest western adventure novel ever. He has said, "*Lonesome Dove* was a critical book but that's not how it was perceived. The romance of the West is so powerful, you can't really swim against the current. Whatever truth about the West is printed, the legend is always more potent." An attempt to correct this misreading would come in a trilogy published between 1993 and 1997.

Texasville (1987) is the sequel to *The Last Picture Show.* The teenagers of the 1966 novel are now planning their thirtieth high school reunion and Thalia's Centenary Celebration. Sonny Crawford, mayor of Thalia and owner of several businesses, plays a minor part in this book. He is slowly losing his mind and spends a great deal of time sitting in the burned-out shell of the picture show imagining he is watching movies. Danny Deck, the protagonist of *All My Friends Are Going to Be Strangers,* is mentioned in chapter thirteen as a screenwriter who has had a large adobe house built near Thalia overlooking a valley know as "The Sorrows" fifteen years earlier, but who is rarely seen there or in town. The story of *Texasville* primarily focuses on the lives of Duane Moore and his wife, Karla. Duane had struck it rich during the oil boom but is now severely in debt. He relieves his growing depression, a depression that grows not so much out of his economic straits as out of sheer boredom, by sitting in his hot tub and shooting holes in a two-story frontier style doghouse with his .44 Magnum. This is a farcical novel about material decadence; sex and drugs are readily available, and credos are worn stenciled on T-shirts. Neither the novel

nor its Hollywood adaptation was well received. The public wanted more Gus and Woodrow adventures, and *Texasville* was a disappointment.

Film Flam: Essays on Hollywood (1987) is a collection of twenty-one essays, most of which were originally published in *American Film* magazine in the 1970s. They are self-deprecating studies of the film industry and the role of the screenwriter. This slim collection (159 pages) drew slim attention. It is of some value to those who seek more information on McMurtry's ties to Hollywood.

Anything for Billy (1988) was a chance for McMurtry to further explore the relationship that he touched on in *All My Friends Are Going to Be Strangers,* that of a writer and his material. Benjamin J. Sippy, the narrator, is a Philadelphia socialite and devotee of dime novels, those immensely popular turn-of-the-century books that featured such titles as *Solemn Sam, the Sad Man of San Saba, Hurricane Nell, Queen of Saddle and Lasso,* and *Sandycraw, Man of Grit.* Indeed, Sippy is such a fervent fan that when his butler returns from a book-buying errand with the bad news that he could find no new publications featuring Sippy's favorite, Mustang Merle, he begins to write his own version of the Wild West in the comfort of his New England home. When the events of the novel begin, Sippy has become the successful author of sixty-five "booklets." Circumstances allow Sippy to leave Philadelphia and journey west to validate his vision. In El Paso, Texas, he encounters Billy Bone (Billy the Kid), a young gunfighter who is determined to live up to his violent reputation. Through traveling with Billy and McMurtry's usual assortment of bizarre characters, Sippy develops a respect for the truth of the West, which lives in marked contrast to the myth fostered by the very dime novels he and others like him have been writing. When Sippy returns to Philadelphia, he is surprised to find that his publisher has no interest in his new outlook and suggests that he try his hand at writing Pinkerton detective stories. "No one wanted my new knowledge—they only wanted my old, silly heroes—or, failing that, Pinkertons." This exemplifies McMurtry's own struggle with the overwhelming power of myth. McMurtry said in an interview with Mervyn Rothstein in 1988, "If you actually read the biography of any of the famous gunfighters, they led very drab, mostly repetitive, not very exciting lives. But people cherish a certain vision, because it fulfills psychological needs. People need to believe that cowboys are simple, strong and free, and not twisted, fantastic and dumb, as many cowboys I've known have been."

The sequel to *All My Friends Are Going to Be Strangers, Some Can Whistle* (1989) brings back the true McMurtry alter ego, Danny Deck. Since his mysterious disappearance eight novels earlier, his survival and whereabouts had been hinted at in *Texasville.* Now he is back, very alive, and very well off, living on the Texas prairie outside of Thalia in his enormous adobe home "Los Dolores." Deck is now wealthy after penning 198 episodes of a hit family sitcom called "Al and Sal." He spends his semiretirement days roaming the rooms of his hilltop estate in a caftan (Deck's girth, as well as his bank account, has swollen), rewriting the difficult opening line of what he hopes is his next novel. A phone call from Deck's twenty-two-year-old daughter, whom he has never seen, sets the events of this story into action. "Mr. Deck, are you my stinkin' daddy?" The caller is T. R. (Tyler Rose), the one and only issue of Deck's brief marriage to Sally. T. R. had seen an article in *Parade* magazine about Deck. The magazine had ranked her father as the "richest writer in the world." T. R., who is working in Houston at a Mr. Burger for minimum wage and raising two children alone, calls not to demand that Deck correct this economic imbalance, but simply to tell him what she thinks of his behavior in "abandoning" her. She hangs up, and Deck is filled with fatherly concerns. He tracks her down,

and after receiving forgiveness, brings her, her children, and a sizable entourage of her friends back to Los Dolores where he can provide her with a life to which she would like to become accustomed.

McMurtry has always favored his female characters. After creating the idealized but hardly ideal Molly in *Leaving Cheyenne,* all of his women from that point on are strong, vital, vivacious, and immensely likeable whether they be mothers, grandmothers, whores, or simply lost children. McMurtry's men, however, never fare as well. They are either unbearably ignorant and violent, living by a code of conduct that no longer applies, or they are dreamy obsessives who are extremely irritating in their helplessness. Both types receive what they lack and sorely need from splendid women who appear at just the right moment in their lives. T. R., and all the things that accompany and therefore create T. R., rescues Danny Deck from his pointlessness.

Some Can Whistle is McMurtry's only father/daughter novel, and it contains some of his finest writing. Early in the novel, having only heard his daughter's voice on the telephone, Deck muses,

> I was beginning to love her voice. If I'm a connoisseur of anything, it's the female voice. Through the years—fifty-one of them now—the voices of women have been my wine: my claret, my Chardonnay, my Chablis. And now I had found a new wine, one with depth and color, bite, clarity, body. I was lapping it up, ready to get drunk on it.

McMurtry has said that he has never written a book about the West that was not elegiac. In *Buffalo Girls* (1990), the elegy is not for the passing of an age alone, but the passing of its most colorful characters as well. Annie Oakley, Wild Bill Hickock, Buffalo Bill Cody, Sitting Bull, Calamity Jane, and Ned Buntline are the historic figures who populate, along with some McMurtry creations, this novel of extinction. Calamity Jane (Martha Jane Canary) writes letters to her daughter Janey, whom she claims was fathered by Wild Bill Hickock and who may or may not have existed, recounting her adventuresome life. Calamity realizes that that era is coming to an end, and when Buffalo Bill Cody reappears in her life, she tries for one more escapade by signing on with Cody's Wild West Show.

Cody, like McMurtry, had a clear sense of what had happened to the West. He knew very well that the characters who bemoan their lost way of life are the very ones responsible for that loss. They are like children who deliberately broke their toys and now weep because they have nothing with which to play. Cody's solution was to re-create the lost times with the very people who lived them, present them in an adventurous traveling extravaganza throughout America and Europe, and thereby preserve it in the collective imagination.

SEQUELS AND PREQUELS

In 1991 McMurtry, who had been working at a breakneck pace (publishing eight books since 1982 in addition to serving as president of American PEN, expanding his book business, and other activities), suffered a massive heart attack and underwent quadruple bypass surgery. While recovering at the Tucson home of writer Diana Ossana, he fell into a severe depression that lasted for close to four years. McMurtry refers to this devastating personal crisis as "the change." In 1997 he said, "Suddenly I found myself becoming an outline, and then what was within that outline vanished." For months, then years, McMurtry did little more than lie on the white couch in Ossana's living room and stare out the window at the Catalina Mountains. He was no longer able to concentrate on the words well enough to read for pleasure, but he could still write every day for close to an hour and a half before returning to the white couch. The work McMurtry managed to create on his old Hermes manual typewriter in

Ossana's kitchen was an unrelenting grim fictional account of his own fragmentation, *Streets of Laredo* (1993).

During this time of recovery, the sequel to *Terms of Endearment* was published. In *The Evening Star* (1992) Aurora Greenway, now in her seventies, is still pursuing inadequate men and is now involving herself in the lives of her three grandchildren, whom she has raised following her daughter, Emma's death from cancer. This is not McMurtry at his best. The novel's six hundred pages are a story of sex as a motivating factor in all the character's lives occasionally sprinkled with sentimental deaths. What notice was given to the book and its Hollywood visualization was slight and harsh.

The first true work to emerge from McMurtry's recovery period was *Streets of Laredo*. The events in this novel take place some twenty years after Woodrow Call returned home at the end of *Lonesome Dove*. Now an old man but still retaining the skills of a former Texas Ranger, Woodrow has been hired by a railroad company to track down and eliminate a fearsome Mexican train robber known as Joey Garza. This sounds like a standard McMurtry western epic, but there is a difference. Where *Lonesome Dove* was heroic and vast, *Streets of Laredo* is savage and austere. The violence is almost self-parody, and the characters are so overdrawn as to be almost cartoon-like. As mentioned earlier, McMurtry was disappointed by what he considered the public's misreading of *Lonesome Dove*. Here, and in two other western novels that follow, he attempts to strip away any romantic notions one may have of the Old West as a result of his Pulitzer Prize–winning book. In the end, Woodrow/McMurtry is shot to pieces, losing an arm and a leg, and left to be cared for by a woman and her children. Ossana, who retyped the work into a computer, remembers that part of the book: "I couldn't even type. I kept thinking that it was Larry. This is how he feels about himself. It was just horribly sad."

Completing *Streets of Laredo* did not lift his

depression; indeed, he was convinced he would never write again. Ossana kept him active during this dangerous period by coaxing him to assist her in the writing of a screenplay based on the life of Charles Arthur "Pretty Boy" Floyd, the Depression Era bank robber. This collaborative effort seemed to bring McMurtry out of the worst of his depression. The novel that grew out of that screenplay (the movie remains unmade), *Pretty Boy Floyd* (1994), tells the story of a poor Oklahoma boy who leaves his family and travels to St. Louis, Missouri, to find work. There, in 1925, he meets Bill "The Killer" Miller and gets involved in an armored car robbery. Despite warnings to lie low for a while, Floyd goes on a wild spending spree, is caught, is convicted of robbery, and spends four years in the state penitentiary. His time in the penitentiary teaches Floyd how to become a better outlaw. On release he meets, through a comic misadventure, and teams up with a rodeo cowboy named George Birdwell. With Birdwell, Floyd puts his improved skills to work in a series of small town bank robberies, vowing to never spend time in jail again. His good looks and reputation for kindness to his victims earn him the nickname "Pretty Boy." After J. Edgar Hoover's G-men gun down John Dillinger in the summer of 1934, Pretty Boy is elevated to the rank of Public Enemy Number One by the headline-hungry Hoover, and his life comes to its predictable close. The novel was fairly well received. The theme is typical of McMurtry's work; it explores how the public's love of and need for mythical heroes is so strong that it can turn a violent, small-time petty crook into a Robin Hood-like "hero of the common man." McMurtry fans were curious, however, about Diana Ossana. Who is she, they wanted to know, to share authorship with a Pulitzer Prize winner? Why would McMurtry need a cowriter? Some critics suspected that McMurtry was trying to enhance the career of a longtime friend, but such was not the case. Ossana's interest, according to the Horowitz interview, was only in reviv-

ing McMurtry's talents, and she offered to keep her name off the book. McMurtry refused. He insisted on recognition of her participation and had her accompany him on the book's promotional tour.

Pretty Boy Floyd was followed by the publication of *The Late Child* (1995). This novel is the sequel to *The Desert Rose,* the weakest effort in the so-called Trash Trilogy. It returns the reader to the hectic life of three-time Miss Las Vegas Showgirl, Harmony. She has just learned that her daughter, Pepper, has died in New York City. Harmony and her five-year-old son, Eddie (the "late" child), decide to go home to Oklahoma via New York, collecting along the way the usual caravan of McMurtry oddballs. Fans and critics were not pleased.

Another curiosity followed later the same year, *Dead Man's Walk* (1995). A prequel to *Lonesome Dove, Dead Man's Walk* is yet another attempt by McMurtry to completely erase the romantic notions of the Old West created by the public's misreading of *Lonesome Dove.* The novel is set in the days of the independent Republic of Texas. Young Woodrow Call and Augustus McCrae have enlisted in the Texas Rangers under the command of a land pirate and self-appointed colonel who is determined to wrest the riches of Santa Fe, in the New Mexico territory, from the control of the Mexicans. What follows is the usual McMurtry recipe for westerns: tests of manhood and unfathomable acts of cruelty and violence. The cast of characters who provide the challenges to the Ranger band includes the supremely vicious Comanche chief, Buffalo Hump (father of *Lonesome Dove*'s Blue Duck); a gruesome Apache, Gomez; and Major Laroche, a Frenchman serving in the Mexican army. The expedition fails, and the surviving Rangers are forced to march across two hundred miles of New Mexico badlands known as la Jornada del Muerto (the dead man's walk). At the end of this journey, they are held prisoner in a leper colony near El Paso. Here the Rangers, and a fat and sassy whore named Matilda Jane Roberts, who has followed the expeditions and somehow survived, are rescued by an English aristocrat, Lady Carey, who is herself ravaged by leprosy. This novel pushes the limits of excess, even for McMurtry. However, by this time, he has a devoted following who flock to read any of his books that chronicle the adventures of Call and McCrae.

McMurtry and Ossana continued their collaborative efforts throughout this period, co-penning the screenplays for *Streets of Laredo* and *Dead Man's Walk,* which were produced by CBS for television in 1996. *Buffalo Girls* and *The Evening Star,* screenplays by McMurtry, were also produced at this time. Another McMurtry/Ossana screenplay resulted in the novel *Zeke and Ned* (1997).

The story told in *Zeke and Ned* is a reworking of actual historic events that were chronicled by Robert J. Conley, historian for the Cherokee Nation of Oklahoma, in his novels *Ned Christie's War* (1991) and *Zeke Proctor, Cherokee Outlaw* (1994). Ezekiel (Zeke) Proctor and Ned Christie were the last of the great Cherokee warriors. Zeke had survived the infamous relocation of American Indians from Georgia to the Indian Territory west of Arkansas, the "Trail of Tears," and now, with his son-in-law Ned, he seeks to preserve the cultural autonomy of his people in the fading days of the nineteenth century. Zeke accidentally shoots the woman he loves, a woman he had intended to bring to his home as a second wife. The family of the woman decrees her death must be avenged, and the stage is set. Warfare within the Cherokee Nation brings on the attempted imposition of white man's law, culminating in a mountaintop standoff with Zeke and Ned on one side and federal marshals on the other. The novel received harsh criticism, especially from members of the Cherokees who felt the book misrepresented their cultural heroes. However, it must be remembered, McMurtry's purpose in his stories of the West is to shed its heroes of mythic ro-

mance and to portray flesh-and-blood men and women who possess human flaws and failings.

Comanche Moon (1997) is both a sequel to *Dead Man's Walk* and a prequel to *Lonesome Dove.* Every novel McMurtry has published since his heart attack, surgery, and depression, except for the two collaborations with Ossana, has been a prequel or sequel. The physical ordeal and its subsequent depression perhaps alerted McMurtry to the fact of his own mortality. He seems to be aggressively trying to tie up loose ends and put the various houses of his characters in order. It is rumored that McMurtry intends to put his own house in order and settle some accounts with his hometown in a collection of essays that was scheduled to be published by Simon & Schuster in November 1999, entitled *Walter Benjamin at the Dairy Queen: Reflections at Sixty and Beyond.*

This novel, the final volume in the *Lonesome Dove* tetralogy, is quite possibly McMurtry's final western. In the Horowitz interview he said, "I am bored to death with the 19th-century West. I wrote more about it than I ever intended to." The story is set in the decade from the late 1850s through the late 1860s and follows Call and McCrae and their Harvard-educated commanding officer, Inish Scull, as they seek a notorious Comanche horse thief, Kicking Wolf. Kicking Wolf steals Scull's prized mount in a humiliating fashion and Scull, in a moment of true cowboy-god hubris, determines to bring in the outlaw and rescue his horse single-handedly. He promotes Call and McCrae to the rank of captain and sends them back to Austin. There, the governor orders the two men to go in search of Scull and return him safely. The usual pursuits and confrontations occur. Buffalo Hump and Blue Duck create difficulties, and a new villain, Ahumado, known as the "Black Vaquero," is introduced. Public and critical response to this book was, for the most part, favorable. Fans of Call and McCrae were pleased to have many of their questions answered regarding the action preceding *Lonesome Dove.*

In 1999 Viking published its first two volumes in the Penguin Lives series. The short (less than two hundred pages) biographies, edited by James Atlas, were projected to present a wide range of figures—from Saint Augustine to Marlon Brando. The initial volumes are the lives of Marcel Proust and Crazy Horse. With the scant information available, McMurtry, who was originally asked to write a volume on General George Armstrong Custer, brings to life the legendary Sioux warrior. Peter Ackroyd, writing for the *New York Times,* January 10, 1999, had this to say about Mc-Murtry's effort: "This is fine writing, and suggests once again that history and biography can best be restored by the creative imagination."

Published a few months after *Crazy Horse, Duane's Depressed* (1999) brings to a conclusion the story that began with *The Last Picture Show* and continued through *Texasville.* In this novel, Duane Moore is sixty-two (McMurtry's age) and a grandfather. Realizing he has spent the better part of his life doing what was expected of him, he retreats to take a long hard look at himself. He decides to give up the use of his pickup truck (an act of supreme rebellion in Texas) and walk wherever he needs to go. This is his first act of letting go and "living deliberately," as he has learned from reading Thoreau. A psychologist, Honor Carmichael, helps him in this process by making Proust's *Remembrance of Things Past* required reading. She explains to Duane that "it's still the greatest catalogue of the varieties of disappointments human beings feel." The novel asks and attempts to answer the question: If the unexamined life is not worth living, what does one do when, upon examination, that life seems worthless? Dr. Carmichael sums it up this way, "People who realize they had the capacity to do more than they've done usually feel cheated," she said. "Even if mainly they have only themselves to blame, they still feel cheated when they come

around a curve in the road and start thinking about the end of their life."

Though it contains the usual assortment of McMurtry's stock-in-trade characters with all of their unusual behavior and ribald humor, *Duane's Depressed* is a subdued book. It is a novel by an author who, if not "in winter," is certainly "in late autumn." McMurtry, as Duane, seems to have reached a point in the process of life when the production may cease and the harvest may be reaped and enjoyed.

A BOOK TOWN

In the late 1990s, McMurtry lived almost full time in Archer City, in a large estate built in the 1920s. It is a home he had admired in his boyhood, and he has filled it with his personal library of well over sixteen thousand books. Since 1988 he has been buying vacant property along South Center Street to house his growing book business. His lifelong dream of creating a book town such as the famous Hay-On-Wye, Wales, is becoming a reality. McMurtry closed the shops he owned in Dallas and Houston and combined that inventory with that of his Archer City shop, the Blue Pig, which was operated by his sister, Sue Deets. The collection, housed in four buildings near the courthouse, is divided into subjects ranging from poetry to westerns and from biography to music. There are enough books to provide each of the small town's residents (population just under two thousand) with 150 books each and leave some left over. The scattered shops, collectively known as Booked Up, attract the serious collector as well as the curious tourist. The resulting economic growth has spawned some oddities—accommodations can be found at the "Lonesome Dove Inn," a bed and breakfast, and the "Texasville Café" serves a good menu of Texas fare. The town's lone Dairy Queen, however, remains the true social hub. McMurtry is the driving force behind a project to restore the Royal Theater, the "picture show" that played a central part in the lives of the characters in the Thalia Trilogy. In an interview with Malcolm Jones for *Newsweek,* McMurtry said, "Susan Sontag tells me that I live in my own theme park."

In 1997 the McMurtry Center of the Arts and Humanities, established by a longtime Wichita Falls resident and patron of the arts, opened on the campus of Midwestern State University in Wichita Falls. The idea for the center grew out of a summer writing program taught to local teenagers by McMurtry and other authors. The center's purpose is to support the study of writing, literature, drama, and art. Enrichment is thereby offered, through McMurtry's efforts and contributions, to the present-day Lonnies, Sonnys, Duanes, and Jacys of Archer City, who would otherwise grow up in a bookless, culturally impoverished, small town in north central Texas.

Selected Bibliography

WORKS OF LARRY MCMURTRY

NOVELS
Horseman, Pass By. New York: Harper, 1961.
Leaving Cheyenne. New York: Harper & Row, 1963.
The Last Picture Show. New York: Dial Press, 1966.
Moving On. New York: Simon & Schuster, 1970.
All My Friends Are Going to Be Strangers. New York: Simon & Schuster, 1972.
Terms of Endearment. New York: Simon & Schuster, 1975.
Somebody's Darling. New York: Simon & Schuster, 1978.
Cadillac Jack. New York: Simon & Schuster, 1982.
The Desert Rose. New York: Simon & Schuster, 1983.
Lonesome Dove. New York: Simon & Schuster, 1985.
Texasville. New York: Simon & Schuster, 1987.
Anything for Billy. New York: Simon & Schuster, 1988.

Some Can Whistle. New York: Simon & Schuster, 1989.
Buffalo Girls. New York: Simon & Schuster, 1990.
The Evening Star. New York: Simon & Schuster, 1992.
Streets of Laredo. New York: Simon & Schuster, 1993.
The Late Child. New York: Simon & Schuster, 1995.
Dead Man's Walk. New York: Simon & Schuster, 1995.
Comanche Moon. New York: Simon & Schuster, 1997.
Duane's Depressed. New York: Simon & Schuster, 1999.

BIOGRAPHIES
Crazy Horse. New York: Viking, 1999.

ESSAYS
In a Narrow Grave: Essays on Texas. Austin: Encino Press, 1968.
"It Is Always We Rambled: An Essay on Rodeo." Santa Barbara: Noel Young, 1974.
"The Texas Moon, and Elsewhere." *Atlantic* 235: 29–36 (March 1975).
"Ever a Bridegroom: Reflections on the Failure of Texas Literature." *Texas Observer,* October 23, 1981.
Film Flam: Essays on Hollywood. New York: Simon & Schuster, 1987.
Walter Benjamin at the Dairy Queen: Reflections at Sixty and Beyond. New York: Simon & Schuster, 1999.

COLLABORATIONS AND OTHERS

Daughter of the Tejas. Greenwich, Conn.: New York Graphic Society, 1965. (Ghostwritten for author Ophelia Ray by Larry McMurtry.)
Pretty Boy Floyd. New York: Simon & Schuster, 1994 (Larry McMurtry and Diana Ossana).
Zeke and Ned. New York: Simon & Schuster, 1997 (Larry McMurtry and Diana Ossana).

BIBLIOGRAPHY

Peavy, Charles D. "A Larry McMurtry Bibliography." *Western American Literature* 8: 235–248 (Fall 1968).

BIOGRAPHICAL AND CRITICAL STUDIES

Adams, Robert M. "The Bard of Wichita Falls." *New York Review of Books,* August 13, 1987: 39–41.

Busby, Mark. "McMurtry, Larry (Jeff)." In *Twentieth-Century Western Writers.* Edited by James Vinson. Detroit: Gale, 1982. Pp. 534–536.

Clifford, Craig Edward. *In the Deep Heart's Core: Reflections on Life, Letters, and Texas.* College Station: Texas A&M University Press, 1985.

Greene, A. C. *The Fifty Best Books on Texas.* Dallas: Pressworks, 1981.

———. "The Texas Literati: Whose Home Is This Range Anyhow?" *New York Times Book Review,* September 15, 1985.

Landless, Thomas. *Larry McMurtry.* Southwest Writers Series. Austin: Steck-Vaughn, 1969.

Neinstein, Raymond L. *The Ghost Country: A Study in the Novels of Larry McMurtry.* Modern Authors Monograph Series 1. Berkeley: Creative Arts, 1976.

Peavy, Charles D. *Larry McMurtry.* Twayne's United States Authors Series 291. Boston: Twayne, 1977.

Reynolds, R. Clay, ed. *Taking Stock: A Larry McMurtry Casebook.* Dallas: Southern Methodist University Press, 1989.

Stegner, Wallace. "Born a Square: The Westerner's Dilemma." *Atlantic* 213: 46–50 (January 1964).

———. "History, Myth, and the Western Writer." *American West* 4.2: 61–62 + (1967).

Stout, Janis P. "Journeying as a Metaphor for Cultural Loss in the Novels of Larry McMurtry." *Western American Literature* 11: 37–50 (1976).

INTERVIEWS

Bennet, Patrick. "Larry McMurtry: Thalia, Houston, and Hollywood." *Talking with Texas Writers: Twelve Interviews.* College Station: Texas A&M University Press, 1980. Pp. 15–36.

Crooks, Alan. "Larry McMurtry—A Writer in Transition: An Essay-Review." *Western American Literature* 7: 151–155 (1972).

Horowitz, Mark. "Larry McMurtry's Dream Job." *The New York Times Magazine,* December 7, 1997.

Jones, Malcolm. "The Poet Lariat." *Newsweek,* January 11, 1999.

Rothstein, Mervyn. "A Texan Who Likes to Deflate the Legends of the Golden West." *New York Times,* November 1, 1988.

FILMS BASED ON THE WORKS OF LARRY MCMURTRY

Buffalo Girls. Screenplay by Larry McMurtry and Cynthia Whitcomb. Directed by Rod Hardy. CBS, 1995.

Dead Man's Walk. Screenplay by Larry McMurtry and Diana Ossana. Directed by Yves Simoneau. CBS, 1996.

The Evening Star. Screenplay by Robert Harling. Directed by Robert Harling. Paramount, 1996.

Hud. Screenply by Irving Ravetch and Harriet Frank Jr. Directed by Martin Ritt. Paramount, 1963.

Larry McMurtry's Streets of Laredo. Screenplay by Larry McMurtry and Diana Ossana. Directed by Joseph Sargent. RHI Entertainment, 1996.

The Last Picture Show. Screenplay by Larry McMurtry and Peter Bogdanovich. Directed by Peter Bogdanovich. Columbia, 1971.

Lonesome Dove. Screenplay by William D. Witliff. Directed by Simon Wincer. CBS, 1989.

Lovin' Molly. Screenplay by Stephen Friedman. Directed by Sidney Lumet. Trimark, 1974.

Terms of Endearment. Screenplay by James L. Brooks. Directed by James L. Brooks. Paramount, 1983.

Texasville. Screenplay by Peter Bogdanovich. Directed by Peter Bogdanovich. Columbia, 1990.

—CHARLES R. BAKER

Tim O'Brien

1946–

*T*IM O'BRIEN IS generally known as a Vietnam War writer, but he is fundamentally a moralist—a moralist who refuses to provide any single, simple morals. He believes in storytelling, but in storytelling as a way to confront the ethical complexity of the real modern world—a complexity that perhaps is best illustrated at war in Southeast Asia but is no less evident at home in the family. For O'Brien, the "true core of fiction" is "the exploration of substantive, important human values." In a 1994 interview O'Brien said, "Fiction in general, and war stories in particular, serve a moral function, but not to give you lessons, not to tell you how to act. Rather, they present you with philosophical problems, then ask you to try to adjudicate them in some way or another." In the same interview, O'Brien said, "All stories have at their heart an essential moral function, which isn't only to put yourself in someone else's shoes, but to go beyond that and put yourself into someone else's moral framework."

O'Brien even goes so far to as to say that style is secondary, teachable, and (almost) an overrated gimmick. O'Brien's style at moments owes an obvious debt to Ernest Hemingway—to the point of intentional parody in *Northern Lights* (1975)—but O'Brien's devices and moral settings come from William Faulkner, Vladimir Na-

bokov, and Kurt Vonnegut. His diction is simple, his sentences are rhythmic, and his characters have distinct speaking voices, but they also represent values. According to O'Brien, "Stylistic problems *can* be solved: by writing better, by recognizing your own faults and getting rid of them. What *can't* be learned, however, is passion for ideas—substance."

Storytelling is another passion, and one interviewer for the *Boston Globe* described O'Brien (who is childless) as discussing his craft "with the same open-eyed delight that other people use to talk about their kids." O'Brien told a *New York Times* reporter that "Storytelling is the essential human activity. The harder the situation, the more essential it is." This storytelling never ends. There is always more to be said about any event. When someone speaks they are often "mostly right. Not entirely." In seeking truth, O'Brien never stops seeking. He revolves ideas and perspectives around and around and around. He revises; he even revised *Going After Cacciato* (1978) after it won the National Book Award. In a 1990 *New York Times* interview O'Brien explained that "As you play with stories you find that whatever is said is not sufficient to the task." Unlike a character in the short story "Loon Point" (in *Esquire,* January 1993), who is silent because "there was nothing she could say that was entirely true," O'Brien keeps writing fiction in an attempt to reach truth or truths. He is an old-fashioned postmodernist.

O'Brien's writing organizes itself around a familiar set of oppositions: war versus peace, love versus hate, men versus women, reality versus imagination, sanity versus insanity, cowardice versus courage, safety versus danger, and change versus stasis. But in each of these cases, O'Brien is finally more interested in the way oppositions break down. For example, although he was against the war and claims he was a terrible soldier who felt only fear, he writes, "Vietnam was more than terror. For me, at least, Vietnam was partly love." One of his more famous lines is from *The Things They Carried* (1990): "I was a coward. I went to the war."

When exploring issues such as courage, love, and the fear of nuclear war, O'Brien holds up the real and symbolic representatives of these issues in different positions and in different lights. He rotates them, places them in varying relationships with each other, and describes them in the speech of different characters. A Vietnamese man in *Going After Cacciato* says, "things may be viewed from many angles. From down below, or from inside out, you often discover entirely new understandings." O'Brien's commitment to understanding every idea and its multiple alternatives means that his novels villainize nobody, but they also sanctify nobody. Steven Kaplan wrote that O'Brien "constantly circles around and around a given theme or idea, but he never conclusively zeroes in on it to offer a final statement." O'Brien develops all the positions he can and leaves his readers to make their own judgments.

O'Brien returns again and again to the complex relationship among reality, the imagination, and language. He examines most extensively the roles of fiction and memory in building the future as well as narrating and making meaning of the past. Separating himself from the word games of William Gass and Jorge Luis Borges, O'Brien main-

tains a primary interest in how humans make their moral choices and a compelling curiosity about truth—not "actual literal truth" but the "emotional qualities" of truth. And perhaps surprisingly, O'Brien believes that "exercising the imagination is the main way of finding truth" and meaning.

Certainly experience and language shape our imaginative lives, but O'Brien also contends that our imagination shapes our realities. In his first book, *If I Die in a Combat Zone* (1973), O'Brien suggests that our decisions are largely guided by the language we use to ask ourselves the questions. In *The Nuclear Age* (1978), O'Brien writes, "Our lives are shaped in some small measure by the scope of our daydreams. If we can imagine happiness, we might find it." In *Tomcat in Love* (1998), his main character (and narrator) is a pathological liar who is always telling at least part of the truth. Tom's imaginative shapings of his experience heavily influence his current and future relationships. In an interview with Larry McCaffery, O'Brien explained, "All of our decision-making—opposing a war, marrying certain people, the jobs we accept or refuse—is at least partly determined by the imaginative faculty." He observed that "Those soldiers who actually did desert were able to imagine a happy ending to it." O'Brien elaborated on this point in a 1994 *Modern Fiction Studies* interview with Eric James Schroeder: "The imagination is a heuristic tool that we can use to help ourselves set goals. We use the outcomes of our imaginings." O'Brien's main interests meet in the matrix of the war: in "The Violent Vet" (*Esquire,* December 1979), he writes, "In memory, in imagination, and in concrete reality, a war goes on and on in its consequences."

Although O'Brien's imagination and his diligence as a writer and reviser are the primary forces behind his success, he says himself that his life experiences, particularly the Vietnam War, influenced—and even brought about—his writing career. Although he takes issue with the limiting designation "war writer," he concedes, "I came to writing because of the war. When I returned from Vietnam, I had something to say." O'Brien expresses his goals in his memoir *If I Die:* "I would write about the army. Expose the brutality and injustice and stupidity and arrogance of wars and men who fight in them." Extending this goal farther, O'Brien celebrates the individual conscience—the side of himself he didn't dare listen to when he succumbed to the draft—while recognizing and not devaluing other, often contrary, responsibilities.

Tobey C. Herzog, whose critical study *Tim O'Brien* (1997) provides the most complete biographical sketch on O'Brien, discussed O'Brien's life in terms of the roles he has fulfilled: as son, soldier, and author. O'Brien has also been a brother, patriot, thinker, reader, friend, teacher, leader, and husband. In his writing, he has explored many of these roles and the way the responsibilities to others and to ourselves have to be negotiated with our individual search for contentedness and meaning. In *Going After Cacciato* O'Brien states, "The real issue is how to find felicity within limits. Within the context of our obligations to other people." In addition to his Vietnam experience, O'Brien's writing has been influenced by his familiarity with the lakes and woods of Minnesota, his childhood love of magic, and his probing of relationships such as the one with his thoughtful, literary-minded, alcoholic father. O'Brien's imagination, though, is the core of his work. His imagination asks questions, wonders what would happen *if,* probes why things are the way they are. These questions lead to scenarios and stories; they open up compelling mysteries and develop into plots that never completely lose their enigmatic qualities.

Some unenigmatic facts. The son of William Timothy O'Brien and Ava Eleanor Schultz O'Brien, William Timothy O'Brien Jr. was born in Austin, Minnesota, on October 1, 1946. Raised in Minnesota, Tim O'Brien graduated summa cum laude and Phi Beta Kappa from St. Paul's Macalaster College with a Bachelor of Arts in political science and a scholarship to start graduate school at Harvard University. At Macalaster, O'Brien was president of the student body his senior year and was mildly involved in Macalaster's already mild version of the antiwar movement. Immediately after graduating he received his draft notice, and he entered the army in August 1968. He was assigned to the 46th Infantry, 198th Infantry Brigade, 5th Battalion, Alpha Company, 3rd squad (as is Paul Berlin in *Going After Cacciato*). O'Brien spent seven months in combat and received the Combat Infantry Badge, a Purple Heart, and the Bronze Star. Sergeant O'Brien finished his 365-day (plus one month) tour of duty in Vietnam as a clerk.

During several years as a graduate student studying government at Harvard University (1970–1976), O'Brien took a year off to work as a general-assignment reporter on the national desk for the *Washington Post* (1973–1974), wrote and published *If I Die in a Combat Zone* and *Northern Lights,* and married Ann Wellard (they were divorced in 1995). He revisited Vietnam, including the My Lai area, in 1994. In addition to teaching at places such as Middlebury College's Breadloaf Writer's Conference, O'Brien has won awards from the Guggenheim Foundation, the National Endowment for the Arts, the Massachusetts Arts and Humanities Foundation, the American Academy of Arts and Letters, and the Vietnam Veterans of America.

O'Brien's work has won many literary awards: two short stories from *Going After Cacciato* won the prestigious O. Henry Memorial Awards (1976 and 1978), and *Going After Cacciato* won the even more prestigious National Book Award in 1979. The story "The Things They Carried" won the National Magazine Award in Fiction (1989), and the novel of that title received the *Chicago Tribune*'s Heartland Prize (1990), the Melcher

Award (1991), and the French *Prix du Meilleur Livre Étranger* (1992). *The Things They Carried* was also a finalist for the Pulitzer Prize (1990) and the National Book Critics Circle Award. The *New York Times* recommended it as one of the ten best works of fiction in 1990. *Time* magazine labeled *In the Lake of the Woods* (1994) the best work of fiction in 1994, and this same best-selling novel received the 1995 James Fenimore Cooper Prize for the best historical novel. *In the Lake of the Woods* has been adapted into a made-for-television movie and was a Book-of-the-Month Club selection.

IF I DIE IN A COMBAT ZONE

O'Brien's first book, *If I Die in a Combat Zone,* is his memoir of his experiences leading up to and in Vietnam and his ruminations about those experiences. Only briefly alluding to the way his ideas of war and manhood were spawned by national self-congratulatory and selective hindsight about World War II, O'Brien relates his physical and mental experiences between August 1968 and March 1970: induction, basic training, advanced infantry training, duties with Alpha Company and at battalion headquarters, and the trip home after being stationed in Vietnam for his 365 days. O'Brien wonders how other war writers such as Ernest Hemingway and World War II correspondent Ernie Pyle managed to write so much about war without answering two compelling questions: (1) When is war right? and (2) What do soldiers think to themselves? These are O'Brien's big issues: moral decisions and the interior life of the individual.

To once-unresolvable arguments about the Vietnam War, O'Brien offers thoughtfulness. One voice says, "No war is worth losing your life for" and another argues that "no war is worth losing your country for." Even after military service, O'Brien does not claim to be an authority; he does not offer answers. He longingly imagines

being able to "integrate it all to persuade my younger brother and perhaps some others to say no to wrong wars." He writes that it would also "be fine to confirm the old beliefs about war: It's horrible, but it's a crucible of men and events and, in the end, it makes more of a man out of you." But he cannot do either one; "none of this seems right." Instead he writes, "Now, war ended, all I am left with are simple, unprofound scraps of truth . . . some men think war is sometimes necessary and others don't and most don't care." He asks, "Is that the stuff for a morality lesson, even for a theme?"

As he discusses the war, he wonders what the issue is, what the deciding priority should be. He suggests that a decision rests on the words in which we couch the question—for example, is the Vietnam War an issue of U.S. imperialism, communist expansion, loyal patriotism, or personal survival? This theme reappears in later works, including his 1998 novel, *Tomcat in Love.* All the words are almost right and also just miss the truth of the situation. Most true statements are "half-truths" that can only be offset with other "half-truths." Thus, he concludes that facts can be accurate but unprofound: the truth of every matter may be that no meaning, no answers, no words, are ever quite final. There is always more to be seen and said.

O'Brien takes his conscience and his thoughts seriously. In this first book, ideas, traditions, and people all pull at him. Unlike one character who "just grinned and gave flippant, smiling, say-nothing answers" such as "it was best not to worry," O'Brien is not flippant. Instead, he is deeply thoughtful. This seriousness about the self—the soul, interiority, and personal responsibility—is not only inspiring but surprisingly pleasant. Our world tends to broadcast flippancy and thoughtlessness; sound bites are necessarily only very partial truths, if that. In a world in which people tend to revere the CEO precept, "do something, even if it's wrong," O'Brien's tendency is to do nothing until he knows what's right. Here is a good man, his reviewers have asserted, a man who struggles with the concepts "right" and "wrong" as well as "heroism" and "cowardice." His honest meditations, the attention and respect he gives his own thoughts, represent the human mind in all its stubbornness and vulnerability. Even in a "good war" such as World War II, according to Paul Fussell in *Wartime,* "things are conventionally asserted to be true which smart people know are false." In Vietnam, O'Brien is profoundly confused: trying to trust in the good will and good intentions of his family, neighbors, and even superior officers, his mind and heart are in ceaseless, dogged turmoil.

In resistance to the mindlessness and anonymity of basic training, O'Brien thinks and talks and tries to "see through ideology" with another thinker, Erik Hansen. While nodding respectfully toward friends who found "easy paths" out of military duty, and wishing he had had the courage to go AWOL before being sent overseas, O'Brien describes his quiet verbal protest. He writes, "Our private conversations were the cornerstone of the resistance, perhaps because talking about basic training in careful, honest words was by itself an insult to army education. Simply to think and talk and try to understand was evidence that we were not cattle or machines." He and Erik are accused of "making some love" when they chat, which goes against one of the implicit lessons of basic training: "There is no thing named love in the world." One of the first things he learns at Alpha Company is that language can be made to control and limit the scope of human emotion and evil-doing (men get "wasted" or "fucked up," not murdered or mangled). O'Brien's thoughtful and humanizing language is an antidote to the vivid but finally euphemistic language of the military.

O'Brien's first work was largely praised by the critics, who appreciated the value he places on communication and accepted the work as a "fictionalized memoir" more often than an "autobiography." In his book *Understanding Tim O'Brien,* however, Steve Kaplan refers to the work as a novel, a collection of short stories, a war memoir, a confession, and even an example of New Journalism. O'Brien himself calls it a "non-fiction personal narrative," which would clearly define the book's relation to fiction if "personal" didn't also imply a singular, internal, and imaginative eye, and if "narrative" were not also a term for the purposeful construction of stories.

Several reviewers described the pleasure of reading a book by "someone exceptional," someone "educated, intelligent, reflective, and thoroughly nice." One surprising characteristic of this "nice" author/narrator is that he confesses but does not excuse his own self-betrayal, and he does not conceal his own awful hatreds and evil brutalities. In the *New York Times Magazine* autobiographical article entitled "The Vietnam in Me," O'Brien writes, "After fire fights, after friends died, there was . . . a great deal of anger—black, fierce, hurting anger—the kind you want to take out on whatever presents itself. . . . I know the boil that precedes butchery." Having "met" such an exceptionally nice author, we hear his antiwar message even more clearly: even reasonable men can feel enough hatred to do these things. O'Brien explores the origins of evil and finds it in himself and others, but he blames the system of war, which creates the necessary conditions: loneliness, attachment to buddies, misunderstanding of the enemy, fear, the Vietnam institution of the "body count" as an index of success, and so on. Concerned that "Evil has no place, it seems, in our national mythology," O'Brien forces his readers to scrutinize evil, to fill in the "ellipses" with which we usually screen it from our attention.

NORTHERN LIGHTS

O'Brien's first novel, *Northern Lights,* is the story of Paul Milton Perry—married, thirty, a minor official for the Department of Agriculture—

and his brother "Harvey the Bull"—ten years younger and a Vietnam veteran with one glass eye. From the older brother's only slightly more binocular perspective, Harvey is the war hero, the outdoorsman, the favorite of their now-deceased but still overbearing father.

The most flawed of O'Brien's novels, *Northern Lights* is gratingly repetitive and yet gains a valuable and expressive texture and depth that would be lost without that forceful, dogged rhythm. After reading pages about cross country skiing through a wilderness area that does not correspond to the old, laminated map the brothers carefully study, one begins to appreciate both the symbolic and physical aspects of their wilderness adventure. While readers can tell what's right and wrong in a conceptual and theoretical sense, perhaps according to precepts that have been passed down to them through the ages, they may not be able to figure out how actual situations correspond to those precepts. Geographically speaking, a map can show someone how to get from the lake to the road, but what does he do if it is not clear how the frozen lake by which he is standing corresponds to any of the lakes on the map? Devoting half a novel to a month of confused skiing tests O'Brien's powers of description, but not beyond endurance. There are surprisingly many kinds of weather and snow, feelings of invigoration and fear and exhaustion and hunger, sounds, thoughts of home, desires and dreams, and phases of coping. Each brother experiences a different parabola of emotion and determination, and somewhere in the middle of the wilderness they exchange roles.

In this first novel, as in his memoir, O'Brien continues to explore the meaning of "heroism." Harvey (the war hero) gives up in the blizzard and Perry (the stick-in-the-mud) is stubborn—and thus heroic. (Harvey's definition of "heroic" is that they are still alive when they might not have been.) Not only do their roles reverse on this trip, but they are also reversed retroactively. In a

rare bit of openness, Harvey describes the past as he remembers it. Instead of being the tough son, the "bull," he sees himself as the child who fearfully did what his father told him to do: when he got a rifle for Christmas he was scared of it, but he used it anyway. Instead of seeing Perry as the son who couldn't swim and was too scared to go on wilderness treks, Harvey remembers Perry as the one who could stand up to their dad: "You said you weren't going to listen to him preach anymore. You just told him. . . . He asked if you were sick, and . . . you said nope, you weren't sick, and you just said you decided not to go listen to him preach anymore. And that was that. I remember. You looked down to eat, calm as could be."

While each man may be heroic at one time or another, neither is a hero. After the wilderness trek, Perry makes a couple of big decisions, but he does not appear in any way to have become a more permanently impressive man. Harvey seems just as flippant as ever, always making plans to do something difficult and heroic or escapist and pleasure-seeking. He never buckles down to any one task. Things are different, but not very. Perceptions may change everything, but their daily lives change only gradually.

Two of the secondary characters in this novel are women, and for the first time O'Brien represents female characters and relationships across gender. Perry's narration depicts his wife, Grace, and his obsession, Addie (who becomes brother Harvey's girlfriend), in limited ways. Grace is pretty, interested in having a child, supportive, talkative, and too nice. Perry finds her easygoing and comfortable, but he does not quite appreciate her. While O'Brien notifies the reader of Perry's fallibility, he includes a long passage in which Grace talks nonstop—a passage too irregular in the text to be much besides parodic and negative. (They are in bed together; O'Brien says he's better at writing dialogue that takes place outside, so maybe that's the problem.) The irresponsible, flighty, thoughtless Addie is more interesting, which brings up the question of why good women such as Grace are so often characterized as more ridiculous than younger and more obviously exciting women.

On the other hand, one potential locus of sanctification in his work is women—not all women, but women such as Grace in *Northern Lights* or Donna (who Tom always calls "Mrs. Robert Kooshof") in *Tomcat in Love.* O'Brien almost reiterates the cultural cliché that associates women with the body or nature and men with the mind or culture. Accepting this commonplace, O'Brien revises it such that these bodily, natural female characters are the ones who truly live because they can accept that life is change. In a very old-fashioned way, these women represent messy, vital life.

While they are compared to the landscape, however, they are not passive and imperialized like that landscape. They are an active form of wilderness, and one that O'Brien's men learn to respect and even emulate. Grace and Donna are heroic, patient, confused about their life paths but ready for movement forward, and enthusiastic about change and experimentation. O'Brien's male characters, such as Perry in *Northern Lights,* have to travel into the wilderness or walk into a gooey life-filled pond to begin to envision and accept their largely unknown futures.

O'Brien's women sometimes represent the unknown that men are attempting to control. *In the Lake of the Woods* depicts John Wade imagining his future and intending to manipulate it into being. His wife, Kathy's, pregnancy is an unwelcome surprise. Although she wants babies more than anything else, she agrees to an abortion. John's spying on Kathy is another way that he tries to feel in control of the relationship (as if knowledge of her possible infidelity might enable him to prevent it). In *The Nuclear Age,* William seems to be able to imagine a future with Bobbi much more vividly than he can with the strong,

radical Sarah, in spite of Sarah's constant reference to their future in Brazil with lots of babies. Bobbi, the blonde stewardess and all-purpose man-trap, can be imagined in a much more conventional setting; if she can be won, happiness can be gained according to a set order of life events. Brazil is an unknown and perhaps therefore unimaginable, and multiple babies would add even more unknowns to William's future. Finally, Mary Anne, the "Sweetheart of the Song Tra Bong" (in *The Things They Carried*) is a girl like Bobbi (sweetly, reassuringly typical) who turns out not only to relish the unfamiliar but becomes alien herself. Bobbi is likely to leave William by the end of *The Nuclear Age,* which shows that her promise as a type is misplaced, but Mary Anne's reversal is even more abrupt and disturbing to the men who witness it.

O'Brien's female characters become more fully imagined in his late novels. While Grace and Addie are less than enigmatic, these later characters have as much personal mystery as his male characters. In *Tomcat in Love,* Mrs. Robert Kooshof is outspoken, desirous, and active, and makes difficult choices with the fullest inklings of the alternative possibilities.

In these ways, O'Brien breaks down the categories of male and female. A soldier and his girlfriend's behaviors are more a difference of geography than gender. He explains that he wrote "The Sweetheart of the Song Tra Bong" in response to the many women who had told him they didn't like war stories. In a 1990 interview with Michael Coffey the author states that "what happened to me as a man in Vietnam could happen to a woman as well." In a later interview with Steven Kaplan he expands on this idea: "Under situations of stress and in situations of incredible danger and trauma, women are capable, as men are, of great evil, of great good, and of all shades in between." As George Bernard Shaw said when asked how he wrote his female characters, "I always assumed that a woman was a person exactly like myself, and that is how the trick is done."

GOING AFTER CACCIATO

While *Northern Lights* reminded reviewers such as Richard Freedman, Roger Sale, and Alasdair Maclean of Hemingway, *Going After Cacciato* may remind readers of Kurt Vonnegut's *Slaughterhouse-Five* and Joseph Heller's *Catch-22.* O'Brien's Paul Berlin lives in the details of future possibilities as much as Vonnegut's Billy Pilgrim lives in the morbid details of his past experiences. While Billy Pilgrim goes to the past, or to an extraterrestrial world, when he becomes "unstuck in time," Paul Berlin's imagination takes him on the 8,600-mile march between Vietnam and Paris when on night watch his "eye came unstuck from the starlight scope." Heller (via Yossarian) repeats the refrain of Snowden's death and only gradually and late in the book reveals the circumstances of this death; O'Brien's Paul Berlin repeatedly remembers that "Billy Boy Watkins had died of fright," and he marks time with the deaths of other squad members such as Pederson, Buff, Frenchy Tucker, and Bernie Lynn. Because of the narrator's position inside the head of a highly imaginative character, and one who is not particularly group-oriented, only gradually can the reader map the chronology of events in both books. A similarity among all three novels is their resolutely truthful depiction of war amid their wild "flights of imagination." Yossarian's tent mate, the dumb but clever Orr, escapes to Sweden; *Catch-22* ends with Yossarian's own attempt to follow Orr. In *Going After Cacciato,* Paul Berlin imagines that his squad follows Cacciato when he walks away from the war: "Each step was an event of imagination."

Berlin's internal life—how his experience limits his imagination and how his imagination determines the future—is the most important theme in *Going After Cacciato.* O'Brien asserts that this internal life is as real a part of the soldier's experience as marching and eating: "In war, the rational faculty begins to diminish . . . and what takes over is surrealism, the life of the imagination. The mind of the soldier becomes part of the experience—the brain seems to flow out of your head, joining the elements around you on the battlefield." He observes, "The life of the imagination is half of war, half of *any* kind of experience."

Yet O'Brien explicitly rejects magical realism as practiced by writers such as Gabriel García Márquez. His surrealism remains true to his experience. When Paul Berlin is imagining an unlikely but potentially appealing alternative journey for himself, he is building it out of past experiences and shaping it via his psychic necessity to create order and make meaning from his overwhelming and awful war experiences—things he has seen as well as things he has done. One critical point of contention about this novel regards the efficacy of the imaginative process. Does anything come of Berlin's imaginative construct? Or, is he left as powerless and confused as the day he stepped off the transport plane and saw—but could make no meaning from—Billy Boy Watkins' death from fright? Interpretation depends largely on how much of the novel one considers real and how much one understands as Berlin's interior construct. In both this and O'Brien's next novel, *The Nuclear Age,* the main characters envision their survival instead of indulging their fears. In a 1994 interview with Eric James Schroeder, O'Brien explains, "The central theme of the novel [*Going After Cacciato*] has to do with how we use our imaginations to deal with situations around us, not just cope with them psychologically but, more importantly, to deal with them philosophically and morally."

O'Brien also continues to explore other themes that he addressed in his earlier work: the nature of courage, the similarities and differences between World War II and the Vietnam War, personal responsibility and volition, language, and the interpretation of the world's details. "True courage" is defined as "how to behave" or "how to act wisely in spite of fear." Paul Berlin deduces a reassuring "corollary: the greater a man's fear, the greater his potential courage." Finding courage in oneself, then, requires "the power of will to defeat fear," but willpower is another inner resource that is difficult to find. He hopes that his body has a "chemical," or a "lone chromosome," or a "piece of tissue that might be touched and sparked," which would "produce a blaze of valor." Instead, he finds himself to be a mass that responds to the mechanisms of momentum: he marches "with no exercise of will, no desire and no determination, no pride, just legs and lungs, climbing without thought and without will and without purpose." If Berlin is counting on his chromosomes to kick in, then he hasn't much active will left. But Lieutenant Sidney Martin, the commanding officer who does things by Standard Operating Procedures, sees Paul Berlin's march and responds to it with joy: "the boy represented so much good—fortitude, discipline, loyalty, self-control, courage, toughness. The greatest gift of God, thought the lieutenant in admiration of Private First Class Paul Berlin's climb, is freedom of will." Even the difference between free will and movement without volition depends on who's looking, where they are standing, and their frameworks of judgment.

O'Brien compares and contrasts the Vietnam War with other wars, particularly the Second World War. He believes that World War II was a necessary war on a political and humanitarian level but that Vietnam was not. From the perspective of the individual soldier, however, all wars are about the same. Doc, one of the more perceptive members of Paul Berlin's errant squad, claims that war "has an identity separate from perception" and that every war, "any war," feels the same from the perspective of the single

necessarily "confused and muddleheaded" soldier. He lectures,

> the common grunt doesn't give a damn about purposes and justice. He doesn't even *think* about that shit. Not when he's out humping, getting his tail shot off. Purposes—bullshit! He's thinking about how to keep breathing. Or he wonders what it'll feel like when he hits that booby trap. Will he go nuts? Will he puke all over himself, or will he cry, or pass out, or scream? What'll it look like—all bone and meat and pus? That's the stuff he thinks about, not purposes.

In other ways, however, the wars are very different. O'Brien writes that the men in Vietnam "did not know even the simple things" that most World War II soldiers did. Soldiers in Vietnam did not know what it was like to win, or to have a specified target, or to capture an area and keep it, or what the rules of engagement were, or what to do with or say to prisoners, or even what to think and feel about their own actions and experiences.

In his memoir, *If I Die*, O'Brien voices some frustration with the irrelevant advice of World War II veterans. In *Going After Cacciato*, Paul Berlin's father's solemn advice consists of, "It'll be all right. You'll see some terrible stuff, sure, but try to look for the good things. Try to learn." And Paul Berlin has as much difficulty gleaning lessons from his war experience as O'Brien does. These lessons tend to be conventional wisdom ("Don't seek trouble, it'll find you soon enough."), painful facts ("It hurts to get shot.") and vague wishes ("Life after death."). What's left are "war stories," stories that try to outdo one another in weirdness and gruesomeness, stories to which Paul Berlin refuses to listen.

War stories trivialize pain, death, fear, the individual, and history—and probably much else—in a way that O'Brien's writing avoids. When Paul Berlin arrives in Vietnam, his first lecture on survival consists of one hour of silence. Not only do these young soldiers need to learn how to overcome the particular nothingness of this war—its "vacuum"—they also seem to need thoughtful silence to maintain their humanness. The words that these men have at their disposal—the incomplete names and nicknames of their fellow soldiers, their understated "weird"'s and "sad"'s, their acronyms and expletives—combined with their complete ignorance of Vietnamese culture and their inability to understand the facial expressions of the Vietnamese or to verbally communicate with them—makes their war stories inadequate, simplistic, commonplace, unprofound, and disturbingly humorous.

O'Brien's passion for tale telling and his careful shaping of sentences allow him to avoid these pitfalls while telling his war stories. He is interested in the truth, but not the facts as they happened. Describing the incessant terror and numbers of dead in Pinkville may be factual, but it doesn't help readers reach the "emotional truth" that O'Brien can achieve by depicting Cacciato calmly washing Buff's face out of his helmet. Doc says, "Facts are one thing" and "interpretation is something else." O'Brien invents details that get readers closer to interpreting the war's meanings than the plain facts could.

THE NUCLEAR AGE

Going After Cacciato's Paul Berlin digs the deepest foxholes in Vietnam, and the Vietcong tunnels in that novel are both friend and enemy, a trap and a safe house—and this distinction does not depend on which side of the war you are on. In *The Nuclear Age* the land is also one's closest friend and a potential enemy. Unlike Paul Perry's father in *Northern Lights,* who had insisted on his building a shelter, William Cowling is gently mocked by his father when he builds a bomb shelter under the Ping-Pong table in the basement. (In "Darkness on the Edge of Town" [in *Feature,* January 1979] Tim O'Brien reports that he did the same in his own basement as a child.) As *The Nuclear Age* begins, William Cowling looks back on the life that has led him toward digging and dynamiting a 12 × 12 × 19-foot bomb shelter in his backyard.

William was a draft dodger and the sad but otherwise convictionless member of a militant antiwar group. After a childhood of nuclear terror and several years of radicalism, he becomes a multimillionaire by selling a mountain of uranium to Texaco. His bomb shelter is meant to save his life and his family's, but he has the urge to use it to kill them all and thus seal their love and lives in a literally rock solid state of permanence. Through these paradoxes, O'Brien symbolically represents the clash between the human desire for permanence, perfect fidelity, "wholeness," and complete knowledge of "now and forever," and the fact that life necessarily involves change, risk, fear, and unknowns. O'Brien seems to conclude that in order to live our lives fully and happily, we must purposely place our faith in things—people and ideas—that are undoubtedly feckless and even false.

The Nuclear Age is written about and was written during the Cold War. William focuses his attention on the facts: "The world is in danger" and "Bad things can happen." His mind pictures the realities of "the wall shadows at Hiroshima," "the ping-ping-ping of submarine sonar," and "the rattlesnakes and butterflies on that dusty plateau at Los Alamos." His first political action is to stand outside a college cafeteria with a sign that reads, "THE BOMBS ARE REAL." When writing this sign, he says, "The language came easily," but it is language that he contends with throughout the book, and language—not a hole in the ground—is where he finds his final, living refuge.

O'Brien suggests—and even laments—that humans maintain their humanity, their zest for life, their hope, by way of metaphors. Scientific realities are too much to confront, but if we read realities as metaphors, we can interpret them without feeling overwhelmed by them. If we can trick ourselves into using our complicated mental mechanisms, then our basic survival instincts—our understandable fear of dying—can be pushed far enough aside to allow us to live. William's wife Bobbi is a poet, and she frustrates him with her willingness to use nuclear terminology to describe their relationship. He asks, "Why this preference for metaphor over the real thing?" William destroys a copy of a poem (he eats it) with the intent to erase the poem's implications, while Bobbi treats physical objects as if they signify meaning in a poetic way (she gives him some blades of grass and says they express "her deepest feelings" for him). Bobbi treats poems as if they are artifacts; she says they don't mean, they are. Bobbi uses radioactive materials as metaphors, but William says to himself, "Uranium is no figure of speech." Real things have meaning in that they bring about real consequences. But by the end of the book, William recognizes his need for metaphor. He will believe "what cannot be believed" and hold to the idea that "E will somehow not quite equal mc^2, that it's a cunning metaphor, that the terminal equation will somehow not quite balance."

O'Brien does more than address the semireflexive issues of poetry and metaphor—the way language changes our reality such that we can live in it without prematurely self-destructing. He is also a thoughtful political writer, and his parsing of the antiwar movement reveals the complexities, paradoxes, and contradictions inherent within this—and perhaps any—political action. In Cuba, William and four friends find themselves enlisted in an army as arbitrary and full of chickenshit as the one they dodged stateside. William's lover Sarah—although she's the most dedicated and thoughtful revolutionary of the group—wants a world of love; she dreams of being a Dallas Cowboys cheerleader who upstages the football game. Her desire for love is so great

that she says, "If necessary, I'll wipe out the world." The infighting among coalitions of the antiwar movement, and even among these five friends in Key West, Florida, highlights the difficulty of resistance. Peacemakers need to make a big bang to get anyone's attention; real bombs require real resistance, and vice versa. They steal weapons for peace but can barely resist using them. They walk a tightrope, contending with a fragile "balance of power" between fighting war and waging war.

They lose. Although William manages to dump crates of rifles and ammo in the ocean, avoiding the direct use of force, the friends lose by becoming participants in the creation of weaponry. They find uranium and sell it for a fortune. They feel guiltless because they "hadn't done much to change the world" but "the world had changed them." They "prospered in a prosperous world." They claim the heroes and the villains all seem to have disappeared, but maybe they have only lost their vision for the moral spectrum. O'Brien suggests that materialism has overtaken the will of people who once were sure of what was right and would act on it—a familiar complaint about the differences between 1969 and 1979 in America. In his short article "We've Adjusted Too Well," O'Brien laments this change. He writes, "We used to *care* about these things. We paid attention, we debated, passion was high." For his characters in *The Nuclear Age,* the world has not become more complicated—they used to spend all night on "convoluted arguments" about "complexities and ambiguities." Ad ditties and investments have simply become more interesting than passion: "The world has been sanitized. Passion is a metaphor." Here O'Brien explores a compelling question of the sixties counterculture: How did a whole passionate generation lose its political edge? How did William become "Mr. Normal"?

William survives his friends. They are somewhat tainted martyrs to their dreams, but William has always been able to envision death much better than he could envision a perfect world. Obsessed with his own mortality since childhood, William avoided the draft primarily out of fear and passivity. He is scared and sad and less politically committed than his friends are. On the other hand, his fear makes him stay in closer touch with the ideal of peace than his friends, who want to use bombs to fight bombs. He can imagine death more vividly than other people, who believe they are "immortal until the very instant of mortality."

O'Brien thus returns to the issues of reality and the imagination in *The Nuclear Age.* William's morbid imagination shapes his life. When young, he imagines the "world-as-it-should-be" but when he's older he commits himself—almost resigns himself—to the job of just imagining his own happiness. In *Going After Cacciato,* Paul Berlin escapes the war by imagining another version of his war story. But Berlin's narrative is not just escape. He is also making sense of his experiences, and this mental achievement gives him the sense of control that he needs. In *The Nuclear Age* William learns to use his imagination to envision survival instead of death; he tells himself (and forces himself to believe) the stories "sane" people live by. But in *The Nuclear Age,* the two worlds are complicated and confusable. No clear division exists between reality and the imagination; the blurring can be disconcerting, but it also makes the imagination more efficacious.

When reality and fantasy are so intertwined so are sanity and insanity. O'Brien sums up the paradox of many post–World War II novels, most obviously *Catch-22:* "If you're sane, you see madness. If you see madness, you freak. If you freak, you're mad." And he asks, "What does one do?" William's friends accept paradoxes and die rich but rebelliously. William's nuclear freeze turns into a meltdown and finally a conviction that in this nuclear age we can survive only via inspired, purposeful self-deception. O'Brien writes, "Among the sane . . . there is no full knowing. If you're sane, you ride without risk, for the risks are not real. And when it comes to pass, some sane asshole will shrug and say, 'Oh well.' " O'Brien's protagonist is insane with self-defeating fears, but what if he is right?

THE THINGS THEY CARRIED

The Things They Carried is O'Brien's most impressively honest work, one in which he reiterates the falseness of war stories and even of truly held memories. This work is a deceptive confession, one couched in such a mixture of fictionalization and factuality that the reader cannot know exactly what O'Brien has seen or done—neither can he, and that is one of his points. In this book O'Brien progresses further in his expression of the radical, mutual dependence of truth and fiction. If in *Going After Cacciato* Paul Berlin gains a sense of control over his real situation via his imagination, and if in *The Nuclear Age,* William Cowling comes to recognize the real power that the human imagination exercises over our collective and individual futures, in *The Things They Carried* O'Brien makes the relationship between truth and fiction even more intimate. Kaplan wrote that O'Brien "destroys the line dividing fact from fiction, and tries to show even more so than in *Cacciato* that fiction (or the imagined world) can often be truer than fact." O'Brien spent five years with the characters in this novel, longer than he did with any of his real war buddies; he dedicated the book to these fictional characters.

Whether we come to understand and control events, we know how we feel about them. *The Things They Carried* seems to reveal how O'Brien has felt: he reaches for the "emotional truth." People really die in Vietnam, but whose fault is that really? If a man physically lets go of the leg of his friend who is really drowning in mud and shit, is he more to blame than the man who watches this happen, or the people who turn their eyes away so they don't have to watch? Or does the blame fall on the lieutenant who followed other people's orders and set up camp in that muddy village toilet? Or on the man who broke the rules and turned on his flashlight for a second to look at his old girlfriend's picture? Or on the order-givers themselves? Or on the terrain? Or on the weather? And does it matter if any of this really happened or not? O'Brien tells us about Kiowa's dreadful, messy drowning as if it's Norman Bowker's story, and he claims that "Norman Bowker" is Norman Bowker's real name. But then O'Brien writes, "That part of the story is my own," leaving it up to his readers to decide if letting go of Kiowa is *O'Brien's* story—his experience—or just O'Brien's *story*—the one he makes up. According to Kaplan, O'Brien's novel is full of stories that happened, did not happen, and might have happened. The future is a contingency, but so is the past.

O'Brien writes that a "true war story" is one to which the reader responds by asking, "Is it true?" He concludes, "If the answer matters, you've got your answer." If "you'd feel cheated if it never happened" then it's probably "pure Hollywood" and "untrue." In Kiowa's case the answer doesn't matter. The truth of this war, and all wars, is found in the ambiguities, not the Silver Star heroics. (This is one reason that the 1998 film *The Thin Red Line* reveals more about real war than *Saving Private Ryan* of the same year.) O'Brien observes, "It's difficult to separate what happened from what seemed to happen," but when someone dies the others cannot rid themselves of the blame. When fictional character Tim O'Brien's fictional daughter asks, "Daddy, tell the truth, did you ever kill anybody?," he writes, "I can say, honestly, 'Of course not,'" but in the next paragraph he adds, "Or I can say, honestly, 'Yes.'" The reader's uncertainty mimics the confusion of the characters themselves.

As in his other books, O'Brien's discussions of one issue usually lead to a discussion of seemingly opposite issues. In *The Nuclear Age,* the discussion of peace involves a discussion of war:

Must the resistance be resistant? In that same novel, O'Brien explicates the ways safety involves danger and how always keeping things the same can be attained only by irrevocably destroying them. In *Going After Cacciato* the experience of the war is largely expressed through the fantasies of Paul Berlin: Can a person best understand a feeling of entrapment via flights of fancy? In *The Things They Carried,* O'Brien's war stories seem necessarily to be mixed up with love stories, and his confrontation with death leads to his coming to terms with life. Is the story of the man who offers a baby water buffalo C rations and then mercilessly kills it a war story or a love story? O'Brien says it's a love story; perhaps anyone who has offered a gift to someone and had it refused can partially understand the way love can turn to spite. Maybe only an armed soldier can understand how spite turns to murderous violence.

Regarding the complex relationship between life and death, O'Brien seems to be repeating the wartime banality "you're never more alive than when you're almost dead." But he tempers this Hemingwayesque tough-guy credo. First, the likelihood of imminent death does not make men into Men as much as it means "jokes are funnier" and "green is greener." Second, war does not affect men only. In "Sweetheart of the Song Tra Bong," a fantastical story about a young man flying his American girlfriend into the jungles to keep him company, a woman is the one who reaches the depths of Kurtz in Joseph Conrad's *Heart of Darkness.* And third, O'Brien shows that war is not the only place to learn about life and death: "You don't have to be in Nam to be in Nam." His final epiphany about life and death is spoken (in his dreams) by a nine-year-old schoolgirl. Linda says, "Once you're alive, you can't ever be dead," and that death is "like being inside a book that nobody's reading."

By likening death to the closing of a book, O'Brien solidifies the relationship between war and stories. In his memoir *With the Old Breed:*

At Peleliu and Okinawa, Eugene Sledge, a U.S. Marine in World War II, writes that the replacements who got "hit before we even knew their names" were "like unread books on a shelf." O'Brien's stories bring his dead friends back to life. In Vietnam, he writes, "We kept the dead alive with stories," and he continues to do that in his written stories. He concludes that "in the spell of memory and imagination" he can "still see" his friends. Nor are they the only ones he is keeping alive: he is "Tim trying to save Timmy's life with a story."

Except for *Northern Lights,* all of O'Brien's novels include separately published short stories, but this structure is most obvious in *The Things They Carried.* O'Brien complicates this popular American genre (think of Ernest Hemingway, Sherwood Anderson, Maxine Hong Kingston, and countless creative writing Master of Fine Arts grads) by making his stories a complex mixture of fact and fiction. O'Brien's "integrated novel," then, not only integrates parts that have their own "internal integrity" but integrates external facts and mental imaginings. "On The Rainy River" appears to be a first-person confession; it begins, "This is one story I've never told before. Not to anyone," and the narrator refers to himself as "Tim O'Brien." Other stories begin with statements such as "This is true" but are told in a self-reflexive form and include statements such as "That's a true story that never happened." The author explains, "A thing may happen and be a total lie; another thing may not happen and be truer than the truth." True war stories have no moral, no clear ending or beginning, and they admit the difficulty of distinguishing between "what happened" and "what seemed to happen." *Minneapolis Star and Tribune* reviewer Dan Carpenter writes,

> O'Brien is inventing a form here. His book evokes the hyperintense personal journalism of Michael Herr and the journalism-as-novel of Norman Mailer, but it is a different animal. It is fiction, even though its main character has the same name as the author . . . If I had to label it, I'd call it an epic prose poem of our time, deromanticizing and demystifying and yet singing the beauty and mystery of human life over its screams and explosions, curses and lies.

If O'Brien is inventing a form, it has precedents far earlier than postmodernism and New Journalism. Perhaps in O'Brien's work, George Orwell meets Sir Philip Sidney. O'Brien takes Orwell's interest in "the politics of the English language" as crucial to the struggle between totalitarianism and freedom, and acts on Sidney's assertion in "The Defence of Poesy" that poetry (or fiction) can express the truth better than fact. Sidney writes that nature's "world is brazen, the poets only deliver a golden." O'Brien puts it differently: most moments are boring, and imagination can distill all the boredom into something meaningful. "You tell lies," he says, "to get at the truth."

IN THE LAKE OF THE WOODS

In his 1994 novel *In the Lake of the Woods,* O'Brien treats the same themes in a different genre: the mystery—a natural genre for a writer so interested in the problems of discovering truth. John Wade has just lost a primary election for the United States Senate. As he attempts to recuperate in the wilderness with his wife, she disappears, and soon the ex-candidate for senator is a murder suspect. While the local police, the neighbors, John Wade himself, and even the book's narrator seem unsure of what has happened, almost all of them make sinister extrapolations from the revelation that cost him the election— his elaborate cover-up of his involvement in the My Lai (or Thuan Yen) massacre, the most notorious U.S. atrocity in Vietnam. O'Brien's chapters alternate between "Hypothesis" (detailed but unconfirmable guesses about what might have been going on in other people's minds) and "Evidence" (short quotations from involved fictional characters and excerpts from a wide variety of existing books and court transcripts). Other chapters stop several places on the spectrum between hypothesis and evidence, but no certainty is offered. And in all these chapters there are footnotes, written by a philosophizing, clue-full but conclusionless investigator (with a tone akin to Nabokov's scholar in *Pale Fire*) who calls himself "a theory man" and is also a "biographer, historian, medium." Kaplan compares this narrator "detective" to "Marlowe in Conrad's *Lord Jim* and the reporter figure in Orson Welles's *Citizen Kane*."

In one footnote, this narrator writes "evidence is not truth. It is only evident." While the nonfictional elements of *In the Lake of the Woods* help us imagine what John Wade might have been capable of, the narrator offers hypothetical reconstructions of what might have happened and challenges readers to notice their own imaginative preferences. As part of the "evidence," John Dominic Crossan, the author of *The Historical Jesus: The Life of a Mediterranean Jewish Peasant* is cited as saying, "If you cannot believe in something produced by reconstruction, you may have nothing left to believe in." Sigmund Freud is represented by his statement that "Whoever undertakes to write a biography binds himself to lying, to concealment, to flummery. . . . Truth is not accessible."

Here as in other works, O'Brien investigates the indivisibility of truth and fiction from several different angles. First, he highlights the struggle between our desire for conclusive knowledge and our fascination with the enigmatic. O'Brien's narrator writes that "solutions only demean the grandeur of human ignorance," "absolute knowledge is absolute closure," and "death itself dissolves into uncertainty, and that out of such uncertainty arise great temples and tales of salvation." Foren-

sic anxiety disperses into epistemological anxiety, plot into philosophy. The conclusion that John Wade—the one man who should know the truth of this story—is able to reach about the mystery of life is that "The only explicable thing . . . was how thoroughly inexplicable it all was." The characters in this novel are "looking for answers to things that cannot be answered, for answers to the unknowable."

O'Brien's novel also discusses the difference between the truth and what we want or need to believe. Our minds seem unable to comprehend the real truths of the world, such as the factuality of sin and evil, so our "quality of abstraction makes reality unreal." As O'Brien writes in *The Nuclear Age*, "Nothing real had ever happened" at Los Alamos. We have to believe things that we are able to live with; we have a "forgetting trick" that erases or "smudge[s]" certain experiences in the mind's eye, changing our potential memories. Kathy and John Wade need to believe certain things about one another, but John doesn't know that Kathy knows he spies on her, John doesn't know the many sides of Kathy's self, and Kathy doesn't know that John mainly lives "in the mirror," where he can purposefully manipulate other people's impressions of him. The narrator asks, "Our own children, our fathers, our wives and husbands: Do we truly know them? How much is camouflage? How much is guessed at?" But in order to have an interpersonal relationship, we need to have some faith in the objects of our affection, so we—like F. Scott Fitzgerald's Jay Gatsby—agree to understand people "just so far" as they want to be understood, believe in them as they would like to believe in themselves, and accept "precisely the impression" of people that they, at their best, would hope to convey.

We not only believe what we need to, but we perform in such a way as to confirm the beliefs and expectations of others. Kathy has never enjoyed being the wife of a politician, but she looks the part and smiles cheerfully when it's expected of her. While she is loyal and a good actress, she also has a multiplicity of identities. She is flexible and adaptive, and as John Wade's cynical campaign manager says, she has "you's galore." The narrator hypothesizes that when (if) her adoring husband killed her, she opened her eyes and saw "twenty years of love dissolving into the certainty that nothing at all was certain." The two characters have lived out John Wade's dream that 1 + 1 = 0 in one way or another. Their union has killed them, or they have disappeared together and are finding happiness in Verona (an ominous address for a happy ending, since it is the setting for Shakespeare's *Romeo and Juliet*). In either case, they were in a fog of performances and appearances, a box of mirrors, surrounded by people trying to discern the truth as much as the Wades were trying to discover it themselves. The wilderness they pass through (or die in) was a "region that bore resemblance to the contours of [John Wade's] own little repository of a soul, the tangle, the overall disarray, qualities icy and wild." If he's a monster, even he doesn't know it.

O'Brien also continues his explication of the ways that safety and danger, change and stasis, and love and war are intrinsically tangled in the human heart. John was obsessed with magic tricks when he was a child, and he continues to be a manipulator in his adulthood, both in his public and his private life. His machinations to keep his wife, however, may directly or indirectly cause her to disappear. The son of an alcoholic father who committed suicide, John goes to war because he wants to be loved, and he even imagines it might help him love himself. Love, or his desire to be loved, also leads him to lie to himself and others, to keep secrets, to spy on his wife, and possibly even to kill her; "Amazing, he thought, what love could do."

Perhaps the most disturbing of O'Brien's novels, *In the Lake of the Woods* seems to have been written during a difficult time in the author's life.

The breakups of his marriage and a subsequent love relationship led O'Brien to write some of his most personally revealing journalism. In the article "The Vietnam in Me" O'Brien describes his self-probing: "I had come to acknowledge, more or less, the dominant principle of love in my life, how far I would go to get it, how terrified I was of losing it. . . . I would risk conscience and rectitude before risking the loss of love." That self-analysis and self-accusation permeate this haunting book.

TOMCAT IN LOVE

After *In the Lake of the Woods,* O'Brien seemed to have signed off as a writer of novels, but in 1998 he published *Tomcat in Love.* Here the main character and narrator's attention to female taxonomy and his defensive confessions are reminiscent of Nabokov's notorious narrator in *Lolita,* Humbert Humbert. Thomas H. Chippering's three main interests are women, words, and himself. Ostensibly the story of his attempt to avenge himself on his ex-wife, Lorna Sue, and her family, Tom reveals his own blind search for love, Lorna Sue's martyr complex, and the absolute and consistent misreading that occurs when men and women attempt to communicate with each other.

Tom's "meticulous" "love ledger" of encounters with women includes categories such as "Hand-holdings: 421. Nuzzlings: 233. Valentines: 98. Marriages: 1. Meaningful gazes: 1,788. Home runs: 4. Near misses: 128." His seductive female students milk him for his writing skills and then self-righteously reject his advances. His insatiable desire for loving attention and his willingness to accept what only looks like adoration allow these young women to strut rings around him, and it probably explains why a man who has written seventeen senior theses in his twenty-four-year teaching career doesn't have higher tallies in that ledger. His self-absorption and needy narcissism lead him to overestimate women's estimations of him. These interpersonal misreadings leave him confused and, at one point, undressed and tied up on a barroom floor.

Like another of Nabokov's characters, John Shade in *Pale Fire,* Thomas Chippering is a linguistics professor, "the Rolvaang Chair in Modern American Lexicology at the University of Minnesota." For Tom, words become laden with all the memories of the situations in which they were used, and his narrative flows according to these verbal associations. He fought in Vietnam, and so "goof," "spider," "wildfire," and "death chant" are heavily loaded words, the nicknames of the Green Berets who claim to have given his life meaning by stalking and threatening him with vengeance. Eventually obliged to resign his tenure, Tom's stint as a day care provider results in three- and four-year-olds quoting Shakespeare and a deep discussion of the "wondrously polytypic word *spot.*"

In *Tomcat in Love,* O'Brien suggests that those who barely fit into the military organization running the Vietnam War are the ones who have been most influenced by it. Mainly assigned to a desk job, Tom was sent on one mission in Vietnam as the companion of six silent and disagreeable Green Berets. After being abandoned by them and then later catching up with them at a beautiful and serene-seeming villa in the jungle, Tom feels betrayed by them for several reasons and in turn betrays them. Hunted down, he responds with uncharacteristic courage to their threats and is told to watch his back "forever." He writes, "Over all these decades . . . I have had to live with the consequences of a single, senseless act of valor." His former companions think of the pursuit as more of a game; they have joined "mainstream America. . . . Death Chant runs this nifty boutique. . . . War's over." Spider says, "For the rest of us, Tommy, the war's history gonzo—but in this really nifty way you've kept it going. That life-and-death edge, man, it gives *meaning* to everything. Keeps you in contact with your own sinnin' self."

Thus, O'Brien "even pokes fun at the Vietnam War," and reviewers tended to like the way O'Brien "lightened up" in "his first comic novel." But the shift to comedy is not as drastic as it might appear. O'Brien's narrative voice has often been limited to the unreliable delusions of a character who gradually comes to be more defined for readers. This time the narrator is less appealing than usual, and in fact "almost too unsufferable to bear," but he's also less imaginative and more like the ordinary reader. O'Brien works hard to build the uneasy sense of identification between the reader and this unpleasantly self-absorbed and selfish main character. Not only does O'Brien create life stories for his novel's characters, but also he has imagined a past for his reader, and he keeps reminding her of it. She too has a "tangled history," her "husband flew off to Fiji in the company of a redhead barely half his age," and she wants revenge, too. O'Brien even writes, "I spotted your ex-husband at one point. Or was he I? In which case, then, who would you be?"

O'Brien's narrator asks parenthetically "If a love dies, how can such love be love? By what linguistic contrivance?" and he thus heralds the entry of O'Brien's big questions about language, love, and war. These things are important to identify but can easily be confused with their opposites. If love is love, then it shouldn't end. If peace is peace, then it cannot lead to war. But it does. Cacciato and his pursuers, for example, witness many hateful atrocities when they leave the war for the supposedly peaceful walk to Paris. *Tomcat in Love* reviewer Jonathan Fasman asserts that O'Brien's narrator expounds "on how words carry extra-definitional penumbras of meaning that vary from person to person." In this novel, "Fiji" reminds readers of their potential identity with a selfish, lovelorn man who loses what he wants and gets something else. For Tim O'Brien, "Vietnam" may remind him of the power of words to control others and maintain individuality, the buddy love and evil vengeance that American soldiers felt there, and the nightmarish catalyst for his creative gift.

Selected Bibliography

WORKS OF TIM O'BRIEN

BOOKS

If I Die in a Combat Zone. New York: Delacorte, 1973. (Quotations cited from the Delta/Seymour Lawrence edition. New York: Delta/Seymour Lawrence, 1989.)

Northern Lights. New York: Delacorte/Seymour Lawrence, 1975.

Going After Cacciato. New York: Delacorte/Seymour Lawrence, 1978.

The Nuclear Age. London: Collins, 1978.

The Things They Carried. Boston: Houghton Mifflin/ Seymour Lawrence, 1990. (Quotations cited from the Penguin edition. New York: Penguin, 1991.)

In the Lake of the Woods. Boston: Houghton Mifflin/ Seymour Lawrence, 1994.

Tomcat in Love. New York: Broadway Books, 1998.

SHORT FICTION

"Speaking of Courage." *Massachusetts Review* 17, no. 2: 243–253 (Summer 1976). (Significantly revised in *The Things They Carried* and discussed in the chapter titled "Notes.")

"The Things They Carried." In *Best American Short Stories 1987.* Edited by Shannon Ravenal and Ann Beattie. Boston: Houghton Mifflin, 1987. Pp. 287–305.

"Loon Point." *Esquire,* January 1993, pp. 90–94.

"Class of '68." *Esquire,* March 1998, p. 160.

"The Streak." *The New Yorker,* September 28, 1998, pp. 88–91.

JOURNALISM AND OTHER SHORT WORKS

"Darkness on the Edge of Town." *Feature,* January 1979, pp. 42–49.

"The Violent Vet." *Esquire,* December 1979, pp. 96–104.

"We've Adjusted Too Well." In *The Wounded Generation: America after Vietnam.* Edited by A. D. Horne. Englewood Cliffs, N.J.: Prentice-Hall, 1981. Pp. 205–207.

"The Vietnam in Me." *New York Times Magazine,* October 2, 1994, pp. 48–57.

BIBLIOGRAPHY

Calloway, Catherine. "Tim O'Brien (1946–): A Primary and Secondary Bibliography." *Bulletin of Bibliography* 50, no. 3: 223–229 (September 1993).

BIOGRAPHICAL AND CRITICAL STUDIES

Bates, Milton. "Tim O'Brien's Myth of Courage." *Modern Fiction Studies* 33, no. 2: 263–279 (Summer 1987).

———. "Toward a Politico-Poetics of the War Story." In his *The Wars We Took to Vietnam: Cultural Conflict and Storytelling.* Berkeley: University of California Press, 1996. Pp. 214–269.

Beidler, Philip D. "The Life of Fiction." In his *Re-Writing America: Vietnam Authors in Their Generation.* Athens: University of Georgia Press, 1991. Pp. 9–103.

Bonn, Maria S. "Can Stories Save Us? Tim O'Brien and the Efficacy of the Text." *Critique: Studies in Contemporary Fiction* 36, no. 1: 2–15 (Fall 1994).

Calloway, Catherine. " 'How to Tell a True War Story': Metafiction in *The Things They Carried.*" *Critique: Studies in Contemporary Fiction* 36, no. 4: 249–257 (Summer 1995).

Couser, G. Thomas. "*Going After Cacciato:* The Romance and the Real War." *Journal of Narrative Technique* 13, no. 1: 1–10 (Winter 1983).

Fasman, Jonathan. "Tomcat in Love." *Times Literary Supplement,* May 14, 1999, p. 24.

Gilliat, Penelope. "Briefly Noted." *The New Yorker,* July 16, 1973, p. 80.

Herzog, Tobey C. "Consideration." In his *Vietnam War Stories: Innocence Lost.* London: Routledge, 1992. Pp. 139–166.

―――. *Tim O'Brien*. New York: Twayne, 1997. (Includes a bibliography.)

Jarraway, David R. " 'Excremental Assault' in Tim O'Brien: Trauma and Recovery in Vietnam War Literature." *Modern Fiction Studies* 44, no. 3: 695–711 (Fall 1998).

Jones, Dale W. "The Vietnams of Michael Herr and Tim O'Brien: Tales of Disintegration and Integration." *Canadian Review of American Studies* 13, no. 3: 309–320 (Winter 1982).

Kaplan, Steven. *Understanding Tim O'Brien*. Columbia: University of South Carolina Press, 1995.

Kinney, Katherine. "American Exceptionalism and Empire in Tim O'Brien's *Going After Cacciato*." *American Literary History* 7, no. 4: 633–653 (Winter 1995).

Myers, Thomas. *Walking Point: American Narratives of Vietnam*. New York: Oxford University Press, 1988.

Nelson, Marie. "Two Consciences: A Reading of Tim O'Brien's Vietnam Trilogy: *If I Die in a Combat Zone, Going After Cacciato,* and *Northern Lights*." In *Third Force Psychology and the Study of Literature*. Edited by B. J. Paris. Rutherford, N.J.: Fairleigh Dickinson University Press, 1986. Pp. 262–279.

Ringnalda, Don. "Tim O'Brien's Understood Confusion." In his *Fighting and Writing the Vietnam War*. Jackson: University Press of Mississippi, 1994. Pp. 90–114.

Schroeder, Eric James. "The Past and the Possible: Tim O'Brien's Dialectic of Meaning and Imagination." In *Search and Clear: Critical Responses to Selected Literature and Films of the Vietnam War*. Edited by W. J. Searle. Bowling Green, Ohio: Bowling Green State University Popular Press, 1988. Pp. 116–134.

Schwininger, Lee. "Ecofeminism, Nuclearism, and O'Brien's *The Nuclear Age*." In *The Nightmare Considered: Critical Essays on Nuclear War Literature*. Edited by N. Anisfield. Bowling Green, Ohio: Bowling Green State University Popular Press, 1991. Pp. 177–185.

Smiley, Jane. "Tomcat in Love." *New York Times Book Review,* September 20, 1998, pp. 11–12.

Taylor, Mark. "Tim O'Brien's War." *Centennial Review* 34, no. 2: 213–230 (Spring 1995).

Tegmark, Mats. *In the Shoes of a Soldier: Communication in Tim O'Brien's Vietnam Narratives.* Uppsala, Sweden: Uppsala, 1998.

Waters, Chris. "Everyman-at-Arms." *New Statesman,* January 4, 1974, pp. 23–24.

Zins, Daniel L. "Imagining the Real: The Fiction of Tim O'Brien." *The Hollins Critic* 23, no. 3: 1–12.

INTERVIEWS

Bruckner, D. J. R. "A Storyteller for the War That Won't End." *New York Times,* April 3, 1990, pp. C15 + .

Caldwell, Gail. "Staying True to Vietnam." *Boston Globe,* March 29, 1990, pp. 69 + .

Coffey, Michael. "Tim O'Brien." *Publisher's Weekly,* February 16, 1990, pp. 60–61.

Kaplan, Steven. "An Interview with Tim O'Brien." *Missouri Review* 14, no. 3: 95–108 (1991).

Lyons, Gene. "No More Bugles, No More Drums." *Entertainment Weekly,* February 23, 1990, pp. 50–52.

McCaffery, Larry. "An Interview with Tim O'Brien." In *Anything Can Happen: Interviews with Contemporary American Novelists*. Edited by T. LeClair. Urbana: University of Illinois Press, 1983. Pp. 262–278.

McNerney, Brian C. "Responsibly Inventing History: An Interview with Tim O'Brien." *War, Literature, and the Arts* 6: 1–26 (Fall/Winter 1994).

Naparsteck, Martin. "An Interview with Tim O'Brien." *Contemporary Literature* 32, no. 1: 1–11 (Spring 1991).

Schroeder, Eric James. "Two Interviews: Talks with Tim O'Brien and Robert Stone." *Modern Fiction Studies* 30, no. 1: 135–164 (Spring 1994).

Schumacher, Michael. "Writing Stories From Life." *Writer's Digest* 71: 34–39 (April 1991).

Weber, Bruce. "Wrestling with War and Love; Raw Pain, Relived Tim O'Brien's Way." *New York Times,* September 2, 1998, p. E1.

FILMS

In the Lake of the Woods. Screenplay by Philip Rosenberg. Directed by Carl Schenkel. Signboard Hill Productions, 1996.

—DANA CAIRNS WATSON

Cynthia Ozick

1928–

I N A CAREER that stretches across the last thirty years of the twentieth century, Cynthia Ozick has established herself as a powerfully original voice for her Jewish-American cultural heritage. Consisting of a dozen books in print—one collection of poems (a special edition), three substantial collections of essays, and eight books of fiction—her work had generated a marked increase in both critical attention and general readership by the late 1990s. Though she has yet to realize the pre-eminence of other Jewish-American writers such as Philip Roth or Bernard Malamud, this renewed interest in her work will help to provide a better appreciation of her artistic achievement.

OZICK'S BACKGROUND

Cynthia Ozick was born on April 17, 1928, in New York City, the second child and only daughter of William and Shiphra Regelson Ozick and the niece of the writer Abraham Regelson. From 1933 to 1941 she attended the local school, P.S. 71, in the Pelham Bay section of the Bronx, where her parents operated a drugstore. From 1942 to 1946 she attended Hunter College High School in Manhattan and then spent three years commuting to the Washington Square campus of New York University. After graduating with a Bachelor of Arts in English and Phi Beta Kappa

honors in 1949, she earned a master's degree in English at Ohio State University with a thesis entitled "Parable in the Later Novels of Henry James." In 1952, after a brief, unhappy stint of college teaching, Ozick married Bernard Hallote, a lawyer, and settled in at their home in New Rochelle, New York, to begin a career as a writer. Apart from the birth of her only child, Rachel, on September 24, 1965, Ozick has sustained her career on a steady, uninterrupted basis for almost fifty years. During that period Ozick has worked in virtually every genre—until age forty, she submitted poems every year to the Yale Series of Younger Poets; in the mid-1990s she tried staging a play based on *The Shawl* (1989)—but her major successes have come with short stories, novels, novellas, and essays. Under the bedazzling influence of Henry James, she began her career in fiction with two huge novels that devoured her entire "young artist" period—the 1950s and the early 1960s. She discarded the first, *Mercy, Pity, Peace, and Love*—a title drawn from William Blake's "The Divine Image"—after seven years of work; she completed the second, *Trust,* which consumed another seven years, on the day of President Kennedy's murder—November 22, 1963—and published it as her first book in 1966.

During the long gestation period of *Trust,* Ozick has said that she underwent significant changes in her own sense of artistic identity: "After *Trust* I became a Jewish writer. I began with an American novel . . . and I ended up with a Jewish one." After her first book, Ozick devoted the great bulk of her work to a broad-ranging consideration of Jewish identity. For many readers, the originality of her imagination on this topic, combined with her exceptional grounding in Jewish history and culture, earns her work a distinguished place alongside the better-known names of the Jewish-American renaissance that marked American fiction in the post–World War II generation—names such as Saul Bellow and Philip Roth.

It is an old adage in literature that there is no drama—no story—without conflict, and Ozick's fiction is no exception. Across the breadth of her work, the idea of Jewish identity comes up against every imaginable kind of disruption, ranging from the prospect of physical annihilation during the Holocaust to the friendly enticement of Gentile-majority America. From her letters and essays, it is clear that these contradictions are very much a part of Ozick's own intellectual history. It was an intellectual history that began very early, in her childhood reading. Although she was brought up in the Conservative (she has sometimes used the word "Orthodox") Jewish tradition, which she understood as prohibiting any commerce with the pagan culture of magic, as a child she imbibed "the secret bliss of the Violet Fairy Book," and in high school she developed a similar hunger for the Hellenistic classics: "It was Latin class, the *Aeneid* in particular, that instigated the profoundest literary feelings." Finally, in college she developed an affinity for Romantic verse, with a senior thesis on Blake, Samuel Coleridge, William Wordsworth, and Percy Shelley, and for mainstream novelists like E. M. Forster, George Eliot, and Henry James. Under these influences that led her to identify with WASP culture rather than her Jewish heritage, she launched her writing career by lavishing fourteen years on *Mercy, Pity, Peace, and Love* and *Trust.*

If the enticement of Gentile culture was a crucial catalyst for Ozick's talent, an impetus of equal force was, paradoxically, the murderous hostility of that same culture toward her Jewish heritage and toward Jewish identity itself. Ozick grew up in New York City as a result of her parents' participation in the huge wave of Jewish immigration seeking escape from the bloody pogroms that swept across Russia for a generation following Czar Alexander II's assassination in 1881—a murder that was blamed on the Jews. In her mother's Russian village, Ozick's great-uncle and his son were tied to horses and dragged across cobblestones until their skulls were broken. Her father, at age five, narrowly escaped being burned alive when, at Easter, a malevolent priest incited a mob to herd the town's Jews into their synagogue for immolation. Another priest who came upon the scene talked the crowd into snuffing out their torches and going home. Though America did offer precious refuge from such horrors, it imposed its own brand of prejudice on Cynthia Ozick during her impressionable grade school years: "In P.S. 71 I am publicly shamed in Assembly because I am caught not singing Christmas carols; in P.S. 71 I am repeatedly accused of deicide." And finally, midway through college, her joyous love affair with two thousand years of Anglo-European culture was brutally interrupted by knowledge of the Holocaust. "I am hammer-struck with the shock of Europe's skull, the bled planet of death camp and war," she recalled in *Art & Ardor: Essays* (1983). The final effect of this dread knowledge was "a revulsion against the values . . . of the surrounding culture itself, . . . whether in the Christian or post-Christian vessels. . . . It is a revulsion against . . . what is called, strangely, Western Civilization."

Besides this enticement/revulsion regarding Western/Christian civilization, two other major sources of conflict undergird Ozick's fictional oeuvre. One involves her status as a woman and the other her status as an artist. Ozick's first awareness of a gender problem came about during a graduate course with the great liberal scholar Lionel Trilling. When he returned her first term paper, it was obvious that he had confused her with the only other woman in the course, an older woman whose mental derangement had caused considerable chaos in Trilling's classroom. Merely on account of her gender, Ozick's identity had been swallowed into that of the "Crazy Lady," as she described in an essay entitled "We Are the Crazy Lady and Other Feisty Feminist Fables" (Spring 1972, *Ms.* Magazine). Later, as she began her writing career, she was sensitized to an oddity concerning women poets: "For many years I had noticed that no book of poetry by a woman was ever reviewed without reference to the poet's sex." In the end, Ozick's hugely ambitious first novel, *Trust,* was crucially—and some critics thought harmfully—affected by this experience of sexism. In the *Ms.* Magazine essay Ozick commented on this point:

> Everything I was reading in reviews of other people's books made me fearful: . . . I was afraid to be pegged as having written a "woman's" novel, and . . . no one takes a woman's novel seriously. . . . So what I left out of my narrator entirely, sweepingly, . . . was any shred of "sensibility." I stripped her of everything, even a name. . . . I wiped the "woman" out of her. And I did it out of fear, out of vicarious, vindictive critical imagination. [ellipses mine]

It turned out that Ozick's forebodings were justified. Although she was fortunate enough to garner reviews in the *New York Times Book Review* and in *Time* magazine, the former—illustrating its text with a naked woman—assigned the narrator a need for "some easy feminine role" that would allow her a "coming to terms with the recalcitrant sexual elements in her life," while the latter described Ozick as "a housewife."

Important as it was, literary sexism was not the only problem Ozick experienced because of her status as a woman. A deeper conflict sprang from the fact that her Jewish heritage, as sacred as it was to her life and work, included male suprem-

acist practices: the insistence, for example, that synagogue worship requires a minimum of ten bar mitzvahed males, no matter how many women are present. At the opposite end of the cultural spectrum, meanwhile, the radical feminist movement proved more hostile than friendly to Ozick's artistic purpose because of its claim for gender apartheid. If taken seriously, the segregation of men and women writers on the basis of inherent "difference" in states of intellect and feeling would prohibit the portrayals of men by women and vice versa, undercutting masterworks ranging from Geoffrey Chaucer's Wife of Bath to Toni Morrison's Paul D. in *Beloved.* Toward both challenges, Ozick's answer has been to assert her independence. Concerning Jewish sexism, Ozick at one point went so far as to suggest that the Torah itself—the essence of Hebrew sacred writ—must be amended to allow woman's equality. And concerning female "difference," Ozick has defined her kind of feminism as "that which opposes segregation. . . . I am, as a writer, whatever I wish to become. I can think myself into a male, or a female, or a stone, or a block of wood. . . . Without disparaging particularity or identity, [literature] universalizes; it does not divide."

Of all the conflicts animating Ozick's life and thought, the most agonizing appears to have involved a contradiction between her calling as a writer and her allegiance, as a Jew, to the Second Commandment. According to Ozick, the most "usefully succinct" definition of a Jew in theological terms is "someone who shuns idols." Unfortunately, however, to be a writer, in her view, was unavoidably to engage in idolatry: "Literature, one should have the courage to reflect, is an idol." An artist must inevitably create an alternative world, one that is in competition with the Creator's, and in so doing she goes whoring after the forbidden gods of Canaan. "The Muses are not Jewish but Greek," she says in her Preface to *Bloodshed and Three Novellas* (1976), and "the story-making faculty itself can be a corridor to the corruptions and abominations of idol-worship." In particular, the goddess of sex—Astarte in ancient Canaan, Aphrodite in Greece, Venus in Rome—keeps reappearing in all the non-Jewish civilizations with power enough to rival that of the One True God of the Hebrews. By contrast, one of Ozick's favorite theologians, Rabbi Leo Baeck, described sexual discipline as definitive of the Jewish ethos (in *This People Israel: The Meaning of Jewish Existence* [1964]): "Purity, in this people [Israel], primarily means that of the sexual life. . . . The battle which this people's soul, in its covenant with God, waged against the people of Canaan. . . was above all a battle for this purity. It continued for centuries." Certainly the overpowering erotic sensibility that animates books like *Trust* and *The Pagan Rabbi and Other Stories* (1971) indicates Ozick's own struggle with the idolatrous gods of nature, which ultimately sustains, in her view, "the issue of Hellenism-versus-Hebraism as the central quarrel of the West."

There is an additional reason Ozick views literature as an idol, namely the fact that the imagination of an artist traffics in evil. "Imagination is more than make-believe, more than the power to invent," she says. "It is also the power to penetrate evil, to take on evil, to become evil, and in that guise it is the most frightening human faculty. Whoever writes a story that includes villainy enters into and becomes the villain." In this guise, the literary imagination veers toward the maw of Moloch, the cannibal god of the Canaanites, in Ozick's judgment. One effect of this misgiving was her reluctance to write imaginatively about the Holocaust, despite its impingement on every one of her books, until her long-delayed publication of *The Shawl* with its harrowing portrayal of life inside a Polish death camp. In the late stages of her writing career, in the mid-1980s, Ozick finally changed her mind about equating the literary imagination with idolatry. "I no longer think of the imagination as a thing to be

dreaded," she stated in an interview with Tom Teicholz. "Only a very strong imagination can rise to the idea of a noncorporeal God. The lower imagination, the weaker, falls to the proliferation of images."

A final conflict in Ozick's life and thought involves contradictory impulses at the heart of the Jewish ethos. On one side is the Jewish "soul-word"—a word corresponding to "soul" in African-American culture, which indicates the cultural value preeminently admired in that culture. (Other ethnic groups have similar words, such as *sissu*—implying stoic endurance—in Finnish; *yamato-damashi*—asserting invincible will power—in Japanese; *dom*—the sacredness of home—in Serbo-Croatian; *genutzat*—"I give you everything I have"—in Armenian; and *machismo*—power or strength—in Hispanic cultures.) The Jewish word *L'Chaim!*, famously meaning "To Life!," comprises both an affirmation of value and a determination to exploit one's life for all it is worth. Contradicting this sentiment, however, are the momentous sufferings of Jewish history, from the enslavement in Egypt through the conquests by the Babylonians, Assyrians, and Romans to the medieval pogroms and the modern Holocaust. So, along with the other conflicts heretofore noted, the conflict between L'Chaim! and the appalling sufferings in Jewish history contributes fundamentally to the dramatic power of Ozick's fictive vision. It all came together in her first, prodigiously ambitious novel, *Trust*.

TRUST: IN SEARCH OF IDENTITY

Concerning *Trust,* in the early 1980s Ozick said "I do know in my deepest sinew that I will never again write so well, that I will never again have that kind of high ambition or monastic patience or metaphysical nerve and fortitude." A decade later, she still maintained that "the energy and meticulous language-love that went into that book drew on sources that were never again so abundant." And yet, though "I do care more for *Trust* than for anything else," she says, it "probably was a towering mistake." What made it a mistake was not any inherent fault in the book but rather her commitment of the most productive years of her youth to an immense project that she hoped would emulate Henry James at his most masterly, not realizing that James himself could not produce such a work until after a long apprenticeship. Worst of all, this long obsession not only forestalled the fruitful apprentice work she should have been doing, but it also nullified any chance for early recognition and support for her work—a crucial need in any young artist's career. As it was, she attracted almost no attention until she published *Trust* in her late thirties, and her definitive niche as a writer had to await her second book, *The Pagan Rabbi,* published when she was forty-two.

Despite Ozick's misgivings, a reliable judgment of *Trust* depends on its internal dynamics rather than its effect on the artist's career. Viewed in that light, there is good reason to credit Ozick's claim, in her Preface to *Bloodshed and Three Novellas,* that *Trust* "was conceived in a style both 'mandarin' and 'lapidary,' every paragraph a poem." Its cast of characters, moreover, is remarkably original and powerfully drawn, and its epic scale rests, in true Jamesian fashion, upon a masterly command of design. And finally, a potent intellect undergirds the whole work, as attested in the sophisticated philosophical, historical, and literary sensibility that animates every page. Given its proper chance, via careful analysis and evaluation, *Trust* could in time emerge from its critical limbo—caused largely by mere lack of readership—to claim the status of Ozick's masterpiece.

The narrative thrust of *Trust* bears out a familiar twentieth-century theme: a young person's search for a father. What distinguishes *Trust* from

James Joyce's *Ulysses,* William Faulkner's *Absalom, Absalom!,* and Robert Penn Warren's *All the King's Men* in this regard is the gender of the seeker, who is alienated both from her wealthy, self-centered mother and from this woman's two husbands, neither of whom is the girl's biological father. Some degree of Ozick's allegorical method persists not only in the mother's name, Allegra, but also in the cultural identities of the two husbands. Husband number one, William, is a quintessential WASP, aloof, dignified, and emotionally dead, while his successor, Enoch Vand, is a Jew who has lost his religious belief because of the Holocaust. In the Jamesian manner, Allegra wants only to ingest the cultural feast of Europe to which Enoch (a former ambassador there) has introduced her, while, ironically, Enoch himself succumbs to his Holocaust horror. The narrator, now twenty-one, recalls an earlier trip to Europe that disclosed both perspectives:

> She [mother] had brought me to see the spires. . . and minarets like overturned goblets, and she promised from this fountain of the world (she called it life, she called it Europe) all spectacle, dominion, energy, and honor. And all the while she never smelled death there. . . . But it was deathcamp gas . . . that plagued his [Enoch's] head . . . and swarmed from his nostrils to touch those unshrouded tattooed carcasses . . . moving in freight cars over the gassed and blighted continent.

Though only ten years old at the time of the trip, the narrator was astute enough to lean toward her stepfather's view in this matter, in one instance making a map of Europe with her vomit and in another framing a similar map from the blood and urine she found on her hotel mattress.

With Enoch's Europe thus polluted by its Hitlerian past, and with William's America (in the 1950s) stultified by its gray flannel conformity, the narrator responds hopefully to a summons from her third father figure, the biological progenitor she hardly knows, to visit him at the abandoned marine museum on Long Island where he is living. Together, the three father figures—WASP, Jew, and, as it turns out, pagan hedonist (he had fathered the girl out of wedlock)—comprise the cultural identities from which the young woman has to choose for her own future pathway. Across the geographical arc that Ozick designates in the book's four sections ("America," "Europe," "Brighton [England]," and "Duneacres [Long Island]"), the narrator pursues her lost father in search of her own identity. Like Joseph Conrad's Kurtz, F. Scott Fitzgerald's Gatsby, and Faulkner's Thomas Sutpen, this mystery man—Gustave Nicholas Tilbeck—is complex and elusive, but in the end he does fulfill his daughter's need, in spectacular fashion. In doing so, he gives positive meaning to a title that otherwise functions in an altogether ironic manner, even to the point of deriding Allegra's corrupting "trust" fund.

As the narrator's pursuit of Tilbeck goes forward, it gradually becomes clear that Ozick deploys his characterization to counterpoint the three other parent figures. As against Allegra's great wealth, he is utterly and happily impecunious; as against Enoch's Hitlerite Europe, his ancestral land is Sweden, a country that saved all of Denmark's Jews during the war; and as against William's priggish Puritan ethos (he calls the narrator "illegitimate issue"), Tilbeck is altogether at ease in his Dionysian eroticism. Moreover, as against Ozick's own deeply held Judaic code (recalling what Rabbi Baeck said about Jewish sexual purity), Tilbeck's libertine role is so powerfully appealing as to overwhelm conventional scruples of any sort, both in the narrator and within the author's lawlessly unrestrained imagination. Here is an instance of what Ozick means in calling literature an idol and in suggesting that the term "Jewish writer" is "an 'oxymoron'—a pointed contradiction, in which one arm of the phrase clashes so profoundly with the other as to annihilate it." To portray the pagan gods so se-

ductively as she does in Tilbeck is to betray the essence of Judaism.

Tilbeck's association with these pagan gods is notably wide ranging. In the climactic scene at Duneacres—the defunct marine museum—he assumes the aspect of the sea-god Poseidon, but along the way he evokes connections with Thor, Loki, Apollo, Zeus, Dionysus, Venus, Mercury, and a nameless "Nile-god." Even Allah and Buddha briefly join the pantheon, the latter in connection with Tilbeck's assertion that he desires nothing (desirelessness being the highest wisdom of the Buddhist sage). But his ultimate identification seems to be with Pan, the supreme god of nature and, therefore, of the immensely creative force associated with sexuality. Next to that primal life force, the celibate Christ and taboo-promulgating Moses pale into arid insignificance, causing the heroine of this bildungsroman to exchange her pallid Judeo-Christian heritage for the philosophy embodied in her final father figure, the man who transmutes the L'Chaim! principle into a neo-pagan worship of Eros.

The grand climax of *Trust* is a sexual encounter that occurs between Tilbeck and, typically, another man's fiancée. Here Ozick's style reaches its most lyrical intensity while festooning itself with multiple mythical associations. Marking the gateway to this scene, for example, is a modern Tree of Forbidden Knowledge:

> Lens upon lens burned in the leaves with a luminosity just short of glass and nearer to vapor. . . . A radiance lifted itself from the shoulders of the tree . . . so that, to see, I had to stare through a tissue of incandescence. . . . I was nymph, naiad, sprite, goddess; I had gifts, powers. . . . [ellipses mine]

Complementing this aura of ancient myth is the indigenous American mythmaking Ozick assigns to the Purse family who lives with Tilbeck at Duneacres. With a brood of children named after Ralph Waldo Emerson, Henry David Thoreau,

Walt Whitman, and Amos Bronson Alcott, the Purses conjoin the American pragmatism implied by their name (Mrs. Purse is an expert mechanic) with the pantheistic nature-worship of the great transcendentalist writers. The Purses' disdain for conventional behavior also reflects their transcendentalist forebears, as evidenced in actions that range from playing tennis without a net to the cuckoldom (by Tilbeck) of the Purse family patriarch. The result is what the narrator had wished for as a young girl, "a different God for America"—a God untainted by the anti-Semitic history of European Christianity and indifferent to the sexual transgression about to unfold.

The narrator's own indifference is a telling sign of growth. Not fornication or adultery but "Sacred Beauty" is her term for this encounter, which indicates her conversion to a value higher than the ethical monotheism of her Judeo-Christian heritage. Another sign of her conversion is her change of attitude concerning her illegitimate birth. Originally shamed and humiliated for being fathered by a seventeen-year-old boy (Allegra had taken Tilbeck as her lover during *her* brief fling with Sacred Beauty two decades earlier), the narrator now comes to full acceptance: "I loved my father." Beyond the narrator's role, moreover, is the appeal of Sacred Beauty for any artist in any medium. Complicating that inference, however, is another conversion experience that comes to light in the closing pages. Enoch Vand, whose despair over the Holocaust had led him to conflate the God of the Jews with Moloch, the god of Death, has now committed himself to total immersion in Orthodox Judaism. Meanwhile, Tilbeck's appeal is weakened in the end by a curious fact that comes to light after his drowned body is retrieved from the sea: he dyed his hair. The implication is that this apostle of desirelessness did desire something after all: eternal youth, which nature provided in the only way it could do so, with an early death. Tilbeck's affinity for youth also implies the lack of maturity that makes his

life utterly irresponsible, to his daughter's profound detriment. So *Trust* ends in a state of ambiguity, with the lure of Sacred Beauty undeniably valorized but unable to free itself from the counterclaims of Mosaic Law. The conflict of "Pan versus Moses," as Enoch Vand framed the question, thus carries over unresolved from Ozick's seven-year struggle in *Trust* to her second major enterprise, the collection of stories she called *The Pagan Rabbi.*

THE STRUGGLES OF THE ARTIST

Of the seven stories in *The Pagan Rabbi and Other Stories,* two—"The Pagan Rabbi" and "The Dock-Witch"—reprise the "Pan versus Moses" conflict, one—"The Suitcase"—deals with ethnic friction, and the remaining four—"Envy; or, Yiddish in America," "The Doctor's Wife," "The Butterfly and the Traffic Light," and "Virility"—comprise various portraits of the artist. Overarching these disparate tales is the theme of Jewish identity, a motif that binds nearly all of Ozick's writing into a unified pattern much in the fashion of Henry James' "figure in the carpet," defined by him as "the primal plan . . . [that] stretches from book to book." Increasingly, as this primal plan plays out, the impression grows of startling originality: from *The Pagan Rabbi* on, only Cynthia Ozick could have written this oeuvre, which resembles no other American fiction.

Unlike *Trust,* which identifies Pan and Moses with different characters, "The Pagan Rabbi" (the book's title story) portrays the Hellenic/Hebraic dichotomy as a conflict within a single man. That man, a learned rabbi named Isaac Kornfeld, poses a mystery that his wife and friend (the story's narrator) will have to solve when he hangs himself from a tree with his prayer shawl. As in *Trust,* the tree evokes lapsarian implications of sex and death, but here these motifs take on a pagan rather than Edenic coloring. Far from leading to a fall, the rabbi's ecstatic coupling with the tree's dryad frees him from the deadly burden of his Jewish heritage. His soul no longer resembles "a dusty old man" bent under a "dusty bag of books" who "passes indifferent through the beauty of the field," ignoring the "Incredible flowers! Of every color!" as he "reads the Law and breathes the dust." The traditional Jewish abhorrence of the unclean likewise dissolves into a love of nature great enough to encompass even the stench coming up the bay, where "the cold brown water covered half the city's turds." And finally, the edict of death pronounced by the God of Genesis means nothing when juxtaposed against the rabbi's pantheistic insight:

> The molecules dance inside all forms, and within the molecules dance the atoms, and within the atoms dance still profounder sources of divine vitality. There is nothing that is Dead. . . . Holy life subsists even in the stone, even in the bones of dead dogs and dead men. Hence in God's fecundating Creation there is no possibility of Idolatry, and therefore no possibility of committing this so-called abomination.

Toward the end, the rabbi's Jewish soul attempts a comeback, claiming that "The sound of the Law is more beautiful than the crickets. The smell of the Law is more radiant than the moss. The taste of the Law exceeds clear water." But the rabbi is too taken with the pagan enticement to listen, leaving the narrator alone to conclude "The Pagan Rabbi" with a soberly antipantheistic gesture: "[At home I] dropped three green house plants down the toilet; after a journey of some miles through conduits they entered [the bay], where they decayed among the civic excrement."

Ozick's other Pan/Moses story, "The Dock-Witch," differs from "The Pagan Rabbi" in having a Christian rather than a Jewish protagonist, a strategy that weakens the conflict by eliminating the Second Commandment as a factor. (In Ozick's view, Christianity risks idolatry by reason of its Trinitarian God and its valorizing of icons.) The title figure, the dock-witch, is another dryad, associated with the wood of the docks and the ships, but her main function is to sacralize the whole of nature. A hint of her sacral purpose occurs when the narrator spots "a pair of rats the size of crouched penguins, one hurrying after the other . . . like a couple of priests late for divine service." Like Tilbeck, she is identified primarily with the sea. When she and the narrator make love, he feels "as though I had dived undersea, with all the ocean pressing on my arched and agonized spine," but she is beyond satiation: "The undersea of her was never satiated, the dive was bottomless, plummeting, vast and vast." Eventually, when she speaks Phoenician, he begins to understand her Canaanite affinities, but it is too late. By reverting to the code that prevailed before the Law of Sinai made civilization possible, the narrator has opened his door to primal chaos. After wrecking his apartment and ravaging his life, the dock-witch sails away at last, transmuted into a wooden figurehead at a ship's prow.

The Gentile enticement takes a sinister turn in "The Suitcase," when a young Jewish woman, Genevieve, becomes involved not with a "Greek" or "Canaanite" tempter but with a German–American of post-Holocaust vintage. Although the lover's ancestry in and of itself is not significant to this story, being German is an issue for this young man's father. An airman in the Kaiser's army, Mr. Hencke came to America before the Hitler era and consequently feels innocent of Nazi atrocities. Nonetheless, his first meeting with Genevieve evokes an immediate hostility, which she does not attribute to his indignation at the fact that both lovers are married with children, but rather as his attempt to break up the romance due to anti-Semitic feelings. In the ensuing conflict, one of the sharpest in Ozick's writing, Mr. Hencke wins in the sense of ending the affair between Genevieve and his son, but she wins the deeper conflict over ethnic identity. Despite his perfectly reasonable claims of innocence—"Who could be blamed for History? . . . History was a Force-in-Itself, like Evolution"—she exposes his guilty feelings. When he claims he will sail tomorrow for Sweden, she torments his conscience:

> "I bet you say Sweden to mislead. I bet you're going to Germany, why shouldn't you? I don't say there's anything wrong with it, why shouldn't you go to Germany?"
> "Not Germany, Sweden. The Swedes were innocent in the war, they saved so many Jews. I swear it, not Germany. . . . I swear it."

Lightening the mood of this bitter encounter is Ozick's satire on contemporary aesthetic criticism. At an art show that Genevieve supervises, one Creighton MacDougal (the then-eminent Dwight MacDonald in actual life) unloads a massive load of verbal garbage on his audience, anticipating by a full decade the hieratic mystifications perpetrated by the Jacques Derrida–Martin Heidegger–Paul de Man cohort.

Of the four tales in *The Pagan Rabbi* devoted to the struggles of the artist, the earliest is "The Butterfly and the Traffic Light," originally published in 1961 and written nearly a decade before that. Here the traffic light, with its narrow range of meanings, signifies the unacceptable limitations of Judaic monotheism: "There ought to be room for Zeus *and* God under one roof . . . . That's why traffic lights won't do for icons! They haven't been conceived in a pluralistic spirit, they're all exactly alike." The other title image, the butterfly, signifies the full perfection of art, a gorgeous but static condition to which the speaker prefers the potentiality of the caterpillar: "The caterpillar is uglier, but in him we can regard the better joy of becoming. The caterpillar's fate is bloom. The butterfly's is waste."

By contrast with this early sketch, the remaining three stories demonstrate the heightened maturity of thought and craft that Ozick had achieved by the end of the 1960s. In "The Doctor's Wife," she combines two of her longtime passions, Chekhov and photography, in a complex web of reference. Like Anton Chekhov, a doctor-artist, the doctor in "The Doctor's Wife" has artistic ambitions; unlike Chekhov, but very much like one of Chekhov's characters, he is a dreamer who fails either to realize his talent or to gain a wife: "He began, quite consciously, to grieve: he thought how imperceptibly, how inexorably, temporary accommodation becomes permanence, and one by one he counted his omissions, his cowardices, each of which had fixed him like an invisible cement." In the end he falls in love not with a woman but with a picture of a woman, thereby conferring superior status on his artistic rival and brother-in-law, a photographer.

Yet another failure of the artist is the subject of "Virility," whose protagonist fails not for lack of merit on her part but on account of sexism within the literary establishment. Here a poet named Edward Gate enjoys universal acclaim until he confesses that the actual author of his poems is his aunt, Rivka, whereupon the critics and reviewers who once called the books (each titled *Virility*) "The Masculine Principle personified," "seminal and hard," now dismiss them as "thin feminine art," "a lace valentine." For penance, Gate, crazed by his guilt, spends the rest of his centenarian's life dressed as a woman.

Like "The Pagan Rabbi," "Envy; or Yiddish in America" ranks among Ozick's most ambitious and original creations. In its main character, the aging immigrant poet Hersheleh Edelshtein, Ozick's triad of recurring themes converge: the pagan enticement, the ordeal of the artist, and the dilemma of Jewish identity. What makes Edelshtein's plight as an artist exceptionally poignant is his entrapment within a rich but dying culture, which leaves him with neither an audience nor a translator for his Yiddish poetry. With the Holocaust having wiped out Yiddish from Europe, and with even Israel having no use for "the language of the bad little interval between Canaan and now," America—and Edelshtein's New York City in particular —remains the only site of possible Yiddish survival. But the young Jews he encounters care nothing for their ancestral tongue, leaving the preservation of tradition in the unlikely hands of Jewish-American writers who were "spawned in America, pogroms a rumor, . . . history a vacuum. . . . They were reviewed and praised, and were considered Jews, and knew nothing."

Yet Edelshtein himself is far from innocent of cultural apostasy. His Jewish roots cannot forestall either his envy of "natural religion, stones, stars, body" or the allure of what Torah calls an abomination—"The love of a man for a boy. Why not confess it?" But in the end, the pagan enticement, which extends to the "[wish] he had been born a Gentile," defers to its opposite counterpart, Gentile hostility, here voiced incongruously by a Christian evangelist: "You people are cowards, you never even tried to defend yourselves. . . . When you were in Europe every nation despised you. When you moved to take over the Middle East the Arab nation, spic faces like your own, your very own blood-kin, began to hate you. . . . You kike, you Yid" (ellipses mine). Edelshtein's retort—"Amalekite! Titus! Nazi!"—encompasses three thousand years of Jewish history, tracing a thread of hatred from Canaan to Rome to the Third Reich to contemporary America. Ironically, the Jewish culture that has survived these millennia of persecution now stands in mortal peril of evisceration from within, owing to the younger generation's loss of belief in the Covenant and loss of interest in the Yiddish heritage. That whole long heritage is voiced in Edelshtein's final outcry: "On account of you [the evangelist, but also the deracinated Jews] I lost everything, my whole life! On account of you I have no translator!"

JEWISH DERACINATION

In *Bloodshed and Three Novellas,* Ozick accords her governing theme, the betrayal of Jewish identity, a new level of coherence and poignancy. At the outset, her Preface rehearses her own anxiety over betraying the Second Commandment by writing stories: "Does the Commandment against idols warn even [against] ink?" Here too, as though to illustrate her point, she ventures a wicked blasphemy: "There *is* a demon in this tale ["Usurpation"] . . . I hope he is not the Creator of the Universe, who admitted Auschwitz into His creation." And she abandons hope of Jewish-Gentile cross-understanding by reason of linguistic incompatibility: "A language, like a people, has a history of ideas. . . . English is a Christian language. When I write English, I live in Christendom. But if my postulates are not Christian postulates, what then? . . . 'Torah' is a stranger in English." So, she says, her readers' incomprehension of her novella "Usurpation (Other People's Stories)" came about because she wrote it "in the language of a civilization that cannot imagine its thesis."

That thesis raises to a new level of urgency and complexity her "Jewish writer" oxymoron. The initial gambit shows the narrator going to hear a famous writer read his story "The Magic Crown" (actually Bernard Malamud's "The Silver Crown"). Moved by writer's envy, she not only usurps his idea of a magic crown that stimulates storytelling, but she also incorporates two Israeli writers into her story—S. Y. Agnon, a preserver of Jewish tradition who in real life won the Nobel Prize in literature in 1966, and the ghost of Tchernikhovsky, a neo-pagan apostate who had lapsed into "pantheism and earth-worship . . . pursuit of the old gods of Canaan." Along the way, she engages in postmodern interaction with her readers—"I looked up one of your stories. It stank, lady. The one called 'Usurpation.' . . . Boring!

Long-winded!"—but the main issue is cultural betrayal in exchange for artistic creativity. "Magic—I admit it—is what I lust after," she says, ". . . oh why can we [Jews] not have a magic God like other peoples?"

Eventually Tchernikhovsky's ghost appears with an offer: "Choose!" "Between what and what?" the narrator replies. To his answer, "God or god. The Name of Names or Apollo," her response is instantaneous: "Apollo." Her reward is equally immediate: "Stories came from me then, births and births of tellings." To judge from Tchernikhovsky's example, there is no punishment for this transgression. On the contrary, his wholly apostate life in the next world is wholly pleasurable as he "eats nude at the table of the nude gods, . . . his youth restored, his sex splendidly erect. . . . and when the Sabbath comes. . . as usual he avoids the congregation of the faithful before the Footstool and the Throne." But though Tchernikhovsky has become a self-idolatrous writer "so audacious and yet so ingenious" as to "fool God and live," he cannot fool the new gods he has chosen. In the last sentence of "Usurpation (Other People's Stories)," they know who he is: "Then the taciturn little Canaanite idols call him, in the language of the spheres, kike."

An artist of sorts is the focus of "An Education," which Ozick says (in the Preface) was "the first story I ever wrote." Initially, the title refers to the classical education of Una Meyer, its main character, but her real education pertains to her observation of a couple named Chimes, whose betrayal of their Jewish heritage may be seen in their change of name (from Chaims, as in L'Chaim!), their name for their daughter (Christina), and their unkosher diet (ham). Moreover, Clement Chimes' graduate study at Union Theological Seminary includes topics such as Martin Heidegger, Paul Tillich, and even Christmas Humphreys on Buddhism, but not a single Jewish theologian. For a while Una envies these people

and their cultural liberation ("you're right in the middle of being alive"—a L'Chaim! moment), but in the end Clement drops out of the seminary and burns his notes. His new career as a poet, however, gets no further than his title page: "SOCIAL CANCER: A DIAGNOSIS IN VERSE AND ANGER, by Clement Chimes, M.A." Like Edelshtein in "Envy," Chimes is a failed writer, but for the opposite reason: not because he participates in a dying minority culture but because his apostasy leaves him with no cultural capital at all from which to create literature.

While "An Education" portrays a farcical instance of Jewish deracination, "A Mercenary" is a hauntingly tragic rendition. Its two main characters in effect exchange birthrights: Stanislav Lushinski repudiates his identity as a Polish Holocaust survivor to become a PM ("Paid Mouthpiece") for a corrupt African dictator at the United Nations, while Morris Ngambe, his assistant, hides his black African heritage under a European veneer acquired during his education at Oxford. Morris, however, eventually sheds that veneer so as to reclaim his birthright, "the dear land itself, the customs, the rites, the cousins, the sense of family," while Lushinski—the "mercenary"—moves in contrary fashion. At the United Nations he gladly votes against Israeli interests and turns his back on the Jews in the gallery. On television talk shows, he implies that his tale of Holocaust horror in childhood was a fabrication, an impression he strengthens by claiming that he murdered someone back there in Poland: "All this was comedy. . . . the audience is elated by its own disbelief. . . . Lushinski is only a story-teller." And his mistress, a Gentile, gently rebukes his dissembling: "You hate being part of the Jews. You hate that." But his past perversely resists its repression. The book on Lushinski's coffee table, Raul Hilberg's masterly *The Destruction of the European Jews,* reveals a telltale hunger for Jewish history. And he is stung when Morris, in New

York ("a city of Jews"), sends him, in Africa, a letter that obliquely calls him "an impersonator. . . . Morris had called him Jew." Thus, once again, a Jew who tries mightily to assimilate is forced back into the Jewish identity of his birth. Like Tchernikhovsky in "Usurpation (Other People's Stories)," called kike by the Canaanite idols though he had fooled the God of the Jews, Lushinski confronts the return of the repressed as the tale ends. Here the blue and white colors, even in his cigarette smoke, signify both the Israeli flag and Holocaust memories as they connect his present self in Africa now to his past self in Poland. In doing so, they reveal, in the penultimate sentence, the name of the man Lushinski had killed and buried in Poland. His victim was none other than his own deepest self:

> And in Africa, in a white villa on the blue coast, . . . smoking and smoking, under the breath of the scented trees, under the shadow of the bluish snow, under the blue-black pillars of the Polish woods, . . . under the stone-white hanging stars of Poland—Lushinski.
> Against the stones and under the snow.

The story from which *Bloodshed and Three Novellas* took its name may have achieved that status because its theological mode of Jewish deracination outweighed the others—sociological in "An Education," political in "A Mercenary," and artistic in "Usurpation (Other People's Stories)." Here a Jewish American's knowledge of the Holocaust produces despair reaching both atheistic and suicidal dimensions. Feebly hoping to revive his faith, Jules Bleilip visits a village of Hasidim and joins a minyan led by an actual Holocaust survivor. Initially, the rebbe, whose fingernails were torn out in a death camp, appears to share Bleilip's feelings: "We were in trains, they drove us into showers of poison, . . . all our prayers are bleats and neighs on the way to a forsaken altar. Little fathers! How is it possible for us to live?" But suddenly he turns on Bleilip:

"Who are you?" To Bleilip's answer, "A Jew. Like yourselves," the rebbe retorts, "Atheist! Devourer! For us, there is the Most High, joy, life. . . . But you! . . . You believe the world is in vain." For Bleilip, a New York intellectual untested by tragic experience, the rebbe's final wisdom carries the weight of a survivor's testimony: "Despair must be earned."

MAKING THE OLD NEW AGAIN

In *Levitation: Five Fictions* (1982), Ozick's third volume of stories/novellas, she reinvigorates her familiar triad of themes—Jewish identity ("Levitation"), the pagan enticement ("Freud's Room," the Puttermesser-Xanthippe stories), and the struggles of the artist ("Shots")—with freshly imagined characters, settings, and dramatic situations. In "Levitation" a Christian minister's daughter marries a Jew named Feingold in an effort at reverse assimilation: he wants to marry a Gentile and she wants to become an "ancient Hebrew." But Feingold's rabid obsession with Jewish history, which to him consists mostly of Christians killing Jews from the time of the Crusades to the Holocaust, produces contrary results among those who listen to his tales of slaughter. While the Jews begin to levitate off the floor in their frenzy of fellow feeling, Feingold's earthbound wife becomes "jaded by atrocity. She is bored by the shootings and the gas." As she relishes instead the memory of Italian peasants dancing, her "ancient Hebrew" mask drops to reveal the ancient nature-worship that is her true religion.

Over half of *Levitation* is given over to "Puttermesser: Her Work History, Her Ancestry, Her Afterlife" and "Puttermesser and Xanthippe." Beginning at age thirty-four in the first segment and moving to forty-eight in the latter one, Puttermesser concludes the series in her mid-fifties with "Puttermesser Paired," which first appeared in

The New Yorker the week of October 8, 1990. The three segments have subsequently been published together as *The Puttermesser Papers* (1997). Of all Ozick's characters, Ruth Puttermesser is most clearly an alter ego of her author. With "a face of a vaguely Oriental cast," she is a bred-in-the-bone New Yorker who exults in studying Hebrew grammar and is determined to spend her afterlife reading all of Ozick's favorite authors—"all of Balzac, all of Dickens, all of Turgenev and Dostoyevsky (her mortal self had already read all of Tolstoy and George Eliot)." Initially, Ozick subjects her creation to postmodern playfulness, intruding at one point to challenge herself: "Hey! Puttermesser's biographer! What will you do with her now?" Ozick's answer to that question is to return to her earlier aesthetic mode, recovering "the old lost power of having a subject." She would "drill through the 'postmodern' and come out on the other side, alive and saved and wise as George Eliot."

Eventually, in "Puttermesser Paired," George Eliot was to figure very prominently, but first Puttermesser had to contend with the pagan enticement. In the novella-length "Puttermesser and Xanthippe," Ozick tried her hand at the then-current mode of "magic realism," which allowed her to appoint Puttermesser mayor of New York and furnish her with a golem. Unlike the Grand Rabbi of Prague's medieval golem, however, who was male and Germanic, Puttermesser's assistant is female and Greek. Now for once Pan and Moses—that is, Puttermesser and Xanthippe —function in harmony, with the latter's magic power effecting a transformation of the city. Rid of its crime, corruption, and debt, New York City thrives. But the golden moment cannot last. Xanthippe's true nature as a sex goddess breaks through at last ("Eros had entered Gracie Mansion") and consumes Puttermesser's whole slate of officers in her sexual fire. In a poignant finish, Puttermesser is forced to chant her beloved creature back to a pile of mud, much in the vein of

the original Grand Rabbi of Prague. *Levitation* as a whole thus assumes a downward configuration: it begins with a levitation and ends in a lapse back into ordinary reality.

Ozick's claim that her favorite period of fiction writing, the nineteenth century, produced "a Judaized novel" that gives "Puttermesser Paired" a special interest. "George Eliot and Dickens and Tolstoy were all touched by the Jewish covenant," she says, "they wrote of conduct and . . . will and commandment." But as far as conduct and commandment are concerned, Puttermesser chooses the wrong phase of George Eliot's life to impersonate, not the period of Eliot's major literary creativity but the time when the aging writer entered a disastrously unconsummated marriage with John Cross, a man twenty years her junior. In the 1990s, Ozick added two more episodes to the saga to make up the 236-page volume *The Puttermesser Papers* (1997). In "Puttermesser and the Muscovite Cousin," the collapse of the Soviet Union allows Puttermesser, now in her sixties, to invite a young relative from Russia to her home, only to find that her cousin Lidia proves far more savvy about acquiring American men and money than does Puttermesser herself. The series closes with "Puttermesser in Paradise," which begins shockingly with Puttermesser being "murdered and raped—in that order"—by a break-in burglar. After suffering some horrible knifework on her head, Puttermesser finds herself in Paradise, where she discovers that because of its timelessness "the secret meaning of Paradise is that it, too, is hell." Without a clock to distinguish past from present, the meaning of experience, and perhaps even the artist's storytelling power (which depends on sequence in time), disappears. So Puttermesser "walks through the white ash of Paradise" and "longs for the plain green earth." Appearing over a fifteen-year time span, the Puttermesser stories resemble John Updike's *Rabbit* novels in their relentless unfolding of their protagonists' aging process and in their many author-protagonist correspondences.

THREATS TO JEWISH HERITAGE

With *The Cannibal Galaxy* (1983), Ozick returned to the novel form that she had abandoned after *Trust* (1966). In showing the miseducation of a child prodigy, Beulah Lilt, Ozick avenges somewhat the "old school hurts" she had suffered during her grade school years when she "had teachers who hurt me, who made me believe I was stupid and inferior" at "book-hating, Jew-hating P.S. 71." And in showing Hester Lilt, Beulah's mother, to be more than a match for the novel's protagonist, Joseph Brill, Ozick portrayed her concept of feminism as full equality between the sexes. But the larger issue in *The Cannibal Galaxy* is the theme implicit in the title, namely the two deadly threats imposed upon the Jewish heritage by the Gentile majority. The more obvious of those threats, the Nazi murder machine, swept away Brill's parents and siblings during his boyhood in Paris and turned Brill's early life to horror. But the greater threat, ironically, is the friendly appeal of Holocaust-free America, whose assimilationist powers may devour the Judaic legacy more totally than Hitler's death camp gas ever could.

As founder and principal of a Jewish school in the American Midwest, Brill betrays his Jewish past regarding both of these threats. For the sake of his "Dual Curriculum," which he hopes will restore the symbiosis between European and Jewish cultures—"the intellectual union of Paris and Jerusalem"—Brill's classrooms eradicate the facts of Gentile persecution from Jewish history. This watered-down Jewish half of the dual curriculum has no chance of surviving the cannibal voracity of the other half, given the enormous magnetic pull of contemporary Gentile culture. The final blow to Brill's dream is his own class

snobbery, bred by his European past, which leads him to lament bringing "a scheme of learning luminous enough for a royal prince" to an unworthy American clientele: "Instead he was educating commoners, weeds, the children of plumbers." In the end, the cannibal galaxy gobbles up his own family: though duly circumcised in infancy, his only son becomes a totally deracinated American businessman, fluent in French but ignorant of all things Judaic. The dual curriculum ends here.

THE GAP BETWEEN IMAGINATION AND REALITY

In *The Messiah of Stockholm* (1987), Ozick converts her three master themes —Jewish identity, the pagan enticement, and the dangerous efficacy of art —into a conflict between imagination and reality. The imagination in this instance belongs to Swedish book critic Lars Andemening, who eschews the "stewpot" of reality—the daily gathering of his fellow journalists to swap gossip and newsbits—in favor of a private dreamlife centered on the fantastic belief that he is the son of Bruno Schulz, in real life a Jewish writer of magic stories who in 1942 was shot to death in his Polish village by a Nazi officer. To confirm this belief, Andemening seeks Schulz's lost novel, *The Messiah,* as a magic totem of the lost father. On the other side of the conflict is the Judaic reality principle, which is principally embodied in Lars' friend and confidante, a bookshop owner named Heidi. Lars fixes upon Schulz's art, whereas Heidi fastens upon his life. For her, as a realist, Bruno Schulz is an obsessive interest not because of his paganized fiction but because of his death by murder, which evokes Jewish history once again: "It was the catastrophe of fact that she wanted, Lars's father gunned down in the gutters of Drohobycz, along with two hundred and thirty other Jews."

Eventually, through Heidi, Lars meets Schulz's

daughter Adela and her mentor Dr. Eklund, who bring Lars the lost *Messiah* in an amphora-like vessel in return for Lars' agreement, as a widely read book critic, to give it a laudatory review. Avidly devouring the work, Lars acquires Schulz's "magic eye," which, with an effect like that of the "magic crown" in "Usurpation (Other People's Stories)," makes him feel "as if copulating with an angel whose wings were on fire." Huge gouts of creative energy shake his being, visions of "crisscrossing rivers, whirlpools twisting their foaming necks, . . . a thousand shoots and sprays bombarding the oceanscape's peaks." But this oceanscape is notably devoid of life. Here his "stewpot" pals reappear as wax dummies, and the Adela of Schulz's manuscript mutates into a Canaanite idol, "made of some artificial dead matter" with eyes that are green jewels, behind whom may be discerned the cannibal god Moloch, devouring human burnt offerings as though this were the Holocaust that the scene adumbrates. At last, the *Messiah* manuscript itself is consumed in fire, and Lars' three friends—Heidi, Dr. Eklund, and Adela—are exposed as impostors who forged *The Messiah* in hopes of profit. Lars's long dream is broken, and he returns chastened to the "stewpot" of ordinary social reality. Even so, the drabness of ordinary life as compared to the excitement of idolatrous Schulz-worship suffices to leave the conflict between imagination and reality unresolved as this novel ends. The conflict thus carries over to Ozick's best-known work of fiction, *The Shawl*.

Originally written in 1977, the two segments of *The Shawl* were published separately in *The New Yorker*—"The Shawl" in 1980 and "Rosa" in 1983—prior to their joint appearance in *The Shawl* in 1989. In *The Shawl,* the gap between imagination and reality widens to Grand Canyon proportions. As a death camp survivor, Rosa Lublin embodies as graphically realistic an experience of Holocaust horror as fiction can make available—a Dantesque nightmare of cold, filth,

starvation, and rapacious, murderous violence. None of Ozick's previous characters had ever sustained so harrowing an immersion in the horrors of "Jewish history." As a survival mechanism against that horror, however, Rosa escapes into an extreme, lifelong fantasy, focused not on a lost father like Lars' Bruno Schulz but on a lost—that is, murdered—daughter, Magda, whose very name suggests the forbidden pagan/Christian realm of Magdelene/Magi/magic. From the moment Magda is hurled into the camp's electric fence, Rosa makes a magic totem of the shawl in which she had last cradled her child, and by such means she transmutes her lost Magda into a living presence that survives to Rosa's old age in America decades later.

Forming a counterweight to Rosa's fantasy life are *The Shawl*'s two other main characters—Stella, her niece and death camp companion, and Persky, an elderly Jewish immigrant from Warsaw whom she meets in a Miami laundromat. Together, these two press the L'Chaim! ethos on Rosa—Stella by begging her "don't be a crazy person! Live your life!" while Persky argues that "it's over. You went through it, now you owe yourself something." In addition, Stella strikes at the idolatry of Rosa's obsession, most notably when she, in New York City, mails the shawl to Rosa in Miami with the warning that Rosa is making a "relic" of her daughter while turning the shawl into an "idol" comparable to "the True Cross." The book ends, however, in ambiguity, with the brightest fantasy in the whole narrative lighting up the closing pages—"The whole room was full of Magda. . . . Magda's hair . . . as yellow as buttercups"—but with Persky coming up the stairs to visit Rosa bearing his reality-based L'Chaim! philosophy.

Apart from his Judaic philosophy, Persky bears one other vital motif through this novella, the theme of class discrimination among Jews. When during their first meeting Rosa mentioned being from Warsaw, Persky delightedly told her that he too came from that heavily Jewish environment, which he had left during the pre-Hitler era. Her retort, "My Warsaw isn't your Warsaw," is meant to draw a sharp line between her aristocratic milieu within a wealthy, cultivated family and Persky's low-class vulgarity: "She imagined what bitter ancient alley, dense with stalls, . . . signs in jargoned Yiddish. . . . The Americans couldn't tell her apart from this fellow with his false teeth and his dewlaps and his rakehell reddish toupee." A further telltale sign of their class difference is her utter ignorance of what Persky and similar New York Jews had learned through their strong ties to the city's gigantic garment industry: "Whatever you wore they would feel between their fingers and give a name to: faille, corduroy, herringbone, shantung, jersey. . . . " The nearly incredible epitome of Rosa's class snobbery occurs when her family is thrust into confinement with other Holocaust victims and her main grievance applies not to Nazi behavior but to this violation of class boundaries: "Can you imagine a family like us . . . who had lived in a house with four floors and a glorious attic. . . . imagine confining us with teeming Moskowiczes and Rabinowiczes and Finkelsteins." Through its bitter sarcasm against class hierarchy, Ozick's most recent novel links itself to her first one, *Trust*, where the spiritual anemia associated with Allegra Vand's wealth plays off against the robust vitality of the low-class Purse family. In *The Shawl*, however, both high- and low-class categories function, shamefully, within the Jewish community.

Although Ozick's literary reputation rests ultimately on her fiction, she has also been a prominent essayist from the 1960s to the 1990s. Published originally in high-brow journals such as *The New Yorker* and *Commentary,* the essays were gathered into three dense volumes: *Art & Ardor: Essays, Metaphor & Memory: Essays* (1989), and *Fame & Folly: Essays* (1996). Her main topic is the work of other artists, to whom she applies extensive study, intensive analysis,

and an irresistibly elegant style. Her full lineup of fellow writers is imposing: Edith Wharton, Virginia Woolf, E. M. Forster, Truman Capote, John Updike, Gershom Scholem, Harold Bloom, I. B. Singer, Bruno Schulz, and Henry James in *Art & Ardor: Essays;* Cyril Connolly, William Gaddis, Italo Calvino, J. M. Coetzee, Primo Levi, Saul Bellow, Theodore Dreiser, George Steiner, Bruno Schulz (again), Sholem Aleichem, S. Y. Agnon, C. N. Bialik, and Henry James (again) in *Metaphor & Memory: Essays;* T. S. Eliot (two essays), Alfred Chester, Anthony Trollope, Isaac Babel, George Steiner (again), Mark Twain, Saul Bellow (again), Salman Rushdie, and Henry James (again) in *Fame & Folly: Essays.* Along with other writers, such as George Eliot, who maintain a pervasive presence in these pages, these names help indicate the complex mixture of interests that Ozick's fiction turned into art. Other essays of special importance in these books are "Justice to Feminism," "Literary Blacks and Jews," and "A Drugstore in Winter" (about her parents) in *Art & Ardor: Essays;* "Washington Square, 1946," "The Muse, Postmodern and Homeless," and "The Question of Our Speech" in *Metaphor & Memory: Essays;* and "Of Christian Heroism" and "Against Modernity" in *Fame & Folly: Essays.*

Because of her late start, the critical response to Ozick has been unusually belated. Though just thirty-eight when her major opus, *Trust,* was published, she was fifty-five when the first substantial response to her work appeared in a seventy-five-page segment of the summer 1983 *Texas Studies in Literature and Language,* edited by William Scheick and Catherine Rainwater. In 1986 Harold Bloom followed with the first book about Ozick, consisting of thirteen book reviews and six essays. In the fall of 1987 Daniel Walden devoted the entire issue of *Studies in American Jewish Literature* to Ozick, and the same year saw the first single-author study of Ozick, Sanford Pinsker's *The Uncompromising Fictions of Cynthia*

Ozick. In 1988 Joseph Lowin's *Cynthia Ozick* appeared, followed in 1989 by Vera Emuma Kielsky's *Inevitable Exiles,* and in 1991 by Lawrence S. Friedman's *Understanding Cynthia Ozick.* In 1993 and 1994, three more books came into print: Elaine M. Kauvar's *Cynthia Ozick's Fiction* (1993), Sarah Blacher Cohen's *Cynthia Ozick's Comic Art* (1994), and my own *Greek Mind/Jewish Soul: The Conflicted Art of Cynthia Ozick* (1994). Perhaps this is the moment to thank the University of Wisconsin Press for allowing me free use of the book in this essay: some repetition of evidence and argumentation, though on a greatly reduced scale, was unavoidable.

Not surprisingly, considering the centrality of Jewish identity in Ozick's writing, the major focus of all these books has been their Jewish cultural ambience. In rendering a final judgment of Ozick's oeuvre, however, I would judge that her Jewish heritage poses no more of an obstacle to her status as an American writer than does Faulkner's Southern regionalism or Hawthorne's Puritan ambience. Her dualities—Pan and Moses, Puttermesser and Xanthippe, Bleilip and the rebbe in "Bloodshed," Lushinski and Morris in "A Mercenary," Edelshtein and the evangelist in "Envy; or, Yiddish in America," Joseph Brill's "Dual Curriculum" in *The Cannibal Galaxy*—reflect an American theme as old as Edgar Allan Poe's William Wilson, Mark Twain's Huck Finn and Tom Sawyer, or the man/horse dichotomy of Updike's *The Centaur.* And her fears of cultural annihilation—whether through hostile violence or friendly assimilation or a younger generation renouncing Yiddish—find an echo in other defenders of a threatened minority heritage such as Toni Morrison, Maxine Hong Kingston, and Scott Momaday. She is most American, perhaps, in the urgency of her theme of identity—the search for, or denial of, one's deepest self—that motivates scenes as various as the narrator's search for a father in *Trust,* Lushinski recalling his buried Polish self in "A Mercenary," and Rosa

fantasizing her ideal of motherhood in *The Shawl.* Thanks to her compelling mastery of narrative, style, and characterization, Cynthia Ozick has transmuted her "Jewish artist" oxymoron into an entirely original literary oeuvre that significantly enriches our national literature.

Note: Since 1982, Ms. Ozick and I have carried on a written correspondence from which I have cited excerpts in this essay.

Selected Bibliography

WORKS OF CYNTHIA OZICK

NOVELS AND SHORT STORIES
Trust. New York: New American Library, 1966.
The Pagan Rabbi and Other Stories. New York: Knopf, 1971.
Bloodshed and Three Novellas. New York: Knopf, 1976.
Levitation: Five Fictions. New York: Knopf, 1982.
The Cannibal Galaxy. New York: Knopf, 1983.
The Messiah of Stockholm. New York: Knopf, 1987.
The Shawl. New York: Knopf, 1989. (Contains "The Shawl" and "Rosa.")
The Puttermesser Papers. New York: Knopf, 1997.

OTHER WORKS
"We Are the Crazy Lady and Other Feisty Feminine Fables." *Ms.* 1: 40–44 (Spring 1972).
Art & Ardor: Essays. New York: Knopf, 1983.
"Notes Toward Finding the Right Question." In *On Being a Jewish Feminist: A Reader.* Edited by Susannah Heschel. New York: Schocken Books, 1983. p. 131.
Metaphor & Memory: Essays. New York: Knopf, 1989.
What Henry James Knew. Bennington, Vt.: Bennington College, 1993.
Fame & Folly: Essays. New York: Knopf, 1996.
Portrait of the Artist as a Bad Character: and Other Essays on Writing. London: Pimlico, 1996.

A Cynthia Ozick Reader. Edited by Elaine M. Kauvar. Bloomington: Indiana University Press, 1996.

BIOGRAPHICAL AND CRITICAL STUDIES

BOOKS

Cohen, Sarah Blacher. *Cynthia Ozick's Comic Art.* Bloomington: Indiana University Press, 1994.

Friedman, Lawrence S. *Understanding Cynthia Ozick.* Columbia: University of South Carolina Press, 1991.

Kauvar, Elaine M. *Cynthia Ozick's Fiction: Tradition and Invention.* Bloomington: Indiana University Press, 1993.

Kielsky, Vera Emuma. *Inevitable Exiles.* New York: Peter Lang, 1989.

Lowen, Joseph. *Cynthia Ozick.* Boston: G. K. Hall & Co., 1988.

Pinsker, Sanford. *The Uncompromising Fictions of Cynthia Ozick.* Columbia: University of Missouri Press, 1987.

Strandberg, Victor. *Greek Mind/Jewish Soul: The Conflicted Art of Cynthia Ozick.* Madison: University of Wisconsin Press, 1994.

ARTICLES

Burstein, Janet Handler. "Cynthia Ozick and the Transgression of Art." *American Literature* 59, no. 1: 85–101 (March 1987).

Chertok, Haim. "Ozick's Hoofprints." *Modern Jewish Studies* Annual 6, published by *Yiddish* magazine 6, no. 4: 5–12 (1987).

Epstein, Joseph. "Cynthia Ozick, Jewish Writer." *Commentary* 77, no. 3: 64–69 (March 1984).

Finkelstein, Norman. "The Struggle for Historicity in the Fiction of Cynthia Ozick." *Lit: Literature, Interpretation, Theory* 1, no. 4: 291–302 (May 1990).

Gitenstein, R. Barbara. "The Temptation of Apollo and the Loss of Yiddish in Cynthia Ozick's Fiction." *Studies in American Jewish Literature* 3: 194–201 (1983).

Krupnick, Mark. "Cynthia Ozick as the Jewish T. S. Eliot." *Soundings: An Interdisciplinary Journal* 74, no. 3–4: 351–369 (Fall–Winter 1991).

Lakritz, Andrew. "Cynthia Ozick at the End of the Modern." *Chicago Review* 40, no. 1: 98–117 (1994).

Rose, Elisabeth. "Cynthia Ozick's Liturgical Postmodernism." *Studies in American Jewish Literature* 9, no. 1: 93–107 (Spring 1990).

Rovit, Earl. "The Two Languages of Cynthia Ozick." *Studies in American Jewish Literature* 8, no. 1: 34–49 (Spring 1989).

Weiner, Deborah Heiligman. "Cynthia Ozick, Pagan vs. Jew (1966–1976)." *Studies in American Jewish Literature* 3:179–183 (1983).

Wilner, Arlene Fish. "The Jewish-American Woman as Artist: Cynthia Ozick and the 'Paleface' Tradition." *College Literature* 20, no. 2: 119–132 (June 1993).

INTERVIEWS

Kauver, Elaine M. *Contemporary Literature* 26, no. 4: 375–401 (Winter 1985).

Rainwater, Catherine, and William J. Scheick. *Texas Studies in Language and Literature* 25, no. 2: 255–265 (Summer 1983).

Teicholz, Tom. "The Art of Fiction" Series (xcv) of the *Paris Review* 29: 167, 182–183 (Spring 1987).

—*VICTOR STRANDBERG*

Upton Sinclair

1878–1968

LIBERTY HILL

*I*N THE CHRONOLOGICAL middle of the journey of his long life, Upton Sinclair had already found international reputation and popularity for fusing journalism and art in the service of democratic social change. On that cool May evening in 1923, he had eighteen novels, nine works of nonfiction, and six plays in print (not to mention the pamphlets). Although a select handful of titles originally had been brought out by commercial publishing houses, all were now published and distributed primarily through his own efforts and those of his second wife, life and literary partner Mary Craig Sinclair. His newest titles would be rapidly translated into an assortment of languages. With the facile assistance of a Chicago printer, he and "Craig," as his wife was known, could sell his books very nearly at cost. (At the end of that journey Sinclair would have authored ninety books and a mountain of other publications.)

Sinclair arguably stood alone as the first major American literary figure to intentionally and successfully address his art to the masses when, on May 15, 1923, he was arrested in the city of Los Angeles for publicly reading from the First Amendment of the U.S. Constitution.

He had traveled just a few dozen miles south that day from his Pasadena home to San Pedro (the port of Los Angeles), supported by friends who were referred to by newspapers for the combination of their affluence and socialism as "parlor pinks." He spoke in defense of the civil liberties of a thousand or so generally nameless workers and members of the Industrial Workers of the World labor union. These so-called Wobblies were being arrested en masse under California's Criminal Syndicalism Act, which denied their right to assemble and speak in conjunction with a maritime and oil workers' strike that was under way in the port at the time; the strike would ultimately fail. They were being rounded up by the Los Angeles Police Department and would be sent via specially commissioned streetcar to what would become in effect a temporary concentration camp built by order of the city council. Their eventual destination would be San Quentin prison.

As he had done in the past and would do again in the future, Sinclair stepped out of the writing room and into the streets. He lent his name to a movement in the same spirit that he applied it to his own work—as a nexus to cooperatively unite two vastly divided sectors of American society in the collective cause of social reform. Sinclair was escorted from the privately owned field (named Liberty Hill by the Wobblies who assembled there to hear speeches and songs), although he had in his pocket the owner's written permission to be there. "I thank you," he was reported to have said to the arresting officer. He was held incommunicado for eighteen hours before his whereabouts were leaked to Craig, who posted his bail.

"I would rather deal with 4,000 I.W.W. than one man like Sinclair, who [sic] I consider one of the worst types of radicals," Los Angeles Police Department chief Louis D. Oaks declared in a written statement. Sinclair characteristically and publicly replied in a letter later reproduced in full in *The Autobiography of Upton Sinclair* (1962)·

> I thank you for this compliment, for to be dangerous to lawbreakers in office such as yourself is the highest duty that a citizen of this community can perform . . . . I am not a giant physically; I shrink from pain and filth and vermin and foul air, like any other man of refinement; also, I freely admit that when I see a line of a hundred policemen with drawn revolvers flung across a street to keep anyone from coming on to private property to hear my feeble voice, I am somewhat disturbed in my nerves. But I have a conscience and a religious faith, and I know that our liberties were not won without suffering, and may be lost again through our cowardice.

The event would eventually lead to the founding of the Southern California Chapter of the American Civil Liberties Union.

HISTORY AS MIRROR

In miniature, the mix of shrewd humor and alarming seriousness demonstrated by his activism on Liberty Hill also characterizes the perpetually problematic place this writer holds in relation to the literary pantheon of a country that continues to share his initials. It was neither the first nor the last time he would be arrested in such highly politicized circumstances. As with his other, numerous direct interventions in the course of nearly four generations of its history, some minor and some quite major indeed, he would pro-

duce his own account of events in one literary form or another.

Nine short months after his arrest, Sinclair opened *The Goslings* (1924)—his essayistic account of the corporate mind control at work in secondary education—with the events of Liberty Hill cast as his personal experience of egregious power abuse at a local level. *The Goslings* was his fourth of six full-length nonfiction books that comprised the so-called Dead Hand series. Sinclair's name for the series was a scornful reference to the "Invisible Hand" that guided Adam Smith's laissez-faire economic philosophy in *The Wealth of Nations*.

These six very readable self-published attacks on capitalist institutions were at the heart of his status as a nationally important public intellectual amid the excesses of post–World War I America. Spanning the decade between his last major literary work, *King Coal* (1917), and his next one, *Oil!* (1927), he used massive, journalistic documentation in the series to "muck rake" just about every institution that could have fostered his posterity as a writer beyond his lifetime.

The Profits of Religion (1918) traces the abuses of institutional religion. By far the most popular and still salient to the contemporary media critic, *The Brass Check* (1920) refers to journalism's corruption at the hands of capital as analogous to prostitution, particularly in regard to its coverage of labor issues. (The same 1920s newspapers he criticizes were, of course, responsible for reviewing his books; it is telling that F. Scott Fitzgerald, once considered the literary poster boy for the excesses of the 1920s, would later refer admiringly to *The Brass Check* in his career-killing confession, *The Crack-Up*.)

The Goose-Step (1923) criticizes the higher education industry that, along with its secondary education subsidary criticized in *The Goslings,* would be ultimately responsible for teaching (or not teaching) Sinclair's work and for providing the historical means to understand it. *Mammonart*

(1925) goes so far as to criticize the industry of canonical culture itself, by defining all art as propaganda and condemning the vast majority of canonical artists for using that power of propaganda to further the interests of the ruling class. Among his handful of exceptions, Sinclair included Euripides, Dante, Miguel de Cervantes, Friedrich Nietzsche, Leo Tolstoy, and particularly Walt Whitman, in whose democratic spirit he said he undertook his study. Finally, forever in search of journalistic simultaneity, in *Money Writes!* (1927) he targeted established, contemporary American novelists, critics, and poets (in short, anyone remaining who might have been able to put in a good word for him).

Four months after the historical events surrounding Sinclair's arrest at Liberty Hill found their way into *The Goslings,* they would take the form of a four-act play. Stylistically experimental (unusual for Sinclair), *Singing Jailbirds* (1924) takes its name from the Wobbly habit of writing and singing songs, even in jail, to strengthen collective will, idealism, and humor. The play was published as the bloody backlash against the failed San Pedro Maritime and Oil Workers' Strike was being exacted. In a lengthy postscript Sinclair painstakingly details the play's factual correspondence to concrete events, concluding with a "breaking news" account of Wobbly Hall being raided and destroyed in June 1924:

> a mob of three hundred men, including policemen and sailors, raids a peaceful entertainment held in the I.W.W. hall at San Pedro, and beats all present with baseball bats and clubs. One little girl is thrown into a vat of boiling coffee, so that the flesh is cooked off her limbs, and she is in hospital, not expected to live.

The play's central action follows the police brutality in the interrogation of Red Adams, to his detention in a holding tank with his fellow Wobblies, to his solitary confinement in the hole, where his mind flees into hallucinations of his wife and comrades. The role most closely corresponding to that of Sinclair, interestingly, takes the form of a priest who is thrown in jail, like Sinclair had been, for speaking his conscience.

Singing Jailbirds would not be produced in the United States until the end of 1928, when four young Greenwich Village playwrights, including Eugene O'Neill and then-radical John Dos Passos, kept it running for several months. In 1927, however, it was successfully produced in Berlin.

That same year the tragic culmination of the San Pedro strike would find its highest literary home in the hauntingly accurate, dramatically distilled denouement of his epic California novel, *Oil!*

First conceived in the heat of those events and deeply rooted in his firsthand experience with the local Los Angeles politics of the day, as documented and researched in the Dead Hand series, *Oil!* stands by itself as a great political novel. Its scope is as locally dependent and as internationally engaged as the subject it tackles—American capital. *Oil!* fits well into the category of what consummate stylist Henry James called a "loose, baggy monster," referring to Tolstoy's *War and Peace* (one of the few works Sinclair would spare the flame in *Mammonart*).

Oil! resists classification, and those who view it within generic prescriptions of literary value may too easily dismiss it as artless because the emotional relationships between characters are often stylized and sometimes flat, particularly those between its centrally positioned emotional observer—the carefully unmacho Bunny Ross, son of an "Angel City" oil baron—and the women he allegedly loves. The deep emotion of *Oil!* functions primarily at the levels of historical reflection and place.

Across the industrial harbor, not two years before and not ten miles from the labor strike on Liberty Hill, a very different sort of strike took place on Signal Hill in Long Beach, California: oil was discovered. The second of three major oil strikes within fifteen miles and as many months, Signal Hill meant instant wealth on a scale unparalleled in world history. But oil also meant oil workers to dangerously tap it from the ground and maritime workers to bring in the instant inventory of lumber required for the derricks that were springing up like giants among the lampposts of the streets of Long Beach. Through the novel's irresistible structure, the Signal Hill oil field discovery in Long Beach (Sinclair calls it Beach City) leads inexorably to the violent aftermath of Liberty Hill in Los Angeles (Sinclair calls it Angel City). Add a third California hill and the full scope of Sinclair's tragedy becomes clear: The Elk Hill naval oil reserves—federal spoils from the patriotic urgency of the War to End All Wars—were illegally transferred to a California oil baron by the Harding administration in 1921. They became a source of federal scandal (not to mention a presidential coronary) whose investigation continued from 1923 to the day *Oil!* was published.

The novel opens—in what is among the most technically masterful prose in Sinclair's stylistically straightforward oeuvre—with Bunny's childhood auto ride into the modern age; his powerful, doting father behind the wheel of an industry so fresh one can still smell the oil beneath it:

> The road ran, smooth and flawless, precisely fourteen feet wide, the edges trimmed as if by shears, a ribbon of grey concrete, rolled out over the valley by a giant hand . . . . "Whoosh!" went the other projectile, hurtling past; a loud, swift "Whoosh!" with no tapering off at the end. You had a glimpse of another man with horn-rimmed spectacles like yourself, with a similar grip of two hands upon a steering wheel, and a similar cataleptic fixation of the eyes. You never looked back; for at fifty miles an hour, your business is with the things that lie before you, and the past is the past—or shall we say the passed are the passed?

Sinclair had personal experience with the Signal Hill oil speculation frenzy. Craig owned a small urban plot of land nearby when the wildcat wells started to gush, sending ordinary people into frantic, self-defeating "community lease" meetings, such as the one young Bunny witnesses in chapter two at the coattails of his father. At that meeting, Bunny meets and admires Wobbly-in-the-making Paul Watkins (who may have been partially inspired by Paul Ware, one of the key organizers of the San Pedro strike). By chapter five he is taking his father to the humble goat ranch of Paul's father on a hunch there might be oil beneath it, thus staging the ideological conflict between his two role models that will propel the narrative from local to international territory, then back again.

Paul's brother, Eli, turns into a self-proclaimed prophet who makes big business out of radio religion (modeled on Aimee Semple MacPherson, who was also the basis for Elmer Gantry, the creation of his friend and protégé Sinclair Lewis, with whom he was in frequent dialogue). Sinclair playfully railroads the University of Southern California as the mind-warping "Southern Pacific University." The reader speeds through even larger vistas as powerfully meticulous oil industry detail unlocks the machinations of the Hollywood film industry; the antilabor, red-baiting press; and even World War I transposed to the 1920s with effortless verisimilitude. "It was literally true," Sinclair's narrator notes simply, "that capitalist industry was a world war going on all the time."

In that true moment of transposed American history, Paul is sent as a soldier to Russia and forced to stay incommunicado after the war is over to protect the interests of capital in the face of the Bolshevik revolution. Finally Paul returns home to the inevitable events of the early 1920s:

> Everywhere confusion, women in hysterics, or sunk upon the floor sobbing. There was not a stick of furniture in the place that had not been wrecked; the chairs had been split with hatchets; the piano had been gutted, its entrails lay tangled on the floor . . . the metal urn or container in which the coffee had

been boiling had been overset, and its steaming contents running here and there . . . The flesh had been cooked off their legs, and they would be crippled for life; one was a ten year old girl known as "the wobbly song bird"; she had a sweet treble, and sang sentimental ballads and rebel songs, and the mob leader had jerked her from the platform, saying, "We'll shut your damned mouth!" . . . Bunny didn't expect to find Paul, but there he lay, flat on his back, with several people bending over him. His left eye was a mass of blood, and seemed as if destroyed by a blow; he lay, limp and motionless, and when Bunny called his name he did not answer.

All the major elements of Sinclair's multifaceted, multigenerational literary achievement are contained within *Oil!*'s ample binding; aspects of every significant work he had undertaken to that point and of every significant work he would undertake from that point forward are somewhere represented.

In the end—although the warm, loving relationship between Bunny and his father and the worshipful and largely unrequited one between himself and arch-Wobbly Paul Watkins are moving in themselves—the novel's tragic heroism cannot be related to the character of any exemplary individual will. Rather, it is to be found in the collective defeat of common sense and purpose. *Oil!*'s is the literary opposite of the Fitzgeraldian view of 1920s America. There is no Great Gatsby here—reflected at the heart of *Oil!* is the neglected spirit of Liberty Hill.

THE DEATH OF THE ARTIST AS A YOUNG MAN

Upton Beall Sinclair Jr. was not born an activist, though he may very well have been born a writer, exhibiting photographic memory and nearly total recall by the age of five; through four generations of American letters, he never made a dime from anything but his labor with the word. He came to be in a Baltimore boardinghouse on September 20, 1878—the Southern son of a Southern son of a long line of Norfolk naval officers—on the heels of the Civil War and Federal Reconstruction. Upton Beall Sinclair Sr., who felt history had sunk his ship, was a poor salesman and an alcoholic.

Also the son of the daughter of the secretary-treasurer of the Western Maryland Railroad, Sinclair was born a poor relation to the robber baronage of American capital. Baltimore was a railroad town on the heels of the Great Railroad Strikes of 1877, the spiritual dawn of the Progressive Era in American history.

Priscilla Harden Sinclair focused her child's interests away from history and onto literature and her father's less worldly calling as a Methodist deacon. Sinclair learned his mother's English literary predilections and her Protestant distaste for liquor (which would last all his days) as his father sank deeper down the bottle. While her sister had married a millionaire banker, Priscilla and her son found a schizophrenic sort of affluence only when visiting relatives for the summer; otherwise life was economically uncertain.

When Sinclair was ten the family moved north to New York City and more boardinghouses. At age fourteen he began his formal education by enrolling in City College; he studied philosophy and literature. New Yorkers Walt Whitman and Herman Melville had both died in the previous year.

As his father's alcoholism worsened, requiring occasional hospitalization (he would finally die because of it in 1911), and as the increasing emotional needs of his mother became more onerous to him, Sinclair turned to a young Episcopal minister named William Wilmerding Moir. Moir taught his adolescent protégés that the repression of sexual desire enhances mental ability.

Sinclair first earned his way out of his father's house by writing racially stereotypical jokes, at a dollar a pop, for the popular magazines of the day. He wrote his first story, about a young Black boy who steals a bird, for $25. In another story, published at the time in his college literary magazine, he wrote about a lazy, drunken Virginia Black man, in apparent reference to his father.

Despite his future radicalism, Sinclair would remain throughout his life a man of his place, class, and times. While he would soon become and remain a passionate and devoted advocate of both multicultural democracy and sexual equality, expressions of his racial and sexual anxieties occasionally continued to surface, even in his mature work.

Turning to the hack-fictional adventures of young men in the Naval Academy, he soon found himself living by the word: singing the praises of U.S. imperialism in the Philippines, Hawaii, Puerto Rico, and Cuba that had been occasioned by the Spanish-American War, and mocking the unwashed agitators of populism.

He took shelter in the idea of his own genius at this time, which he believed could elevate him above historical concerns, as he believed it had his three adolescent heroes: Percy Shelley, Shakespeare's Hamlet, and Jesus. (The borders between fact and fiction were never a sticking point for Sinclair.)

When he first came to the dismissive attention of the New York literary world, he was still one half step removed from the sense of politics that would preoccupy his greatest works. Although steeped in the works of the radical (and radically subjective) individualists of the Western European canon, collective consciousness was far from his mind. He considered himself a pure artist.

Meta H. Fuller—whom he met while writing a self-described literary masterpiece in a cabin in the woods and married in the fall of 1900— agreed. (They had also agreed not to sleep together, but he was eventually forced to concede on that point.) In 1901 he returned to New York City, borrowed money from a relative after a series of publishers rejected *Springtime and Harvest* (1901), and published it himself, selling very

few copies. In the depths of December, Meta gave birth to his only son, David. His activities in politics at the time were restricted to the confines of New York's Tammany Hall.

Through a chance encounter in 1902, he was formally exposed to socialism, albeit by the upper echelons of its most affluent practitioners (among them the millionaire publisher Gaylord Wilshire). Sinclair's Protestant predisposition and his current economic impasse infused the fortuitous discovery of this newfound belief with the essential, psychological elements of a religious conversion. The experience would be cast about in various forms for several years before finding its first genuine literary expression. So, too, would the increasingly miserable personal experiences of Sinclair's marriage.

In the meantime, in what amounted to a publicity stunt, Sinclair convinced a publishing house to release *The Journal of Arthur Stirling* (1903) as if the narrator, who kills himself in the end, had actually written it. It was not merely a joke; in a very real sense Sinclair was psychologically exorcising the subjective poet from his as yet undefined literary designs. The press was not amused. Four months later the publication of *Prince Hagen* (1903) took his recent discovery of Friedrich Nietzsche (decades before his English translation) into the corruption of Tammany Hall through Wagnerian fantasy. Teddy Roosevelt was launching his 1904 election campaign to legitimate his presidency. The word of the day was "reform."

In August 1904, some months before Roosevelt's election, Sinclair published *Manassas,* an extensively researched novel of the Civil War. Its main character, ubiquitous Alan Montague, brushes shoulders with everyone from Jefferson Davis to John Brown as Sinclair set out to critically exorcise the injustice of slavery at the roots of his Southern past.

Slavery, as Sinclair would quickly discover through his newfound appetite for the facts, was not confined to the South; neither was it confined to the past.

THE BIRTH OF A PUBLIC INTELLECTUAL

Even as Sinclair sought to redefine himself as an Easterner, his new sense of politics was drawing him to the populist traditions (and audiences) of the West.

Sinclair's discovery of the *Appeal to Reason*—a Kansas-based journal deeply rooted in the populist and socialist traditions of the radical, abolitionist "Free State" activists of the 1850s—first allowed him to come into contact with a mass readership. He began to see these primarily Western workers and farmers as his audience. By 1904, when Sinclair had officially joined the Socialist Party and had become an avid reader of the journal, the *Appeal to Reason* had a circulation of several hundred thousand; it also exposed him to Jack London and other like-minded writers and thinkers who published in its well-read, mass-appealing pages. Sinclair first published a series of articles in that year on the unsuccessful 1904 Chicago meatpacking strike, which would become the historical center of the one book among ninety for which Upton Sinclair is remembered: *The Jungle* (1906).

Years later, he would begin his "Dead Hand" critique of American journalism in *The Brass Check* with his personal experience of *The Jungle*'s publication (just as he would use his experience at Liberty Hill to introduce *The Goslings*):

> There was a strike of the wage-slaves of the Beef Trust in Chicago, and I wrote for the "Appeal to Reason" a broadside addressed to these strikers. . . . This broadside was taken up by the Socialists of the Stockyards district, and thirty thousand copies were distributed among the defeated strikers. . . . I ceased to oppose social wickedness with the fragile weapon of poetry, with visions and inspirations and consecrations; instead, I took a sharp sword of

contemporary fact, and thrust it into the vitals of one of those monstrous parasites which are sucking the life-blood of the American people.

The Chicago stockyards were the first fully realized manifestation of mass production the world had ever known; Sinclair, through a combination of journalistic acumen, political awakening, and personal despair, became its first poet. What the whaling industry had metaphysically foreboded to Melville before the Civil War, the meat industry materially demonstrated to Sinclair in its aftermath. Earlier that year in an article published in the mainstream magazine, *Collier's*, entitled "Our Bourgeois Literature," Sinclair insists that art, rather than transcending the social structure, depends on it.

As he was pitching the novel to publishers, the editor of the *Appeal to Reason* dared him to write a *Manassas* for wage slavery and gave him $500 for serialization rights. He took it, put a down payment on a New Jersey farm for his wife and new child, and—in a spirit not dissimilar to Ishmael's "hypos" as he takes himself a'whaling to better understand the workings of this great Democracy in *Moby Dick*—set off for the Chicago heartland. Once in "Packingtown," he put himself in the position of a meatpacking worker for seven weeks and investigated through observation.

What he observed was hard for publishers to swallow at first. The novel, already appearing serially in the *Appeal to Reason*, had been accepted with a $500 advance by the Macmillan Company. When they saw the manuscript, though, Sinclair was told to cut out some of the bloodier details. He refused. Four other publishers rejected the book as well, until Jack London called from the pages of the *Appeal to Reason* for America's Socialists to publish it themselves. Sinclair raised $4,000 that way, and once he had had the plates made on his own, Doubleday, Page, and Company accepted it on condition that the "facts" be investigated. They first relied on a reporter from the *Chicago Tribune* who reported back that virtually every detail of the reality portrayed in Sinclair's novel was false. When it was discovered by Doubleday's own investigator that the reporter had based his own discoveries not on observation but on a 32-page report from the publicity department of the Armour and Company meatpackers, Doubleday agreed to publish *The Jungle* with the facts as Sinclair had presented them. The only concession on Sinclair's part may have been his abandoning of the easily recognizable, alliterative names for Armour, Swift, and Morris, the three offending members of the Chicago Beef Trust. (They became Durham, Brown, and Jones, respectively.)

The rest is American history; it earned Sinclair his place in the index of virtually every high school textbook that covers the period. The novel became an overnight best-seller, drawing the attention of President Teddy Roosevelt and prompting federal regulation of the industry in the form of the Pure Food and Drug Act of 1906.

However, as Sinclair would succinctly note in *The Brass Check,* conditions for the workers remained as bad as ever. Meat in *The Jungle* is primarily a metaphor to communicate the plight of the modern wage-slave; that fact was lost to the middle-class metabolism of the day. "I aimed at the public's heart," said Sinclair, "and by accident I hit it in the stomach."

While any treatment of Upton Sinclair, whether literary or historical, must focus significant attention on *The Jungle,* its use as a template for understanding Sinclair's artistic, social, and political achievements as a whole may be not only misleading but also misrepresentative of both the novel and Sinclair. *The Jungle* is Sinclair's exception, not his rule, but not because it is superior from a literary point of view, as many tend to assume (*Oil!* and *King Coal,* his 1917 novel of the Ludlow Massacre, as well as *Boston,* his 1928 novel of the Sacco and Vanzetti trial, are

among its literary peers). Rather, it is exceptional among Sinclair's work because its narrative point of view directly assumes the eyes of the oppressed.

In the vast majority of his other novels, the narrator's vision is mediated through the point of view of someone, such as Bunny Ross in *Oil!,* who has at least one foot in the world of privilege and represents the peaceful nexus of possible cooperation between the two divided halves of society. However, during *The Jungle*'s composition—for the first and perhaps only time in his life—Sinclair allowed himself to personally identify with America's subaltern laborers through unmediated journalistic content. The correspondence between his life and theirs was immediate, as he recalls in his *Autobiography:*

> I repaired on Christmas Day, and started the first chapter of *The Jungle* . . . . Externally, the story had to do with a family of stockyard workers, but internally it was the story of my own family. Did I wish to know how the poor suffered in wintertime in Chicago? I had only to recall the previous winter in the cabin, when we had only cotton blankets, and had put rugs on top of us, and cowered shivering in our separate beds. It was the same with hunger, with illness, with fear. Ona was [Meta], speaking Lithuanian but otherwise unchanged. Our little boy was down with pneumonia that winter, and nearly died, and the grief of that went into the book.

The action of *The Jungle* closely follows the systemic disillusionment, disruption, dismemberment, and destruction of a peasant Lithuanian immigrant family by a Chicago meatpacking industry that profits from its labor. It is written in a third-person prose that meticulously describes a series of concrete health and safety violations perpetrated by the corporate "packers" as recorded through the ingenuous eyes of the economic head of that family, the uneducated, physically powerful Jurgis Rudkin. Jurgis is a working man who, until this moment in his history, has conquered every conceivable adversity by simply working harder.

The opening chapter—the marriage of Jurgis and Ona (based on details of a Lithuanian wedding Sinclair carefully observed)—represents the last moment of hope and joy in the novel. The next six chapters reconstruct the systemic injustice and graft of the packing plants that have brought their large, extended family to this brink of the abyss. (The family's belief in the inviolability of Lithuanian gift-giving customs pushes them gently over the edge.) The entire family works harder and harder to stay afloat in the next series of chapters, amid the mortgage scams and the environmental poisons. Meanwhile they unwittingly feed their babies with the chalk-water in "Packingtown" stores that masquerades as milk. Their earnest attempts to work faster and harder are factored into the companies' bottom lines by the foremen and bosses, until inevitable accidents leave them crippled by misery and despair.

In chapter sixteen—the structural center of the novel—Jurgis winds up in jail on Christmas Day (the same day Sinclair began to write). He has attacked Ona's boss in a drunken rampage after learning that his wife had been driven to surreptitious prostitution. She is about to give birth to Jurgis' child. (Male humiliation through capitalists sexually preying on women workers was a common trope among turn-of-the-century Socialists, who bemoaned men's impotence to be real patriarchs for their own women. It also belied an anxiety about women being workers.)

Here is the structural heart of *The Jungle,* the fullest literary expression of Sinclair's conversion to socialism and, perhaps, the spiritual end to his marriage as well. (The marriage was not dissolved until 1913, when he married Craig.) At this moment in the story, Jurgis abandons his personal cares and attachments and—in a "conversion through inversion" reminiscent of Dante's *Divine Comedy*—begins his ascent toward the purgatory of socialism through a descent into crime and corruption.

Sinclair, in total identification with his character, turns that seminal literary corner, curiously, not in his own words, but in those of Oscar Wilde:

These midnight hours were fateful ones to Jurgis; in them was the beginning of his rebellion, of his outlawry and his unbelief . . . . So wrote a poet, to whom the world had dealt its justice—

"I know not whether Laws be right,
    Or whether Laws be wrong;
All that we know who lie in gaol
    Is that the wall is strong.
And they do well to hide their hell,
    For in it things are done
That Son of God nor son of Man
    Ever should look upon!"

Ironically, it is this novel's subaltern viewpoint—clearly distinguishable as "fictional"—that has given *The Jungle* a critical legitimacy as something universal and beyond the politics of historical circumstance and has set it apart in the minds of many as his only work of literary value. Consequently, from the time it was printed critics have had trouble with the last third of the novel, in which Jurgis converts to an anarchic vision of socialism. This problematic section is usually dismissed as an idiosyncratic appendix of authorial propaganda and the rest of the book is considered for the formal elements of its tragic descent.

Although the political speaker is not Sinclair but an incidental character, the final lines of *The Jungle* are unambiguous: "—So spoke an orator upon the platform; and two thousand pairs of eyes were fixed upon him, and two thousand voices were cheering his every sentence . . . [']—and Chicago will be ours! *Chicago will be ours!* CHICAGO WILL BE OURS!' "

The Socialists felt a very real chance of winning in Chicago in 1906; Sinclair himself was running (nominally) as a Socialist for Congress in New York.

GOING WEST

Ironically, now for the first time in his life, Sinclair had some capital of his own; he was twenty-eight years old, a public intellectual, and the author of an international blockbuster. Days before that hopeful election day in 1906 (on which neither he nor the Chicago Socialists would prevail), Sinclair staked his claim for idealism in real estate. He sank the lion's share of his royalties ($30,000) into a several-storied former boys' boarding school just across the Hudson from New York City, in Englewood, New Jersey. It was fortuitously named Helicon Hall (after the putative home of the muses in Ancient Greece) by, as Sinclair put it, "an aesthetic-minded pedagogue."

In a social experiment that would culminate twenty-eight years later in the depths of the Great Depression within a hair's breadth of his becoming the governor of California on a platform of cooperative agrarian and industrial reform, Sinclair began his literary, spiritual, political, and physical migration west. On All Saints' Day, he and Meta took their five-year-old son those dozen miles across the river and joined several score more of "decent literary folk" and their thirteen children in the foundation of Helicon Home Colony.

The newspapers of the day made much of the move, mostly ridicule, as Sinclair set out to address the problems of domesticity that he was facing by forming a company, issuing stock, and inviting investors into a collective project. (He ended up paying nine-tenths of the purchase price himself.) Through advertisements he attracted like-minded families from the New York professional class to join him. In its legal structuring, the colony was no different than an apartment co-op, with a board, membership, meetings, and services. Its amenities were centrally located in a manner similar to that of a hotel. In the creation of a home colony engendered with his own social contradictions, Sinclair sought social comfort for his family that did not conflict with his social beliefs. Meta had not been faring well under the poor, isolated conditions of their married life in the rented farm place where he had written *The Jungle.* She discovered Charlotte Perkins Gilman's *Women and Economics* and passed it on to Sinclair. As a consequence of her unhappiness, Sinclair's attention was drawn to the vast extent of domestic labor involved in maintaining a household and raising a child—an obvious reality to which most of the contemporaries of his sex remained oblivious. While Sinclair would clearly apply what Meta had passed on to him about socializing housework to the advancement of his career as an intellectual and as an activist, the idea apparently did not alter his own behavior enough to save their marriage. In *The Brass Check,* thirteen years after the colony's demise and seven years after his and Meta's divorce, Sinclair still inadvertently invokes the project's (and his own) many social contradictions. He describes Helicon as:

> an attempt to solve the problem of the small family of moderate means, who have one or two children and are not satisfied with the sort of care these children get from ignorant servant-maids, nor with the amount of play-space they can find in a city apartment . . . . The economic importance of the idea, if it could be made to work, would be beyond exaggerating. There are twenty million families in America, maintaining twenty million separate kitchens, with twenty million stoves and twenty million fires, twenty million sets of dishes to be washed, twenty million separate trips to market to be made. The waste involved in this is beyond calculation; I believe that when our system of universal

dog-eat-dog has been abolished, and the souls of men and women have risen upon the wings of love and fellowship, they will look back on us in our twenty million separate kitchens as we look upon the Eskimos in their filthy snow-huts lighted with walrus-blubber.

Helicon Hall was undoubtedly exclusive, as the capitalist papers of the day, from the *New York Times* on down, were gleefully quick to point out. There were complicated discussions about who could be denied admittance and for what reasons, as well as on what adjusted terms women members would be allowed to vote and on how servants could also be intellectual and cultural peers to the members. (This last problem was addressed through the recruitment of college students, which attracted the janitorial services of the future Nobel Prize winner Sinclair Lewis, among others.) As Sinclair himself would point out, it was a cooperative of consumption, not of production. It is also true that freedom from domestic labor was meant to free both men and women for intellectual production. And as such it was profoundly feminist. Among its members were the suffrage worker Frances Maule Bjorkman and the novelist Grace MacGowan Cooke. And while she would later dissociate her work from the Helicon Colony, Sinclair specifically acknowledged its genesis in the ideas of Charlotte Perkins Gilman that Meta exposed him to. Whatever the contradictions between his personal and his public sense of politics in this regard, Sinclair's strong association with the issues of temperance, birth control, and healthful eating would continue to closely ally him with the feminist movement for many decades to come.

At three o'clock on a March morning in 1907, the Helicon Hall caught fire and burned to the ground under mysterious circumstances. With it went Sinclair's and all the other members' manuscripts, including Sinclair's detailed documentation of fraud in Andrew Carnegie's steel trust, the destruction of which Sinclair maintained was a likely motive for sabotage. (He indicated that a stick of dynamite had been found lodged in the foundation of Helicon Hall a few weeks before.) One man, a carpenter, was killed. Sinclair himself was laid up for several weeks with burns and glass cuts on the soles of his feet. Investigators concluded that either foul play or criminal negligence had been the fire's source and the colony's company was fined for lack of safe egress. And so the experiment ended amid dark rumors of social anarchism, "free love," and insurance fraud murmured on the streets of Englewood. (As a matter of fact, Sinclair wound up losing several thousand dollars as well as aiding several families put into dire straits.) During those brief six months at Helicon Hall, Sinclair apparently had a brief respite from the chronic stomach problems that plagued him all his life. When all was said and done, by 1920, in *The Brass Check,* he remembered the experience fondly: "Our children had a little world of their own, and did their own work and lived their own community life, and were happier than any fourteen children I have seen before or since. Also we had a social life which no one who took part in will forget."

While Sinclair continued to write and publish (he never stopped producing prose, no matter his emotional state), he was largely consumed by the dysfunction of his marriage. He fell back on literary threads that had been fruitfully broken with *The Jungle* when Allan Montague appeared again in *The Metropolis* (1908) and *The Moneychangers* (1908), as the son of the original Allan Montague of *Manassas.*

Sinclair's testifying before Congress in 1906 in connection with the Pure Food and Drug Act had awakened his interest in healthful eating. Homeless following the Helicon fire, Sinclair, Meta, and their son had spent the winter in Bermuda and adopted a vegetable diet. He coauthored *Good Health and How We Won It* (1909) with former Helicon colonist and journalist Michael Williams, advocating yogurt, vegetables, and the avoidance of stimulants and fried meats in a time when such prescriptions were far from commonplace. He traveled in the West, visiting Lawrence, Kansas, Utah, and California. On the verge of a nervous breakdown, he went to Carmel, California, to live temporarily with the poet George Sterling. In 1910, in an effort to find his health and balance through fasting, he went to a spa in Alabama, where he met another writer and fellow Southerner, Mary Craig Kimbrough, who would share his interest in health and much else. In 1911, joining a Delaware health colony, he published a book on controlled fasting and confined his social activism to getting arrested for playing tennis on Sunday.

Love's Pilgrimage (1911) is a detailed, lyrical novel of his now-total estrangement from Meta, in which he took great pains to represent her point of view as well as his own. In February 1912 he left Meta, taking his son with him to Europe. He sued for and obtained a divorce in Holland. On April 21, 1913, Upton Sinclair and Mary Craig Kimbrough were married in Fredericksburg, Virginia. He would soon receive legal custody of his son.

ACROSS THE GREAT DIVIDE

At first, Sinclair and Craig remained East in New York City, but Sinclair's activism was no longer confined to tennis. He set his sites on the king of capitalism, John D. Rockefeller, as news of the 1914 Easter night Ludlow Coal Massacre drew his attention West to the Colorado Fuel and Iron Company, which in turn was owned by Rockefeller's Standard Oil in New York. Craig (who had not been politically active previously) joined his cause. Angered by the virtual news blackout on what had escalated into what amounted to a small war in Huerfano County, Colorado, they

organized a picket in front of Standard Oil. Sinclair got himself arrested and locked up in the notorious "Tombs," using the opportunity to fill in reporters on the details of the massacre; Craig bailed him out, as she would again a decade later after Liberty Hill. They also became involved in protecting the civil liberties of anarchist students holding demonstrations outside Rockefeller's Tarrytown, New York, estate, just across the river from the former Helicon Hall.

In May, while Craig kept up the fight in New York, Sinclair went to Ludlow. He arrived in the immediate wake of a class war that had raged for ten days after Rockefeller's men and state militia opened fire on a striking mine workers' tent city with machine guns, killing three women and eleven children. Federal troops had only just disarmed the miners at President Wilson's demand. Wobbly leader Big Bill Haywood declared that the country was now engaged in "an irreconcilable class struggle."

Sinclair stood literally and figuratively on the Great Divide where the Rockies meet the Sangre de Cristo Mountains in southeastern Colorado, near the high country border with northern New Mexico. The major work of literature that would finally emerge from this visit confronts the great rifts in America society head on, and does not resolve them.

The first draft of *King Coal* was written in Mississippi in 1915. By agreeing to live within the Jim Crow plantation bosom of Craig's family, Sinclair was attempting to make amends for the "scandal" of their marriage (to her father in particular, a paternally racist judge with jurisdiction over the local Black population). In November, Sinclair went to California—alone. In what would consummate a lifetime commitment, Craig finally followed him there, to the state where they would live out their days, until her death in 1961.

George Brett, the same editor at Macmillan who had rejected *The Jungle,* rejected Sinclair's first version of *King Coal* as well; the characters were not convincing and there was too much un-incorporated detail about the strike. This time it was Craig, not Sinclair, who responded. She agreed to collaborate on the rewrite, and on that basis, Brett agreed to read it again and eventually to accept it (though it never fully satisfied him).

Not surprisingly, considering the intimate shifting that preceded it and its deep collaborative origins within his and Craig's relationship, *King Coal* is probably Sinclair's most emotionally so-phisticated novel. At least when viewed in tra-ditional terms of characters and the relationships between them, it is formally well wrought and courageously unresolved in a way that Sinclair's other novels are not, which is not to say it intends to stand independent of history. As with each of Sinclair's greatest works, it brings unsung his-torical events with it through journalistically wit-nessed detail, and casts them into an aesthetically reflective form that cannot be unwritten or sub-sequently revised as long as the book is read.

Dedicated to Craig, "To whose persistence in the perilous task of tearing her husband's manu-script to pieces, the reader is indebted for the ab-sence of most of the faults from this book," *King Coal* follows Hal Warner, an upper-class college student on break, through a sentimental education in which the reader (and perhaps Sinclair himself) learns more about this country's great divisions than the character does himself and, unlike that earnest young man left attempting to bridge the gap, is left without a simple answer. Although it is not revealed until the third of the novel's four books, Hal is both the son and the brother of a coal magnate. He attempts to discover the truth of labor by getting a job at the mine of his college friend's father, the founder and funder of the uni-versity they both attend. At first he is turned away for looking educated, like a union "agitator." Then he succeeds under the assumed name of "Joe Smith." As he begins to overcome his class and racial prejudices, the mostly immigrant workers' plight reveals itself, as does the com-pany-store corruption that controls the town and mines in absolute dictatorship. While his omis-sion of all but incidental and pejorative references to native, Hispanic villagers (who acted both as strikers and as scabs in the Ludlow conflict) points to a deeper contradiction between his in-tellectual understanding of racism and his need to identify labor with whiteness, Sinclair boldly confronts the racial divisions at stake in the mines and consequently their relative stakes in the union movement:

> The Americans and English and Scotch looked down upon the Welsh and the Irish; the Welsh and the Irish looked down upon the Dagoes and Fren-chies; the Dagoes and Frenchies looked down upon Polacks and Hunkies, those in turn upon Greeks, Bulgarians and "Monty-negroes," and so on through the races of Eastern Europe, Lithuanians, Slovaks, and Croatians, Armenians, Roumanians, Rumelians, Ruthenians—ending up with Greasers, niggers, and last and lowest, Japs.

Though the "General Fuel Company" openly mocks state and federal laws, Hal gets himself elected as a "check-weighman" or federally man-dated watchdog for the workers to assure them-selves they aren't being cheated on their pay-loads. At that moment he switches sides in the class war taking shape. He also finds himself dan-gerously attracted across class barriers to Mary Burke, an Irish girl in the coal camp (whose psy-chological richness and irony are due in large measure to Craig); but Hal is in love with a girl of his own class at school in "Western City." Af-ter the two women finally meet, the terms of class war point, with deep misogyny, to another divide articulated, disturbingly, in the words of "Red" Mary, whom Hal has emotionally abandoned:

> "I'd read about fine ladies in books, ye see; but I'd never been spoke to by one, I'd never had to swal-low one, as ye might say. But there I did—and all at once I seemed to know where the money goes that's wrung out of the miners. I saw why people

were robbin' us, grindin' the life out of us—for fine ladies like that, to keep them so shinin' and soft! . . . My God, Joe [Hal]—d'ye know what she seemed to me like? Like a smooth, sleek cat that has just eat up a whole nest full of baby mice, and has the blood of them all over her cheeks!"

. . . Hal could not have said anything now, if he had wished to. He knew that this was what he had come to seek! This was the naked soul of the class war!

A fatal mine explosion lights the spark and he and Mary become leaders of the strike, but not lovers; ultimately his capitalist brother and the high society girl he loves compel him back to his class. He leaves the mines and "Red" Mary (who would have abandoned the cause to escape the misery) with a self-transfigured resolve that the reader receives skeptically, even if Hal does not. The unresolved plot ultimately leaves the reader with the grim, unaided metaphor for class struggle that Edstrom, the battered, veteran organizer, bequeaths to Mary: "They travel in long columns, millions and millions of them. And when they come to a ditch, the front ones fall in, and more and more of them on top, till they fill up the ditch, and the rest cross over. We are ants, Mary."

King Coal never got the initial attention it deserved, however. Even as it was being published in 1917, the country's attention was drawn outside itself to the events of the First World War. President Wilson's containment of a highly localized labor war three years before no longer felt intellectually salient. And the Bolshevik revolution brewing in Russia would soon raise the stakes of the game.

ANGLE OF INCIDENCE EQUALS ANGLE OF REFLECTION

Sinclair initially came out in favor of World War I. But by the end of *Jimmie Higgins* (1919), his novel of a rank-and-file Socialist who goes overseas to fight as an American soldier, the criticism of America's role in attempting to suppress the Russian Revolution, (revisited by Paul Watkins in *Oil!*) was already in place. He continued to explore the class war in America in such lesser-known works as the experimental (low-selling) *100%* (1920) and on through the "Red Terror" repression of the 1920s. Its ultimate articulation, wedged between the publication of *Oil!* and the stock market crash of 1929 that began the Great Depression, came in *Boston* (1928), the last of Sinclair's major novels from a literary point of view.

The Boston establishment had already drawn Sinclair's attention and visit through its unusual reception of *Oil!* They banned it, but not for its volatile political content. Rather (ostensibly, at least) on the basis of its sexual content (not very erotic mentions of birth control and "petting parties"), they forbade its sale throughout Massachusetts. This prompted Sinclair to instruct his Chicago printer to reissue a special "Fig Leaf Edition" that humorously covered up the offending passages; he went to Boston to hawk it himself.

At 12:30 A.M., August 23, 1927, two working-class Italian immigrants were executed by the State of Massachusetts. In fact, Nicola Sacco and Bartolomeo Vanzetti were convicted for their alleged involvement in a robbery; in spirit, they were officially murdered for their political belief in anarchism. (The trial was not officially declared unfair until the execution's fiftieth anniversary.)

Sacco and Vanzetti were first arrested in 1920. In 1922, the year before his stand on Liberty Hill, Sinclair had met and visited with Vanzetti in prison. Sinclair maintains he began the work, so large it had to be bound in two volumes, within hours of the execution. He wrote it in nine months, in a white heat of anger that only sharpened its documentary acumen.

Perhaps applying the gender lessons he learned in *King Coal,* Sinclair chose a woman for his main character, Boston blue blood and ex-governor's widow Cornelia Thornwall. Just as the young Hal Warner posed as a miner, the aging Cornelia tries to support herself free of the paternalistic wealth that has kept her down. Learning the lessons of labor by finding employment at a cordage factory, she first meets Bart Vanzetti and remains on hand to witness as the metaphoric equivalent of the rope wraps around his neck: "The guards stepped back, and the warden gave the signal; the executioner moved the switch, and the body of Bartolomeo Vanzetti leaped as the others had done. Nineteen hundred and fifty volts were estimated to be sufficient for this less robust person, a dreamer and a man of words rather than of action."

If all of Sinclair's major fiction draws its aesthetic power from the mirror of history, *Boston's* relation to that mirror is nearest to total, simultaneous identity. He makes no claims, fictional or otherwise, about Sacco's or Vanzetti's guilt or innocence. Ultimately, the novel does not reflect the facts of the case, but the facts of the trial. "*Boston* does not fit orthodox library categories, which insist on the boundary between fiction and non-fiction . . . ." wrote the public intellectual Howard Zinn in his introduction to the fiftieth anniversary reissue of the novel. "It puts the straight lines of neutral type in the lawbooks under a microscope, where they show up as rows of trenches in the war of class against class."

COOPERATION

During the Great Depression, without any initial political change on his own part, Sinclair's ideas grew increasingly acceptable to the swelling majority of economically vulnerable lower- and middle-class Americans. Since *The Jungle,* he had always managed to successfully direct his ideas to a mass audience, but always through his persona as an earnest literary figure on the intellectual margins. Suddenly, after five decades of hopeful struggle, Upton Sinclair became a popular political figure in his own right.

While continuing, as always, to write during the early 1930s, his novels would never again achieve the literary force of *Oil!* and *Boston.* He was also exploring the issues of extrasensory perception, in *Mental Radio* (1930), and alcoholism, in *The Wet Parade* (1931).

Perhaps another major work would have eventually come, as it had in the past, but instead, in August 1933, a Santa Monica hotel owner acting as an official of the central committee for the California Democratic Party nominated Sinclair to run for governor of California on the Democratic ticket. The following month he officially switched from the Socialist to the Democratic Party and, in a spirit of cooperation between divided social classes, committed himself to working within the two-party electoral system he had so effectively critiqued in the past. His candidacy very nearly changed the face of American history and very certainly changed the face of its politics; it also fundamentally altered Sinclair's artistic relation to both.

In October, availing himself of his rapid self-publishing and distribution savvy, Sinclair released his first 10,000 copies of the nominally fictional *I, Governor of California and How I Ended Poverty* (1933), introducing the twelve steps he would take, at the moment he took office, to "end poverty in California." The plan and movement both became known as EPIC. EPIC clubs sprang up from grassroots all over the state. He began printing the weekly *EPIC News,* which at a nickel a copy with paid advertisement was a publication miracle in its own right. (By the election its circulation would reach two million.) In

August 1934 Sinclair swept the Democratic primary in a landslide of nearly half a million votes. The race drew both national and international attention.

Until this point his EPIC platform had been one of government-imposed agrarian and industrial reform, providing cooperative working colonies for the unemployed through the taxation of capitalist institutions. But after the primaries, he made the necessary capitalist contributions voluntary in order to appeal to a broader constituency.

The newspapers and Hollywood launched an unprecedented campaign to defeat him through movie trailers and cartoons such as one depicting him as Stalin, Hitler, and Mussolini's crackpot counterpart. Franklin Roosevelt distanced his "New Deal" and himself from Sinclair's campaign. Sinclair was narrowly defeated by Republican-machine politician Frank Merriam.

In 1936 Sinclair returned to fiction with *Co-op*, an imagined implementation of his moderated EPIC ideas in the fictional California town of San Sebastian. Fascinating for its collective structure in which no single point of view prevails, its tale of the dispossessed, migratory Jett family at least superficially anticipates the Joads of Steinbeck's *The Grapes of Wrath*.

Even as *The Flivver King* (1937) became instrumental in the United Automobile Workers pickets against Henry Ford, Sinclair's causes began to travel closer to the liberal bank of the political mainstream. The American communists had opposed EPIC and ridiculed Sinclair for being too idealistic about class collaboration, and he partially blamed them for his defeat. In addition, Stalin's purges in Russia were contributing to a more general, intellectual crisis in the American Left. By 1939 Sinclair was, himself, increasingly anticommunist as well as anti-fascist, in close accord with the mood of the country throughout World War II and into the Cold War and beyond.

THE BIRTH OF A POPULAR AUTHOR

At sixty years old, Upton Sinclair got what can best be described as a second wind. Between 1938 and 1948 he interpreted and contextualized international history from 1913 to 1946 for the pleasure and education of a popular audience through ten novels' worth of dime-store appearances by Lanny Budd—a globetrotting sophisticate of his son's generation—at every crucial moment of world decision. The Lanny Budd novels, which came to be known as the World's End series, were commercially published best-sellers, one and all. (Although Sinclair kept the right to publish them himself, as always.) The anticipatory thrill for each installment only increased for Lanny's eager readers, themselves embroiled in the turmoil of World War II, as the historical events described crept physically closer to readers' contemporary, journalistic reality. Volume number three, *Dragon's Teeth* (1942), about the Treaty of Versailles, earned him the Pulitzer Prize. (Ironically, in 1931 Sinclair had been nominated for the Nobel Prize, for the full span of his work, by such international luminaries as Albert Einstein, George Bernard Shaw, John Dewey, Bertrand Russell, and Frederick Schiller; his candidacy was refused.)

A CHANGING OF THE GUARD

Nine decades after his own birth in a Baltimore boarding house and that of the Progressive movement in a great workers' uprising, Upton Sinclair died in a New Jersey nursing home, on November 25 of that tumultuous year when a New Left would put its indelible stamp on history: 1968.

He had written quite a few more books after the World's End series, including a couple on the nuclear age that are only now receiving critical consideration. At age eighty-three, five months after Craig's death, he had married Mary Hard

Willis, only to see her die, too, six years later. In 1966 he was finally convinced to leave his beloved California to be closer to his son in the East.

In the year Sinclair died, two gold-medal American athletes at the Olympic Games raised their fists in the gesture of Black Power. COINTELPRO, the FBI's counterintelligence program, was instigated to infiltrate and manipulate activist groups. Chicago police beat up anti–Vietnam War demonstrators outside the Democratic Convention, and both Robert Kennedy and Martin Luther King Jr. were assassinated. The Chicano movement was taking shape in Los Angeles and feminists were disrupting the Miss America pageant; it was the year before Stonewall.

John Steinbeck, whose younger literary vision of California and its politics became so closely intertwined with Sinclair's, also died in that watershed year of 1968. And perhaps most poetically fitting, forty-five years after the incomparable writer Upton Sinclair was arrested under its purview for reading the U.S. Constitution to a bunch of Wobblies, California's notorious Criminal Syndicalism Act was quietly dropped from the books as well.

Selected Bibliography

WORKS OF UPTON SINCLAIR

NOVELS

Springtime and Harvest. New York: The Sinclair Press, 1901.

The Journal of Arthur Stirling. New York: D. Appleton, 1903.

Prince Hagen. Boston: L. C. Page, 1903.

Manassas. New York: Macmillan, 1904.

The Jungle. New York: Doubleday & Page, 1906. (Quotations cited from University of Illinois edition. Urbana: University of Illinois, 1988. This edition has excellent historical annotations and is of particular use to those interested in subaltern studies.)

The Metropolis. New York, Moffat & Yard, 1908.

The Moneychanges. New York: B. W. Dodge, 1908.

Love's Pilgrimage. New York: Mitchell Kennerley, 1911.

Sylvia. Philadelphia: John C. Winston, 1913.

Sylvia's Marriage. Philadelphia: John C. Winston, 1914.

King Coal. New York: Macmillan, 1917. (Quotations cited from the Bantam Classics edition. New York: Bantam Books, 1994.)

Jimmie Higgins. New York: Boni and Liveright, 1919.

100%. Pasadena: Upton Sinclair, 1920.

They Call Me Carpenter. New York: Boni and Liveright, 1922.

Oil! New York: Albert & Charles Boni, 1927. (Quotations cited from the University of California edition. Berkeley: University of California, 1997. Jules Tygiel's foreword is a good read.)

Boston. New York: Albert & Charles Boni, 1928. (Quotations cited from the fiftieth anniversary Robert Bentley edition. Cambridge, Mass.: Robert Bentley, 1978. Howard Zinn's introduction is valuable on many levels.)

Mountain City. New York: Albert & Charles Boni, 1930.

Roman Holiday. New York: Farrar & Rinehart, 1931.

Co-op. New York: Farrar & Rinehart, 1936.

No Pasaran! Pasadena: Upton Sinclair, 1937.

The Flivver King. Pasadena: Upton Sinclair, 1937. (Edition of particular interest for U.S. labor studies: Charles H. Kerr edition. Chicago: Charles H. Kerr, 1984.)

World's End. New York: Viking, 1940.

Between Two Worlds. New York: Viking, 1941.

Dragon's Teeth. New York: Viking, 1942.

Wide Is the Gate. New York: Viking, 1943.

A World to Win. New York: Viking, 1946.

Presidential Mission. New York: Viking, 1947.

One Clear Call. New York: Viking, 1948.

O Shepherd, Speak! New York: Viking, 1949.

The Coal War. Boulder: Colorado Associated University, 1976.

NONFICTION

The Industrial Republic. New York: Doubleday, Page, & Co., 1907.

Good Health and How We Won It. New York: Frederick A. Stokes, 1909.

The Fasting Cure. New York: Mitchell Kennerley, 1911.

The Profits of Religion. Pasadena: Upton Sinclair, 1918.

The Brass Check. Pasadena: Upton Sinclair, 1920.

The Book of Life. New York: Macmillan, 1921.

The Goose-Step. Pasadena: Upton Sinclair, 1923.

The Goslings. Pasadena: Upton Sinclair, 1924.

Mammonart. Pasadena: Upton Sinclair, 1925.

Money Writes! New York: Albert & Charles Boni, 1927.

Mental Radio. New York: Albert & Charles Boni, 1930.

The Wet Parade. New York: Farrar & Rinehart, 1931.

American Outpost. New York: Farrar & Rinehart, 1932.

Upton Sinclair Presents William Fox. Los Angeles: Upton Sinclair, 1933.

I, Governor of California and How I Ended Poverty. New York: Farrar & Rinehart, 1933.

I, Candidate for Governor, and How I Got Licked. New York: Farrar & Rinehart, 1935.

Telling the Word. London: T. Werner Laurie, 1939.

The Cup of Fury. Great Neck: Channel, 1956.

The Autobiography of Upton Sinclair. New York: Harcourt, Brace, & World, 1962.

PLAYS

Plays of Protest. New York: Mitchell Kennerley, 1912.

Hell. Pasadena: Upton Sinclair, 1923.

Singing Jailbirds. Pasadena: Upton Sinclair, 1924.

A Giant's Strength. Monrovia, Calif.: Upton Sinclair, 1948.

PAMPHLETS, ARTICLES, AND COLLECTIONS

Our Bourgeois Literature. Chicago: Charles H. Kerr, 1905.

A Home Colony. New York: Jungle Publishing, 1906.

The Cry for Justice. Philadelphia: John C. Winston, 1915.

McNeal-Sinclair Debate on Socialism. Girard, Kans.: Appeal, 1921.

The Candidacy of Upton Sinclair for the Nobel Prize. 1932.

Immediate Epic. Los Angeles: End Poverty League, 1934.

Terror in Russia? New York: Richard R. Smith, 1938.

Upton Sinclair Anthology. Culver City, Calif.: Murray & Gee, 1947.

BIBLIOGRAPHIES

Ahouse, John. *Upton Sinclair: A Descriptive, Annotated Bibliography.* Los Angeles: Mercer & Aitchison, 1994. (Invaluable for a synoptic overview of Sinclair's work. A pleasure to read in and of itself.)

Gaer, Joseph. *Upton Sinclair: Bibliography and Biographical Data.* New York: Burt Franklin, 1935. (Historically interesting.)

Gottesman, Ronald, and Charles Silet. *The Literary Manuscripts of Upton Sinclair.* Columbus: Ohio State University Press, 1972.

Lilly Library. *Catalogue of the Upton Sinclair Archives.* Bloomington: The Lilly Library/Indiana University, 1963. (Overview of and reproductions from definitive archive for books, manuscripts, and other material.)

BIOGRAPHICAL, CRITICAL, AND HISTORICAL STUDIES

Allen, James Preston. "Oil!" *Random Lengths,* November 14–27, 1997.

Almeida, Arthur A. "Liberty Hill Shone as San Pedro Labor Beacon." *California Historian* 3: 44 (Spring 1998).

———. "Veterans of Dock Wars Reminisce." *California Historian* 3: 44 (Spring 1998).

Blinderman, Abraham, ed. *Critics on Upton Sinclair.* Coral Gables: University of Miami Press, 1975.

Bloodworth, William A., Jr. *Upton Sinclair.* Boston: G. K. Hall, 1977.

Coodley, Lauren. "Toward a Reinterpretation of Upton Sinclair." Master's thesis, Sonoma State University, 1997.

Davis, Mike. *City of Quartz.* London: Verso, 1990.

Dell, Floyd. *Upton Sinclair: A Study in Social Protest.* New York: George Doran, 1927.

Dreiser, Theodore. "Upton Sinclair." *The Upton Sinclair Quarterly* 9: 2 (Summer 1985).

Harris, Leon. *Upton Sinclair: American Rebel.* New York: Thomas Crowell, 1975.

Irving, Paul. "Southern California ACLU Born on 4th and Beacon Streets." *Random Lengths,* April 4–17, 1991.

Knox, George. "The Complete Story of Helicon Hall."

Uppie Speaks 3: 1–3 (March, June, September 1979).

Kongshaug, Erik. "What's In a Name?" *Random Lengths,* July 9–22, 1999.

McWilliams, Carey. "Writers of the Western Shore." *Westways,* January 1979.

Mitchell, Greg. *The Campaign of the Century.* New York: Random House, 1992.

Mookerjee, R. N. *Art for Social Justice: The Major Novels of Upton Sinclair.* Metuchen, N.J.: Scarecrow Press, 1988.

Rohde, Stephen F. "The Muckraker and the Spirit of Protest at Liberty Hill Live On." *Los Angeles Times,* May 18, 1998.

Sinclair, Mary Craig. *Southern Belle.* New York: Crown, 1957. (Current edition of special interest: Oxford: University of Mississippi Press, 1999. Revisits Sinclair's famous biography/autobiography from a feminist perspective.)

Starr, Kevin. *Endangered Dreams: The Great Depression in California.* New York: Oxford University Press, 1996.

Vinsel, Arthur R. "Digging Up Liberty Hill." *Random Lengths,* May 1–14, 1998.

Yoder, Jon. *Upton Sinclair.* New York: Ungar Publishing, 1975.

— *ERIK KONGSHAUG*

Robert Stone

1937–

ROBERT STONE HAS WRITTEN that "the first law of heaven is that nothing is free," and there are reasons enough to believe that he came by this hard truth early and ungently. Born on August 21, 1937, in New York City to a schizophrenic mother and an absent father, by the age of six the young Stone found himself boarded in St. Ann's Marist academy in Manhattan—a quasi orphanage, in his case—where physical and psychological brutality on the part of both students and priests was daily fare. Some of the grueling particulars of his life at this school of hard knocks are recounted in his autobiographical short story "Absence of Mercy," printed in *Bear and His Daughter: Stories,* in 1997; but nearly every page of his fiction is permeated with the sense that life is a continual struggle "red in tooth and claw." When his mother was well enough, Stone lived with her, taking trips to make "new starts" in various parts of the country, at least one of which ended with a stay in a homeless shelter. Despite, or perhaps in part because of, such early dislocations of the spirit, the boy began to write stories that from the start garnered attention and praise, and which were obviously a welcome outlet for his stifled ambitions and for the active imagination that had hitherto served largely as a refuge.

Expelled from St. Ann's in his senior year for spreading athcism, Stone indulged his imaginative infatuation with the sea by joining the navy in 1955, witnessing some combat during the Suez crisis and doing a journalistic stint in Antarctica before his hitch expired. Back in civilian life, he began working for the New York *Daily News* and also attended classes at New York University, where he met his wife, Janice Burr, in a creative writing course. Married in late 1959, the newlyweds arrived in New Orleans soon after with no clear prospects, working various jobs and living from paycheck to paycheck. It was the era in the South of the emerging Civil Rights movement as well as the violent backlash against it, both of which Stone observed at close hand and eventually transposed to his fiction.

After the birth of their first child, the Stones moved back to New York and again took up various odd and temporary jobs. After reading *The Great Gatsby*, Stone determined to write a novel himself and so set to work on *A Hall of Mirrors,* which would be published in 1967. Before his labors had progressed very far, he sent a sample of the book to the writing program at Stanford University, which promptly awarded him a $2,500 stipend and a place in a writing workshop. While in residence in the Bay Area from 1962 to 1964 he made the acquaintance of the novelist Ken Kesey and began to indulge in hallucinogenic drugs at Kesey's compound, an experience that Stone credits for some of the more surreal effects in his early works. He also found a more

295

conservative benefactor in Wallace Stegner, who extended Stone's stipend at Stanford for an extra year. Then, in 1964 Stone was awarded a Houghton Mifflin Literary Fellowship; for an unpublished author, he was now doing rather well. Still, Stone has always been a slow and meticulous writer, and his first novel was not completed until his various grants expired; it took shape gradually, with a stint at a writer's colony, the birth of a second child, a move back to New York, and some temporary jobs for the tabloid press along the way.

A HALL OF MIRRORS

In retrospect, the long gestation of *A Hall of Mirrors* may have benefited the work in ways other than the refinement of its prose, for the book seems not a snapshot of any particular year in the sixties but rather a surprising distillation of many of that decade's disparate elements; it captures the period's early idealism and subsequent inebriated solipsism, its celebration of sensual pleasures and confrontations over social and political issues. And thus, although *A Hall of Mirrors* possesses some of the phantasmagoric aspects fairly typical of the fiction by the era's young writers, it tempers such extravagances with a more serious and tough-minded depiction of America's racism, economic exploitation, and spiritual emptiness than that delivered in the romps of, say, Tom Wolfe or Kurt Vonnegut.

The novel focuses on Rheinhardt, a burned-out, cynical ex-musician and sometime deejay, and Geraldine Crosby, an occasional prostitute from Appalachia, both of whom drift into New Orleans escaping past careers of aimless and dangerous failure. Their first efforts at gainful employment in the "Big Easy" are anything but, for Rheinhardt, who intends to get a job at a radio station, goes on a series of benders that propels him to skid row, while the only work Geraldine can find is more of the same in the French Quarter. Eventually, Rheinhardt ends up in a soup kitchen whose officiating "clergyman" is Farley the Sailor, a con-man with a long record of enterprising and outrageous scams whom Rheinhardt knew previously in New York. Farley, partly for old times' sake and partly for fear of exposure by Rheinhardt, gets the protagonist a job in the chemical plant of Matthew J. Bingamon, a powerful right-wing industrialist. It is while working one of the deadening shifts at this plant that Rheinhardt and Geraldine, who has been sent to the factory after being arrested for vagrancy, see each other through apertures in an elevator shaft. Later, they meet at the plant's bus stop, ride home together, and begin an affair fueled largely by desperation, evasion, and drugs.

Rheinhardt manages to gain a job interview at WUSA, Bingamon's ultraconservative radio station, where he quickly catches on to the editorial drift and skillfully puts together a scattering of wire reports into a subtly racist newscast. Bingamon, impressed by Rheinhardt's talent, hires him and explains in general terms the national aspirations of his organization and the major political changes he is planning to foment through his radio station and other outlets. The protagonist tries to tell himself that the propagandizing newscasts expected of him will be just another of his "routines," but the voice of his conscience is not stilled; in the following weeks Rheinhardt attempts to detach himself from his work by adopting a cynical stance whose ultimate purpose is to mask the depth of his own self-betrayal.

The novel now shifts its focus to Morgan Rainey, the introverted and socially awkward son of a prominent Louisiana family, who is currently working as a kind of census taker (a job Stone performed) in the black slums in and around New Orleans. After a few discouraging visits to various ramshackle dwellings, Rainey is told by his superiors to contact the black hotel operator Lester Clotho, who is charged with escorting him safely though the most dangerous neighborhoods. Clotho is an ambiguous figure. On the one hand, he is politically connected with, performs favors for, and presumably receives payments from, the white, racist power brokers of the city. On the other hand, he takes it upon himself to introduce Rainey to several of his tenants and to reveal—or to have them reveal—their appalling stories of suffering and oppression, all the while encouraging the obvious signs of compassion that Rainey begins to exhibit. Clotho tells Rainey, "Everybody has to aspire toward concern."

Rainey is also a tenant in the building where Rheinhardt and Geraldine live, and when the young man begins prodding the protagonist about the political effects of the radio station and his part in it, Rheinhardt's guilt lends a nasty edge to his cynicism. Claiming that do-gooders like Rainey "leav[e] a thick odorous film of piety on everything near them," he advises the young idealist to "despair and die right now while you're among friends." Geraldine is angered by this cruelty, but Rheinhardt has already begun to sever the bonds between them, feeling himself unable—or knowing himself unwilling—to fulfill her emotional needs. Eventually he cooks up an argument between them and strikes her; when he later returns to their apartment, she has fled.

Rainey, however, is not so easily discouraged, for though he is all too conscious of his own mental and physical shortcomings, he feels, because of certain traumas suffered in youth, that he has a covenant with God that enjoins him to undertake large if undefined humanitarian efforts. Thus, when he discovers that the survey he is carrying out will be used by a right-wing state attorney as grounds for launching a race-baiting political crackdown on welfare "cheats," Rainey decides he must do something to stop it. His resolve foreshadows a violent reprisal against the powers that be, for as he tells Geraldine: "Even though my weak life is lost I set myself against them and I shall not be moved."

In the novel's third section, which takes place during a huge stadium rally planned and promoted by Bingamon, the novel's tone changes from the grim to the manic. It begins with a comic catalogue worthy of the eighteenth-century novelist Tobias Smollett, introducing the various reactionary celebrities who are to be featured speakers, and continues in this humorous vein by contrasting the fervor of the true believers with the amoral detachment of the two fakirs, "Father" Farley and Rheinhardt—the former expected to offer prayers and a sermon, the latter to emcee the spectacular. While the tension builds toward curtain time, we find Rainey wandering the black precincts again and having a final mystical (or merely hallucinogenic) encounter with Clotho, which prompts his steps toward the rally—at which, he has learned, Bingamon intends to stage manage a race riot for political gain. Once at the coliseum parking lot, he meets an old-time leftist railroad worker named Prothwaite sitting in a truck full of explosives, who intends to crash the gates and cause mayhem inside. After some mutual explanation, Rainey convinces the union man to let him occupy the passenger seat in the death van.

Inside the coliseum, things are quickly spiraling out of control: the white crowd is seething with hate from the speakers' rhetoric, and blacks—both those placed by Bingamon and enraged intruders from the surrounding ghetto—have been sighted in the stands. As the pageant stumbles along, angry bullhorns interrupt, the crashing of chairs can be heard, and pistol shots ring out. It is at this moment that Rheinhardt, befuddled by booze and pot, is ordered to soothe the multitudes. The oration he actually delivers, however, is a potent mixture of irony and empathy: a conscious parody clearly meant to mock the racist audience, it is simultaneously an inspired act of psychic ventriloquism that articulates the basic fears and fantasies embedded in American racism and jingoism:

Americans, . . . our shoulders are broad and sweaty but our breath is sweet. When your American soldier fighting today drops a napalm bomb on a cluster of gibbering chinks, it's a bomb with a heart. In the heart of that bomb, mysteriously but truly present, is a fat old lady on her way to see the world's fair. This lady is as innocent as she is fat and motherly. This lady is our nation's strength. This lady's innocence if fully unleashed could defoliate every forest in the torrid zone. This lady is a whip to niggers! This lade is chinkbane! Conjure with this lady and mestizos, zambos, Croats and all such persons simply disappear. Confronted with her, Australian abos turn to the wall and die. Latins choke on their arrogant smirks, Nips disembowel themselves, the teeming brains of gypsies turn to gum. This lady is Columbia my friends. Every time she tells her little daughter that Jesus drank carbonated grape juice—then, somewhere in the world a Jew raises quivering gray fingers to his weasely throat and falls dead.

Patriots, there is danger! Listen to the nature of the menace! They're trying to take that fat old woman off her Greyhound Bus. Men of valor, she may never reach the world's fair. In one of the dark fields of the Republic a gigantic leering coon with a monstrously distended member is waiting in a watermelon patch. He is obscenely nude save only for a helmet emblazoned with a Red Star.

It is at this pass that Prothwaite's van comes crashing into view and soon after explodes, severely injuring Rainey. With the stadium beginning to burn, Rheinhardt and Farley decide to make their escape, managing to kill Bingamon in the process. When Rheinhardt finally reaches the open, he hears Geraldine's voice desperately calling to him from within the arena, but cannot find her amid the chaos.

Geraldine has indeed come to the rally, hoping in some way to win Rheinhardt back. Later that night, dazed and wandering, she is picked up by the police and, alone in a cell for the night, hangs herself with a chain. Rheinhardt rouses himself to come and identify the body, but his anxiety to escape from the New Orleans police trumps any higher impulses he might have to make a Rainey-like stand. We last see him about to board a Grey-

hound for Denver, bitter with the knowledge of his own moral impotence.

After the publication of *A Hall of Mirrors,* which was awarded the William Faulkner Foundation Prize for the best first novel of 1967, Stone lived in England and worked as a freelance writer; a stint in Vietnam provided him with material for his next novel, *Dog Soldiers* (1974). The author was awarded a Guggenheim Fellowship in 1971; in the early seventies Stone began a teaching career, serving as a writer-in-residence at Princeton and later as a faculty member at Amherst College. The list of his academic posts would eventually grow to include Stanford, Harvard, the University of California at Irvine, and New York University, among others.

His long-awaited second novel was somewhat ahead of its time, in that the American literary establishment did not seriously take up the Vietnam War as a subject until later in the decade. But *Dog Soldiers* also clarifies Stone's debt to the past, with its themes and obsessions inherited from Herman Melville, Joseph Conrad, and Graham Greene. (Although Stone claims to despise the works of Greene, his vituperative 1978 review of Greene's *The Human Factor* suggests, rather, an acute anxiety of influence.) Stone shares with these novelists the convictions that safety is either an illusion or a trap, that whatever genuine transcendence the world allows is to be found only beneath the shadow of mortal risk, and that the brute forces of necessity will have their final say no matter how artful our dodging. As Stone himself has declared, in his essay "The Reason for Stories: Toward a Moral Fiction": "Things happen ruthlessly, without mercy; the elemental force of things bears down upon us. From one moment to the next we hardly know what's going on, let alone what it all means. Civilization and its attendant morality are not structures, they're more like notions, and sometimes they can seem very distant notions. They can blow away in a second." Stone, like his novelist forebears, pursues a search for God through a world that God has abandoned, wringing small, hard-won redemptions from an irredeemably cold and empty world.

DOG SOLDIERS

Whereas many of the Vietnam novels that followed Stone's play up the disconcerting voyage between the safe, unheroic normality of America and the psychedelic violence and perilous extremes of war-torn Vietnam, *Dog Soldiers* makes the more provocative claim that the homeland is every bit as twisted, dangerous, and amoral as the foreign battlefield, and that to a certain extent the former has been made so by our misguided involvement in the latter. John Converse, a reporter for his father-in-law's tabloid who is in Vietnam to practice journalism and search for book ideas, drifts into a drug-smuggling operation, agreeing to transport three kilos of heroin to California where his wife, Marge, will pick it up and hand it on to others. This uncharacteristic action is spurred in part by a recent negative epiphany concerning his own identity and place within the cosmic order: "One bright afternoon, near a place called Krek, Converse had watched with astonishment as the world of things transformed itself into a single overwhelming act of murder. In a manner of speaking, he had discovered himself. Himself was a soft shell-less quivering thing encased in a hundred and sixty pounds of pink sweating meat. It was real enough. It tried to burrow into the earth. It wept." Marge's motivations for getting involved with the heroin operation are almost as obscure as her husband's, though she does seem to resemble Geraldine from *A Hall of Mirrors* in that from time to time she exhibits a kind of death wish, as if hoping her final payoff will be a bullet and oblivion.

Converse approaches Roy Hicks, an ex-Marine who will be sailing back to Oakland on a decom-

missioned aircraft carrier, and asks him to transport the heroin. Hicks' self-image is more exalted than Converse's, for he thinks of himself as a modern-day samurai whose combination of quick instincts, mental discipline, and worldly knowledge will carry him victorious through any dangers instigated by the world of petty crooks. Though he gets drunk the night before his meeting with Marge, Hicks' cockiness seems in part justified when, arriving at her apartment in Oakland, he foils the efforts of two thugs—Danskin and Smitty—who were poised to make off with the drugs and possibly kill Marge. Thrown together by a situation they cannot fully grasp, much less control, Marge and Hicks escape to a cabin he owns in the canyons above Los Angeles. While they are holed up, Hicks develops an attachment to Marge that seems to spring as much from his conception of himself as a latter-day knight as it does from any knowledge of Marge: "In the end there were not many things worth wanting—for the serious man, the samurai. But there were some. In the end, if the serious man is still bound to illusion, he selects the worthiest illusion and takes a stand. The illusion might be of waiting for one woman to come under his hands. Of being with her and shivering in the same moment." They make love once, but the extent to which Marge shares her new protector's feelings is not immediately clear. After a botched attempt to sell the heroin, which simultaneously burns their last bridge in Los Angeles, they head out into the desert toward a remote hippie ashram at which Hicks once was an acolyte.

Meanwhile, Converse himself has landed back in Oakland only to find himself immersed in a world of trouble. As he attempts to elude unknown pursuers through a crowded department store, we are given another clue as to his motive for involving himself in the drug trade—the glamour of a life where everything is on the line: "In the short length of time during which he could force himself to reflect on the matter, he felt certain that it was preferable to be chased through Macy's as a scourge to the poor and a poisoner of children than as a hapless, cowardly concerned citizen. It was more chic, probably even in God's eyes." Eventually captured by Danskin and Smitty, Converse is taken back to his apartment, injected with drugs, and tortured over the kitchen stove in an attempt to discover the heroin's whereabouts—about which he is wholly ignorant. They finally relent and leave, only to return later in the company of their superior, a corrupt federal agent named Antheil, who explains that they will all be going hunting for Hicks, and that Converse will be taken along as leverage to convince his wife to give up the drugs.

The remote, mountain-top ashram to which Marge and Hicks have fled is led by a middle-aged guru named Dieter, whose congregation apparently undertook a genuine quest for enlightenment until at some point "succumb[ing] to the American dream"—the temptation to smooth and streamline the hard, steep road to nirvana, in their case with large amounts of drugs. By the time the fugitives arrive, the community is long scattered, but the paraphernalia of sixties spirituality and countercultural experimentation is everywhere to be seen, including a network of lights and speakers in the surrounding forest. Dieter, like Clotho in *A Hall of Mirrors,* is an equivocal figure—at times he seems significantly wiser than Hicks and Marge, though at other times he merely appears to peddle self-pitying psychobabble. Not long after the couple have arrived there, their pursuers make their way up the mountain. Converse, ascending between his captors on what he fears may be his last day, feels "intensely aware and alive, the way he had felt in the moment when he decided to buy the dope"—suggesting again that terror may be the modern world's most readily available antidote to ennui and a chronic sense of detachment from reality. For her part, Marge is ready to give up the heroin, even though she knows the pursuers' promises of subsequent

safety are probably lies: "We did this—John and I. I won't have anybody else fucked up over it." Hicks allows her to take the packet down the mountain, but only after he secretly removes the drugs and fills the container with sand. His plan is to circle around unseen but heavily armed, surprise Antheil, and rescue "the love of [his] life, no shit," getting away with the heroin as well. Dieter has ridiculed Hicks as the "Furor Americanus," but Hicks tells him that his bloody and pyrotechnic caper will stand as "the revolution until the revolution comes along." Passing down the mountain through an Indian cave that the commune once used as a gathering place, he traverses a kind of mausoleum of the sixties, a physical symbol of that decade's vanished hopes and ideals:

> The walls were the solid stone of the mountain, rising to a vault forty feet above and covered to an improbable height with a Day-Glo detritus of old highs.
> There Are No Metaphors, it said—in violet—on one wall. Everywhere he turned the light there were fossilized acid hits, a riot of shattered cerebration, entombed. The floor was littered with filter tips and aluminum film cans, there were mattresses reverting to the slime, spools of tape and plastic pill bottles. A few light brackets and speakers were strung with rusted copper wire over supporting pegs set in the stone. The unnatural colors had hardly faded at all.

Stone wrote in "The Reason for Stories" that "the early to mid-'70s still seem to me, in retrospect, like a creepy, evil time. A lot of bills from the '60s were coming up for presentation. *Dog Soldiers* was my reaction to that period." Indeed, the novel presents materialism, cynicism, nihilism, and violence as the symptoms of an idealistic ethos dying a painful and ignominious death.

In the ensuing firefight at the foot of the mountain Hicks manages to free Converse and Marge, though he himself is seriously wounded. Danskin and Smitty are killed, but Antheil and his accomplice, a Mexican policeman, survive. Hicks tells the husband and wife to take his car while he either finishes off or holds off their pursuers and, though wounded and bleeding, promises to meet them after retreating along a difficult route. Along that route he encounters Dieter back at the ashram, who grabs the heroin away from him. Convinced by his long and jaded experience since leaving the commune that this is just one more betrayal by another craven impostor, he shoots Dieter, only to discover that the guru had intended to hurl the heroin over the cliff, an intention that garners from Hicks a measure of grudging respect. Meanwhile, when Converse and Marge arrive at the place of rendezvous, Marge insists, despite Converse's objections, that they try to find Hicks—"It's not a matter of what I want. I have to"—and eventually come upon his corpse. Stone presents Hicks' last hours of genuine fortitude and laughable self-romanticizing in a lengthy tour de force of interior monologue. (Indeed, it is during his final march across the desert that Hicks most closely attains the true control of mind over matter that has mostly eluded him through the novel.) Tying a white Kleenex of surrender to the pack of heroin for the approaching Antheil to find, Converse and Marge drive away, though any prospect of their escaping from jeopardy—physical, moral, emotional—is tentative at best.

Dog Soldiers won the National Book Award in 1975 and was made into a movie called *Who'll Stop the Rain* (1978), which featured Nick Nolte as Hicks and Tuesday Weld as Marge. That film, written by Stone in collaboration, is better regarded than *WUSA* (1970), the film version of *A Hall of Mirrors* (with a screenplay by Stone).

A FLAG FOR SUNRISE

Stone's next novel, *A Flag for Sunrise* (1981), is a tale of disastrous conjunction—or rather collision. Holliwell, an American anthropologist, is to deliver a paper in the Latin American country of Compostela, a mildly sinister polity bordering on the gothically sinister nation Tecan, where a reactionary kleptocracy is kept in power by a ruthless Guardia Nacional. Before Holliwell can leave, however, he is approached by an old acquaintance from the CIA—for whom Holliwell did some work in Vietnam—and asked to make a side trip to Tecan to observe the political goings-on at a Devotionist mission on the coast. Holliwell refuses, but the encounter fosters in him a feeling of dread as he boards his plane for what he conceives to be "a world far from God, a few hours from Miami." In this book there is much talk about God—or rather, about the terrifying absence of God.

The mission Holliwell was asked to spy on is inhabited by only two people, the young, beautiful, and headstrong nun, Justin, and the increasingly feeble, alcoholic, and visionary Father Egan. As all its parishioners have been scared away by threats from the Guardia's sadistic Lieutenant Campos, the mission now serves no practical purpose and has been ordered closed and evacuated by Devotionist superiors. Justin, whose Catholic faith has attenuated, or rather evolved, into a purely secular desire to aid the wretched of Tecan, is disgusted by what she sees as the uselessness of her existence. Thus, when she is approached by a priest who has been working with Tecan's rebel movement in the mountains, she gratefully puts herself and the mission at the disposal of the revolution. Their understanding is sealed at a festival in the nearby town, where the local object of veneration is a permanently coffined Christ, a symbol perhaps of the unavailability of redemptive possibilities in Tecan as a whole. But if Christ is unrisen, there are signs aplenty of Satan walking on Earth. Egan, reluctantly disposing of the body of a woman whom Lieutenant Campos has killed, is amazed at the ease with which a human life can be completely erased, and feels "as though he [has] gained a thoroughly new insight into the processes of the world." Indeed, such appalling insights await the reader of *A Flag for Sunrise*.

Also into the bloody world of Tecan steps Pablo Tabor, an American sailor in the Coast Guard whose amphetamine addiction leads him to desert both the service and his family in a burst of irrational violence. He strikes out southward for what he hopes will be a career better suited to his megalomaniacal sense of self and personal destiny. Pablo's motto is never to let anyone "turn him around," a definition of betrayal that, under the influence of uppers, can become frighteningly broad. On one level, Pablo is no more than an ignorant, murderous, drug-addicted punk, but he does in fact share one thing with Justin—a burning desire for an absolutist vocation (though one of vainglory rather than service). Thus, having arrived in a Caribbean port, he puts an urgent question to a bartender: "What do you think is the use of me?" The bartender thinks the query hilarious, yet has a ready answer: "De use of you, mon? Same as everbody. Put one foot to front of de other. Match de dolluh wif de day. . . . Purpose of you and me to be buried in de ground and das hard enough to do." Before the novel's end, Holliwell, Justin, and Pablo will, each in his or her own way, attempt to raise their heads—however briefly and falteringly—above this despairing vision of life as a mere mundane plodding toward extinction; they will attempt to prove, or merely find, or more merely glimpse the "use" of themselves.

Holliwell's Latin American excursion begins inauspiciously. His lecture, delivered drunk and extempore, is disastrous for him though a delight for the reader. Its real subject is the United States, and although the professor warns his audience that "Mickey Mouse will see [them] dead," he also declares that America's "secret culture, the non-exportable one, is dying. It's going sour and we're going to die of it. We'll die of it quietly around our own hearths while our children laugh at us. So, no more Mickey Mouse, *amigos*. The world is free for Latinate ideologies and German ismusisms . . . temples of reason, the Dialectic, you name it." Because this performance is seen by members of various death-squads present in the audience as an endorsement of communism, Holliwell decides to decamp for Tecan, though he cannot escape political discussions as his vehicle passes through *scenes* of repression and terror. A fellow passenger, for instance, wonders "whether the people down here have to live this way so that we can live the way we do":

> "We have to believe [the answer is] no, don't we?" Cole asked. "We couldn't face up to it otherwise. Because if most of the world lives in this kind of poverty so that we can have our goodies and our extra protein ration—what does that make us?"
> "It makes us vampires," Holliwell said. "It makes us all the cartoon figures in the Communist press."

While this issue is never settled definitively, one of the implicit arguments of *A Flag for Sunrise* is that America is a country that refuses openly to acknowledge the violent sources of its dream of sanitized security. As another passenger puts it, the safe civilians back home have forgotten "the price of salt . . . and the ten pains of death."

Pablo finds himself in Tecan after a stint aboard a gun-running yacht, where he is employed by a kind of piratical family that means to use him for his muscle and then kill him. Pablo figures out the fate that awaits him and strikes first, but not before he has made a foray ashore where his attempt at larceny interrupts the intended victim's suicide attempt. The dying man—a world-weary survivor of the Holocaust—delivers unto Pablo a prophecy at gunpoint: "Your name rolls, Pablo. It's your skull down there—white and round. It shines in the clear light . . . eight fathoms under the fan coral. Your skull is the counter . . . it's the only ball in this game, Pablo." (This broken allusion to *The Tempest* is no accident, for the play is a motif running throughout the novel. But whereas in

Shakespeare's drama shipwreck on a tropical shore leads eventually to personal and political reconciliation, the reigning spirit in Tecan is Caliban rather than Prospero.) Pablo comes away convinced that he has been given powerful insight into the workings of the world and the future arc of his own destiny, and goes on to kill his shipmates and deliver the guns single-handedly, scuttling the yacht on a Tecan coral reef and barely surviving with his head above water.

As it happens, the dangerous beauty of coral is another of the book's central images, for one of Holliwell's first acts in the vicinity of the mission is to go diving to view a reef whose "icy, fragile beauty" and "perfection provoke[s] a recognition" of something "lost and forgotten" in the downward drift of his life. Venturing ever deeper, however, he feels a "terror . . . [strike] the sea, an invisible shadow, a silence within a silence." He manages to surface safely, but the dive is clearly an emblem for his larger situation, since he will soon find himself involved in the shark-infested political waters he had vowed to avoid, lured there by Justin's dangerous beauty. Soon consumed by love for—and curiosity about—the nun and her whole-souled engagement, he comes to think of her as a "Lady of sorrows . . . creature of marvel . . . a unicorn to be speared, penned and adored." They eventually make love, but immediately afterward the professor understands that the nun has "eluded him after all." Long the distanced observer, Holliwell finds that he cannot now possess that one being for whom he would cast aside all caution to wholly enter and occupy.

On the night the shipwrecked Pablo stumbles upon the ancient site of human sacrifice at which Father Egan preaches to bands of roving hippies, the priest is in the midst of a debate with a local child-murderer whose God combines elements of the Old Testament, Central American antiquity, and the Demogorgon; enamored of blood offerings, He is thus well suited to rule over tyrant-ridden Tecan. Pablo listens to it all in a feverish delirium brought on by his wound and his drugs,

and later gives ear to Egan's sermon on attenuated providence until he experiences a self-centered revelation:

> "I do feel it," he declared, nodding furiously. "Fuckin'-A."
> "It's the world moving in time," Father Egan explained to him. "One gets these little epiphenomenal jolts. Petty spookery in a way. But underneath it all—there is something." He clapped Pablo lightly on the shoulder. "It's in the moment. Take it in your hands, my boy."
> Tabor stared wide-eyed into the fire. In the dancing flames he saw dragons, winged horses, a choir of demiurges and such things.
> "It was all meant to be," he said in a choked voice. "It was all meant to be like this." He put his hand to his face and shook his head. He felt happy.

Tecan's political apocalypse soon follows. As Justin is intent on leaving with the guerrillas, Holliwell, who has been cowed by Campos into telling all he knows of the nun, says his anguished good-byes and allows her to put him aboard a small boat with the wounded and babbling Pablo. Once out in the open water, though, he becomes increasingly alarmed by Tabor's intermittently threatening pronouncements and the knife he has strapped to his leg. Finally, after much indecision, he steals the blade from the sleeping sailor and, telling him that he too will teach him an important philosophical lesson—entitled "the abridgment of hope"—stabs him and gives his body at last to the keeping of the coral.

The revolution having yet neither failed nor succeeded, Justin is captured by the Guardia and tortured to death by Lieutenant Campos. During the course of her horrific execution by inches, she feels herself in proximity to something like the perpetually unavailable God of Father Egan:

> You after all? Inside, outside, round and about. Disappearing stranger, trickster. Christ, she though, so far. Far from where?
> But why always so far?
> *"Por qué?"* she asked. There was a guy yelling. Always so far away. You. Always so hard on the

kid here, making me be me right down the line. You old destiny. You of Jacob, you of Isaac, of Esau.

Let it be you after all. Whose after all I am. For whom I was nailed.

So she said to Campos: "Behold the handmaiden of the Lord."

Holliwell eventually drifts onto the shore of an island, complete with a vacationing American family as a symbol of returning safety. It is unclear, however, how useful physical safety will be to a man who has "learned what empty places were in him," for the professor "had undertaken a little assay at the good fight and found that neither good nor fight was left to him. Instead of quitting while he was ahead, he had gone after life again and they had shown him life and made him eat it." He has also garnered some toxic truths about his species and the cosmos as well, since he "get[s] the joke now. . . . We're all the joke. We're the joke on one another. It's our nature." And as for his encounter with evil—"the absence of evil was the greatest horror," for even dizzying moral depths, like those of coral, possess a kind of hazardous sublimity. It is not the vision of the abyss that truly terrifies, but the suspicion that the world lacks any spiritual dimension—that it stretches flat, monotonous, and blood-soaked all the way to the horizon.

A flood of official recognition came Stone's way in response to *A Flag for Sunrise,* including the *Los Angeles Times* Book Prize, the John Dos Passos Prize for literature, and the American Academy and Institute of Arts and Letters Award. It is said that no prophet is honored in his own time, but, appearing as it did at the beginning of a decade in which the consequences of American involvement abroad would make frequent headlines, Stone's highly praised novel can be seen as that rarest of occurrences, the Jeremiad that falls on listening ears.

CHILDREN OF LIGHT

Like the protagonists of *A Flag for Sunrise,* those in Stone's 1986 novel *Children of Light* seem to be on a collision course, though in the later novel there is something even more decidedly chosen about the smash-up, something suicidally deliberate about their steerings toward disaster. Gordon Walker, a Hollywood screenwriter and occasional actor, finds himself, amid the wreckage of his marriage, longing for the company of his old lover, Lee Verger (real name Lu Anne Bourgeois), a brilliant actress in feature films who has long waged a battle against a mental illness that in some ways is also the foundation of her considerable talent. Walker has just come off a successful stage production of *King Lear,* in which he played the title role, but his use of alcohol and drugs has been slowly spiraling out of control; and by the time he decides to visit Lu Anne—who is starring in a movie rendition of Kate Chopin's *The Awakening,* for which Walker has written the screenplay—his ability to think clearly and choose wisely is deeply in question. Against the advice of his agent and what friends remain to him—and despite warnings that, because of his drug-soaked reputation, he will be barely tolerated on the Baja set—he inevitably begins to make his way south along the coast, drawn to the risky transcendence of life's otherwise downward momentum that only Lu Anne's presence can provide.

Meanwhile, at the seaside hotel where *The Awakening* is taking shape, Lu Anne has gone off her medication for the sake of her craft and appears on the brink of disintegration. Her husband, who has kept Lu Anne's insanity tenuously at bay with a combination of love, counseling, and pharmaceuticals, is decamping, unable to face another of her spectacular breakdowns. The picture's director cares only for getting the best performance possible from Lu Anne and does not concern himself with the psychic cost such an effort will inevitably exact from his star. Indeed, Lu Anne has already begun to hallucinate the presence of what she calls her Long Friends, spirits of the dead who, though man-sized and insectlike, are not so much immediately frightening as chronically badgering, intent on criticizing Lu Anne's behavior and belittling her talents.

It is an implicit assumption throughout *Children of Light* that despair is the natural default setting of all who see life clearly, who are not able to palliate it with obsessive labors, aggressive egoism, or drugs. While the Long Friends are Lu Anne's constant reminder that life's trajectory is inevitably a downward one, Gordon has long lost all redemptive illusions, refusing suicide only because "the luxury of abandoning hope was not available to him. Hope might make a fool of him and compound his grief, but he was bound to it as much as the next man. For his sons, himself, even his marriage." In his screenplay, Gordon has written that Chopin's Edna commits suicide because she "senses a freedom the scope of which she has never known. She has come beyond despair to a kind of exaltation." Upon reading it, however, Lu Anne's reaction is to murmur "Really, now, Gordon," for she "had never found anything beyond despair except more despair."

And yet there is one spot of blinding brightness amid the funereal gloom, for the most poignant aspect of this cocaine-smothered novel is that Lu Anne and Gordon's effect on each other is very like that of an ecstasy-inducing drug, in both a beneficent and destructive sense. Their proximity endows them with a bliss that consumes, with a genuine high that is too intense to last. Thus, at the peak of his rapture Gordon thinks "that this [is] his golden girl and that she [is] in his arms and that they [can] never have peace or a quiet moment or a half hour's happiness." In fact, their rediscovered gladness evaporates in an eye blink when talk of the children they have both failed to spiritually nourish sends Lu Anne into a despairing frenzy:

> Her face was pressed against his chest, her mouth was open in a scream of pain, but not a sound came out of her. Panting, he held on. . . . This time she only kept on screaming, and in the single moment that his grip relented she drove him off the bed and

clear across the room and into the beige cloth-covered wall. He hung on to her all the way. His body absorbed her unvoiced scream until he felt he could hardly contain, without injury, the force of her grief and rage.

After a dinner party thrown by the film's producer, at which several subplots are rather comically resolved, a drug-addled Lu Anne contrives to bolt the set. If the novel is Stone's latter-day *Wuthering Heights,* Walker, who follows despite dreadful foreboding, is a left-coast Heathcliff choosing his Cathy—though it means losing all the world to keep her. "Are you going to tell me where we're going?" he asks, to which she replies, "Morning. . . . We're going where it's morning." Their actual destination is a pig-stall atop a mountain—once a movie location—which Stone intends for us to take as a modern analogue of Lear's hut on the heath. Frolicking upon this dubious height, Walker realizes that "the philosophy whose comforts [Lu Anne] represented was Juggernaut," but also "that he was happy. That [this] was why he had come, to be with her in harm's way and be happy." As with Conrad and Greene, so with Stone the evanescent happiness of life seems to reveal itself only in proximity to deadly menace.

What occurs next is a modern, skeptical echo of Lear's agonies and epiphanies in the storm, for the lovers scourge themselves and come to hard recognitions during the course of a hurricane that is as much internal as meteorological.

> "We'll begin from here," Walker said. "We'll mark time from this mountain."
>
> "Who will, Gordon? You and me?"
>
> "Absolutely," Walker burbled happily. "Baptism! Renewal! Rebirth!"
>
> Lu Anne pointed through the rain toward the road they had climbed. "It'll be all down from here, Gordon."
>
> "Christ," Walker said, "you threw my coke away. I had at least six grams left."
>
> "Takes the edge off baptism, renewal and rebirth, doesn't it? When you're out of coke?"

The Mexican police break up Walker and Lu Anne's imitation of "unaccommodated man" and send them back to the set, but on the brink of safety Lu Anne—out of recklessness, being drugged, or out of the suicidal impulse that seems to claim so many of Stone's female protagonists—dashes into the rip-tide and breakers despite the exhausted Gordon's desperate attempts to prevent her and then pull her out. To the reader, nothing has seemed more firmly prepared for Lu Anne than an untimely death, but Walker escapes with at least one hopeful doubt: "As surely as there was water hidden in the desert, there was mercy. Her crazy love was mercy. It might have saved her."

In a brief coda Walker confronts a hostile audience of acquaintances who have attended Lu Anne's memorial service. We find that he has given up drinking and drugs and reunited with his wife and is attempting to work steadily again. It is difficult to know exactly how to take this—are we to see Walker as having learned the valuable lesson of sobriety from the tragedy of Lu Anne's death, or are we to understand that without his soul mate in the world, life's highs and lows have all been reduced to a bourgeois, workaday mean that he cannot singly transcend? Atop their heath, Walker tried to assert that "living is better than dying. Morally. Don't you think?" It is difficult to know whether to praise Walker for a spiritual progress or to charge him with a failure to keep the faith.

OUTERBRIDGE REACH

Owen and Anne Browne, the protagonists of the 1992 novel *Outerbridge Reach,* are a couple nearing forty whose domestic history is closely bound to the Vietnam War, in which Owen played an active but secretive role, and which they fondly remember as a time in which their private lives were characterized by youthful energy, lofty dreams, and an intense love for each other. Such

feelings made them, and to a certain extent keep them, outsiders amidst their own generation. Now, twenty years later, they present an outwardly happy and stable face to the world, though both husband and wife are troubled by currents of disappointment and claustrophobia rising from the depths. "On the other side of darkness, [Browne] imagined freedom. It was a bright expanse, an effort, a victory. It was a good fight or the right war—something that eased the burden of self and made breath possible. Without it, he felt as though he had been preparing all his life for something he would never live to see."

When the playboy owner of the conglomerate for which Owen works disappears amid rumors of shady business dealings, Browne is unexpectedly chosen to take his place in a round-the-world solo regatta, piloting one of the company's new boats, about which he has been writing advertising copy. Feeling that the race may be just the medicine to salve his midlife discontents, Browne quickly agrees to go. Anne, despite serious misgivings about both the man and the enterprise, supports his decision. Had she not,

> She would always have stood between him and the sky-blue world of possibility. She would be responsible for every boring, repetitious day as things went on and the two of them grew ever more middle-aged, disappointed and past hope. Their lives would be like everyone else's and it would always be her fault.

For not the first time in Stone's novels, the lure of a life of absolutes—and escape from the ordinary—prove temptations too alluring to pass up.

As the corporation has already engaged a documentary filmmaker to record the scion's circumnavigation, Owen and Anne now find themselves the reluctant stars of a movie in the making. Strickland is a world-wizened, well-traveled cynic who prides himself on being able to draw out his subjects' basest motivations and most fatal confusions. His specialty is exposing "the bottom line. . . . The difference between what people say they're doing and what's really going on," and his talk about his own craft alternates between protestations of objectivity and prideful assertions of his ability to deftly manipulate reality to serve his chosen aesthetic purpose. It is not long before the Brownes sense the disdain of the man whom they must allow, camera in hand, into their private lives, and begin treating him with a good deal of suspicion. But Strickland's feelings are in fact a bit more complicated, for while he does see Owen as a "dorky fucking citizen," his view of Anne is tinged by curiosity and desire.

Not long into Owen's voyage there are ambiguous signs to interpret: dolphins escort his boat but disappear when he takes out Strickland's video camera; favorable winds are followed by doldrums; a cloud of disgusting insects, blown off the African coast, defiles his decks. On his one previous solo cruise, Browne had experienced hallucinations, and it is in fact not long before the aspects of sea and sky, the music he plays at night, the rhythms of his own body, begin to take on an exhilarating yet disturbing intensity, a brilliance that might illuminate but also threatens to blind. In particular, a shortwave religious program that he continually picks up seems to be full of portentous prophecies and warnings that may or may not apply to his lonely battle against the elements and himself, but which definitely sets his mind stumbling toward precincts both high and deep.

Back on shore, Anne, much to her own surprise, drifts into an affair with Strickland, whose feelings for Anne surpass his usual aesthetic and aggressive interest in his many sexual conquests. The author appears to suggest that Anne is pushed toward adultery by the same smoldering discontents, broadening of horizons, and quickening of the senses that Brown is experiencing at sea. Thus, she shares an intimacy of imitation with her absent husband in the midst of her betrayal, for she "feel[s] more and more like going

to sea herself. . . . The fact was they had been wasting their lives. She had been bored sick without knowing it. Owen had been right about the race. It had opened up life." For his part, Strickland, beyond being in love, is also engaged in a kind of crusade, for he believes that he has already succeeded in freeing Anne from a middle-class rut that he feels dishonors her human potential.

Out at sea, Browne discovers that his boat, constructed on the cheap by the floundering corporation, is literally coming apart at the seams, and from here on in the disintegration of the craft and its captain proceed in tandem. In his mind, the shoddy construction is a sign both of national decline and the absurdity of his own heroic pretensions: "*Res sacrum perdita* [the holy things are lost]. He could not remember the origin of the phrase. Sold our pottage, overheated the poles, poisoned the rain, burned away the horizon with acid. Despised our birthright. Forgot everything, destroyed and laughed away our holy things. . . . There is a justice here, Browne thought. He had been trying to be someone else." It is at this point that Owen comes across an uncharted volcanic island and maneuvers his craft into the shelter of its flooded caldera, there to ponder his fate and identity. Unwilling to give up the idea of himself as one of life's winners, he succumbs to the temptation of filing false position reports—in effect claiming to have sailed around the world while actually sneaking back to New York the short way round. Befuddled by solitude and self-doubt, he engages in rationalizations he would never entertain ashore: "It could all be looked at as philosophy, Browne decided—as a question of reality and perception. Everyone had to believe his informing story. Everyone had to endure his own secret. That was survival."

Browne explores his desolate island, exhilarated at times by the thought of the double life he will lead like Conrad's Nostromo; but the increasingly intense hallucinations he suffers warn us that his mind will not tolerate such levels of moral torque. Writing "Be true to the dreams of your youth"—Melville's credo—on the side of an abandoned whaling shack with an instrument that leaves no visible mark, Browne's decision to merely masquerade as the man he wishes to be robs him of his self-conception and of any chart that might allow him safely to navigate his life: "On this ocean, Browne thought, goodbye to almanacs and hope in Stella Maris and the small rain down. This is a game beyond me." Browne leaves the island and begins his clandestine backtracking toward the race's finish line, but, beset by shame, despair, self-loathing, and a sense of attenuated identity, he commits suicide by stepping into the sea. Before doing so, however, he manages to affirm a few hard facts about himself and life: "The truth's my bride, my first and greatest love. . . . It was horrible . . . to employ the godly instruments of rectitude—compass, sextant, rule—in lying. It eroded the heart and soul. . . . Single-handed, he thought, I'll make myself an honest man."

Back home, the reports of Browne's approach cause Anne to realize that, despite her love for Strickland, she cannot live with herself if she abandons Owen. She, too, has wandered beyond her depth, but, possessing perhaps a greater fund of strength and courage than her husband, she can fight her way to shore. When Browne's abandoned boat washes up in Brazil, both Anne and Stickland rush to the scene, the filmmaker more determined than ever to complete his documentary, which he swears to Anne will not be a scathing exposé of either Owen or herself. Anne, however, does not trust him, for she knows his first loyalty is to the corrosive power of his skeptical art. When Strickland steals Owen's false logs and the video he shot while on board, Anne goes to her father, a kingpin of the New York docklands, who has a pair of heavies steal back the material and cripple Strickland's hands in the process. The novel concludes a year or so later with Anne her-

self preparing to enter the next solo circumnavigation race—an act that will involve contrition, reparation, expiation, and, not least, further personal and philosophical exploration, since, as Anne concludes, "The ocean encompassed everything, and everything could be understood in terms of it. Everything true about it was true about life in general."

In 1987 Stone won a five-year, $250,000 Strauss Living Award; he also brought out a collection of his short stories entitled, after one of the stories, *Bear and His Daughter*. The tales, only seven in number, are fine pieces of writing but do not represent any radical departure for Stone—indeed, their characters and plots will seem familiar to anyone who has read the novels. They are almost all marked by a looming sense of catastrophe—from the first page one feels that the protagonists are in terrible danger; the fact that this danger results from their own obsessions or omissions does not interfere with anxious empathy that Stone always manages to evoke on their behalf. Also like the novels, the stories contain a number of truly funny passages side by side with the darker material. *Bear and His Daughter* makes it clear that, though Stone has chosen to expend his greatest energies on the novel, he is equally adept at the more compact genre of the short story.

DAMASCUS GATE

Perhaps the most surprising aspect of Stone's novel *Damascus Gate,* published in 1998, is its Dickensian plotting, in which a multitude of seemingly disparate souls collide with and carom off each other amid the frenetic and dangerous tides of modern-day Jerusalem. Stone makes a concerted attempt to paint the Holy City as, morally and politically, nothing less than the center of the world, the place where "religion . . . is something that's happening now, today," because "the monuments of Jerusalem [do] not belong to the past. They [are] of the moment and even the future." One of the techniques by which this is accomplished is the juxtaposition of ancient Hebrew terms like *tikkun, talmud, sefirot,* and *ayin* with acronyms out of modern newspapers—IDF, PKF, UNRWA. This, coupled with Stone's depiction of how the fiercest and most ancient religious passions are confused with and compromised by the latest political expediencies (without the former loosing their terrible power to alight the mind), all serve to evoke Jerusalem as a cauldron that has been boiling over for at least three millennia, and which always promises to explode tonight.

The protagonist, freelance journalist Christopher Lucas, is a familiar figure in Stone's oeuvre—a more-or-less baffled American seeker, a lone man losing the sense of his life's coherence, a skeptical quipster. He is the son of a Jewish father and a gentile mother, a man of no current faith who is yet drawn inevitably toward the city of many faiths for a journalistic assignment that turns into a religious pilgrimage. Ostensibly researching a book on the "Jerusalem syndrome," the modern psychiatric term for a type of religious mania that strikes devout Christian and Jewish visitors to the city, causing them to feel called to messiahship (or, in its milder form, discipleship)—he eventually discovers that "because of who he was. . . . He himself suffered from the Jerusalem Syndrome."

The object of his more secular yearnings is Sonia, an American of mixed black and white heritage whose parents were communists. She is now a Sufi, a cabaret singer, and a veteran of relief agency work in the world's hot spots of misery and starvation. Sonia is a seeker much less conflicted than Lucas—she is actively looking for a spiritual answer and is willing to follow the call of a cult about which the reporter is more than a bit suspicious. Yet she is neither the giddy groupie nor the true believer, filtering most of the

spiritual dogmas she hears through the communist sympathies that she continues to carry and honor. This cautious balance is attractive to both the reader and Lucas, for Sonia occupies a middle ground between what Stone suggests are the only two options open to U.S. citizens in the Holy Land—either that of retaining fully one's American eclecticism and thus remaining "the slave of possibility"—Lucas' situation—or of becoming zealous fanatics in whatever creed one chooses to adopt. Indeed, by highlighting repeatedly the American provenance of Jerusalem's faith-crazed Jews, Christians, and Muslims—a grim, ongoing joke—Stone makes a serious point about the sorry spiritual and political state of the contemporary United States.

The cult to which Sonia has attached herself—and with which Lucas tags along in pursuit of her and his story—preaches a syncretic gospel that attempts to see all religions, and especially all gnostic traditions within those religions, as possessing one of the keys to a benign apocalypse that will halt history and issue in a new heaven and new earth. On the one hand, the assertions of the unlikely cult leader, De Kuff—an elderly ex-musician from Louisiana—sound facile and vague:

> All mysteries are the same mystery! . . . Whether we worship the Holy Ancient One, whether we worship the *sefirot,* we are the same. There is one truth! There is one belief! There is one holiness! And at the birth of things to come, we all, through birth, through *partsufim,* we all stood at Sinai. There is not Israel! There is only Israel! The mystery is one! You are one faith! You are all believers in one heart! Not to believe together is to cease to be!

At the same time, though, the ubiquitous hatreds aroused by the many conflicting faiths of Stone's Jerusalem are so raw and so seemingly intractable that such a message cannot help but strike a note of hopeful relief in the novel's readers. It certainly does so for the small band of followers who wind up accompanying De Kuff on a journey to the source of the Jordan and then back to the city, where he expects to fulfill his messianic destiny. It is an unlikely and rag-tag bunch, to be sure, but depending on how you count, there appear to be twelve of them, a subtle hint from the author that the band may have a respectable pedigree as things go in the Holy Land.

The cult, far from single-handedly bringing about the End of Days, is in fact the pawn of various zealot factions—Jewish and Christian— who are attempting to blow up the mosque atop the Temple Mount, an action that they believe will, according to their bent, either bring King Jesus back in glory or begin a war that will finally remove the Arabs from Israel. Involved either in league or in opposition to this conspiracy are various Israeli secret service agencies, the Communist Party, assorted soldiers of fortune, and various field operatives of the United Nations, all of which give rise to complications of plot too intricate to synopsize. The main point is that Stone demonstrates through their many collisions and collusions that in Jerusalem the spiritual and the political, the ancient and the postmodern, are never far apart.

One such complication involves both Lucas and Sonia in a trip to the Gaza strip, which Stone presents as the locus of a truly harrowing misery. His evocation of the desperation of mind that comes with being politically repressed and personally humiliated on a daily basis is utterly convincing. And yet whatever partisan political message Gaza's agony sends is, if not muted, then partially subsumed by larger historical tragedies. The morning of his trip to Gaza, Lucas visits Yad Vashem, the Israeli Holocaust museum, and weeps at "a fallen universe of shame." Later, after near-death encounters with both enraged Arabs and militant Jews, Lucas decides that while it is possible to find a "cheap equivalence" between the two sites, it remains true that "the chain of circumstance connecting the two shaped the underlying reality. Blind champions would forever turn the wheels in endless cycles of outrage and redress, an infinite round of guilt and grief. Instead of justice, a circular darkness."

As Lucas gets caught up in the peripatetic cult and is drawn, half purposely, half puppetlike, closer to the dangerous secret of the Temple Mount conspiracy, his religious condition vacillates. At times he is in skeptical, disgusted rebellion against both the Almighty and the land He has blighted: "But in the invisible roaring giant of this land we must believe, the dread Ancient One. . . . This Alice in Wonderland character on the throne of being, a cosmic psychopath in a spinning layered chariot. . . . Not me, Lucas thought. *Non serviam* [I shall not serve]." Like Greene's characters, however, he is drawn to larger causes and larger truths through personal commitments. When Sonia, after seeing Lucas soften somewhat toward De Kuff and his ministry, allows him into her sleeping bag at last, he finds there "the place of understanding . . . in whose depths is the place of wisdom" and clears a space in his heart for a tentative faith in whatever her band can manage to shake loose from heaven. Yet spiritual progress can also mean an increase in terror. As friends start to die and hidden forces and deceits begin to reveal themselves, Lucas begins a trembling that is half piety and half panic: "What he was experiencing, he thought, might be described as fear of the Lord. This emotion, it was written, was the beginning of wisdom. Of course it had been rash of him to refer to the Almighty as an invisible winged paperweight. He wondered if wisdom might not be, at long last, presenting itself to him."

In the end, after the flowering of the conspiracy and the Golgotha of their long-shot savior, Lucas and Sonia both manage to escape with shaken but workable faiths. No longer expecting the world's cold walls of stone to come tumbling down, Sonia now envisions a more personal salvation:

"The Temple is inside," she said. "The Temple is the Law."

"A lot of people," Lucas said, "think that's been the way too long. They want the real thing."

"Sure," she said. "And the fulfillment of prophecy. Me, I think they're wrong. Lots of places have temples. Utah has a temple. Amritsar. Kyoto. The Temple has to be in the heart. When everybody builds it there, maybe then they can think about Beautiful Gates and the Holy of Holies."

A quieter, more modest pilgrimage this may be, but it is nevertheless one that Sonia feels must be followed in Jerusalem, and so she declines Lucas' request that she marry him and follow him to morally cooler lands (where the Mossad, the Israeli intelligence agency, has strongly suggested he go). His love for her is, in the keen, clarifying quality of the misery it causes him, the most palpably real aspect of his life; but his future is not a total loss, for Lucas has, through his rough experience, discovered a way in which the religious and the erotic, the personal and the eternal, come together: "A thing is never truly perceived, appreciated or defined except in longing. A land in exile, a God in His absconding, a love in its loss. And . . . everyone loses everything in the end. But . . . certain things of their nature cannot be taken away while life lasts. Some things can never be lost utterly that were loved in a certain way."

Stone's world is one in which "nothing is free"—this goes double for love and wisdom. Interestingly, the one text within *Damascus Gate* that seems to best exemplify the workings of Stone's cosmos is not the Old Testament or the Koran or the Kabbala, but a more modern and unlikely classic.

"Well," Lucas said, "if [life is] not *The Wind in the Willows,* maybe it's *Alice in Wonderland.*"

"But why *Alice in Wonderland?*"

"Well, because *Alice in Wonderland* is funny. It's funny but it has no justice. Or meaning, or mercy."

"Right," [Helen] said. "But it's got logic. There's a chess game behind it."

She had him there.

As Conrad's Marlow puts it, in *Heart of Darkness,* "Droll thing life is—that mysterious arrangement of merciless logic for a futile purpose. The most you can hope from it is some knowledge of yourself—that comes too late—a crop of inextinguishable regrets." Stone would likely agree, but it is the inexorable logic of all Stone's novels that our passionate longing to transcend our God-forsaken condition, to seek out sufficient meaning within a seemingly indifferent universe, drives us relentlessly toward those high ramparts of bliss and enlightenment whose admission fee is always reckoned in blood and regret.

Selected Bibliography

NOVELS AND SHORT STORIES
Bear and His Daughter: Stories. Boston: Houghton Mifflin, 1997.
Children of Light. New York: Knopf, 1986.
Damascus Gate. New York: Houghton Mifflin, 1998.
Dog Soldiers: A Novel. Boston: Houghton Mifflin, 1974.
A Flag for Sunrise: A Novel. New York: Knopf, 1981.
A Hall of Mirrors. Boston: Houghton Mifflin, 1967.
Outerbridge Reach. New York: Ticknor and Fields, 1992.

ANTHOLOGY
The Best American Short Stories: 1992 (with Katrina Kenison). Boston: Houghton Mifflin, 1992.

ESSAYS AND ARTICLES
"East-West Relation." *Harper's* (November 1989), pp. 63–67.
"Everything Possible, Nothing Sacred." *New York Times,* March 15, 1992.
"Finding Mercy in a God-Forsaken World." *Times Literary Supplement,* November 15, 1996, p. 23.
"The Genesis of Outerbridge Reach." *Times Literary Supplement,* June 5, 1992, p. 15.
"Gin and Nostalgia." (Review of *The Human Factor* by Graham Greene.) *Harper's* (April 1978), pp. 78–83.

"Havana Then and Now." *Harper's* (March 1992), pp. 36–46.

"A Higher Horror of the Whiteness: Cocaine's Coloring of the American Psyche." *Harper's* (December 1986), pp. 49–54.

"Itchy Feet and Pencils: A Symposium" (with Russell Banks, Jan Morris, and William Styron). *New York Times Book Review,* August 18, 1991, pp. 1, 23–25.

"Keeping the Future at Bay: Republicans and Their America." *Harper's* (November 1988), pp. 57–66.

"Me and the Universe." *Triquarterly* 65: 229–234 (Winter 1986).

"The Reason for Stories: Toward a Moral Fiction." *Harper's* (June 1988), pp. 71–76.

"We Couldn't Swing with It: The 'Intrepid Four.' " *Atlantic* (June 1968), pp. 57–64.

CRITICAL AND BIOGRAPHICAL STUDIES

Bloom, James D. "Cultural Capital and Contrarian Investing: Robert Stone, Thom Jones, and Others." *Contemporary Literature* 36: 490–507 (Fall 1995).

Elliott, Emory. "History and Will in *Dog Soldiers, Sabbatical,* and *The Color Purple.*" *Arizona Quarterly* 43: 197–217 (Autumn 1987).

Finn, James. "The Moral Vision of Robert Stone: The Transcendent in the Muck of History." *Commonweal* 120: 9–14 (November 5, 1993).

Fredrickson, Robert S. "Robert Stone's Decadent Leftists." *Papers on Language and Literature* 32: 315–334 (Summer 1996).

Garren, Samuel B. "Stone's 'Porque No Tiene, Porque Le Falta.' " *Explicator* 42: 61–62 (Spring 1984).

Karagueuzian, Maureen. "Irony in Robert Stone's *Dog Soldiers.*" *Critique: Studies in Modern Fiction* 24: 65–73 (Winter 1983).

Moore, L. Hugh. "The Undersea World of Robert Stone." *Critique: Studies in Modern Fiction* 11: 43–56 (1969).

Parks, John G. "Unfit Survivors: The Failed and Lost Pilgrims in the Fiction of Robert Stone." *CEA Critic* 53: 52–57 (Fall 1990).

Pink, David, and C. Lewis. "An Interview with Robert Stone." *Salmagundi* 108: 119–139 (Fall 1995).

Sale, Roger. "Robert Stone." In *On Not Being Good Enough: Writings of a Working Critic.* New York: Oxford University Press, 1979.

Shelton, Frank W. "Robert Stone's *Dog Soldiers:* Vietnam Comes Home to America." *Critique: Studies in Modern Fiction* 24: 74–81 (Winter 1983).

Solotaroff, Robert. *Robert Stone.* Twayne's United States Authors Series, No. 632. New York: Twayne, 1994.

Weber, Bruce. "An Eye for Danger." *New York Times Magazine,* January 19, 1992, pp. 18–24.

—CATES BALDRIDGE

Peter Taylor

1917–1994

A GOOD GENERAL RULE to keep in mind while reading the stories and novels of Peter Taylor is that things in them are often not what they seem. At its most extreme, as in his 1986 Pulitzer Prize–winning novel, *A Summons to Memphis,* this quality in Taylor's work can show itself in the form of a classic unreliable narrator, whose observations warrant the reader's vigorous skepticism. At its mildest, it requires only that the reader enter into his narrators' good-natured sense of humor, a tendency to laugh at the human capacity for self-deception. This laughter does not mock the subjects of his tales so much as enfold the reader, narrator, and characters in a web of understanding and sympathy. But beyond these two levels of disjunction is a subtler one that invites the reader to misread multilayered narratives that often take on different and even opposing meanings as the layers are peeled away.

On the surface of much of his work, which spans a writing life of nearly sixty years, Taylor seems to focus admiringly on a remembered world of upper-class Tennesseans from the 1920s to the 1940s. In stories ranging from "A Long Fourth" (1946) to "The Old Forest" (1979), details like big houses, servants, the country-club whirl, all the trappings of a way of life that today seems distant if not particularly exotic, are observed by a narrator who is certainly an insider. This insider status distinguishes Taylor's work

from that of another writer who took the upper class (of about the same era if not locale) as his subject, F. Scott Fitzgerald. Because Fitzgerald's narrators are always explicitly or at least implicitly interlopers in the world of the rich, the reader does not have to work very hard to discover the disillusionment that is just below the glittering surface. That disillusionment is there in Taylor as well, but it is deeper and more complex, growing out of the mature understanding of a narrator looking back on his youthful naiveté; differences between Taylor's generation and that of his parents; changes over time in racial and class sensitivities; the distinctions between country ways and city ways; and inequalities between the sexes. Because Taylor's narrators seem so much a part of their world, as do for instance the upper-class narrators of Henry James, and because in Taylor they seem at first so enamored of or at least amused by their world, the disillusionment is more hidden and thus easier for the reader to miss.

EARLY LIFE

This upper-South, upper-class society of the first part of the twentieth century is the world into which Peter Matthew Hillsman Taylor was born, on January 8, 1917. Although the place of his birth was Trenton, Tennessee, a country town in the western third of the state where his father, Matthew Hillsman Taylor, had grown up on a farm, Taylor spent his boyhood in the cities of the upper South. His mother, Katherine Baird (Taylor) Taylor, the daughter of a Tennessee governor who was later a United States senator, grew up both in Nashville and Washington, although she too had roots in the country—in eastern Tennessee. Peter Taylor's father was a lawyer whose forebears had also been politically active in the state. He moved his family often between the cities of Nashville and Memphis, and upon becoming president of an insurance company in 1926, moved his wife and four children, of which Peter was the last, to St. Louis. Taylor's family returned to Memphis from St. Louis in 1932, and he attended Central High School, from which he graduated in 1935.

In just these few biographical details are hints of the subjects of many of Taylor's stories and novels—the interplay of rural and urban lives ("What You Hear From Em" and "The Hand of Emmagene"), for instance, or the distinctions between Nashville and Memphis ("The Captain's Son," *A Summons to Memphis*). The St. Louis boyhood is the milieu for Taylor's first novel, *A Woman of Means*. The death of his maternal grandfather while serving in the U.S. Senate and the funeral train that took the senator back to Tennessee form the basis of Taylor's final novel, *In the Tennessee Country*; a long story from late in Taylor's life, "The Oracle at Stoneleigh Court," focuses on the members of a family from Tennessee who follow a relation to Washington because he has been elected to Congress.

Perhaps two-thirds of all Taylor's narratives grow out of the decades of his Tennessee and St. Louis youth and early manhood, and many of the rest ("1939," "*Je Suis Perdu*," "Dean of Men," "The Gift of the Prodigal") draw directly on experiences from elsewhere later in his life. But even when the fictional details closely parallel the biographical ones, Taylor carefully arranges and examines the elements of his story to draw some larger meaning out of them. In an interview a year before his death (published in *The Craft of Peter Taylor*; all other interviews cited here can be found in the collection of interviews edited by Hubert H. McAlexander), Taylor told Christopher P. Metress:

> You see, things can be true on two levels. That's what I always seem to discover as I write my stories. For instance, I'm now writing a story about my two sisters and the two men they married. Growing up, I would listen to stories about them, and the stories they would tell about each other. All four of them were quite important to me. And so I'm starting with the stories I know, the stories I heard. But as I think about them, as I write down the stories, I'm not restricted to only that kind of truth. There's a second kind of truth, the one that I arrive at after thinking through the events. And it's this second level of truth where things get interesting.

Taylor dedicated his *Collected Stories*, published in 1969, to his mother, "the best teller of tales I know and from whose lips I first heard many of the stories in this book." He told Stephen Goodwin in a 1973 interview that his early story "A Spinster's Tale" (1938) is "right out of my mother's mouth. My mother was rather prim and puritanical—old maidish, we used to say, at least she had that side of her—and that story is really hers. . . . The language in the story was my mother's too—it's more Victorian, more elevated than the language in most of my stories."

But even in this his first mature work, written when Taylor was only twenty-one and still an undergraduate, there is far more going on than the recounting of an old maid's memories of her youth (beginning, of course, with the fact that, unlike the story's narrator, his mother might have been old-maidish but was obviously no spinster).

In the story the narrator tells of the months that follow the death of her mother in a large Nashville house with several servants, in which the girl's father and high-school-age brother also live. The girl, though past puberty, has been sheltered from the world and has not faced the implications of becoming a woman. On a day six months after her mother's death, she notices a figure passing the house, a drunken man her father calls Old Speed. He fills her with horror, a fear she tries to face as she begins to notice him passing the house several times a week. Her loneliness in the big house is somehow linked to her fear of this Speed, and it grows as she begins to detect in her brother (who tends to a more genteel form of drunkenness) and her father (whose Saturday afternoon ritual of a toddy with his brothers has grown into something more alcoholic since his wife's death) certain qualities of Speed himself. The story builds with a Jamesian sort of psychological complexity to a climax in which the narrator seems to be accepting certain aspects of womanly responsibility, for example with regard to the running of the household. But then she fails as a woman in her father's eyes when she overreacts to Old Speed's drunkenly approaching the house during a downpour by calling the police. "I regret that the bluecoats were called," is all her father says when he returns home.

Her father believes that she has been harsh and unsympathetic, but she concludes that "despite the surge of pity I felt for the old man on our porch that afternoon, my hatred and fear of what he had stood for in my eyes has never left me." This is a story she tells years later, and we have of course seen it through her eyes. Still, the title of the story urges us to part company with its narrator. After all, this is "A Spinster's Tale," and her mixture of loneliness and fear, her identifying her father and brother's sympathy for Speed as sympathy with the brutality of his drunkenness has turned into a lifetime of holding herself back

from life. The story can also be read as a clash between the nineteenth-century or Victorian values of Taylor's mother and the more lax values of the modern South of Taylor's youth.

COLLEGE AND POSTGRADUATE YEARS

Upon graduating from high school, Taylor won a scholarship to Columbia University to study writing, a plan that in those Depression years did not appeal to Taylor's father, who wanted him to attend Vanderbilt University in Nashville and become a lawyer. Instead of choosing either option, Taylor worked his way to England on a freighter, waiting until the spring semester of 1936 to enter college, at Southwestern in Memphis. There his freshman composition teacher was Allen Tate, the first of the many important American poets with whom he would become friends. Tate was impressed by his student and encouraged him to enroll at Vanderbilt the next fall to study with another accomplished poet and literary figure, John Crowe Ransom. While at Vanderbilt Taylor met a brilliant older student, Randall Jarrell, who would become one of the most important friends of his life—and who himself became a significant poet and critic.

The following spring, in 1937, Taylor published his first two stories, "The Party" and "The Lady Is Civilized," in a short-lived literary magazine called *River*, based in Oxford, Mississippi. (The great Mississippi short-story writer Eudora Welty published one of her first stories in *River* at the same time.) That spring Ransom was lured away from Vanderbilt to teach at Kenyon College in Gambier, Ohio. Jarrell followed him in the fall, but Taylor dropped out of college for a year, selling real estate in Memphis, and enrolled at Kenyon himself in the fall of 1938. There Taylor roomed with another brilliant student drawn to Kenyon by Ransom, a Bostonian named Robert

Lowell. Lowell would become a preeminent American poet and one of the most famous literary men of his generation.

At Kenyon Taylor worked hard at his fiction, writing "A Spinster's Tale," "Sky Line," and "The Fancy Woman," each of which would be published in *The Southern Review,* edited in Baton Rouge, Louisiana, by Robert Penn Warren and Cleanth Brooks. A story published in 1939 in *Hika,* the student literary magazine at Kenyon College, would be republished in *The New Yorker* in 1948.

Years later, Taylor wrote "1939," a story drawn almost directly from his experience at Kenyon and his friendship with Robert Lowell. It begins, "Twenty years ago, in 1939, I was in my senior year at Kenyon College." Although much of the story recounts a Thanksgiving trip to New York and Boston taken by the character based on Taylor himself and a character based on Lowell, the beginning and end of the story convey the texture of life at Kenyon for Taylor and a group of writing students who lived together in a house apart from the rest of the student body. These characters in the story also hold themselves apart emotionally from the other students and are reviled by them in their turn. Taylor tells how "from the windows of their house the writing students could look down on the dormitory students who passed along the sidewalk, and could make our comment on what we considered their silly affectations— on their provincial manners and their foppish, collegiate clothing." He also describes the writing students' feelings of independence, even from each other, and the sense each of them has that he might leave Kenyon at any time. In fact, as the two main characters set out on their trip, the question they keep repeating to each other is whether they will even return to Kenyon after Thanksgiving or instead launch themselves as writers in the real world beyond the campus. The experiences they have on the holiday—especially their visit to New York City to see girls they know who turn out to be more worldly or emotionally mature than they are—convince them that the answer to the question is, as the rhythm of the train they ride back to Ohio seems to suggest: "Not yet, not yet, not yet." Although this story was written two decades after Taylor's student days at Kenyon, it shows that the conflict between being a part of or apart from the milieu he lives in and observes was an incipient theme of Taylor's fiction.

Not only did Taylor and Lowell remain at Kenyon, graduating in the spring of 1940, they decided to go on to graduate school together at Louisiana State University, where *The Southern Review* was located and where they could study under Warren and Brooks. Lowell had married Jean Stafford, on whom one of the girls the students visited in "1939" is based and who would become a celebrated novelist and short-story writer. The three of them settled in Baton Rouge, with Stafford writing and doing secretarial work at *The Southern Review* while the men went to classes and themselves continued to write. But by Thanksgiving of 1940, Taylor quit to work harder at his fiction. In June 1941 Taylor was drafted and spent the next thirty-three months at an army post near Chattanooga. During this time his story "The Fancy Woman" was selected for *The Best American Short Stories of 1942.*

Taylor spoke of "The Fancy Woman" (in interviews with Goodwin and J. William Broadway) as a story written in deliberate opposition to "A Spinster's Tale." Lowell had chided him about the latter story, Taylor tells Broadway: "Why do you write about such nicey-nice people? To show [Lowell] I said to myself, I'm going to write a story about a woman who is so corrupt that she can't recognize innocence when she sees it. And I wrote the first sentence without any idea what the story would be. 'He wanted no more of her drunken palaver.' That was 'The Fancy Woman,' a story about the discovery of evil, really."

The spinster and the fancy woman (a polite euphemism for a prostitute) are indeed opposites: youth vs. maturity, innocence vs. experience, idealism vs. cynicism, city vs. country, upper class vs. middle class, a revulsion toward alcohol vs. drunkenness. And yet despite Taylor's assertion of the fancy woman's corruption, there are some striking similarities in the two characters. Like Elizabeth who will become the spinster, Josephine the fancy woman finds herself deeply isolated from the other characters in the story. In both stories the isolation is caused by the position of women in a milieu dominated by men and complicated by misunderstandings of relations between the sexes and between classes. Josephine is spending a week in the country in the house of her rich boyfriend. Three couples from Memphis society join them in the country, well aware of what she is, although Josephine is sometimes able to persuade herself that she is being treated as a social equal. These couples, free of the moral bonds of their social set in the city, themselves drink too much and misbehave with each other's spouses, including Josephine in the fun. The next day her boyfriend's attractive sons visit this party, and Josephine supposes that they, too, are interested in playing these dangerous games. She implies as much to the younger of the sons, with disastrous results. At the end of the story she cowers in her room with a bottle of whiskey, "listening and just waiting for [her boyfriend] to break the door, and wondering what he'd do to her." The bad behavior of the society couples and her lover do not justify Josephine's behavior, but in the end it is hard not to feel sympathy for her. For all her exterior toughness, the fancy woman is as powerless as the spinster.

The other important event during Taylor's years in the army was meeting Eleanor Ross, a North Carolinian doing postgraduate work at Vanderbilt. They were introduced by Allen Tate and six weeks later, on June 4, 1943, were married near Sewanee, Tennessee. Eleanor Ross Tay-lor would herself become an accomplished and critically admired poet. The marriage lasted more than fifty years, until Peter Taylor's death in 1994.

A story called "Rain in the Heart" (published in *Sewanee Review* in 1945) undoubtedly draws many of its details and all of its emotional power from the early days of their marriage. In the story a sergeant stationed during wartime in an unnamed city that is certainly Chattanooga leaves camp at the end of a day of drills to visit his new bride. The story is narrated in the third person, but there is as much fidelity between the author's point of view and that of his main character here as in anything Taylor ever wrote. This uncharacteristic straightforwardness almost certainly comes from the depth and unambiguousness of Taylor's feelings about his subject. The story has three sections. In the first, as the sergeant readies himself to leave the camp for the night, he observes the other soldiers' rough manners and hears the sexual innuendo in their banter. In the second section, he is on his way home, where his wife awaits him. After he alights from a second bus to wait for the trolley that will take him the rest of the way, he has a protracted conversation with a garrulous country woman, a cleaning woman with greasy hair and a sour personality. In the third section he arrives home, discovering about his new wife that "just as her voice was softer, her appearance was fairer even than he had remembered." This observation contrasts with a thought the sergeant has in the first section of the story: "How unreal to him were these soldiers and their hairy bodies and all their talk and their rough ways. How temporary. How different from his own life, from his real life with her."

Class differences are clearly a major component of this story, but here (unlike "A Spinster's Tale" and "The Fancy Woman") they do not complicate the story so much as make its meaning clearer. The class differences between himself and the soldiers and the people he meets while riding home are part of what isolates the couple from the rest of the world. His wife feels this too, telling him when he arrives, "I know you are tired. You're probably not so tired from soldiering as from dealing with people of various sorts all day." Later, when it rains and then the rain ends, she says, "I'm sorry it stopped . . . hasn't the rain made us seem even more alone up here?" Later still, as they prepare for bed, the sergeant feels unsettled, thinking of his day, of the need to return to camp in the morning, and of the fighting he might take part in on a battlefield that was now distant and almost abstract. He waivers between feeling grateful for the happiness and completeness of his marriage and feeling that even this happiness was dwarfed by the sense that "no moment in his life had any relation to another." But then the rain starts again, sealing him off with his wife from the rest of the world, and the story concludes, "It's much better now."

In February 1944 Taylor was shipped overseas to England but did not see battle. He was discharged from the army in December 1945 and beginning in April 1946, went to work briefly for the book publisher Henry Holt in New York. The Taylors rented an apartment in Greenwich Village, but by the fall he had accepted a teaching job in the English department at the Woman's College of the University of North Carolina, in Greensboro, from which Mrs. Taylor had graduated before going to Vanderbilt. Randall Jarrell was also teaching at Greensboro, and together the Taylors and Jarrell and his wife bought and moved into a duplex.

FIRST COLLECTION

By this time, early 1947, Taylor had published ten stories in six journals. It was time for Taylor to publish a collection, and in March 1948 *A Long Fourth and Other Stories* appeared, with an introduction by Robert Penn Warren that is as per-

ceptive a critical introduction to Taylor's work as anything written in the half century that followed:

Peter Taylor's stories are officially about the contemporary, urban, middle-class world of the upper South, and he is the only writer who has taken this as his province. This world which he delineates so precisely provides a special set of tensions and complications. For instance, the old-fashioned structure of family life still persists, disintegrating slowly under the pressures of modernity. . . . Lost simplicities, the role of woman, the place of the Negro—these are topics which properly appear in the drama of this urban world. It is a world vastly uncertain of itself and the ground of its values, caught in a tangle of modern commercialism and traditions and conventions gone to seed, confused among pieties and pretensions.

This new world, Warren continues, "invites satire, but in the whole effect, [Taylor] stops somewhere short of satire, Rather, he presents an irony blended of comedy and sympathetic understanding. . . . We find an awareness of character beyond what explicitly appears." And then, in the most insightful and often-quoted sentence anyone has written about him, Warren asserts that "Peter Taylor has a disenchanted mind, but a mind that nevertheless understands and values enchantment." He elaborates this thought by saying that Taylor's "family affections and loyalties are real, and the memories compelling. It is sad that they cannot exist without being entangled with shoddiness, stupidity, and even cruelty."

The title story of the collection embodies virtually all of these perceptions of Warren's. The central subject of the story is the third, after class and the role of women, of the major concerns of Taylor's work—that is, race. The story follows a Nashville doctor, his wife, Harriet, and their two grown but unmarried daughters, Helena and Kate, over a long Fourth of July weekend as they prepare for and to some extent endure the visit of the only son, who will enter the army at the end of the visit. Helping the family prepare for the arrival of Son, as he is called, is Mattie, their black cook, and B.T., her nephew, who lives in a shack behind their place and does outside work for the family. Set against the racial prejudice Harriet shows toward B.T. from the first line of the story, the narrative reveals that he has decided to leave the household, something that deeply distresses Mattie. Harriet reacts sympathetically at first, "taking the weeping Mattie (her old friend) in her arms." But when Mattie tells her that B.T. is going to work in an airplane factory because of the war and adds, "Miss Harriet, it's like you losin' Mr. Son," Harriet reacts violently. "'Mattie!' she declaimed. 'How dare you'? That will be just exactly enough from you!'" Harriet is so upset at what she regards as Mattie's impertinence that she retires to her bedroom, where "not since a little girl had such rage been known to her bosom. . . . "

Son arrives from New York, where he writes "disturbing articles in magazines, displaying his peculiar, radical ideas." With him is a woman friend, who appears to share these unspecified ideas. Finally, at a family dinner on the eve of the Fourth, the subject of race bursts forth, with Harriet and her daughters mightily defending the old racial order against Son and his friend. The paternalistic nostrums of the three women get a pointed test the following evening, when B.T. quarrels with Mattie out in the shack and afterward the doctor implores Harriet to go to Mattie to calm her. When Harriet balks, her husband says, "Harriet, why should this be so hard for you?" The story continues: "There was no sympathy in the question, and actually he did not seem to want an answer to this precise question. He seemed to be making a larger and more general inquiry into her character than he had ever done before."

Despite the way this story unfolds, entering only into Harriet's thoughts, there is little doubt in the reader's mind that we, too, along with Harriet are to distance ourselves from misapprehensions about race. But it is the story's subtlety that Harriet is not portrayed as evil or even wholly unsympathetic. Taylor gives her every chance before he condemns her for her stupidity and cruelty, to use Warren's words.

This collection contained seven stories, among them "The Fancy Woman," "A Spinster's Tale," and "Rain in the Heart." It received favorable reviews in major literary and general interest magazines such as *The New Yorker, The New Republic, Commonweal, Partisan Review*, and *Saturday Review*. Given this critical welcome—including that of the fine short-story writer J. F. Powers and the respected writer and critic Elizabeth Hardwick—and the nature of American publishing, according to which a writer of stories is always expected to "graduate" to the novel, it was not long before a novel was forthcoming.

A WOMAN OF MEANS

A Woman of Means appeared in 1950. It is a very short novel, and although it is beautifully written, with an uncharacteristic stylistic spareness, it lacks the richness and complexity of Taylor's greatest stories. The reviews were generally not encouraging (*Saturday Review* called it "as slight in effect, in content, and in quality as it is slight in form"), although Robert Penn Warren praised it in *The New York Times*. One reviewer, Thomas Wilcox, wrote that "when you try to construe the few events his novel describes you find that no single interpretation will account for everything you have learned and that finally you must credit all the explanations—some of them seemingly contradictory—the characters separately entertain." In his introduction to his 1993 volume, *Critical Essays on Peter Taylor*, which includes the Wilcox review and others cited throughout this essay, Hubert H. McAlexander rightly points out that "this insight illuminates many works of the Taylor canon."

The novel is narrated by Quint Dudley, a boy whose mother died giving birth to him and whose father works as a traveling salesman for a hardware company based in St. Louis. Quint's father takes the boy on the road with him, leaving him for the summers with his maternal grandmother on a farm in Tennessee. The father gets promoted to vice president of the company, and so the two move to St. Louis, where, before long, his father meets and marries a very rich woman—the title's woman of means. Ann is the daughter of a St. Louis beer magnate and lives in an Italianate mansion her father had built for her after her own mother's death. Quint's stepmother has two spoiled daughters who are themselves independently wealthy. Quint and his father settle into this grand household, and before long his father rises to president of the company. Quint, used to a nomadic life with a new school every year, eventually settles into the country day school that his new wealth requires of him, even winning the school's award for best boy. But at the moment when everything about Quint's life ripens to perfection, it begins to spoil. By the book's end his father has been fired as president of the hardware company and is back on the road, his stepmother has descended into madness, and his stepsisters are making plans to have the mansion razed. In the last scene Quint stands in the center of the library of the great house, "weeping bitter tears."

Why has all this happened? The novel suggests a number of reasons. Quint's father's naked ambition is to blame; Ann tells Quint that his father has married her only for her money. Or is it the spoiled Ann, inheritor of too much wealth, who is herself to blame? Quint's father accuses Ann of marrying him because she has always wanted a son, a role that Quint fills. Or is the fault Quint's, because he forms an Oedipal attachment to his stepmother? And why, finally, does Ann go mad? One of Ann's daughters attributes her mother's downfall to big-city life. Indeed, would Quint have been better off raised not in the city but back on his grandmother's farm in Tennessee, as the older woman has urged? As Wilcox observed, no clear answer emerges to any of these questions.

The reception of *A Woman of Means* undoubtedly affected the course of Taylor's writing life. He did not write another novel for more than thirty-five years, instead devoting himself to writing stories and plays. But in addition to the disappointment of mediocre reviews, 1950 also brought encouragement. That year, Taylor was awarded a Guggenheim Fellowship, and his story "Their Losses," published in *The New Yorker* in March, was selected for the annual O. Henry collection of the year's best short stories.

SOCIETAL PORTRAITS

"Their Losses" led off Taylor's next book, a collection of eight stories and a play called *The Widows of Thornton*, which was published in 1954 and represented some of his strongest work to date. Four of the stories ("Their Losses," "What You Hear from Em?" "A Wife of Nashville," and "Cookie") would be reprinted in 1969 in *The Collected Stories of Peter Taylor*. Three more ("Bad Dreams," "Porte-Cochere," and "Two Ladies in Retirement") appeared in what was in effect a second volume of collected stories, *The Old Forest*, in 1985. Hubert McAlexander, in his 1993 *Critical Essays* introduction, calls this book "Taylor's most unified collection, in which most of the stories [are] meaningfully linked by the characters' ties to the town of Thornton and by the recurring theme of women displaced by cultural change." One of the book's reviewers, Richard Hayes, described it as "the portrait of a complex society held in the most fastidious dramatic suspense; the past impinging upon and molding the present, the present rebelling against the tyranny of the past, the noisy warring of both in the abused heart."

Probably no story in the collection embodies Hayes' description as clearly as "The Dark Walk," the long work that ends the collection. As the story opens, Sylvia Harrison is, in a foreshadowing of what is to come, alone with her children at a Colorado resort while her husband, Nate, is back home in Chicago tending to his business. Both Sylvia and Nate come from towns in middle Tennessee, Sylvia from Thornton and Nate from Cedar Springs, where they first lived after being married. Nate's career requires that they move in 1922 to Memphis, and for the next ten years the couple and their four children move from city to larger city, ending up in Chicago, where Nate is president of a wire-manufacturing company. During all these moves Sylvia insists that every bit of inherited family furniture—much more than they can use in the houses they rent—be moved with them, and it becomes Sylvia's job and pride to make these moves efficiently. We are told that both the hauling about of unneeded furniture and reluctance to buy a home are attributable to the couple's resolve to move back to Tennessee someday. In 1939 Nate dies, and Sylvia soon decides to move the family home, although for her nearly grown children Chicago is now in fact home.

As the time draws near to move, Sylvia finds herself visited repeatedly by two men. One, her rich, elderly landlord, tries to convince her to stay in Chicago and is apparently trying to court her; the other, an old black servant who has been with the family since Cedar Springs, petitions Sylvia to return to his hometown with the family. On the day of the move, the two men arrive at her house and nearly get into a fight. As Sylvia tries to sort this out, she realizes that the men each represent a part of Nate's personality—the landlord his modern, urban, businessman side, the servant his old-fashioned, backward-looking, Tennessee side. She realizes that the furniture, which includes oversize family portraits and paintings depicting scenes from Tennessee history, has been Nate's comfort, not hers. She sends it back to Tennessee with the old servant and moves her family into an apartment overlooking Lake Michigan, for which she buys "only what was new and useful and pleasing to the eye."

Although the story is in places overly sche-

matic and underdramatized, and was not reprinted in later collections, it embodies not only the main concerns of *The Widows of Thornton* but the main themes of Taylor's oeuvre—the tensions between the past and the present, between country and city, blacks and whites, male and female. Sylvia's affirmation of her own freedom from all of these concerns presages the ending of one of Taylor's greatest works, another novella or long story called "The Old Forest" (1979), in which the woman who is to be the narrator's wife says, "Power, or strength, is what everybody must have some of if he—if she—is to survive in any kind of world." Breaking free of the family furniture, of a binding connection to the past, is Sylvia's source of power.

During the 1950s the Taylors, who by 1955 had two children, a daughter and a son, lived in Greensboro and later in Gambier, Ohio, while Taylor was on the faculty of his alma mater, Kenyon College. In 1957 he went to teach at Ohio State, having spent part of 1955 and 1956 in Paris on a Fulbright grant. The family also spent the summers of 1956 and 1958 in Italy, settling in Rome for the fall of 1958. One story from these travels, "*Je Suis Perdu*," published in *The New Yorker* in 1958 as "A Pair of Bright Blue Eyes," is taken directly from the family's experience in Paris. In it the father of a young family that is gathering itself to leave Paris after having spent a year there acknowledges his helpless attachment to his children and his wife. The title comes from an incident in a Paris movie theater in which the narrator and his daughter are separated, and he hears the child calling out "*Je suis perdue*" before he recognizes the voice as his daughter's. The story is divided into two parts, headed "L'Allegro" and "Il Penseroso." In the first section the family seems utterly happy as it goes about its morning rituals on the last day before it is to leave Paris; in the second section the father walks through the Jardin du Luxembourg trying to nurse a little despair over leaving Paris. But then he sees his daughter and his son out on a walk with their maid and realizes that even his moods are no longer his own now that he has children. He is lost like his little daughter in the theater, but lost happily in love.

DARKER THEMES

Happy Families Are All Alike was the title of his next book of stories, published in 1959 and dedicated to his son (born in 1955) as his previous collection had been dedicated to his daughter (born in 1948). Of the ten stories published in this collection (including "*Je Suis Perdu*"), the best known and perhaps the most successful is "Venus, Cupid, Folly and Time," which won first prize in the O. Henry competition for 1959 and has been widely anthologized ever since.

The story tells of an elderly brother and sister who live alone on "the most splendid street" in the fictional city of Chatham. To call them eccentric is mild; the narrator refers to them as foolish. They have taken down parts of their once-impressive family home so as to lower the taxes on it. Their only source of income seems to be the bland-tasting figs he grows and the garish paper flowers she makes, which they sell to their neighbors. Although they are an embarrassment to the neighborhood, they are tolerated because they give a party each year for the young people from the nicest families in the city, and nobody is willing to cross them and forgo this social distinction. At the party the old people, who dress bizarrely (and sometimes not at all) throughout the rest of the year, dress beautifully and dance together at the party. For what turns out to be the last such party they will ever give, a character named Ned and his sister, Emily, decide to play a joke on their hosts: they invite the siblings' former paperboy, Tom, to crash the party and, pretending to be Ned, kiss and fondle Emily in the presence of the old couple. Ned himself simply slips in with the other young people to enjoy the fun. The house is be-

strewn with paper flowers and an odd perfume, and at various places in the house are displayed under special lighting things like a plaster copy of Rodin's statue *The Kiss*, a plaque depicting the mythical Leda and the swan, and a print of a painting by Bronzino called *Venus, Cupid, Folly and Time*. In this sexually suggestive and otherwise bizarre setting, Ned finds himself growing more and more uncomfortable as Tom kisses his sister. The story's climax comes when Ned bursts out with, "Don't you know? . . . Can't you tell? Can't you see who they are? They're brother and sister!" Of course, they are not brother and sister, but the old couple are. They believe that Ned is the uninvited guest and lock him in an upstairs bathroom. When his parents arrive to get Ned and Emily, the old couple refuse to believe they have mistaken Ned for their former paperboy. "Why, *we* know nice children when we see them," they say.

In an interview in 1985, Taylor was asked to tell in one word what the story is about: "That's easy. Incest." But then he adds another word of elaboration: "Social incest." In an interview two years later with Barbara Thompson, he elaborated further: "It is a story about incest—not just the brother and sister, but all the young people. It's a form of incest to only want to marry within your own class, your own background exactly. That was the world I had grown up in."

In these and an earlier interview, Taylor spoke of the story as a departure from his earlier work in two ways: first, in that its main elements were all made up, rather than taken from his own experiences or stories he had been told from life; and second, in that he worked the story out systematically, almost as an allegory, with characters and situations devised to make it work as a story. "I knew exactly what I was saying," he told Goodwin in 1973. His skill as a storyteller had grown to the extent that in "Venus, Cupid, Folly and Time"—unlike "The Dark Walk," apparently formed of materials closer to his own experience—his scheme for the story is well hidden. "Venus, Cupid," the made-up story, paradoxically has a more organic structure, as would his great long stories to come, such as "In the Miro District" and "The Old Forest."

During the 1960s Taylor returned to teaching at Greensboro, taught a term at Harvard, and spent a year on a Rockefeller grant. His great friend Randall Jarrell, with whom his family had shared a duplex in Greensboro, died in 1965. Taylor and many of Jarrell's other friends believed the death was a suicide. Both of Taylor's parents and a sister also died during the decade. In 1967 Taylor moved to the University of Virginia, where he would teach until his retirement in 1983.

In 1964 Taylor's fourth collection of stories, *Miss Leonora When Last Seen*, was published. In addition to the title story, the collection had four new stories—"Reservations," "An Overwhelming Question," "At the Drugstore," and "A Strange Story"—and nine stories plus a one-act play reprinted from earlier collections. McAlexander, in his 1993 study, notes that "more critics of this collection than of any other discovered deeply pessimistic strains in the fiction." Indeed, two of the stories deal with feelings of futility and even despair. "Reservations" is about a honeymooning couple who tell each other about the reservations with which they have entered the marriage. At the end of the story they look to the future with a hopefulness that is clearly delusory. And in "At the Drugstore," the narrator returns home with his family to the house in which he grew up and confronts a deeply antisocial side of himself that seems to make a kind of ruse of family life. The critic John Thompson, who had been a fellow writing student at Kenyon with Taylor and Lowell, offers in his review of *Miss Leonora* what McAlexander calls "the darkest reading of Taylor ever presented":

> The warm [family] circle is a desperate one, surrounded by a cold vacuum and surrounding a cold vacuum. There is no outside alternative to this family circle but emptiness, and within it, at its center, is emptiness. The circle itself survives by exclusion, exclusion of two things, thought and feeling.

This assessment is unduly pessimistic; yet it serves as a corrective for readers tempted to take a title like *Happy Families Are All Alike*—from the famed opening sentence of Tolstoy's *Anna Karenina*—at face value. As with Tolstoy, it is unhappy families that are the real subject of Taylor's work.

THE COLLECTED STORIES

In August 1969 Taylor reached the culmination of his three decades as a writer with the publication of *The Collected Stories of Peter Taylor*. These twenty-one stories, drawn from as far back in his career as "A Spinster's Tale" and "The Fancy Woman," and including five stories that had not previously been collected ("Dean of Men," "First Heat," "There," "The Elect," and "Mrs. Bilingsby's Wine"), elicited a number of reviews that attempted to place him as a writer and sum up his work thus far. The novelist Joyce Carol Oates called the *Collected Stories* "one of the major books of our literature," although in her review she never quite explains why. The writer and critic R. V. Cassill wrote that "in the fascinating configurations of this whole collection, we see how the world spins out from Tennessee and closes its vast circles there—how history itself must be the accumulation of minutiae like those recorded here." Stephen Goodwin wrote that Taylor "demands of us our best emotions and leads us to some of our clearest discoveries—and never encourages our hope that these emotions and discoveries may be lasting."

But perhaps the clearest and most cogent summing-up of Taylor's stories came in an essay by Jan Pinkerton, included in McAlexander's volume of essays on the author, in which Pinkerton confronts the ways in which Taylor was sometimes misread as a regional writer with a slavish devotion to the past and a persistent regret over the breakup of the family. As for Taylor's supposed nostalgia, Pinkerton makes a distinction between such characters as Aunt Munsie in "What You Hear from Em," who hopes for the return of those who have left Thornton for the city, and the author himself:

> The character who mourns the past is usually shown by the author, through a variety of narrative techniques, to be limited in perception, to be ignoring obvious truths of the past, to be fantasizing an ideal age that never existed. . . . He views the nostalgic stances of his characters with often-critical detachment, although ultimately he bestows the sympathy he always gives his imperfect human beings.

As for his supposed role as mourner of the decline of the family, Pinkerton writes: "He often records the discontinuities of contemporary family life, but he does not imply that families of the past were superior or preferable; . . . he makes clear [that] even a seemingly stable family facade has always been blighted by the basic and constant flaws in human nature." Pinkerton finds Taylor to be more than a regional writer because, on the one hand, so many of his themes are ones he does not share with other Southern writers, and, on the other hand, those he does share, such as the role of manners and the importance of rootedness, he makes use of in what Pinkerton sees as a heretical way.

> In a society with divisions between class, race, and sex, a social code can achieve a formal rapport between these divisions, but yet—as Taylor demonstrates with frequency and poignancy—it can exclude a more intimate rapport among those for whom such communion would relieve the loneliness and misunderstanding that bring misery to so many of Taylor's characters.

As for questions of rootedness, "The Southerners Taylor writes about . . . are those who stagnated because they did not move on, who fell into worship of an unreal past because they did not keep themselves refreshed with new ideas." Pinkerton concludes that Taylor is "a Southern writer who distrusts the past, a conservative writer who believes in change; those who see him as a stereotyped regionalist are themselves blinded by their clichéd responses to setting and style."

By the time his *Collected Stories* appeared, Taylor had published nearly fifty short stories, many of them of such quality as to put him among the very best writers of short fiction in the country. Still, he was known primarily, as many of the reviews of the book noted, as a writer's writer, and had never gained a wide audience or broad recognition. In 1973 Taylor remarked in an interview, "I feel that I've done what I want to do as a short story writer."

PLAYS

At about the time the *Collected Stories* appeared, Taylor began to focus on drama, a form in which he had always had an interest. His one-act play, *The Death of a Kinsman*, had been included in two story collections. He had also written two book-length plays over the years, *Tennessee Day in St. Louis* (1957) and *A Stand in the Mountains*, which was published by *Kenyon Review* in 1968 but did not appear in book form until 1985. *A Stand in the Mountains* contains a beautifully written prose preface giving the history of Owl Mountain, the play's fictional setting, based on the mountain resort of Monteagle, Tennessee. The play itself, which is probably Taylor's most successful dramatic work, explores the violent disintegration of a family at the summer retreat against the backdrop of the state's intention of building a four-lane highway up the mountain. In the early 1970s Taylor began writing short ghost plays, seven of which were published in 1973 as *Presences*.

All the pieces appeared first in literary quarterlies, and none of them is considered to be among Taylor's most successful works. Topical subjects like the Vietnam war, radical politics, and generational disputes often come to the fore in these dramatic pieces, as Taylor called them. As Albert J. Griffith has noted, their primary value is to illuminate the methods of the stories. Although broad themes of the individual's need to accommodate himself to the social context and the problems of families appear in the short plays, the form dictates against at least two elements that make Taylor's stories so successful. One is the use of a narrator's or central character's point of view as a means to give unity and integrity to the perceptions offered; the other is Taylor's comfortable, seemingly meandering story-telling style—what Griffith calls Taylor's "digressive-progressive narrative technique"—which the relatively linear nature of drama prevents. As Griffith puts it, "The relatively straightforward objective thrust of the plays has its artistic effectiveness, too, but it is better for hammering home abstract messages than for proceeding delicately from nuance to nuance of barely discovered meaning."

LATER STORIES

In 1974 Taylor suffered a heart attack, and he would not again be in robust health for the remainder of his life. Nonetheless, he recovered from the attack to begin one of the richest decades of his creative life, one undoubtedly spurred by his brush with death. (Taylor dedicated his next book to his heart doctor, thanking him "for an extension of time.") One of his best collections, the first since *Happy Families Are All Alike* in 1959 to publish all stories that had not previously been in book form, appeared in 1977, called *In the Miro District and Other Stories*. The title story is one of the richest he ever wrote, and two other stories in the collection, "The Captain's Son" and "The Hand of Emmagene," are also extraordinary. It would become a commonplace in Taylor criticism to say, as Stephen Goodwin had first written about the *Collected Stories*, that Taylor's stories had the amplitude of novels. This is unquestionably true of "In the Miro District," a story that ranges across time from 1811 until the late 1930s, that moves from violent historical events such as earthquakes and kidnappings to the subtle ways in which power is deployed within families. "In the Miro District" is the story of a well-brought-up Nashville boy and his maternal grandfather, a man who rode with Nathan Bedford Forrest in the Civil War and later survived a kidnapping that left his law partner murdered. The parents have thrust the old man and the boy together, hoping they will develop a rapport that they themselves have not achieved with either generation. In a series of increasingly serious incidents in which the old man discovers the teenage boy misbehaving in his parents' house while they are away, the grandfather finally abandons any notion of his own freedom within the family and succumbs to the wishes of his daughter and son-in-law that he live with them in their big Nashville house. Summary cannot do justice to the story's strange, elliptical nature and the complexity of the feelings of the boy and his grandfather.

"The Captain's Son" is another long, complicated story that combines the odd and subtle strains of family life, as an immensely rich boy from Memphis marries an upper-crust girl from Nashville and moves in with her and her family, pursuing no career but drink. "The Hand of Emmagene" is a short story in verse lines, a form Taylor called the story poem or "stoem," because it was neither fiction nor poetry, but in his mind a new form. The story has the measured, inevitable unfolding of a fable, but one that turns gothic at the end, as a woman from the country tries to accommodate her values to those of the city, with tragic results.

The following year, 1978, Peter Taylor was awarded the Gold Medal for the Short Story from the American Academy and Institute of Arts and Letters, arguably the most prestigious award available to an American writer short of the Nobel Prize, as it comes from the country's most distinguished writers and artists and is awarded only twice a decade. But even with this award Taylor still had not achieved the public recognition he clearly deserved. It was not until the publication of his next book, *The Old Forest and Other Stories*, in 1985, when Taylor was almost seventy years old, that the public acclaim that would reach him during the last decade of his life began. Only two new stories appeared in this book, the title story and "The Gift of the Prodigal," but the other eleven stories (plus the play *The Death of a Kinsman*), drawn from the whole of his career, had not been published in the *Collected Stories* (which was still in print); therefore, the new book amounted to a companion volume. Once again, this gave critics the chance to introduce readers to his work and offer an overview of his career. Critics writing for such broad-circulation national publications as *Time, Newsweek,* and *USA Today* let out all the stops. The novelist Anne Tyler called him "the undisputed master of the short story form." Jonathan Yardley, the literary critic for *The Washington Post,* wrote that "Taylor can be compared to no one except himself; he is, as every word in this book testifies, an American master." "Compared to *The Old Forest,*" Yardley said, "almost everything else published by American writers in recent years seems small, cramped, brittle, inconsequential." Most observers felt that the outpouring of enthusiasm for this book in part rode the wave of a new golden age of the American short story. Many critics, like Yardley, noted the marked difference between Taylor's long, leisurely, lush,

mature stories and the prevailing minimalist style of such writers as Raymond Carver.

But the burst of favorable criticism was not only long overdue, it was appropriate for this particular book. Of all Taylor's long stories, going back to "The Dark Walk," none is as complex or as fully realized as "The Old Forest," which *The New Yorker* had published in 1979. It is perhaps Taylor's greatest story. It is narrated, like many of Taylor's later stories, by a man past middle age looking back at his youth. Nat Ramsey, the narrator, tells of events leading up to his marriage in 1937 to a girl from his own social class in Memphis—once again, the country-club set. The male members of this set, as the narrator tells us, are fascinated by girls from a lower social class, whom they refer to snottily but wittily as "demimondames." These intelligent, beautiful, energetic, free-spirited working girls are prototypes for the New Woman, who would emerge in America after World War II. In the week before his wedding, Nat explains, he was involved in a traffic accident while riding with one of these girls, Lee Ann Deehart. If discovered, her being with him just as his wedding approached would of course be embarrassing to everyone concerned; but when Lee Ann flees the scene into a nearby woods (known in Memphis as the Old Forest), her action does not alleviate the difficult situation but compounds it, for she seems to have disappeared. The marriage cannot go on until she is found; it soon becomes clear that no harm has befallen her but that she is for some reason hiding from Nat. Much of the action of the story involves Nat's attempts to find her by talking to her friends. Finally, he is forced to confess everything to the woman he is to marry, Caroline Braxley, and she takes charge of finding Lee Ann.

By way of these events, Taylor with great subtlety gets to the heart of the subjects that have long been of interest to him: questions of class and the status of women in a male-dominated society especially, but also the ways in which individuals are bound by history and society and must make accommodations to them in order to move on with their lives. The story evokes with real vividness Nat and Caroline's world, the world of Lee Ann and her friends, and a dark juke-joint world that plays an unexpected role in the story's unfolding. Finally, he makes the Old Forest itself into a bold, unforgettable symbol of chaos, of feminine mystery, and finally of a primordial need for freedom.

A SUMMONS TO MEMPHIS

In the spring of the following year Taylor won the PEN/Faulkner award for *The Old Forest*; in the fall he published his second novel, *A Summons to Memphis*. That book was nominated for the American Book Award (which the National Book Award was briefly called), but Taylor withdrew the nomination because he objected to the format for the award, which seemed to him to pit writer against writer. Still, the novel would be amply rewarded the following spring, when it won both the Ritz-Paris Hemingway Award for the best novel published in English anywhere in the world, and the Pulitzer Prize. The book received widespread favorable reviews, with one notable exception, a condescending notice in *The New Yorker* by the novelist John Updike, who characterized Taylor as "having spent a lifetime tracing teacup tempests among genteel Tennesseans." Certain reviewers seemed to misread the book as a straightforward first-person narration, missing the profound unreliability of its narrator, Phillip Carver, and failing to recognize the book's almost numbing circularity as a sign of Phillip's haplessness and sterility.

The story's structure is familiar from other Taylor works: the narrator looks back on the events of his youth and young manhood from middle age. A rare-book collector and book editor in New York, Phillip lives an orderly life (so

he says, although they have recently separated briefly) with a companion named Holly Kaplan. He recounts how, when he was a child, his family moved from their country town first to Nashville and then, after the betrayal of his lawyer father by a client, from the genteel Nashville to the Deep South Memphis. (The distinctions between the two cities is a feature of "The Captain's Son," as well.) In retrospect, Phillip blames the move to Memphis for a series of problems the family has had ever since: his mother's illness, the spinsterhood of his two sisters, and the breakup of his one-time engagement to the love of his life. Phillip himself had fled Memphis after returning from World War II. Two years after the death of their mother, Phillip's sisters call him back from New York to Memphis to prevent their father's second marriage. He agrees to return to Memphis, where he finds that his sympathy migrates to his father. Nevertheless, the sisters manage to prevent the marriage. Phillip gets a similar summons when his father decides to become reconciled to the man who betrayed him so many years before and altered all of their lives. Once again Phillip returns home, and once again a decision to act is thwarted, this time by the death of his father's betrayer. Phillip goes back to New York, and he and his father begin a warm series of telephone communications, which continue until his father dies the following spring. As the novel ends, he imagines his own end with Holly, "puttering amongst our papers and books until when the dusk of some winter day fades into darkness we'll fail to put on the lights in these rooms of ours, and when the sun shines the next morning there will be simply no trace of us." Although Taylor is not one to sentimentalize the past, the meaning of home and family, nevertheless this gloomy vision, the prospect of modern urban man utterly cut off from these elements of life, is his darkest view of the world yet.

Between the publication of *The Old Forest* and *A Summons to Memphis*, Taylor suffered the first of a series of strokes; he retired from teaching at the University of Virginia in 1983. But he continued to write up until the last months before his death in the fall of 1994. In his last years he would say to his friends, "All I can do anymore is write." He published three long stories in the early 1990s; these stories came out in book form in *The Oracle at Stoneleigh Court* in 1992. The title story and the third of the three new long stories, "The Witch of Owl Mountain Springs: An Account of Her Remarkable Powers," both deal in a realistic setting with older women who claim or are thought to have special powers. Another of the long stories, "Cousin Aubrey," formed the beginning of Taylor's last published work, the novel *In the Tennessee Country*. Written in the last years of his life, it tells the story of a famous art historian who looks back on his life and regrets that he has not been an artist instead, a path he urges upon his son. This character is unreconciled to his life near its end; Peter Taylor, by contrast, lived the life that his character did not, that of the artist. Taylor died in Charlottesville in the fall of 1994, within a few weeks of the novel's publication.

Selected Bibliography

WORKS OF PETER TAYLOR

SHORT STORIES AND NOVELS

A Long Fourth and Other Stories. New York: Harcourt Brace, 1948.

A Woman of Means. New York: Harcourt Brace, 1950.

The Widows of Thornton. New York: Harcourt Brace, 1954. (Related stories.)

Happy Families Are All Alike. New York: McDowell, Oblensky, 1959. (Stories.)

Miss Leonora When Last Seen and Fifteen Other Stories. New York: Ivan Oblensky, 1963.

The Collected Stories of Peter Taylor. New York: Farrar, Straus & Giroux, 1969.

In the Miro District and Other Stories. New York: Knopf, 1977.

The Old Forest and Other Stories. New York: Dial, 1985.

A Summons to Memphis. New York: Knopf, 1986.

The Oracle at Stoneleigh Court: Stories. New York: Knopf, 1993.

In the Tennessee Country. New York: Knopf, 1994.

PLAYS

Tennessee Day in St. Louis. New York: Random House, 1957.

Presences: Seven Dramatic Pieces. Boston: Houghton Mifflin, 1973.

A Stand in the Mountains. New York: Frederic C. Beil, 1985.

BIBLIOGRAPHY

Wright, Stuart. *Peter Taylor: A Descriptive Bibliography, 1935–87*. Charlottesville: University Press of Virginia, 1988.

CRITICAL AND BIOGRAPHICAL STUDIES

Bell, Madison Smartt. "Less Is Less: The Dwindling American Short Story." *Harper's*, April 1986, pp. 64–69.

————. "Time and Tide in the Southern Short Story." *Chronicles: A Magazine of American Culture*, March 1991.

Boatwright, James, ed. "A Garland for Peter Taylor on His Sixtieth Birthday." *Shenandoah* 28: 4–85 (Winter 1977).

Griffith, Albert J. *Peter Taylor*. (Twayne's United States Authors Series, No. 169.) New York: Twayne, 1970; rev. ed, 1990.

Hamilton, Ian. *Robert Lowell: A Biography*. New York: Random House, 1982.

Kuehl, Linda Kandel. "Voices and Victims: A Study of Peter Taylor's *In the Miro District*." Ph.D. diss., Lehigh University, 1988.

McAlexander, Hubert H., ed. *Critical Essays on Peter Taylor*. New York: G. K. Hall.

Robinson, David M. "Tennessee, Taylor, the Critics and Time." *Southern Review* 23: 281–294 (Spring 1987).

Robinson, James Curry. *Peter Taylor: A Study of the*

Short Fiction. (Twayne's Studies in Short Fiction, No. 3.) Boston: Twayne, 1988.

Stephens, C. Ralph, and Lynda B. Salamon, eds. *The Craft of Peter Taylor.* Tuscaloosa: University of Alabama Press, 1995.

Sullivan, Walter. "The Last Agrarian: Peter Taylor Early and Late." *Sewanee Review*, 95: 308–317 (Spring 1987).

Updike, John. "Summonses, Indictments, Extenuating Circumstances." *New Yorker,* November 3, 1986, pp. 158–165.

Warren, Robert Penn. "Introduction." *A Long Fourth and Other Stories.* New York: Harcourt Brace, 1948, pp. vii–x.

Wilson, Robert. "A Subversive Sympathy: The Stories of Peter Taylor and the Illusions They Bring to Life." *Atlantic Monthly*, September 1997, pp. 108–112.

INTERVIEWS

McAlexander, Hubert H., ed. *Conversations with Peter Taylor.* Jackson: University Press of Mississippi, 1987.

FILMS BASED ON THE WORKS OF PETER TAYLOR

Delayed Honeymoon. Television drama based on the story "Reservations." *U.S. Steel Hour.* September 1961.

The Old Forest. Written and directed by Steven J. Ross. Memphis State University, 1984.

—*Robert Wilson*

Charles Wright
1935—

CHARLES WRIGHT BEGAN writing during a tectonic shift in twentieth-century poetry. In the 1950s, a fissure had opened between New Critics, whose principles derived from the intricate linguistic patterns of English Renaissance poetry, and a wide array of groups announcing their own renaissances under banners belonging to the Deep Image, New York, Black Mountain, Beat, or Confessional schools. The most obvious difference between the poetry sanctioned by New Critics and the poetry promoted by their opponents had to do with traditional concepts of versification. As has been pointed out ad infinitum, New Critics advocated meter, stanza, and rhyme as the proper containers for the mind's and the world's flux; they believed poems should be "verbal icons" and "well-wrought urns." Other critics such as Donald Davie speculated in the 1950s that the shift away from traditional versification and syntax by Modernists and their Postmodernist epigones arose from a disbelief in or at least disenchantment with "the conscious mind's intelligible structure." Although Charles Wright, a Southerner born in 1935, learned from the New Critical agendas of fellow Southerners such as John Crowe Ransom and Allen Tate, he strayed from their camp out of a commitment to subconscious and transcendental experiences that strain linguistic intelligibility to the breaking point.

In his appraisals of New Formalist and New Narrative poets who resuscitated interest in traditional verse forms after the New Critics were discredited in the 1960s, Wright has been dismissive. His attitude harks back to Modernists like James Joyce, who once justified his avant-garde experiments by saying: "One great part of every human existence is passed in a state which cannot be rendered sensible by the use of wide-awake language, cutanddry grammar and goahead plot." It was not Joyce, however, but Joyce's imitator and great champion Ezra Pound who served as Wright's original model. Reading Pound for the first time in 1959, Wright was entranced by his imagistic lyrics and by the kaleidoscopic array—or disarray—of his *Pisan Cantos* (1948). Wright's stylistic evolution followed Pound's: from short lyrics (often divided into stanzas of syllabic, unrhymed lines) to long sequences that mix sensuous description and discursive rumination. With Pound as his guide, he merged the visual precision of Chinese poetry and the epic scope of Dante's *Divine Comedy,* the Oriental devotion to "the world of the ten thousand things" (a phrase Wright used as the title for his 1990 *Poems, 1980–1990*) and the Occidental preoccupation with an extraterrestrial *paradiso.* Wright's principal alter ego is an iconoclastic pilgrim shuttling between Eastern and Western cultures, offering snapshots of and commentaries on the artifacts and landscapes he discovers.

Wright has acknowledged debts to American poetry's founding mother, Emily Dickinson, and founding father, Walt Whitman, quipping that he wanted to write Whitman's poems in Dickinson's room. If he emulated Dickinson by brooding monastically on sin, redemption, and God, and by examining divine mysteries and designs in what he could see from his window, he followed Whitman's example by cataloging the world's diversity on the open road. Regarding his relationship with his own generation of American poets, Wright has expressed similar divided loyalties:

My generation seems somehow caught between the generation of those born in the twenties [Richard Wilbur, Howard Nemerov, Anthony Hecht, James Dickey, James Merrill, Allen Ginsberg, John Ashbery, et al.] and those born in the forties, which is another huge generation. . . . Those of us born in the thirties, there are very few of us. Mark Strand once said, "Charles, we're a generation of three: me and you and [Charles] Simic." Well, that's not true, it's just that we're all good friends. . . . But in that joke is a kernel of truth, in that those of us in the thirties are kind of squeezed in. We don't really have a generation: we're either tacked onto the end of the twenties or tacked onto the beginning of the forties.

The fact that Strand was born in Canada and Simic in Yugoslavia must have made Wright's generational feelings about his American peers even more problematic.

With regard to his immediate elders, Wright shared the greatest affinity with Deep Image poets such as Robert Bly, James Wright, W. S. Merwin, and Galway Kinnell. These poets, heavily influenced by South American and European brands of surrealism, dedicated themselves to a style that yoked mythical archetype with everyday life, dream with reality, fairy tale with historical fact, id with ego. As Wright has pointed out, the surrealism imported from Spanish poetry, such as that of Pablo Neruda and Cesar Vallejo, took hold in America because of the social and political upheavals in the 1960s.

Nothing out of Breton was more surreal than watching tanks carrying dead and bleeding bodies, easing through the supper hour as millions swallowed the image along with their Hamburger Helper. The young poets were mirrors of the times. . . . American Surrealism's high-water mark was about a ten-year period, say 1965 to 1975, whose other high-water marks were found in marijuana smoking and the Vietnam War.

The American Surrealism that attracted Wright the most had a Zen inflection. He declared in an interview: "The two people in the generation above me I feel closest to are W. S. Merwin and Peter Matthieson. . . . They are both practicing Zen Buddhists, which I am not, but there's something about that particular quest that fascinates me." The quest, as Wright articulated it, was a meditative one for "that still, small, pinpoint of light at the center of the universe." For the most part, Wright has eschewed political and social involvement out of a devotion to his religious and aesthetic goals. Wright yearns for divine states of being and divine beings themselves, and he laments that they remain elusive, unattainable, and ineffable. Wright's *via negativa* through absence, darkness, and solitude, as well as the sardonic and whimsical way he shrugs off his disillusionments, link him with Strand and Simic. But while all three share a penchant for dolorous musing, surreal imagery, and black comedy, Wright's language is more rhetorically lush than the often deadpan diction favored by his two friends.

Few poets have mapped out their careers as deliberately as Wright has. In 1971, after completing his first major collection, *The Grave of the Right Hand* (1970), he conceived of a Dantesque plan to write a trilogy of trilogies. It took him twenty-eight years to complete. *Hard Freight* (1973), *Bloodlines* (1975), and *China Trace* (1977) composed the first of the three trilogies. These were collected in *Country Music: Selected Early Poems* (1982), which won the National Book Award. The second trilogy included *The Southern Cross* (1981), *The Other Side of the*

River (1984), and *Zone Journals* (1988). Along with their coda, *Xionia,* the books were published in *The World of the Ten Thousand Things: Selected Poems 1980–1990.* The third trilogy contained *Chickamauga* (1995), *Black Zodiac* (1997), and *Appalachia* (1998). Together, the volumes formed a Modernist epic that charted an exotic journey through many different times and places, amassing impressions and reflections into what amounted to Wright's spiritual autobiography.

If the long, discontinuous sequence "is the decisive form toward which all the developments of modern poetry have tended," as M. L. Rosenthal has argued in *The Modern Poetic Sequence,* Wright is one of its most capable practitioners. Unlike epic poets of the past, who trace heroic action according to a logical storyline, Wright traces the wanderings of his own mind according to the randomness of its associations. "My plots do not run narratively or linearly, but synaptically, from one nerve spark to another, from one imagistic spark to another," he has said. As in music, to which his poems often allude, his sequences follow their Modernist forebears by introducing and then playing variations on certain motifs—moon, sun, wind, night, water, stars—in order to register fluctuations of mood and idea. He compulsively returns to his roots in Tennessee and North Carolina; to his residences in California, Montana, and Virginia; and to his sojourns in Italy in order to explain his religious and artistic impulses. His music, with its crescendos and diminuendos, is a deliberate mimesis of natural and mental cycles. Painting, especially Paul Cézanne's (which he frequently celebrates), also offers an analogy for his sequential methods. Like Cézanne returning to Mont St. Victoire to depict its different shades and lights, or Monet returning to the same cathedral and water lilies, Wright revisits familiar landscapes and familiar subjects— God, language, salvation—to record the way time and perspective alter them.

Wright noted in his journal that he wanted his poems "to sing and to tell the story of my life,"
but he also asserted, contradictorily, that "a life is not a story" and that "the poet's 'life' consists of only those things that are not good enough to go into his poems." In addition to underscoring his ambivalence toward traditional narrative, his statements point to the sort of "life" he wanted to evince in his poems. Unlike the Confessional poets, he chose to stress luminous or numinous moments, epiphanies or "spots of time," rather than the more mundane business of working at a job, socializing with friends, or managing one's love life. His avoidance of narrative has posed a problem for those who would like to classify him alongside Robert Penn Warren, James Dickey, and Dave Smith as a "Southern poet." Although he once said, "The South means a great deal to me. The look of it, the 'idea' of it, the history of it as I knew it," his sense of Southernness never prompted him to join the hallowed tradition of Southern storytellers. The narrative elements in Wright's poems are usually brief anecdotes that emerge like islands in a stream of similes and metaphors; the characters are usually ghosts of dead painters, poets, musicians, parents, friends, and acquaintances who have become *genii loci* associated with particular landscapes. Of the flesh-and-blood people who appear, Wright is the most frequent.

WRIGHT'S EARLY YEARS

Wright was born on his father's thirty-first birthday, August 25, 1935, in a Tennessee Valley Authority hospital located in Pickwick Dam, Tennessee. He was the first baby delivered in the new facility. His parents named him after his great-grandfather, Charles Ferdinand Penzel, who hailed from minor landowning nobility in Asch, Bohemia. Dismayed by the privileges he had forfeited because of primogeniture (he was a second son) and by the possibility of military service during one of the Austro-Hungarian empire's many wars, Penzel emigrated to America at the age of sixteen. Five years after settling in Little Rock, Arkansas, Penzel was asked to organize a company of Confederate volunteers. According to family legend, during the Civil War battle of Chickamauga, a Yankee shot him in the mouth as he yelled "Charge!" (His great-grandson recalled this incident in his poem "Arkansas Traveller" and obliquely in "Chickamauga.") With the ball lodged permanently in his jaw, Penzel survived the war and later prospered in the wholesale grocery business.

Wright's maternal ancestors were mainly farmers, ministers, and ferrymen who lived in northern Virginia for two hundred years. His mother, Mary Winter Wright, was the exception. She was born on the Mississippi delta after her mother left Virginia to become a governess near the end of the nineteenth century. Mary had literary ambitions and wrote short stories as a student at the University of Mississippi. For literary as well as romantic reasons, she dated William Faulkner's younger brother, Dean, who died in his famous brother's plane when it crashed. In 1934 she married Wright's father, an employee of Arkansas Power and Light. The writer William Percy—the future uncle of Walker Percy—was a guest at the wedding and commented to Mr. Wright: "Sir, you have plucked the fairest flower in the delta." In addition to a passion for literature, Mary's family had musical talents, which were passed on to Charles' first cousins, the legendary rock musicians Johnny and Edgar Winter. Charles was one of the only members of his family who could not play an instrument or carry a tune. Nevertheless, his love of music inspired some of his best poems.

For ten years Charles Wright's father worked on damsites for the Tennessee Valley Authority as a civil engineer, which was the reason that Charles was born in a TVA hospital. Charles' view of his life as a nomadic pilgrimage began early; as his father's jobs changed, he moved from one damsite to another. At the age of six

months, Charles was transplanted from Pickwick Dam to Knoxville, Tennessee, so his father could work on the Cherokee Dam. After a year in Knoxville, the family moved to Corinth, Mississippi (from there Mr. Wright commuted to the Mussel Shoals Dam in Alabama). Before long, the Wrights returned to Knoxville, only to uproot once again in 1941 when Charles' father got a job on the Fontana Dam. For two years they lived in rural Hiwassee Village, North Carolina, which consisted of a commissary, a school, and a community hall. One spur to remembering these boyhood homes in poems such as "Dog Creek Mainline" was the fact that some of the small villages constructed for TVA crews and their families had vanished from maps. Absences would haunt Wright's memory and writing throughout his career.

After Hiwassee, where Wright began to show a keen interest in nature and landscape, his family settled in Oak Ridge, Tennessee. From 1943 to 1945 his father worked on the top-secret Manhattan Project that developed the first nuclear weapons. At the end of World War II, the Wrights bought a house in Kingsport, Tennessee. Initially, Wright's father worked for the Eastman construction company; later, he started his own construction company. Here the Wrights remained and here, while in the fifth grade, Charles came to a sudden realization about himself that would eventually affect his poetry: "I learned with something of an awesome finality . . . how I would fit into a group. . . . It has continued to this day pretty much unchanged from the fifth grade: always of the group, but never at its center; always at the edges observing and commenting, never inside making it do whatever it was that the group did." If storytellers commanded attention from a position in the group's center, Wright would become the artist of visual detail and pithy statement on the periphery.

It was also during his years in Kingsport that Wright began to cultivate his taste for country music. The Carter Family, one of his favorite singing groups, lived only ten miles from his house. He also listened attentively to Earl Scruggs, Lester Flatt, Roy Acuff, and Merle Travis. Although country music's usual soap opera of adultery, divorce, heartbreak, and revenge exerted little influence on Wright's later subject matter, its religious concerns with death, loss, resurrection, and salvation had an enduring appeal. To aid the gestation of his ambitious autobiographical sequence "Tattoos" in his third book, *Bloodlines,* he listened to country music for six months, and he paid tribute to the genre by entitling his first collection of selected poems *Country Music.* The music affected his appreciation of other poets as well. Emily Dickinson was the first poet who spoke to him with down-home intimacy because her rhythms and themes—what he called her "White Soul"—resembled those in the country music songs he once listened to as a boy.

Dickinson also appealed to Wright because of her immersion in the Bible, hymnals, and prayer books. Wright's own immersion came at the Sky Valley school and summer camp near Hendersonville, North Carolina, which was run by the "evangelical daughter" of the Episcopal Bishop of South Carolina. Anne Perry and her husband, Jim, had become conscientious objectors during World War II and tried to impart their lofty spiritual values to the children under their care. Wright spent his twelfth, thirteenth, and fourteenth summers at the Perrys' camp, and his fifteenth year (1950–1951) at their school, which enrolled only eight students—seven boys and one girl. Disgruntled by the school's size, Wright told his parents he didn't want to return for his last two years of high school. But rather than go to a public institution, from 1951 to 1953 he attended an Episcopal boarding school, Christ School, in Arden, North Carolina. "Jesus Tech," as the students nicknamed it, had the benefit of being larger—it had 143 students. Nevertheless, it was extremely strict. Finding a roll of LifeSavers stashed in Wright's dresser drawer, the school

prefect punished Wright by making him wait on tables, remain on campus, and dig up an oak tree.

Christ School was not all misery. Wright was able to nurture his appetite for tobacco (he proudly smoked a pipe), alcohol (he occasionally tippled), fancy cars (he liked to look at them), and girls (whom he rarely courted because of shyness). His poor eyesight and lack of size notwithstanding, Wright got a chance to play on the first-string varsity basketball and baseball teams. His contributions, however, were minimal. In his senior year, the basketball team tallied no wins. During his junior-year season with the baseball team, he got only one hit. (He improved substantially as a senior, batting over .320.) After graduating from Christ School in May 1953, Wright abandoned organized religion, only to return to it constantly in his writing. His experiences at the two Episcopal schools provided much of the material for his first two books of poetry. In his other books he adapted the language of Christianity to his spiritual concerns, which were marked more by doubt and ambivalence than belief. His experiences at Sky Valley led directly to such poems as "Sky Valley Rider," "Northhanger Ridge," "The Other Side of the River," and "Blackwater Mountain." Along with the precepts of Episcopalianism, Wright continued to absorb the melancholic tunes and tales of country music, especially those by Merle Travis and Hank Snow. Reflecting on this formative period, Wright acknowledged: "I was formed by the catechism in Kingsport, the evangelical looniness at Sky Valley Community in North Carolina, and by the country songs and hymns . . . I kept hearing on the radio back in Tennessee."

LITERARY BEGINNINGS

Wright got his first practical training as a writer in the summer of 1953 when he took a job as a police reporter for the *Kingsport Times-News.* Each evening he scouted the police blotter for such calamities as drownings, shootings, and automobile accidents. Seeing his name in print above his modest articles was a heady experience, and it led to his decision to become a journalist and novelist. Away from the newspaper, Wright did little to advance his literary ambitions. He usually played golf. But on his dinner breaks at work, while eating sandwiches made soggy by the afternoon heat in his '52 Oldsmobile, he read comics, and at his mother's urging, nearly all of Faulkner's novels and two collections of Eudora Welty's stories. He also read Hemingway, whose pared-down lyricism he considered an antidote to Faulkner's baroque flourishes. Later, in his own writing, he would effectively marry the two styles.

With his stint as a cub reporter behind him, Wright attended Davidson College, where he partied at his fraternity, played more golf, went on road trips to women's colleges, took ROTC, and did passably well in his courses (he got a B average) but otherwise experienced what he called "four years of amnesia." He continued to write in a class taught by a Shakespeare professor, but the stories he composed were negligible—usually moody descriptions of landscapes in the purple prose of another literary idol, Thomas Wolfe. He showed little propensity for poetry, his main concentration being history, but he did win a literary competition as a senior and eagerly collected his prize, a collection of Hemingway's stories. His most significant accomplishment came in the form of a diploma and commission from the U.S. Army Intelligence Corps, which he earned one summer at Fort Benning, Georgia. Before reporting on November 2, 1957, to Fort Holabird, Maryland, he spent three weeks in New York. It was during this trip that he bought a book that would change his life—the 1957 New Directions edition of the *Selected Poems of Ezra Pound.*

Although Wright put off reading Pound's poems, his interest in poetry continued to percolate at the Presidio's Army Language School in Monterey, California (here he studied Italian in prep-

aration for overseas duty). With Jack Kerouac's *On the Road* and Allen Ginsberg's *Howl* all the rage in the San Francisco area, Wright channeled his romantic yearnings into a notebook at night and on weekends. In early January 1959, he flew from Fort Dix, New Jersey, to Paris, and later took a train to Verona, Italy. Over the next three years he worked in Verona for the 430th CIC Detachment on security for military installations. His friend Harold Schimmel, a former Cornell English major, having borrowed and returned the *Selected Poems of Ezra Pound,* urged Wright to read the book and visit Catullus' legendary villa on Lake Garda's peninsula of Sirmione, which Pound had memorialized in one of his poems. Wright dutifully read Pound's "Blandula, Tenulla, Vagula," and in March 1959 made his momentous visit to the villa. He later recalled

the late March sun pouring through the olive trees, reflecting off their silver and quicksilver turns in the lake wind, the lake itself stretched out below me and into the distance, the pre-Alps above Riva cloud-shouldered and cloud-shadowed, the whole weight of history and literature suddenly dropping through the roof of my . . . world in one of those epiphanic flashes that one is fortunate enough to have in one's lifetime now and then if one is ready. I was ready.

In "Blandula, Tenulla, Vagula," utilizing the biblical diction he favored in his early poems, Pound had questioned orthodox ideas of heaven and outlined his quest for an earthly paradise:

What hast thou, O my soul, with paradise?
Will we not rather, when our freedom's won,
Get us to some clear place wherein the sun
Lets drift in on us through the olive leaves
A liquid glory?

The poem launched Wright's own quest for Sirmione-like paradises, and it converted him to poetry.

Knowing little about Pound's controversial political and economic theories at the time, Wright responded almost entirely to the visual and auditory aspects of his poetry. Wright found the *Pisan Cantos* especially moving because as in "Blandula, Tenulla, Vagula," Pound wrote about places in Italy Wright knew; for the next two years he wrote imitations of the *Pisan Cantos*. Even though he recognized the flaws in Pound's epic work, his admiration for *The Cantos* (1975) never wavered. "It remains one of the most spectacular and gorgeous literary wrecks, in English, of the century," he declared in 1992, "and the lyrical songs that continue to rise from the wreckage, and the incredible music and visions of many of its parts continue to seduce us toward that same shore and those same shoals." Wright's trilogy of trilogies would attest to the seduction of Pound's visions as well as to an awareness of the "shoals" on which the Mussolini-adoring Pound foundered. Pound's bad example helped steer Wright away from lengthy forays into politics.

UNIVERSITY TRAINING

Following four years of Army Intelligence work, three of which were spent in Italy, Wright entered the University of Iowa's creative writing program in 1961. His entrance was unusual. He was twenty-six and he had originally applied to the regular graduate program. For some reason, nobody had bothered to read the poems he had sent to gain admission into the writing workshop. Unfazed by the oversight, Wright simply showed up and never left. The workshop, whose reputation had been established by former teachers such as Robert Lowell and John Berryman, was one of the most prestigious in the country. Recent graduates included Donald Justice (who was a teacher when Wright arrived), Philip Levine, W. D. Snodgrass, and Flannery O'Connor. Despite the program's status, classes were held in a group of World War II-vintage Quonset huts. In these humble abodes, Wright's teachers, Paul Engle and Justice, provided him with the most intense

educational experience of his life. Wright found Justice especially helpful. "For several years, everything I knew about poetry I knew through him or because of him," he later said. Justice, who was open-minded, enthusiastic, and savvy, introduced his student to John Cage, William Carlos Williams, Wallace Stevens, W. H. Auden, Gerard Manley Hopkins, and John Crowe Ransom. "I was the blackboard and he was the chalk," Wright remarked.

Wright's fellow students also took chalk to his blackboard. Harboring a low opinion of Pound, the Beats, and the Black Mountain poets, they guided him toward Elizabeth Bishop, James Wright, James Merrill, Philip Larkin, Richard Wilbur, W. D. Snodgrass, Berryman, and Lowell. "It was the era of the Great Schism, the Academics versus the Beats," Wright recalled. At first submitting to the Academics' New Critical principles, Wright wrote mostly in conventional forms and never abandoned his conviction that poetry was composed of lines with a definite—not necessarily metric—integrity. Among those students who would establish reputations comparable to Wright's were Marvin Bell and Mark Strand. As a newly appointed teacher in the Iowa program, Strand directly influenced Wright's career by encouraging him to compose prose poems and translate the Italian poet Eugenio Montale.

With the aid of two Iowa Italianists, between 1961 and 1963 Wright translated Montale's "Mottetti," a sequence of twenty poems to an unnamed lover, and later translated Montale's book *La Bufera e Altro*. Wright credited Montale for teaching him something about the hermetic method. Montale, along with Giuseppe Ungaretti and Dino Campana, belonged to the Hermetic movement of Italian poets that prized hard-edged images and obscure associations. Wright found in Montale's weltanschauung a confirmation of his own point of view:

In his world of time as the steady destroyer, of existence as entropy, the steady process of decay, like the darkness, surrounds us from the inside out. Any relief from that, in him, becomes an intercession, a kind of grace beyond our ability to explain or understand. The mysteries beat just under the surface of everything. He hears that beating, he sees the flashes of light.

Wright also translated Montale's fellow hermeticist, Campana, because he was drawn to his reputation as a romantic pilgrim with a "desperate reaching and yearning for what he felt but couldn't write down or understand truly." Campana's longer prose pieces offered one model for Wright's later verse journals.

Wright received his Master of Fine Arts degree in 1963 and returned to Italy for two years, this time as a Fulbright scholar rather than as an Army Intelligence officer. (Experiences from his second visit worked their way into "The Southern Cross," "Roma I," and "Roma II.") At the University of Rome he studied Dante and Montale with an engaging teacher named Maria Sampoli. He read *The Inferno* in both Italian and English. Many years later, while living in Laguna Beach, California, he continued to immerse himself in Dante by reading a canto a day in the Singleton edition of *The Divine Comedy*.

In 1965 Wright returned to the University of Iowa to begin a Ph.D. dissertation in English. During the 1965–1966 academic year, Wright got to know fellow students Jon Anderson and James Tate (the latter became a lifelong friend). Wright flourished in Iowa's friendly, competitive, intensely literary atmosphere, but as his comments about being a blackboard indicated, he also felt poorly educated. Before coming to Iowa, he had received no criticism of his poems. Furthermore, he had read nothing but Pound, Eliot, e.e. cummings, Dylan Thomas, and some Montale and Dino Campana in Italian, and he could not distinguish an iambic pentameter line. Nevertheless, Wright curtailed his doctoral plans to take a teaching job at the University of California, Irvine. There he met the photographer Holly Mc-

Intire, whom he married in 1969. A year before his nuptials, he embarked for Italy again, this time as a Fulbright lecturer on Thoreau, Emerson, and Melville at the University of Padua. It was on this trip that he and his friend James Tate arranged to meet Pound, who unfortunately had left Italy to receive an honorary degree from his alma mater, Hamilton College. Wright did see Pound walking or dining with Olga Rudge in the Piazza San Marco and once stood next to him under the porticos of San Marco. The fact that Wright never introduced himself to Pound or his other idol, Montale, was a measure of his humble respect for them.

Not long after Wesleyan University Press published *The Grave of the Right Hand* in 1970, Wright revealed similar humility by dismissing it as an "apprentice volume" and including only a handful of its prose poems in *Country Music*. The prose poems introduced significant themes that resonated throughout his trilogies—the contrast between an unimaginative childhood in the American South and an imaginative adulthood in the European South, the recuperation of sacred landscapes through memory, the journey along a *via negativa* toward illumination—but many of the other poems in the volume deserved preservation as well. In these poems, echoes of Pound and Montale can be detected, but it was the stark, plain-spoken, cryptic expressions of alienation and gloom of his two teachers, Justice and Strand, that Wright emulated most overtly. Wastelands dominate Wright's landscapes, whether they be in the American East (Tennessee, North Carolina), the American West (California, Montana), or the Mediterranean (Italy). Winter, night, rain, fog, frigid winds, graves, stones, owls, bats, menacing moons, dead or mad writers, fiery ship burials, poisonous plants, and disembodied body parts contribute to the grotesquerie. Like Eliot in *The Waste Land,* Wright documents a dismal stage in a quest for redemption. Floundering in various graves, he entertains hope of a radiant *paradiso,* and at the end of the penultimate poem, "Addendum," he declares auspiciously: "Where the fire ripens . . . / The path will open, the Angel beckon, / And we will follow. For light is all."

"The Night Watch," a central poem in *The Grave of the Right Hand,* delineates Wright's typical journey from existential woe toward meditative quiet and luminous afflatus. The poem begins with a waking from sleep and fog:

I can hear
The fog start to rise, the slow
Memory of an ocean,

And I, like a ship, begin
To stir, to lurch in its swell,
And to move outward, beyond

The steel jetty, the lighthouse,
The red-flagged channel buoys,
—Beyond, at last, sleep even—

Into a deeper water,
Pale, oracular, its waves
Motionless, seagulls absent.

Mnemosyne, Wright's invigorating muse, leads him from internal and external fog to an Eliotic still-point, an absence of motion and distracting stimuli, where he can listen to the oracles—the voices of past masters—that facilitate his poems. The ocean, for Wright as for St. John, offers up the dead in an apocalypse, but Wright's voice eschews the bard's apocalyptic yawp. Clear diction, natural images, and neat syllabic tercets resembling haikus (each line has seven syllables) modulate the oracular voice that is the journey's telos.

THE FIRST TRILOGY

Following the soft-spoken, hermetic lucubrations of his first book, Wright in his second, *Hard Freight,* grappled with his literary mentors, his Southern upbringing, and his present experience in a more forthright way. His "Homage to Ezra Pound" demonstrates what he had learned from Pound's imagistic principles by literally following his master on a walk through Venice: "Past San Sebastiano, past / The Ogni Santi and San Trovaso, down / The Zattere and left / Across the tiered bridge to where / —Off to the right, half-hidden— / The Old Dogana burns in the spring sun." "Homage to Arthur Rimbaud" recounts a similar literary pilgrimage with similar feelings of attraction and repulsion. If Pound was a "cold-blooded father of light," so was Rimbaud. "For almost a hundred years / We've gathered outside your legend (and been afraid / Of what such brilliance affords)," Wright says of Rimbaud. As one of the moths drawn to the brilliance of these self-destructive poets, Wright is no naif. He is fully cognizant of how perilous the incandescent imagination can be.

In "The New Poem," which became a popular anthology piece, Wright offered what some regarded as his aesthetic manifesto. Reacting against injunctions from peers like Marvin Bell, who advocated a new kind of poem that would rectify the sociopolitical ills of the Vietnam era in America, Wright composed a set of directives that specified what the new poem should not or would not do, and in doing so he upheld the poet's right to be an apolitical aesthete. The new poem, he declared, "will not resemble the sea. / It will not have dirt on its thick hands. / It will not be part of the weather." Neither would the new poem have any spiritual or didactic purposes: "It will not attend our sorrow / It will not console our children. / It will not be able to help us." Was Wright siding with the "art-for-art's-sake" writers like Oscar Wilde, who was the subject of two poems in *Hard Freight*? The book, after all, was a compendium of homages to other artists, and many of its poems were based on paintings and photographs. But in their naturalism and religious bent, many also ran counter to his manifesto. In the sequence of poems addressed to his infant son, "Firstborn," Wright is openly didactic, consolatory, and earthbound. His purpose is ethical; he instructs his suffering child to attach himself to the ground, the weather, the daily and seasonal cycles:

> Indenture yourself to the land;
> Imagine you touch its raw edges
> In all weather, time and again;
>
> Imagine its colors; try
> To imitate, day by day,
> The morning's growth and the dusk,
>
> The movement of all their creatures;
> Surrender yourself, and be glad;
> This is the law that endures.

In the dense textures of poems like "Dog Creek Mainline," "Blackwater Mountain," "Sky Valley Rider," and "Northhanger Ridge," Wright again contradicts the dicta of "The New Poem" by retracing his roots to the soil of Tennessee and North Carolina.

In *Bloodlines,* his next collection, Wright tracked down his origins in the American South more deliberately. He wrote elegies for grandparents and parents who seemed remote not only because they were dead, but also because they had lived in places and times so different from his current location in California. Wright's remembrances of times past occasionally begin with Proustian epiphanies, such as when camellia blossoms falling in his backyard in Laguna Beach remind him of camellias at one of his Southern homes in "Tattoos." What follows is a sequence of twenty reminiscences, each comprising three five-line stanzas that skip back and forth between references to dead parents, artistic exaltations in Italy, childhood illnesses and sexual traumas, and nearly fatal adult accidents. Indelibly engraved on his memory, these experiences are the "tattoos" that define him. Inspired by "Tattoos" in a contrapuntal way is another sequence, "Skins," whose twenty free-form sonnets express a desire to shed all those indelible impressions that determine one's identity. Biological and environmental destiny, however, stymies Wright's religious prayers for self-metamorphosis. He tells himself: "What you are is what you will be / Until the end, no matter / What prayer you answer to." In the last poem of the sequence, Wright portrays himself as a puzzled pilgrim "walking to and fro on the earth, knowing / That nothing changes, or everything," and one devoted to recording his erratic trail before it, too, vanishes. What emerges from *Bloodlines* is a series of glimpses into Wright's religious, rural, inward personality that he has tried to escape and transform to no avail. His identity haunts him like the memory of his twelve-year-old face reflected on a window in his family's house in Tennessee. In the poem "Rural Route" he writes: "I back off, and the face stays. / I leave the back yard, and the front yard, and the face stays. / I am back on the West Coast, in my studio / My wife and my son asleep, and the face stays." He may slough skin, addresses, and personae, but in his memory they always remain as if fossilized in amber.

Wright completed his first trilogy in November 1976 with *China Trace,* which differed from his two previous books by being conceived as a unified sequence rather than a collection of individual lyrics and shorter sequences. He considered each poem, even those one or two or three lines long, as a chapter in a fragmentary autobiography that traced his abandonment of childhood, disillusionments with orthodox religion, travels to exotic lands, encounters with art, and hoped-for apotheosis among the stars. His title referred to a pilgrim's road ("trace" can mean road or path) as well as the trace of Chinese poems, specifically those from the T'ang Dynasty translated by Pound and Arthur Waley, that informed his book. To approximate the brevity and subject matter of Chinese lyrics, Wright assigned himself an arbitrary limit of twelve lines in which to convey "one man's relationship to the endlessness, the ongoingness, the everlastingness of what's around him . . . in the natural world." He emphasized the Oriental preoccupation with this world rather than the Christian's with the next world. He shifted his focus away from the transcendent and toward the quotidian (at one point he considered calling his book *Quotidiana*).

Despite this intended thematic shift, Wright continued to write poems that yearned for Christian transcendence, that denied conventional beliefs in salvation and God, and that lamented the loss of religious consolation. In the first poem, "Childhood," Wright offers one of many valedictions to his early beliefs in heaven and hell. The "beads from a broken rosary," he claims, have fallen away, but what falls away rises again, slightly altered or well-preserved, in memory. The things of this world are fleeting and fill Wright with regret, but low spirits give him all the more reason to continue his unorthodox Christian quest for "The wafer of blood in its chalk robes, // The bright nail of the east I usher my body toward." Confronted by intimations of divinity and immortality, Wright assumes a familiar posture. In "1975" he says: "I turn in the wind / Not knowing what sign to make, or where I should kneel." Wandering through remembered landscapes in Italy, his native South, and California, he hopes to receive the mystic's sacred wound that will open him to God's love and miracles. "I want to be bruised by God," he says in "Clear Night." "I want to be strung up in a strong light and singled out." In "Cloud River," he prays for "something immense and unspeakable to uncover its face." What usually appears, however, is the poet's face rather than God's face, the poetic word rather than the Christian Word.

THE SECOND TRILOGY

Because Wright felt more emotionally and intellectually involved in *China Trace* than in his previous books, he was disappointed that some of the reviews faulted the new poems for their lack of ambition, accessibility, and narrative coherence. Wright maintained that a "subnarrative" unified the poems. In 1971, after going to a John Cage concert with Donald Justice in Irvine, Wright decided to follow Cage's example by assigning himself a series of difficult exercises that would make his next book more ambitious. Wright listed his self-imposed instructions to an interviewer: "Number one was [to compose a poem resembling] a watercolor, two was [to compose a poem resembling] the blues. Three was to write a seasonal poem and four was to write a childhood poem unlike any I had done before. Five was to write a poem that was basically commentary. Six was to write an abstract of a poem that wasn't there. Seven was to write a poem from a photograph—Ezra Pound in his garden in San Ambrogio." He also planned to write a poem without verbs, a poem with a verb in every line, a poem borrowing images from Dante, a poem completed at a single sitting, several poems recalling occasions with people who had not attended them, one with a highfalutin statement and commentary, one with no point of reference, one that was an "Ars Poetica," another based on a photograph that substituted Wright's friends for the people actually in the photograph, another "deliberately retrograde in manner or location," and finally one written during a three-day Modern Language Association (MLA) conference. The guidelines, as arbitrary and quirky as they were, helped Wright produce one of his most compelling books.

Fortunately, Wright refused to let his assignments bind him like straitjackets. His first poem, "Homage to Paul Cézanne," was less an imitation of a Cézanne watercolor than a lengthy elegy for Wright's parents and artistic ancestors. The poem began fortuitously after Christmas in 1976, when he looked up from his television set and saw in a field some torn sheets of notebook paper made luminous by the evening light. The first line that came to him was "In the fading light the dead wear our white shirts to stay warm," which he later transmogrified into the stunning opening: "At night, in the fish-light of the moon, the dead wear our white shirts / To stay warm, and litter the fields." The poem diverged from the *pictura poesis* exercise to become a long, highly intricate meditation on the way the beloved dead interact with the living through memory. Wright said in an interview

> I've been trying to write poems ... the way a painter might paint a picture ... using stanzas in the way a painter will build up blocks of color, each disparate and often discrete, to make an overall representation that, taken in its pieces and slashes and dabs, seems to have no coherence, but seen in its totality, when it's finished, turns out to be a very recognizable landscape. . . . Cézanne is someone who does this, in his later work, to an almost magical perfection.

He had been using this Modernist technique for years, but he had never acknowledged his debt to Cézanne so extensively before "Homage." In addition to honoring Cézanne, Wright in *The Southern Cross* paid tribute to the baroque mellifluence and jarring discontinuities of Hart Crane, most directly in "Portrait of the Artist with Hart Crane." "Southern Cross" was a title taken from a section of Crane's *The Bridge* (1930), which suggested to Wright his lost boyhood in the South (the Southern Cross constellation cannot be seen in the northern hemisphere), his persistent attraction to a distant faith symbolized by the cross, and his perennial theme of time past crossed with time present.

Passages through time and space distinguished both the content and style of Wright's next book, *The Other Side of the River*. The meandering lines, which often broke in the middle of the page, dropped one line, and kept going in a "lowrider" to the margin, mimed the journeys to familiar haunts in California, Montana, Tennessee, North Carolina, and Italy. As at the end of *China Trace,* Wright speculated on his future destination in a nebulous otherworld, not in the stars but across an unspecified river resembling the mythical Styx. Recalling his religious training in the South, he proclaimed in his first poem, "Lost Bodies": "If I had it all to do over again / I'd be a Medievalist." Genuflections to his Christian education and to the Christian-saturated culture of medieval and Renaissance Italy, however, provoke iconoclastic dismissals. Mnemosyne remains his muse, yet increasingly he admits to the flaws and failures of memory. After proselike accounts of his father training him how to use a jackhammer, of friends sucking gin from a watermelon outside Nashville in 1957, and of his job reporting for the *Kingsport Times-News* in 1953, Wright exclaims: "Nothing you write down is ever as true as you think it was." Working against his heartfelt recollections is his realization that "There is no metaphor for any of this," and that memory and language conceal as much as they reveal. Nevertheless, his inventive metaphors, surreal pathetic fallacies, and incantatory rhythms never fail to transform what he does remember—whether true or false—into something dazzlingly rich and strange.

In 1983, one year after publishing *Country Music,* Wright accepted a position at the University of Virginia and settled permanently in Charlottesville (in 1988 he would become UVA's Souder Family Professor of English). His next collection, *Zone Journals,* reflected his geographical move as well as his ongoing stylistic move toward the discursive expansiveness of prose. His new poems, which stretched in length from one page to forty pages, aspired to the frank, "unliterary" spontaneity of journals. Even so, his "journals" were as fastidiously crafted and "literary" as his previous poems. They meditated on art and religion and paid homage to numerous artistic ghosts (Li Po, Dante, Petrarch, Leonardo da Vinci, Fulke Greville, Sir Philip Sidney, John Keats, Edgar Allen Poe, Pablo Picasso, Mark Rothko, Dickinson,

Pound). The "zones" he explored were geographical (California, Virginia, England, Italy) as well as psychological. Focusing on "language and landscape, and how they coexist in each other, and speak for, and to, each other," as Wright said of his journal poems, he continued to find his guiding principles in Pound's *Cantos,* Eliot's *Four Quartets* (1943), and other sequences in the Modernist canon.

Helen Vendler argued that Wright in *Zone Journals* demonstrated a "deepening concentration that aims at either obliteration or transcendence, blanks or mysticism," but that "he remains bound to the materiality and the temporal rhythm of language, whereas both Eastern nothingness and Western transcendence, at their utmost point, renounce as meaningless both materiality and time." For Wright, mystical concentration, which proceeded from nothingness to transcendence, and materiality were related. A Dantesque ghost confirmed this relation in "A Journal of the Year of the Ox":

> *Brother, remember the way it was*
> *In my time: nothing has changed:*
> *Penitents terrace the mountainside, the stars hang*
> *   in their bright courses*
> *And darkness is still the dark:*
> *   concentrate, listen hard,*
> *Look to the nature of all things.*

A visual and auditory attentiveness to the things of this world was still the goal of Wright's self-obliteration, self-transcendence, and prayerlike poems.

As an elegist of sacred places and sacred concepts, Wright memorialized a place he knew well as a boy in Kingsport, Tennessee: the Cherokee nation's ceremonial ground on the Holston River's Long Island. Although his *Zone Journals* are not as steeped in political history as Pound's *Cantos* or Lowell's *Notebook* (1969), they bear witness to the Cherokees' defeat, obliquely comparing their sacred, haunted ground to Wright's

ancestral ground in Virginia and the artistic shrines to which he makes pilgrimage in Italy. In the middle of *Zone Journals,* he records a relatively contemporary journey to Italy when his family and Mark Strand's family shared a farmhouse outside Padua for two months in the summer of 1985. In the middle of this section, he describes a room in Ferrara's Palazzo Schifanoia whose Renaissance frescoes divide existence into a tripartite hierarchy: everyday life, allegorical life, and ideal life. *Zone Journals,* like Wright's other books, is a vestigial allegory: an autobiographical journey through everyday life that aims at elusive spiritual ideals—whether they belong to Native Americans, contemporary poets, or Renaissance painters.

THE THIRD TRILOGY

Given the title of Charles Wright's next book of poems, *Chickamauga,* one might expect a withdrawal from spiritual concerns and a more direct engagement with the nightmares of history. The battle of Chickamauga in September 1863 near Georgia's West Chickamauga creek was one of the bloodiest of the Civil War; no other battle had a higher percentage of casualties per army. For the most part, however, Wright skirts history and politics in order to dwell on his aesthetic concerns with the way writing issues from reading, art from previous art. The titles highlight his penchant for collaborating with tradition's dead masters: "Lines After Rereading T. S. Eliot," "Reading Lao Tzu Again in the New Year," "After Reading Wang Wei, I Go Outside to the Full Moon," "Reading Rorty and Paul Celan One Morning in Early June," "After Reading Tu Fu, I go Outside to the Dwarf Orchard." Lines from other writers abound in these highly textured, inter-textual poems. Wright usually acknowledges his sources, but sometimes—for instance when he borrows phrases from Rainer Maria Rilke,

Sylvia Plath, and Dylan Thomas—he covers his tracks. He mentions by name Pseudo-Dionysus, Blaise Pascal, William Blake, Elizabeth Bishop, Franz Kafka, Federico García Lorca, Campana, Montale, Simic, Sappho, and a host of others. Fond of such constructions as "Lao Tzu says, more or less," "as Anna Akhmatova says," "as Blake reminds us," "as Kafka has told us," "as Lorca has taught us to say," "Sappho once said—more or less—," Wright avoids sounding like a stuffy name-dropper by deflating his idols with easygoing humor and world-weary skepticism.

The horrors of the American Civil War remain in the background of *Chickamauga* just as the horrors of the English Civil War remain in the background of Eliot's *Four Quartets.* These public conflicts, like their private correlatives, have a similar effect: they spur the two poets toward a still point at the center of the turning world. For Wright, meditative calm is attainable only for a moment, if at all. "The gill net of history will pluck us soon enough / From the cold waters of self-contentment," Wright asserts in his title poem. If history's guns and gill nets loom on the horizon, they do not prevent him from lavishing attention on the pastoral landscape that surrounds him. Here Wright wanders, registering a melancholy appreciation of earth's splendors as they flare and falter. As he searches for the mystic's "*Purgatio, illuminatio, contemplatio*" that will lift him beyond the burdens of language, everyday work, nature's cycles, and history, he acknowledges in "An Ordinary Afternoon in Charlottesville" that mystical and philosophical ideals lose their luster as inevitably as autumn leaves. Disillusioned, he circumvents despair with a whimsical sense of humor and a love of words, physical realities, and metaphysical ideas that endure despite their cyclical nature.

As Wright neared the end of his epic series of trilogies, not all critics were clapping. His most vociferous detractor was the poet David Mason, who griped in the *Hudson Review:* "Going over most of his work in preparation to review *Chickamauga* . . . I found very little that would justify paying hard-earned money to acquire it. Most of his poems are so flat and passive that they should have been left in a drawer. . . . His ideas are uninteresting, his poems undramatic, his language is only intermittently charged or lyrical." Mason, however, represented a minority opinion. Wright's next book, *Black Zodiac,* won both the National Book Critics Circle Award and the Pulitzer Prize. In it, Wright gave an overview of the final phase of his project and its difficulties: "Journal and landscape /—Discredited form, discredited subject matter—/ I tried to resuscitate both." He again resuscitates the old forms and old subjects in collages of weather reports, landscape sketches, autobiographical anecdotes, reflections on art and artists, and religious confessions. His "black zodiac" denotes another *via negativa,* another journey through sensory deprivation toward mystical illumination, another passage through the dark toward the light, so it should come as no surprise that Wright declares: "St. John of the Cross, Julian of Norwich, lead me home." Although Wright's tenebrous pilgrimage is interrupted by moments of quiet praise for the creation and its ineffable origin, he is more open about his depressions than in previous volumes. Sometimes as he catalogs his ailments, he echoes the sardonic confessionalism of Robert Lowell: "Melancholia's got me, / Pains in the abdomen, pains down the left leg and crotch. // Slurry of coal dust behind the eyes, / Massive weight in the musculature, dark blood, dark blood. / I'm sick and tired of my own complaints." Gloom hovers over his poems like a dark star. "Out of any two thoughts I have, one is devoted to death," he laments in "Meditation on Form and Measure." His nostalgic reminiscences of Oak Ridge, Sky Valley, Monterey, and Verona do little to dispel his anguish.

The annual cycle of the zodiac in Wright's penultimate trilogy is more a torture wheel than an array of constellations bestowing different personality traits on earthlings. He refers to "February . . . / Wordlessness of the wrong world," "Spring's via Dolorosa," "June . . . a migraine above the eyes," "Summer a holding pattern" of "heat, haze, humidity," "September . . . / Like an early page from The Appalachian Book of the Dead," "Autumn . . . pushing through like a cold front from the west, / Drizzle and dropped clouds, wired wind," "October, the exponential negative," and "December's chill redaction." Rather than submit to despair, Wright struggles from his zodiacal rack toward a complex affirmation: "I'll take as icon and testament / The daytime metaphysics of the natural world, / Sun on tie post, rock on rock." In bleaker times, when a "shapeless, unfingerprintable dread" presses down on him, he contemplates giving up words altogether and simply apprehending the world's vagaries in silence. He tries to cheer himself by professing that "The happy life is the darkened life" and by seeking out the "Occasional void through which the supernatural flows." Still, he can never wholly eradicate his doubts, depressions, and vacillations.

The title of the last book in Wright's series of trilogies, *Appalachia,* indicates a happier return to his rural origins in the South. Living in sight of the Appalachian mountains west of his home in Charlottesville, he proclaims, "All forms of landscape are autobiographical." His new poems revisit old lansdcapes, whether in Virginia, Italy, or the American west, that contain the gists of his identity. Saint John of the Cross, Saint Teresa of Avila, Saint Thomas Aquinas, and other divines attend his forays, which, compared to those in *Black Zodiac,* seem more likely of reaching satisfactory destinations. As if glancing furtively over his shoulder at the *Divine Comedy*'s majesterial progression from *inferno* to *purgatorio* to *paradiso* (he says of his concluding trilogy "This is an end without a story"), Wright chooses to emphasize sublimity rather than acedia. His

metaphysical riddles—"What God is the God behind the God who moves the chess pieces?"; "What mask is the mask behind the mask / The language wears and the landscape wears'?"—have the effect of Zen koans, catapulting the mind beyond reason's limits toward an apprehension of divine mysteries. Unsurprisingly, he glimpses his *paradiso* more like Pound than Dante, more like a Buddhist than a Christian. "Do not move. / Let the wind speak. / That is Paradise," Pound wrote in a draft for one of his final *Cantos*. His early lyric, "Blandula, Tenulla, Vagula," located paradise in a similarly terrestrial place—in Sirmione where sun drifted through olive leaves and glinted off lake waves. Wright perceives a similarly modest paradise among the same elements. "South wind and a long shine," he says in "Appalachian Book of the Dead III," make up his "small-time paradiso." The Egyptian Book of the Dead, to which Wright refers, was a religious manual full of elaborate rituals designed to facilitate a dead Egyptian's quest for immortality. Wright's trilogies record a similar quest and, in their ambitious scope and splendid craftsmanship, go a long way toward fulfilling it.

Selected Bibliography

WORKS OF CHARLES WRIGHT

POETRY

The Voyage. Iowa City: Patrician Press, 1963.

6 Poems. London: David Freed, 1965.

The Dream Animal. Toronto: House of Anansi, 1968.

Private Madrigals. Madison, Wis.: Abraxas Press, 1969.

The Grave of the Right Hand. Middletown, Conn.: Wesleyan University Press, 1970.

The Venice Notebook. Boston: Barn Dream Press, 1971.

Backwater. Santa Ana, Calif.: Golem Press, 1973.

Hard Freight. Middletown, Conn.: Wesleyan University Press, 1973.

Bloodlines. Middletown, Conn.: Wesleyan University Press, 1975.

China Trace. Middletown, Conn.: Wesleyan University Press, 1977.

Colophons. Iowa City: Windhover Press, 1977.

Wright, a Profile. Iowa City: Grilled Flowers Press, 1979.

Dead Color. Salem, Ore.: Charles Seluzicki, 1980.

The Southern Cross. New York: Random House, 1981.

Country Music: Selected Early Poems. Middletown, Conn.: Wesleyan University Press, 1982.

Four Poems of Departure. Portland, Ore.: Trace Editions, 1983.

The Other Side of the River. New York: Vintage/Random House, 1984.

5 Journals. New York: Red Ozier Press, 1986.

A Journal of the Year of the Ox. Iowa City: Windhover Press, 1988.

Zone Journals. New York: Farrar, Straus & Giroux, 1988.

The World of the Ten Thousand Things: Poems, 1980–1990. New York: Farrar, Straus & Giroux, 1990.

Chickamauga. New York: Farrar, Straus & Giroux, 1995.

Black Zodiac. New York: Farrar, Straus & Giroux, 1997.

Appalachia. New York: Farrar, Straus & Giroux, 1998.

PROSE

Halflife: Improvisations and Interviews, 1977–87. Ann Arbor: University of Michigan Press, 1988.

Quarter Notes. Ann Arbor: University of Michigan Press, 1995.

TRANSLATED WORKS

The Storm and Other Things, by Eugenio Montale. Oberlin, Ohio: Field Translation Series, 1978.

Motets, by Eugenio Montale. Iowa City: Windhover Press, 1981.

Orphic Songs, by Dino Campana. Oberlin, Ohio: Field Translation Series, 1984.

BIOGRAPHICAL AND CRITICAL STUDIES

BOOKS

Andrews, Tom. *The Point Where All Things Meet: Essays on Charles Wright.* Oberlin, Ohio: Oberlin College Press, 1995.

Contemporary Authors Autobiography Series, Volume 7. Detroit: Gale, 1988. Pp. 287–303.

Contemporary Authors, New Revision Series, Volume 62. Pp. 447–450.

Parini, Jay. *Some Necessary Angels.* New York: Columbia University Press, 1997. Pp. 181–200.

Poulin, A., Jr., ed. *Contemporary American Poetry.* 6th ed. Boston: Houghton Mifflin, 1996. Pp. 732–734.

Stitt, Peter. *Uncertainty & Plenitude: Five Contemporary Poets.* Iowa City: University of Iowa Press, 1997. Pp. 145–182.

Upton, Lee. *The Muse of Abandonment: Origin, Identity, Mastery in Five American Poets.* Lewisburg, Pa.: Bucknell University Press, 1998. Pp. 23–53.

ARTICLES

Most of the important reviews of Charles Wright's books are collected in Tom Andrews' *The Point Where All Things Meet.* Others include:

Jackson, Richard. "Worlds Created, Worlds Perceived." *Michigan Quarterly Review* 17: 555–556 (Fall 1978).

Kinzie, Mary. "Haunting." *American Poetry Review* 11: 40–41 (September/October 1982).

Longenbach, James. "Poetry in Review." *Yale Review* 83: 148–151 (October 1995).

Mason, David. "Poetry Chronicle." *Hudson Review* 49: 166–167 (Spring 1996).

McClatchy, J. D. "Recent Poetry: New Designs on Life." *Yale Review* 65: 103–105 (Autumn 1975).

Morris, John. "Making More Sense than Omaha." *Hudson Review* 27: 106–107 (Spring 1974).

———. "The Songs Protect Us in a Way." *Hudson Review* 27: 453–455 (Autumn 1975)

Muske, Carol. "Ourselves as History." *Parnassus: Poetry in Review* 4: 116–121 (Spring-Summer, 1976).

Ramsey, Paul. "American Poetry in 1973." *Sewanee Review* 82: 399 (Spring 1974).

—HENRY HART

Index

Index

*Arabic numbers printed in bold-face type refer
to extended treatment of a subject.*

349

"Elementary Scene, The" (Jarrell), **II,** 387, 388, 389
Elements of Style, The (Strunk), **Supp. I, Part 2,** 670
"Eleonora" (Poe), **III,** 412
Eleuthriambos (Lee), **IV,** 158
"Elephants" (Moore), **III,** 203
"Elevator Boy" (Hughes), **Retro. Supp. I,** 200; **Supp. I, Part 1,** 326
Eleven Essays in the European Novel (Blackmur), **Supp. II, Part 1,** 91, 111
Eleven Poems on the Same Theme (Warren), **IV,** 239–241
"El-Hajj Malik El-Shabazz" (Hayden), **Supp. II, Part 1,** 379
Eli (biblical person), **Supp. I, Part 2,** 690
"Eli, the Fanatic" (Roth), **Supp. III, Part 2,** 407–408
Elias, Robert H., **I,** 520; **Supp. I, Part 2,** 627
Elijah (biblical person), **III,** 347
Elinor Wylie (Gray), **Supp. I, Part 2,** 730
"Elinor Wylie: Heroic Mask" (Kohler), **Supp. I, Part 2,** 730
"Elinor Wylie: The Glass Chimaera and the Minotaur" (Wright), **Supp. I, Part 2,** 730
Elinor Wylie: The Portrait of an Unknown Lady (Hoyt), **Supp. I, Part 2,** 730
"Elinor Wylie's Poetry" (Tate), **Supp. I, Part 2,** 730
"Elinor Wylie's Shelley Obsession" (Cluck), **Supp. I, Part 2,** 730
Eliot, Charles W., **I,** 5; **II,** 345; **Supp. I, Part 2,** 479
Eliot, Charles William, **Retro. Supp. I,** 55
Eliot, Charlotte Champe Stearns, **I,** 567
Eliot, George, **I,** 375, 458, 459, 461, 467; **II,** 179, 181, 191–192, 275, 319, 324, 338, 577; **IV,** 311, 322; **Retro. Supp. I,** 218, 220, 225; **Supp. I, Part 1,** 370, **Part 2,** 559, 579; **Supp. IV,**

Part 1, 31, 297, **Part 2,** 677; **Supp. V,** 258
Eliot, Henry Ware, **I,** 567
Eliot, John, **Supp. I, Part 2,** 484, 485
Eliot, Mrs. T. S. (Valerie Fletcher), **I,** 568, 583
Eliot, Mrs. T. S. (Vivienne Haigh Haigh-Wood), **I,** 568
Eliot, Samuel, **Supp. I, Part 2,** 479
Eliot, T. S., **I,** 48, 49, 52, 59, 60, 64, 66, 68, 105, 107, 215–216, 236, 243, 256, 259, 261, 266, 384, 386, 395, 396, 399, 403, 430, 433, 441, 446, 475, 478, 479, 482, 521, 522, 527, 567–591; **II,** 65, 96, 158, 168, 316, 371, 376, 386, 529, 530, 532, 537, 542, 545; **III,** 1, 4, 5, 6, 7–8, 9, 10, 11, 14, 17, 20, 21, 23, 26, 34, 174, 194, 195–196, 205–206, 216, 217, 220, 236, 239, 269, 270–271, 277–278, 301, 409, 428, 432, 435, 436, 453, 456–457, 459–460, 461–462, 464, 466, 471, 476, 478, 485, 488, 492, 493, 498, 504, 509, 511, 517, 524, 527, 539, 572, 575, 586, 591, 594, 600, 613; **IV,** 27, 74, 82, 83, 95, 122, 123, 127, 129, 134, 138, 140, 141, 143, 191, 201, 213, 237, 331, 379, 402, 403, 418, 419, 420, 430, 431, 439, 442, 491; **Retro. Supp. I,** 51–71, 74, 80, 89, 91, 171, 198, 210, 283, 289, 290, 292, 296, 298, 299, 311, 324, 359, 411, 413, 414, 416, 417, 420, 428; **Supp. I, Part 1,** 257, 264, 268, 270, 274, 275, 299, **Part 2,** 387, 423, 455, 536, 554, 624, 659, 721; **Supp. II, Part 1,** 1, 4, 8, 20, 30, 91, 98, 103, 136, 314; **Supp. III, Part 1,** 9, 10, 26, 31, 37, 41, 43, 44, 48, 62–64, 73, 91, 99–100, 105–106, 273, **Part 2,** 541, 611, 612, 617, 624; **Supp. IV, Part 1,** 40, 47, 284, 380, 404, **Part 2,** 436; **Supp. V,** 79, 97, 101, 338, 343, 344

Eliot's Early Years (Gordon), **Retro. Supp. I,** 55
Elisha (biblical person), **III,** 347
"Elizabeth" (Longfellow), **I,** 502
Elizabeth Appleton (O'Hara), **III,** 362, 364, 375–377
"Elizabeth Bishop," **Supp. I, Part 1,** 96
Elizabeth Bishop (Stevenson), **Supp. I, Part 1,** 97
"Elizabeth Bishop in Brazil" (Brown), **Supp. I, Part 1,** 96
"Elizabeth Bishop, or the Power of Reticence" (Paz), **Supp. I, Part 1,** 97
"Elizabeth Bishop's 'Natural Heroism' " (Spiegelman), **Supp. I, Part 1,** 97
Elizabeth I, Queen, **I,** 284; **II,** 139; **Supp. I, Part 1,** 100, 111, 114, 115, 116, 118
"Elizabeth Gone" (Sexton), **Supp. II, Part 2,** 674, 681
Elizabeth Lloyd and the Whittiers (ed. Currier), **Supp. I, Part 2,** 705
Elizabethan literature, **I,** 177, 384, 569; **II,** 14–15, 18, 74; **III,** 77, 83, 145, 152, 397; **IV,** 155, 309; **Supp. I, Part 1,** 365, **Part 2,** 719
Elk Heads on the Wall (Ríos), **Supp. IV, Part 2,** 540
"Elk Song" (Hogan), **Supp. IV, Part 1,** 406
Ellen Rogers (Farrell), **II,** 42–43
Eller, Ernest, **Supp. I, Part 2,** 497
Ellerman, Winifred, **II,** 533; **Supp. I, Part 1,** 258–259, 275; *see also* McAlmon, Mrs. Robert (Winifred Ellerman)
Ellery Queen's Mystery Magazine, **Supp. IV, Part 2,** 466
Ellington, Duke, **Supp. IV, Part 1,** 360
Elliot, Charles, **Supp. V,** 161
Elliott, George B., **III,** 47, 289, 478
Elliott, Karin, **III,** 407
Ellis, Albert, **Supp. IV, Part 2,** 527
Ellis, Charles, **Supp. I, Part 1,** 99

"Eros at Temple Stream"
(Levertov), **Supp. III, Part 1,**
278–279
"Eros Turannos" (Robinson), **III,**
510, 512, 513–516, 517, 518
"Errand" (Carver), **Supp. III, Part
1,** 149
Erskine, Albert, **IV,** 261
Erskine, John, **I,** 223
Erstein, Hap, **Supp. IV, Part 2,**
589, 590
"Escape" (MacLeish), **III,** 4
Espey, John, **III,** 463, 468, 478
Esprit (publication), **III,** 352, 355,
356, 358
Esquire (magazine), **I,** 139; **II,** 78,
97, 98, 591; **III,** 38, 351; **IV,** 97,
461; **Retro. Supp. I,** 98, 113,
114, 115; **Supp. I, Part 1,** 50,
295, 329, **Part 2,** 664; **Supp. IV,
Part 1,** 102, 198, 201, 205, 383,
Part 2, 678; **Supp. V,** 237, 238
Essais (Renouvier), **II,** 344–345
*Essay Concerning Human
Understanding, An* (Locke), **I,**
554; **II,** 8, 348–349
Essay on American Poetry
(Brown), **Supp. I, Part 1,** 156
"Essay on Aristocracy" (Paine),
Supp. I, Part 2, 515
Essay on Man (Pope), **II,** 111;
Supp. I, Part 2, 516
Essay on Our Changing Order
(Veblen), **Supp. I, Part 2,** 629,
642
Essay on Projects (Defoe), **II,**
104
Essay on Rime (Shapiro), **I,** 430;
Supp. II, Part 2, 702, 703,
708–711
"Essay on the Character of
Robespierre" (Paine), **Supp. I,
Part 2,** 515
*Essay on the Chinese Written
Character* (Fenollosa), **III,** 474
"Essay Toward a Point of View,
An" (Brooks), **I,** 244
Essays (Emerson), **II,** 1, 7, 8, 12–
13, 15, 21
Essays in Anglo-Saxon Law
(Adams), **I,** 5
Essays in London (James), **II,** 336

Essays in Radical Empiricism
(James), **II,** 356–357, 355
*Essays on the Nature and
Principles of Taste* (Alison),
Supp. I, Part 1, 151
*Essays, Speeches, and Public
Letters by William Faulkner*
(Meriweather, ed.), **Retro.
Supp. I,** 77
Essays to Do Good (Mather), **II,**
104; **Supp. II, Part 2,** 461,
467
Essential Keats (Levine, ed.),
Supp. V, 179
"Essential oils are wrung"
(Dickinson), **I,** 471
"Essential Oils—are wrung"
(Dickinson), **Retro. Supp. I,** 43,
46
"Essentials" (Toomer), **Supp. III,
Part 2,** 486
*Essentials: A Philosophy of Life in
Three Hundred Definitions and
Aphorisms* (Toomer), **Supp. III,
Part 2,** 486
"Essentials of Spontaneous Prose"
(Kerouac), **Supp. III, Part 1,**
227–228
Essex Gazette (newspaper), **Supp.
I, Part 2,** 683, 684
Esslin, Martin, **I,** 95
Estess, Sybil, **Supp. IV, Part 2,**
449, 452
Esther (Adams), **I,** 9–10, 20
"Esthétique du Mal" (Stevens), **IV,**
79; **Retro. Supp. I,** 300, 311,
312
"Estoy-eh-muut and the
Kunideeyahs (Arrowboy and the
Destroyers)" (film), **Supp. IV,
Part 2,** 560
"Estrangement, Betrayal &
Atonement: The Political Theory
of James Baldwin" (Daniels),
Supp. I, Part 1, 70
Esty, William, **III,** 358; **Supp. I,
Part 1,** 198
"Etching, An" (Masters), **Supp. I,
Part 2,** 458
*Eternal Adam and the New World
Garden, The* (Noble), **Supp. I,
Part 1,** 70

"Eternal Goodness, The"
(Whittier), **Supp. I, Part 2,** 704
"Eternity, An" (Williams), **Retro.
Supp. I,** 423
"Eternity Is Now" (Roethke), **III,**
544–545
"Ethan Brand" (Hawthorne), **II,**
227
Ethan Frome (Wharton), **IV,** 316–
317, 327; **Retro. Supp. I,** 372–
373
Ethics (Spinoza), **IV,** 12
Etulain, Richard, **Supp. IV, Part 2,**
597, 601, 604, 606, 607, 608,
610, 611
Euclid, **III,** 6; **III,** 620
"Euclid Alone Has Looked on
Beauty Bare" (Millay), **III,** 133
Eudora Welty Society, **Retro.
Supp. I,** 354
Eudora Welty Writers' Center,
Retro. Supp. I, 354
Eugene Onegin (Pushkin), **III,** 246,
263
Eugene Onegin (Pushkin; trans.
Nabokov), **Retro. Supp. I,** 266,
267, 272
Eugénie, Empress, **IV,** 309
Eugénie Grandet (Balzac), **II,** 328
"Eugénie Grandet" (Barthelme),
Supp. IV, Part 1, 47
Eumenides (Aeschylus), **Retro.
Supp. I,** 65
Eureka (Poe), **III,** 409, 424, 428–
429
Euripides, **I,** 325; **II,** 8, 282, 543;
III, 22, 145, 398; **IV,** 370;
Supp. I, Part 1, 268, 269, 270,
Part 2, 482; **Supp. V,** 277
"Euripides—a Playwright" (West),
IV, 286
"Euripides and Professor Murray"
(Eliot), **Supp. I, Part 1,** 268
"Europe" (Ashbery), **Supp. III,
Part 1,** 7–10, 13, 18
"Europe! Europe!" (Ginsberg),
Supp. II, Part 1, 320, 322
*Europe of Trusts, The: Selected
Poems* (Howe), **Supp. IV, Part
2,** 420, 422, 426
Europe without Baedeker (Wilson),
IV, 429

La Farge, John, **I,** 1, 2, 20; **II,** 322, 338; **Retro. Supp. I,** 217

La Farge, Oliver, **Supp. IV, Part 2,** 503

"La Figlia che Piange" (Eliot), **Retro. Supp. I,** 63

La Follette, Robert, **I,** 483, 485, 492; **III,** 580

La Fontaine, Jean de, **II,** 154; **III,** 194; **IV,** 80

La France, Marston, **I,** 426

La France en Liberté (publication), **Supp. III, Part 2,** 618, 621

La Hood, Marvin J., **II,** 100

La kabbale pratique (Ambelain), **Supp. I, Part 1,** 273, 275

La Motte-Fouqué, Friedrich Heinrich Karl, **III,** 77, 78

La Rochefoucauld, François de, **I,** 279; **II,** 111

"La Rose des Vents" (Wilbur), **Supp. III, Part 2,** 550

La Salle and the Discovery of the Great West (Parkman), **Supp. II, Part 2,** 595, 598, 605–607

La Terre (Zola), **III,** 316, 322

"La Tigresse" (Van Vechten), **Supp. II, Part 2,** 735, 738

La Traviata (Verdi), **III,** 139

La Turista (Shepard), **Supp. III, Part 2,** 440

Labaree, Leonard, **II,** 123

"Labours of Hercules, The" (Moore), **III,** 201

Lacan, Jacques, **Supp. IV, Part 1,** 45

Lachaise, Gaston, **I,** 434

"Lackawanna" (Merwin), **Supp. III, Part 1,** 350

Lackawanna Elegy (Goll, trans. Kinnell), **Supp. III, Part 1,** 235, 243–244

Laclède, Pierre, **Supp. I, Part 1,** 205

"Lacquer Prints" (Lowell), **II,** 524–525

Ladder of Years (Tyler), **Supp. IV, Part 2,** 657, 671–672

Ladder, The (publication), **Supp. IV, Part 1,** 365

Ladies Almanack (Barnes), **Supp. III, Part 1,** 37–39, 42

Ladies' Home Journal (magazine), **III,** 54, 491; **Supp. I, Part 2,** 530

"Ladies in Spring" (Welty), **Retro. Supp. I,** 353

"Ladies in Spring" (Welty), **IV,** 276–277

Lady Audley's Secret (Braddon), **Supp. I, Part 1,** 35, 36

"Lady Barberina" (James), **Retro. Supp. I,** 227

"Lady Bates" (Jarrell), **II,** 380–381

Lady Chatterley's Lover (Lawrence), **III,** 170; **IV,** 434

"Lady from Redhorse, A" (Bierce), **I,** 203

"Lady in the Lake, The" (Chandler), **Supp. IV, Part 1,** 129

Lady in the Lake, The (Chandler), **Supp. IV, Part 1,** 127, 129–130

Lady in the Lake, The (film), **Supp. IV, Part 1,** 130

"Lady in the Pink Mustang, The" (Erdrich), **Supp. IV, Part 1,** 270

"Lady Is Civilized, The" (Taylor), **Supp. V,** 315

Lady Is Cold, The (White), **Supp. I, Part 2,** 653

"Lady Lazarus" (Plath), **Supp. I, Part 2,** 529, 535, 542, 545

Lady of Aroostook, The (Howells), **II,** 280

"Lady of the Lake, The" (Malamud), **Supp. I, Part 2,** 437

Lady Sings the Blues (film), **Supp. I, Part 1,** 67

"Lady Wentworth" (Longfellow), **II,** 505

"Lady with the Heron, The" (Merwin), **Supp. III, Part 1,** 343

"Lady's Maid's Bell, The" (Wharton), **IV,** 316

Lafayette, Marquis de, **I,** 344, 345; **II,** 405–406; **Supp. I, Part 2,** 510, 511, 683

Laforgue, Jules, **I,** 386, 569, 570, 572–573, 575, 576; **II,** 528; **III,** 8, 11, 466; **IV,** 37, 79, 80, 122; **Retro. Supp. I,** 55, 56

"Lager Beer" (Dunbar), **Supp. II, Part 1,** 193

Laguna Woman (Silko), **Supp. IV, Part 2,** 557, 560–561

Laing, R. D., **Supp. I, Part 2,** 527

Laird, C. G., **II,** 318

"Lake Isle of Innisfree" (Yeats), **Retro. Supp. I,** 413

"Lake, The" (Bradbury), **Supp. IV, Part 1,** 101

L'Alouette (Anouilh), **Supp. I, Part 1,** 286–288

Lamb, Charles, **III,** 111, 207

Lamb, Wendy, **Supp. IV, Part 2,** 658

Lambert, Mary, *see* Paine, Mrs. Thomas (Mary Lambert)

"Lame Shall Enter First, The" (O'Connor), **III,** 348, 351, 352, 355, 356–357, 358

"Lament" (Wilbur), **Supp. III, Part 2,** 550

"Lament for Dark Peoples" (Hughes), **Retro. Supp. I,** 199

"Lament for Saul and Jonathan" (Bradstreet), **Supp. I, Part 1,** 111

"Lament of a New England Mother, The" (Eberhart), **I,** 539

"Lamentations" (Glück), **Supp. V,** 83, 84

Lamia (Keats), **II,** 512; **III,** 523

Lamm, Martin, **III,** 407

Lamont, Corliss, **II,** 52

Lamp for Nightfall, A (Caldwell), **I,** 297

Lampoon (magazine), **Retro. Supp. I,** 319

Lampoon (publication), **III,** 52, 600; **IV,** 218

Lampton, Jane, *see* Clemens, Mrs. John Marshall (Jane Lampton)

"Lance" (Nabokov), **Retro. Supp. I,** 266

Lancelot (Percy), **Supp. III, Part 1,** 384, 395–396

Lancelot (Robinson), **III,** 513, 522

New Criterion, The (publication), **Supp. III, Part 2,** 611, 613; **Retro. Supp. I,** 108
New Criticism, **I,** 267, 273, 276, 280, 281, 282, 283, 517; **III,** 591; **IV,** 236, 237, 331, 433
New Criticism, The (Ransom), **III,** 497–498, 499, 501
New Critics, **Supp. II, Part 1,** 87–88, 90, 103, 106–107, 135, 136, 137, 318, **Part 2,** 416, 639, 698, 703, 713
"New Day, A" (Levine), **Supp. V,** 182
New Dictionary of Quotations, A (Mencken), **III,** 111
New Directions, **Retro. Supp. I,** 423, 424, 426, 428, 430
New Directions (publication), **Supp. III, Part 2,** 624
New Directions in Poetry and Prose (publication), **Supp. IV, Part 2,** 639
New Directions Number Seven (journal), **Retro. Supp. I,** 426
New Eclectic (magazine), see *Southern Magazine*
"New England" (Lowell), **II,** 536
"New England" (Robinson), **III,** 510, 524
"New England Bachelor, A" (Eberhart), **I,** 539
New England Courant (newspaper), **II,** 106
New England: Indian Summer (Brooks), **I,** 253, 256
New England Primer (children's educational publication), **Supp. I, Part 1,** 310
"New England Sabbath-Day Chace, The" (Freneau), **Supp. II, Part 1,** 273
New England Saints (Warren), **Supp. I, Part 1,** 123
New England Tragedies, The (Longfellow), **II,** 490, 505, 506
New England Weekly Review (publication), **Supp. I, Part 2,** 684
"New Englander, The" (Anderson), **I,** 114
New Era in American Poetry, The

(Untermeyer), **Supp. I, Part 2,** 402
New Found Land: Fourteen Poems (MacLeish), **III,** 12–13
New Freeman (publication), **II,** 26
New Hampshire: A Poem with Notes and Grace Notes (Frost), **II,** 154–155; **Retro. Supp. I,** 132, 133, 135
"New Hampshire, February" (Eberhart), **I,** 536
New Industrial State, The (Galbraith), **Supp. I, Part 2,** 648
New Journalism, The (ed. Wolfe and Johnson), **Supp. III, Part 2,** 570, 579–581, 583, 586
"New Journalism, The" (Wolfe), **Supp. III, Part 2,** 571
New Leader (publication), **III,** 292; **Supp. I, Part 1,** 50
New Left, The: The Anti-Industrial Revolution (Rand), **Supp. IV, Part 2,** 527
"New Life" (Glück), **Supp. V,** 90
New Life, A (Malamud), **Supp. I, Part 2,** 429–466
"New Life at Kyerefaso" (Sutherland), **Supp. IV, Part 1,** 9
"New Light on Veblen" (Dorfman), **Supp. I, Part 2,** 650
New London Telegraph (newspaper), **III,** 387
New Masses (publication), **II,** 450; **III,** 434, 582; **IV,** 476; **Retro. Supp. I,** 137, 202, 203, 303, 423; **Supp. I, Part 1,** 331; **Supp. III, Part 2,** 618
"New Medea, The" (Howells), **II,** 282
New Music (journal), **Supp. IV, Part 1,** 82
"New Name for Some Old Ways of Thinking, A" (James), **II,** 353
New Native American Novel, The: Works in Progress (Bartlett), **Supp. IV, Part 1,** 335
"New Natural History, A" (Thurber), **Supp. I, Part 2,** 619
New Negro, The (anthology), **Retro. Supp. I,** 199

New Negro, The (Locke), **Supp. II, Part 1,** 176
New Negro, The: An Interpretation (Locke), **Supp. IV, Part 1,** 170
New Negro movement, **Supp. II, Part 1,** 233
New Numbers (magazine), **III,** 471
New Orleans Crescent (newspaper), **IV,** 194, 334
New Orleans Sketches (Faulkner), **Retro. Supp. I,** 80
New Orleans Times-Picayune (newspaper), **II,** 56; **Retro. Supp. I,** 80
New Path to the Waterfall, A (Carver), **Supp. III, Part 1,** 138–140, 147, 149
"New Poem, The" (Wright), **Supp. V,** 339, 340
"New Poems" (MacLeish), **III,** 19
"New Poetry Handbook, The" (Strand), **Supp. IV, Part 2,** 626
New Poetry, The (eds. Monroe and Henderson), **Supp. I, Part 2,** 387
New Poetry of Mexico (trans. Strand), **Supp. IV, Part 2,** 630
New Poets, The: American and British Poetry Since World War Two (Rosenthal), **Supp. I, Part 2,** 548–549
New Poets of England and America (eds. Hall, Pack, and Simpson), **Supp. IV, Part 2,** 621
New Radicalism in America, The (1889–1963): The Intellectual as a Social Type (Lasch), **Supp. I, Part 1,** 27
New Republic (magazine), **I,** 170, 230, 231, 232, 233, 294; **II,** 430, 562; **III,** 171, 292, 452; **IV,** 427; **Retro. Supp. I,** 15, 19, 79, 131; **Supp. I, Part 1,** 174, 332, **Part 2,** 609, 647, 709; **Supp. II, Part 1,** 139, 140, 142; **Supp. III, Part 2,** 612; **Supp. IV, Part 1,** 22, 208, 286, 351, **Part 2,** 527, 653, 657; **Supp. V,** 319
"*New Republic* Moves Uptown, The" (Cowley), **Supp. II, Part 1,** 142

Once (Walker), **Supp. III, Part 2,** 519, 522, 530

Once at Antietam (Gaddis), **Supp. IV, Part 1,** 285

"Once by the Pacific" (Frost), **II,** 155; **Retro. Supp. I,** 122, 137

"Once More, the Round" (Roethke), **III,** 529

"Once More to the Lake" (White), **Supp. I, Part 2,** 658, 668, 673–675

Ondaatje, Michael, **Supp. IV, Part 1,** 252

One (magazine), **III,** 36; **Supp. IV, Part 1,** 365

"One Arm" (Williams), **IV,** 383

One Arm, and Other Stories (Williams), **IV,** 383

"One Art" (Bishop), **Supp. I, Part 1,** 72, 73, 82, 93, 94–95, 96

"One Art: The Poetry of Elizabeth Bishop, 1971–1976" (Schwartz), **Supp. I, Part 1,** 81, 97

"One Blessing had I than the rest" (Dickinson), **Retro. Supp. I,** 45

One Boy's Boston, 1887–1901 (Morison), **Supp. I, Part 2,** 494

"One Coat of Paint" (Ashbery), **Supp. III, Part 1,** 26

"One Dash-Horses" (Crane), **I,** 416

One Day (Morris), **III,** 233–236

One Day, When I Was Lost (Baldwin), **Supp. I, Part 1,** 48, 66, 67

"One Dead Friend" (Kumin), **Supp. IV, Part 2,** 441

One Flew Over the Cuckoo's Nest (Kesey), **III,** 558

"One for the Rose" (Levine), **Supp. V,** 181, 190

One for the Rose (Levine), **Supp. V,** 178, 179, 181, 187, 189–191

"One Friday Morning" (Hughes), **Supp. I, Part 1,** 330

One Hundred Days in Europe (Holmes), **Supp. I, Part 1,** 317

"$106,000 Blood Money" (Hammett), **Supp. IV, Part 1,** 345, 346

$106,000 Blood Money (Hammett), **Supp. IV, Part 1,** 345

"One Is a Wanderer" (Thurber), **Supp. I, Part 2,** 616

"One Last Look at the Adige: Verona in the Rain" (Wright), **Supp. III, Part 2,** 603

One Man in His Time (Glasgow), **II,** 178, 184

"One Man to Stand for Six Million" (Hicks), **Supp. I, Part 2,** 453

"One Man's Fortunes" (Dunbar), **Supp. II, Part 1,** 211, 212–213

One Man's Initiation (Dos Passos), **I,** 476–477, 479, 488

"One Man's Meat" (White), **Supp. I, Part 2,** 655

One Man's Meat (White), **Supp. I, Part 2,** 654, 669, 676

"One More Song" (Lindsay), **Supp. I, Part 2,** 400–401

"One More Thing" (Carver), **Supp. III, Part 1,** 138, 144

"One More Time" (Gordon), **II,** 200

One Nation (Stegner), **Supp. IV, Part 2,** 599, 608

"ONE NIGHT STAND" (Baraka), **Supp. II, Part 1,** 32

"One of Our Conquerors" (Bourne), **I,** 223

One of Ours (Cather), **I,** 322–323; **Retro. Supp. I,** 1, 3, **13–15,** 20

"One of the Missing" (Bierce), **I,** 201–202

"One Person" (Wylie), **Supp. I, Part 2,** 709, 724–727

"One Sister have I in our house" (Dickinson), **Retro. Supp. I,** 34

"One Song, The" (Strand), **Supp. IV, Part 2,** 619

"One Summer in Spain" (Coover), **Supp. V,** 40

One Time, One Place: Mississippi in the Depression, a Snapshot Album (Welty), **Retro. Supp. I,** 339, 343, 344

1 × 1 (One Times One) (Cummings), **I,** 430, 436, 438–439, 441, 446, 447, 448

"One Touch of Nature" (McCarthy), **II,** 580

"One Trip Abroad" (Fitzgerald), **II,** 95

"One Way" (Creeley), **Supp. IV, Part 1,** 150–151

One Way to Heaven (Cullen), **Supp. IV, Part 1,** 170, 172

"One Way to Spell Man" (Stegner), **Supp. IV, Part 2,** 601

One Way to Spell Man (Stegner), **Supp. IV, Part 2,** 595, 598, 601, 609

"One Who Skins Cats, The" (Gunn Allen), **Supp. IV, Part 1,** 331

"One Winter I Devise a Plan of My Own" (Ríos), **Supp. IV, Part 2,** 549

One Writer's Beginnings (Welty), **Retro. Supp. I,** 339, 340, 341, 343, 344, 355–356

O'Neale, Sondra, **Supp. IV, Part 1,** 2

O'Neil, Elizabeth Murrie, **Retro. Supp. I,** 427

O'Neil, Joseph E., **II,** 509

O'Neill, Eugene, **I,** 66, 71, 81, 94, 393, 445; **II,** 278, 391, 427, 585; **III,** 151, 165, **385–408; IV,** 61, 383; **Supp. III, Part 1,** 177–180, 189; **Supp. IV, Part 1,** 359, **Part 2,** 587, 607; **Supp. V,** 277

O'Neill, Eugene, Jr., **III,** 403

O'Neill, James, **III,** 386

O'Neill, James, Jr., **III,** 386

O'Neill, Mrs. Eugene (Carlotta Monterey), **III,** 403

O'Neill, Oona, **III,** 403

O'Neill, Shane, **III,** 403

One-Way Ticket (Hughes), **Retro. Supp. I,** 206, 207, 208; **Supp. I, Part 1,** 333–334

Only a Few of Us Left (Marquand), **III,** 55

Only Dark Spot in the Sky, The (Dove), **Supp. IV, Part 1,** 244

"Only in the Dream" (Eberhart), **I,** 523

"Only Path to Tomorrow, The" (Rand), **Supp. IV, Part 2,** 524

"Only Rose, The" (Jewett), **II,** 408

"Only Son of the Doctor, The" (Gordon), **Supp. IV, Part 1,** 305, 306

Pritchard, John P., **Supp. I, Part 1,** 173, **Part 2,** 426
Pritchard, William H., **Retro. Supp. I,** 131, 141; **Supp. IV, Part 1,** 285, **Part 2,** 642
Pritchett, V. S., **II,** 587, 608; **Supp. II, Part 1,** 143
"Privatation and Publication" (Cowley), **Supp. II, Part 1,** 149
"Private History of a Campaign That Failed" (Twain), **IV,** 195
"Private Theatricals" (Howells), **II,** 280
Privilege, The (Kumin), **Supp. IV, Part 2,** 442–444, 451
"Problem from Milton, A" (Wilbur), **Supp. III, Part 2,** 550
"Problem of Being, The" (James), **II,** 360
"Problem of Housing the Negro, The" (Du Bois), **Supp. II, Part 1,** 168
Problems and Other Stories (Updike), **Retro. Supp. I,** 322, 329
Probst, Leonard, **IV,** 401
Processional (Lawson), **I,** 479
Proclus, **Retro. Supp. I,** 247
Prodigal Parents, The (Lewis), **II,** 454–455
"Prodigal, The" (Bishop), **Supp I, Part 1,** 90, 92
"Proem" (Crane), **I,** 397
"Proem, The: By the Carpenter" (O. Henry), **Supp. II, Part 1,** 409
"Profession of a New Yorker" (Krutch), **Supp. I, Part 2,** 681
Profession of Authorship in America, 1800–1870, The (Charvat), **Supp. I, Part 1,** 148
"Professor" (Hughes), **Supp. I, Part 1,** 330
"Professor, The" (Bourne), **I,** 223
Professor at the Breakfast Table, The (Holmes), **Supp. I, Part 1,** 313, 316
"Professor Clark's Economics" (Veblen), **Supp. I, Part 2,** 634
Professor of Desire, The (Roth), **Supp. III, Part 2,** 403, 418–420

"Professor Veblen" (Mencken), **Supp. I, Part 2,** 630
Professor's House, The (Cather), **I,** 325–336; **Retro. Supp. I,** 16
Proffer, Karl, **III,** 266
Profile of Vachel Lindsay (ed. Flanagan), **Supp. I, Part 2,** 402
Profits of Religion, The (Sinclair), **Supp. V,** 276
"Prognosis" (Warren), **IV,** 245
Progressive (publication), **Supp. I, Part 1,** 60
"Project for a Trip to China" (Sontag), **Supp. II, Part 2,** 454, 469
"Project for *The Ambassadors*" (James), **Retro. Supp. I,** 229
"Projection" (Nemerov), **III,** 275
"Projective Verse" (Olson), **Supp. III, Part 1,** 30; **Supp. III, Part 2,** 555, 556, 557, 624; **Supp. IV, Part 1,** 139, 153
Prokofiev, Sergey Sergeyevich, **Supp. IV, Part 1,** 81
"Prolegomena, Section 1" (Pound), **Supp. III, Part 2,** 615–616
"Prolegomena, Section 2" (Pound), **Supp. III, Part 2,** 616
Proletarian Literature in the United States (Hicks), **Supp. I, Part 2,** 609–610
"Prologue" (MacLeish), **III,** 8, 14
"Prologue to OurTime" (Mumford), **Supp. III, Part 2,** 473
"Prometheus" (Longfellow), **II,** 494
Prometheus Bound (Lowell), **II,** 543, 544, 545, 555
Promise, The (Buck), **Supp. II, Part 1,** 124
Promise of American Life, The (Croly), **I,** 229
"Promise This—When You Be Dying—" (Dickinson), **Retro. Supp. I,** 44, 46
Promised Land, The (Porter), **III,** 447
Promised Lands (Sontag), **Supp. III, Part 2,** 452
Promises: Poems 1954–1956 (Warren), **IV,** 244–245, 249, 252

Promises, Promises (musical), **Supp. IV, Part 2,** 575
Proof, The (Winters), **Supp. II, Part 2,** 786, 791, 792–794
Proofs and Theories: Essays on Poetry (Glück), **Supp. V,** 77, 79, 92
"Propaganda of History, The" (Du Bois), **Supp. II, Part 1,** 182
Propertius, Sextus, **III,** 467
"Prophecy of Samuel Sewall, The" (Whittier), **Supp. I, Part 2,** 699
"Prophetic Pictures, The" (Hawthorne), **II,** 227
"Proportion" (Lowell), **II,** 525
"Proposal" (Carver), **Supp. III, Part 1,** 149
Proposals Relating to the Education of Youth in Pensilvania (Franklin), **II,** 113
"Proposed New Version of the Bible" (Franklin), **II,** 110
Prose and Poetry of Elinor Wylie, The (Benét), **Supp. I, Part 2,** 730
"Prose for Departure" (Merrill), **Supp. III, Part 1,** 336
"Prose Poem as an Evolving Form, The" (Bly), **Supp. IV, Part 1,** 64
"Prose Style in the Essays of E. B. White" (Fuller), **Supp. I, Part 2,** 681
"Proserpina and the Devil" (Wilder), **IV,** 358
"Prosody" (Shapiro), **Supp. II, Part 2,** 710
Prospect, The (journal), **Supp. I, Part 2,** 520
Prospect before Us, The (Dos Passos), **I,** 491
Prospect of Peace, The (Barlow), **Supp. II, Part 1,** 67, 68, 75
"Prospective Immigrants Please Note" (Rich), **Supp. I, Part 2,** 555
Prospects on the Rubicon (Paine), **Supp. I, Part 2,** 510–511
Prospectus of a National Institution, to Be Established in the United States (Barlow), **Supp. II, Part 1,** 80, 82

Spring Tides (Morison), **Supp. I, Part 2,** 494

Springer, Marlene, **Supp. I, Part 1,** 225

Springfield Daily Republican (newspaper), **I,** 453, 454

"Springfield Magical" (Lindsay), **Supp. I, Part 2,** 379

Springfield Republican (newspaper), **Retro. Supp. I,** 30

Springtime and Harvest (Sinclair), **Supp. V,** 280

Spruance, Raymond, **Supp. I, Part 2,** 479, 491

Spy, The (Cooper), **I,** 335, 336, 337, 339, 340; **Supp. I, Part 1,** 155

Spy, The (Freneau), **Supp. II, Part 1,** 260

Squanto, **Supp. I, Part 2,** 486

"Square Business" (Baraka), **Supp. II, Part 1,** 49

Square Root of Wonderful, The (McCullers), **II,** 587–588

Squaring Off: Mailer vs. Baldwin (Weatherby), **Supp. I, Part 1,** 69

Squires, Radcliffe, **II,** 222; **IV,** 127, 142, 143

S.S. Gliencairn (O'Neill), **III,** 387, 388, 405

S.S. San Pedro (Cozzens), **I,** 360–362, 370, 378, 379

"St. Augustine and the Bullfights" (Porter), **III,** 454

St. Elmo (Wilson), **Retro. Supp. I,** 351–352

"St. Francis Einstein of the Daffodils" (Williams), **IV,** 409–411

St. George and the Godfather (Mailer), **III,** 46

"St. George, the Dragon, and the Virgin" (Bly), **Supp. IV, Part 1,** 73

St. Jean de Crèvecoeur (Mitchell), **Supp. I, Part 1,** 252

St. John, David, **Supp. V,** 180

St. John, Edward B., **Supp. IV, Part 2,** 490

St. John, James Hector, *see* Crèvecoeur, Michel-Guillaume Jean de

St. Louis Daily Globe-Democrat (newspaper), **Supp. I, Part 1,** 200

St. Louis Globe-Democrat (newspaper), **I,** 499

St. Louis Post-Dispatch (newspaper), **IV,** 381; **Supp. I, Part 1,** 200

St. Louis Republic (newspaper), **I,** 499

St. Louis Woman (Bontemps and Cullen), **Supp. IV, Part 1,** 170

St. Mawr (Lawrence), **II,** 595

St. Nicholas (magazine), **II,** 397; **Retro. Supp. I,** 99, 341

Stade, George, **I,** 449; **Supp. IV, Part 1,** 286

Staël, Madame de, **II,** 298

"Staff of Life, The" (Miller), **III,** 187

Stafford, Jean, **Supp. V,** 316, *see* Lowell, Mrs. Robert (Jean Stafford)

Stafford, William, **I,** 543; **Supp. IV, Part 1,** 72, **Part 2,** 642

"Stage All Blood, The" (MacLeish), **III,** 18

Stalin, Josef, **Supp. V,** 290

Stalin, Joseph, **I,** 261, 490; **II,** 39, 40, 49, 564; **III,** 30, 298; **IV,** 372, 376

"Stalking the Billion-Footed Beast: A Literary Manifesto for the New Social Novel" (Wolfe), **Supp. III, Part 2,** 586

Stallman, R. W., **I,** 70, 405, 425, 426, 427

Stamberg, Susan, **Supp. IV, Part 1,** 201

Stanard, Mrs. Jane, **III,** 410, 413

Stand, The (King), **Supp. V,** 139, 140–141, 144–146, 148, 152

Stand in the Mountains, A (Taylor), **Supp. V,** 324

Stand Still Like the Hummingbird (Miller), **III,** 184

Stander, Lionel, **Supp. I, Part 1,** 289

Standish, Burt L. (pseudonym), *see* Patten, Gilbert

Standish, Miles, **I,** 471; **II,** 502–503

Stanford, Ann, **Retro. Supp. I,** 41;

Supp. I, Part 1, 99, 100, 102, 103, 106, 108, 109, 113, 117, 123; **Supp. IV, Part 2,** 637

Stanford, Donald E., **II,** 217, 222; **IV,** 165, 166

Stanford, Leland, **I,** 196, 198

Stang, Joanne, **IV,** 401

Stanton, Frank L., **Supp. II, Part 1,** 192

Stanton, Robert J., **Supp. IV, Part 2,** 681

"Stanzas from the Grande Chartreuse" (Arnold), **Supp. I, Part 2,** 417

Stanzas in Meditation (Stein), **Supp. III, Part 1,** 13

Staples, Hugh B., **II,** 557; **III,** 550

Star Child (Gunn Allen), **Supp. IV, Part 1,** 324

Star Is Born, A (film), **Supp. IV, Part 1,** 198

Star Rover, The (London), **II,** 467

Starbuck, George, **Supp. I, Part 2,** 538; **Supp. IV, Part 2,** 440

"Stare, The" (Updike), **Retro. Supp. I,** 329

"Starfish, The" (Bly), **Supp. IV, Part 1,** 72

"Staring at the Sea on the Day of the Death of Another" (Swenson), **Supp. IV, Part 2,** 652

Starke, Aubrey Harrison, **Supp. I, Part 1,** 350, 352, 356, 360, 362, 365, 370, 371, 373

"Starlight" (Levine), **Supp. V,** 188

Starr, Ellen Gates, **Supp. I, Part 1,** 4, 5, 11

Starrett, Vincent, **I,** 425, 426

"Starry Night, The" (Sexton), **Supp. II, Part 2,** 681

"Stars" (Frost), **II,** 153

"Stars of the Summer Night" (Longfellow), **II,** 493

"Stars over Harlem" (Hughes), **Retro. Supp. I,** 207

Star-Spangled Girl, The (Simon), **Supp. IV, Part 2,** 579

"Star-Splitter, The" (Frost), **Retro. Supp. I,** 123, 133

"Starting from Paumanok" (Whitman), **IV,** 333

"Starved Lovers" (MacLeish), **III,** 19

Vasse, W. W., **III,** 478

Vaudeville for a Princess (Schwartz), **Supp. II, Part 2,** 661–662

Vaughan, Henry, **IV,** 151

"Vaunting Oak" (Ransom), **III,** 490

Veblen, Andrew, **Supp. I, Part 2,** 640

Veblen, Mrs. Thorstein (Ellen Rolfe), **Supp. I, Part 2,** 641

Veblen, Oswald, **Supp. I, Part 2,** 640

Veblen, Thorstein, **I,** 104, 283, 475–476, 483, 498, 511; **II,** 27, 272, 276, 287; **Supp. I, Part 2,** 628–650; **Supp. IV, Part 1,** 22

Veblen (Hobson), **Supp. I, Part 2,** 650

Veblenism: A New Critique (Dobriansky), **Supp. I, Part 2,** 648, 650

"Veblen's Attack on Culture" (Adorno), **Supp. I, Part 2,** 650

Vechten, Carl Van, **Retro. Supp. I,** 199

Vedas, **IV,** 183

Vega, Lope de, **Retro. Supp. I,** 285; **Supp. III, Part 1,** 341, 347

Vegetable, The (Fitzgerald), **Retro. Supp. I,** 105

Vegetable, The, or From President to Postman (Fitzgerald), **II,** 91

Vein of Iron (Glasgow), **II,** 175, 186, 188–189, 191, 192, 194

Veinberg, Jon, **Supp. V,** 180

Velie, Alan R., **Supp. IV, Part 2,** 486

"Velvet Shoes" (Wylie), **Supp. I, Part 2,** 711, 714

Vendler, Helen H., **IV,** 96; **Retro. Supp. I,** 297; **Supp. I, Part 1,** 77, 78, 92, 95, 97, **Part 2,** 565; **Supp. IV, Part 1,** 245, 247, 249, 254, 257, **Part 2,** 448; **Supp. V,** 78, 82, 189, 343

"Venetian Blind, The" (Jarrell), **II,** 382–383

Venetian Glass Nephew, The (Wylie), **Supp. I, Part 2,** 707, 709, 714, 717–719, 721, 724

Venetian Life (Howells), **II,** 274, 277, 279

Venice Observed (McCarthy), **II,** 562

Ventadorn, Bernard de, **Supp. IV, Part 1,** 146

"Ventriloquists' Conversations" (Gentry), **Supp. IV, Part 1,** 236

Venus and Adonis (film), **Supp. IV, Part 1,** 82

"Venus, Cupid, Folly and Time" (Taylor), **Supp. V,** 322–323

Venus in Sparta (Auchincloss), **Supp. IV, Part 1,** 25

"Veracruz" (Hayden), **Supp. II, Part 1,** 371, 373

Verga, Giovanni, **II,** 271, 275

Verhaeren, Emile, **I,** 476; **II,** 528, 529

Verlaine, Paul, **II,** 529, 543; **III,** 466; **IV,** 79, 80, 86, 286; **Retro. Supp. I,** 56, 62

Vermeer, Jan, **Retro. Supp. I,** 335

"Vermeer" (Nemerov), **III,** 275, 278, 280

Vermont Notebook, The (Ashbery), **Supp. III, Part 1,** 1

"Vernal Ague, The" (Freneau), **Supp. II, Part 1,** 258

Verne, Jules, **I,** 480; **Retro. Supp. I,** 270

Vernon, John, **III,** 550

Verplanck, Gulian C., **Supp. I, Part 1,** 155, 156, 157, 158

Verrazano, Giovanni da, **Supp. I, Part 2,** 496, 497

"Verse for Urania" (Merrill), **Supp. III, Part 1,** 329, 330

Verses (Wharton), **Retro. Supp. I,** 362

"Verses for Children" (Lowell), **II,** 516

"Verses Made at Sea in a Heavy Gale" (Freneau), **Supp. II, Part 1,** 262

Verses, Printed for Her Friends (Jewett), **II,** 406

"Version of a Fragment of Simonides" (Bryant), **Supp. I, Part 1,** 153, 155

Verulam, Baron, *see* Bacon, Francis

Very, Jones, **III,** 507

"Very Proper Gander, The" (Thurber), **Supp. I, Part 2,** 610

"Very Short Story, A" (Hemingway), **II,** 252; **Retro. Supp. I,** 173

"Vesalius in Zante" (Wharton), **Retro. Supp. I,** 372

Vesey, Denmark, **Supp. I, Part 2,** 592

"Vespers" (Auden), **Supp II, Part 1,** 23

"Vespers" (Glück), **Supp. V,** 88

Vested Interests and the Common Man, The (Veblen), **Supp. I, Part 2,** 642

"Vesuvius at Home" (Rich), **Retro. Supp. I,** 42

"Veteran, The" (Crane), **I,** 413

"Veteran Sirens" (Robinson), **III,** 512, 524

"Vetiver" (Ashbery), **Supp. III, Part 1,** 26

"Via Dieppe-Newhaven" (Miller), **III,** 183

Vicar of Wakefeld, The (Goldsmith), **I,** 216

Vickery, John, **II,** 608

Vickery, Olga W., **II,** 76

Victim, The (Bellow), **I,** 144, 145, 147, 149, 150, 151, 152, 153, 155, 156, 158, 159, 164; **IV,** 19

"Victor" (Mumford), **Supp. II, Part 2,** 476

Victoria, Queen, **II,** 191, 490

Victorian Knight-Errant: A Study of the Early Literary Career of James Russell Lowell (Howard), **Supp. I, Part 2,** 426

Victorian literature, **II,** 499, 507–508, 590; **III,** 4, 87, 109, 189, 509, 510; **IV,** 230, 321, 435; **Supp. I, Part 1,** 29, 35–37, **Part 2,** 552, 656

"Victory at Sea" (television series), **Supp. I, Part 2,** 490

"Victory comes late—" (Dickinson), **Retro. Supp. I,** 45

Victory in Limbo: Imagism 1908–1917 (Harmer), **Supp. I, Part 1,** 275

"Victory of the Moon, The" (Crane), **I,** 420

Vidal, Gore, **II,** 587; **IV,** 383; **Supp. IV, Part 1,** 22, 35, 92, 95, 198, **Part 2,** 677–696

Wanderings of Oisin (Yeats), **Supp. I, Part 1,** 79
Waniek, Marilyn Nelson, **Supp. IV, Part 1,** 244
"Wanted: An Ontological Critic" (Ransom), **III,** 498
"Wanting to Die" (Sexton), **Supp. II, Part 2,** 684, 686
Waples, Dorothy, **I,** 348, 357
Wapshot Chronicle, The (Cheever), **Supp. I, Part 1,** 174, 177–180, 181, 196
Wapshot Scandal, The (Cheever), **Supp. I, Part 1,** 180–184, 187, 191, 196
"War" (Kingston), **Supp. V,** 169
War and Peace (Tolstoi), **I,** 6, 7; **II,** 191, 205, 291; **IV,** 446; **Supp. V,** 277
"War Between Men and Women, The" (Thurber), **Supp. I, Part 2,** 615
War Bulletins (Lindsay), **Supp. I, Part 2,** 378–379
"War Diary, A" (Bourne), **I,** 229
War Dispatches of Stephen Crane, The (Crane), **I,** 422
War Games (Morris), **III,** 238
War in Heaven, The (Shepard and Chaikin), **Supp. III, Part 2,** 433
"War Is Kind" (Crane), **I,** 419
War Is Kind (Crane), **I,** 409; **III,** 585
War of the Classes (London), **II,** 466
"War Poems" (Sandburg), **III,** 581
"War, Response, and Contradiction" (Burke), **I,** 283
"War Widow, The" (Frederic), **II,** 135–136
Ward, Aileen, **II,** 531
Ward, Artemus (pseudonym), *see* Browne, Charles Farrar
Ward, Douglas Turner, **Supp. IV, Part 1,** 362
Ward, Henry, **Supp. I, Part 2,** 588
Ward, J. A., **IV,** 235
Ward, Lester, **Supp. I, Part 2,** 640
Ward, Lynn, **I,** 31
Ward, Mrs. Humphry, **II,** 338
Ward, Nathaniel, **Supp. I, Part 1,** 99, 102, 111, 116
Ward, Samuel, **II,** 22

Ward, Theodora, **I,** 470, 473; **Retro. Supp. I,** 28
Ward, William Hayes, **Supp. I, Part 1,** 371
"Ward Line, The" (Morris), **III,** 220
Warfel, Harry R., **III,** 243; **Supp. I, Part 1,** 148, 366, 373
Warner, Charles Dudley, **II,** 405; **IV,** 198
Warner, John R., **III,** 193
Warner, Oliver, **I,** 548
Warner, Susan, **Retro. Supp. I,** 246
Warner, W. Lloyd, **III,** 60
"Warning" (Hughes), **Supp. I, Part 1,** 343
"Warning" (Pound), **III,** 474
"Warning, The" (Creeley), **Supp. IV, Part 1,** 150
"Warning, The" (Longfellow), **II,** 498
Warning Hill (Marquand), **III,** 55–56, 60, 68
Warnke, Frank J., **Supp. I, Part 1,** 199
Warren, Austin, **I,** 265, 268, 271, 287, 473; **II,** 246; **IV,** 166; **Supp. I, Part 1,** 123, **Part 2,** 423, 426
Warren, Earl, **III,** 581
Warren, Gabriel, **IV,** 244
Warren, Mrs. Robert Penn (Eleanor Clark), **IV,** 244
Warren, Robert Penn, **I,** 120, 190, 211, 517, 520; **II,** 57, 76, 217, 228, 253, 390; **III,** 134, 310, 382–383, 454, 455, 482, 485, 490, 496, 497, 502; **IV,** 121, 122, 123, 125, 126, 142, 236–259, 261, 262, 279, 284, 340–341, 458; **Retro. Supp. I,** 40, 41, 73, 90; **Supp. I, Part 1,** 359, 371, 373, **Part 2,** 386, 423, 706; **Supp. II, Part 1,** 139; **Supp. III, Part 2,** 542; **Supp. V,** 261, 316, 318, 319, 333
Warren, Rosanna, **IV,** 244
Warrington Poems, The (Ríos), **Supp. IV, Part 2,** 540
Warrior, Robert Allen, **Supp. IV, Part 1,** 329
"Warrior, The" (Gunn Allen), **Supp. IV, Part 1,** 326

Wars I Have Seen (Stein), **IV,** 27, 36, 477
Warshawsky, Isaac (pseudonym), *see* Singer, Isaac Bashevis
Warshow, Robert, **Supp. I, Part 1,** 51
Wartime (Fussell), **Supp. V,** 241
"Was" (Creeley), **Supp. IV, Part 1,** 155
"Was" (Faulkner), **II,** 71
"Was Lowell an Historical Critic?" (Altick), **Supp. I, Part 2,** 423
"Wash" (Faulkner), **II,** 72
Washington, Booker T., **Supp. I, Part 2,** 393; **Supp. II, Part 1,** 157, 160, 167, 168, 171, 225
Washington, George, **I,** 453; **II,** 313–314; **Supp. I, Part 2,** 399, 485, 508, 509, 511, 513, 517, 518, 520, 599
Washington, D.C. (Vidal), **Supp. IV, Part 2,** 677, 684, 686–687, 690
Washington Post (newspaper), **Supp. IV, Part 1,** 205, 207, 227, **Part 2,** 657
Washington Post Book World (Lesser), **Supp. IV, Part 2,** 453
Washington Square (James), **II,** 327, 328; **Retro. Supp. I,** 215, 220, **222–223**
"Washington Square, 1946" (Ozick), **Supp. V,** 272
Waskow, Howard J., **IV,** 354
Wasp (publication), **I,** 192, 196, 197
Wasserman, Earl R., **Supp. I, Part 2,** 439, 440, 453
Wasserman, Jakob, **Supp. I, Part 2,** 669
Wasserstein, Wendy, **Supp. IV, Part 1,** 309
Wasserstrom, William, **I,** 263
Wasson, Ben, **Retro. Supp. I,** 79, 83
Waste Land, The (Eliot), **I,** 107, 266, 298, 395, 396, 482, 570–571, 572, 574–575, 577–578, 580, 581, 584, 585, 586, 587; **III,** 6–8, 12, 196, 277–278, 453, 471, 492, 586; **IV,** 122, 123, 124, 140, 418, 419, 420; **Retro. Supp. I,** 51, 60, **60–62,** 63, 64,

"Yankee Gallimaufry" (Baker), **Supp. I, Part 1,** 198
Yankee in Canada, A (Thoreau), **IV,** 188
Yankey in London (Tyler), **I,** 344
"Yánnina" (Merrill), **Supp. III, Part 1,** 329
Yarboro, Chelsea Quinn, **Supp. V,** 147
Yardley, Jonathan, **Supp. V,** 326
Yates, Norris W., **IV,** 235; **Supp. I, Part 2,** 626
Yates family, **II,** 173
Yatron, Michael, **Supp. I, Part 2,** 402, 478
"Year, The" (Sandburg), **III,** 584
"Year of Mourning, The" (Jeffers), **Supp. II, Part 2,** 415
"Year of the Double Spring, The" (Swenson), **Supp. IV, Part 2,** 647
Year's Life, A (Lowell), **Supp. I, Part 2,** 405
"Years of Birth" (Cowley), **Supp. II, Part 1,** 149
Years of My Youth (Howells), **II,** 276
"Years of Wonder" (White), **Supp. I, Part 2,** 652, 653
Years With Ross, The (Thurber), **Supp. I, Part 2,** 619, 681
Yeats, John Butler, **III,** 458
Yeats, William Butler, **I,** 69, 172, 384, 389, 403, 434, 478, 494, 532; **II,** 168–169, 566, 598; **III,** 4, 5, 8, 18, 19, 20, 23, 29, 40, 205, 249, 269, 270–271, 272, 278, 279, 294, 347, 409, 457, 458–460, 472, 473, 476–477, 521, 523, 524, 527, 528, 533, 540, 541, 542, 543–544, 591–592; **IV,** 89, 93, 121, 126, 136, 140, 271, 394, 404; **Retro. Supp. I,** 59, 66, 127, 141, 270, 283, 285, 286, 288, 290, 311, 342, 350, 378, 413; **Supp. I, Part 1,** 79, 80, 254, 257, 262, **Part 2,** 388, 389; **Supp. II, Part 1,** 1, 4, 9, 20, 26, 361; **Supp. III, Part 1,** 59, 63, 236, 238, 253; **Supp. IV, Part 1,** 81, **Part 2,** 634; **Supp. V,** 220
Yellow Book (publication), **I,** 421; **III,** 508
"Yellow Girl" (Caldwell), **I,** 310
"Yellow Gown, The" (Anderson), **I,** 114
Yellow House on the Corner, The (Dove), **Supp. IV, Part 1,** 244, 245, 246, 254
"Yellow River" (Tate), **IV,** 141
"Yellow Violet, The" (Bryant), **Supp. I, Part 1,** 154, 155
"Yellow Woman" (Keres stories), **Supp. IV, Part 1,** 327
"Yellow Woman" (Silko), **Supp. IV, Part 2,** 567–568
"Yentl the Yeshiva Boy" (Singer), **IV,** 15, 20
Yerkes, Charles E., **I,** 507, 512
Yerma (opera) (Bowles), **Supp. IV, Part 1,** 89
"Yes and It's Hopeless" (Ginsberg), **Supp. II, Part 1,** 326
Yes, Mrs. Williams (Williams), **Retro. Supp. I,** 423
"Yet Do I Marvel" (Cullen), **Supp. IV, Part 1,** 165, 169
Yet Other Waters (Farrell), **II,** 29, 38, 39, 40
Yevtushenko, Yevgeny, **Supp. III, Part 1,** 268
Yohannan, J. D., **II,** 20, 24
Yonge, Charlotte, **II,** 174
"Yore" (Nemerov), **III,** 283
"York Beach" (Toomer), **Supp. III, Part 2,** 486
Yorke, Dorothy, **Supp. I, Part 1,** 258
Yoshe Kalb (Singer), **IV,** 2
Yost, Karl, **III,** 144
"You All Know the Story of the Other Woman" (Sexton), **Supp. II, Part 2,** 688
"You, Andrew Marvell" (MacLeish), **III,** 12–13
"You Are in Bear Country" (Kumin), **Supp. IV, Part 2,** 453, 455
"You Are Not I" (Bowles), **Supp. IV, Part 1,** 87
You Came Along (film), **Supp. IV, Part 2,** 524
"You *Can* Go Home Again" (TallMountain), **Supp. IV, Part 1,** 324–325
"You Can Have It" (Levine), **Supp. V,** 188–189
You Can't Go Home Again (Wolfe), **IV,** 450, 451, 454, 456, 460, 462, 468, 469, 470
"You Can't Go Home Again: James Baldwin and the South" (Dance), **Supp. I, Part 1,** 70
You Can't Keep a Good Woman Down (Walker), **Supp. III, Part 2,** 520, 525, 531
"You Can't Tell a Man by the Song He Sings" (Roth), **Supp. III, Part 2,** 406
"You Don't Know What Love Is" (Carver), **Supp. III, Part 1,** 147
"You, Dr. Martin" (Sexton), **Supp. II, Part 2,** 673
You, Emperors, and Others: Poems 1957–1960 (Warren), **IV,** 245
"You, Genoese Mariner" (Merwin), **Supp. III, Part 1,** 343
"You Have Left Your Lotus Pods on the Bus" (Bowles), **Supp. IV, Part 1,** 91
You Have Seen Their Faces (Caldwell), **I,** 290, 293–294, 295, 304, 309
You Know Me Al (comic strip), **II,** 423
You Know Me Al (Lardner), **II,** 26, 415, 419, 422, 431
"You Know What" (Beattie), **Supp. V,** 33
You Touched Me! (Williams and Windham), **IV,** 382, 385, 387, 390, 392–393
"You Wouldn't Believe It" (Broyard), **Supp. I, Part 1,** 198
Young, Alfred F., **Supp. I, Part 2,** 525
Young, Art, **IV,** 436
Young, Brigham, **Supp. IV, Part 2,** 603
Young, Charles L., **II,** 24
Young, Edward, **II,** 111; **III,** 415, 503
Young, Philip, **II,** 270, 306, 318; **Retro. Supp. I,** 172
Young, Stark, **III,** 408
Young, Thomas Daniel, **III,** 502
"Young" (Sexton), **Supp. III, Part 2,** 680

A Complete Listing of Authors in *American Writers*

Veblen, Thorstein	Supplement I
Vidal, Gore	Supplement IV
Vonnegut, Kurt	Supplement II
Walker, Alice	Supplement III
Warren, Robert Penn	Volume 4
Welty, Eudora	Volume 4
Welty, Eudora	Retrospective Supplement I
West, Nathanael	Volume 4
Wharton, Edith	Volume 4
Wharton, Edith	Retrospective Supplement I
White, E. B.	Supplement I
Whitman, Walt	Volume 4
Whitman, Walt	Retrospective Supplement I
Whittier, John Greenleaf	Supplement I
Wilbur, Richard	Supplement III
Wilder, Thornton	Volume 4
Williams, Tennessee	Volume 4
Williams, William Carlos	Volume 4
Williams, William Carlos	Retrospective Supplement I
Wilson, Edmund	Volume 4
Winters, Yvor	Supplement II
Wolfe, Thomas	Volume 4
Wolfe, Tom	Supplement III
Wright, Charles	Supplement V
Wright, James	Supplement III
Wright, Richard	Volume 4
Wylie, Elinor	Supplement I
Zukofsky, Louis	Supplement III